Bali, Lombok & Nusa Tenggara

North Bali p253
Central Mountains p237
West Bali p274
Ubud Region p160
East Bali p203
Kuta & Southwest Beaches p64
South Bali & the Islands p115
Gili Islands p312
Lombok p283
Nusa Tenggara p334

Virginia Maxwell,
Mark Johanson, Sofia Levin, MaSovaida Morgan

PLAN YOUR TRIP

NORMAN ONG/SHUTTERSTOCK ©
PURA TANAH LOT P277

SONY HERDIANA/SHUTTERSTOCK ©
BALINESE DANCER P416

ON THE ROAD

Welcome to Bali, Lombok & Nusa Tenggara

Blessed with rich cultures, magnificent landscapes and some of the world's best beaches, this string of tropical islands is as seductive as it is paradisiacal.

Island of the Gods

The rich and diverse culture of Bali plays out at all levels of life, from the exquisite flower-petal offerings placed everywhere, to the processions of joyfully garbed locals shutting down major roads as they march to one of the myriad temple ceremonies, to the otherworldly traditional music and dance performed island-wide. Almost everything has spiritual meaning. The middle of Bali is dominated by the dramatic volcanoes of the central mountains and hillside temples such as Pura Luhur Batukau (one of the island's estimated 10,000 temples), while the tallest peak, Gunung Agung, is the island's spiritual centre.

One Island, Many Destinations

On Bali you can lose yourself in the chaos of Kuta or the sybaritic pleasures of Seminyak and Kerobokan, surf wild beaches in the south or just hang out on Nusa Lembongan. You can go family-friendly in Sanur or enjoy a romantic getaway on the Bukit Peninsula. And you can visit Ubud, the heart of Bali and a place where the culture of the island is most accessible. Wherever you go on this magical island, one thing is sure: you're bound to be beguiled.

Lombok & the Gilis

The 2018 earthquakes may have wreaked havoc on the island of Lombok and its near neighbour, the Gili Island group, but the enchantment of these places remains palpable. The fortitude of locals as they came together to regroup, rebuild, and write a new chapter in their lives has been inspirational and though the road ahead will be long and the challenges many, the mood remains defiantly cheerful. After all, with bone-white beaches, prismatic undersea realms and terraced rice fields tumbling down Indonesia's second-tallest volcano, who wouldn't be eager to pick up the pieces here and give it another go?

Nusa Tenggara

There's no lack of variety on the islands that make up this archipelago east of Bali. With a surfeit of unspoiled sandy beaches, world-class diving and surfing spots, hot springs, spectacular waterfalls and plenty of hiking opportunities, this is a great destination for active tourists keen to diverge off the beaten track. It's also culturally fascinating, with hundreds of traditional villages where animist rituals and tribal traditions continue to thrive.

Contents

UNDERSTAND

SURVIVAL GUIDE

SPECIAL FEATURES

Why I Love Bali

By MaSovaida Morgan, Writer

When I first arrived in Bali, my imaginings of a peaceful paradise were thwarted by a more frenetic scene. Instagram has a way of up-selling reality – admittedly, those initial ideas hinged on what I saw while scrolling down my phone screen. I eventually found picture-perfect vistas, but also discovered an interstitial serenity amid the bustle that helped me reconcile Bali's dual identities of tourism-driven hubbub and tranquil utopia. Welcoming dreamers and doers, this land quickens an inherent spirituality within all who visit its shores. Every step (over an offering to the gods) feels like a prayer.

For more about our writers, see p480

Above: Rice fields in Ubud (p160)

Bali, Lombok & Nusa Tenggara

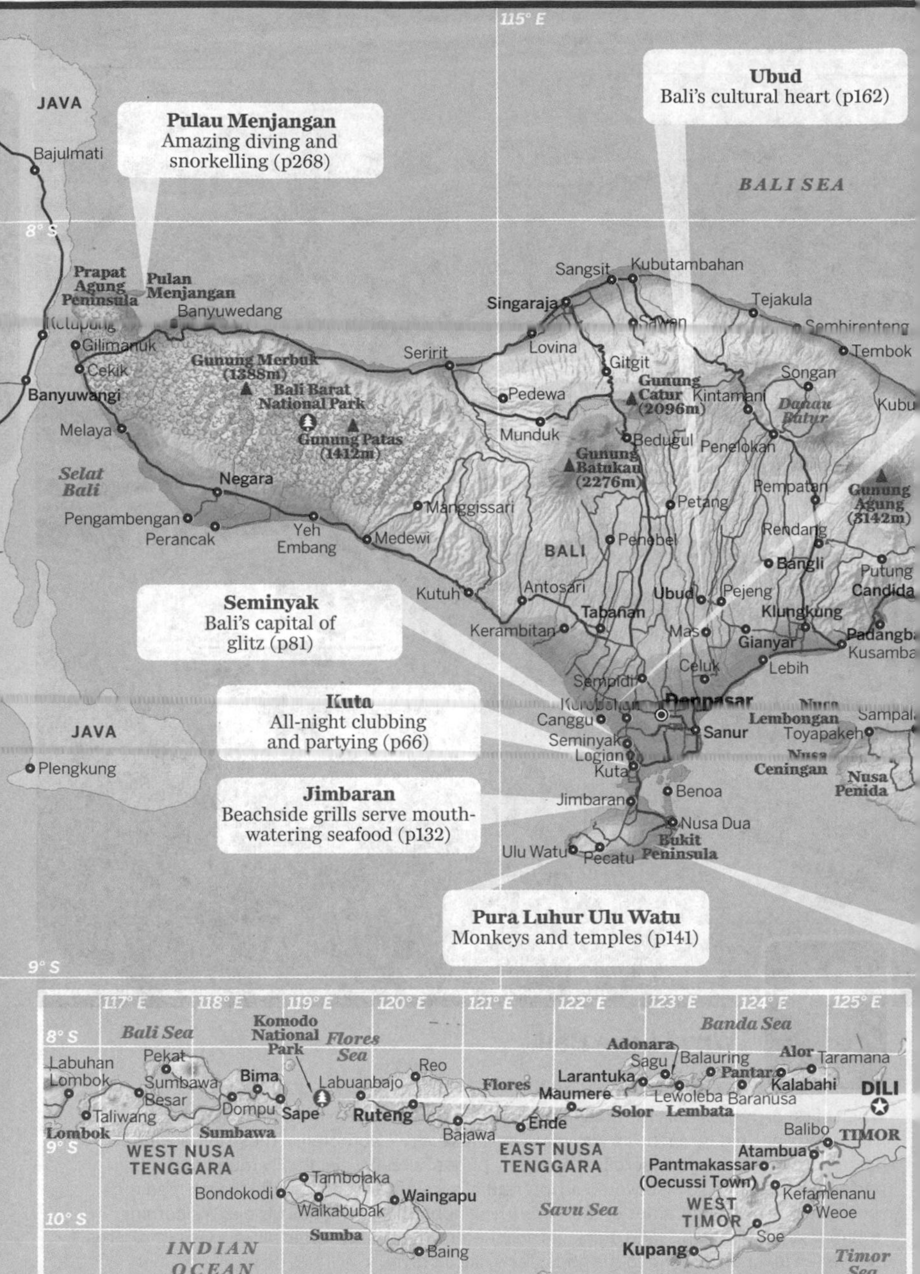

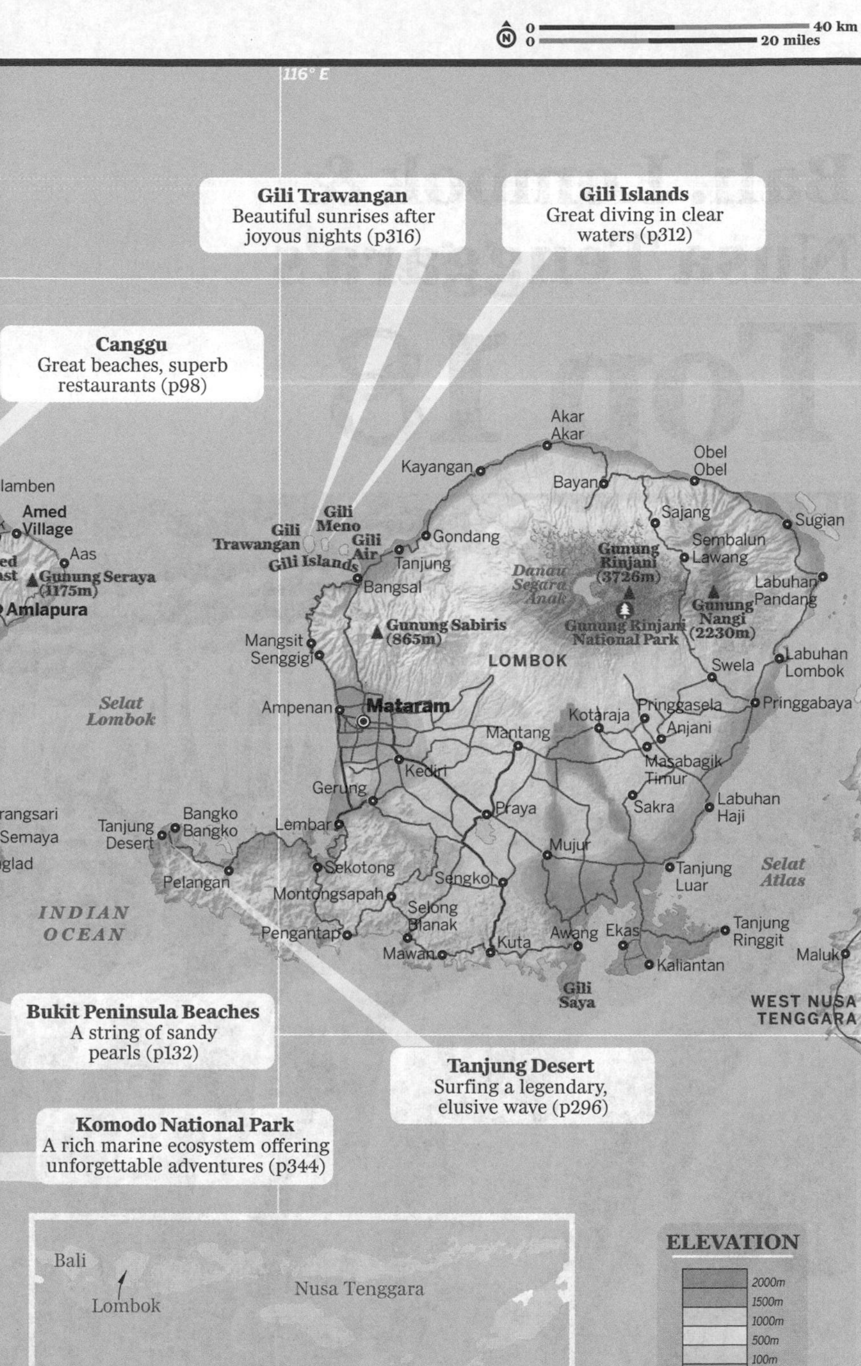

0 40 km
0 20 miles
116° E
Gili Trawangan
Beautiful sunrises after joyous nights (p316)
Gili Islands
Great diving in clear waters (p312)
Canggu
Great beaches, superb restaurants (p98)
Akar Akar
Obel Obel
Kayangan
Bayan
Tulamben
Amed Village
Sajang
Sugian
Gili Meno
Gili Trawangan
Gili Air
Gili Islands
Gondang
Sembalun Lawang
Aas
Gunung Seraya (1175m)
Tanjung
Bangsal
Danau Segara Anak
Gunung Rinjani (3726m)
Labuhan Pandang
Amlapura
Gunung Nangi (2230m)
Gunung Rinjani National Park
Gunung Sabiris (865m)
Mangsit
Senggigi
LOMBOK
Labuhan Lombok
Swela
Selat Lombok
Ampenan
Mataram
Pringgasela
Pringgabaya
Kotaraja
Anjani
Mantang
Masabagik Timur
Kediri
Gerung
Sakra
Labuhan Haji
Praya
Karangsari
Semaya
Tanjung Desert
Bangko Bangko
Lembar
Mujur
Tanjung Luar
Selat Atlas
Sekotong
Pelangan
Sengkol
Montongsapah
Selong Blanak
INDIAN OCEAN
Tanjung Ringgit
Pengantap
Awang
Ekas
Kuta
Mawan
Kaliantan
Maluk
Gili Saya
WEST NUSA TENGGARA
Bukit Peninsula Beaches
A string of sandy pearls (p132)
Tanjung Desert
Surfing a legendary, elusive wave (p296)
Komodo National Park
A rich marine ecosystem offering unforgettable adventures (p344)
Bali
Lombok
Nusa Tenggara
Bali, Lombok & Nusa Tenggara
ELEVATION
2000m
1500m
1000m
500m
100m
0

Bali, Lombok & Nusa Tenggara's Top 18

1

Bali's Processions

1 There you are sipping a coffee at a cafe in, say, Kuta or Ubud, when there's a crash of the gamelan and traffic screeches to a halt as a crowd of elegantly dressed people comes flying by bearing pyramids of fruit, tasselled parasols and a furred, masked Barong (mythical lion-dog creature) or two. It's a temple procession (p414), disappearing as suddenly as it appeared, leaving no more than a fleeting sparkle of gold-and-white silk and hibiscus petals in its wake. Dozens occur daily across Bali.

Bukit Peninsula Beaches

2 A little plume of white sand rises out of the blue Indian Ocean and fills a cove below limestone cliffs clad in deep green tropical beauty. It sounds idyllic, and it is. The west coast of the Bukit Peninsula (p132) in south Bali is dotted with these very beaches, such as Balangan Beach, Bingin and Padang Padang. Families run surfer bars built on bamboo stilts over the tide, where the only views are the breaks, just metres away. Grab a lounger and be lulled by the waves. Below: Balangan Beach (p136)

TROPICAL STUDIO/SHUTTERSTOCK ©

2

MARIUS DOBILAS/SHUTTERSTOCK ©

Sybaritic Spas

3 Whether it's a total fix for the mind, body and spirit, or simply the desire for a bit of serenity, visitors to Bali spend many happy hours (sometimes days) being massaged, scrubbed, perfumed, pampered, bathed and blissed out. Sometimes all this attention to your well-being happens on the beach or in a garden – think Ubud's Taksu Spa (p169) – other times it's in stylish, even lavish, surroundings. The Balinese massage techniques of stretching, long strokes, skin rolling and palm-and-thumb pressure result in an all-over feeling of calm; it's the perfect holiday prescription.

Luxe Stays

4 On an island that honours art and serenity, is it any wonder you'll find some of the world's finest hotels and resorts? From blissful retreats like Katamama (p93) on south Bali's beautiful beach in Kerobokan to perches on cliffs above the dazzling white sands that dot the Bukit Peninsula, these stylish hotels are as lovely outside as they are luxurious inside. Further resorts by vaunted architects can be found in Ubud's river valleys and in remote idyllic coastal locations right round the island. Above: Mandapa (p181)

Bali's Dive Sites

5 Legendary Pulau Menjangan (p268) thrills, one tank after another. It offers multiple types of diving around a protected island renowned for its coral walls. And that's just one of Bali's great dive sites. Under the waves at Nusa Penida, you can feel small as a manta ray blocks out the sun's glow overhead, its fluid movement causing barely a disturbance in the surrounding waters as it glides past. And just when you think your dive can't get more dramatic, you turn to find a 2.5m sunfish motionlessly hovering, checking you out. Top: Nusa Penida (p157)

Ubud

6 The artistic heart of Bali exudes a compelling spiritual appeal. The streets are lined with galleries where artists, both humble and great, create. Beautiful performances showcasing the island's rich culture grace a dozen stages nightly. Museums honour the works of those who have been inspired here over the years, while people walk the rice fields to find the perfect spot to sit in lotus position and ponder life's endless possibilities. Ubud (p162) is a state of mind and a beautiful state of being. Top: Performance at Ubud Palace (p162)

7

8

Kuta's Never-Ending Night

7 It starts with stylish cafes and bars in Seminyak, open-air places where everything seems just that bit more beautiful amid the post-sunset glow and pulsing house beats. Maybe you move down to action at Double Six beach. Later, the legendary clubs of Kuta (p78) draw you in, with international DJs spinning their sets to packed dance floors. Some time before dawn, Kuta's harder, rawer clubs such as Sky Garden Lounge (p78) suck you in like black holes, spitting you out hours later into an unsteady daylight, shattered but happy. Top left: Beach bar in Kuta (p66)

Canggu's Beaches

8 Canggu (p98) is more of an idea and really less of a distinct place, given that the area was all rice fields just a few years ago. But now it's a label that denotes sandy fun and frolic on beaches such as Batu Bolong (p99), pounding surf offshore and nights you hope will never end at a fast-expanding collection of creative cafes and superb restaurants. Find your own faves and make Canggu your Canggu. See what cool new place opens just as you turn your back.

Surfing Bali

9 If it's a month containing the letter 'r', go east; during other months, go west to fabled breaks like Padang Padang (p140). Simplicity itself. On Bali you have dozens of great breaks in each direction. This was the first place in Asia where surfing took off and, like the perfect set, it shows no signs of calming down. Surfers buzz around the island on motorbikes with board racks, looking for the next great break. Waves blown out? Another spot is just five minutes away. Don't miss classic surfer hangout Balian Beach. Above: Padang Padang (p140)

Kuta Beach

10 Tourism on Bali began here, and is there any question why? A sweeping arc of sand curves from Kuta into the misty horizon northwest to Echo Beach. Surf that started far out in the Indian Ocean crashes to shore in long symmetrical breaks. You can stroll the 12km of sand (p66), enjoying a foot massage and cold beer with thousands of your new best friends in the south, or find a hip hang-out or even a plot of sand to call your own up north.

Bali's Food

11 'Yum!' It's virtually impossible not to say this when you step into a classic warung (food stall) for lunch to find dozens of freshly made dishes on the counter awaiting you. It shouldn't surprise that this fertile island provides a profusion of ingredients that combine to create fresh and aromatic dishes. Local specialities such as *babi guling* (roast suckling pig that's been marinated for hours in spices) will have you lining up again and again. Try lunch at one of the excellent Balinese cafes in Denpasar like Warung Lembongan (p119).

Balinese Dance

12 The antithesis of Balinese mellow is Balinese dance (p416), a discipline that demands methodical precision. A performer of the Legong spends years learning minutely choreographed movements from her eyeballs to her toes. Each movement has a meaning and the language flows with a grace that is hypnotic. Clad in silk and ikat, the dancers tell stories rich with the very essence of Balinese Hindu beliefs and lore. Performances occur regularly at temples like Pura Dalem Ubud (p191) and Pura Taman Saraswati. Top: Performance at Pura Ulun Danu Bratan (p245)

Seminyak

13 People wander around Seminyak (p81) and ask themselves if they are even in Bali. Of course! On an island that values creativity like few other places, the capital of glitz is where you'll find inventive boutiques run by local designers, the most eclectic and interesting collection of restaurants, and little boutique hotels that break with the island clichés. Expats, locals and visitors alike idle away the hours in its cafes, at ease with the world and secure in their enjoyment of life's pleasures. Above: Mama San (p88)

Jimbaran Seafood

14 Enormous fresh prawns marinated in lime and garlic and grilled over coconut husks. Tick. A hint of post-sunset pink on the horizon. Tick. Stars twinkling overhead. Tick. A comfy teak chair on the beach while your toes play in the sand. Tick. An ice-cold beer. Tick. A strolling band playing the Macarena. OK, maybe not a tick. But the beachside seafood grills such as Warung Ramayana (p135) in Jimbaran are a don't-miss evening out, with platters of seafood that arrived fresh that morning to the market just up the beach.

Komodo National Park

15 This constellation of islands (p344) is one of the world's greatest natural treasures. Its marine ecosystem is so rich that Unesco has declared it a protected Biosphere Reserve as well as a World Heritage Site, and its islands are home to flora and fauna including the extraordinary *ora* (Komodo dragon). It's paradise for active travellers, offering world-class hiking, snorkelling, diving and nature watching. Bottom: Komodo dragon (p348)

14

15

Underwater Gilis

16 Taking the plunge? There are few better places for high-level diving than the Gilis, encircled by coral reefs teeming with life, such as at Meno Wall (p325), and visited by pelagics such as cruising manta rays. Scuba diving is a huge draw – there are numerous professional schools and all kinds of courses taught (from absolute beginner to nitrox specialist). With easy access from beach to reef, snorkelling is also available, and you're very likely to see turtles. Want to take snorkelling to the next level? Try freediving; it's sweeping the Gilis. Above: Meno Wall (p325)

Pura Luhur Ulu Watu

17 Just watch out for the monkeys. One of Bali's holiest temples, Pura Luhur Ulu Watu (p141) is perched on tall cliffs in the southwest corner of the island. In the 11th century a Javanese priest first prayed here and the site has only become holier since. Shrines and sacred sites are strung along the edge of the limestone precipice. Gaze across an ocean rippled by swells that arrive with metronomic precision. Sunset dance performances delight while those monkeys patiently await a banana – or maybe your sunglasses. Top right: Kecak (p417) performance

Snorkelling

18 Bali has oodles of places where you can slip on fins and a mask and enter another beautiful world. Swim a short distance from shore and see the eerie ghost of a sunken freighter at Tulamben (p234) or hover a few metres over the marine life around the beautiful reef wall at Pulau Menjangan. The mangroves of Nusa Lembongan lure a rainbow of fish that gather in profusion. Or simply make your way into the calm waters off a beach, such as Sanur, and see what darts off into the distance.

Need to Know

For more information, see Survival Guide (p439)

Currency
Rupiah (Rp)

Language
Bahasa Indonesia, Balinese and Sasak (Lombok). Islands of Nusa Tenggara also have their own languages.

Visas
Visas are easily obtained on arrival, but can be a hassle to arrange if you hope to stay longer than 30 days.

Money
ATMs are common in most towns but not in villages. Credit cards are accepted at more expensive establishments.

Mobile Phones
Cheap local SIM cards (from 5000Rp with no calling credit) are sold everywhere. Data speeds of 3G and faster are the norm across Bali and Lombok. Any modern mobile phone will work.

Time
Indonesia Central Time (GMT/UTC plus eight hours)

When to Go

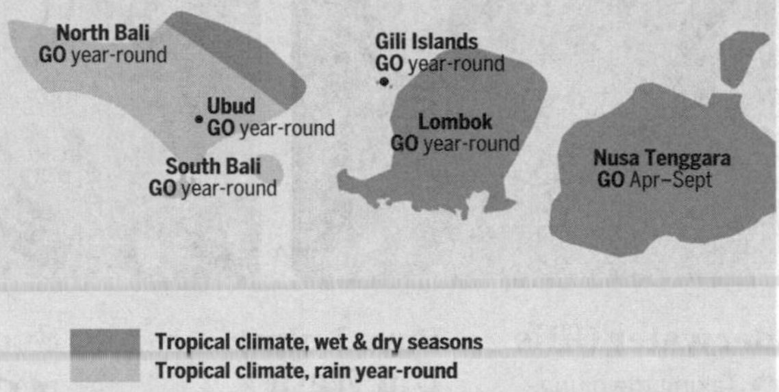

North Bali
GO year-round

Ubud
GO year-round

South Bali
GO year-round

Gili Islands
GO year-round

Lombok
GO year-round

Nusa Tenggara
GO Apr–Sept

Tropical climate, wet & dry seasons
Tropical climate, rain year-round

High Season
(Jul, Aug & Dec)

- Accommodation rates increase by 50% or more.
- Many hotels are booked far ahead; the best restaurants need to be booked in advance.
- Christmas and New Year are equally expensive and crowded.

Shoulder
(May, Jun & Sep)

- Coincides with the best weather (drier, less humid).
- You may find a good room deal, and last-minute bookings are possible.
- Best time for many activities, including diving.

Low Season
(Jan–Apr, Oct & Nov)

- Deals everywhere, good airfares.
- Rainy season – though rainfall is never excessive.
- Can do most activities except volcano treks.

Useful Websites

Bali Advertiser (www.baliadvertiser.biz) Bali's expat journal with insider tips and good columnists.

Bali Discovery (www.balidiscovery.com) Weekly summary of news, plus hotel deals.

The Beat Bali (http://thebeatbali.com) Comprehensive listings for nightlife, music and events.

Lombok Guide (www.thelombokguide.com) Comprehensive site covering main areas of interest.

Gili Life (www.facebook.com/Gililife) Local culture and news.

Sumba Information (www.sumba-information.com) Vast compendium of information about Sumba in Nusa Tenggara.

Lonely Planet (www.lonelyplanet.com/indonesia) Destination information, hotel bookings, traveller forum and more.

Important Numbers

The international access code can be any of three versions; try all three.

Indonesia country code	✆62
International access code	✆001/008/017
Police	✆110
Fire	✆113
Medical emergency	✆119

Exchange Rates

Australia	A$1	10,500Rp
Canada	C$1	11,300Rp
Euro	€1	17,500Rp
Japan	¥100	13,300Rp
New Zealand	NZ$1	9600Rp
UK	UK£1	19,300Rp
US	US$1	14,800Rp

For current exchange rates, see www.xe.com.

Daily Costs: Bali

Budget: Less than US$80

- Room at guesthouse or homestay: less than US$50
- Cheap food and drink, meals: under US$5
- Beaches: free

Midrange: US$80–250

- Room at midrange hotel: US$50–150
- Great night out eating and drinking: from US$20
- Spa treatment: US$10–40

Top end: More than US$250

- Room at top-end hotel or resort: over US$150
- Lavish evening out: over US$40
- Car and driver per day: US$60

Daily Costs: Lombok

Budget: Less than US$25

- Dorm at a hostel: US$7–10
- Food and drink at a warung: under US$5
- Snorkel rental: US$3

Midrange: US$25–100

- Bungalow with air-con: US$20–60
- Night out eating and drinking: US$20
- Massage: US$7–15

Top end: More than US$100

- Room at top-end hotel or resort: over US$100
- Fine dining with wine: over US$25
- Car and driver per day: US$60

Opening Hours

Typical opening hours are as follows:

Banks 8am–2pm Monday to Thursday, 8am–noon Friday, 8am–11am Saturday

Government offices 8am–3pm Monday to Thursday, 8am–noon Friday (although these are not standardised)

Post offices 8am–2pm Monday to Friday, longer in tourist centres

Restaurants & cafes 8am–10pm daily

Shops & services catering to visitors 9am–8pm or later daily

Arriving in Bali, Lombok & Nusa Tenggara

Ngurah Rai International Airport, Bali A taxi to Kuta is 80,000Rp, to Seminyak it's 130,000Rp and to Ubud it's 300,000Rp.

Lombok International Airport A taxi is 150,000Rp to Kuta, 180,000Rp to Mataram, 300,000Rp to Senggigi and 350,000Rp to Bangsal.

El Tari Airport, West Timor Taxis from the airport to Kupang cost 70,000Rp. An ojek (motorcycle taxi) will cost 30,000Rp.

Gilimanuk, West Bali A bus trip from the depot close to the ferry port to Denpasar's Ubung terminal costs 45,000Rp; bemos (minivans) charge 5000Rp more.

For much more on **getting around**, see p451

First Time Bali, Lombok & Nusa Tenggara

For more information, see Survival Guide (p439)

Checklist

➡ Make certain your passport will be valid for six months after your date of arrival in Indonesia. This regulation is strictly enforced.

➡ Download Bali mapping data to the Google Maps app so you can navigate with your phone offline. In Nusa Tenggara printed maps are more useful.

➡ Inform your ATM and credit card issuers of your trip so you won't get locked out.

What to Pack

➡ Plug converter for Indonesia

➡ Insect spray and sunscreen; both are essential but can be hard to find or expensive locally

➡ Small umbrella

➡ A water bottle

Top Tips for Your Trip

➡ At the beach, don't swim near any water flowing into the ocean. You don't want to know what's in that water. And don't swim anywhere at all unless you've checked conditions carefully – strong rips can be deadly.

➡ Use the handy website Refill My Bottle (www.refillmybottle.com) to identify hotels and restaurants where you can refill your bottle with safe drinking water for free or for a negligible fee.

➡ Travel slowly; the people of this region are relaxed, so you can be too.

What to Wear

➡ Women topless at the beach or pool is offensive. Wandering around in a bathing suit elsewhere is not acceptable.

➡ Casual wear, shorts, cottons, short-sleeve shirts, sandals etc are all fine during the day.

➡ At fine-dining restaurants you should dress more formally (long pants for men; dresses, skirts or long pants for women).

➡ Some nightspots ban men in singlets.

➡ Don't wear clothing featuring alcohol branding – many locals find this offensive.

Sleeping

Bali and Lombok have a huge range of accommodation for any budget; options on Nusa Tenggara are more limited. If visiting in August or during the Christmas/New Year period, book well in advance.

Homestays & Guesthouses Family-run accommodation gives a true taste of local life.

Hostels Geared towards divers and surfers in Lombok and the Gilis.

Hotels Can range from simple thatch bungalows by the beach to boutique bungalows, or multistory buildings, set in lush gardens with a pool and restaurant.

Resorts This region (and Bali in particular) has some of the world's best and most affordable resorts.

Villas Often come with private pool, transport and maid service, making for a sybaritic stay.

Cash

The unit of currency is the rupiah (Rp). Coins of 50Rp, 100Rp, 200Rp, 500Rp and 1000Rp are in circulation. Notes come in 1000Rp (rare), 2000Rp, 5000Rp, 10,000Rp, 20,000Rp, 50,000Rp and 100,000Rp denominations.

Bargaining

Bargaining can be an enjoyable part of shopping in this region. Try following these steps:

➡ Have some idea of the item's worth.

➡ Establish a starting price – ask the seller for their price.

➡ Your first offer can be from one-third to two-thirds of that price.

➡ If you don't like the price, walk – the vendor may go lower.

➡ When you name a price, you're committed – you must buy if your offer is accepted.

Tipping

Restaurants Tipping a set percentage is not expected, but if service is good, 5000Rp or 10% or more is appropriate.

Services Hand cash directly to individuals (drivers, porters, people giving you a massage, bringing you beer at the beach etc); 5000Rp to 10,000Rp or 10% to 20% of the total is generous.

Hotels Most midrange and all top-end hotels add 21% to the bill for tax and service.

Spas Not mandatory, though 5% to 10% is appreciated.

Seminyak Beach (p81)

Etiquette

Indonesia is a pretty relaxed place, but there are a few rules of etiquette.

Body language Use both hands when handing somebody something. Don't show displays of affection in public or talk with your hands on your hips (it's seen as a sign of aggression).

Clothing Avoid showing a lot of skin, although many local men wear shorts. Don't go topless if you're a woman at any pool or beach.

Photography Before taking photos of someone, ask – or mime – for approval.

Places of worship Be respectful in sacred places. Remove shoes and dress modestly when visiting temples and mosques.

Eating

Bali is a splendid destination for food. The local cuisine, whether truly Balinese or influenced by the rest of Indonesia and Asia, draws from the bounty of fresh local foods and is rich with spices and flavours. Savour this fare at roadside warungs (simple local cafes) or top-end restaurants, and for tastes further afield, you can choose from restaurants offering some of the best dining in the region.

Food in Nusa Tenggara isn't quite as creative, but you'll have no trouble sourcing tasty meals. In Lombok and the Gilis, opt for simply prepared, freshly caught fish and seafood.

What's New

Pura Lempuyang

Perched on a hilltop on the side of Gunung Lempuyang, this temple's status as a tourism hotspot is a recent phenomenon, courtesy of safety issues associated with visiting the similarly sacred Pura Besikah. The complex comprises seven temples on the steep mountain slope and is one of the most important religious sites in east Bali. (p226)

Munduk's Majestic Waterfalls

Ready to chase waterfalls? The secret's out – new development has created easier access to sets of once-secluded cascades such as Banyu Wana Amertha. A visit to these falls, in the island's central mountains, is an adventure through lush rainforest and offers a glimpse into a truly local way of life. (p248)

Omnia

This modern mega day club at the bottom of the Bukit Peninsula is Bali's hottest place to dance to bumping hip-hop beats. Saddle up under the geometric architecture of the imposing outdoor bar and enjoy views of waves crashing into the jagged cliffs below. (p143)

Freediving

Holding one's breath while diving is becoming a popular alternative to scuba diving and snorkelling, especially near Jemeluk in east Bali and on the Gili Islands. (p228)

Digital Nomad Digs

New community-driven working and living spaces like Outsite in Canggu are making it ever easier for location-independent entrepreneurs and creatives to dwell productively in paradise. (p100)

Full Circle

Contemporary Australian cafe style has arrived in Ubud with a vengeance courtesy of this sleek coffee roastery. (p184)

Love Anchor Market

The weekend bazaar at Love Anchor, Canggu's hipster dining and retail complex, is a one-stop shop for traditional Balinese souvenirs and handmade wares by local creatives. (p104)

Mandalika Resort Area

Construction on the US$3 billion Mandalika Resort Area near Kuta in south Lombok is now in full force, with plans to turn it into a sandy playground for the rich and famous. (p309)

Pulau Moyo

Three years ago there was only one hotel on this West Sumbawan island paradise; now there are a half-dozen budget and mid-range accommodations, as well as two dive schools. (p340)

Gili Gede

New fast boat connections to Bali and Gili Trawangan and some of the best snorkelling in the region have contributed to the growing popularity of this island off Lombok's southwestern peninsula. (p297)

Kerewe Beach

Affordable accommodation options have opened in this celebrity hideaway spot in West Sumba, opening up its world-class beaches and surf breaks to all. (p392)

For more recommendations and reviews, see lonelyplanet.com/indonesia

If You Like...

Beaches

Seminyak Beach This wide stretch of sand boasts great surf for both swimmers and surfers. Don't miss sunset. (p81)

Jimbaran Beach Mellow surf, clean sand and lots of eateries make this a great spot to claim a sun lounger and spend a day. (p132)

Padang Padang Beach Great white sands and some of the best surfer-watching you'll find anywhere. (p140)

Nusa Lembongan Beaches Little coves of dreamy sand you can walk between, plus fab swimming. (p150)

Gili Island beaches The beaches are uniformly gorgeous, with white sand, nice snorkelling and a timeless traveller vibe. (p312)

Selong Blanak An idyllic Lombok bay and beach that astounds first-time visitors. (p311)

Senggigi Crescents of still-virgin sands lined with perky palms beckon travellers north from Lombok's original resort town. (p291)

Kuta The surrounding bays at this Lombok beach have enough pearly white sands to keep you busy for a week. (p304)

West Sumba One sensational scalloped beach after another. (p388)

Temples

Pura Luhur Batukau One of Bali's most important temples is a misty, remote place that's steeped in ancient spirituality. (p250)

Pura Taman Ayun A beautiful moated temple with a royal past; part of Unesco's recognition of Bali's rice-growing traditions. (p279)

Pura Lempuyang Older than most Balinese temples, this spectacularly sited *pura* on the slopes of Mount Lempuyang is one of the holiest sites of worship on the island. (p226)

Pura Luhur Ulu Watu As significant as it is popular, this temple has sweeping views, sunset dance performances and resident monkeys. (p141)

Nightlife

Seminyak Beach clubs where the cocktails somehow taste better when you can hear the surf. (p89)

Kuta All raw energy and a mad mix of party-goers enjoying every aspect of Bali hedonism. (p308)

Legian Beach bars and beanbags on the sand where the glow of sunset segues into the twinkle of stars. (p78)

Echo Beach A necklace of ephemeral beach bars runs along the sand going west; some have raves. (p105)

Gili Trawangan The place for pounding beats and party vibes just about every night (and day!) of the week. (p316)

Senggigi Sunset cocktails at a beachfront bar morphs into raucous karaoke nights. (p291)

Culture

Dance Rigid choreography and discipline are hallmarks of beautiful, melodic Balinese dance. (p418)

Gendang beleq Dance performances featuring big drums and warlike characters can be enjoyed during festivals in Senggigi, Lombok. (p418)

Gamelan The ensemble orchestra creates its unforgettable music with bamboo and bronze instruments at performances and celebrations. (p418)

Genggong Musicians in Lombok use a simple set of instruments, including a bamboo flute, a *rebab* (two-stringed bowed lute) and knockers in village performances. (p418)

Painting Balinese and Western styles merged in the 20th century and the results are often extraordinary. See some of the best in Ubud's museums. (p419)

Offerings Artful and ubiquitous in Bali. (p414)

Ikat Vividly coloured handwoven textiles featuring geometric and slightly wavy patterns are a regional passion; head to East Sumba to source collector-quality examples. (p422)

Diving & Snorkelling

Gili Trawangan World-class dive shops and an abundance of turtles are the key to Gili T's underwater pleasures. (p316)

Gili Gede See why the south-western Gilis now lure informed snorkellers away from their cousins to the north. (p297)

Belongas Two famed sites, Magnet and Cathedrals, entice advanced divers with the chance to spot schooling mobula rays. (p311)

Gili Kondo Have the crystalline water all to yourself when you snorkel at this 'secret gili' near the port of Labuhan Lombok. (p303)

Tulamben The wreck of the USAT *Liberty* is among the most popular dive sites on Bali. (p234)

Komodo National Park A rich marine ecosystem that affords divers unforgettable underwater adventures in a remote location. (p344)

Alor Archipelago Uncrowded dive sites where you can explore completely unspoiled reefs with vibrant soft and hard coral. (p372)

Top: Pura Taman Ayun (p279)

Bottom: Traditional Balinese offerings (p423)

Month by Month

TOP EVENTS

Pasola, February & March

Galungan, varies

Indonesian Independence Day, 17 August

Ubud Writers & Readers Festival, October

Bali Arts Festival, June to July

February

The rainy season pours on and Bali starts to hum again after the January pause following the holiday high season. Accommodation bargains abound at this time.

Bau Nyale Festival

The ritual harvesting of *nyale* (sea worms) takes place on Pantai Seger near Lombok's Kuta. The evening begins with poetry readings, continues with gamelan music performances and carries on until the dawn, when the *nyale* start appearing. Can also be held in March. (p304)

Pasola

Held annually in Lamboya, this West Sumbanese tournament between two teams of spear-wielding, ikat-clad horsemen is one of the most extravagant (and bloodiest) harvest festivals in Asia. Also held in Wanokaka in March.

March

As the rainy season comes to an end, there's a lull in the crowds – this is low season for tourism, especially around Nyepi when even many non-Balinese flee the silence.

Nyepi (Day of Silence)

Bali's major Hindu festival, Nyepi celebrates the end of the old year and the start of the next. It's marked by inactivity – a strategy to convince evil spirits that Bali is uninhabited so they'll leave the island alone for another year. For the Balinese, it's a day for meditation and introspection. The rules are more relaxed for foreigners as long as you don't leave your residence or hotel. Nyepi is actually a fantastic time to be in Bali – there are colourful festivals the night before, and there's something inspiring about being forced to do nothing. (p414)

April

The islands dry out after the rainy season and there's a small but noticeable uptick in visitors. This is another month when insiders recommend visiting.

Bali Spirit Festival

A hugely popular yoga, dance and music festival from the people behind the Yoga Barn in Ubud. There are more than 100 workshops and concerts, plus a market and more; tack on one of the pre- or post-retreats or other events to get more mileage from the experience. It's usually held in early April but may begin in late March. (p176)

Ubud Food Festival

At this three-day foodie festival, diverse and delicious Indonesian cuisine takes centre stage. Events include cooking demonstrations, workshops, forums, markets, food tours and film screenings. (p176)

June

The airport is getting busier, but much of what makes May a good month to visit also applies in June. Crowds of surfers and sun chasers descend upon the Bukit breaks.

Bali Arts Festival

This is the premier event on Bali's cultural calendar. Based at the Taman Wedhi Budaya arts centre in Denpasar, the festival is a great way to see traditional Balinese dances such as the Legong, Gambuh, Kecak, Barong and Baris, as village-based groups compete fiercely for local pride. Held mid-June to mid-July. (p118)

July

After August, July is the second-busiest month for visitors to Bali. Don't expect to have your pick of places to stay, but do plan to enjoy the energy of crowds on holiday.

Bali Kite Festival

In south Bali scores of kites soar overhead much of the year. Often huge (10m-plus), they fly at altitudes that worry pilots. There's a spiritual connection to their flight: it is believed the kites urge the gods to provide abundant harvests. During this festival (p128) the skies fill with huge creations.

Surf Contests

The exact names and sponsorships change every year but you'll find top international surf contests being held throughout July or August down at Padang

Top: Ceremony at Pura Tirta Empul (p198)
Bottom: Bali Kite Festival (p128), Sanur

Padang Beach. Peak tourist season coincides with peak wave season.

August

The busiest time on Bali sees an ever-increasing number of visitors each year. Book your room and tables far, far in advance and expect crowds.

Indonesian Independence Day

Celebrated across Indonesia, 17 August is the day Indonesia's independence from the Dutch was declared in 1945. Flags fly high and you'll encounter legions of school kids marching with great enthusiasm on Bali's main roads. Traffic is snarled (as it is days before for rehearsals) and lots of fireworks are shot off.

Ubud Village Jazz Festival

Annual two-day jazz festival featuring an international line-up of performers. (p176)

GALUNGAN & KUNINGAN

One of Bali's major festivals, Galungan celebrates the death of a legendary tyrant called Mayadenawa. Celebrations culminate with the Kuningan festival, when the Balinese say thanks and goodbye to the gods.

Every village in Bali celebrates Galungan and Kuningan in grand style, and visitors are welcome to join in.

The 210-day *wuku* (or *pawukon*) calendar is used to determine festival dates. Dates for future Galungan and Kuningan celebrations are as follows:

Year	Galungan	Kuningan
2019	22 Jul	5 Jan & 3 Aug
2020	19 Feb & 16 Sep	29 Feb & 26 Sep
2021	14 Apr & 10 Nov	24 Apr & 20 Nov

October

The skies darken more often with seasonal rains, but mostly the weather is pleasant and the islanders bustle about their normal business. Outside of Ubud, crowds are few.

Ubud Writers & Readers Festival

One of the country's premier literary events, this festival hosts scores of writers and readers from around the world in a celebration of writing – especially that which touches on Bali. Each year there is a theme and famous authors whose works address the topic attend. (p176)

Bali Vegan Festival

Aiming to inspire converts to the vegan lifestyle, this three-day festival includes talks, cooking demonstrations, workshops and films in Ubud and Canguu. (p176)

November

It's getting wetter, but not really so wet that you can't enjoy the islands to the fullest. Crowd-wise, this is usually a quiet month, which means you can find great accommodation bargains.

Perang Topat

This 'rice war' on Lombok is fun. It takes place at Pura Lingsar just outside Mataram and involves a costumed parade, and Hindus and Wektu Telu pelting balls of *ketupat* (sticky rice) at each other. Can also be held in December.

December

Visitors rain on Bali ahead of the Christmas and New Year holidays. Most hotels and restaurants are booked out and everybody is busy; in the south, the energy can seem manic.

Peresean

Martial arts Lombok-style. Competitors, stripped to the waist, spar with rattan sticks and cowhide shields. Contests are typically held in Mataram late in the month, but you can catch bouts on just about any major holiday. (p290)

Itineraries

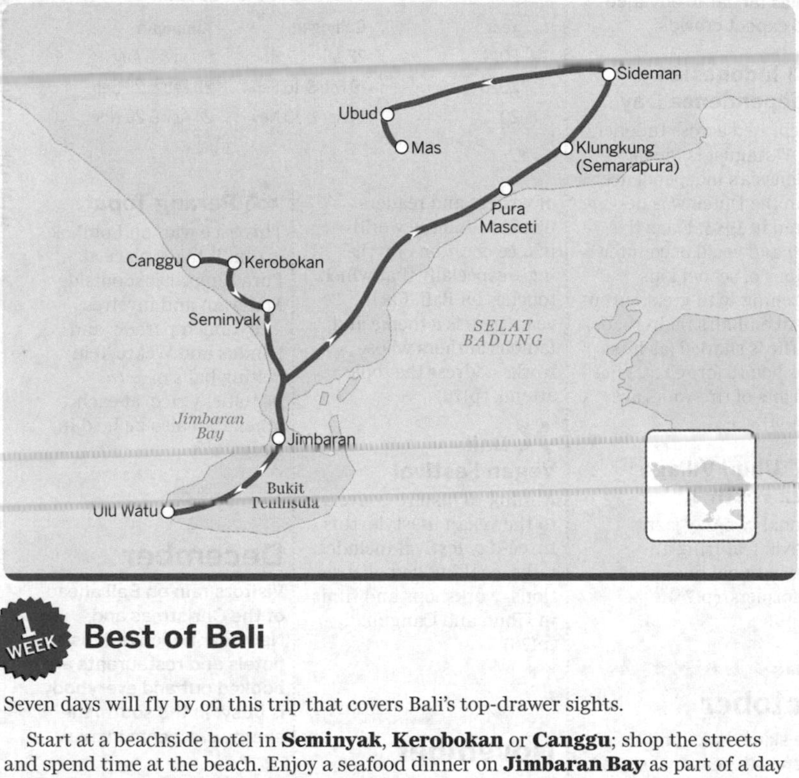

Best of Bali

Seven days will fly by on this trip that covers Bali's top-drawer sights.

Start at a beachside hotel in **Seminyak**, **Kerobokan** or **Canggu**; shop the streets and spend time at the beach. Enjoy a seafood dinner on **Jimbaran Bay** as part of a day trip to the monkey-filled temple at **Ulu Watu**.

In the east, take the coast road to wild beaches like the one near **Pura Masceti**, followed by the town of **Klungkung (Semarapura)**, once the royal seat of Bali's most important kingdom. Head north up to **Sideman**, which combines rice terraces with lush river valleys and cloud-shrouded mountains. Then go west to **Ubud**, the crowning glory on any itinerary.

To spoil yourself, stay in one of Ubud's many hotels with views across rice fields and rivers. Sample the offerings at a spa before you try one of the myriad great restaurants. Bali's rich culture is most celebrated and most accessible in Ubud and you'll be captivated by nightly dance performances. Check out local craft studios, including the woodcarvers of **Mas**. Hike through the surrounding rice fields to river valleys, taking a break in museums bursting with paintings.

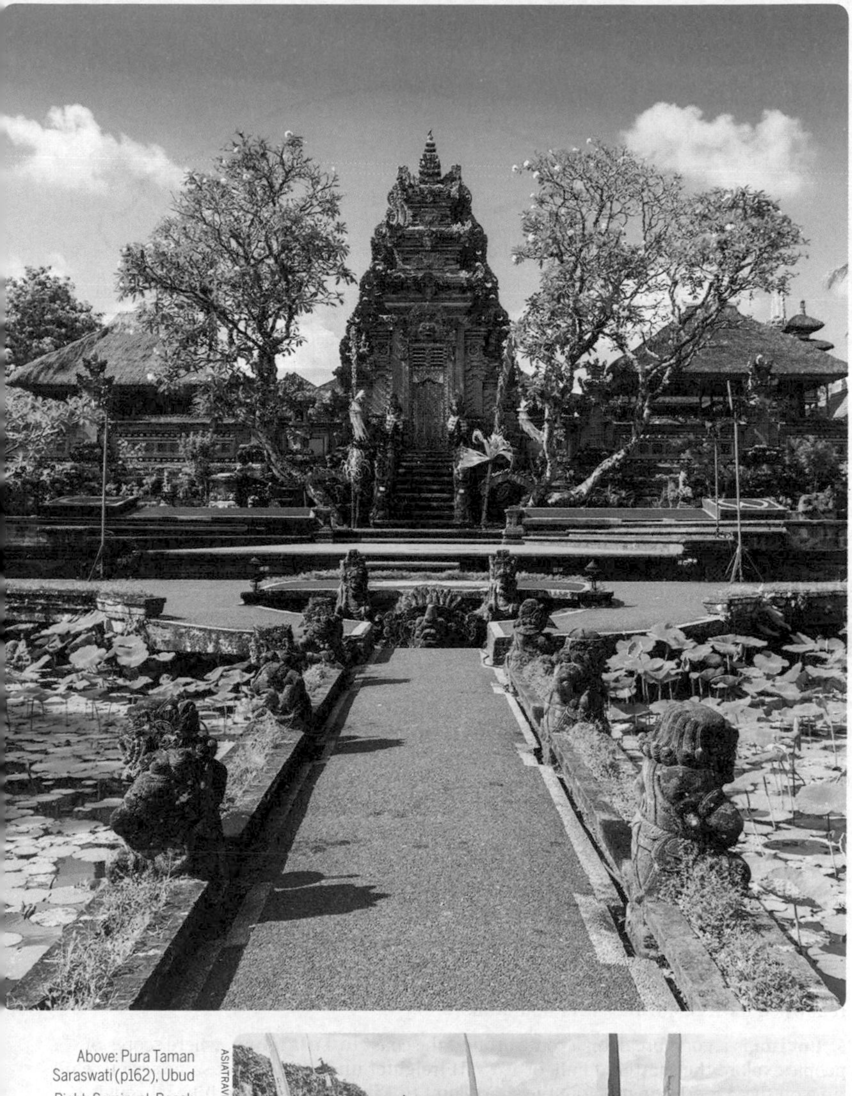

Above: Pura Taman Saraswati (p162), Ubud
Right: Seminyak Beach (p81)

ASIATRAVEL/SHUTTERSTOCK ©

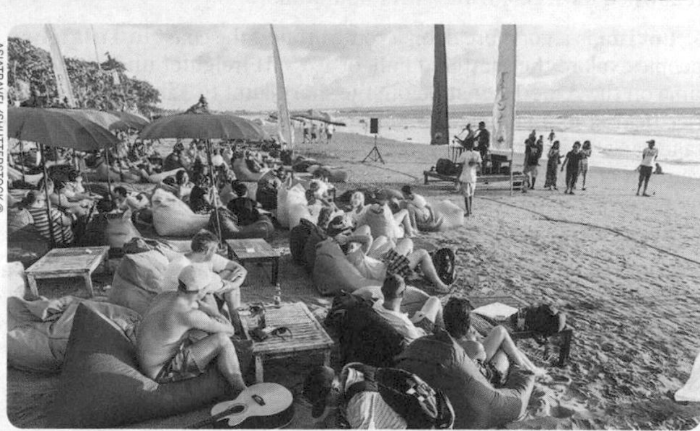

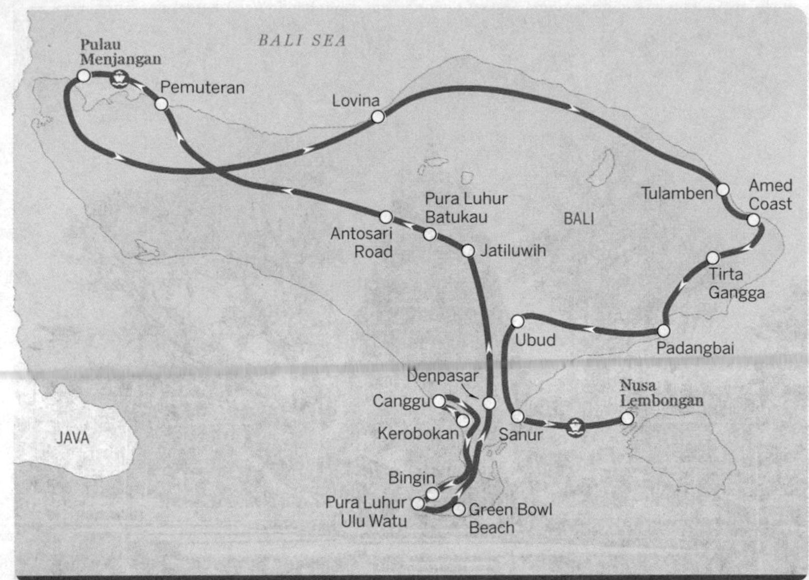

Bali at a Slow Pace

Find accommodation close to the beach in **Kerobokan**. Be sure to get to the trendy restaurants and cafes of **Canggu** before you leave this part of south Bali behind. Maybe you can learn how to surf, or at least brush up on your skills, before you head south to **Bingin** and its cliff-side inns overlooking the surf. Make the short drive down to Bukit Peninsula's spiritual centre (and monkey home) **Pura Luhur Ulu Watu** and explore the secluded beaches at the bottom of Bali, such as **Green Bowl Beach**.

Take a trip through **Denpasar** and stop at the excellent local restaurants and museum. Next, Bali's ancient rice terraces will exhaust your abilities to describe green. Sample these in a drive up to the terraces of **Jatiluwih** followed by the lyrical **Pura Luhur Batukau**. Make your way over the mountains via the **Antosari Road**, pausing at a remote hotel on the way. Head west to **Pemuteran**, where the hotels and resorts define relaxation. Dive or snorkel nearby **Pulau Menjangan** in Bali Barat National Park. It's renowned for its coral and sheer 30m wall.

Lovina is a good break on a route around the coast to **Tulamben**, where scores of people explore the shattered hulk of a WWII freighter underwater. Get some serious chill time on the **Amed Coast** before the short jaunt to **Tirta Gangga** and hikes through rice fields and up jungle-clad hills to remote temples. Continue to **Padangbai** and then take back roads to **Ubud**. Find your favourite cafe and let the world wander past, or rid yourself of travel kinks at a spa. You might consider staying at one of the iconic family homestays, taking gentle walks through rice fields by day and marvelling at dance performances at night.

When you're ready and rested, get a fast boat from **Sanur** to **Nusa Lembongan**. This little island has its own buzz, with a string of hotels – from basic to semiposh – lining its sands. It's a timeless travellers' scene with a backdrop of excellent surfing and splendid snorkelling and diving.

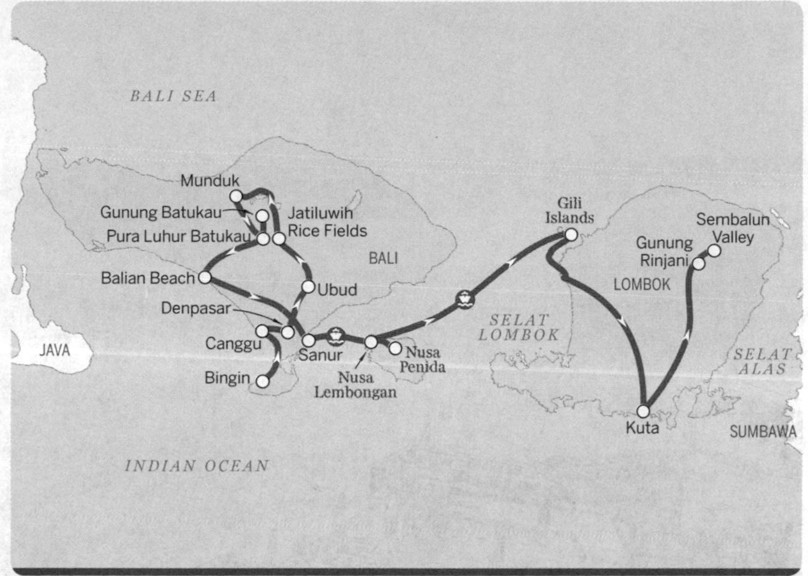

Total Bali & Lombok

You'll visit six islands and countless beaches on a trip that takes you to the most interesting sites and places across Bali, Lombok and the Gilis.

Begin your trip at **Bingin**. Settle back in the sand and let the jet lag vanish. Then move to **Canggu** for Bali's hippest scene. Transit through **Denpasar** for a purely Balinese lunch and head up the hill to **Ubud** to get a taste of traditional Balinese culture over two or three days. Next, visit the **Jatiluwih Rice Fields**, centuries old rice terraces that have received Unesco World Heritage status in recognition of their ancient rice-growing culture.

Next, head west to the village of **Munduk**, which looks down to the north coast and the sea beyond. Go for a walk in the area and enjoy waterfalls, truly tiny villages, wild fruit trees and the sinuous ribbons of rice paddies lining the hills. Then head south to the wonderful temple of **Pura Luhur Batukau** and consider a trek up Bali's second-highest mountain, **Gunung Batukau**. Recover with some chill-out time on popular **Balian Beach**, just west.

Next, bounce across the waves from **Sanur** to **Nusa Lembongan**, the island hiding in the shadow of **Nusa Penida**. The latter is visible from much of the south and east – it makes a good day trip. Take in the amazing vistas from its cliffs and dive under the waves to check out the marine life.

Head to the **Gili Islands** on the direct boat from Nusa Lembongan for more tranquil time circumnavigating the three islands above and below the idyllic sapphire waters fringing them. Take a boat to Senggigi, but ignore the resorts and head south. Still off the beaten path, the south coast near Lombok's **Kuta** has stunning beaches and surfing to reward the intrepid. The seldom-driven back roads of the interior will thrill the adventurous and curious, with tiny villages where you can learn about the amazing local handicrafts. Many of these roads travel through the foothills of sacred **Gunung Rinjani**, the volcanic peak that shelters the lush and remote **Sembalun Valley**.

WERNERMUELLERSCHELL/SHUTTERSTOCK ©

Above: Ulu Watu (p141)

Left: Beach swing, Gili Air (p329)

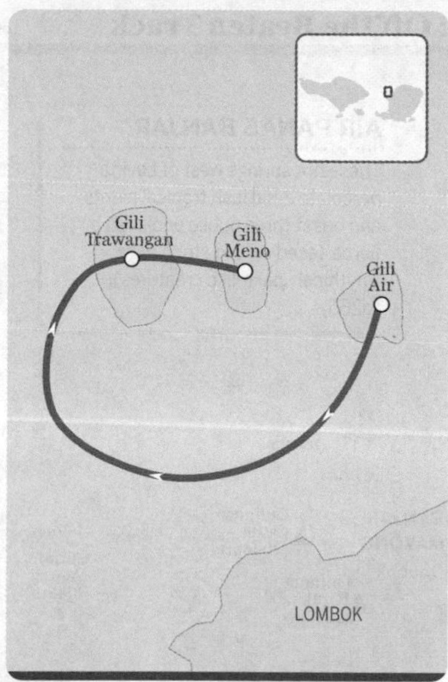

1 WEEK Gili Islands in One Week

These three little dots of white sand off Lombok can easily occupy your entire trip, with their top-class options for diving, dining, partying and sunbathing. The ideal place to get to grips with island life is **Gili Air**, where the main beachfront strip is perfect tropical lounging territory. You can while away a day or two doing nothing but chilling with a book, taking a cooling dip, perfecting your asanas at a yoga school or feasting on inexpensive fresh seafood.

Next up is **Trawangan**, where there's much more action. The perfect day here could start with a morning dive at a site such as Shark Point, followed by a healthy vegan lunch and an afternoon snooze. Then take a gentle stroll round the sandy lanes of the island, slipping in a sunset cocktail on the west coast. After dinner, feel the beat at one of Trawangan's parties.

The final stop is **Gili Meno**, where, once you've secured the perfect place to stay (including at some new upscale choices), there's little to do except ponder the sheer desert-isle-ness of the place. If you can drag yourself away from the beach, try snorkelling out to the underwater sculpture Nest or egret-spotting on the inland lake.

2 WEEKS Surfing Bali

Ease into a tour of Bali's best surf in the **Kuta** area. The surf break Halfway Kuta is the best scene for beginners; **Legian Beach** has more powerful breaks. North of **Kerobokan**, on the northern extremity of the bay, **Batu Bolong** (often called Canggu) has a nice beach with light-coloured sand and a chilled party scene.

Next, head west to classic surfer hangout **Balian Beach**, where there are a few peaks near the mouth of Sungai Balian (Balian River). Further up the south coast of western Bali is a soft left called **Medewi**, a point break that can give a long ride right into the river mouth.

End the circuit in south Bali, where surfing sparked tourism on the island. **Balangan** is a fast left over a shallow reef; **Bingin** has short but perfect left-hand barrels. **Padang Padang's** super-shallow, left-hand reef break is a very demanding break that only works over about 6ft from mid- to high tide (if you can't surf tubes, backhand or forehand, don't go out). **Ulu Watu**, the most famous surfing spot in Bali, has about seven different breaks (observe where other surfers paddle out and follow them).

Bali, Lombok & Nusa Tenggara: Off the Beaten Track

AROUND ANTOSARI & MAYONG

Take the road between Antosari and Mayong and you'll pass rice paddies and terraces, fragrant spice-growing villages, coffee plantations and an eminently Instagrammable rice-growing valley near Subuk. (p251)

AIR PANAS BANJAR

These hot springs west of Lovina percolate amid lush tropical plants and boast three public pools fed by fierce-faced carved stone *naga* (mythical snake-like creatures). (p265)

KEROBOKAN

Kerobokan has more than its fair shares of tourists, but wander a couple of kilometres east of its infamous jail and you'll discover tourist-free streets lined with shops making and selling a fascinating array of local products. (p92)

SIKKA

One of Flores' first Portuguese settlements, this charming seaside village 6km off the Trans-Flores Hwy south of Maumere has a handsome 19th-century cathedral. (p365)

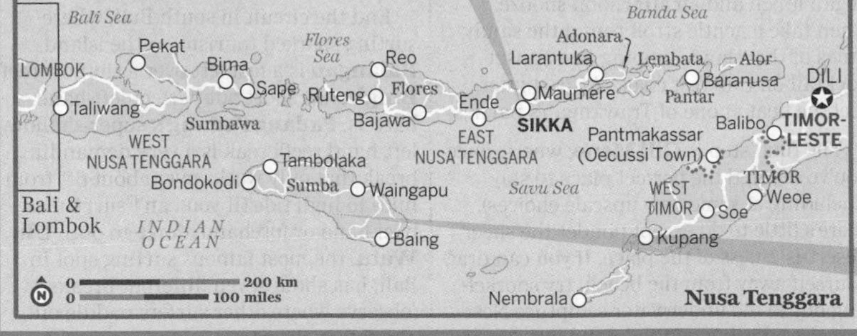

TABANAN TO THE COAST

The rarely traversed route from Tabanan to Gilimanuk passes villages producing traditional pottery, a secluded beach at Yeh Gangga and the village of Kerambitan, known for its dance troupe, musicians and 17th-century palace. (p278)

GELUMPANG

Located in the fertile green foothills of Gunung Agung, the farming village of Gelumpang is home to a restaurant and cooking school that receives rave reviews from food-focussed travellers. (p225)

PEJENG

Once the ancient capital of a powerful Balinese kingdom, temple-rich Pejeng is now part of greater Ubud and an easy ride or walk from the centre of town. (p179)

SOUTHWEST GILIS

Untouched corals and a wealth of marine life make the waters in this little-visited group of islands a perfect destination for those who enjoy crowd-free snorkelling. (p312)

SOUTH CENTRAL SUMBA

It can be a hard slog to reach this remote region, but if you're a keen surfer the trip will be worth it because the waves at Pantai Tarimbang, 95km southwest of Waingapu, are terrific. (p387)

Plan Your Trip
Activities

This region is an incredible place to get outside and play – enjoy exceptional diving and surfing, and hikes through rice fields or up volcanoes. Indoors, you can learn to cook local meals, make yourself a souvenir or bend into new shapes in the pursuit of bliss.

Best Experiences

Top Surfing

In Bali, surfing at world famous Ulu Watu is an experience that every serious surfer needs to tackle once. Its surrounds, including Padang Padang and Bingin, are great too. In Lombok, remote Tanjung Desert is home to a left-handed tube that has been described as the best wave in the world.

Top Diving & Snorkelling

Pulau Menjangan on Bali is spectacular, whether you're just drifting or following a wall. Tulamben's sunken WWII freighter and coral-encrusted reefs are also popular spots. Jemeluk in Amed is accruing a reputation as a freediving hotspot. Southwest Lombok has healthy reefs teeming with marine life and the waters off the Gili Islands are famed for their extraordinary coral and marine life.

Top Hiking

On Bali, Munduk's lush, spice-scented, waterfall-riven landscape is a stunner. There are beautiful walks lasting from one hour to one day in Ubud and its rice-field surrounds. Tirta Gangga is great for emerald rice terraces, gorgeous views and temples. On Lombok, communities, hotels and businesses are still recovering from the 2018 earthquakes (p299), but the climb up 3726m-high Gunung Rinjani and the Sembalun Valley on its slopes draws hikers from around the world.

Courses

Opportunities for specialised courses and workshops abound in Bali, where you can learn everything from woodcarving and batik to jewellery making and traditional dance. These two centres in Ubud are worth checking out for a range of cultural activities:

ARMA (p171) Classes in painting, batik, woodcarving, dance, Hinduism and architecture.

Pondok Pekak Library & Learning Centre (p171) Huge range of courses, from dance and music to woodcarving and Bahasa Indonesia.

Cooking

If you want to carry on enjoying the tastes of Indonesia after you go home, Bali has several cooking schools where you can learn everything from how to shop in the markets and the basics of Indonesian cuisine to advanced cooking techniques. Many are taught by chefs with reputations well beyond Bali and you get to eat what you make! Here are some of the best.

Southwest Beaches

Warung Eny (p95) Learn how to cook Balinese dishes from the owner, Eny, at her tiny warung (food stall) in Kerobokan.

South Bali & the Islands

Bumbu Bali Cooking School (p147) Classes run by long-time resident and cookbook author Heinz von Holzen from his excellent South Bali restaurant.

Balinese Cooking Class (p127) Beachfront Balinese cooking in Sanur.

Ubud

Casa Luna Cooking School (p173) Half-day courses cover cooking techniques, ingredients and the cultural background of the Balinese kitchen.

Balinese Farm Cooking School (p197) Vegetarian, vegan and omnivore courses taught by locals in a village north of Ubud.

East Bali

Bali Asli (p225) Restaurant and cooking school near Amlapura that combines spectacular views with some of the best food in Bali.

Smiling Buddha Restaurant (p234) Organic Balinese dishes in Aas.

North Bali

Warung Bambu (p262) Market trips and classic Balinese dishes in Pemaron, near Lovina.

Santai Warung (p270) Excellent Indonesian restaurant that offers cooking classes in Pemuteran.

ART & DESIGN CLASSES IN UBUD

Ubud is a veritable hotbed of cultural workshops and courses and enrolling in one is a great way to take a piece of Bali home with you. Check out the following course providers:

Nirvana Batik Course (p173) Batik techniques taught over one to five days.

Studio Perak (p173) Balinese-style silversmithing.

Ida Bagus Anom (p200) Traditional mask carving, south of town.

Wayan Karja Painting (p173) Learn painting and drawing classes from a celebrated local artist.

Threads of Life Indonesian Textile Arts Center (p171) Textile-appreciation courses run by a well-respected gallery.

Cycling

Cyclists are increasingly common on Bali's busy roads. The main advantage of touring Bali by bike is the quality of the experience – you can be totally immersed in the environment, hearing the wind rustling in the rice paddies or the sound of a gamelan practising while catching the scent of flowers. The island's back roads more than make up for the traffic-clogged streets of the south.

Some people are put off cycling in a tropical location, but when you're riding on level ground or downhill, the breeze really moderates the heat.

Bali

Denpasar, south through Sanur in the east, and Kerobokan to Kuta in the west suffer from lots of traffic and narrow roads. But across the rest of the island you can find many rides that reward with lush tropical beauty. For something really different, try the still-lonely lanes of Nusa Penida.

Popular tours start high in the central mountains at places such as Kintamani or Bedugul. The tour company takes you to the top and then you ride down relatively quiet mountain roads, soaking up the lush scenery, village culture and tropical scents.

The cost including bicycle, gear and lunch is US$40 to US$80. Transport to/from south Bali and Ubud hotels is usually included; hotel pick-up in Kuta can be as early as 6.30am. Tours usually run from 8.30am to 4pm and involve a lot of coasting and stopping. Not all companies provide helmets; make sure yours does.

Companies to consider:

Archipelago Adventure (☎0851 0208 1769, mobile 0812 3850517; www.archipelago-adventure.com; adult/child from US$55/45) Offers a huge and interesting range of tours. On Bali, there are rides around Jatiluwih and Danau Buyan, and mountain biking on trails from Kintamani.

Bali Bike-Baik Tours (☎0361-978052; www.balibike.com; tours from 500,000Rp) Tours run downhill from Kintamani. The emphasis is on cultural immersion and there are frequent stops in tiny villages and at rice farms.

Bali Eco Cycling (☎0361-975557; www.baliecocycling.com; adult/child from US$50/30) Tours start at Kintamani and take small roads through lush scenery south to Ubud; other options focus on rural culture.

Banyan Tree Cycling Tours (p173) Enjoy day-long tours of remote villages in the hills above Ubud. It's locally owned by Bagi and very popular. The tours emphasise interaction with villagers; there is also an extreme cycling tour.

Bung Bung Adventure Biking (p226) Based in Tirta Gangga, these tours follow back roads in fecund east Bali that are ignored by other tours.

C.Bali (p242) Offers excellent bike tours in and around Gunung Batur and the lake. The antidote to cookie-cutter bike tours.

Lombok

Lombok is good for touring by bicycle. In the populated areas, the roads are flat and well paved, and the traffic across the island is less chaotic than on Bali.

East of Mataram are several attractions that would make a good day trip: south to Banyumulek via Gunung Pengsong and then back to Mataram, for example. Some coastal roads have hills and curves like a roller coaster. Try going north from Senggigi to Pemenang along the spectacular paved road, and then (if you feel energetic) return via the steep climb over the Pusuk Pass.

Bicycles are available for hire on the Gili Islands as a means to get around; Trawangan (p316) is best suited for exploration.

Equipment

Serious cyclists will want to pack personal gear they consider essential. Bali Bike Hire (p98) stocks top-end gear not found elsewhere. Casual riders can rent bikes and helmets in many locations but they are often in poor condition; when in doubt ask at your accommodation.

Diving & Snorkelling

With their warm water, extensive coral reefs and abundant marine life, Bali and Nusa Tenggara offer excellent diving and snorkelling adventures. Reliable dive schools and operators throughout the region (particularly in Bali, in the Gilis and in Labuan Bajo in Flores) can train complete beginners or arrange challenging trips that will satisfy the most experienced divers.

Snorkelling gear is available near all the most accessible spots but it's worthwhile bringing your own and checking out some of the less-visited parts of the coasts.

Where to Dive & Snorkel

Bali

Bali's most spectacular diving and snorkelling locations draw people from near and far. Skilled divers will enjoy the challenges of Nusa Penida (p157), as well as the schools of manta rays and 2.5m sunfish, but novices and snorkellers will be in over their heads. Spectacular 30m walls await off Pulau Menjangan (p268) and are good for

TOP CYCLING SPOTS IN BALI

You can't get too lost on an island as small as Bali. The following are areas good for exploring on two wheels.

LOCATION	DETAILS
Bukit Peninsula	Explore cliffs, coves and beaches along the west and south coasts; beach promenade at Nusa Dua; avoid the congested area by the airport
Central Mountains	Ambitious routes; explore Danau Bratan, Danau Buyan and Danau Tamblingan; ride downhill to the north coast via Munduk and to the south via small roads from Candikuning
East Bali	The coast road is lined with beaches; north of the coast is uncrowded with serene rice terraces; the Sideman area has lodges good for cyclists
North Bali	Lovina is a good base for day trips to remote waterfalls and temples; the northeast coast has resorts popular with cyclists circumnavigating Bali
Nusa Lembongan	Small, with beaches that make good goals for each ride; cross the cool narrow suspension bridge and explore Nusa Ceningan
Nusa Penida	For serious cyclists who bring bikes; nearly traffic-free, with remote vistas of the sea, sheer cliffs, white beaches and lush jungle
Ubud	Many tour companies are based here; narrow mountain roads lead to ancient monuments and jaw-dropping rice-terrace views
West Bali	Rice fields and dense jungle rides in and around Tabanan, Kerambitan and Bajera; further west, small roads off the main road lead to mountain streams, deserted beaches and hidden temples

Cyclist, Lombok (p283)

divers and snorkellers of all skills and ages. Tulamben (p234), with its sunken WWII freighter, is another site for both divers and snorkellers with good swimming skills.

Lombok

Southwest Lombok boasts healthy reefs teeming with marine life. Divers and snorkellers need good swimming skills here.

Gili Islands

Divers and snorkellers of all skills and ages head here to enjoy all types of diving and snorkelling in beautiful waters. Some sites may require advanced skills.

Komodo & Rinca Islands

These isolated islands have some of the most exhilarating scuba diving in Indonesia, if not the world. It's a region swept by strong currents and cold upswells, created by the convergence of the warmer Flores Sea with the cooler Selat Sumba (Sumba Strait). These conditions create a rich plankton soup that feeds an astonishing variety of marine life. Manta rays and whales are drawn here during their migration from the Indian Ocean to the South China Sea, dolphins are common in the waters between Komodo and Flores and you're likely to spot white-tip and reef sharks more fearful of you than you are of them. Coral is almost pristine. Liveaboards ply these waters between April and September when diving is at its finest. Dive shops in Labuan Bajo (p349) on Flores can organise trips and equipment hire.

Sumbawa

Good reefs with a plunging wall can be found all around Pulau Moyo (p340).

Alor Archipelago

With unspoiled reefs and vibrant soft and hard coral intact, diving Alor is a special experience. You'll encounter wall dives, slopes, caves, pinnacles, reefs and impressive muck diving. For more information, see p373.

Equipment

If you are not picky, you'll find all the equipment you need in Bali, the Gilis and Lombok (the quality, size and age of the equipment can vary). If you bring your own, you can usually get a discount on your dive. Some small, easy-to-carry things to bring from home include

RESPONSIBLE DIVING

Bear in mind the following tips when diving and help preserve the ecology and beauty of reefs:

- Never use anchors on reefs, and take care not to run boats aground on coral.
- Avoid touching or standing on living marine organisms or dragging equipment across the reef.
- Be careful with your fins. Even without contact, the surge from fin strokes near the reef can damage delicate organisms. Don't kick up clouds of sand, which can smother organisms.
- Practise and maintain proper buoyancy control. Major damage can occur from reef collisions.
- Do not collect or buy coral or shells, or loot marine archaeological sites.
- Ensure that you take home all your rubbish and any other litter you may find as well. Plastics are a serious threat to marine life.
- Do not feed the fish.
- Minimise your involvement with marine animals. *Never* ride on the backs of turtles.

protective gloves, spare straps, silicone lubricant and extra globes/bulbs for your torch/flashlight. Tanks and weight belts are usually included in the cost of the dive. Other equipment to consider bringing:

Mask, snorkel & fins Many people bring these as they are not too big to pack and you can be sure they will fit you. Snorkelling gear rents from about 50,000Rp per day and is often shabby.

Thin, full-length wetsuit For protection against stinging animals and possible coral abrasions. Bring your own if you are worried about size. If diving off Nusa Penida, you'll need a wetsuit thicker than 3mm, as up-swells bring up 18°C water from the deep.

Regulators & BCVs Most dive shops have decent ones. (BCVs are also known as BCDs or buoyancy control devices.)

Dive Operators

Major dive operators in tourist areas can arrange trips to the main dive sites in their regions. Distances can be long, so it's better to sleep relatively close to your diving destination.

For a local trip, count on US$60 to US$100 per person for two dives, which includes all equipment. Note that it is becoming common to price dives in euros.

Wherever there is decent local diving there are dive shops. Usually you can count on some reefs in fair condition being reachable by boat. Recommended sites with shops include the following:

Bali

- Amed (p228)
- Lovina (p259)
- Nusa Lembongan (p152)
- Nusa Penida (p157)
- Padangbai (p216)
- Pemuteran (p267)
- Sanur (p120)
- Tulamben (p234)

Lombok

- Kuta (p304)
- Senggigi (p291)

Gili Islands

- Gili Air (p329)
- Gili Meno (p325)
- Gili Trawangan (p316)

Sumbawa

- Pulau Moyo (p340)
- Pantai Lakey (p342)

Flores

- Labuan Bajo (p350)

Choosing a Dive Operator

In general, diving here is safe, with a good standard of staff training and equipment maintenance. There are decompression chambers in Sanur in Bali and at Rumah

Sakit Harapan Keluarga (p458) in Mataram in West Lombok. Here are a few things to consider when selecting a well-set-up and safety-conscious dive shop.

Are its staff fully trained and qualified? Ask to see certificates or certification cards – no reputable shop will be offended by this request. Guides must reach 'full instructor' level to teach. To guide certified divers on a reef dive, guides must hold at least 'rescue diver' or preferably 'dive master' qualifications.

Do they have safety equipment on the boat? At a minimum, a dive boat should carry oxygen and a first-aid kit. A radio or mobile phone is also important.

Is the boat's equipment OK and its air clean? This is often the hardest thing for a new diver to judge. To test this, smell the air: open a tank valve a small way and breathe in. Smelling dry or slightly rubbery air is OK. If it smells of oil or car exhaust, that tells you the operator doesn't filter the air correctly.

When the equipment is put together, are there any big air leaks? All dive centres get some small leaks in equipment some time; however, if you get a *big* hiss of air coming out of any piece of equipment, ask to have it replaced.

Is the organisation conservation-oriented? Good dive shops explain that you should not touch coral or take shells from the reef, and they work with local fishing people to ensure that certain areas are protected. Some even clean beaches.

Learn to Dive

If you're not a qualified diver and you want to try scuba diving in this part of the world, you have several options, including packages that include lessons and cheap accommodation in a pretty place.

COURSE	DETAILS	COST
Introductory/ orientation	Perfect for novices to see if diving is for them	US$60-100
Basic certification	Three- or four-day limited courses for the basics; popular at resorts	US$300-400
Open Water certification	The international PADI standard, recognised everywhere	US$350-500

Guided Tours

Standardised organised tours are a convenient and popular way to visit a few places in Bali. There are dozens and dozens of operators who provide a similar product and service. Much more interesting are specialised tour companies that can take you far off the beaten track, offer memorable experiences and otherwise show you a different side of Bali. You can also easily arrange your own custom tour.

Standard Day Tours

Tours are typically in white minibuses with air-con, which pick up/drop off at your hotel. Prices typically range from 250,000Rp to 700,000Rp for what are essentially similar tours, so it pays to shop around. Consider the following:

- Will lunch be at a huge tourist buffet or somewhere more interesting?
- How much time will be spent at tourist shops?
- Will there be a qualified English-speaking guide?
- Are early morning pick-ups for the convenience of the company, which will then dump you at a central point to wait for another bus?

Specialist Tours

Many Bali tour operators offer experiences that vary from the norm. These can include cultural experiences hard for the casual visitor to find, such as cremations or trips to remote villages where life has hardly changed in decades. Often you'll avoid the clichéd tourist minibus and travel in unusual vehicles or in high comfort.

Hanafi (p80) This legendary tour guide operates from Kuta. Customises trips of all kinds, whether for families or couples. Gay friendly too.

JED (p449) Community-based, it organises highly regarded tours of small villages, some overnight.

Suta Tours (☎0361-462666, 0361-466783; www.sutatour.com; prices vary) Arranges standard tours and also trips to cremation ceremonies and temple festivals, market tours and other custom plans.

Hiking & Trekking

You could travel through this region for a year and still not see all the islands have to offer, but their relatively small size means that you can nibble off a bit at a time, especially as day hikes and treks are easily arranged. Guides can help you surmount volcanoes, while tour companies will take you to remote regions and emerald-green valleys of rice terraces. In terms of what to pack, you'll need good boots for mountain treks and solid hiking sandals for walks.

Where to Hike

Bali

Bali is very walkable. No matter where you're staying, ask for recommendations and set off for discoveries and adventures. Ubud (p162), the Sideman area and Munduk (p248) are obvious choices. The adjoining lakes of Danau Tamblingan and Danau Buyan (p247) are great places to explore and feature two different groups of great local guides. Even from busy Kuta or Seminyak, you can just head to the beach, turn right and walk north as far as you wish alongside the amazing surf while civilisation seems to evaporate.

For strenuous treks that verge on mountain climbing, consider Gunung Agung (p211) or Gunung Batur (p239). Note that at the time of writing Agung had an official Level 3 (standby) alert, with an exclusion zone of 4km around its crater, and Batur wasn't accessible due to an official exclusion zone having been put in place due to concerns about potential eruptions). There are varying routes, none of which take longer than a day. Bali does not offer remote wilderness treks beyond the volcano climbs and day trips within Bali Barat National Park (Taman Nasional Bali Barat). For the most part, you'll make day trips from the closest village, often leaving before dawn to avoid the clouds and mist that usually blanket the peaks by mid-morning. No treks require camping gear.

Lombok

Gunung Rinjani draws trekkers from around the world. Besides being Indonesia's second-tallest volcano, it holds cultural and spiritual significance for the various people of the region. And then there's its stunning beauty: a 6km-wide cobalt blue lake nestled beneath the rim of the vast caldera. Expert advice is crucial on the mountain – people die on its slopes every year. You can organise explorations of Gunung Rinjani at Sembalun Valley, Senaru and Tetebatu. See p299 for information on the impact of the 2018 earthquakes.

Sumbawa

Massive, climbable Gunung Tambora (2722m), which once had an explosion so large it changed the climate of the planet, is the main draw here. From its summit there are spectacular views of the 6km-wide caldera, which contains a two-coloured lake, and also of endless ocean vistas that stretch as far as Gunung Rinjani.

Komodo & Rinca Islands

Komodo National Park (p345) offers excellent hiking opportunities. As well as short walks there's a long trek and a range of adventure treks that are up to 10km long. One trek climbs the 538m-high Gunung Ara, which offers expansive views from the summit.

Flores

Climbing breathtakingly beautiful Gunung Inerie (2245m), a volcano just 10km from Bajawa, is difficult but rewarding.

HIKING HIGHLIGHTS: BALI

One of Bali's great joys is hiking. You can have good experiences across the island, often starting right outside your hotel. Hikes can last from an hour to a day.

LOCATION	DETAILS
Danau Buyan & Danau Tamblingan	Natural mountain lakes, few people, great guides
Gunung Agung	Sunrises and isolated temples
Gunung Batukau	Misty climbs amid the clouds, with few people
Gunung Batur	Hassles but other-worldly scenery
Munduk	Lush, spice-scented, waterfall-riven landscape
Sideman area	Rice terraces, lush hills and lonely temples; comfy lodging for walkers
Bali Barat National Park	Remote, wild scenery, wildlife
Tirta Gangga	Rice terraces, gorgeous views, remote mountain temples
Ubud	Beautiful walks from one hour to one day; rice fields and terraces, river-valley jungles and ancient monuments

Komodo National Park (p344)

Equipment

Guides may be able to supply a few bits of gear, but don't count on it – bring your own. Depending on the hike, consider bringing the following:

➡ Torch/flashlight

➡ Warm clothes for higher altitudes (it can get pretty chilly up there)

➡ Waterproof clothes because rain can happen at any time and most of the mountains are misty at the least

➡ Good hiking sandals, shoes or boots – you definitely won't find these items locally

Safety Guidelines for Hiking & Trekking

Before embarking on a hiking or trekking trip, consider the following points to ensure a safe and enjoyable experience:

➡ Pay any fees and carry any permits required by local authorities; often these fees will be rolled into the guide's fee, meaning that it's all negotiable.

➡ Be sure you are healthy and feel comfortable walking for a sustained period.

➡ Obtain reliable information about environmental conditions along your intended route – the weather can get quite wet and cold in the upper reaches of the volcanoes.

➡ Confirm with your guide that you will only go on walks/hikes within your realm of experience.

➡ Carry the proper equipment. Depending on the trek and time of year this can mean rain gear or extra water. Carry a torch/flashlight; don't assume the guide will have one.

Rafting

Rafting is popular in Bali, usually as a day trip from either south Bali or Ubud. Operators pick you up, take you to the put-in point, provide all the equipment and guides, and return you to your hotel at the end of the day. The best time is during the wet season (November to March) or just after. At other times, water levels can be too low.

Some operators use the Sungai Ayung (Ayung River), near Ubud, where there are between 25 and 33 Class II to III rapids (ie potentially exciting but not perilous). The Sungai Telagawaja (Telagawaja River) near Muncan in east Bali is also popular. It's

HIKING HIGHLIGHTS: LOMBOK

Like the island itself, Lombok has walks and hikes that are often remote, challenging or both.

LOCATION	DETAILS
Air Terjun Sindang Gila	One of many waterfalls on Rinjani's northern slopes
Gilis	Beach-bum circumnavigations
Gunung Rinjani	Superb for trekking; climb the 3726m summit then drop into a crater with a sacred lake and hot springs
Sembalun Valley	Garlic-scented hikes on the slopes of Rinjani
Tetebatu	Rice field walks that lead to pounding waterfalls

more rugged than the Ayung and the scenery is more wild.

Discounts on published prices are common, so do ask. Consider the following operators:

Bio (☎0361-270949; www.bioadventurer.com; adult/child from 950,000/850,000Rp) Get closer to the water on an individual river board or a tube. Tours go to west Bali.

Mason Adventures (Bali Adventure Tours; ☎0361-721480; www.masonadventures.com; Adventure House, Jl Ngurah Rai Bypass; rafting trips from 695,000Rp) Sungai Ayung; also has kayak trips.

Mega Rafting (☎0361-246724; www.megaraftingbali.com; adult/child from US$79/69) Trips on the Sungai Ayung.

Sobek (☎0361-729016; www.balisobek.com; rafting from US$52) Trips on both the Sungai Ayung and Sungai Telagawaja.

Spas & Massages

Bali brims with salons and spas where you can heal, pamper, rejuvenate or otherwise focus on your personal needs, physical and mental. Visiting a spa is at the top of the itinerary for many travellers and the wellness industry grows every year. Expect the latest trends from many practitioners and prepare to try some new therapies. You may also wish to seek out a *balian* (traditional healer).

Walk down any street in Seminyak or Ubud and you'll find plentiful options for massages, full-body scrubs, fish spas and hair masques. If air-con and privacy aren't your top priority, you can score a real bargain. If you're seeking a more luxurious experience, head to a hotel or more upmarket spa. Here are a few suggestions to get you started:

Taksu Spa (p169) Spend a few hours enjoying a massage and relaxing over lunch at this Ubud haven.

Sundari Day Spa (p93) A Kerobokan favourite that offers healing rituals alongside the usual luxuries.

Jari Menari (p84) Be spoiled at the branch in Tanjung Benoa or the Seminyak original.

Jamu Wellness (p127) Delicious scrubs and rubs, as well as facials and hair-removal in Sanur.

Surfing

Surfing kick-started tourism in Bali in the 1960s, and the region has never looked back. Many locals have taken to surfing, and the grace of traditional dancing is said to influence their style.

Surfing Bali

Swells come from the Indian Ocean, so the surf is on the southern side of the island and, strangely, on the northwest coast of Nusa Lembongan, where the swell funnels into the strait between there and the Bali coast.

In the dry season (around April to September), the west coast has the best breaks, with the trade winds coming in from the southeast; this is also when Nusa Lembongan is at its best. In the wet season, surf the eastern side of the island, from Nusa Dua around to Padangbai. If there's a north wind – or no wind at all – there are also a couple of breaks on the south coast of the Bukit Peninsula.

Note that the best breaks almost always have good beaches of the same name.

To reach the breaks, many will rent a motorbike with a surfboard rack while others will hire a surfboard-carrying-capable car with a driver. Either option is easily accomplished.

Balangan
Follow Jl Pantai Balangan and its surfer crash pads until you reach the parking area overlooking the Balangan beach cafes. Balangan (p136) is a fast left over a shallow reef, unsurfable at low tide, but good at mid-tide with anything over a 4ft swell; with an 8ft swell, it's magic.

Balian
There are a few peaks near the mouth of Sungai Balian (p278) (Balian River) in western Bali. The best break here is an enjoyable and consistent left-hander that works well at mid- to high tide if there's no wind. Choose from guesthouses simple to luxe.

Batu Bolong
North of Kerobokan, on the northern extremity of the bay, Batu Bolong (p99), often called Canggu, has a nice beach with light-coloured sand, many surfers and a cool party scene. An optimum size for Batu Bolong is 5ft to 6ft. There's a good right-hander that you can really hook into, which works at high tide.

Bingin
Accessible down a cliff, this spot (p137) can get crowded. It's best at mid-tide with a 6ft swell, when it manufactures short but perfect left-hand barrels. The cliffs backing the beach are lined with plenty of accommodation options.

Impossibles
Just north of Padang Padang, this challenging outside reef break (p140) has three shifting peaks with fast left-hand tube sections that can join up if the conditions are perfect.

Keremas & Ketewel
These two beaches are northeast of Sanur (p124). They're both right-hand beach breaks, which are dodgy at low tide and close out over 6ft. The surf is fairly consistent year-round and you can night surf at the Hotel Komune (p215) surf resort.

Kuta Area
For your first plunge into the warm Indian Ocean, try the breaks at Kuta's beach. At full tide, go out near the life-saving club at the southern end of the beach road. At low tide, try the tubes around Halfway Kuta (p70), probably the best place in Bali for beginners to practice. Start at the beach breaks if you are a bit rusty, but treat even these breaks with respect.

Further north, the breaks at Legian Beach (p66) can be pretty powerful, with

Bali & Lombok Surf Breaks

Surfer, Sumbawa (p336)

lefts and rights on the sandbars off Jl Melasti and Jl Padma.

For more serious stuff, go to the reefs south of the beach breaks, about a kilometre out to sea. Kuta Reef (p70), a vast stretch of coral, provides a variety of waves. You can paddle out in around 20 minutes, but the easiest way to get there is by boat. The main break is a classic left-hander, best at mid- to high tide, with a 5ft to 6ft swell, when it peels across the reef and has a beautiful inside tube section.

Medewi

Along the south coast of western Bali is a soft left called Medewi (p280). It's a point break that can give a long ride right into the river mouth. This wave has a big drop, which fills up then runs into a workable inside section. There's accommodation here.

Nusa Dua

During the wet season, there are some fine reef breaks on the eastern side of the island. The reef off Nusa Dua (p146) has very consistent swells. The main break is 1km off the beach to the south of Nusa Dua – go past the golf course and look for the remaining shred of Gegar Beach up against the huge Mulia resort, where there will be some boats to take you out. There are lefts and rights that work well on a small swell at low to mid-tide. Further north, in front of Club Med, there is a fast, barrelling right reef break called **Sri Lanka**, which works best at mid-tide.

Nusa Lembongan

In the Nusa Penida group, this island is separated from the southeast coast of Bali by Selat Badung (Badung Strait).

The strait is very deep and generates huge swells that break over the reefs off the northwest coast of Lembongan. Shipwrecks (p150), clearly visible from the beach, is the most popular break, a longish right that gets a good barrel at mid-tide with a 5ft swell.

A bit to the south, Lacerations (p150) is a very fast, hollow right breaking over a very shallow reef – hence the name. Still further south is a smaller, more user-friendly left-hander called Playgrounds (p150). Remember that Lembongan is best with an easterly wind, so it's dry-season surfing.

Padang Padang

Just Padang (p140) for short, this super-shallow, left-hand reef break is off a very popular beach and just below some rickety accommodation joints where you can crash *and* watch the breaks. Check this place carefully before venturing out. It's a very demanding break that only works over about 6ft from mid- to high tide.

If you can't surf tubes, backhand or forehand, don't go out. After a ledgy take-off, you power along the bottom before pulling up into the barrel. Not a wave for the faint-hearted and definitely not one to surf when there's a crowd (such as you'll find during high-profile surf contests throughout the year).

Sanur

Sanur Reef (p125) has a hollow wave with excellent barrels. It's fickle and doesn't even start until there is a 6ft swell, but anything over 8ft will be world-class, and anything over 10ft will be brown-boardshorts material. There are other reefs further offshore and most of them are surfable.

Hyatt Reef, over 2km from shore, has a shifty right peak that can give a great ride at full tide. The classic right is off the Grand Bali Beach Hotel.

Serangan

The development at Pulau Serangan (Turtle Island) has caused huge disruption on the southern and eastern sides of the island; paradoxically, these changes to the shape of the shore have made the surf here much more consistent. In addition, the causeway has made the island more accessible, and several warung face the water, where waves break right and left in anything over a 3ft swell.

South Coast

The extreme south coast, around the end of the Bukit Peninsula (p132), can be surfed any time of the year provided there is a northerly wind, or no wind at all – get there very early to avoid onshore winds. The peninsula is fringed with reefs, and big swells are produced, but access is a problem; the shoreline is all cliff (getting down to **Nyang-Nyang** requires traversing more than 500 steps).

Ulu Watu

When Kuta Reef is 5ft to 6ft, Ulu Watu (p142), the most famous surfing break in Bali, will be 6ft to 8ft with bigger sets. It's way out on the southern extremity of the bay and consequently picks up more swell than Kuta.

Teluk Ulu Watu (Ulu Watu Bay) is a great set-up for surfers – local boys will wax your board, get drinks for you and carry the board down into the cave, which is the usual access to the waves. There are popular cafes, and accommodation for every budget.

Ulu Watu has about seven different breaks. The **Corner** is straight in front of you to the right. It's a fast-breaking, hollow left that holds about 6ft. The reef shelf under this break is extremely shallow, so try to avoid falling head first. At high tide, the **Peak** starts to work. This is good from 5ft to 8ft, with bigger waves occasionally right on the Peak itself. You can take off from this inside part or further down the line. It's a great wave.

Another left runs off the cliff that forms the southern flank of the bay. It breaks outside this in bigger swells, and once it's 7ft, a left-hander pitches right out in front of a temple on the southern extremity. Out behind the Peak, when it's big, is a *bombora* (submerged reef) appropriately

ALTERNATIVE ACTIVITIES

Feel like getting active but want to try something a bit different? There are a number of possibilities:

Canyoning Cunca Wulang Cascades (p352), 30km southeast of Labuan Bajo in Flores, is a popular canyoning destination.

Caving There are two caves worth exploring near Labuan Bajo (p352): Gua Batu Cermin and Gua Rangko. Both are easily accessed and can be visited with or without guides.

Kitesurfing Head to the Ekas Peninsula in southwestern Lombok and to Pantai Lakey in East Sumbawa.

WILD BALI

When some people think of the wild in Bali, they think pink-faced Australians downing Bintangs 'till dawn in Kuta. They're not wrong, but there's another wild side to the island that **Aaranya Wildlife Odysseys** (☎in Australia 1300 585 662; www.aaranya.com.au; prices vary), an expat-owned and science-based tour company, is introducing to travellers: the actual nature.

On custom, week-long trips to off-the-beaten-track areas of Bali and over to Nusa Penida, the company explores the far-flung habitats of fascinating critters such as the endemic, critically endangered Bali starling and reptiles such as monitor lizards and yellow-lipped sea krait. Tour leaders are prominent field researchers and wildlife biologists who specialise in Bali's fauna – and particularly its reptiles – offering deep knowledge of ecological landscapes across the island and beyond. Activities alongside the pros include snorkelling (or scuba diving for those who are certified), trekking, cave exploration and birdwatching, most of which are best suited to those in good physical condition. Itineraries and prices are flexible to accommodate wish lists, travel dates, locations, activities, the level of accommodation and the number of guests.

Email is the best way to inform the team about your interests, and fear not: after a hard day of adventuring there's also plenty of Bintang.

called the **Bommie**. This is another big left-hander and it doesn't start operating until the swell is about 10ft. On a normal 5ft to 8ft day, there are also breaks south of the Peak.

Observe where other surfers paddle out and follow them. If you are in doubt, ask someone. It's better having some knowledge than none at all. Climb down into the cave and paddle out from there. When the swell is bigger you will be swept to your right. Don't panic – it is an easy matter to paddle around the white water from down along the cliff. Coming back in you have to aim for the cave. When the swell is bigger, come from the southern side of the cave because the current runs to the north.

Surfing Lombok

Lombok has some superb surfing and the dearth of tourists means that breaks are generally uncrowded.

Gerupuk

This giant bay 7km east of Kuta boasts four surf breaks, so there's always some wave action no matter what the weather or tide. **Bumbang** is extremely dependable: best on an incoming tide, this right-hander over a flat reef is good for all levels and can be surfed year-round. **Gili Golong** excels at mid- to high tide between October and April. **Don-Don** needs a bigger swell to break but can be great at any time of year. Finally **Kid's Point** (or Pelawangan) only breaks with big swells, but when it does it's barrels all the way. You need to hitch a boat ride to each wave.

Mawi

About 18km west of Kuta, the stunning bay of Mawi has a fine barrelling left with a late take-off and a final tube. It's best in the dry season, from May to October, with easterly offshore winds and a southwest swell. There are sharp rocks and coral underwater, and the rip tide is very fierce – take great care.

Tanjung Desert

Located in an extremely remote part of Lombok, Tanjung Desert is a legendary if elusive wave that has been voted the 'best wave in the world' by *Tracks* magazine. Only suitable for very experienced surfers, it's a fickle beast, in a region known for long, flat spells.

On its day, this left-handed tube can offer a 300m ride, growing in size from take-off to close-out (which is over razor-sharp coral). Tanjung Desert only really performs when there's a serious ground swell – May to September offers the best chance. Wear a helmet and boots at low tide.

Ekas

This remote bay in southeastern Lombok has two user-friendly breaks. **Outside Ekas** is a long, hollow wall that breaks left below a cliff face and is ideal for more experienced surfers. **Inside Ekas** is suitable for surfers of all abilities, breaking long inside the bay. Peak swells are from April to November, but it's pretty consistent and surfable year-round.

The Ekas Peninsula is also a hub for kite and wind surfing.

Surfing the Gili Islands

Much better known as a diving mecca, Gili Trawangan also boasts a surf spot off the island's southern tip. It's a quick right-hander that breaks in two sections, one offering a steeper profile, over rounded coral. It is best surfed December to March or on a windless high season day.

Surfing Sumbawa

Well off the beaten track, Sumbawa's southwest coast has white beaches with renowned surf, while in the southeast, the **Lakey Peak** and **Lakey Pipe** waves are year-round surf magnets.

Directly south of Maluk is **Supersuck**, consistently rated as the best left the world. Surfers descend regularly from Hawaii's North Shore to surf here – which should tell you something – and many life-long surfers have proclaimed it the finest barrel of their lives. It really pumps in the dry season (May to October).

Surfing Rote

Stunning Pantai Nemberala is home to the world-renowned **T-Land** break, a legendary left. The surf season here peaks between June and September.

Equipment: Pack or Rent?

A small board is usually adequate for the smaller breaks, but a few extra inches on your usual board length won't go astray. For the bigger waves – 8ft and upwards – you'll need a 'gun'. For a surfer of average height and build, a board around the 7ft mark is perfect.

If you try to bring more than two or three boards into the country, you may have problems with customs officials, who might think you're going to try to sell them.

There are surf shops in Kuta and elsewhere in south Bali. You can rent boards of varying quality (from around 100,000Rp per day) and get supplies at most popular surf breaks. If you need repairs, ask around: there are lots of places that can help.

Other recommended equipment:

- Solid luggage for airline travel
- Board-strap for carrying
- Tough shoes for walking down rocky cliffs
- Your favourite wax if you're picky
- Wetsuit (a spring suit or shorty will be fine) and reef booties
- Wetsuit vest, rashvest or other protective cover from the sun, reefs and rocks
- Surfing helmet for rugged conditions (and riding a motorbike)

Yoga

There are so many ways to relax the mind, body and spirit in Bali. For many, merely stepping foot on the island is enough to lower stress levels, but if you want to take it a step further then a yoga class is a good chance to practise some pranayama (breathing techniques) and get bendy. Yoga studios are a little less common than the all-pervasive spas (some of which also offer yoga), but there is an increasing number of options available.

Choose your class by the style and level on offer: restorative or yin classes are great if you're new to yoga or relaxation is your aim. It can be a good idea to start with a slow flow in Bali's humid climate, even if you're an experienced yogi.

Ubud is undeniably Bali's hotspot for all things yoga, where the Bali Spirit Festival (p176) is a major drawcard every year. The Festival was born at the Yoga Barn (p170) – the Bali epicentre for all things yogic. Studios are constantly popping up in Ubud, where Radiantly Alive (p170) and Intuitive Flow (p171) are among the best.

In Kerobokan, Jiwa Yoga (p93) specialises in Bikram-style hot yoga for those who want to get *really* sweaty.

The Seminyak Yoga Shala (p84) offers vigorous Ashtanga classes or Hatha style, which are more approachable for the visiting yoga sampler.

For yoga with stunning views, check out Blue Earth Village (p228) in East Bali or Sanur's Power of Now Oasis (p127).

Even if you aren't staying at a swish hotel, many hotels allow you to sample the lifestyle with a drop-in class. If you're up with the birds on a Saturday morning, join the yoga class (and access the spa facilities) at W Bali – Seminyak (p94). Try out ecolodge life at Serenity Eco Guesthouse (p100) in Canggu, or take a post-surf class at Hotel Komune (p215) in Keramas.

Plan Your Trip

Travel with Children

Travelling with children in this part of the world is an enriching experience. Locals consider kids part of the community, and everyone has a responsibility towards them. Children of all ages will enjoy both the attention and the many diversions that will make their holiday as special as that of the adults.

Best Regions for Kids

Kuta & Legian, Bali Though crowded, crazy and sometimes sleazy, beachfront resorts near the sand as well as surf lessons and all manner of cheap souvenirs will entice kids and teens.

Nusa Dua, Bali Huge beachside resorts with kids' programs, a reef-protected beach and modest traffic.

Sanur, Bali Beachside resorts, a reef-protected beach, light traffic and proximity to many kid-friendly activities.

Ubud, Bali There are many things to see and do (walks, monkeys, markets and shops). Evenings may require greater creativity to keep younger kids amused, although many will be entranced by the dance performances.

Senggigi, Lombok Modest, quiet hotels on the beach; limited traffic; reef-protected beach with gentle waves.

Gili Air, Gili Islands The smallest of the Gilis; gentle surf; many tourist amenities and activities such as snorkelling.

Bali, Lombok & Nusa Tenggara for Kids

Children are a social asset when you travel here, especially in Bali, where locals will display great interest in any visiting child they meet. You will have to learn how to say your child's age and gender in Bahasa Indonesia – *bulan* is month, *tahun* is year, *laki-laki* is boy and *perempuan* is girl. You should also make polite enquiries about the other person's children, present or absent.

The obvious drawcards for kids are the diverse outdoor adventures available. But there are also many cultural treats that kids will love.

Dance

A guaranteed snooze right? Wrong. Check out an evening Barong dance at the Ubud Palace (p191) or Pura Dalem Ubud (p191), two venues that look like sets from Tomb Raider right down to the flaming torches. Sure, the Legong style of Balinese might be tough going for fidgety types, but the Barong has monkeys, monsters, a witch and more.

Markets

If young explorers are going to temples, they will need sarongs. Give them 100,000Rp at a traditional market and let 'em loose.

Vendors will be truly charmed as the kids try to bargain and assemble the most colourful combo.

Temples

Pick the fun ones. Goa Gajah (p196) in Bedulu has a deep cavern where hermits lived and which you enter through the mouth of a monster. Pura Luhur Batukau (p250) is in dense jungle in the Gunung Batukau area with a cool lake and a rushing stream.

Children's Highlights

Best Beaches

Kuta Beach (p66) Surf schools.

Sanur Beach (p125) Kids will get their kicks in the gentle surf.

Batu Bolong Beach (p99) Where the cool kids of all ages hang out.

Best Water Fun

Pulau Menjangan, north Bali (p268) The best snorkelling on the island.

Weekuri Lagoon, West Sumba What could be better than renting a black rubber ring and floating in the cool, crystal water.

Rice fields walks, Ubud For something different, walk amid muddy water filled with ducks, frogs and other fun critters.

Best Frolicking

Bali Treetop Adventure Park, Candikuning (p246) Kids can make like monkeys.

Waterbom Park, Tuban (p71) A huge aquatic playground.

Best for Animals

Ubud Monkey Forest, Ubud (p166) Monkeys and temples!

Bali Bird Park, south of Ubud (p202) Amazing birds and reptiles.

Dolphin watching, Lovina (p258) Boat rides to see dolphins on Bali's north coast.

Best Cool Old Things

Tirta Empul, north of Ubud (p440) Kids will love the *Indiana Jones*–like pools at the ancient water palace and park.

Ubud Monkey Forest (p166)

Planning

The critical decision is deciding where to base yourselves.

Where to Stay

There's a huge range of accommodation options for families.

➡ A hotel with a swimming pool, air-con and a beachfront location is fun for kids and very convenient, and still provides a good break for parents. Fortunately, there are plenty of choices.

➡ Many larger resorts in Bali have special programs for kids that include lots of activities during the day and evening. Better ones have special supervised pool areas and other fun kids' zones.

➡ Many hotels and guesthouses, at whatever price range, have a 'family plan', which means that children up to about 12 years old can share a room with their parents free of charge. The catch is that hotels may charge for extra beds, although many offer family rooms, which can accommodate four or more.

➡ A family might really enjoy a villa-style unit in the southwest beaches region in Bali. Within

STAYING SAFE

The main danger to kids – and adults for that matter – is traffic and bad footpaths in busy areas.

The sorts of facilities, safeguards and services that Western parents regard as basic may not be present. Not many restaurants provide highchairs, places with great views might have nothing to stop your kids falling over the edge, and shops often have breakable things down low.

Given the ongoing presence of rabies on Bali, be sure to keep children away from stray dogs and cats.

For any activity, it's worth checking out conditions carefully. Just because that rafting company sells tickets to families doesn't mean they are well set up to cater to the safety needs of children.

your own small private compound you'll have a pool and often more than one TV. Cooking facilities mean you can prepare familiar foods while the relative seclusion makes naps easy.

➡ Many hotels can arrange a babysitter during the day or evening.

➡ Hotel staff are usually very willing to help and improvise, so always ask if you need something for your children.

➡ At family homestays and guesthouses, especially in Ubud, young travellers might just feel part of the family as they watch offerings being made and people their own age going about their daily business.

What to Pack

Huge supermarkets and stores, such as Carrefour in south Bali, stock almost everything you'd find at similar shops at home, including many Western foods. Nappies (diapers), Western baby food, packaged UHT milk, infant formula and other supplies are easily purchased in Bali but can be harder to source in Nusa Tenggara.

Babies & Toddlers

➡ A front or back sling or other baby carrier: poorly maintained streets and paths are not suited to prams and pushchairs.

➡ A portable changing mat, hand-wash gel and so on (baby changing facilities are a rarity).

➡ Kids' car seats: cars, whether rented or chartered with a driver, are unlikely to come with these.

Six to Twelve Years

➡ Binoculars for young explorers to zoom in on wildlife, rice terraces, temples, dancers and so on.

➡ A camera or phone that shoots video to inject newfound fun into 'boring' grown-up sights and walks.

Eating with Kids

Eating out as a family is one of the joys of travelling here. Kids are often treated like deities by doting staff who will clamour to grab yours (especially young babies) while parents enjoy some quiet time together.

Bali, especially, is so relaxed that kids can just be kids. There are plenty of top-end eateries in Seminyak and elsewhere where kids romp nearby while their parents enjoy a fine meal.

If your children don't like spicy food, show caution in offering them the local cuisine. For older babies, bananas, eggs, peelable fruit and *bubur* (rice cooked to a mush in chicken stock) are all generally available. Many warungs (food stalls) will serve food without sauces upon request, such as plain white rice, fried tempe or tofu, chicken, boiled vegetables and boiled egg. Otherwise, kid-pleasers like burgers, chicken fingers, pizza and pasta are widespread, as are fast-food chains in south Bali.

Plan Your Trip
Eat & Drink Like a Local

Food, glorious food – or perhaps food, laborious food? Cooking the delectable dishes of this region is time-consuming, but no effort is required to enjoy the results. That's one of the best things about travelling here: the variety and quality of the cuisine is hard to beat.

Food Experiences

Meals of a Lifetime

Bali Asli (p225), Amlapura Ultra-fresh *nasi campur* and spectacular views over rice terraces are on offer at this hybrid restaurant and cooking school.

Sardine (p94), Kerobokan Amid the south Bali hubbub, an oasis set on a private rice field; exquisite seafood, great bar.

Hujon Locale (p184), Ubud Will Meyrick's stylish and casual farm-to-table eatery is emphatically and deliciously on-trend.

Warung Goûthé (p103), Canguu Bali's best casual French lunch, daily specials are just that.

El Bazar (p307), Kuta (Lombok) Authentic tastes from around the Mediterranean enjoyed in trendy surrounds.

Coco Beach (p294), Senggigi A secluded beachside setting, fresh seafood and simply marvellous madras curry.

Ruby's (p332), Gili Air The namesake chef here excels at everything from burgers to green curries.

Sari Rasa (p364), Ende Regulars can't get enough of the *ayam goreng* (fried chicken) topped with spiced, grated coconut.

Depot Bambu Kuning (p376), Kupang One of the best places in West Timor to try succulent *se'i babi* (smoked pork).

The Year in Food

Wet season (October–April)

Tropical fruit delights – rambutan, dragon fruit, salak, durian, mangosteen, pineapple, banana, mango, guava and lychee – are lush and abundant. April ushers in the Ubud Food Festival, a three-day event showcasing the diversity and innovation of Indonesian cuisine.

Dry season (May–September)

Enjoy year-round staples like papaya and coconut. The end of the rice harvest season is celebrated with a festival from 1 May to 30 June, when towns raise flags, erect shrines and prepare traditional regional dishes in honour of Dewi Sri, the goddess of rice and fertility.

Cheap Treats

The most common place for dining out is a warung, the traditional street-side eatery. There's one every few metres in major towns and at least one or two in most small villages. They are cheap, no-frills hang-outs with a relaxed atmosphere; you may find yourself sharing a table with strangers as you watch the world go by. The food is fresh and different at each, and is usually displayed in a glass cabinet at the entrance where you can create your own *nasi campur* (rice dish) or just order the house standard.

At warungs, the range of dishes is endless. Some local favourites include *babi kecap* (pork stewed in sweet soy sauce), *ayam goreng* (fried chicken), *urap* (steamed vegetables with coconut), *lawar* (salad of chopped coconut, garlic and chilli with pork or chicken meat and blood), fried tofu or tempe in a sweet soy or chilli sauce, fried peanuts, salty fish or eggs, *perkedel* (fried corn cakes), and various *sate* made from chunks of goat meat, chicken and pork. In Lombok, *ayam taliwang* (whole split chicken roasted over coconut husks served with tomato-chilli-lime dip) is a favourite; in West TImor, locals can't eat enough succulent *se'i babi*.

Local Specialities

Rice

Rice is the staple dish in this part of Indonesia and is revered as a gift of life from the gods. It is served generously with every meal – anything not served with rice is considered a *jaja* (snack). Rice acts as the medium for the various fragrant, spiced foods that accompany it, almost like condiments, with many dishes chopped finely to complement the dry, fluffy grains and for ease of eating with the hand. On Bali, a dish of steamed rice with mixed goodies is known as *nasi campur*. It's the island's undisputed 'signature' dish, eaten for breakfast, lunch and dinner. In other parts of the region, *nasi goreng* (fried rice) is equally popular.

There are as many variations of *nasi campur* as there are warungs. Just like a sandwich in the West can combine any number of fillings, each warung serves its own version according to budget, taste and whatever ingredients are fresh at the market. The secret to a good *nasi campur* is often in the cook's own base, which flavours the pork, chicken or fish, and the sambal, which may add just the right amount of heat to the meal at one place, or set your mouth ablaze at another. There are typically four or five dishes that make up a single serving, including a small portion of pork or chicken (small because meat is expensive), fish, tofu or tempe (fermented soy-bean cake), egg, various vegetable dishes and crunchy *krupuk* (flavoured rice crackers).

Beef seldom features because the Balinese believe cows are sacred. The 'side dishes' are arrayed around the centrepiece of rice and accompanied by the warung's signature sambal (paste made from chillies, garlic or shallots, and salt). The food is not usually served hot, because it would have been prepared during the morning.

Sambal

Locals certainly like a spicy kick with their meals, and food on Lombok can be particularly fiery. Balinese cuisine is mild but locals relish a dollop of fiery sambal on the side of every dish. Taste it to gauge the temperature before ploughing in. If you're averse to spicy food, request '*tanpa sambal*' (without chilli paste); better for most, though, is *tamba* (more) sambal!

One other note on Balinese sambal: if your request results in a bottle of the generically sweet commercial gloop, ask for 'Balinese sambal'. This latter request can open many more doors to eating joy because every Balinese cook has their own favourite way of creating sambal. If you add the many sambals adopted from other parts of Indonesia, especially

PRICE RANGES

In this book, the following price ranges represent the average cost of a main course or meal.

$ less than 60,000Rp (under US$4)

$$ 60,000–250,000Rp (US$4–17)

$$$ more than 250,000Rp (over US$17)

Above: *Nasi campur*
Right: *Gado gado* (p56)

Lombok, you could get one of many variations, including the following:

Sambal bajak A Javanese sambal, this is a creamy tomato-based sauce that is redolent with crushed chillies, yet gets smoothed out with palm sugar and shallots and then fried. Very common.

Sambal balado Chillis, shallots, garlic and tomatoes are sautéed in oil for a literally hot sambal. Often fried up fresh on the spot.

Sambal matah A raw Balinese sambal made from thinly sliced shallots, tiny chilies, shrimp paste and lemongrass. Divine.

Sambal plecing A Lombok sambal, this one takes hot chillies and puts them in a tomato base, letting the heat sneak up on you.

Sambal taliwang Another Lombok sambal made with special peppers, garlic and shrimp paste. One of the few true culinary highlights of Bali's neighbour and a favourite on Bali, where spicy Lombok-style chicken is adored.

Celebratory Dishes

On Bali, food is not just about enjoyment and sustenance. Like everything in Balinese life, it is an intrinsic part of the daily rituals and a major part of ceremonies to honour the gods. The menu varies according to the importance of the occasion. By far the most revered dish is *babi guling* (suckling pig), presented during rites-of-passage ceremonies such as a baby's three-month blessing, an adolescent's tooth filing or a wedding.

Babi guling is the quintessential Bali experience. A whole pig is stuffed with chilli, turmeric, ginger, galangal, shallots, garlic, coriander seeds and aromatic leaves, basted in turmeric and coconut oil and skewered on a wooden spit over an open fire. Turned for hours, the meat takes on the flavour of the spices and the fire-pit, giving a rustic smoky flavour to the crispy crackling. Short of being invited to a ceremonial feast, you can enjoy *babi guling* at stands, warungs and cafes across Bali.

Bebek or *ayam betutu* (smoked duck or chicken) is another ceremonial favourite. The bird is stuffed with spices, wrapped in coconut bark and banana leaves, and cooked all day over smouldering rice husks and coconut husks.

Often served at marriage ceremonies, *jukut ares* is a light, fragrant broth made from banana stem and usually contains chopped chicken or pork. The satay for special occasions, *sate lilit,* is a fragrant combination of good-quality minced fish, chicken or pork with lemongrass, galangal, shallots, chilli, palm sugar, kaffir lime and coconut milk. This is wrapped onto skewers and grilled.

In Flores, *tapa kolo* (rice cooked over coals in bamboo, bulked out with chicken or pork) is a popular festive dish.

Sasak Cuisine

Lombok's Sasak people are predominantly Muslim, so Bali's porky plethora does not feature in their diet of fish, chicken, vegetables and rice. The fact that 'lombok' means chilli in Bahasa Indonesia makes sense, because Sasaks like their food spicy.

Ares is a dish made with chilli, coconut juice and banana-palm pith; sometimes it's mixed with chicken or meat. *Sate pusut* is a delicious combination of minced fish, chicken or beef flavoured with coconut milk, garlic, chilli and other spices and wrapped around a lemongrass stick and grilled.

Meat-Free Fare

Indonesia is a dream come true for vegetarians. Tofu and tempe are part of the staple diet, and many tasty local favourites just happen to be vegetarian. Try *nasi saur* (rice flavoured with toasted coconut and accompanied by tofu, tempe, vegetables and sometimes egg), *urap* (a delightful blend of steamed vegetables mixed with grated coconut and spices), *gado gado* (tofu and tempe mixed with steamed vegetables, boiled egg and peanut sauce) and *sayur hijau* (leafy green vegetables, usually *kangkung* – water spinach – flavoured with a tomato-chilli sauce).

In addition, the way *nasi campur* is served means it's easy to request no meat, instead enjoying an array of fresh stir-fries, salads, tofu and tempe. When ordering curries and stir-fries such as *cap cay,* diners can usually choose meat, seafood or vegetarian.

Western-style vegetarian pasta and salads are on the menu in many restaurants and a few purely vegetarian eateries cater for vegans.

MARKETS

Pasar (markets) offer a glimpse of the variety and freshness of local produce, often brought from the mountains within a day or two of being harvested, sometimes sooner. The atmosphere is lively and colourful with baskets loaded with fresh fruits, vegetables, flowers, spices and varieties of red, black and white rice. There are trays of live chickens, dead chickens, freshly slaughtered pigs, sardines, eggs, colourful cakes, ready-made offerings and base, and stalls selling *es cendol* (colourful iced coconut drink), *bubur* (rice porridge) or *nasi campur* for breakfast.

There's no refrigeration, so things come in small packages and what you see is for immediate sale. Bargaining is expected.

How to Eat & Drink

Locals usually eat with their right hand, which is used to give and receive all good things. The left hand deals with unpleasant, sinister elements (such as ablutions). It's customary to wash your hands before eating, even if you use a spoon and fork; local restaurants always have a sink outside the restrooms. If you choose to eat the local way, use the bowl of water provided at the table to wash your hands after the meal, as licking your fingers is not appreciated.

If you're invited to a local home for a meal, your hosts will no doubt insist you eat more, but you may always politely pass on second helpings or refuse food you don't find appealing.

When to Eat

Many locals save their appetite for lunch. They might kick-start the day with a cup of rich, sweet black coffee and a few sweet *jaja* (snacks) at the market: colourful temple cakes, glutinous rice cakes, boiled bananas in their peels, *pisang goreng* (fried banana) and *kelopon* (sweet-centred rice balls). Popular fresh fruits include snake fruit, named after its scaly skin, and jackfruit, which is also delicious stewed with vegetables.

The famous *bubuh injin* (black-rice pudding with palm sugar, grated coconut and coconut milk), which most tourists find on restaurant dessert menus, is actually a breakfast dish and a fine way to start the day. A variation available at the morning market is the nutty *bubur kacang hijau* (green mung-bean pudding), fragrantly enriched with ginger and pandanus leaf and served warm with coconut milk.

The household or warung cook usually finishes preparing the day's dishes mid-morning, so lunchtime happens around 11am when the food is freshest. This is the main meal of the day. Leftovers are eaten for dinner, or by tourists who awake late and do not get around to lunch until well and truly after everyone else has had their fill. Dessert is a rarity; for special occasions, it consists of fresh fruit or gelato-style coconut ice cream.

Where to Eat

Bali has myriad eating options: every cuisine, every style, every budget. The diversity, quality and value make it a top dining destination.

Restaurants Bali is a magnet for talented chefs, especially young ones, as the cost of doing business is low. In south Bali and Ubud you'll find the kinds of casual, innovative eateries that wouldn't be out of place in Sydney or San Francisco. On Lombok, head to Kuta or Gili T.

Cafes There are relaxed Western-style cafes all over Bali, Lombok and the Gilis but not many elsewhere in Nusa Tenggara. Coffee is often made from local beans.

Warungs Local food stalls serve great-tasting fare on a budget. In Nusa Tenggara, the terms warung and *rumah makan* (restaurant) are often interchangeable.

Fast-Food Vendors Locals of all stripes gather around simple food stalls in markets and on village streets and wave down *pedagang* (mobile traders) who ferry sweet and savoury snacks around by bicycle or motorcycle.

Above: Balinese beachside restaurant

Left: Traditional Balinese sweets

CAHAYA IMAGES/SHUTTERSTOCK ©

THE SIX FLAVOURS OF BALI

Compared with that of other Indonesian islands, Balinese food is more pungent and lively, with a multitude of layers making up a complete dish. A meal will contain the six flavours (sweet, sour, spicy, salty, bitter and astringent), which promote health and vitality and stimulate the senses.

There's a predominance of ginger, chilli and coconut, as well as the beloved candlenut (often mistaken for the macadamia, which is native to Australia). The biting combination of fresh galangal and turmeric is matched by the heat of raw chillies, the complex sweetness of palm sugar, tamarind and shrimp paste, and the clean, fresh flavours of lemongrass, musk lime, kaffir lime leaves and coriander seeds.

There are shades of south Indian, Malaysian and Chinese flavours, stemming from centuries of migration and trading with seafaring pioneers. Many ingredients were introduced in these times: the humble chilli was brought by the fearless Portuguese, the ubiquitous snake bean and bok choy by the Chinese, and the rice substitute cassava by the Dutch. In true Balinese style, village chefs selected the finest and most durable new ingredients and adapted them to local tastes and cooking styles.

Drinks

If there's a beach there's likely a beer vendor nearby to sell you a cold one while the sand tickles your toes. If you'd like something more posh, stylish and popular, beach venues can be found from Seminyak to Kerobokan and Canggu. No matter where you are, though, you're likely not too far from a typically mellow Bali cafe, where fresh juices, great coffee and various adult drinks will be on offer.

Beer

Beer drinkers are well catered for in Bali thanks to Indonesia's ubiquitous crisp, clean national lager, Bintang. Bali Hai beer sounds promising, but isn't.

Wine

Wine connoisseurs had better have a fat wallet. The abundance of high-end eateries and hotels has made fine vino from the world's best regions widely available but it is whacked with hefty taxes. Medium-grade bottles from Australia go for US$50.

Of the local producers of wine, the least objectionable is Artisan Estate, which overcomes the import duties by bringing crushed grapes from Western Australia. Hatten Wine, based in north Bali, has gained quite a following among those who like its very sweet pink rosé. Two Islands also has a following.

Local Booze

At large social gatherings, Balinese men might indulge in *arak* (fermented wine made from rice or palms or...other materials) but generally they are not big drinkers. Watch out for adulterated *arak*, which is rare but can be poisonous.

Fresh Juice

Local nonalcoholic refreshments are available from markets, street vendors, some warungs and many cafes. They are tasty and even a little psychedelic (in colour) – and without the hangover! One of Bali's most popular drinks is *cendol*, an interesting mix of palm sugar, fresh coconut milk and crushed ice.

Coffee & Tea

Many Western eateries sell imported coffees and teas alongside local brands, some of which are very good. The most expensive – and most overhyped – is Indonesia's peculiar *kopi luwak*. Around 200,000Rp a cup, this coffee is named after the cat-like civet *(luwak)* indigenous to Sulawesi, Sumatra and Java that feasts on ripe coffee cherries. Entrepreneurs initially collected the intact beans found in the civet's droppings and processed them to produce a supposedly extra-piquant brew. But now that interest in coffee *luwak* has exceeded all reason, trouble abounds, from fraudulent claims to documented animal mistreatment.

Regions at a Glance

Bali and Nusa Tenggara are home to disparate and highly distinctive regions. In Bali, most of the tourism action occurs in the coastal towns and islands on the island's southern coast and in Ubud, a magical town in the interior. Those wanting to head off the well-beaten tourist trail will want to explore the countryside and coastlines of east Bali, west Bali and north Bali, as well as the stunning volcanic spine of the central mountains.

To the east of Bali is the archipelago of Nusa Tenggara, which incorporates Lombok, the Gili Islands, Sumbawa, Komodo and Rinca Islands, Sumba, Flores, Rote and the Alors. Sharing a land mass on the eastern edge of the archipelago with the independent nation of Timor-Leste is the Indonesian region of West Timor, a magical place almost untouched by modern mass tourism.

Kuta & Southwest Beaches

Beaches
Nightlife
Shopping

Kuta Beach

Kuta's famous sweep of wave-pounded sand extends for 12km past Legian, Seminyak, Kerobokan and Canggu, before ending near Pererenan Beach. All along the sand are beach bars and vendors where the atmosphere is always merry.

Party 'Til Dawn

Restaurants and cafes in Seminyak, Kerobokan and Canggu are some of the best on Bali. Some have gorgeous sunset views, while bars and clubs have a vaguely sophisticated air. Nightlife becomes manic in Kuta, where the party goes all night.

Seminyak's Shops

Shopping in Seminyak and Kerobokan is reason enough to visit Bali – the choice is extraordinary.

p64

South Bali & the Islands

Beaches
Surfing
Diving

Balangan Beach

Beaches can be found right around south Bali: little coves of white sand like Balangan and Bingin are idyllic and inspire one to just chill on a beach chair and watch the gorgeous surf.

Ulu Watu Breaks

You can't say enough about the surf breaks on the west coast of the Bukit Peninsula; Ulu Watu is famous the world over, and its multitude of breaks are world-renowned. Cool guesthouses let you stay near the action.

Underwater Nusa Penida

The best diving is at the islands. Nusa Penida has challenging conditions and deep-water cliffs, and you might even see large creatures, such as manta rays winging their way along.

p115

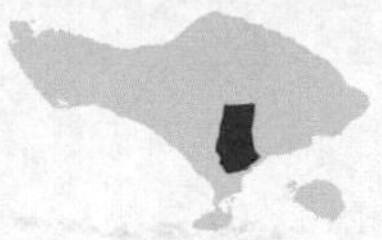

Ubud Region

Culture
Indulgence
Walks

Dancers & Artists

Ubud is the nexus of Balinese culture. Each night there are a dozen performances of traditional Balinese dance, music, puppets and more. It's also home to talented artists, including superb woodcarvers who make the masks for the shows.

Spas

Spas of every stripe, often with traditional medicine sessions and yoga classes, are the soul of Ubud indulgence. Services for mind and body abound, with near limitless options.

Explore Nature

The rice fields surrounding Ubud are some of Bali's most picturesque. You can walk for an hour or an entire day, enjoying river valleys, small villages and the enveloping natural beauty.

p160

East Bali

Beaches
Hikes
History

Amed

Beaches are found along much of Bali's east coast, and the best beach action is found in the northeast corner of the island, along the laid-back stretch of fishing villages collectively known as Amed.

Rice Field Hikes

Some of Bali's most alluring rice fields and landscapes are found in the east. You're spoilt for choice around Sideman and Tirtaa Gangaa, where there are walks aplenty through verdant green hills and valleys.

A Tragic Past

The town of Klungkung (Semerapura) has the moving remains of a palace lost when its king, his family and courtiers committed ritual suicide rather than surrender to the Dutch in 1908.

p203

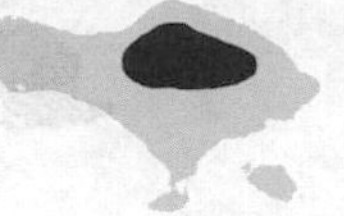

Central Mountains

Hikes
Culture
Solitude

Munduk Hikes

The centre of the island offers hikes around volcanoes and lakes. Trails radiating from Munduk include these natural highlights along with misty walks through spice plantations and jungle to waterfalls.

Top Temple

Pura Luhur Batukau never fails to touch the spirit of those who visit this important temple. It is a mystical – and misty – place to contemplate Bali's beliefs and to commune with nature.

Remote Walks

Cooler than the rest of Bali, the mountains have a solitary air. A visit to Pura Luhur Batukau can be followed by retreats to remote lodges, treks through volcanic mountains and wanderings around the lakes Danau Buyan and Danau Tamblingan.

p237

North Bali

Resorts
Chilling
Diving

Pemuteran's Resorts

The crescent of beach hotels at Pemuteran is the real star of north Bali. Beautifully built, the hotels form a fine human-scale resort area, and they're close to Pulau Menjangan.

Lovina's Quiet

Settle onto a mat on Lovina's tan and grey sand, pick up a book and let the day drift past at your low-cost, quiet getaway. Even the surf is mellow: much of the north coast is protected by reefs.

Pulau Menjangan

Pulau Menjangan lives up to its many superlatives. A 30m coral wall close to shore delights both divers and snorkellers with a cast of fish and creatures that varies from sardines to whales.

p253

West Bali

Surfing
Beaches
Rice Fields

Medewi Breaks

The breaks at Balian Beach have a following, and a small surfer community has sprung up with simple guesthouses and somewhat posher retreats. Hang out with locals who know the waters well. Further west, Medewi is even more remote.

Balian Beach

Balian Beach is the main strand in the west, and it makes a good place to hang even if you're not surfing. Enjoy the range of accommodation, from hip to simple to posh.

Tabanan

Unesco has given Bali's *subak* system of rice-field irrigation World Heritage Site status. The area around Tabanan has some of the most beautiful rice fields, plus a nice little museum and the nearby temple of Pura Taman Ayun.

p274

Lombok

Hiking
Coastline
Tropical Chic

Gunung Rinjani

A majestic volcano, Gunung Rinjani's very presence overshadows all of northern Lombok. Hiking trails sneak up Rinjani's astonishing caldera, where you'll find a shimmering crater lake, hot springs and a smoking mini-cone.

South Coast

Lombok's southern coastline is nature in the raw. There's absolutely nothing genteel about the magnificent shoreline, which is pounded by oceanic waves that make it a surfer's mecca. Empty beaches allow for exceptional swimming in cyan seas.

Sire

For total immersion in tropical chic, the Sire area offers some gorgeous resorts that combine a bamboo and thatched motif with pampering.

p283

Gili Islands

Diving
Beaches
Chilling

Coral Reefs

The Gilis' coral reefs teem with fascinating sea life, and you're almost guaranteed to see turtles. There are dozens of dive shops ready and waiting with a wide array of courses, from beginner to technical and advanced.

Gili Air Beaches

Pack your sunscreen, mat, some water and a good book and head out in the morning to walk around Gili Air. Along the way stop at each and every beach that catches your fancy.

Gili Meno

We've all dreamed of finding the ultimate beach: a vision of palm trees, blinding white sands and a turquoise sea, plus a bamboo shack selling cool drinks and fresh fish. Yours might just be an obscure corner on Meno.

p312

Nusa Tenggara

Nature
Diving
Village Culture

Komodo National Park

Home to extraordinary flora and fauna as well as natural and marine landscapes perfect for hiking, diving and snorkeling, this garland of islands is much more than the home of the legendary lizard of the same name.

Alor Archipelago

There are plenty of top-drawer dive destinations in this part of Indonesia, but few are as rewarding (and deserted) as the crystal-clear bays of the Alors.

West Timorese Villages

A paucity of Western tourists means that villages in this mountainous region have retained their traditional tribal dialects, laws and distinctive beehive-shaped houses.

p334

On the Road

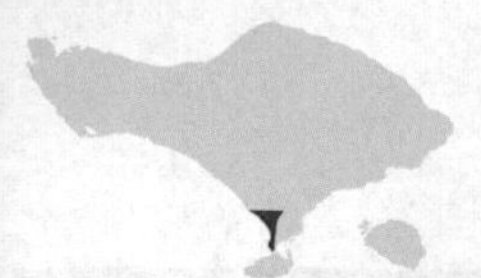

Kuta & Southwest Beaches

Includes ➡

Best Places to Eat

- ➡ Sardine (p94)
- ➡ Ginger Moon (p88)
- ➡ Sangsaka (p94)
- ➡ One Eyed Jack (p103)
- ➡ Warung Goûthé (p103)

Best Places to Stay

- ➡ Oberoi (p86)
- ➡ Samaya (p86)
- ➡ Alila Seminyak (p94)
- ➡ Katamama (p93)
- ➡ Hotel Tugu Bali (p102)

Why Go?

Crowded and frenetic, the swathe of south Bali hugging the amazing ribbon of beach that runs north almost from the airport is the place many travellers begin and end their visit to the island.

In Seminyak and Kerobokan there is a bounty of restaurants, cafes, designer boutiques, spas and the like that rivals anywhere in the world, while Kuta and Legian are the choice for rollicking clubs, cheap singlets and carefree family holidays. North around Canggu is Bali's most exciting region, where great beaches vie with enticing cafes and compelling nightlife.

Renowned shopping, all-night clubs, fabulous dining, cheap beer, sunsets that dazzle and relentless hustle and bustle are all part of the experience. But just when you wonder what any of this has to do with Bali – the island supposedly all about spirituality and serenity – a religious procession appears and shuts everything down. And then you know the answer.

When to Go

➡ Bali's ever-increasing popularity means that the best time to visit Kuta, Seminyak and their neighbours is outside high season (July, August and the weeks around Christmas and New Year). Holidays in other parts of the world mean that visitor numbers spike and it can require actual effort to organise tables in the best restaurants, navigate trendy shops and get a room with a view.

➡ Many prefer April to June and September, when the weather is drier and slightly cooler, and the crowds manageable.

➡ To surf this side of Bali, or just revel in the surf culture, visit during Bali's west coast surfing season: April to September.

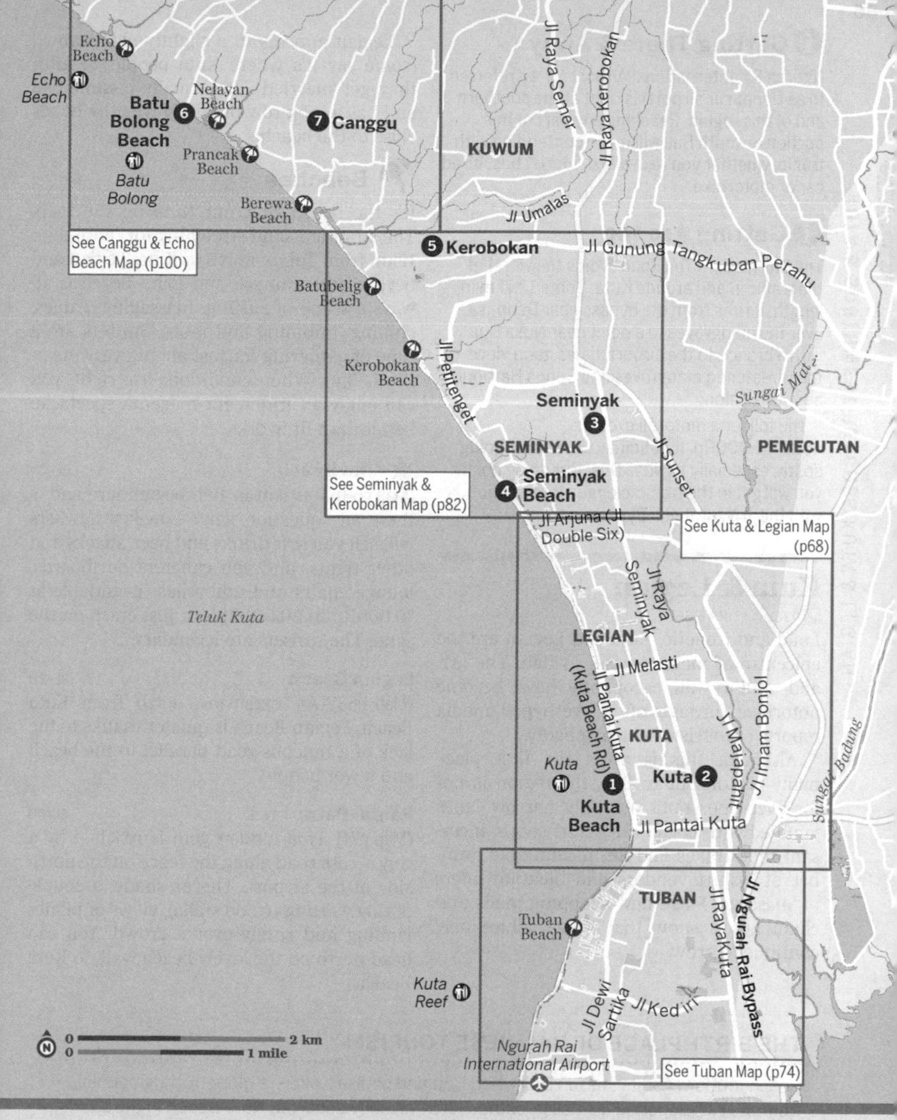

Kuta & Southwest Beaches Highlights

❶ **Kuta Beach** (p66) Lolling around on Bali's original tourist magnet.

❷ **Kuta Nightlife** (p78) Raving through the night in the manic clubs and legendary nightlife scene of Kuta.

❸ **Seminyak** (p81) Ignoring your resolve while shopping in the myriad boutiques and designer outlets.

❹ **Seminyak Sunsets** (p90) Revelling in a technicolour sunset with a beer from a beach vendor or swanky bar.

❺ **Kerobokan** (p94) Savouring a meal at one of the many fabulous and world-class restaurants.

❻ **Batu Bolong Beach** (p99) Joining the hip beach and surf scene, while debating where to have a refreshment.

❼ **Canggu** (p98) Making a delightful discovery, be it food, drink or commerce, amid rice fields and villas on the twisting and confounding lanes.

Getting There & Away

Ngurah Rai International Airport (often referred to as Denpasar airport) is right at the southern end of this region. Reaching any part of this portion of south Bali will mean contending with traffic, whether you're in a taxi, tourist bus, hired car or motorbike.

Getting Around

The Bali Madara Toll Road avoids the worst of the traffic in and around Kuta. Some 12.7km in length, it runs from the bypass near Denpasar over the mangroves to a point near Nusa Dua with a branch to the airport. It has good views of the threatened mangroves and Benoa Harbour as you sail along.

The toll for a motorbike/car is 4500/11,000Rp. It definitely saves time going south, especially to Nusa Dua. But going north you will get in the traffic-clogged intersection with the Jl Ngurah Rai Bypass.

Kuta & Legian

0361 / POP 46,660

Loud and frenetic, Kuta and Legian are the epicentre of mass tourism in Bali. The grit and wall-to-wall cacophony have become notorious through often overhyped media reports of tourists behaving badly.

Although this is often the first place many visitors hit in Bali, the region is not for everyone. Kuta has ugly narrow lanes jammed with cheap cafes, surf shops, incessant motorbikes and an uncountable number of T-shirt vendors and bleating offers of 'massage'. Flash new shopping malls and chain hotels show that Kuta's allure may continue to grow.

Legian appeals to a slightly older crowd (some say it's where Kuta people go after they get married). It's equally commercial and has a long row of family-friendly hotels close to the beach.

Beaches

It's the beach that put Kuta on the map. The strand of sand stretching for more than 12km from Tuban north to Kuta, Legian and beyond to Seminyak and Echo Beach is always a scene of surfing, massaging, games, chilling, imbibing and more. Sunsets are a time of gathering for just about everyone in south Bali. When conditions are right, you can enjoy an iridescent magenta spectacle: better than fireworks.

★Kuta Beach BEACH

(Map p68) Tourism in Bali began here and is there any question why? Low-key hawkers will sell you soft drinks and beer, snacks and other treats, and you can rent surfboards, lounge chairs and umbrellas (negotiable at 10,000Rp to 20,000Rp), or just crash on the sand. The sunsets are legendary.

Legian Beach BEACH

(Map p68) An extension north from Kuta Beach, Legian Beach is quieter thanks to the lack of a raucous road parallel to the beach and fewer people.

Pantai Patra Jasa BEACH

(Map p74) This hidden gem is reached by a tiny access road along the fence on the north side of the airport. There's shade, a couple of tiny warungs (food stalls), views of planes landing and rarely ever a crowd. You can head north on the lovely beach walk to Kuta Beach.

THE BIRTHPLACE OF BALINESE TOURISM

Beach tourism got its start in Bali when Bob and Louise Koke – a globetrotting couple from the US – opened a small guesthouse on virtually deserted Kuta Beach in the 1930s. The guests, mostly from Europe and the US, were housed in thatched bungalows built in an idealised Balinese style. In a prescient move, Bob taught the locals to surf, something he'd learned in Hawaii.

Kuta really began to change in the late 1960s when it became a stop on the hippie trail between Australia and Europe. By the early 1970s it had relaxed losmen (small Balinese hotels) in pretty gardens, friendly places to eat, vendors peddling magic mushrooms and a delightfully laid-back atmosphere. Enterprising Balinese seized the opportunity to profit from the tourists and surfers, often in partnership with foreigners seeking a pretext to stay longer.

Legian, the village to the north, sprang up as an alternative to Kuta in the mid-1970s. At first it was a totally separate development, but these days you can't tell where one ends and the other begins.

TEMPLE FESTIVALS

Temple festivals in Bali are quite amazing, and you'll come across them quite unexpectedly, even in the most remote corners of the island. Each of the thousands of temples on the island has a 'temple birthday' known as an *odalan*. These are celebrated once every Balinese year of 210 days or every 354 to 356 days on the *saka* calendar (one of the two Balinese calendars).

Odalan are very big deals indeed and even the loneliest temple will suddenly spring to life around these special days. People from villages will travel far to attend, and grumbling business owners in south Bali will automatically give employees time off.

The most obvious sign of a temple festival is a long line of women in traditional costume, walking gracefully to the temple with beautifully arranged offerings piled in huge pyramids, which they carry on their heads.

Meanwhile, the various *pemangku* (temple guardians and priests for temple rituals) suggest to the gods that they should come down for a visit.

All night long there's activity, music and dancing – it's like a great country fair, with food, amusements, gambling, colour and confusion. Finally, as dawn approaches, the entertainment fades away, the *pemangku* suggest to the gods that it's time they made their way back to heaven and the people wind their weary way back home.

Double Six Beach BEACH

(Map p68) The beach becomes less crowded as you go north from Legian until very popular Double Six Beach, which is alive with pick-up games of football and volleyball all day long. It's a good place to meet partying locals. Watch out for water pollution after heavy rains.

Kuta Reef Beach BEACH

(Pantai Segara; Map p74) Some still call this beach 'Pantai Jerman', a legacy of some long-forgotten early surfing tourist. It's nicely low-key, with beer vendors and surfboard rentals.

Tuban Beach BEACH

(Map p74) Tuban's beach is a mixed bag. There are wide and mellow stretches of sand to the south but near the Discovery Mall it disappears entirely.

Sights

Bali Sea Turtle Society HATCHERY

(Map p68; 0811 388 2683; www.baliseaturtle.org; Kuta Beach; site 24hr, turtle releases 4.30pm Apr-Oct) The Bali Sea Turtle Society is a conservation group working to protect olive ridley turtles. It's one of the more responsible turtle hatcheries in Bali, and re-releases turtle hatchlings into the ocean from Kuta Beach. Join the queue to collect your baby turtle in a small plastic water bath, pay a small donation, and join the group to release them. Signs offer excellent background info.

Stop by an hour before the release time to ensure activity is on for the day.

Dream Museum Zone MUSEUM

(Map p68; 0361-849 6220; www.facebook.com/dmzbali/; Jl Nakula 33X; 110,000Rp, child under 3 free; 9am-10pm;) Fun for the whole family, this museum features a collection of around 120 interactive life-size murals that come to life – or rather, can be viewed in 3D – once photographed. It's divided into 14 sections so you can take your pick from Indonesia, Jurassic Park, Egypt and others.

Memorial Wall MONUMENT

(Map p68; Jl Legian) This memorial wall reflects the international scope of the 2002 bombings, and people from many countries pay their respects. Listing the names of the 202 known victims, including 88 Australians and 35 Indonesians, it is starting to look quite weathered. Across the street, a car park is all that is left of the destroyed Sari Club, site of the bombing.

Mads Lange's Tomb HISTORIC SITE

(Map p74; Jl Tuan Langa) Mads Lange, a Danish copra trader and 19th-century adventurer, set up a successful trading enterprise near modern-day Kuta in 1839. He mediated profitably between local rajahs (lords or princes) and the Dutch, who were encroaching from the north. His business soured in the 1850s and he died suddenly, just as he was about to return to Denmark. His restored tomb is near where he used to live in a quiet, tree-shaded area by the river. Lange bred Dalmatians and today locals assume that any dog with a hint of black and white has some of this blood.

Kuta & Legian

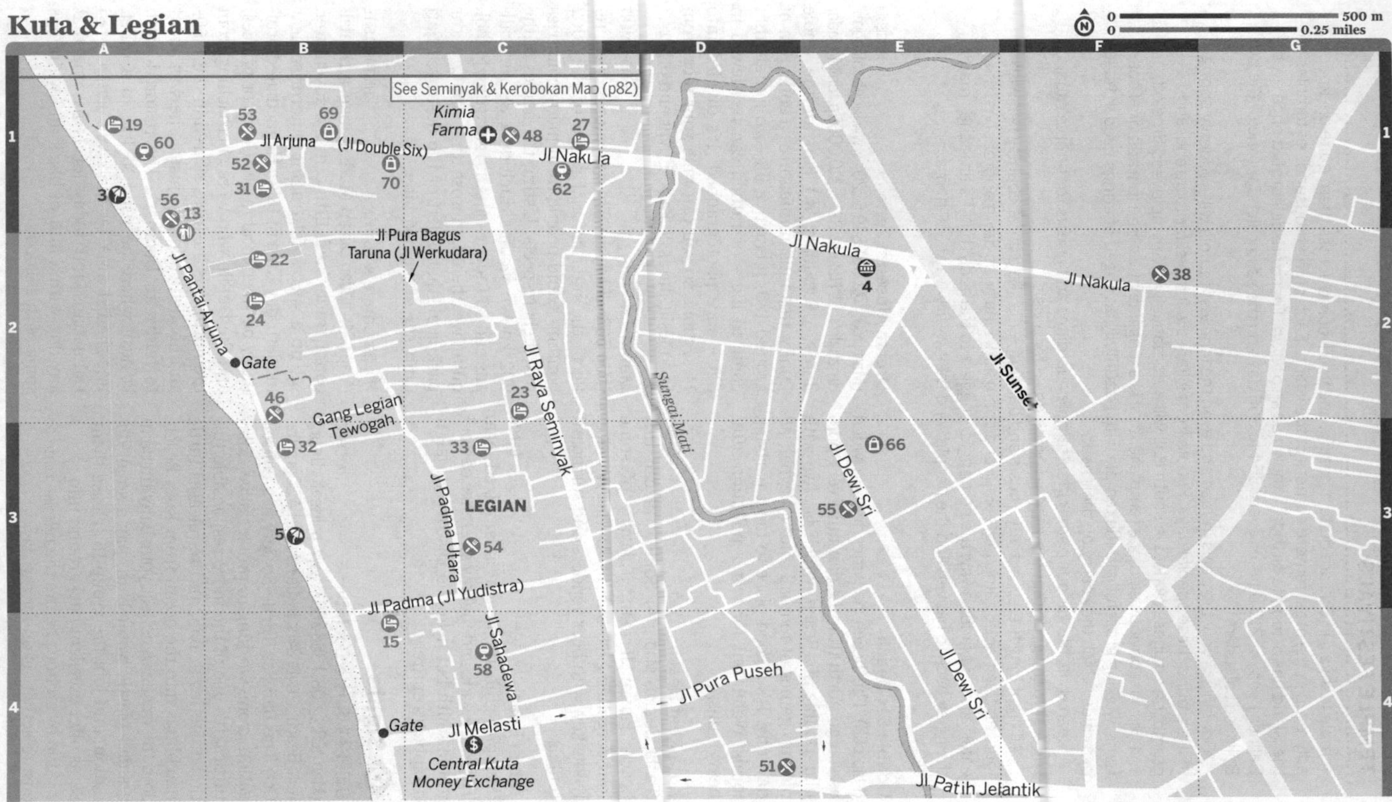
0 500 m
0 0.25 miles
See Seminyak & Kerobokan Map (p82)
Kimia Farma
Jl Arjuna
(Jl Double Six)
Jl Nakula
Jl Pura Bagus Taruna (Jl Werkudara)
Jl Pantai Arjuna
Gate
Gang Legian Tewogah
Jl Raya Seminyak
Sungai Mati
Jl Sunset
Jl Dewi Sri
LEGIAN
Jl Padma Utara
Jl Padma (Jl Yudistra)
Jl Sahadewa
Jl Pura Puseh
Jl Melasti
Central Kuta Money Exchange
Jl Patih Jelantik
A
B
C
D
E
F
G
1
2
3
4
19
60
53
69
52
31
70
48
27
62
3
56
13
22
24
4
38
46
23
32
33
66
55
5
54
15
58
51

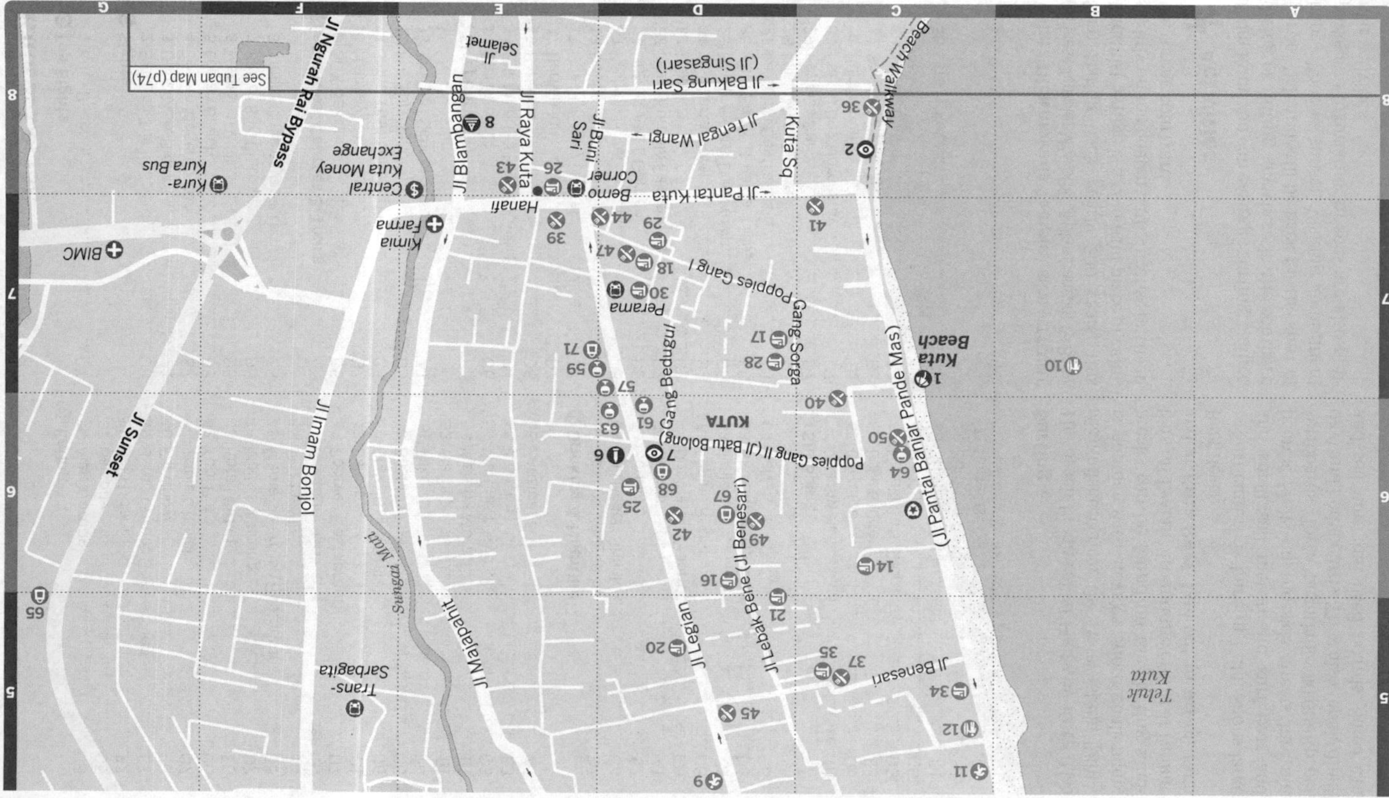
See Tuban Map (p74)
Jl Ngurah Rai Bypass
Jl Sunset
Jl Imam Bonjol
Sungai Mati
Jl Majapahit
Jl Blambangan
Jl Selamet
Jl Raya Kuta
Jl Buni Sari
Jl Bakung Sari
(Jl Singasari)
Jl Tengal Wangi
Kuta Sq
Jl Pantai Kuta
Bemo Corner
Hanafi
Kimia Farma
Central Kuta Money Exchange
Kura-Kura Bus
BIMC
Perama
Poppies Gang I
Gang Sorga
Gang Bedugul
Poppies Gang II (Jl Batu Bolong)
KUTA
Jl Legian
Jl Lebak Bene (Jl Benesari)
Jl Benesari
(Jl Pantai Banjar Pande Mas)
Beach Walkway
Kuta Beach
Teluk Kuta
Trans-Sarbagita
A
B
C
D
E
F
G
5
6
7
8
1
2
6
7
8
9
10
11
12
14
16
17
18
20
21
25
26
28
29
30
34
35
36
37
39
40
41
42
43
44
45
47
49
50
57
59
61
63
64
65
67
68
71

Kuta & Legian

Top Sights
1 Kuta Beach ... C7

Sights
2 Bali Sea Turtle Society ... C8
3 Double Six Beach ... A1
4 Dream Museum Zone ... E2
5 Legian Beach ... B3
6 Memorial Wall ... D6
7 Site of Sari Club ... D6
8 Vihara Dharmayana Temple ... E8

Activities, Courses & Tours
9 5GX Bali ... D5
10 Halfway Kuta ... B7
11 Jamu Traditional Spa ... C5
12 Pro Surf School ... C5
13 Rip Curl School of Surf ... A1

Sleeping
14 Bali Bungalo ... C6
15 Bali Mandira Beach Resort ... B4
16 Bendesa ... D6
17 Berlian Inn ... D7
18 Cheeky Piggy Hostel ... D7
19 Double-Six ... A1
20 Fashion Hotel ... D5
21 Hotel Ayu Lili Garden ... D5
22 Hotel Kumala Pantai ... B2
23 Island ... C2
24 Jayakarta Hotel ... B2
25 Kayun Hostel Downtown ... D6
26 Kuta Bed & Breakfast Plus ... E8
27 La Costa Central ... C1
28 Mimpi Bungalows ... D7
29 Poppies Bali ... D7
30 Puri Agung Homestay ... D7
31 Puri Damai ... B1
32 Sari Beach Hotel ... B3
33 Sri Beach Inn ... C3
34 Stones ... C5
35 Un's Hotel ... C5

Eating
36 Ajeg Warung ... C8
37 Balcony ... C5
38 Balé Udang ... F2
39 Bemo Corner Coffee Shop ... E7
40 Fat Chow ... C6
41 Jamie's Italian ... C7
42 Kopi Pot ... D6
43 Kuta Market ... E8
44 Made's Warung ... D7
45 Mama's German Restaurant ... D5
46 Mozzarella ... B2
Plantation Grill ... (see 19)
47 Poppies Restaurant ... D7
48 Saleko ... C1
49 Stakz Bar & Grill ... D6
50 Sushi Tei ... C6
51 Take ... D4
52 Warung Asia ... B1
53 Warung Murah ... B1
54 Warung Yogya ... C3
55 Wooyoo ... E3
56 Zanzibar ... A1

Drinking & Nightlife
57 Apache Reggae Bar ... D7
58 Bali Beach Shack ... C4
59 Bounty ... E7
60 Cocoon ... A1
Double-Six Rooftop ... (see 19)
61 Engine Room ... D6
62 Jenja ... C1
63 Sky Garden Lounge ... D6
64 Velvet ... C6

Shopping
Beachwalk ... (see 50)
65 Carrefour ... G5
66 Luke Studer ... E3
67 Naruki Surf Shop ... D6
68 Rip Curl ... D6
69 Sriwijaya Batik ... B1
70 Summer Batik ... B1
71 Surfer Girl ... E7

Vihara Dharmayana Temple BUDDHIST TEMPLE
(Chinese Temple; Map p68; Jl Blambangan; 8am-8pm) Dating back nearly 200 years, this Buddhist temple is a colourful place of calm, slightly off the beaten path. Incense burns in the serene courtyard.

Activities

From Kuta, you can easily go surfing, sailing, diving or rafting anywhere in the southern part of Bali and still be back for the start of happy hour at sunset. Visiting amusement parks and luxuriating in spas are also popular activities.

Surfing

The beach break called **Halfway Kuta** (Map p68), offshore near the Hotel Istana Rama, is popular with novices. More challenging breaks can be found on the shifting sandbars off Legian, around the end of Jl Padma, and at **Kuta Reef**, 1km out to sea off Kuta Reef Beach.

Surf culture is huge in Kuta. Shops large and small sell megabrand surf gear and boards. Stalls on the side streets hire out surfboards (for a negotiable 50,000Rp per day) and bodyboards. They also repair dings and sell new and used boards. Some can arrange transport to nearby surfing spots. Used boards in good shape average US$200.

Waterbom Park WATER PARK
(Map p74; ☎0361-755676; www.waterbom-bali.com; Jl Kartika Plaza; adult/child 535,000/385,000Rp; ⊙9am-6pm) This watery amusement park covers 3.8 hectares of landscaped tropical gardens. It has assorted water slides (a couple dozen in total, including the 'Climax'), swimming pools, a FlowRider surf machine and a 'lazy river' ride. Other indulgences include a food court, a bar and a spa.

Pro Surf School SURFING
(Map p68; ☎0361-751200; www.prosurfschool.com; Jl Pantai Kuta 32; lessons per day from 675,000Rp) Right along Kuta Beach, this well-regarded school has been getting beginners standing for years. It offers all levels of lessons, including semi-private ones, plus gear and board rental. There are dorm rooms (from 150,000Rp), a pool and a cool cafe.

Rip Curl School of Surf SURFING
(Map p68; ☎0361-735858; www.ripcurlschoolofsurf.com; Jl Arjuna; lessons from 700,000Rp) Usually universities sell shirts with their logos; here it's the other way round: the beachwear company sponsors a school. Lessons at all levels are given across the south; there are special courses for kids. It has a location for kitesurfing, windsurfing, diving, wakeboarding and stand-up paddle boarding (SUP) in Sanur.

Jamu Traditional Spa SPA
(Map p68; ☎0361-752520, ext 165; www.jamutraditionalspa.com; Jl Pantai Kuta, Alam Kul Kul; 1hr massage from 350,000Rp; ⊙9am-7pm) In serene surrounds at a resort hotel you can enjoy a massage in rooms that open onto a pretty garden courtyard. If you've ever wanted to be part of a fruit cocktail, here's your chance – treatments involve tropical nuts, coconuts, papayas and more, often in fragrant baths.

5GX Bali AMUSEMENT PARK
(Reverse Bungy; Map p68; ☎0878 6063 5464; 99 Jl Legian Kaja; per person 250,000-350,000Rp; ⊙11am-3am) Designed in New Zealand, this light-up purple fairground ride is suspended on elastic ropes between two towers, and with either two or three passengers inside, it is catapulted vertically at about 200km/h, then left to bounce around, rotating wildly and sending the occupants into fits of laughter and terror. It's almost as fun just to watch.

Upside Down World AMUSEMENT PARK
(☎0361-847 3053; www.upsidedownworldgroup.com; Jalan Bypass Ngurah Rai 726; adult/child 100,000/50,000Rp; ⊙9am-9pm; 👪) Fun for the whole family, Upside Down World features themed rooms with decor positioned the wrong way up. Strike a pose and see the hilarious results on your camera screen. From everyday rooms such as a kitchen to a special Balinese room with ornate carvings, your imagination is the only limit when it comes to these gravity-defying antics.

Sleeping

Kuta, Legian and Tuban have hundreds of places to stay. Tuban and Legian have mostly midrange and top-end hotels – the best places for budget accommodation are Kuta and southern Legian. Almost every hotel has air-con and a pool. Dozens of generic midrange chain hotels are appearing throughout the area. Many are very inconveniently located.

Any place west of Jl Legian won't be more than a 10-minute walk to the beach.

Kuta

★ **Hotel Ayu Lili Garden** HOTEL $
(Map p68; ☎0361-750557; ayuliligardenhotel@yahoo.com; off Jl Lebak Bene; r with fan/air-con from 195,000/250,000Rp; ❄📶🏊) In a *relatively* quiet area near the beach, this vintage family-run hotel has 22 bungalow-style rooms. Standards are high and for a little bit extra you can add amenities such as a fridge.

★ **Kuta Bed & Breakfast Plus** GUESTHOUSE $
(KBB; Map p68; ☎0818 568 364, 0821 4538 9646; kutabnb@gmail.com; Jl Pantai Kuta 1E; r from 100,000Rp; ❄📶) There are nine comfortable rooms in this excellent guesthouse right across from Bemo Corner – it has all the basics. It's a 10-minute walk from the beach and a 10-minute ride from the airport. It has a wonderful rooftop with views over the Kuta skyline; nightlife is close too.

Cheeky Piggy Hostel HOSTEL $
(Map p68; ☎0361-475 3919; Poppies Lane I; dm/r 75,000/170,000Rp; ❄📶🏊) In a tourist-thronged location in the back alleys of Kuta, this homely and intimate hostel is a top place to meet fellow travellers. There's a small pool, free pancakes and cheap beer.

Kayun Hostel Downtown HOSTEL $
(Map p68; ☎0361-758442; www.kayun-downtown.com; Jl Legian; dm from 100,000Rp; ❄📶🏊)

In the heart of Kuta, close to all the nightlife, this hostel is the place to be if you're here to party. Set in an elegant colonial building, it has a sense of style and a small plunge pool. Dorm rooms have between four and 20 beds, with curtains for privacy.

Mimpi Bungalows HOTEL $
(Map p68; 0361-751848; mimpibungalowkuta@gmail.com; Gang Sorga; r 300,000-600,000Rp;) The cheapest of the 12 bungalow-style rooms here are the best value (and are fan only). Private gardens boast orchids and shade, and the pool is a good size.

Bendesa HOTEL $
(Map p68; 0361-754366; www.bendesaaccommodation.com; off Poppies Gang II; r from 200,000Rp;) The 42 rooms here are in a three-storey block overlooking a pleasant-enough pool area. The location manages to be quiet amid the greater hubbub. The cheapest rooms have cold water (some with bathtubs) and fan. There's wi-fi in some rooms near the lobby.

Berlian Inn HOTEL $
(Map p68; 0361-751501; off Poppies Gang I; s/d from 135,000/210,000Rp;) A stylish cut above other budget places, the 27 rooms in the two-storey buildings here are pleasingly quiet, with ikat bedspreads and an unusual open-air bathroom design. Pricier rooms have air-con and hot water.

Puri Agung Homestay GUESTHOUSE $
(Map p68; 0361-750054; off Gang Bedugul; r with fan/air-con from 120,000/200,000Rp;) Hungover travellers will appreciate the 12 dark, cold water–only rooms at this attractive little place that features a tiny grotto-like garden. Nonvampires can find more light on the top floor. Run by a charming family; a novelty as chains take over Kuta.

★ **Un's Hotel** HOTEL $$
(Map p68; 0361-757409; www.unshotel.com; Jl Benesari; r with fan/air-con 380,000/490,000Rp;) A hidden entrance sets the tone for the secluded feel of Un's, a two-storey place with bougainvillea spilling over the pool-facing balconies. The 30 spacious rooms in a pair of blocks (the southern one is quieter) feature antiques and comfy cane loungers. It's close to the beach.

Bali Bungalo HOTEL $$
(Map p68; 0361-755109; www.bali-bungalo.com; off Jl Pantai Kuta; r 270,000-600,000Rp;) Large rooms close to the beach yet away from irritations are a big part of the appeal of this older 40-room hotel. It's well maintained and there are statues of prancing horses to inspire horseplay in the pool. Rooms are in two-storey buildings and have patios/porches; not all have wi-fi.

Fashion Hotel HOTEL $$
(Map p68; 0361-849 6688; www.fashionbalilegian.com; Jl Legian 121; r from 420,000Rp;) The once-gaudy Love F Hotel in the heart of the Kuta strip got a face lift and recently re-opened as the Fashion Hotel Legian – but the sleek, modern design is still suitably over the top. Strut your stuff down the catwalk in the lobby, where mirrors and lighting effects are designed to make you feel like a model.

There's a rooftop Jacuzzi and a bar with nightly parties.

Poppies Bali HOTEL $$$
(Map p68; 0361-751059; www.poppiesbali.com; Poppies Gang I; r 1,980,000-2,130,000Rp;) This Kuta institution has a lush, green setting for its 20 thatch-roofed cottages with outdoor sunken baths. Bed choices include kings and twins. The pool is surrounded by stone sculptures and water fountains in a garden that almost makes you forget you are in the heart of Kuta.

Stones RESORT $$$
(Map p68; 0361-300 5888; www.stoneshotelbali.com; Jl Pantai Kuta; r incl breakfast from US$110;) Looming across the road from Kuta Beach, this vast resort boasts a huge pool, a vertical garden and 308 rooms in five-storey blocks. The design is hip and contemporary, and high-tech features abound. It's one of the growing number of megahotels along this strip and affiliated with Marriott. Some rooms have bathtubs on the balcony.

Legian

La Costa Central HOTEL $
(Map p68; 0812 8041 7263; Jl Nakula; r incl breakfast 280,000Rp;) In a multistorey building off a relatively quiet side street in Legian, this comfy and economical hotel will wow backpackers with its sparkling clean rooms, lush garden and refreshing swimming pool. Rooms contain midrange amenities such as minifridge and bath products, and staff members are kind and helpful. Those seeking a bit more privacy will prefer the 3rd floor.

OFF THE BEATEN TRACK

LEGIAN BYWAYS

Dodging cars, motorcycles, touts, dogs and dodgy footpaths can make walking through Tuban, Kuta and Legian seem like anything but a holiday. It's intense and can be stressful. You may soon be longing for uncrowded places where you hear little more than the rustling of palm fronds and the call of birds.

Think you need to book a trip out of town? Well, think again. You can escape to the country without leaving the area. Swaths of undeveloped land and simple residential areas where locals live often hide behind the commercial strips.

In Legian, take any of the narrow *gang* (alleys) into the area bounded by Jl Legian, Jl Padma, Jl Padma Utara and Jl Pura Bagus Taruna and soon you'll be on narrow paths that go past local houses and the occasional simple warung or shop. Wander at random and enjoy the silence accented by, yes, the sound of palm fronds and birds.

Sri Beach Inn GUESTHOUSE $
(Map p68; 0361-755897; Gang Legian Tewngah; r with fan/air-con from 200,000/350,000Rp;) Follow a series of paths into the heart of old Legian; when you hear the rustle of palms overhead, you're close to this guesthouse in a garden with five rooms. More money gets you hot water, air-con and a fridge. It offers cheap monthly rates.

★**Puri Damai** GUESTHOUSE $$
(Map p68; 0361-730665; www.puridamai.com; Jl Werkudara; apt 1-/2-bedroom US$70/140;) An elegant choice tucked away near Double Six Beach, this exquisite little hotel is run by Made, the doyen of the Made's Warung empire. The 12 units are sizeable apartments with full kitchens, dining and living areas, terraces and balconies. The compact compound is lush and the furniture is relaxed tropical.

Island GUESTHOUSE $$
(Map p68; 0361-762722; www.theislandhotelbali.com; Gang Abdi; dm/r incl breakfast from 150,000/300,000Rp;) One of Bali's few flashpacker options, Island is a real find – literally. Hidden in the attractive maze of tiny lanes west of Jl Legian, this stylish place with a sparkling pool lies at the confluence of Gang 19, 21 and Abdi. It has a deluxe dorm room with 12 beds.

Sari Beach Hotel HOTEL $$
(Map p68; 0361-751635; www.thesaribeach.com; off Jl Padma Utara; r incl breakfast US$65-80;) Follow your ears down a long *gang* to the roar of the surf at this good-value beachside hotel that defines mellow. It feels like a time warp from the 1980s but is perfect for a no-frills beach holiday. The 21 rooms have patios and the best have big soaking tubs. Grassy grounds boast many little statues and water features.

Jayakarta Hotel RESORT $$
(Map p68; 0361-751433; www.jayakartahotelsresorts.com; Jl Pura Bagus Taruna; r incl breakfast 1,100,000-2,400,000Rp;) The Jayakarta fronts a long and shady stretch of beach. The palm-shaded grounds, several pools and various restaurants make it a favourite with groups and families. Hair-braiders by the pool give kids that holiday look. The 331 rooms are large and in two- and three-storey blocks. Wi-fi is not in every room.

Hotel Kumala Pantai HOTEL $$
(Map p68; 0361-755500; www.kumalapantai.com; Jl Werkudara; r incl breakfast 1,100,000-3,800,000Rp;) The 173 rooms are large, with marble bathrooms featuring separate shower and tub. The three-storey blocks are set in lush grounds across from popular Double Six Beach. Many rooms have fridges and microwaves; ask for one.

Double-Six RESORT $$$
(Map p68; 0361-730466; www.double-six.com; Double Six Beach 66; r incl breakfast from 3,900,000Rp;) A colossus five-star resort, Double-Six takes a leaf out of the Vegas book of extravagance. Fronted by a luxurious 120m pool, the 146 spacious rooms all overlook the beach, and have 24-hour butler service, and TVs in the bathrooms; some rooms have balcony hot tubs. It has an enormous rooftop bar (p78), plus several restaurants including the noted Plantation Grill (p77).

Bali Mandira Beach Resort HOTEL $$$
(Map p68; 0361-751381; www.balimandira.com; Jl Padma 2; r US$150-360;) Gardens filled with bird-of-paradise flowers set the tone at this 191-room, full-service resort

with four-storey blocks and individual garden units. Cottages have updated interiors, and the bathrooms are partly open-air. A dramatic pool at the peak of a stone ziggurat (which houses a spa) offers sweeping ocean views, as does the cafe.

Tuban

There is a string of large hotels along the sometimes-nonexistent Tuban Beach. These places are popular with groups; many have extensive activities geared to children.

Patra Jasa Bali Resort & Villas RESORT **$$$**
(Map p74; ☎0361-935 1161; www.thepatrabali.com; Jl Ir H Juanda; r incl breakfast 1,300,000-2,500,000Rp; ❄📶🏊) At the far-south end of Tuban near Kuta Reef Beach, this low-key resort is very quiet, yet close to the action thanks to the beach walk. The spacious grounds have two pools and sprawling gardens. The 228 rooms have a standard charm; the villas have nice sea views from their terraces.

Tuban

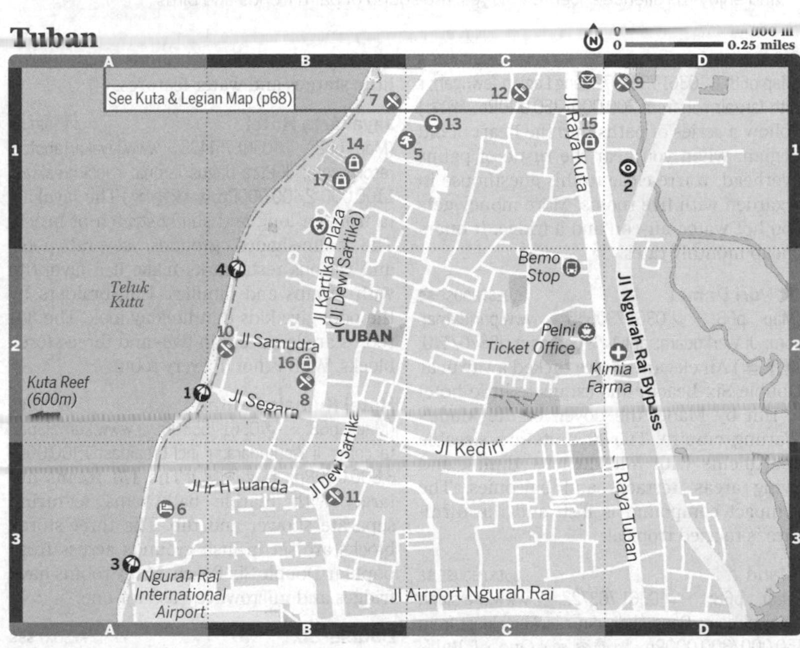

Tuban

Sights
1 Kuta Reef Beach A2
2 Mads Lange's Tomb D1
3 Pantai Patra Jasa A3
4 Tuban Beach B2

Activities, Courses & Tours
5 Waterbom Park C1

Sleeping
6 Patra Jasa Bali Resort & Villas A3

Eating
7 B Couple Bar 'n' Grill B1
8 Kafe Batan Waru B2
9 Kuta Night Market D1
10 Pantai B2
11 Pisgor B3
12 Warung Nikmat C1

Drinking & Nightlife
13 DeeJay Cafe C1

Shopping
14 Discovery Mall B1
15 Joger C1
16 Lippo Mall Kuta B2
17 Periplus Bookshop B1
Sogo .... (see 17)

Eating

There's a profusion of dining options here. Cheap tourist cafes with Indonesian standards, sandwiches and pizza are ubiquitous.

Find laid-back travellers' cafes by wandering the *gang* and looking for crowds. For quick snacks and 4am beers, 24-hour Circle K stores are everywhere.

Beware of big-box restaurants on Jl Sunset. Heavily promoted, they suffer from traffic noise and are aimed at tourists.

Kuta

Ajeg Warung BALINESE $

(Map p68; ☎0822 3777 6766; Kuta Beach; mains from 20,000Rp; ⏲8am-10pm) This simple stall with shady tables is right on Kuta Beach. It dishes up some of the freshest local fare you'll find, with views of the surf. Enter the beach where Jl Pantai Kuta turns north and walk south 100m along the beach path.

Bemo Corner Coffee Shop CAFE $

(Map p68; ☎0812 397 3313; www.facebook.com/bemocappucino; Jl Pantai Kuta 10A; mains from 40,000Rp; ⏲7am-8pm) An attractive oasis just off the madness of Jl Legian, this sweet little open-fronted cafe serves excellent coffee drinks, smoothies and casual fare such as sandwiches and huge trad breakfasts with eggs, bacon, sausage etc.

Wooyoo ICE CREAM $

(Map p68; ☎0822 3652 7735; Jl Dewi Sri 18F; treats from 20,000Rp; ⏲10am-10pm) In a hot tropical place, what is better than ice cream? The soft-serve treats here come from a well-known Korean brand renowned for its rich, creamy swirls. Enjoy in a cup, cone or on sweet 'snail' bread. Toppings include sweet popcorn, chocolate bits and churros. The dining area has a woodsy, open style.

Kuta Night Market INDONESIAN $

(Map p74; Jl Blambangan; mains 15,000-25,000Rp; ⏲6pm-midnight) This is an enclave of stalls and plastic chairs. It bustles with locals and tourism workers chowing down on hot-off-the-wok treats, grilled goods and other fresh foods.

Kuta Market MARKET $

(Map p68; Jl Raya Kuta; ⏲6am-4pm) Not big but its popularity ensures constant turnover. Look for some of Bali's unusual fruits here, such as the mangosteen.

★ **Take** JAPANESE $$

(Map p68; ☎0361-759745; www.take.ramarestaurantsbali.com; Jl Patih Jelantik; mains 70,000-300,000Rp; ⏲11am-midnight; 📶) Flee Bali for a relaxed version of Tokyo just by ducking under the traditional curtain over the doorway at this ever-expanding restaurant. Hyper-fresh sushi, sashimi and more are prepared under the keen eyes of a team of chefs behind a long counter. The head chef is a stalwart at the Jimbaran fish market in the early hours.

★ **Poppies Restaurant** INDONESIAN $$

(Map p68; ☎0361-751059; www.poppiesbali.com; Poppies Gang I; mains 50,000-135,000Rp; ⏲8am-11pm; 📶) Opening its doors in 1973, Poppies was one of the first restaurants established in Kuta (Poppies Gang I is even named after it). It's popular for its elegant garden setting and a menu of upmarket Balinese, Western and Thai cuisine. The *rijstaffel* (selection of dishes served with rice) and seafood is popular.

Fat Chow ASIAN $$

(Map p68; ☎0361-753516; www.fatchowbali.com; Poppies Gang II; mains from 65,000Rp; ⏲9am-11pm; 📶) A stylish, modern take on the traditional open-fronted cafe, Fat Chow serves Asian-accented fare at long picnic tables, small tables and lounges. The food is creative, with lots of dishes for sharing. Among the favourites: crunchy Asian salad, pork buns, Tokyo prawns and authentic pad Thai.

Sushi Tei SUSHI $$

(Map p68; ☎0361-849 6496; www.sushitei.co.id; Jl Pantai Kuta, Beachwalk, 2nd fl; mains 40,000-100,000Rp; ⏲11am-11pm) Let the beach breezes waft across your cheeks at this upscale sushi outlet with views of the surf. The menu is long on sushi and quality is high. Watch for incredible-value specials. There's a good drinks list and sunset happy hour.

Balcony INTERNATIONAL $$

(Map p68; ☎0361-757409; www.thebalconybali.com; Jl Benesari 16; mains 50,000-170,000Rp; ⏲6am-11pm) The Balcony has a breezy tropical design and sits above the din of Jl Benesari below. Get ready for the day with something from the long breakfast menu. At night choose from pasta, grilled meats and a few Indo classics. It's all nicely done and the perfect place for an impromptu date night.

KUTA COWBOYS UNSADDLED

You see them all around Bali's southern beaches: young men who are buff, tattooed, long-haired and gregariously courtly. Long known as 'Kuta cowboys', they turn the Southeast Asian cliché of a younger local woman with an older Western man on its ear. For decades women from Japan, Australia and other nations have found companionship on Bali's beaches that meets a need, be it romantic, adventurous or otherwise.

The dynamic between these foreign women and Balinese men is more complex than a simple exchange of money for sexual services (which is illegal in Bali): although the Kuta cowboys do not receive money directly for sex, their female companions tend to pay for their meals, buy gifts and may even pay other expenses such as rent.

This well-known Bali phenomenon is detailed in the entertaining documentary *Cowboys in Paradise* (stream it online). Director Amit Virmani says he got the idea for the film after he talked to a Balinese boy who said he wanted 'to sex-service Japanese girls' when he grew up. The result looks at the lives of the Kuta cowboys and explores the economics and emotional costs of having fleeting dalliances with female tourists on a schedule.

Made's Warung INDONESIAN $$
(Map p68; ☎0361-732130; www.madeswarung.com; Jl Pantai Kuta; mains from 60,000Rp; ⏲8am-11pm) Made's was the original tourist warung in Kuta and its Westernised Indonesian menu has been much copied. Classic dishes such as *nasi campur* (rice with a choice of side dishes) are served in an open-fronted setting that harks back to when Kuta's tourist hot spots were lit by gas lantern.

Kopi Pot CAFE $$
(Map p68; ☎0361-752614; www.kopipot.com; Jl Legian; mains from 43,000Rp; ⏲7am-11pm; 📶) Shaded by trees, Kopi Pot is a favourite, popular for its coffees, milkshakes and many desserts. The multilevel, open-air dining area and bar sits back from noxious Jl Legian.

Mama's German Restaurant GERMAN $$
(Map p68; ☎0361-761151; www.bali-mamas.com; Jl Legian; mains from 65,000Rp; ⏲24hr) Once you get used to the local serving staff in full German dirndl, you might almost think you're in a sweatier version of Munich. The menu is authentic German, with a vast selection of sausages, roasts and pork steaks from the restaurant's own private butcher. (Non-wurst choices include burgers, noodles, pizza etc.) Quaff draught Bintang by the litre.

Stakz Bar & Grill AUSTRALIAN $$
(Map p68; ☎0361-762129; Jl Benesari; mains 40,000-140,000Rp; ⏲8am-midnight; 📶) From Vegemite on toast and a flat white for brekkie, a potato-cake roll or meat pie in the afternoon, and an Aussie burger with the lot (including beetroot, egg and pineapple) for dinner, Stakz is pure Aussie fare. Patrons mob the bar from the morning; the tattoo outpaces the clothing count.

Jamie's Italian ITALIAN $$$
(Map p68; ☎0361-762118; www.jamieoliver.com; Jl Pantai Kuta; mains from 245,000Rp; ⏲noon-11pm) One of 40 worldwide, this outlet of Jamie Oliver's chain has the expected creative and seasonal menu. The dishes bust clichés and also, possibly, your wallet. Burgers are priced the same as you'd get in NYC. There are tables inside and out. Service and presentation is polished.

Legian

Saleko INDONESIAN $
(Map p68; ☎0361-738170; Jl Nakula 4; mains from 15,000Rp; ⏲8am-1am Mon-Sat, 9am-1am Sun; 🌶) If you haven't tried Masakan Padang food yet, you haven't eaten proper Indonesian. Saleko is a great place to sample this simple, delicious and cheap Sumatran street food. Spicy grilled chicken and fish dare you to ladle on the volcanic sambal – not de-spiced for timid tourist palates. For vegetarians there's also tasty tofu, cooked jackfruit and flavourful eggplant.

All dishes are halal; there's no alcohol.

Warung Murah INDONESIAN $
(Map p68; ☎0361-732082; Jl Arjuna; mains 20,000-35,000Rp; ⏲8am-11pm) Lunch goes swimmingly at this authentic warung specialising in seafood. An array of grilled fish awaits; if you prefer fowl over fin, the *sate ayam* (satay chicken) is succulent and a bargain. Hugely popular at lunch; try to arrive right before noon. Don't miss the sambal.

Warung Yogya INDONESIAN $
(Map p68; ☎0812 3995 5321; Jl Padma Utara; mains from 25,000Rp; ⏰8am-10pm) Hidden in the heart of Legian, this simple warung is spotless and has a bit of mod style. It serves up hearty portions of local food for prices that would almost tempt a local.

Warung Asia ASIAN $
(Map p68; www.warungasia.com; Jl Werkudara 5; mains from 50,000Rp; ⏰1.30-10.30pm; 📶) Staffed by waiters cheery even by Bali standards, this popular upstairs warung serves both Indo classics and Thai fare. It gets boozy and raucous at night.

Mozzarella ITALIAN, SEAFOOD $$
(Map p68; ☎0361-751654; www.mozzarella-resto.com; Jl Padma Utara; mains 70,000-200,000Rp; ⏰7am-11pm; 📶) The best of the beachfront restaurants on Legian's car-free strip, Mozzarella serves Italian fare that's more authentic than most. Fresh fish also features; service is rather polished and there are various open-air areas for moonlit dining, plus a more sheltered dining room. A great spot for a quiet beachfront breakfast.

Balé Udang INDONESIAN $$
(Mang Engking; Map p68; ☎0815 2904 0654; www.baleudang.com; Jl Nakula 88; mains from 45,000Rp; ⏰11am-10pm) Serving the food of Indonesia, this large restaurant is a metaphor for the islands themselves, with various thatched dining pavilions set amid ponds and water features. The long menu focuses on fresh seafood. Service is snappy, but friendly.

Zanzibar INTERNATIONAL $$
(Map p68; ☎0361-733529; Jl Arjuna; mains 50,000-120,000Rp; ⏰7am-11pm) This popular patio fronts a busy strip at Double Six Beach. Sunset is prime time; the best views are from the tables on the 2nd-floor terrace. Dishes include the 'nasi family' and the 'burger bunch'. If it's crowded, the many nearby competitors will do just fine.

Plantation Grill MODERN AUSTRALIAN $$$
(Map p68; ☎0361-734300; www.plantationgrillbali.com; 4th fl, Double-Six Hotel, Double Six Beach 66; mains 200,000-850,000Rp; ⏰6pm-midnight) The gaudy sign outside leaves no doubt that this posh hotel restaurant springs from the empire of Australian chef Robert Marchetti. Inside you'll find a luxurious tropical setting meant to evoke a 1920s fantasy. The menu features big steaks and seafood with some wildly priced specials such as lobster Thermidor (855K!). Sling bar is an intimate retreat for a fantasy cocktail.

Tuban

★Pisgor INDONESIAN $
(Map p74; Jl Dewi Sartika; treats from 2000Rp; ⏰10am-10pm) All sorts of goodness emerges from the ever-bubbling deep-fryers at this narrow storefront near the airport. The *pisang goreng* (banana fritters) are not to be missed and you can enjoy more esoteric fare such as *ote-ote* (vegetable cakes). Get a mixed bag and munch away with raw chillies for extra flavour.

Warung Nikmat INDONESIAN $
(Map p74; ☎0361-764678; Jl Bakung Sari 6A; mains 15,000-30,000Rp; ⏰8am-9pm) This long-running Javanese favourite is known for its array of authentic Indonesian dishes, including beef *rendang* (curry), *perkedel* (fritters), prawn cakes, *sop buntut* (oxtail soup) and various curries and vegetable dishes. Get there before 2pm for the best selection.

Pantai SEAFOOD $$
(Map p74; ☎0361-753196; Jl Wana Segara; mains 50,000-150,000Rp; ⏰10am-11pm; 📶) It's location, location, location at this beachside bar and grill. The food is stock tourist fare (seafood, Indo classics, pasta etc) but the setting overlooking the ocean is idyllic. Each year it gets a bit more stylish and upscale, but it still avoids pretence. It's on the beachfront walk, well behind the Lippo Mall Kuta.

B Couple Bar 'n' Grill SEAFOOD $$
(Map p74; ☎0361-761414; Jl Kartika Plaza; mains 60,000-200,000Rp; ⏰11am-midnight) A vibrant mix of upscale local and international tourists tuck into Jimbaran-style grilled seafood at this slick operation. Pool tables, TV sports and live music add to the din while flames flare in the open kitchens.

Kafe Batan Waru INDONESIAN $$
(Map p74; ☎0361-897 8074; www.batanwaru.com; Jl Kartika Plaza, Lippo Mall Kuta; mains from 60,000Rp; ⏰11am-11pm) The Tuban branch of the noted Ubud restaurant is a slicked-up version of a warung, albeit with excellent and creative Asian and local fare. There's also good coffee, baked goods and kid-friendly items. It has a high-profile spot in front of the glam Lippo Mall (p79).

Drinking & Nightlife

Sunset on the beach is popular, with a drink at a sea-view cafe or beachside beer vendor. Later, the legendary nightlife action heats up. Many spend the early evening at a hipster joint in Seminyak before working their way south to oblivion.

Stylish Seminyak clubs are popular with gay and straight crowds. Kuta and Legian have a mixed crowd.

The Beat (www.beatmag.com) has listings.

★Velvet BAR

(Map p68; ☎0361-846 4928; Jl Pantai Kuta, Beachwalk, level 3, Kuta; ⏲11am-late) The sunset views can't be beat at this large terrace bar and cafe at the beach end of the Beachwalk mall. It morphs into a club after 10pm Wednesday to Sunday. Grab a lounger for two.

★Double-Six Rooftop BAR

(Map p68; ☎0361-734300; www.doublesixrooftop.com; Double Six Beach 66, Legian; ⏲3-11pm; 📶) Sharks swimming in aquarium-lined walls, suave lounges, a commanding location and tiki torches: this ostentatious bar above the Double-Six hotel could be the villain's lair from a Bond film. Amazing sunset views are best enjoyed from the circular booths – the minimum 1,000,000Rp spend to reserve one is redeemable against food, and perfect for groups. Drinks here are pricey.

★Jenja CLUB

(Map p68; ☎0361-882 7711; www.clubjenja.com; TS Suites, Jl Nakula 18, Legian; ⏲10pm-4am Wed & Thu, to 5am Fri & Sat) A very slick, high-concept nightclub in the TS Suites hotel, spread over several levels. DJs rev it up with disco, R&B, funk, soul and techno.

> **DON'T MISS**
>
> **SUNSET DRINKING**
>
> Bali sunsets regularly explode in stunning displays of reds, oranges and purples. Sipping a cold one while watching this free show to the beat of the surf is the top activity at 6pm. Genial local guys offer plastic chairs on the sand and cheap, cold Bintang (20,000Rp).
>
> In Kuta, head to the car-free south end of the beach; in Legian, the best place is the strip of beach that starts north of Jl Padma and runs to the south end of Jl Pantai Arjuna.

The crowd is a mix of well-heeled locals and expats. The restaurant serves upscale fare, good for sharing.

Bali Beach Shack BAR

(Map p68; ☎0819 3622 2010; www.balibeachshack.com; Jl Sahadewa, Legian; ⏲3-11pm Tue-Sun) A fab open-air bar, with nightly crowds for live music and vivacious drag shows. The music spans pop to country.

Sky Garden Lounge CLUB

(Map p68; www.skygardenbali.com; Jl Legian 61, Kuta; from 99,000Rp; ⏲5pm-4am) A multi-level palace of flash, the Sky Garden flirts with height restrictions from its rooftop bar, where all of Kuta twinkles around you. Look for top DJs, a ground-level cafe and paparazzi-wannabes. Possibly Kuta's most iconic club, with hourly drink specials and a buffet. Attracts backpackers, drunken teens, locals on the make etc.

Engine Room CLUB

(Map p68; ☎0361-755188; www.engineroombali.com; Jl Legian 89, Kuta; ⏲6pm-4am) Open to the street, this lurid club features go-go dancers in cages as a come-on. As the evening progresses almost everyone dances and clothing gets shed. It's a wild party, with four hedonistic venues playing music that includes hip-hop, trap and rap.

Cocoon CLUB

(Map p68; ☎0361-731266; www.cocoon-beach.com; Jl Arjuna, Legian; ⏲10am-midnight) A huge pool with a view of Double Six Beach anchors this sort-of high-concept club (alcohol-branded singlets not allowed!), which has parties and events around the clock. Beds, loungers and VIP areas surround the pool; DJs spin theme nights.

Bounty CLUB

(Map p68; Jl Legian, Kuta; ⏲10pm-3am) Set on a faux sailing boat amid a mini-mall of food and drink, the Bounty is a vast open-air disco that pumps all night to hip-hop, techno, house and party tracks. Foam parties, go-go dancers, drag shows and cheap shots add to the rowdiness.

Apache Reggae Bar BAR

(Map p68; Jl Legian 146, Kuta; ⏲8pm-2am) One of the rowdier spots, Apache jams in locals and visitors, many of whom are on the make. The music is loud, but that pounding you feel the next day is from the boozy drinks served in huge plastic jugs.

DeeJay Cafe CLUB
(Map p74; ☎0361-758880; Jl Kartika Plaza 8X, Kuta Station Hotel, Tuban; ⊙1am-11am) The choice for closing out the night (or starting the day). House DJs play tribal, underground, progressive, trance, electro and more. Expect a hardcore crowd of ravers.

Shopping

Kuta has a vast concentration of cheap, tawdry shops (top-selling souvenirs include penis-shaped bottle openers), and flashy surf-gear emporiums. As you head north along Jl Legian, the quality improves and you start finding cute boutiques, especially near Jl Arjuna (which has wholesale fabric, clothing and craft stores, giving it a bazaar feel). Continue into Seminyak for absolutely fabulous shopping.

★ **Luke Studer** SPORTS & OUTDOORS
(Map p68; ☎0361-894 7425; www.studersurfboards.com; Jl Dewi Sri 7A, Legian; ⊙9am-8pm) Legendary board-shaper Luke Studer works from this large and glossy shop. Short boards, retro fishes, single fins and classic longboards are sold ready-made or custom-built.

Sriwijaya Batik TEXTILES
(Map p68; ☎0878-6150 0510; Jl Arjuna 19, Legian; ⊙9am-6pm) Makes batik and other fabrics to order in infinite colours. Great browsing.

Surfer Girl CLOTHING
(Map p68; ☎0361-752693; www.surfer-girl.com; Jl Legian 138, Kuta; ⊙9.30am-11pm) A local legend, this vast store for girls of all ages has a winsome logo that says it all. Clothes, gear, bikinis and plenty of other stuff in every shade of bubblegum ever made.

Rip Curl SPORTS & OUTDOORS
(Map p68; ☎0361-754455; www.ripcurl.com; Jl Legian 62, Kuta; ⊙9am-11pm) Cast that mopey black stuff aside and make a bit of a splash! Bali's largest arm of the surfwear giant has a huge range of beachwear, swimsuits and surfboards.

Beachwalk MALL
(Map p68; www.beachwalkbali.com; Jl Pantai Kuta, Kuta; ⊙10.30am-10.30pm Sun-Thu, 10am-midnight Fri & Sat) This vast open-air mall, hotel and apartment development across from Kuta Beach is filled with international chains: from Gap to Starbucks. Water features course amid the generic retail glitz. Dig deep for the odd interesting find.

LOCAL KNOWLEDGE

FOLLOW THE PARTY

Bali's most infamous clubs cluster in about a 300m radius of Sky Garden Lounge. The distinction between drinking and clubbing is blurry at best, with one morphing into another as the night wears on (or the morning comes up). Most bars are free to enter, and often have special drink promotions and happy hours that run at various intervals until after midnight. Savvy partygoers follow the specials from venue to venue and enjoy a massively discounted night out. Look for cut-price-drinks coupon fliers.

Bali club ambience ranges from the laid-back vibe of the surfer dives to high-concept nightclubs with long drink menus and hordes of prowling staff. Sex workers have proliferated at some Kuta clubs.

Lippo Mall Kuta MALL
(Map p74; ☎0361-897 8000; www.lippomalls.com; Jl Kartika Plaza, Tuban; ⊙10am-10pm) This large mall in south Bali only adds to the traffic chaos on Tuban's under-engineered streets. A huge Matahari department store is joined by scores of international chains, restaurants and a supermarket.

Sogo DEPARTMENT STORE
(Map p74, Tuban; ☎0361-769555; Jl Kartika Plaza, Discovery Mall; ⊙10am-10pm) Stylish Japanese department store that has an international cult following.

Summer Batik TEXTILES
(Map p68; ☎0361-735401; Jl Arjuna 45, Legian; ⊙9.30am-5pm) Although most other outlets have left, Jl Arjuna still has a few batik wholesalers hanging on amid the construction boom in chain hotels. This one is a riot of colour with thousands of samples in a tight little space.

Discovery Mall MALL
(Map p74; ☎0361-755522; www.discoveryshoppingmall.com; Jl Kartika Plaza, Tuban; ⊙10am-10pm, to 10.30pm Sat & Sun) Swallowing up a significant section of the shoreline, this huge, hulking and popular enclosed Tuban mall is built on the water and filled with shops of every kind, including the large Centro and trendy Sogo department stores.

DON'T MISS

KUTA'S FAVOURITE STORE

The mobs out the front look like they're making a run on a bank. Inside it's simply pandemonium. Welcome to **Joger** (Map p74; ☎0361-752523; www.jogerjelek.com; Jl Raya Kuta; ⏰10am-8pm), a Bali retail legend that is the most popular store in the south. No visitor from elsewhere in Indonesia would think of leaving the island without a doe-eyed plastic puppy (4000Rp) or one of the thousands of T-shirts bearing a wry, funny or simply inexplicable phrase (almost all are limited edition). Warning: conditions inside the cramped store are simply insane.

Carrefour MALL
(Map p68; ☎0361-847 7222; Jl Sunset, Kuta; ⏰8am-10pm) This large outlet of the French discount chain combines lots of small shops (books, computers, bikinis) with one huge hypermarket. It's the place to stock up on staples and there's a large ready-to-eat section and food court as well. The downside, however, is inescapable: it's a mall.

Periplus Bookshop BOOKS
(Map p74; ☎0361-769757; Jl Kartika Plaza, Discovery Mall, 1st fl, Tuban; ⏰10am-10pm) Large selection of new books.

Naruki Surf Shop SPORTS & OUTDOORS
(Map p68; ☎0361-765772; Jl Lebak Bene, Kuta; ⏰10am-8pm) One of dozens of surf shops lining the lanes of Kuta, sells a huge range of boards at popular prices.

Information

EMERGENCY

Tourist Police Station (Map p74; ☎0361-224111; 170 Jl Kartika; ⏰24hr)

Tourist Police Post (Map p68; ☎0361-784 5988; Jl Pantai Kuta; ⏰24hr) A second tourist police office right across from the beach; the officers have a gig that is sort of like a Balinese *Baywatch*.

MEDICAL SERVICES

BIMC (Map p68; ☎0361-761263; www.bimcbali.com; Jl Ngurah Rai 100X; ⏰24hr) On the bypass road just east of Kuta, near the Bali Galeria shopping mall. It's a modern clinic that can do tests, hotel visits and arrange medical evacuation. Visits can cost US$100 or more. It has a branch in Nusa Dua.

Kimia Farma (Map p68; ☎0361-755622; Jl Pantai Kuta 102; ⏰24hr) Part of a local chain of pharmacies, this is well-stocked and carries hard-to-find items, such as that antidote for irksome revellers in the morning: earplugs. Also has branches at **Tuban** (Map p74; ☎0361-757472; Jl Raya Kuta; ⏰24hr) and **Legian** (Map p68; ☎0361-734970; Jl Legian 504; ⏰24hr).

MONEY

Central Kuta Money Exchange (Map p68; ☎0361-762970; www.centralkutabali.com; Jl Raya Kuta 168; ⏰8am-6pm) This trustworthy place deals in numerous currencies. Has many locations, including a branch in **Legian** (Map p68; Jl Melasti; ⏰8.30am-9pm) and counters inside some Circle K convenience stores.

POST

Postal agencies that can send mail are common.

Main Post Office (Map p74; ☎0361-754012; Jl Selamet; ⏰7am-2pm Mon-Thu, to 11am Fri, to 1pm Sat) On a little road east of Jl Raya Kuta, this small and efficient post office is well practised in shipping large packages.

TOURIST INFORMATION

There's no useful official tourist office. Places that advertise themselves as 'tourist information centres' are usually commercial travel agents, or worse: time-share apartment sales operations.

TRAVEL AGENCIES

Hanafi (Map p68; ☎0821 4538 9646; www.hanafi.net; Jl Pantai Kuta) This legendary tour guide operates from Kuta. Customises trips of all kinds, whether for families or couples, and runs the charming Kuta Bed & Breakfast Plus (p71) as well. Gay friendly.

Getting There & Away

BEMO

Bemos (minibuses) travel between Kuta and the Tegal terminal in Denpasar – the fare should be around 10,000Rp. The route goes from Jl Raya Kuta near Jl Pantai Kuta, looping past the beach, then on Jl Melasti and back past **bemo corner** (Map p68) for the trip back to Denpasar.

There's a **bemo stop** (Map p74) off Jl Raya Kuta for infrequent bemo service between Kuta and Tuban.

BUS

For public buses to anywhere in Bali, you'll have to go to the appropriate terminal in Denpasar first. Tourist shuttles are widely advertised on backstreets.

Perama (Map p68; ☎0361-751551; www.peramatour.com; Jl Legian 39; ⏰7am-10pm) The main tourist shuttle-bus operation in town;

it may do hotel pick ups and drop-offs for an extra 10,000Rp (confirm with staff when making arrangements). It usually has at least one bus a day to destinations including Lovina (125,000Rp, 4½ hours), Padangbai (75,000Rp, three hours) and Ubud (60,000Rp, 1½ hours).

Trans-Sarbagita (Map p68; ☎0811 385 0900; Jl Imam Bonjol; 3000Rp; ⏰5am-9pm) Bali's public bus service has four routes that converge on the central parking area just south of Istana Kuta Galleria. Destinations include Denpasar, Sanur, Jimbaran and Nusa Dua.

Kuta is a hub for the highly useful **Kura-Kura tourist bus** (Map p68; ☎0361-757070; www.kura2bus.com; Jl Ngurah Rai Bypass, ground fl, DFS Galleria; rides 20,000-80,000Rp, 3-/7-day pass from 150,000/250,000Rp; 📶) service.

BOAT

Pelni Ticket Office (Map p74; ☎0623 6175 5855, 0361-763963; www.pelni.co.id; Jl Raya Kuta 299; ⏰8am-noon & 1-4pm Mon-Fri, 8am-1pm Sat) Source for schedules and tickets for the national shipping line.

Getting Around

TO/FROM THE AIRPORT

A minivan from the airport costs 200,000Rp to Tuban, 250,000Rp to Kuta and 260,000Rp to Legian. When travelling *to* the airport, get a metered taxi for savings. A motorbike taxi will usually cost about half of a regular taxi.

TAXI

In traffic, a ride from Kuta to Seminyak can top 150,000Rp and take more than 30 minutes; walking the beach will be quicker.

Seminyak

☎0361 / POP 6140

Fabulous Seminyak is the centre of life for hordes of the island's expats, many of whom own boutiques, design clothes, surf, or do seemingly nothing at all. It may be immediately north of Kuta and Legian, but in many respects, not the least of which is its intangible sense of style, Seminyak feels almost like it's on another island.

It's a dynamic place, home to scores of restaurants and clubs and a wealth of creative, designer shops and galleries. World-class hotels line the beach, and what a beach it is – as wide and sandy as Kuta's but less crowded.

Seminyak seamlessly merges with Kerobokan, which is immediately north – in fact the exact border between the two is as fuzzy as most other geographic details in Bali. You could easily spend your entire holiday in Seminyak.

Beaches

Kuta Beach morphs into Legian, then Seminyak. Because of the limited road access, the sand in Seminyak tends to be less crowded than in Kuta. This also means that it's less patrolled and the water conditions are less monitored. The odds of encountering dangerous rip tides and other hazards are ever-present, especially as you head north.

★Seminyak Beach BEACH

A lounger and an ice-cold Bintang on the beach at sunset is simply magical. A good stretch can be found near Pura Petitenget, and it tends to be less crowded than further south in Kuta.

Sights

BIASA ArtSpace GALLERY

(☎0361-730308; www.biasagroup.com; Jl Raya Seminyak 34; ⏰9am-9pm) FREE Founded in 2005, BIASA ArtSpace showcases the work of up-and-coming Indonesian and international artists. The gallery has a line-up of rotating exhibitions in a variety of art forms, from painting and photography to sculpture and installation art. The upper floor houses a mini library and a restoration studio.

Pura Petitenget HINDU TEMPLE

(Jl Petitenget) This is an important temple and the scene of many ceremonies. It is one of a string of sea temples that stretches from Pura Luhur Ulu Watu on the Bukit Peninsula north to Pura Tanah Lot in western Bali. Petitenget loosely translates as 'magic box'; it was a treasured belonging of the

SEMINYAK'S CURVING SPINE

The thriving heart of Seminyak is along meandering Jl Kayu Aya (aka Jl Oberoi/Jl Laksmana). It heads towards the beach from bustling Jl Basangkasa and then turns north through a part of Seminyak along Jl Petitenget. The road is lined with a profusion of restaurants, upscale boutiques and hotels as it winds through Seminyak and into Kerobokan. Footpaths have hugely improved window-shopping and cafe-hopping; now it's the drivers stuck in traffic who fume.

Seminyak & Kerobokan

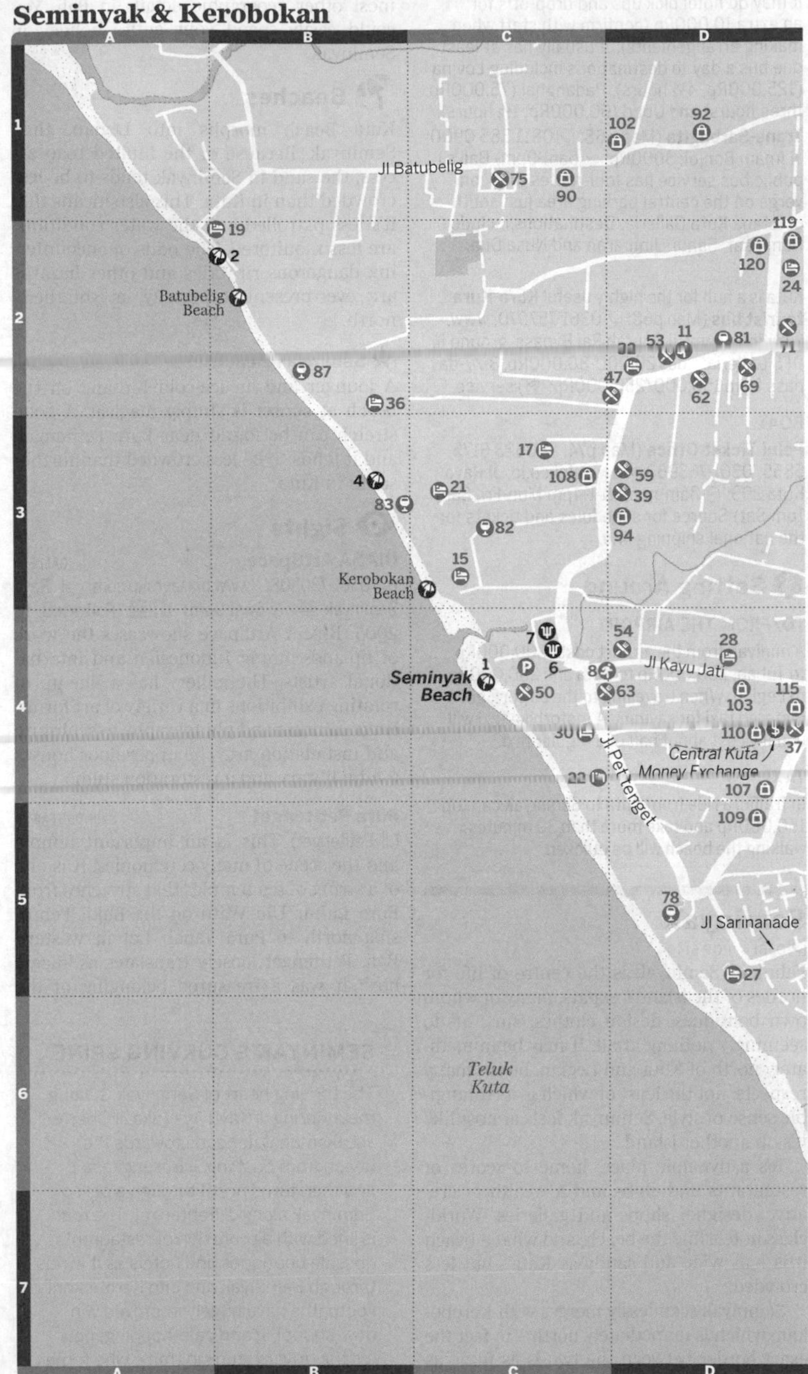

Nook (150m)
Bali Bike Hire (2km)
Central Kuta Money Exchange
Reza Art 2 (300m)
Jl Gunung Tangkuban Perahu
Sari Kembar (650m)
Jl Petitenget
KEROBOKAN
Jl Raya Kerobokan
Jl Raya Mertanadi
Bali Bike Rental
Jl Pangkung Sari
Kimia Farma
ChannelOne
My Basket Bali (700m); Rainbow Tulungagung (700m); Yoga Batik (700m); Victory Art (1km)
Jl Braban
Jl Sunset
Jl Kayu Aya (Jl Laksmana & Jl Oberoi)
Jl Basangkasa
SEMINYAK
Jl Sarinande
Jl Kunti
Jl Drupadi
Jl Plawa
Jl Camplung Tanduk (Jl Dhyana Pura & Jl Abimanyu)
Jl Raya Seminyak
Seminyak Beach
See Kuta & Legian Map (p68)
500 m
0.25 miles

Seminyak & Kerobokan

Top Sights
1 Seminyak Beach C4

Sights
2 Batubelig Beach B2
3 BIASA ArtSpace G7
4 Kerobokan Beach B3
5 Kerobokan Jail G1
6 Pura Masceti C4
7 Pura Petitenget C4

Activities, Courses & Tours
8 Bodyworks C4
9 Chill H6
10 Jari Menari G5
11 Jiwa Bikram D2
12 Prana H6
13 Seminyak Yoga Shala G4
14 Sundari Day Spa F1

Sleeping
15 Alila Seminyak C3
16 Brown Feather E1
17 Buah Bali Villas C3
18 Casa Artista E5
19 Grand Balisani Suites B2
20 Inada Losmen G6
21 Katamama C3
22 Legian C4
23 Luna2 Studiotel E6
24 M Boutique Hostel D2
25 Mutiara Bali E4
26 Ned's Hide Away G6
27 Oberoi D5
28 Pradha Villas D4
29 Raja Gardens F7
30 Samaya C4
31 Sarinande E6
32 Taman Ayu Cottage D2
33 Villa Bunga E1
34 Villa Karisa F6
35 Villa Kresna E6
36 W Bali – Seminyak B2

Eating
37 Bali Bakery D4
38 Barbacoa F1
39 Biku D3
40 Bintang Supermarket G7
41 Café Moka G5
Café Seminyak .... (see 40)
42 Corner House F4
43 Divine Earth G4
44 Earth Cafe & Market F4
45 Fat Gajah G5
46 Ginger Moon E4
47 Gourmet Cafe D2
48 Grocer & Grind E4
49 Gusto Gelato & Coffee G3
50 La Lucciola C4
51 L'Assiette G4
52 Mama San F4
53 Merah Putih D2
54 Motel Mexicola D4
55 Nalu Bowls G6
56 Naughty Nuri's G3
57 Pasar Kerobokan G1
58 Rolling Fork H6
59 Saigon Street D3
60 Sangsaka E3
61 Sardine F1
62 Sarong D2

legendary 16th-century priest Nirartha, who refined the Balinese religion and visited this site often.

The temple is renowned for its anniversary celebrations on the Balinese 210-day calendar. It is right next to Pura Masceti.

Pura Masceti HINDU TEMPLE
(Jl Petitenget) An agricultural temple where farmers pray for relief from rat infestations, and savvy builders make offerings of forgiveness before planting yet another villa in the rice fields.

Activities

★ Jari Menari SPA
(☎0361-736740; www.jarimenari.com; Jl Raya Basangkasa 47; massages from 435,000Rp; ⊙9am-9pm) Jari Menari is true to its name, which means 'dancing fingers': your body will be one happy dance floor. The all-male staff use massage techniques that emphasise rhythm. It also offers massage classes (from US$170).

Prana SPA
(☎0361-730840; www.pranaspabali.com; Jl Kunti 118X; massages from 510,000Rp; ⊙9am-10pm) A palatial Moorish fantasy that is easily the most lavishly decorated spa in Bali, Prana offers everything from basic hour-long massages to facials and all manner of beauty treatments.

Seminyak Yoga Shala YOGA
(☎0361-730498; www.seminyakyogashala.com; Jl Basangkasa; classes from 140,000Rp) No-nonsense yoga studio with daily classes in several styles including ashtanga, Mysore and yin yang.

Bodyworks SPA
(☎0361-733317; www.bodyworksbali.com; Jl Kayu Jati 2; massage from 295,000Rp; ⊙9am-10pm) Get waxed, get your hair done, get the kinks

63 Sea Circus C4
Shelter Cafe .... (see 55)
64 Sisterfields E4
65 Taco Beach Grill H6
66 Ultimo E4
67 Wacko Burger F6
68 Warung Aneka Rasa F4
69 Warung Eny D2
70 Warung Ibu Made G4
71 Warung Kita D2
72 Warung Sobat G1
73 Warung Sulawesi F2
74 Warung Taman Bambu H6
75 Watercress C1

Drinking & Nightlife
76 40 Thieves F1
77 Bali Joe F6
78 Ku De Ta D5
79 La Favela F4
80 La Plancha E7
81 Mirror D2
82 Mrs Sippy C3
83 Potato Head B3
84 Red Carpet Champagne Bar F4
85 Revolver E4
86 Ryoshi Seminyak House of Jazz G7
87 Warung Pantai B2
88 Zappaz E4

Entertainment
Upstairs Lounge Cinema Club .... (see 43)

Shopping
89 Ashitaba G5
90 Ayun Tailor C1
91 Bamboo Blonde F4
92 Bathe D1
93 Biasa G7
94 Carga D3
95 Cotton Line by St Isador F4
96 Divine Diva F4
97 Domicil G6
98 Drifter Surf Shop E4
99 Geneva Handicraft Centre F3
100 Indivie G6
101 JJ Bali Button G1
102 Kevala Home D1
103 Kody & Ko D4
Lily Jean .... (see 115)
104 Lucy's Batik G4
105 Lulu Yasmine F4
106 Mercredi F1
107 Milo's D4
108 Namu C3
109 Niconico D5
110 Periplus Bookshop D4
111 Pourquoi Pas G4
112 Prisoners of St Petersburg F4
113 Purpa Fine Art Gallery G4
Quarzia Boutique .... (see 107)
114 Sandio G4
115 Seminyak Village D4
116 Souq G4
117 Thaikila F4
118 Theatre Art Gallery G6
119 Tribali D2
120 Tulola D2
Uma & Leopold .... (see 44)
White Peacock .... (see 115)
121 You Like Lamp G3

rubbed out of your joints – all this and more is on the menu at this uber-popular spa in the heart of Seminyak.

Chill SPA
(☎0361-734701; www.chillreflexology.com; Jl Kunti; treatments per hr from 250,000Rp; ⏰10am-10pm) The name says it all. This Zen place embraces reflexology; treatments include full-body pressure-point massage.

Surf Goddess SURFING
(☎0858 997 0808; www.surfgoddessretreats.com; per week incl private room from US$2495) Surf holidays for women that include lessons, yoga, meals and lodging in a posh guesthouse in the backstreets of Seminyak.

Sleeping

Seminyak has a wide range of accommodation, from world-class beach resorts to humble hotels hidden on backstreets. This is also the start of villa-land, which runs north from here through the vanishing rice fields beyond Canggu. For many, a private villa with its own pool is a holiday dream.

Oodles of midrange chain hotels across south Bali add Seminyak to their names even when they're as far away as Denpasar.

Inada Losmen GUESTHOUSE $
(☎0361-732269; putuinada@hotmail.com; Gang Bima 9; s/d from 150,000/180,000Rp) Buried in a *gang* behind Bintang Supermarket, this budget champ is a short walk from clubs, the beach and other Seminyak joys. The 12 rooms are small and somewhat dark.

Ned's Hide-Away GUESTHOUSE $
(☎0361-731270; waynekelly1978@gmail.com; Gang Bima 3; r with fan/air-con from 180,000/300,000Rp; ❄📶) While its standards have slipped, Ned's remains a good budget choice with 16 rooms, some basic and others more plush. Wi-fi is only available in reception.

Raja Gardens GUESTHOUSE $$

(☎0361-934 8957; www.jdw757.wixsite.com/rajagardens; off Jl Camplung Tanduk; r with fan/air-con from 500,000/700,000Rp; ❄📶🏊) Here since 1980, this old-school guesthouse has spacious, grassy grounds with fruit trees and a quiet spot located almost on the beach. The eight rooms are fairly basic but there are open-air bathrooms and plenty of potted plants. The large pool is a nice spot to lounge by, and it's generally a mellow place.

Villa Kresna BOUTIQUE HOTEL $$

(☎0361-730317; www.villakresna.com; Jl Sarinande 17; r/villa from 800,000/1,130,000Rp; ❄📶🏊) The beach is only 50m from this cute, idiosyncratic property tucked away on a small *gang*. The 22 art-filled units are mostly suites, which have a nice flow-through design with both public and private patios. A small, sinuous pool wanders through the property.

Sarinande HOTEL $$

(☎0361-730383; www.sarinandehotels.com; Jl Sarinande 15; r incl breakfast 630,000-680,000Rp; ❄📶🏊) The 26 excellent-value rooms here are in older two-storey blocks set around a small pool; the decor is a bit dated but everything is well maintained. Amenities include fridges, satellite TV and DVD players, and there's a cafe. The beach is a three-minute walk away.

Mutiara Bali HOTEL $$

(☎0361-734966; www.mutiarabali.com; Jl Braban 77; r/villa from 1,125,000/2,900,000Rp; ❄📶🏊) The 17 private villas here are good value, each with an open lounge area looking out to a private plunge pool. The hotel-style rooms have all the usual amenities plus deep balconies for lounging.

★Oberoi HOTEL $$$

(☎0361-730361; www.oberoihotels.com; Jl Kayu Aya; r incl breakfast from 4,600,000Rp; ❄@📶🏊) The beautifully understated Oberoi has been a refined Balinese-style beachside retreat since 1971. All accommodation options have private verandahs, and as you move up in price, additional features include walled villas, ocean views and private pools. From the cafe that overlooks the almost-private sweep of beach to the numerous luxuries, this is a place to spoil yourself.

★Samaya VILLA $$$

(☎0361-731149; www.thesamayabali.com; Jl Kayu Aya; villa from US$725; ❄📶🏊) Understated yet cultured, the Samaya is one of the best bets for a villa right on the beach in south Bali. It boasts 52 villas in a luxurious contemporary style, each featuring a private pool. Some units are in a compound away from the water. The food, from breakfast onwards, is superb.

STREET NAME VARIATIONS

A small lane or alley is known as a *gang*, and most of those in Bali lack signs or even names. Some are referred to by the name of a connecting street, eg Jl Padma Utara is the *gang* going north of Jl Padma.

Meanwhile, some streets in Kuta, Legian and Seminyak have more than one name. Many streets were unofficially named after a well-known temple and/or business place. In recent years there has been an attempt to impose official – and usually more Balinese – names on the streets. But the old names are still common and some streets may have more than one.

Following are the old (unofficial) and current official names, from north to south.

OLD (UNOFFICIAL)	CURRENT (OFFICIAL)
Jl Oberoi/Jl Laksmana	Jl Kayu Aya
Jl Raya Seminyak	Northern stretch: Jl Basangkasa
Jl Dhyana Pura/Jl Abimanyu	Jl Camplung Tanduk
Jl Double Six	Jl Arjuna
Jl Pura Bagus Taruna	Jl Werkudara
Jl Padma	Jl Yudistra
Poppies Gang II	Jl Batu Bolong
Jl Pantai Kuta	Jl Pantai Banjar Pande Mas
Jl Kartika Plaza	Jl Dewi Sartika
Jl Segara	Jl Jenggala
Jl Satria	Jl Kediri

Casa Artista GUESTHOUSE $$$
(☎0361-736749; www.casaartistabali.com; Jl Sari Dewi 17; r incl breakfast US$175-195; ❄☜≋) You can literally dance for joy at this cultured guesthouse where the owner, a professional tango dancer, offers lessons. The 12 compact rooms, with names such as Passion and Inspiration, are in an elegant two-storey house surrounding a pool. Some have crystal chandeliers; breakfast is served on your patio.

Legian HOTEL $$$
(☎0361-730622; https://lhm-hotels.com/legian-bali/en; Jl Pantai Kaya Aya; ste/villa incl breakfast from US$600/900; ❄@☜≋) The Legian is flash and brash – one of the reasons it's a fave with people who use their own jets to reach Bali. All 79 rooms claim to be suites, even if some are just large rooms (called 'studios'). On a little bluff right on the beach, the views are panoramic. The design mixes traditional materials with contemporary flair.

Luna2 Studiotel BOUTIQUE HOTEL $$$
(☎0361-730402; www.luna2.com; Jl Sarinande 20; r incl breakfast US$280-450; ❄☜≋) Is it Mondrian? Is it Roy Lichtenstein? We're not sure which modern artists are the inspiration for this eye-popping hotel, but we can say the results astound. The 14 boldly decorated studio apartments feature kitchens, gadgetry, balconies and access to a rooftop bar looking over the ocean. A 16-seat cinema shows movies, and the pool is a full 25m.

Pradha Villas VILLA $$$
(☎0361-735446; www.pradhavillas.com; Jl Kayu Jati 5; villa from 3,100,000Rp; ❄☜≋) Ground zero for Seminyak: the 11 villas are a short walk to some of the best restaurants and the beach. Units vary in size but each is a private walled compound with a swimming pool. Jacuzzis add an extra romantic touch; wake up to a custom-prepared breakfast by the gracious staff.

Villa Karisa HOTEL $$$
(☎0361-739395; www.villakarisabali.com; Jl Drupadi 100X; r 1,310,000-2,800,000Rp; ❄☜≋) It's like visiting the gracious friends in Bali you wish you had. Ideally located on a little *gang* off busy Jl Drupadi, this large villa-style inn has a row of rooms filled with antiques and many comforts. Guests gather in the common room or around the luxurious 12m pool. Enjoy Javanese antique style in the 'Shiva' room.

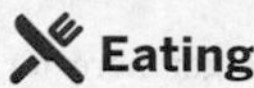

Eating

Jl Kayu Aya is the focus of Seminyak eating (despite the hokey nickname 'Eat St') but there are great choices for every budget virtually everywhere. Note that some restaurants morph into clubs as the night wears on. Conversely, some bars and clubs also have good food. Meanwhile, you're never far from top-notch coffee as Seminyak has a thriving cafe culture.

Warung Taman Bambu BALINESE $
(☎0361-888 1567; Jl Plawa 10; mains from 28,000Rp; ⊙10am-10pm; ☜) This classic warung may look simple from the street but the comfy tables are – like the many fresh and spicy dishes on offer – a cut above the norm. There's a small stand for *babi guling* (spit-roast pig) right next door.

Warung Aneka Rasa INDONESIAN $
(☎0812 361 7937; Jl Kayu Aya; mains from 25,000Rp; ⊙7am-7pm) Keeping things real in the heart of Seminyak's upmarket retail strip, this humble warung cooks up all the Indo classics in an inviting open-front cafe. It's a refuge from the buzz.

Bali Bakery CAFE $
(☎0361-738033; www.balibakery.com; Jl Kayu Aya, Seminyak Sq; mains 40,000-70,000Rp; ⊙7.30am-10.30pm; ☜) The best feature of the Seminyak Sq open-air mall is this bakery with its shady tables and long menu of baked goods, salads, sandwiches and other fine fare. It's a good place to linger before heading back out to shop.

Warung Ibu Made INDONESIAN $
(Jl Basangkasa; mains from 15,000Rp; ⊙7am-7pm) The woks roar almost from dawn to dusk amid the constant hubbub on this busy corner of Jl Raya Seminyak, where several stalls cook food fresh under the shade of a huge banyan. Refresh yourself with the juice of a young coconut.

Café Seminyak CAFE $
(☎0361-736967; Jl Raya Seminyak 17; mains 50,000-90,000Rp; ⊙7am-10pm) Right in front of the busy Bintang Supermarket, this cute and casual place has excellent smoothies and sandwiches made with freshly baked bread.

Café Moka CAFE $
(☎0361-731424; www.cafemokabali.com; Jl Basangkasa; treats 15,000-35,000Rp; ⊙7am-10pm; ❄) Enjoy French-style baked goods (fresh baguettes!) at this popular bakery and cafe.

Many escape the heat and linger here for hours over little French treats. The bulletin board spills over with notices for villa rentals.

Bintang Supermarket SUPERMARKET $
(☎0361-730552; www.bintangsupermarket.com; Jl Raya Seminyak 17; ⏰7.30am-10.30pm) Always busy, this large supermarket is the grocery favourite among expats, who appreciate its good prices and broad range of food, including good fruit and veg. It sells affordable sunscreen, insect spray and other sundries as well.

★ **Shelter Cafe** AUSTRALIAN $$
(☎0813 3770 6471; www.sheltercafebali.com; Jl Drupadi; mains 55,000-95,000Rp; ⏰8am-6pm; 📶) This second-storey cafe brims daily with the young, beautiful people of Seminyak, their coffee strong, their acai bowls piled high (those are actually from Nalu Bowls (p88), the acai bar downstairs). With an extensive menu of healthy fare, it's the top brunch spot in Seminyak, and a cultural hub and host of things like pop-up fashion stores and parties on weekends.

★ **Sisterfields** CAFE $$
(☎0361-738454; www.sisterfieldsbali.com; Jl Kayu Cendana 7; mains 85,000-140,000Rp; ⏰7am-10pm; 📶) Trendy Sisterfields does classic Aussie breakfasts such as smashed avocado, and more-inventive dishes such as salmon Benedict and maple-roasted-pumpkin salad. There are also hipster faves such as pulled-pork rolls and shakshuka poached eggs. Grab a seat at a booth, the counter or in the rear courtyard. There are several other good places for coffee nearby.

★ **Ginger Moon** ASIAN $$
(☎0361-734533; www.gingermoonbali.com; Jl Kayu Aya 7; mains 65,000-195,000Rp; ⏰noon-11pm; 📶👪) Australian Dean Keddell is one of scores of young chefs lured to Bali to run restaurants. His creation is an appealing, airy space, with carved wood and palms. The menu features a 'Best of' list of favourites, served in portions designed for sharing and grazing. Top picks include cauliflower pizza and a special chicken curry. There's a good kids menu.

Mama San FUSION $$
(☎0361-730436; www.mamasanbali.com; Jl Raya Kerobokan 135; mains 90,000-200,000Rp; ⏰noon-3pm & 6.30-11pm; ❄📶) One of Seminyak's most popular restaurants, this stylish warehouse-sized space is split into levels, with photographs hanging from exposed brick walls. The menu has an emphasis on creative dishes from across Southeast Asia. A long cocktail list provides liquid balm for the mojito set and has lots of tropical-flavoured pours.

Sea Circus INTERNATIONAL $$
(☎0361-738667; www.seacircus-bali.com; 22 Jl Kayu Aya; mains from 75,000Rp; ⏰7.30am-10pm; 🖉) Adorned in cartoonish, pastel circus murals, this fabulous spot offers up fresh and delicious dishes inspired by cuisines in Asia, Australia and the Americas. Brunch is hugely popular and includes favourites like acai bowls, chilli scrambled eggs and the 'hangover happy meal'; the cocktails, taco bar and dinner selections, including a summer tuna poke bowl, are also exquisite.

Nalu Bowls HEALTH FOOD $$
(☎0812 3660 9776; www.nalubowls.com; Jl Drupadi; 60,000-80,000Rp; ⏰7.30am-6pm) Inspired by Hawaii's culture and tropical ingredients, this chain of acai bowl establishments has made a big splash in Bali. The flagship Seminyak restaurant occupies just a small bar downstairs from Shelter Cafe, but the line sometimes extends down the block for the fresh fruit and smoothie bowls topped with homemade granola and bananas.

Fat Gajah ASIAN $$
(☎0851 0168 8212; Jl Basangkasa 21; dumplings 52,000-110,000Rp; ⏰11am-11pm; 📶) Fat Gajah is all about dumplings and noodles, prepared with mostly organic ingredients. They come fried or steamed with innovative fillings such as beef *rendang*, black-pepper crab, kimchi tuna or lemongrass lamb. There's a range of small Asian plates. The spare dining room is very appealing.

Motel Mexicola MEXICAN $$
(☎0361-736688; www.motelmexicolabali.com; Jl Kayu Jati 9; mains from 60,000Rp; ⏰11am-1am) Not your average taqueria, Motel Mexicola is an extravaganza that channels a tropical version of a nightclub. The huge space is decked out in kitschy neon and palm trees. Food is secondary to drinks: soft corn tortilla tacos filled with tempura prawn or shredded pork, along with meaty mains. Cocktails, served in copper kettles, are a treat on a balmy evening.

Divine Earth VEGAN $$
(☎0361-731964; www.divineearthbali.com; Jl Raya Basangkasa 1200A; mains 70,000-140,000Rp; ⊙7am-11pm; ❄📶✍) 🌿 A sibling of the much-loved Earth Cafe, this organic vegetarian restaurant also does tasty vegan and raw food. It's perhaps better known for its Upstairs Lounge Cinema Club (p90), where you can bring your food and drink to watch classic, art-house and documentary films.

Corner House CAFE $$
(☎0361-730276; www.cornerhousebali.com; Jl Laksmana 10A; mains 35,000-125,000Rp; ⊙7am-11pm; 📶) With polished concrete floors, dangling light bulbs, distressed walls and vintage-style furniture, this cavernous cafe is almost a Seminyak cliché. A popular brunch spot, it does great coffee, big breakfasts, homemade sausage rolls and steak sandwiches. There's also a small shady courtyard and a relaxed, breezy upstairs dining area.

Rolling Fork ITALIAN $$
(☎0361-733 9633; Jl Kunti 1; mains from 80,000Rp; ⊙8.30am-11pm; 📶) A gnocchi-sized little trattoria, Rolling Fork serves excellent Italian fare. Breakfast features gorgeous baked goods and excellent coffees. Lunch and dinner include authentic and tasty homemade pastas, salads, seafood and more. The open-air dining room has an alluring retro charm; the Italian owners provide just the right accent.

Taco Beach Grill MEXICAN $$
(☎0361-854 6262; www.tacobeachgrill.com; Jl Kunti 6; mains 70,000-120,000Rp; ⊙10am-11pm; 📶) As sprightly as a chilli-accented salsa, this open-fronted casual cafe is known for its *babi guling* tacos. Obviously merging Bali's iconic suckling pig with Mexican flavours is a good thing. Expect the usual south-of-the-border standards plus good juices, smoothies and margaritas. Offers hotel and villa delivery.

Wacko Burger BURGERS $$
(☎0821 4401 0888; www.wackoburger.com; Jl Drupadi 18; mains from 50,000Rp; ⊙noon-9.30pm) It's like you died and went to comfort-food heaven. The burgers here are beloved as are the onion rings, fries, shakes and more. There are all manner of toppings and condiments to choose from. The tables are in an open-air covered patio with actual rice-field views.

Ultimo ITALIAN $$
(☎0361-738720; www.balinesia.co.id; Jl Kayu Aya 104; mains 70,000-180,000Rp; ⊙4pm-1am) This vast and always popular restaurant thrives in a part of Seminyak that's as thick as a good risotto with eateries. Choose a table overlooking the street action, out the back in one of the gardens or inside. Ponder the surprisingly authentic menu and then let the army of staff take charge.

Earth Cafe & Market VEGETARIAN $$
(☎0851 0304 4645; www.earthcafebali.com; Jl Kayu Aya; mains 60,000-100,000Rp; ⊙7am-11pm; 📶✍) 🌿 The good vibes are organic at this vegetarian cafe and store. Choose from creative salads, sandwiches or wholegrain vegan and raw-food goodies. It's most famous for its six-course 'Planet Platter'. The beverage menu includes fresh juices and detox mixes.

Grocer & Grind CAFE $$
(☎0361-730418; www.grocerandgrind.com; Jl Kayu Jati 3X; dinner mains from 85,000Rp; ⊙7am-10pm; ❄📶) You might think you're at a sleek Sydney cafe, but look around and you're unmistakably in Bali. Classic sandwiches, homemade Aussie pies, salads and big breakfasts are popular at this south Bali chain.

La Lucciola FUSION $$$
(☎0361-730838; Jl Petitenget; mains 120,000-400,000Rp; ⊙9am-11pm) A sleek beachside restaurant with good views across a lovely lawn and sand to the surf from its 2nd-floor tables. The bar is popular with sunset-watchers, most of whom move on to dinner here. The menu is a creative melange of international fare with Italian flair.

Drinking & Nightlife

Like your vision at 2am, the division between restaurant, bar and club blurs in Seminyak. Although it lacks massive clubs where you can greet the dawn (or vice versa), stalwarts can head south to the rough edges of Kuta and Legian in the wee hours.

Numerous bars line Jl Camplung Tanduk, though noise-sensitive locals complain if things get too raucous.

★ **La Favela** BAR
(☎0812 4612 0010; www.lafavela.com; Jl Kayu Aya 177X; ⊙5pm-late; 📶) An alluring, mysterious entry seduces you into full bohemian flair at La Favela, one of Bali's coolest and most original nightspots. Themed rooms lead you on a confounding tour from dimly lit

SEMINYAK SUNSETS

At the beach end of Jl Camplung Tanduk you have a choice: turn left for a beachy frolic at the string of beach bars, both simple and plush; or turn right for trendy beach clubs such as Ku De Ta, or cheery vendors offering cheap Bintang, a plastic chair and maybe some amateur guitar music.

speakeasy cocktail lounges and antique dining rooms to graffiti-splashed bars. Tables are cleared after 11pm to make way for DJs and a dance floor.

It's equally popular for its garden restaurant, which has a Mediterranean-inspired menu.

★Revolver CAFE
(☎0851 0088 4968; www.revolverespresso.com; off Jl Kayu Aya; coffee 28,000-55,000Rp, mains from 55,000Rp; ⏰7am-midnight; 📶) Wander down a tiny *gang* and push through narrow wooden doors to reach this matchbox coffee bar that does an excellent selection of brews. There are just a few tables in the creatively retro room that's styled like a Wild West saloon; nab one and enjoy tasty fresh bites for breakfast and lunch.

Ryoshi Seminyak House of Jazz BAR
(☎0361-731152; www.ryoshibali.com; Jl Raya Seminyak 17; ⏰noon-midnight, music from 9pm Mon, Wed & Fri) The Seminyak branch of the Bali chain of Japanese restaurants has live jazz three nights a week on an intimate stage under a traditionally thatched roof. Expect some of the best local and visiting talent.

Red Carpet Champagne Bar BAR
(☎0361-737889; www.redcarpetchampagnebar.com; Jl Kayu Aya 42; ⏰1pm-4am) Choose from more than 200 types of champagne at this over-the-top glam bar on Seminyak's couture strip. Waltz the red carpet and toss back a few namesake flutes while contemplating a raw oyster and displays of frilly frocks. It's open to the street (but elevated, darling) so you can gaze down on the masses.

40 Thieves BAR
(☎0878 6226 7657; www.facebook.com/40thieves.bali; Jl Petitenget 7; ⏰8pm-2am Mon-Thu, to 4am Fri & Sat; 📶) A New York–style speakeasy, this hidden bar is perched above Mad Ronin, a Japanese ramen restaurant, in the trendy area of Seminyak. The atmospheric venue, which is peppered with memorabilia such as old maps and vintage bicycles, attracts a good mix of expats, tourists and locals. There is no signage, so enquire at Mad Ronin if you get lost.

La Plancha BAR
(☎0878 6141 6310; www.laplancha-bali.com; off Jl Camplung Tanduk; ⏰9am-11pm) The most substantial of the beach bars along the beach walk south of Jl Camplung Tanduk, La Plancha has its share of ubiquitous brightly coloured umbrellas and beanbags on the sand, plus a typical beach menu (pizzas, noodles etc). After sunset, expect DJs and beach parties.

Ku De Ta CLUB
(☎0361-736969; www.kudeta.net; Jl Kayu Aya 9; ⏰8am-late; 📶) Ku De Ta teems with Bali's beautiful people (including those whose status is purely aspirational). Scenesters perfect their 'bored' look over drinks during the day while gazing at the fine stretch of beach. Sunset brings out crowds, who dine on eclectic fare at tables. The music throbs with increasing intensity through the night. Special events are legendary.

Bali Joe GAY & LESBIAN
(☎0361-300 3499; www.balijoebar.com; Jl Camplung Tanduk; ⏰4pm-3am; 📶) One of several lively LGBTIQ venues along this strip. Drag queens and go-go dancers rock the house nightly.

Zappaz BAR
(☎0361-742 5534; Jl Kayu Aya 78; ⏰11am-midnight) Brit Norman Findlay tickles the ivories nightly at this cheerful piano bar, where he's been not-quite perfecting his enthusiastic playing for years and years. An enthusiastic cover band lures in gleeful crowds. Skip the food.

☆ Entertainment

Upstairs Lounge Cinema Club CINEMA
(☎0361-731964; www.divineearthbali.com/cinema; Jl Raya Basangkasa 1200A; ⏰films 8pm) State-of-the-art screenings of new, classic, arthouse and unusual movies in a comfy and small cinema. Admission is free with any food purchase from the downstairs Divine Earth (p89) cafe.

🛍 Shopping

Seminyak has it all: designer boutiques (Bali has a thriving fashion industry), retro-chic stores, slick galleries, wholesale emporiums and family-run workshops.

The best shopping starts on Jl Raya Seminyak at Bintang Supermarket and runs north through Jl Basangkasa. The retail strip branches off into Jl Kayu Aya and Jl Kayu Jati while continuing north on Jl Raya Kerobokan into Kerobokan. Avoid stepping into a yawning pavement cavern.

★Souq HOMEWARES
(☎0822 3780 1817; www.souqstore.co; Jl Basangkasa 10; ⏰8am-8pm) The Middle East meets Asia at this glossy high-concept store with Bali-designed housewares and clothing. It has a small cafe with healthy breakfast and lunch choices plus good coffee and cold-pressed juices.

★Drifter Surf Shop FASHION & ACCESSORIES
(☎0361-733274; www.driftersurf.com; Jl Kayu Aya 50; ⏰9am-11pm) High-end surf fashion, surfboards, gear, cool books and brands such as Obey and Wegener. Started by two savvy surfer dudes, the shop stocks goods noted for their individuality and high quality.

★Ashitaba ARTS & CRAFTS
(☎0361-737054; Jl Raya Seminyak 6; ⏰9am-9pm) Tenganan, the Aga village of east Bali, produces the intricate and beautiful rattan items sold here. Containers, bowls, purses and more (from 50,000Rp) display the very fine weaving.

★Indivie ARTS & CRAFTS
(☎0361-730927; www.indivie.com; Jl Raya Seminyak, Made's Warung; ⏰10am-11pm) The works of young designers based in Bali are showcased at this intriguing and glossy boutique.

Bamboo Blonde CLOTHING
(☎0361-731864; www.bambooblonde.com; Jl Kayu Aya 61; ⏰10am-10pm) Shop for frilly, sporty or sexy frocks and formal wear at this cheery designer boutique (one of 11 island-wide). All goods are designed and made in Bali.

Theatre Art Gallery ARTS & CRAFTS
(☎0361-732782; Jl Raya Seminyak; ⏰9am-8pm) Specialises in vintage and reproduction *wayang* puppets used in traditional Balinese theatre. Just looking at the animated faces peering back at you is a delight.

Thaikila CLOTHING
(☎0361-731130; www.thaikila.com; Jl Kayu Aya; ⏰9am-9pm) 'The dream bikini of all women' is the motto of this local brand that makes a big statement with its tiny wear. The swimwear is French-designed and made right in Bali. If you need something stylish for the beach, come here.

Kody & Ko ART
(☎0361-737359; www.kodyandko.com; Jl Kayu Jati 4A; ⏰9am-9pm) The polychromatic critters in the window set the tone for this vibrant shop of art and decorator items. There's a large attached gallery with regular exhibitions.

Uma & Leopold CLOTHING
(☎0361-737697; www.umaandleopold.com; Jl Kayu Aya 77X; ⏰9am-9pm) Luxe clothes and little frilly things to put on before slipping off... Designed in Bali by a French couple.

Lily Jean CLOTHING
(☎0811 398 272; www.lily-jean.com; Jl Kayu Jati 8, Seminyak Village, 1st fl; ⏰9am-10pm) Selling mostly Bali-made items, this designer shop combines international allure with local motifs.

Seminyak Village MALL
(☎0361-738097; www.seminyakvillage.com; Jl Kayu Jati 8; ⏰9am-10pm; 📶) Rice fields just a few years ago, this air-con mall deserves a compliment for being discreetly placed back from the street. The selection of shops is refreshingly local, with some notable names, such as Lily Jean, on the three levels. The small carts leased to up-and-coming Balinese designers is a nice touch.

Prisoners of St Petersburg FASHION & ACCESSORIES
(☎0361-736653; Jl Kayu Aya 42B; ⏰10am-10pm) Some of Bali's hottest young designers are behind this eclectic and ever-evolving hip collection of women's wear and accessories.

Biasa CLOTHING
(☎0361-730766; www.biasagroup.com; Jl Raya Seminyak 36; ⏰9am-9pm) This is Bali-based designer Susanna Perini's premier shop. Her line of elegant tropical wear for men and women combines cottons, silks and embroidery.

Milo's CLOTHING
(☎0361-822 2008; www.milos-bali.com; Jl Kayu Aya 992; ⏰10am-8pm) The legendary local designer of silk finery has a lavish shop in the heart of designer row. Look for batik-bearing, eye-popping orchid patterns.

Niconico CLOTHING
(☎0361-738875; www.niconicoswimwear.com; Jl Kayu Aya; ⏰9am-9pm) German designer Nico Genge has a line of intimate clothing, resort

wear and swimwear that eschews glitz for a slightly more subtle look. Among his many Seminyak shops, this one has both the full collection and an art gallery upstairs.

Sandio SHOES
(☎0361-737693; www.facebook.com/sandio.bali; Jl Basangkasa; ⏰10am-8pm) Shoes and sandals, from formal to casual, at great prices. Replace the one you lost riding your scooter.

Domicil HOMEWARES
(☎0818 0569 8417; www.domicil-living.com; Jl Raya Seminyak 56; ⏰10am-10pm) Facade meets merchandise: everything is designed with flair at this appealing housewares shop.

Quarzia Boutique CLOTHING
(☎0361-736644; Jl Kayu Aya; ⏰10am-9pm) Casual cotton clothes designed with colour and flair; worn with attitude and authority.

White Peacock HOMEWARES
(☎0361-733238; Jl Kayu Jati 1; ⏰9am-8pm) Styled like a country cottage, this is the place for cute cushions, throw rugs, table linens and more.

Lulu Yasmine CLOTHING
(☎0361-736763; www.luluyasmine.com; Jl Kayu Aya; ⏰9am-10pm) Designer Luiza Chang gets inspiration for her elegant line of women's clothes from her worldwide travels.

Periplus Bookshop BOOKS
(☎0361-736851; Jl Kayu Aya, Seminyak Sq; ⏰8am-10pm) A large outlet of the island-wide chain of lavishly fitted bookshops. In addition to design books numerous enough to have you fitting out even your garage with 'Bali Style', it stocks bestsellers, magazines and newspapers.

Lucy's Batik TEXTILES, CLOTHING
(☎0361-736098; www.lucysbatikbali.com; Jl Basangkasa 88; ⏰9.30am-9pm) Great for both men and women, Lucy's is a good spot to shop for the finest batik. Shirts, dresses, sarongs and bags are mostly handwoven or hand-painted. It also sells material by the metre.

Cotton Line by St Isador TEXTILES
(☎0361-738836; Jl Kaya Aya 44; ⏰9am-9pm) The workshops upstairs spew forth lovely bed linens, pillows and other items made of fabrics imported from across Asia.

Divine Diva CLOTHING
(☎0361-732393; www.divinedivabali.com; Jl Kayu Aya 1A; ⏰9am-7pm) A simple shop filled with Bali-made breezy styles for larger figures. You can custom order from the on-site tailors.

Information

DANGERS & ANNOYANCES

Seminyak is generally more hassle-free than Kuta and Legian. But it's worth reading up on the warnings, especially those regarding surf and water pollution.

MEDICAL SERVICES

Kimia Farma (☎0361-735860; Jl Raya Kerobokan 140; ⏰8am-11pm) Located at a major crossroads, this outlet of Bali's best chain of pharmacies has a full range of prescription medications.

MONEY

ATMs can be found along all the main roads.

Central Kuta Money Exchange (www.centralkutabali.com; Jl Kaayu Aya, Seminyak Sq; ⏰8.30am-9.30pm) Reliable currency exchange.

POST

Post Office (☎0361-761592; Jl Raya Seminyak 17, Bintang Supermarket; ⏰8am-8pm) Convenient and friendly.

Getting There & Away

The Kura-Kura tourist bus (p81) has a route linking Seminyak with Umalas in the north and Kuta in the south, however it runs infrequently.

Metered taxis are easily hailed. A trip from the airport with the airport taxi cartel costs about 250,000Rp; a regular taxi to the airport costs about 150,000Rp. You can beat the traffic, save the ozone and have a good stroll by walking along the beach; Legian is only about 15 minutes away. **Blue Bird** (☎0361-701111; www.bluebirdgroup.com) has the most reliable taxi service.

Kerobokan

☎0361 / POP 13,815

Continuing seamlessly north from Seminyak, Kerobokan combines some of Bali's best restaurants and shopping, lavish lifestyles and still more beach. Glossy new resorts mix with villa developments. One notable landmark is the notorious Kerobokan Prison.

Beaches

Kerobokan Beach BEACH
Backed by flash resorts and trendy clubs, Kerobokan's beach is surprisingly quiet. A lack of access keeps away crowds because all the roads running west from Jl Petitenget

dead-end in developments. You can reach the sand from Seminyak Beach in the south or by walking down from Batubelig Beach. There are beach vendors and loungers just north of the W Bali hotel.

The most direct access, however, is by waltzing through the Potato Head (p96) beach club or the W Bali (p94) hotel. The surf is more thunderous here than to the south, so be careful when swimming.

Batubelig Beach BEACH

The sand narrows here but there are some good places for a drink, both grand and simple. Easily reached via Jl Batubelig, this is a likely place to start a walk along the curving sands northwest to popular beaches as far as Echo Beach.

About 500m north, a river and lagoon flow into the ocean, sometimes up to 1m deep – after rains it may be much deeper. In this case, take the little footbridge over the lagoon to La Laguna (p103) bar, where you can call a taxi.

Activities

★Sundari Day Spa SPA

(0361-735073; www.sundari-dayspa.com; Jl Petitenget 7; massages from 250,000Rp; 10am-10pm) This much-recommended spa strives to offer the services of a five-star resort without the high prices. The massage oils and other potions are organic, and there's a full menu of therapies and treatments on offer.

Jiwa Yoga YOGA

(0361-841 3689; https://jiwabali.com; Jl Petitenget 78; classes from 150,000Rp; 9am-8pm) In a convenient location, this no-frills place offers several different types of yoga, including Bikram, hot flow and yin.

Sleeping

M Boutique Hostel HOSTEL $

(0361-473 4142; www.mboutiquehostel.com; Jl Petitenget 8; dm from 125,000Rp;) A contemporary choice for flashpackers, M Boutique's beds are capsule dorms, which come with the benefit of privacy. Each has shutter blinds, a drop-down table, a reading light and an electrical plug. The neatly trimmed lawn and small plunge pool add charm.

Brown Feather GUESTHOUSE $$

(0361-473 2165; www.brownfeather.com; Jl Batu Belig 100; r 500,000-800,000Rp;) On the main road, but backing onto rice paddies, this small hotel exudes a Dutch-Javanese colonial charm. Rooms mix simplicity with old-world character, such as wooden writing desks and washbasins made from old Singer sewing machines. For rice-field views, go for room 205 or 206. There's a small, attractive pool and free bicycle rental, too.

Grand Balisani Suites HOTEL $$

(0361-473 0550; www.balisanisuites.com; Jl Batubelig; r US$85-220;) Location! This elaborately carved complex is right on popular Batubelig Beach. The 96 rooms are large and have standard teak furniture plus terraces (some also have great views). Wi-fi is limited to public areas.

Villa Bunga HOTEL $$

(0361-473 1666; www.villabunga.com; Jl Petitenget 18X; r 500,000-550,000Rp, apt from 600,000Rp;) An excellent deal in the heart of Kerobokan, this hotel has 13 rooms set in two-storey blocks around a small pool. Rooms are small but modern and have fridges.

Taman Ayu Cottage HOTEL $$

(0361-473 0111; www.thetamanayu.com; Jl Petitenget; r incl breakfast 660,000-960,000Rp;) This great-value hotel has a fabulous location. Most of the 52 rooms are in two-storey blocks around a pool shaded by mature trees. Everything is a bit frayed around the edges, but all is forgotten when the bill comes. Family rooms and villas are available.

★Buah Bali Villas VILLA $$$

(0361-847 6626; www.thebuahbali.com; Jl Petitenget, Gang Cempaka; villa from 4,600,000Rp;) This small development has only seven villas, which range in size from one to two bedrooms. Like the many other nearby villa hotels, each unit has a private pool in a walled compound and a nice open-air living area. The location is superb: local hot spots are a five-minute walk away.

★Katamama BOUTIQUE HOTEL $$$

(0361-302 9999; www.katamama.com; Jl Petitenget 51; r from 3,500,000Rp;) The same architectural derring-do that makes Potato Head much copied is on display at the club's hotel. However here the details are lavish and artful. Designed by Indonesian Andra Matin, it has 57 suites in a confection of Javanese bricks, Balinese stone and other indigenous materials. There are huge windows, lavish seating areas and private terraces and balconies.

★Alila Seminyak RESORT $$$
(☎0361-302 1888; www.alilahotels.com; Jl Taman Ganesha 9; r from 5,500,000Rp; ❄📶🏊) This sprawling resort has a prime position right at the junction of Seminyak and Kerobokan beaches (and nightlife). A whopping 240 rooms come in various flavours. The cheapest have garden views, but as you rise up through the rate card you get beach views and more room. The colour scheme is a sandy palette of beige and tan.

W Bali – Seminyak RESORT $$$
(☎0361-473 8106; www.wretreatbali.com; Jl Petitenget; r incl breakfast from 4,900,000Rp; ❄@📶🏊) Like many W hotels, the usual too-cute-for-comfort vibe is at work here (how 'bout an 'extreme wow' suite?), but the location on a wave-tossed stretch of sand and the views are hard to quibble with. Stylish, hip bars, restaurants and smiling staff abound. The pricey rooms all have balconies, but not all have ocean views.

The Woobar is a great spot for a sundowner; happy-hour two-for-one cocktails come with a free pizza (from 4pm to 6pm).

Eating

Gusto Gelato & Coffee GELATO $
(☎0361-552 2190; www.gusto-gelateria.com; Jl Raya Mertanadi 46; gelato from 25,000Rp; ⏰10am-10pm; 🌿📶) Bali's best gelato is made fresh throughout the day, with unique flavours such as rich Oreo, surprising and delicious tamarind and *kamangi* (lemon basil). The classics are here as well. It gets mobbed in the afternoons.

Biku FUSION $
(☎0361-857 0888; www.bikubali.com; Jl Petitenget 888; mains 40,000-95,000Rp; ⏰8am-11pm; 📶👶) Housed in a 150-year-old teak *joglo* (traditional Javanese house), wildly popular Biku retains the timeless vibe of its predecessor. The menu combines Indonesian and other Asian with Western influences in a cuisine Biku calls 'tropical comfort food'. The burgers get rave reviews as do the desserts. Be sure to book ahead. There's a good kids' menu.

It's also popular for high tea (11am to 5pm; 110,000Rp per person). It can be served Asian-style – with samosa, spring rolls etc, and green or oolong tea – or traditional – with cucumber sandwiches etc.

Gourmet Cafe CAFE $
(☎0361-473 7324; www.balicateringcompany.com; Jl Petitenget 77A; snacks from 30,000Rp; ⏰7am-9pm; ❄) Like a gem store of treats, this upscale deli-cafe run by the Bali Catering Company serves an array of fanciful little delights. Many spend all day battling the temptation of the mango ice cream; others succumb to the croissants from the in-house bakery.

Pasar Kerobokan MARKET $
(Fruit Market; cnr Jl Raya Kerobokan & Jl Gunung Tangkuban Perahu; ⏰5am-10pm) Bali's numerous climate zones (hot and humid near the ocean, cool and dry up the volcano slopes) mean that pretty much any fruit or vegetable can be grown within the island's small confines. Vendors sell them all here, including unfamiliar fruits such as nubby mangosteens. A string of stalls prepare assorted tasty snacks and there's a small night market.

★Sangsaka INDONESIAN $$
(☎0812 3695 9895; www.sangsakabali.com; Jl Pangkung Sari 100; mains 80,000-180,000Rp; ⏰6pm-midnight Tue-Sun) On a Kerobokan backstreet, this casual restaurant serves well-nuanced versions of Indonesian dishes drawn from across the archipelago. Many are cooked over various types of charcoal, which vary depending on the origin of the dish. The dining area is done up in the usual vintage-wood motif, with just a touch more polish than usual. It has a good bar.

★Saigon Street VIETNAMESE $$
(☎0361-897 4007; www.saigonstreetbali.com; Jl Petitenget 77; mains 50,000-175,000Rp; ⏰11am-1am; 📶) Modern, vibrant and packed, this Vietnamese restaurant lures in the buzzing masses with its swanky neon decor. Creative Vietnamese dishes include peppery betel leaves filled with slow-cooked octopus, and there's an impressive rice-paper roll selection, along with curries, *pho* (rice-noodle soup) and grilled meats cooked on aromatic coconut wood. Cocktails include the 'bang bang' martini, a chilled bit of boozy splendour. Book ahead.

★Sardine SEAFOOD $$
(☎0811 397 8111; www.sardinebali.com; Jl Petitenget 21; dinner mains from 200,000Rp; ⏰11.30am-4pm & 6-11pm; 📶) Seafood fresh from the famous Jimbaran market is the star at this elegant yet intimate, casual yet stylish restaurant. It's in a beautiful bamboo pavilion, with open-air tables overlooking a private sunflower garden and a lovely koi

DON'T MISS

KEROBOKAN'S WARUNGS

Although seemingly upscale, Kerobokan is blessed with many a fine place for a truly authentic local meal. Top choices include:

Warung Eny (☎0361-473 6892; warungeny@yahoo.com; Jl Petitenget 97; mains from 35,000Rp; ⏰8am-11pm) The eponymous Eny cooks everything herself at this tiny open-front warung nearly hidden behind various potted plants. The seafood, such as large prawns smothered in garlic, is delicious and most ingredients are organic. Also offers excellent cooking classes.

Warung Sulawesi (☎0821 4756-2779; Jl Petitenget 57B; mains from 35,000Rp; ⏰7am-8pm) Here you'll find a table in a quiet family compound and enjoy fresh Balinese and Indonesian food served in classic warung style. Choose rice, then pick from a captivating array of dishes that are always at their peak at noon. The long beans – yum!

Warung Kita (Jl Petitenget 98A; mains from 25,000Rp; ⏰9am-7.30pm Mon-Sat) A Javanese halal classic. Choose your rice (we prefer the fragrant yellow), then pick from a delectable array that includes tempeh in sweet chilli sauce, *sambal terung* (spicy eggplant), *ikan sambal* (spicy grilled fish) and other daily specials. Most of the labels are in English.

Sari Kembar (☎0361-847 6021; Jl Teuku Umar Barat 99; mains from 15,000Rp; ⏰8am-10pm) One of Bali's best places for *babi guling* (spit-roast pig stuffed with chilli, turmeric, garlic and ginger) is back off this busy street about 1.5km east of the junction with Jl Raya Kerobokan. Besides the succulent marinated pork, there's melt-in-your-mouth crackling, duck stuffed with cassava leaves, sausage and more. It's dead simple and amazingly good.

Warung Sobat (☎0361-731256; Jl Pengubengan Kauh 27; mains 37,000-100,000Rp; ⏰11am-10.30pm; 📶) Set in a bungalow-style large open-sided brick space, this old-fashioned restaurant excels at fresh Balinese seafood with an Italian accent (lots of garlic!). Prices are extraordinary, as you can see from the value-minded expats who pack the place every night.

pond. The inventive bar is a must and stays open until 1am. The menu changes to reflect what's fresh. Booking is vital.

Merah Putih INDONESIAN $$
(☎0361-846 5950; www.merahputihbali.com; Jl Petitenget 100X; mains 80,000-200,000Rp; ⏰noon-3pm & 6-11pm) Merah Putih means 'red and white', which are the colours of the Indonesian flag. That's perfect for this excellent restaurant, which celebrates food from across the archipelago. The short menu is divided between traditional and modern – the latter combining Indo flavours with diverse foods. The soaring dining room has a hip style and the service is excellent.

Sarong FUSION $$
(☎0361-473 7809; www.sarongbali.com; Jl Petitenget 19X; mains 120,000-180,000Rp; ⏰6.30-10.45pm; 📶) Sarong is an elegant affair. The cuisine spans Asia, and its small plates are popular with those wishing to pace an evening and enjoy the commodious bar. No children allowed. Dine outside under the stars.

Watercress CAFE $$
(☎0851 0280 8030; www.watercressbali.com; Jl Batubelig 21A; mains from 75,000Rp; ⏰7.30am-11pm; P📶) A hit with the hipster set, this leafy roadside cafe does a roaring trade. As well as hearty breakfasts and gourmet burgers, it features healthy mains and salads. Excellent coffee, beer on tap and cocktails are other reasons to stop by. The small garden area out front is nice.

Naughty Nuri's INDONESIAN $$
(☎0361-934 7391; www.naughtynurisseminyak.com; Jl Raya Mertanadi 62; mains from 60,000Rp; ⏰11am-10pm) Inspired by the overhyped Ubud original, this Nuri's works to promote the concept and has a much larger outdoor component. Remarkably, it has become a must-see stop for visitors from across Indonesia, who tuck into the not-especially tender pork ribs. The original's trademark kick-ass martinis remain.

L'Assiette FRENCH $$
(☎0361-735840; www.lassietterestaurantbali.wordpress.com; Jl Raya Mertanadi 29; mains from

140,000Rp; ⏲10am-11pm Mon-Sat; 📶) The huge quiet garden behind this airy cafe is the perfect place to enjoy a *salade niçoise* or any of the other fresh and tasty, classic French-cafe fare served here. Perhaps a *steak frites* or a terrine will strike your fancy. If not, there are Asian-accented dishes too. It shares space with Pourquoi Pas antique shop.

Barbacoa LATIN AMERICAN $$$
(☎0361-739235; www.barbacoa-bali.com; Jl Petitenget 14; mains 180,000-250,000Rp; ⏲noon-midnight; 📶) Barbacoa is an impressive space with soaring timber ceilings, colourful mosaic-tiled floors and rice-field views (for now). The food is all about grilled meats; the restaurant's walls are lined with firewood to cook up its menu of Latin American dishes.

Drinking & Nightlife

Some of Kerobokan's trendier restaurants have stylish bar areas that stay open late, while the beach club Mrs Sippy is the daytime drinking hotspot.

★**Mrs Sippy** CLUB
(☎0361-335 1079; www.mrssippybali.com; Jl Taman Ganesha; cover 100,000Rp; ⏲10am-9pm) This Mediterranean-style beach club pretty much has it all – booze, international DJs, a saltwater swimming pool and three levels of diving platforms. It's not currently a late-night spot (the neighbours have complained too much for that), but it offers the best daytime and early-evening parties in south Bali.

★**Potato Head** CLUB
(☎0361-473 7979; www.ptthead.com; Jl Petitenget 51; ⏲10am-2am; 📶) Bali's highest-profile beach club is one of the best. Wander up off the sand or follow a long drive off Jl Petitenget and you'll find much to amuse, from an enticing pool to restaurants like the swanky Kaum and zero-waste Ijen, plus a pizza garden, lots of lounges and patches of lawn for chillin' the night away under the stars.

Mirror CLUB
(☎0811 399 3010; www.mirror.id; Jl Petitenget 106; ⏲11pm-4am Wed-Sat) This club is big with south Bali expats, who may own those designer shops you were in a few hours before. The interior is sort of like a cathedral out of *Harry Potter*, albeit with an unholy amount of lighting effects. Mainstream electronica blares forth.

Warung Pantai BAR
(Batubelig Beach; ⏲8am-9pm) A bunch of drinking shacks line this inviting stretch of beach just north of the W Bali hotel including Pantai, which offers up cheap drinks, mismatched tables and splendid surf and sunset views.

Shopping

★**Purpa Fine Art Gallery** ART
(☎0819 9940 8804; www.purpagallerybali.com; Jl Mertanadi 22; ⏲10am-6pm Mon-Sat) This long-time gallery has shown some of Bali's very best artists going back to the most notable names of the 1930s, such as Spies, Snell and Lempad. It has regular special exhibits.

★**Bathe** BEAUTY, HOMEWARES
(☎0812 384 1825; www.facebook.com/bathestore; Jl Batu Belig 88; ⏲10am-7pm) Double-down on your villa's romance with handmade candles, air diffusers, aromatherapy oils, bath salts and homewares that evoke the feel of a 19th-century French dispensary. It's in a cluster of upscale boutiques.

Tulola JEWELLERY
(☎0361-473 0261; www.shoptulola.com; Jl Petitenget; ⏲11am-7pm) This is the jewellery shop of noted Balinese-American designer Sri Luce Rusna. High-end items are created in Bali and displayed in this exquisite boutique.

Ayun Tailor CLOTHING
(☎0821 8996 5056; Jl Batubelig; ⏲10am-6pm) Ayun is an excellent tailor. Buy batik or other fabric at one of Bali's many textile emporiums and she'll turn it into an outfit for a man, woman or child. Bring along a shirt you love and she can copy it. Great rates.

Mercredi HOMEWARES
(☎0812 4634 0518; https://mercredi.business.site; Jl Petitenget; ⏲9am-9pm) Fashionable cushions to turn your tired sofa into a spry fashion statement are but some of the goods on sale in this stylish shop of well-designed housewares.

Kevala Home HOMEWARES
(☎0361-473 5869; www.kevalaceramics.com; Jl Batubelig; ⏲9am-7pm) Designed and made in Bali, the top-end ceramics here are exquisite examples of the art.

Geneva Handicraft Centre ARTS & CRAFTS
(☎0361-733542; www.genevahandicraft.com; Jl Raya Kerobokan 100; ⏲9am-8pm) Tourist vans

OFF THE BEATEN TRACK

HANDICRAFT HOTSPOT

East of Seminyak and Kerobokan, a series of streets is lined with all manner of interesting shops selling and manufacturing housewares, baubles, fabric and other intriguing items. Head east of Kerobokan jail for about 2km on Jl Gunung Tangkuban Perahu and then turn south on – get this – a street with the same name.

This particular *jalan* has been called 'the street of amazement' by a shopaholic friend; look for an array of stores with vintage seaman's gear and primitive art. South, it becomes Jl Gunung Athena, with housewares and art, and then heads east as Jl Kunti II, where it ends at the busy intersection with Jl Sunset and Jl Kunti.

Yoga Batik (0813 5309 3344; Jl Gunung Athena 17; 10am-6pm Mon-Sat) A huge variety of the iconic Indonesian fabric.

Rainbow Tulungagung (0812-594 0391; Jl Gunung Athena 1; 8am-10pm Mon-Sat) Handicrafts made from marble and stone. The soap dispensers are easily carried home.

My Basket Bali (0361-994 3683; https://my-basket-bali.business.site; Jl Gunung Athena 39B; 10am-5pm Mon-Fri) If it can be woven from fibre, it's here. Baskets that look as good as they are practical.

Victory Art (0812 3681 67877; Jl Gunung Tangkuban Perahu; 8am-5pm) As much spectacle as store, this corner place is jammed with intriguing works of new art. All manner of primitive faces gaze out from the array of merchandise that's inspired by indigenous cultures from across Indonesia.

flock to the big space out front of this multifloor emporium of Indonesian handicraft. And with good reason, quality is good and prices are fair and fixed.

Tribali JEWELLERY
(0818 0541 5453; Jl Petitenget 12B; 9am-6pm Mon-Sat) Rustic jewellery and accessories with a luxe hippy vibe are shown in earthy display cases.

Carga HOMEWARES
(0361-847 8180; https://carga.business.site; Jl Petitenget 886; 9am-9pm) This beautiful shop is set back from the cacophony of Jl Petitenget in a vintage house shaded by palm trees. The homewares are sourced across Indonesia and range from elegant to whimsical.

Pourquoi Pas ANTIQUES
(Jl Raya Mertanadi 29; 9am-8pm) Owned by the French family behind the cafe L'Assiette (p95), this adjoining antique store is filled with treasures from across the archipelago and Southeast Asia.

Namu CLOTHING
(0361-279 7524; www.namustore.com; Jl Petitenget 23X; 9am-8pm) Designer Paola Zancanaro creates comfy and casual resort wear for men and women that doesn't take a holiday from style. The fabrics are lusciously tactile; many are hand-painted silk.

JJ Bali Button ARTS & CRAFTS
(www.jjbalibutton.com; Jl Gunung Tangkuban Perahu 5; 9am-5pm Mon-Sat) Zillions of beads and buttons made from shells, plastic, metal and more are displayed in what at first looks like a candy store. Elaborately carved wooden buttons cost 800Rp. Kids may have to be bribed to leave.

You Like Lamp HOMEWARES
(0813-3868 0577; Jl Raya Mertanadi 52; 9am-5pm Mon-Sat) Why yes, we do. All manner of endearing little paper lamps – many good for tea lights – are sold here cheap by the bagful. Don't see what you want? The staff working away on the floor will rustle it up immediately.

Information

Central Kuta Money Exchange (www.central-kutabali.com; Jl Raya Kerobokan 51; 8.30am-9.15pm) Reliable currency exchange.

Getting There & Away

Although the beach may seem tantalisingly close, few roads or *gang* actually reach the sand from the east. Note also that Jl Raya Kerobokan can come to a fume-filled stop for extended periods.

The Kura-Kura tourist bus (p81) has a route linking Seminyak with Umalas in the north and Kuta in the south, however it runs infrequently.

Metered taxis can be hailed. Blue Bird (www.bluebirdgroup.com) has the most reliable service.

Getting Around

Bali Bike Rental (0855 7467 9030; www.balibikerental.com; Jl Raya Kerobokan 71; rental per day from US$10; 8am-7pm) An alternative to the thousands of freelance motorbike renters in Bali. For the extra money, you get a motorbike in prime shape along with extras such as clean helmets, roadside assistance and more. Faster, more powerful motorcycles are also available.

CANGGU REGION

The Canggu region, north and west of Kerobokan, is Bali's fastest-growing area. Much of the growth is centred along the coast, anchored by the endless swathe of beach, which, despite rampant development, remains fairly uncrowded. Kerobokan morphs into Umalas inland and Canggu to the west, while neighbouring Echo Beach is a big construction site.

Cloistered villas lure expats who whisk past the remaining rice farmers on motorbikes or in air-con comfort. Traffic may be the ultimate commoner's revenge: road building is a decade behind settlement. Amid this maze of too-narrow lanes you'll find creative cafes, trendy restaurants and appealing shops. Follow the sounds of the surf to great beaches such as the one at Batu Bolong.

To stay current with the constant flurry of new openings, check out www.canggu guide.com.

Getting There & Around

You'll need your own wheels to get here, whether it's a car and driver, a motorbike or a taxi. The beach areas usually have a taxi monopoly that will charge upwards of 150,000Rp for a ride to Seminyak.

Bad, narrow and clogged roads will keep you stuck in traffic often during daylight. When possible, walk on the beach as a shortcut.

Umalas

0361

Expat villas and Balinese compounds mix with rice fields north of Kerobokan. Look for surprises such as a cute warung or a delightfully oddball shop on the back roads.

Tours

★**Bali Bike Hire** CYCLING

(0361-202 0054; www.balibikehire.com; Jl Raya Semer 61; rental per day from 60,000Rp) Run by people passionate about bikes, here you can choose from a variety of top-quality rides. It offers plenty of advice for navigating Bali's often tortuous roads, and leads various excellent guided tours by bike.

Eating

Go exploring the small roads east of Jl Raya Kerobokan and you'll discover lots of interesting warungs serving a variety of cuisines.

★**Nook** INTERNATIONAL $$

(0361-847-5625; www.facebook.com/nookbali; Jl Umalas I; mains 50,000-160,000Rp; 8am-11pm;) Sublimely positioned among the rice fields, this casual, open-air cafe is popular for its creative takes on Asian and Western fare. It has a modern vibe mixed with tropical flavours, plus good breakfasts and burgers. Get a table on the back wooden terrace.

Bali Buda CAFE $$

(0361-844 5935; www.balibuda.com; Jl Banjar Anyar 24; mains from 23,000Rp; 8am-10pm;) This appealing outlet of the Ubud original has all the excellent baked goods and organic groceries you'd expect. The small cafe serves healthy juices and smoothies, plus an array of mostly vegetarian fare. Stop in for breakfast on your way to visit Tanah Lot (sane people visit the temple before noon).

Shopping

Reza Art 2 ANTIQUES

(0821 9797 4309; Jl Mertasari 99; 10am-6pm) Oodles of lamps in many sizes mix with nautical antiques and junk (think old ship telegraphs and rudder wheels) in this shop that's more treasure hunt than retail establishment.

Canggu

0361 / POP 7090

More a state of mind than a place, Canggu is the catch-all name given to the villa-filled stretch of land between Kerobokan and Echo Beach. It's packed with an ever-more alluring collection of businesses, especially casual cafes. Three main strips have emerged, all running down to the beaches: two along meandering Jl Pantai Berawa and one on Jl Pantai Batu Bolong.

Beaches

The beaches of the Canggu area continue the sweep of sand that starts in Kuta. Their personalities vary from hip hang-out to sparsely populated – the latter can often be found a mere 10-minute amble away from the crowded areas.

★ Batu Bolong Beach BEACH
(parking motorbike/car 2000/5000Rp) The beach at Batu Bolong is the most popular in the Canggu area. There's almost always a good mix of locals, expats and visitors hanging out in the cafes, surfing the breaks or watching it all from the sand. There are rental loungers, umbrellas and beer vendors.

You can also rent surfboards (100,000Rp per day) and take lessons. Overlooking it all is the centuries-old Pura Batumejan complex.

Berawa Beach BEACH
(parking motorbike/car 2000/3000Rp) Greyish Berawa Beach ('Brawa Beach' on many signs) has a couple of surfer cafes by the pounding sea. The grey volcanic sand here slopes steeply into foaming water. Overlooking it all behind Finn's Beach Club is the vast estate of fashionista Paul Ropp.

Prancak Beach BEACH
A couple of drinks vendors and a large parking area are the major amenities at this beach, which is rarely crowded. The large temple is Pura Dalem Prancak. Berawa Beach is an enjoyable 1km walk along the wave-tossed sands. It's known for pick-up volleyball games.

Nelayan Beach BEACH
A collection of fishing boats and huts marks the very mellow stretch of sand at Nelayan Beach, which fronts 'villa-land'. Depending on the river levels, it can be an easy walk from here to Prancak and Batu Bolong beaches.

Sights

Pura Batumejan HINDU TEMPLE
(Jl Pantai Batu Bolong) Overlooking Batu Bolong Beach is the centuries-old Pura Batumejan complex, which has a striking pagoda-like temple.

BEACH WALK

You can usually walk the 4km of sand between Batubelig Beach and Echo Beach in about one to two hours. It's a fascinating stroll and you'll see temples, tiny fishing encampments, crashing surf, lots of surfers, cool cafes and outcrops of upscale beach culture. The only catch is that after heavy rains some of the rivers may be too deep to cross, especially the one just northwest of Batubelig. In any case, put your gear in waterproof bags in case you have to do some fording.

It's easy to find taxis at any of the larger beaches if you don't want to retrace your steps.

Pura Dalem Prancak HINDU TEMPLE
(Jl Pantai Prancak) This large temple is often the site of ceremonies.

Activities

Very popular for surfing, the Canggu area beaches draw a lot of locals and expat residents on weekends. Access to parking areas usually costs 5000Rp and there are cafes and warungs for those who work up an appetite in the water or watching others in the water.

Finn's Recreation Club HEALTH & FITNESS
(☎0361-848 3939; www.finnsrecclub.com; Jl Pantai Berawa; adult/child day pass 450,000/300,000Rp; ⏲6am-9pm) Bali's expats shuttlecock themselves silly at Finn's Recreation Club, a New Age version of something you'd expect to find during the Raj. The vast, perfectly virescent lawn is manicured for croquet. Get sweaty with tennis, squash, polo, cricket, bowling, the spa or the 25m pool. Many villa rentals include guest passes here. The garish **Splash Waterpark** is popular.

Amo Beauty Spa SPA
(☎0361-907 1146; www.amospa.com; Jl Pantai Batu Bolong 69; massages from 230,000Rp; ⏲8am-10pm) With some of Asia's top models lounging about it feels like you've stumbled into a *Vogue* shoot. In addition to massages, services range from haircare to pedicures and unisex waxing. Book ahead.

Sleeping

Canggu has all types of places to stay. Guesthouses self-billed as 'surf camps' have proliferated. For longer-term lodging, besides searching online, check the bulletin board at Warung Varuna (p102).

Serenity Eco Guesthouse GUESTHOUSE $
(☎0361-846 9257, 0361-846 9251; www.serenityecoguesthouse.com; Jl Nelayan; dm/s/d incl breakfast 175,000/205,000/495,000Rp; ❄📶🏊) This hotel is an oasis among the sterility of walled villas, run by young and inexperienced (though lovable) staff members. Rooms range from shared-bath singles to nice doubles with bathrooms (some with fans, others with air-con). The grounds are eccentric; Nelayan Beach is a five-minute walk. There are yoga classes (from 110,000Rp) and you can rent surfboards and bikes. This place makes an effort to minimise its carbon footprint.

Big Brother Surf Inn GUESTHOUSE $
(☎0812 3838 0385; www.big-brother-surf-inn-canggu.bali-tophotels.com/en; Jl Pantai Berawa 20; r US$40; ❄📶🏊) This sleek take on a traditional Balinese guesthouse has clean lines and plenty of minimalist white. The six rooms are airy and have outdoor sitting areas overlooking a garden with barbecue facilities and a pool. It's in a quiet location back off the road; despite the name, your high jinks are unlikely to end up on a reality TV show.

Canggu Surf Hostel HOSTEL $
(☎0813 5303 1293; www.canggusurfhostels.com; Jl Raya Semat; dm 100,000-160,000Rp, r 400,000Rp; ❄📶🏊) This well-equipped hostel has a split personality: two locations, with the other just around the corner on Jl Pantai Berawa. There are eight-, six- and four-bed rooms plus private rooms. Enjoy multiple public spaces, pools, kitchens and lockable surfboard storage.

Widi Homestay HOMESTAY $
(☎0819 3626 0860; widihomestay@yahoo.co.id; Jl Pantai Berawa; r from 250,000Rp; ❄📶) There's no faux-hipster vibe here with fake nihilist bromides, just a spotless, friendly, family-run homestay. The four rooms have hot water and air-con; the beach is barely 100m away.

★ **Sedasa** BOUTIQUE HOTEL $$
(☎0361-844 6655; www.sedasa.com; Jl Pantai Berawa; r incl breakfast 700,000-890,000Rp; ❄📶🏊) Both intimate and stylish, Sedasa has an understated Balinese elegance. The 10 large rooms overlook a small pool and have designer furniture. The beanbags on the rooftop make a good place to relax with a book. Downstairs there's an organic cafe. It's a five-minute walk to the beach, and there's free bike rental and a shuttle into Seminyak.

Canggu & Echo Beach

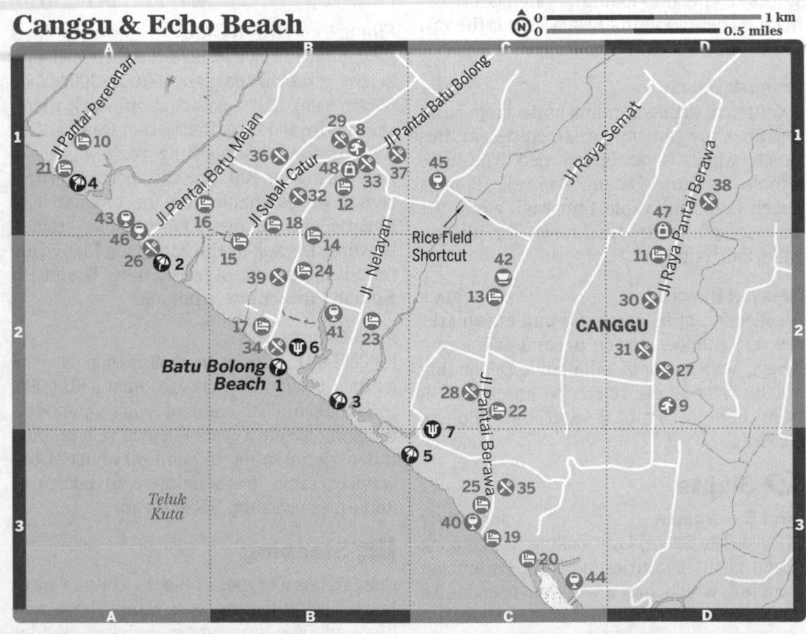

Outsite CO-LIVING **$$**
(www.outsite.co; Jl Pantai Batu Bolong 45; r from US$50;) Aimed at Bali's ever-growing slew of digital nomads, Outsite's five traditional Javanese-style bungalows and atmospheric pool offer a cosy place to recharge between bursts of productivity. Nestled against a rice field, it's a peaceful and inspiring place for a working holiday – wi-fi is fast and stable, and the included breakfast smoothie bowls are a delicious way to start the day. Two-night minimum stay required; Outsite members save on nightly rates.

Calmtree Bungalows GUESTHOUSE **$$**
(0851 0074 7009; www.thecalmtreebungalows.com; Jl Pantai Batu Bolong; r from 640,000Rp;) Right in the middle of the heart of Batu Bolong, this family-run compound has 10 traditional-style units around a pool. Inside the thatched walls you'll find rustic style fused with a touch of modern. The bathrooms are open-air. There's no air-con but there are nets and fans – think of it as atmospheric. Great staff.

Coconuts Guesthouse Canggu GUESTHOUSE **$$**
(0878 6192 7150; www.facebook.com/pg/coconutsguesthouse; Jl Pantai Batu Bolong; r from US$75;) The five breezy rooms at this contemporary guesthouse are very comfortable. Some have lovely views of the (surviving) rice fields, and all have fridges and a relaxed motif. Enjoy sunsets from the rooftop lounge area or take a dip in the 10m pool. Batu Bolong Beach is a 700m walk.

Legong Keraton HOTEL **$$**
(0361-473 0280; www.legongkeratonhotel.com; Jl Pantai Berawa; r 820,000-1,400,000Rp;) The Canggu boom has caught up with this well-run 40-room beachfront resort. The grounds are shaded by palms and the pool borders the beach. The best rooms are in bungalow units facing the surf. Long isolated, the hotel is now in the centre of the action.

Canggu & Echo Beach

Top Sights
1 Batu Bolong Beach B2

Sights
Berawa Beach .... (see 19)
2 Echo Beach A2
3 Nelayan Beach B2
4 Pererenan Beach A1
5 Prancak Beach C3
6 Pura Batumejan B2
7 Pura Dalem Prancak C3

Activities, Courses & Tours
8 Amo Beauty Spa B1
9 Finn's Recreation Club D2

Sleeping
10 Andy's Surf Villa A1
11 Big Brother Surf Inn D2
12 Calmtree Bungalows B1
13 Canggu Surf Hostel C2
14 Coconuts Guesthouse Canggu B2
15 Echo Beach Resort B2
16 Echoland A1
17 Hotel Tugu Bali B2
18 Koming Guest House B1
19 Legong Keraton C3
20 Lv8 Resort Hotel C3
21 Pondok Nyoman Bagus A1
22 Sedasa C2
23 Serenity Eco Guesthouse B2
24 Slow B2
25 Widi Homestay C3

Eating
26 Beach House A2
Betelnut Cafe .... (see 12)
27 Bungalow D2
28 Creamery C2
29 Deus Ex Machina B1
Dian Cafe .... (see 26)
30 Green Ginger D2
31 Indotopia D2
32 Mocca B1
33 Monsieur Spoon B1
34 Old Man's B2
35 One Eyed Jack C3
36 Shady Shack B1
37 Warung Bu Mi B1
38 Warung Goûthé D1
39 Warung Varuna B2

Drinking & Nightlife
40 Finns Beach Club C3
41 Gimme Shelter Bali B2
42 Hungry Bird C2
Ji .... (see 17)
43 La Brisa A1
44 La Laguna C3
45 Pretty Poison C1
46 Sand Bar A1

Shopping
Dylan Board Store .... (see 33)
47 It Was All a Dream D1
48 Love Anchor B1

★**Hotel Tugu Bali** HOTEL $$$
(☎0361-473 1701; www.tuguhotels.com; Jl Pantai Batu Bolong; r incl breakfast from US$400; ❄@🛜≋) Right at Batu Bolong Beach, this exquisite hotel blurs the boundaries between accommodation and a museum-gallery, especially the Walter Spies and Le Mayeur Pavilions, where memorabilia from the artists' lives decorates the rooms. There's a spa and a high-style beachfront bar, Ji. The stunning collection of antiques and artwork begins in the lobby and extends throughout the hotel.

Slow BOUTIQUE HOTEL $$$
(☎0361-209 9000; http://theslow.id; Jl Pantai Batu 97; r from 2,400,000Rp; ❄🛜≋) Raising the design bar in Canggu with its 'tropical brutalism' style, the Slow's aesthetic is defined by elegant spaces with clean lines, natural colour schemes, abundant hanging foliage and the owner's edgy personal art collection. Rooms are expansive, with every modern comfort.

Lv8 Resort Hotel RESORT $$$
(☎0361-894 8888; www.lv8bali.com; Jl Discovery 8; r from 3,000,000Rp; ❄🛜≋) Right on a bend in the lagoon and fronting Berawa Beach, this light and airy resort makes the most of its long and narrow location. Even the smallest of the 124 rooms are large, with balconies and sitting areas. Some have sweeping ocean views while others have private plunge pools.

Eating

★**Creamery** ICE CREAM $
(☎0819 9982 5898; www.facebook.com/CreameryBali; Jl Pantai Berawa 8; sundaes from 35,000Rp; ⊙11.30am-10.30pm) Learn the meaning of true small batch ice cream at this cheery shop that churns its creations one serving at a time using liquid nitrogen. House-created sundaes are decadent in their simplicity – build your own if you're feeling creative, or enjoy an ice cream sandwich or milkshake for something a bit tamer.

Warung Varuna INDONESIAN $
(☎0818 0551 8790; www.facebook.com/warungvaruna; Jl Pantai Batu Bolong 89A; mains 20,000-40,000Rp; ⊙8am-10.30pm) The best deal for great local fare close to the beach, Varuna combines excellent Balinese fare with a surfer sensibility. The nasi goreng (fried rice) comes in several creative variations; there are also juices, smoothies and jaffles. It has good, hearty Western breakfasts. The bulletin board has many listings for villa and room rentals.

Warung Bu Mi INDONESIAN $
(☎0857 3741 1115; www.facebook.com/warungbumi; Jl Pantai Batu Bolong 52; meals 25,000-40,000Rp; ⊙8am-10pm) Classic Balinese warung-style food. Choose your style of rice (we like the local fave: nutty red) and then go down the line picking from various dishes. Don't pass up the corn fritters. It has long tables amid a simple, clean interior.

Bungalow CAFE $
(☎0361-844 6567; www.bungalowlivingbali.com; Jl Pantai Berawa; mains from 40,000Rp; ⊙8am-6pm Mon-Sat; ❄) Set just far enough back from the road to avoid the fumes, this cafe reflects the retro-chic design sensibilities of its parent housewares emporium. Relax amid distressed-wood surrounds on the verandah and choose from a vast range of coffee drinks, juices, smoothies, sandwiches, salads and desserts.

Indotopia VIETNAMESE $
(☎0822 3773 7760; www.facebook.com/IndotopiaCanggu; Jl Pantai Berawa 34; mains from 40,000Rp; ⊙8am-10pm; 🛜) Otherwise known as 'Warung Vietnam', this place serves bowls of *pho* that are simply superb. Lots of rich beefy goodness contrasting with perfect noodles and fragrant greens. Prefer something sweeter? Go for the Saigon banana crepes.

Betelnut Cafe CAFE $
(☎0821 4680 7233; Jl Pantai Batu Bolong; mains from 50,000Rp; ⊙8am-10pm; ❄🛜🌿) There's a hippy-chic vibe at this thatched cafe with a mellow open-air dining room upstairs. The menu leans towards healthy, but not too healthy – you can get fries. There are juices and lots of mains featuring veggies. It has good baked goods and nice shakes.

Monsieur Spoon CAFE $
(www.monsieurspoon.com; Jl Pantai Batu Bolong; snacks from 25,000Rp; ⊙6.30am-9pm; ❄) Beautiful French-style baked goods (the almond croissant, wow!) are the speciality at this small Bali chain of cafes. Enjoy pastries, sandwiches on picture-perfect bread and fine coffees at a table in the garden or inside.

Green Ginger ASIAN $
(☎0878 6211 2729; www.elephantbali.com/green-ginger; Jl Pantai Berawa; meals from 55,000Rp; ⊙8am-9pm; 🛜🌿) An attractive

little restaurant on the fast-changing strip in Canggu, Green Ginger specialises in fresh and tasty vegetarian and noodle dishes from across Asia.

★ **Mocca** CAFE $$
(☎0361-907 4512; www.facebook.com/themocca; Gg Nyepi; mains 60,000-90,000Rp; ⏰7am-10pm) Tucked away from the bustle of Jl Batu Bolong, this Canggu gem is equal parts charming cafe and boho concept store. Between the downstairs garden and upstairs open-air patio, both decked in potted palms and reclaimed wood furnishings, there isn't a bad seat in the house. Stellar service and a broad, multi-cuisine menu make it easy to linger for hours.

★ **One Eyed Jack** JAPANESE $$
(☎0819 9929 1888; www.oneeyedjackbali.com; Jl Pantai Berawa; small plates 45,000-90,000Rp; ⏰5pm-midnight) *Izakaya,* the style of Japanese dining that encourages groups of friends to enjoy drinks and shared plates of food, is exemplified by this wonderful small restaurant. The chef is a veteran of internationally acclaimed Nomu; the dishes are superb. Tiny taco-style appetisers, chicken *tsukune* sliders and barbecue-pork buns will have you ordering seconds. Don't miss the tea-based cocktails.

★ **Warung Goûthé** BISTRO $$
(☎0878 8947 0638; www.facebook.com/warung-gouthe; Jl Pantai Berawa 7A; mains from 60,000Rp; ⏰9am-5pm Mon-Sat) Superbly prepared and presented casual meals are the hallmark of this open-front cafe. The very short menu changes each day depending on what's fresh. The French owners can take a simple chicken sandwich and elevate it to magnificent and memorable. The desserts alone should cause you to stop in whenever you are nearby.

★ **Deus Ex Machina** CAFE $$
(Temple of Enthusiasm; ☎0811 388 150; www.deuscustoms.com; Jl Batu Mejan 8; mains 60,000-170,000Rp; ⏰7am-11pm; 📶) This surreal venue amid Canggu's rice fields has many personas. If you're hungry, it's a restaurant-cafe-bar; for shoppers, it's a fashion label; if you're into culture, it's a contemporary-art gallery; for music lovers, it's a live-gig venue (Sunday afternoons) for local punk bands; for bikers, it's a custom-made motorcycle shop; if you want your beard trimmed, it's a barber…

Old Man's INTERNATIONAL $$
(☎0361-846 9158; www.oldmans.net; Jl Pantai Batu Bolong; mains from 50,000Rp; ⏰7am-midnight) You'll have a tough time deciding just where to sit down to enjoy your drink at this popular coastal beer garden overlooking Batu Bolong Beach. The self-serve menu is aimed at surfers and surfer-wannabes: burgers, pizza, fish and chips, salads. Wednesday nights are an institution, while Fridays (live rock and roll) and Sundays (DJs) are also big.

Drinking & Nightlife

★ **La Laguna** COCKTAIL BAR
(☎0812 3638 2272; www.lalagunabali.com; Jl Pantai Kayu Putih; ⏰9am-midnight; 📶) A sibling of Seminyak's La Favela (p89), La Laguna is one of Bali's most alluring bars. It combines a beatnik look with Moorish trappings and sparkling tiny lights. Explore the eclectic layout, and sit on a couch, sofa bed, a table inside or a picnic table in the garden. The drinks are good and the food is delicious (mains from 80,000Rp).

To arrive in style, walk along the beach and then take the footbridge right over the lagoon.

Ji BAR
(☎0361-473 1701; www.jiatbalesutra.com; Jl Pantai Batu Bolong, Hotel Tugu Bali; ⏰5-11pm) Easily Canggu's most alluring bar, Ji is a fantasy of historic Chinese and Balinese wood carving and rich decor. From the terrace on the 1st floor there are fine views you can enjoy with exotic cocktails, sake and Japanese bites.

Pretty Poison BAR
(☎0812 4622 9340; www.prettypoisonbar.com; Jl Subak Canggu; ⏰4pm-midnight) Pretty Poison's bar overlooks an old-school '80s skate bowl, so a surfboard isn't the only board you to need to pack. Run by longtime Aussie expat and surfer Maree Suteja, it's a great place to hang out, with cheap beers and bands. Being Canggu, there's logo wear for sale. It's close to the chaotic comedy of the rice-field shortcut.

Hungry Bird CAFE
(☎0898 619 1008; www.facebook.com/hungrybirdcoffee; Jl Raya Semat 86; ⏰8am-5pm Mon-Sat; 📶) One of the few genuine third-wave coffee roasters in Bali, Hungry Bird does superb single-origin brews. The Javanese owner is incredibly knowledgeable on the subject, and roasts beans on-site from all over Indonesia; cupping sessions are possible if you

call ahead. The food's also excellent (organic eggs and baked goods) and perfect for brunch.

Gimme Shelter Bali BAR
(☎0812 3804 8867; www.facebook.com/gimmeshelterbali; Jl Lingkar Nelayan 444; ⏲7pm-3am) The perfect hang-out for those who like their music with an extra dose of loud, Gimme Shelter regularly stages alternative gigs by the island's rock and roll, rockabilly and punk bands. This is one of the only venues in Canggu that stays open past midnight.

Finns Beach Club BAR
(☎0361-844 6327; www.finnsbeachclub.com; Jl Pantai Berawa; ⏲9am-11pm; 📶) An enormous spectacle built from soaring bamboo, Finns dominates the beachfront. There's a huge pool and driving sound system. Hipster types fill seating areas and groups seeking tans frame the pool. Day loungers require a pricey minimum spend of 500,000Rp; the price includes a towel. There's a big bar and various treats like 'nitro ice cream'. Food spans the casual gamut (mains from 135,000Rp).

Note that the grilled corn on the menu for 65,000Rp inside can be had from the cheery vendor on the sand for the (already inflated) tourist price of 10,000Rp.

Shopping

★**Love Anchor** MARKET
(☎0822 3660 1648; www.loveanchorcanggu.com; Jl Pantai Batu Bolong 56; ⏲8am-midnight Mon-Fri, bazaar 9am-5pm Sat & Sun) Built in a traditional *joglo* style, this wood- and palm-tree-laden Canggu village is the trifecta of hipster retail, food and shopping. You can kick back with a Bintang or fuel up on everything from pizzas and burgers to smoothies and vegan-friendly fare before browsing boutiques and surf shops.

The open-air weekend bazaar (9am to 5pm Saturday and Sunday) is a one-stop shop for everything from Balinese souvenir essentials (circular rattan purse, anyone?) to chic custom leather goods and delicate jewellery hand-made by local artisans.

It Was All A Dream FASHION & ACCESSORIES
(☎0811 388 3322; Jl Pantai Berawa 14B; ⏲10am-7pm) Great-quality leather bags, fun sunglasses, vintage jeans, jersey basics, embroidered kaftans and more. This hip boutique has original pieces at reasonable prices. It's run by a French-American pair of expat designers.

Dylan Board Store SPORTS & OUTDOORS
(☎0819 9982 5654; www.dylansurfboards.com; Jl Pantai Batu Bolong; ⏲10am-8pm) Famed big-wave rider Dylan Longbottom runs this custom surfboard shop. A talented shaper, he creates boards for novices and pros alike. He also stocks plenty of his own designs that are ready to go.

Information

ATMs, basic shops and markets can be found on Canggu's main strip, Jl Pantai Berawa.

Getting There & Away

The airport taxi cartel charges 250,000Rp for a taxi.

You can reach the Canggu area by road from the south by taking Jl Batubelig west in Kerobokan almost to the beach and then veering north past various huge villas and expat shops along a curved road. It's much longer to go up and around via the traffic-clogged Jl Raya Kerobokan.

Getting to the Canggu area can cost 150,000Rp or more by taxi from Kuta or Seminyak. Don't expect to find taxis cruising anywhere, although any business can call you one.

Getting Around

This is good motorbike country – many of the impromptu roads are barely wide enough for one car, let alone two. The narrow road called the 'rice-field shortcut' is a perfect example of the complete lack of adequate road planning and construction in the Canggu area. There are websites devoted to photos of vehicles that have plunged into the rice after they tried to treat it as a two-lane road.

Note that street names are ad hoc: 'Jl Pantai Berawa' comprises a tangle of seemingly separate roads.

Echo Beach

☎0361

One of Bali's most popular surf breaks, Echo Beach has reached critical mass in popularity; surf shops abound. Construction has not been kind to the area and there's an unsightly dormant resort complex just to the east. If it seems too crowded here, walk along the sands 200m east for quietude.

Sunsets – and big waves – draw crowds who enjoy drinks coloured by the rosy glow.

Beaches

Echo Beach BEACH
(Pantai Batu Mejan) Surfers and those who like to watch them flock here for the high-tide left-hander that regularly tops 2m. The greyish sand right in front of the developments can vanish at high tide, but you'll find wide strands east and west. Batu Bolong Beach is 500m east.

Sleeping

Echo Beach Resort APARTMENT $$
(☎0878 7881 1440; www.echobeach.co.id; Jl Mundu Catu; apt from 900,000Rp; ❄📶🏊) Soaring above nearby villas, this apartment complex has nine one-bedroom units that come in various flavours. Some have ocean views, others have private pools. All have kitchen facilities. The compound is quiet and the decor is light-coloured and spartan. There is a good roof deck with sweeping water views. The beach is a 300m walk.

Koming Guest House GUESTHOUSE $$
(☎0819 9920 0996; www.komingguesthouse.com; Jl Munduk Catu; r from 500,000Rp; ❄📶🏊) Surrounded by other villas, this one has four rooms on two floors. The bottom ones have direct access to the pool. The upstairs pair have terraces with glimpses of the ocean. All have fridges and basic furnishings. Watch out for some tiled bathrooms that are not recommended after a night out.

Echoland GUESTHOUSE $$
(☎0361-887 0628; www.echolandbali.com; Jl Pantai Batu Mejan; dm from 180,000Rp, r with fan/air-con from 435,000/500,000Rp; ❄📶🏊) There are 17 private rooms plus dorms in this compact two-storey compound about 300m from the beach. The rooftop lounge has a nice cover for shade and predictably good views. Yoga classes are offered from 80,000Rp per hour.

Eating

Samadi Bali HEALTH FOOD $
(☎0812 3831 2505; www.samadibali.com; Jl Padang Linjong 39; lunch mains 46,000-80,000Rp; ⏲8am-7pm; ❄📶🖉) A guesthouse, yoga studio, holistic treatment centre and organic cafe rolled into one, Samadi Bali is the quintessential wellness stop in the heart of trendy Canggu. The popular Samadi Sunday Organic Market is a great spot to stock up on chemical-free produce and products. The menu in the health-conscious cafe covers the globe, from Indian thalis to Spanish gazpacho.

Dian Cafe INDONESIAN $
(☎0813 3875 4305; Jl Pura Batu Mejan; mains from 30,000Rp; ⏲8am-10pm) Old-school Indonesian and Western standards are served up cheap at this open-air cafe just a few metres from the beach.

Shady Shack VEGETARIAN $$
(☎0819 1639 5087; www.facebook.com/theshadyshackbali; Jl Tanah Barak 53; mains 50,000-95,000Rp; ⏲7.30am-10pm; 🖉) Under big trees, this charming cafe evokes the feel of a simple colonial country house in the Caribbean. There are tables in the garden as well as the woodsy dining room with huge open windows. The menu is a long list of bowls, wraps and juices. Most are vegan and/or veggie. Try the blueberry muesli, beautiful haloumi burger or gorgeous desserts.

Beach House CAFE $$
(Echo Beach Club; ☎0361-747 4604; www.echobeachhouse.com; Jl Pura Batu Mejan; mains 55,000-95,000Rp; ⏲7am-11pm; 📶) An Echo Beach icon, this seafront restaurant-bar has front-row seats (tables, sofas, picnic tables) to enjoy the surf action. There's an impressive display of skewered meats and seafood ready to grill, as well as a tasty breakfast and lunch menu. Evening barbecues are popular, especially on Sundays when there's live music.

Drinking & Nightlife

Enjoying a drink while watching the surf break is an Echo Beach tradition. Just west of the main cafe cluster, a string of ephemeral beach bars have appeared that are little more than bamboo shacks. They offer beanbags on the sand and cold beer. Note that an upscale development could sweep them away overnight.

La Brisa INTERNATIONAL
(☎0811 394 6666; www.labrisabali.com; Jl Pantai Batu Mejan, Gang La Brisa; ⏲7am-11pm Mon-Sat, from 11am Sun; 📶) The newest member of Bali's trendy La family – La Plancha, La Favela, La Sicilia and La Laguna – La Brisa is nestled along the sands of Echo Beach in Canggu. Constructed using reclaimed wood from old fishing boats, this ocean-themed restaurant and bar is aptly decorated with fishing nets, fishing rods, seashells and antique buoys.

Sand Bar BAR
(Echo Beach; ⏰10am-late) This barely there bar is just west of the main cluster of Echo Beach businesses. It serves cold beer and cheap drinks until predawn on many nights. Sit on beanbags, chairs or sand. On some nights bands play until after midnight.

Going west along the beach you'll find a long series of bamboo beach bars with simple food and cheap beer.

ℹ Getting There & Away

A local taxi cooperative will shuttle you to Seminyak and the south for 150,000Rp or more.

Pererenan Beach

☎0361

The bookend of the vast sweep of sand that begins near the airport, Pererenan Beach is rapidly changing as villas and other buildings appear amid the vanishing rice fields, all the way back to the Tanah Lot road. Before long it will be indistinguishable from the Echo Beach area.

Pererenan Beach BEACH
The most northern of the Canggu-area beaches, laid-back Pererenan is next in the sights of developers. Villas, guesthouses and beach bars are found near the dark tanned sands and decent waves. It's an easy 300m walk west from Echo Beach across sand and rock formations (or about 1km by road). Vendors sell beer and rent loungers and surfboards.

Andy's Surf Villa BUNGALOW $$
(☎0818 567 538; www.andysurfvilla.com; Jl Pantai Pererenan; r 450,000-700,000Rp; ❄📶🏊) Five small bungalows surround a compact courtyard and are watched over by a charming Balinese family; 12 people can rent the entire complex and throw a nonstop party. The beach is 200m away.

Pondok Nyoman Bagus GUESTHOUSE $$
(☎0361-848 2925; www.facebook.com/PondokNyomanBagus; Jl Pantai Pererenan; r 500,000-700,000Rp; ❄📶🏊) Just behind Pererenan Beach, this popular guesthouse has 14 rooms with terraces and balconies, all set in a modern two-storey building that boasts a rooftop infinity pool and a restaurant with average food and sensational sea views.

ℹ Getting There & Away

With traffic on the Tanah Lot road, it can take well over an hour to reach Seminyak from here. Taxis will cost upwards of 150,000Rp.

ALINA_DANILOVA/SHUTTERSTOCK ©

Best Beaches

Bali and the many islands of Nusa Tenggara are fringed by beaches, with sand from white to black and surf from wild to tame. They draw visitors in droves for sunbathing, yoga, running, surfing, snorkelling, diving and good times aplenty. With so many to chose from, you'll find one – or several – for any mood.

Contents

Above Kuta (p66) coastline

1

2

1. Balangan Beach (p136) 2. Kuta Beach (p304), Lombok
3. Gili Trawangan (p316)

Beaches

There are so many great beaches in this part of Indonesia that it's best to just categorise them by region. Within each of these five areas, you'll find many different patches of sand to enjoy.

Tuban to Echo Beach

Stretching some 12km from just north of the airport all the way northwest to Pererenan Beach (p106), this is the beach that made Bali famous. This multifaceted playground has multiple personalities, including surfer, hip, family, lonely, boozy and more.

Bukit Beaches

The cliffs on the west coast of the Bukit Peninsula (p132) often shelter little coves of beautiful white sand, like that found at Balangan, Bingin and Padang Padang. It can be hard to reach these sands (and their neighbours) but the rewards include incredible views of the surf breaks, nameless little bamboo warungs selling Bintang, and sublimely beautiful water.

East Coast Beaches

A vast crescent of black sand that started up the volcanic slopes of Gunung Agung sweeps from north of Sanur to the east side of the island (p203). Some beaches here are empty, others have surfers, while still more have temples and slices of local Bali life.

South Lombok Beaches

The best Kuta Beach isn't on Bali. Along Lombok's south coast (p304) running east and west from that Kuta, you'll discover a dozen gorgeous bays ringed with white sand and, often, not much else.

Gili Beaches

The Gili Islands (p312) – Trawangan, Meno and Air – are each ringed by beautiful sands. Walk the big loop, sample at the beach buffets, try some offshore snorkelling and just enjoy.

1

2

AARON LIM/SHUTTERSTOCK ©

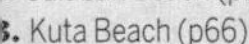

1. Suluban Beach (p142), Ulu Watu 2. Tanjung Desert (p296) 3. Kuta Beach (p66)

3

Surfing

Surfing is the top reason many come to this region and surf culture is part of its modern fabric. Surfer lifestyle here might be low key, but the breaks are not.

Kuta Beach

Kuta Beach (p66), Bali's original surf beach, is still a winner. You can't help but be drawn to this vast sweep of sand, where surfers of all stripes are drawn to the nonstop breaks right offshore. And you can easily learn to surf here. Schools abound and there are classes all day long.

Ulu Watu

You'll find Bali's most legendary surfing at Ulu Watu (p141). It's really the climax of a string of breaks that march down the west coast of the Bukit Peninsula. The conditions are challenging and you can spend days just sussing out the scene.

Nusa Lembongan

Nusa Lembongan (p150) off Bali is an excellent place for days of riding. Breaks – accessed by boat – are offshore, past the reefs. And there are cheap places to stay with good views of the action, so you can pick your moment to plunge in.

Tanjung Desert

Tanjung Desert (Desert Point; p296) on Lombok wins plaudits, and that's not just from surfers congratulating themselves for trekking out to this remote spot. Fickle (its season is a short one: May to September), this break is tough for even the most experienced and a reward for all.

Supersuck

Supersuck (p337), on Sumbawa's southwest coast, is consistently rated as the best left break in the world. It's so good that surfers descend regularly from Hawaii's North Shore to surf here.

KRISTINA VACKOVA/SHUTTERSTOCK ©

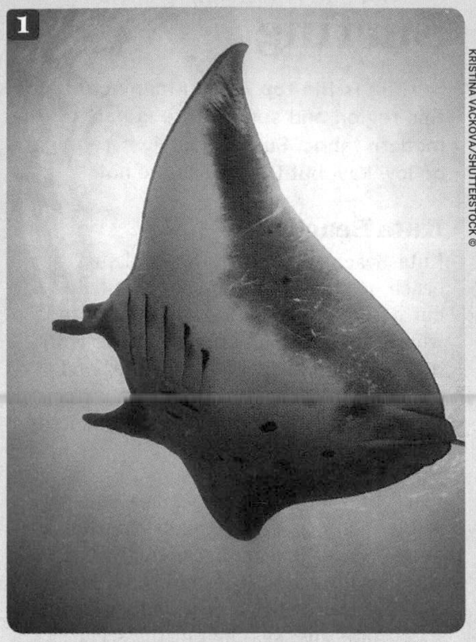

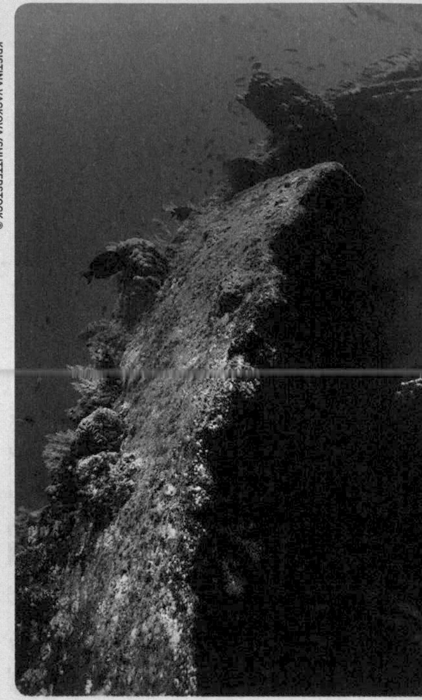

1. Manta ray, Nusa Penida (p157) **2.** Diver explores the *Liberty* shipwreck (p234), Tulamben **3.** Gili Trawangan (p316) **4.** Coral, Pulau Menjangan (p268)

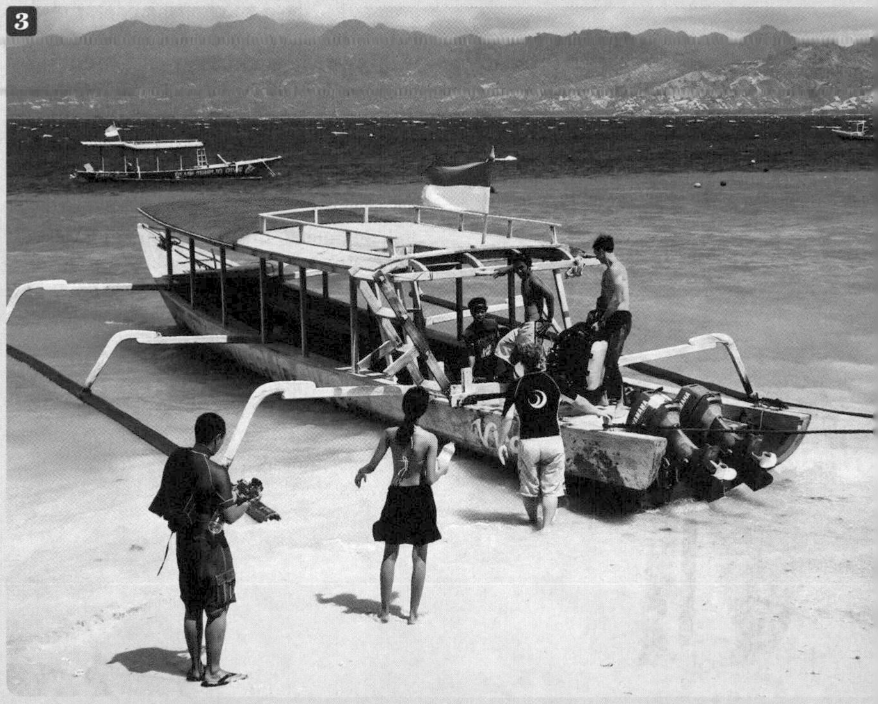

2

DUDAREV MIKHAIL/SHUTTERSTOCK ©

4

Diving

The islands have great diving and a whole bunch of great dive shops to support your explorations. From simple wall dives to challenging open-water observations of massive creatures, you'll find something here to fit your skills and desires.

Tulamben

Tulamben (p234) seems like a mere village along the coast road of east Bali – until you notice all the dive shops. The big attraction here lies right offshore: an old ship, the *Liberty*, sunk during WWII. You can dive and snorkel the wreck from offshore.

Gili Trawangan

Gili Trawangan (p316) is a fabulous centre for diving and snorkelling. Great places to explore the depths abound in the waters around all three Gilis. Freediving is popular here, you can snorkel right off the beaches and there are reefs in all directions.

Nusa Penida

Seldom-visited Nusa Penida (p157) is surrounded by what could be an underwater theme park. Conditions can be challenging – the services of an excellent dive shop are essential – but you might see huge, placid sunfish and manta rays.

Pulau Menjangan

Pulau Menjangan (p268) is Bali's best-known dive and snorkel area and has a dozen superb dive sites. The diving is excellent – iconic tropical fish, soft corals, great visibility (usually), caves and a spectacular drop-off. It's best visited as part of an overnight jaunt to Pemuteran.

Komodo & Rinca Islands

Diving the waters around these islands (p344) where the Flores Sea and Selat Sumba (Sumba Strait) merge showcases an astonishing variety of marine life and corals.

Sea life, Pulau Menjangan (p268)

Marine Life

There is a rich variety of coral, seaweed, fish and other marine life in the coastal waters off the islands; in fact Indonesia's entire marine territory was declared a manta ray sanctuary in 2014. Much of the marine life can be appreciated by snorkellers, but you're only likely to see the larger marine animals while diving.

Dolphins

Dolphins (p435) can be found right around the islands and have been made into an attraction off Lovina. But you're just as likely to see schools of dolphins if you take a fast boat between Bali and the Gilis, or dive near Komodo and Rinca Islands in Nusa Tenggara.

Sharks

Sharks (p435) are always dramatic and there are very occasional reports of large ones, including great whites, throughout the region, although they are not considered a massive threat. In the Gilis, reef sharks are easily spotted at Shark Point.

Sea Turtles

Sea turtles (p435) are common but greatly endangered. Long considered a delicacy by the Balinese, it is a constant struggle by environmentalists to protect them from poachers. Still, you can find them, especially in the Gilis.

Fish of All Kinds

Smaller fish and corals can be found at a plethora of spots around the islands. Everybody's favourite first stop is Bali's Menjangan. Fish as large as whale sharks have been reported, but what thrills scores daily are the coloured beauty of an array of corals, sponges, lacy sea fans and much more. Starfish abound and you'll easily spot clownfish and other polychromatic characters.

South Bali & the Islands

Includes ➡

Best Places to Eat

- Bumbu Bali 1 (p148)
- Depot Cak Asmo (p119)
- Men Gabrug (p119)
- Deck Cafe & Bar (p155)

Best Places to Stay

- Temple Lodge (p138)
- Belmond Jimbaran Puri (p134)
- Sofitel Bali Nusa Dua Beach Resort (p146)
- Rock'n Reef (p141)
- Alila Villas Uluwatu (p144)
- Tandjung Sari (p128)

Why Go?

You won't have seen Bali if you haven't fully explored south Bali. The island's capital, Denpasar, sprawls in all directions from the centre with traditional markets, busy malls, great eating and lashings of Balinese history and culture, even as it threatens to absorb Seminyak, Kuta and Sanur.

The Bukit Peninsula (the southern part of south Bali) has multiple personalities. In the east, Tanjung Benoa is a beach-fronted playground of package resorts while Nusa Dua attempts to bring order out of chaos with an insulated pasture of five-star hotels. The south coast sees posh cliff-side resorts, but the west side is where the real action is. Small coves and beaches dotted with edgy guesthouses and luxe eco-resorts enjoy a cool vibe and fab surfing.

To the east, Nusa Penida dominates the horizon, but in its lee you'll find Nusa Lembongan, the ultimate island escape from the island of Bali.

When to Go

- The best time to visit south Bali is outside the high season of July, August and the weeks around Christmas and New Year's Day. Visitor numbers spike during high season and rooms from Bingin to Tanjung Benoa and Sanur to Nusa Lembongan may be filled. Many prefer April to June and September when crowds are manageable.
- Surfing is best at the world-class breaks along the west coast of the Bukit Peninsula from February to November, with May to August being especially good.
- To surf at the breaks in Nusa Lembongan, aim for October to March.

South Bali & the Islands Highlights

1. **Jimbaran** (p132) Picking a lobster for the grill at one of the many beachfront seafood joints.
2. **Bingin** (p137) Finding a perfectly retro-chic place to stay the night in the back lanes.
3. **Ulu Watu** (p142) Surfing Bali's ultimate breaks and an internationally revered swell magnet.
4. **Sanur** (p124) Watching as a full moon climbs over Nusa Penida, casting a mysterious glow over land and sea.
5. **Denpasar** (p117) Savouring the best US$2 meal you've ever had.
6. **Nusa Lembongan** (p150) Escaping one island (Bali) for a more peaceful, smaller one, with an ideal mix of fun and frolic.
7. **Nusa Penida** (p157) Swimming with manta rays and other large fish in the challenging waters off this mysterious island.

Getting There & Away

In most of south Bali, you're never far from the airport. Other access depends on the often-jammed roads, although the toll road offers a quick trip between Sanur and Nusa Dua. Fast boats serve Nusa Lembongan and the islands.

DENPASAR

0361 / POP 962,900

Sprawling, hectic and ever-growing, Bali's capital has been the focus of a lot of the island's growth and wealth over the last five decades. It can seem a daunting and chaotic place, but spend a little time on its tree-lined streets in the relatively affluent government and business district of Renon and you'll discover a more genteel side.

Denpasar might not be a tropical paradise, but it's as much a part of 'the real Bali' as the rice paddies and clifftop temples. This is the hub of the island for nearly a million locals and here you will find their shopping malls and parks. Most enticing, however, are the authentic restaurants and cafes aimed at the burgeoning middle class.

History

Denpasar, which means 'next to the market', was an important trading centre and the seat of local rajas (lords or princes) before the colonial period. The Dutch gained control of northern Bali in the mid-19th century, but their takeover of the south didn't start until 1906. After the three Balinese princes destroyed their own palaces in Denpasar and made a suicidal last stand – a ritual *puputan* – the Dutch made Denpasar an important colonial centre. As Bali's tourism industry expanded in the 1930s, most visitors stayed at one or two government hotels in the city.

The northern town of Singaraja remained the Dutch administrative capital until after WWII, when it was moved to Denpasar because of the new airport; in 1958, some years after Indonesian independence, the city became the official capital of the province of Bali. Recent immigrants have come from Java and all over Indonesia, attracted by opportunities in schools, business, construction and the enormous tourist economy. Denpasar's edges have merged with Sanur, Kuta, Seminyak and Kerobokan.

Sights

★Bajra Sandhi Monument MONUMENT

(Monument to the Struggle of the People of Bali; 0361-264517; Jl Raya Puputan, Renon; adult/child 20,000/10,000Rp; 9am-6pm) The centrepiece to a popular park, this monument is as big as its name. Inside the vaguely Borobudur-like structure are dioramas tracing Bali's history. Note that in the portrayal of the 1906 battle with the Dutch, the King of Badung is literally a sitting target. Take the spiral stairs to the top for 360-degree views.

Museum Negeri Propinsi Bali MUSEUM

(0361-222680; Jl Mayor Wisnu; adult/child 50,000/25,000Rp; 7.30am-3.30pm Sat-Thu, to 1pm Fri) Think of this as the British Museum or the Smithsonian of Balinese culture. It's all here, but unlike those world-class institutions, you have to work at sorting it out – the museum could use a dose of curatorial energy (and some new light bulbs). Most displays are labelled in English. The museum comprises several buildings and pavilions, including many examples of Balinese architecture, housing prehistoric pieces, traditional artefacts, Barong (mythical lion-dog creatures), ceremonial objects and rich displays of textiles.

Museum staff members often play music on a bamboo gamelan to magical effect; visit in the afternoons when it's uncrowded. Ignore 'guides' who offer little except a chance to part with US$5 or US$10.

The **main building** has a collection of prehistoric pieces downstairs, including stone sarcophagi, and stone and bronze implements. Upstairs there are traditional artefacts, including items still in everyday use. Look for the intricate wood-and-cane carrying cases for transporting fighting cocks, and tiny carrying cases for fighting crickets.

The **Northern Pavilion** is built in the style of a Tabanan palace. It houses dance costumes and masks, including a sinister *rangda* (widow-witch), a healthy-looking Barong and a towering Barong Landung (tall Barong) figure.

The spacious verandah of the **Central Pavilion** is inspired by the palace pavilions of the Karangasem kingdom (based in Amlapura), where rajas held audiences. The exhibits are related to Balinese religion and include ceremonial objects, calendars and priests' clothing.

In the **Southern Pavilion** there are rich displays of textiles, including *endek* (a Balinese method of weaving with predyed threads), double ikat, *songket* (silver- and gold-threaded cloth, handwoven using a floating weft technique) and *prada* (the application of gold leaf or gold or silver thread on traditional Balinese clothes).

Puputan Square PARK

(Jl Gajah Mada) This bit of urban open space commemorates the heroic but suicidal stand of the rajas of Badung against the invading Dutch in 1906. A monument depicts a Balinese family in heroic pose, brandishing the weapons that were so ineffective against the Dutch guns. The woman also has jewels in her left hand, as the women of the Badung court reputedly flung their jewellery at the Dutch soldiers to taunt them.

The park is popular with locals at lunchtime and with families near sunset. Vendors sell chicken satay and other snacks plus drinks. On weekends it can fill with kite-flyers of all ages.

Pura Maospahit TEMPLE

(off Jl Sutomo) Established in the 14th century, at the time the Majapahit arrived from Java, this temple was damaged in a 1917 earthquake and has been heavily restored since. The oldest structures are at the back of the temple, but the most interesting features are the large statues of Garuda and the giant Batara Bayu (God of Wind).

Pura Jagatnatha HINDU TEMPLE

(Jl Surapati) FREE The state temple, built in 1953, is dedicated to the supreme god, Sanghyang Widi. Part of its significance is its statement of monotheism. Although the Balinese recognise many gods, the belief in one supreme god (who can have many manifestations) brings Balinese Hinduism into conformity with the first principle of Pancasila – the 'Belief in One God'.

The *padmasana* (temple shrine) is made of white coral and consists of an empty throne (symbolic of heaven) on top of the cosmic turtle and two *naga* (mythical snake-like creatures), which symbolise the foundation of the world. The walls are decorated with carvings of scenes from the Ramayana and Mahabharata.

Two major festivals are held here every month, during the full moon and new moon, and feature *wayang kulit* (leather shadow puppet) performances.

Taman Wedhi Budaya CULTURAL CENTRE

(☎0361-222776; off Jl Nusa Indah; ⏰8am-3pm Mon-Thu, to 1pm Fri-Sun) This arts centre is a sprawling complex in the eastern part of Denpasar. Its lavish architecture houses an art gallery with an interesting collection. However, it's only worth dropping by if there's an event on. From mid-June to mid-July, the centre comes alive for the Bali Arts Festival, with dances, music and craft displays from all over Bali.

Book tickets at the centre for more popular events.

Activities & Courses

Kube Dharma Bakti MASSAGE

(☎0361-749 9440; Jl Serma Mendara 3; massage per hr 100,000Rp; ⏰9am-10pm) Many Balinese wouldn't think of having a massage from anyone but a blind person. Government-sponsored schools offer lengthy courses to certify blind people in reflexology, shiatsu massage, anatomy and much more. In this airy building redolent with liniments you can choose from a range of therapies.

Indonesia Australia Language Foundation LANGUAGE

(IALF; ☎0361-225243; www.ialf.edu; Jl Raya Sesetan 190) The best place for serious courses in Bahasa Indonesia.

Festivals & Events

★Bali Arts Festival PERFORMING ARTS

(www.baliartsfestival.com; Taman Wedhi Budaya; ⏰mid-Jun–mid-Jul) This annual festival, based at Taman Wedhi Budaya arts centre, is an easy way to see a wide variety of traditional dance, music and crafts. The productions of the Ramayana and Mahabharata ballets are grand and the opening ceremony and parade in Denpasar are spectacles. Tickets are usually available before performances; schedules are online and at the Denpasar tourist office.

The festival is the main event of the year for scores of village dance and musical groups. Competition is fierce, with local pride on the line at each performance ('our Kecak is better than your Kecak', etc). To do well here sets a village on a good course for the year. Some events are held in a 6000-seat amphitheatre, a venue that allows you to realise the mass appeal of traditional Balinese culture.

Sleeping

Denpasar has many new midpriced chain hotels, but it's hard to think of a compelling reason to stay here unless you want to revel in the city's bright lights. Most visitors stay in the tourist towns of the south and visit Denpasar as a day trip.

Nakula Familiar Inn GUESTHOUSE $
(☎0361-226446; www.nakulafamiliarinn.com; Jl Nakula 4; r 200,000-300,000Rp;) The eight rooms at this sprightly urban family compound, a longtime traveller favourite, are clean and have small balconies. There is a nice courtyard and cafe in the middle. Tegal–Kereneng bemos go along Jl Nakula.

Inna Bali HOTEL $$
(☎0361-225681; http://inna-bali-denpasar.denpasararea-hotels.com/en; Jl Veteran 3; r 400,000-1,000,000Rp;) The Inna Bali has simple gardens, a huge banyan tree and a certain nostalgic charm; it dates from 1927 and was once the main tourist hotel on the island. Room interiors are standard, but many have deeply shaded verandahs. Ongoing renovations have added an attractive colonial facade, including a decent sidewalk cafe. The hotel is a good base for the **Ngrupuk parades** that take place the day before the Nyepi festival, as they pass in front. Get the veteran employees talking – they have many stories.

Eating

Denpasar has a good range of Indonesian and Balinese food, and savvy locals and expats each have favourite warungs (food stalls) and restaurants here. New places open regularly on Jl Teuku Umar, while in Renon there is a phenomenal strip of eating places on Jl Cok Agung Tresna between Jl Ramayana and Jl Dewi Madri and along Letda Tantular.

★**Depot Cak Asmo** INDONESIAN $
(☎0361-256246; Jl Tukad Gangga; mains from 15,000Rp; ⊙9.30am-11pm) Join the government workers and students from the nearby university for superb dishes cooked to order in the bustling kitchen. Order the buttery and crispy *cumi cumi* (calamari) battered in *telor asin* (a heavenly mixture of eggs and garlic). Fruity ice drinks are a cooling treat. An English-language menu makes ordering a breeze. It's halal, so there's no alcohol.

There are two more restaurants with the same name, both located in Denpasar, that are part of the same chain.

★**Men Gabrug** BALINESE $
(☎0361-7070 8415; Jl Drupadi; snacks from 10,000Rp; ⊙9am-6pm Mon-Sat) A favourite sweet treat for Balinese of all ages is *jaje laklak* – disks of rice flour cooked in an open-air cast-iron pan and redolent of coconut. One of the best places to get them is at this family-run outlet where the cooking takes place right on the street.

Be sure to get the perfect accompaniment: *rujak kuah pindang,* which is made fresh when you order it and combines young vegetables with chillies and fish sauce.

Bakso Supra Dinasty BALINESE $
(☎0812-3488 8712; Jl Cok Agung Tresna; mains from 15,000Rp; ⊙8am-10pm) One taste of the soup assembled to order out of the steaming vats at this small stall and you'll agree that the name (translated: Meatball Super Dynasty) is fully deserved. The broth is rich and the meatballs are filled with flavour.

Warung Wardani INDONESIAN $
(☎0361-224398; Jl Yudistira 2; nasi campur from 35,000Rp; ⊙8am-4pm) Don't be deceived by the small dining room at the entrance: there's another vastly larger one out the back. The top-notch *nasi campur* (rice with side dishes) draws in the masses for lunch daily.

Warung Bundaran Renon BALINESE $
(☎0361-234208; Jl Raya Puputan 212; meals from 40,000Rp; ⊙9am-5pm) A slightly upscale *babi guling* (spit-roast pig) place with excellent plate lunches of same. It feels a bit like a suburban house and there's a shady patio.

Pondok Kuring INDONESIAN $
(☎0361-234122; Jl Raya Puputan 56; meals from 20,000Rp; ⊙10am-9.30pm) The foods of the Sundanese people of west Java are the speciality here. Highly spiced vegetables, meat and seafood draw flavours from an array of herbs. Deceptively simple, the *lalapan* is excellent. This glossy restaurant has an arty dining room and a lovely and quiet garden out back.

Warung Lembongan INDONESIAN $
(☎0361-221437; Jl Cok Agung Tresna 6C; meals 17,000-25,000Rp; ⊙8am-10pm) Silver folding chairs at long tables are shaded by a garish green awning out front. These are details you will quickly forget after you have the house speciality: chicken lightly fried yet delicately crispy like the top of a perfect crème brûlée. The other speciality is a spicy *sop kepala ikan* (fish soup).

Ayam Goreng Kalasan INDONESIAN $
(☎0361-472 2938; Jl Cok Agung Tresna 6; mains 15,000-25,000Rp; ⊙8am-10pm) The name here says it all: fried chicken (*ayam goreng*) named for a Javanese temple (Kalasan) in a region renowned for its fiery, crispy chicken. Note the hint of lemongrass imbued by a long marination before cooking.

Denpasar

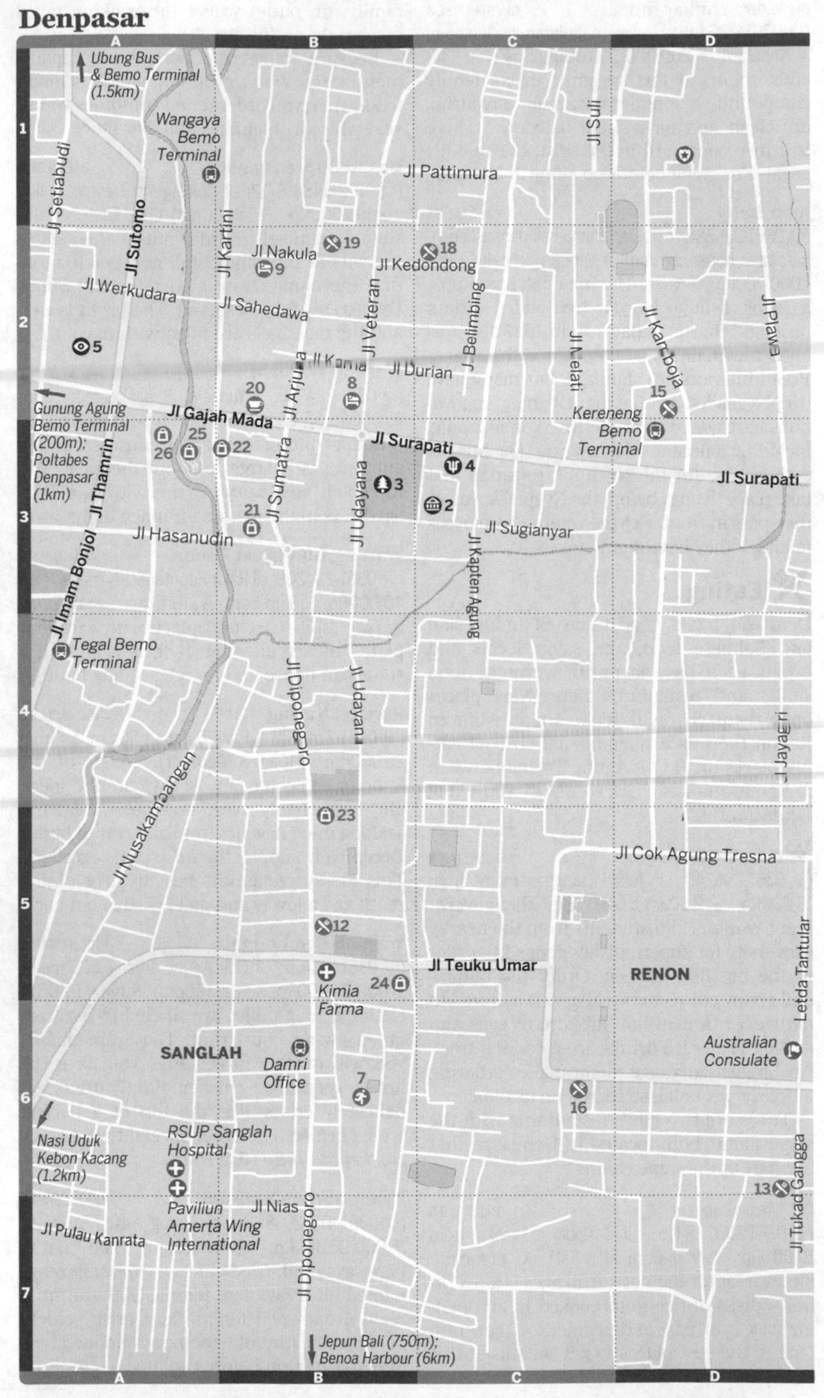
Ubung Bus & Bemo Terminal (1.5km)
Wangaya Bemo Terminal
Jl Pattimura
Jl Suli
Jl Setiabudi
Jl Sutomo
Jl Kartini
Jl Nakula
19
18
9
Jl Kedondong
Jl Werkudara
Jl Sahedawa
Jl Veteran
Jl Belimbing
Jl Kamboja
Jl Plawa
5
Jl Karna
Jl Durian
Jl Kelati
Jl Arjuna
20
8
15
Gunung Agung Bemo Terminal (200m); Poltabes Denpasar (1km)
Jl Gajah Mada
25
26
22
Jl Surapati
Kereneng Bemo Terminal
4
Jl Thamrin
Jl Sumatra
Jl Udayana
3
2
Jl Surapati
21
Jl Hasanudin
Jl Sugianyar
Jl Imam Bonjol
Jl Kapten Agung
Tegal Bemo Terminal
Jl Diponegoro
Jl Udayana
Jl Jayagiri
Jl Nusakambangan
23
Jl Cok Agung Tresna
12
Jl Teuku Umar
Kimia Farma
24
RENON
Letda Tantular
SANGLAH
Damri Office
Australian Consulate
7
16
Nasi Uduk Kebon Kacang (1.2km)
RSUP Sanglah Hospital
Paviliun Amerta Wing International
Jl Nias
Jl Pulau Kanrata
Jl Diponegoro
13
Jl Tukad Gangga
Jepun Bali (750m); Benoa Harbour (6km)

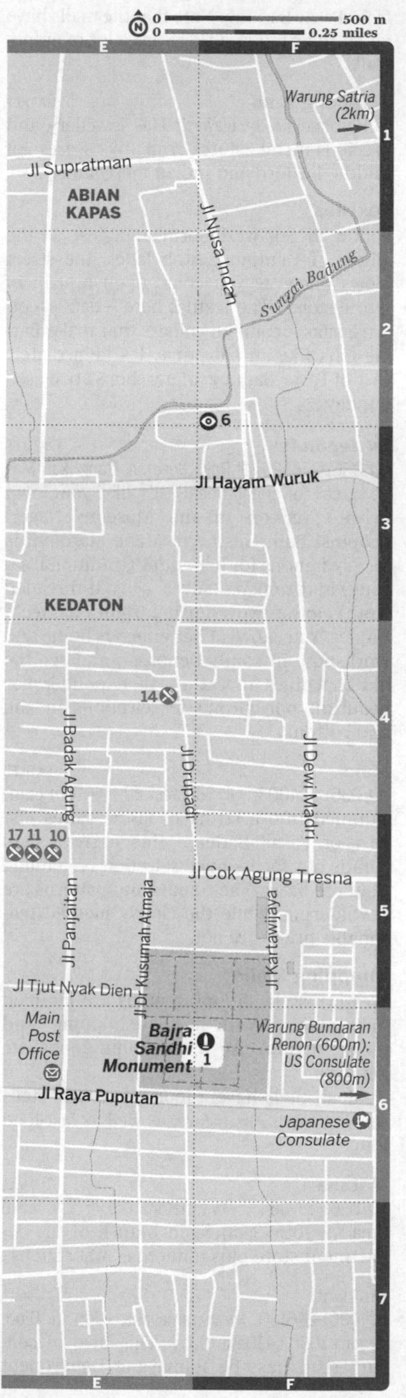

Denpasar

Top Sights

1 Bajra Sandhi Monument F6

Sights

2 Museum Negeri Propinsi Bali C3
3 Puputan Square B3
4 Pura Jagatnatha C3
5 Pura Maospahit A2
6 Taman Wedhi Budaya F2

Activities, Courses & Tours

7 Kube Dharma Bakti B6

Sleeping

8 Inna Bali B2
9 Nakula Familiar Inn B2

Eating

10 Ayam Goreng Kalasan E5
11 Bakso Supra Dinasty E5
12 Café Teduh B5
13 Depot Cak Asmo D6
14 Men Gabrug E4
15 Pasar Malam Kereneng D2
16 Pondok Kuring C6
17 Warung Lembongan E5
18 Warung Satria C2
19 Warung Wardani B2

Drinking & Nightlife

20 Bhineka Djaja B2

Shopping

21 Kampung Arab B3
22 Maju B3
23 Mal Bali B5
24 Matahari B5
25 Pasar Badung A3
26 Pasar Kumbasari A3

Nasi Uduk Kebon Kacang INDONESIAN $
(☎0812 466 6828; Jl Teuku Umar 230; meals 12,000-25,000Rp; ⏰9am-11pm) Open to the street, this spotless cafe serves up Javanese treats such as *nasi uduk* (sweetly scented coconut rice with fresh peanut sauce) and *lalapan* (a simple salad of fresh lemon basil leaves). Chicken dishes win raves.

Pasar Malam Kereneng MARKET $
(Kereneng Night Market; Jl Kamboja; meals from 10,000Rp; ⏰6pm-5am) Dozens of vendors dish up food until dawn at this excellent night market.

Warung Satria INDONESIAN $
(☎0361-235993; Jl Kedondong; mains 15,000-25,000Rp; ⏰9am-9pm) On a quiet street; try the seafood satay served with a shallot sambal. Otherwise, choose from the immaculate

displays, but don't wait too long after lunch or it will all be gone. There is a **second location** (☎0361-464602; Jl Supratman; mains 15,000-25,000Rp; ⏰10am-8pm) near the junction where the main road to Ubud branches off from the bypass, east of the centre of Denpasar.

Café Teduh INDONESIAN $
(☎0361-221631; off Jl Diponegoro; mains 12,000-25,000Rp; ⏰10am-10pm Sun-Fri, to 11pm Sat; 📶) Hidden down a tiny lane, Café Teduh is a little oasis with hanging orchids, trees, flowers and ponds with fountains. Try *ayam dabu-dabu* (grilled chicken with chilli paste, tomatoes, shallots, lemongrass and spices) or *nasi bakar cumi hitam* (rice and marinated squid wrapped in banana leaf and grilled).

Drinking & Nightlife

★**Bhineka Djaja** COFFEE
(☎0361-224016; Jl Gajah Mada 80; coffee 7000Rp; ⏰9am-3pm Mon-Sat) Home to Bali's Coffee Co, this storefront sells locally grown beans and makes a mean espresso, which you can enjoy at the two tiny tables while watching the bustle of Denpasar's old main drag.

Shopping

Markets

Denpasar's largest traditional markets are in a fairly compact area that makes visiting them easy, even if navigating their crowded aisles across multiple floors is not. Like other aspects of Balinese life, the big markets are in flux. Large chain supermarkets are biting into their trade and the evolving middle class say they prefer the likes of Carrefour because it has more imported goods. But the public markets aren't down yet. This is where you come for purely Balinese goods, such as temple offerings, ceremonial clothes and a range of foodstuffs unique to the island, including numerous types of mangosteen.

Pasar Badung MARKET
(☎0361-224361; Jl Gajah Mada; ⏰24hr) Busy in the mornings and evenings, Bali's largest food market is a great place to browse and bargain, with food from all over the island, including fruits and spices.

Pasar Kumbasari MARKET
(Jl Gajah Mada; ⏰8am-6pm) Handicrafts, a plethora of vibrant fabrics and costumes decorated with gold are just some of the goods at this huge market across the river from Pasar Badung. Note that the malls have taken their toll and there are a lot of empty stalls.

Kampung Arab MARKET
(Jl Hasanudin & Jl Sulawesi) Has jewellery and precious-metal stores run by scores of Middle Eastern and Indian merchants.

Textiles

Follow Jl Sulawesi north and, just as the glitter of Kampung Arab fades, the street glows anew as you come upon a strip of fabric stores. The textiles here – batiks, cottons, silks – come in colours that make Barbie look like an old purse. It's immediately east of Pasar Badung. Many shops are closed Sunday.

★**Jepun Bali** TEXTILES
(☎0361-726526; Jl Raya Sesetan, Gang Ikan Mas 11; ⏰call for appointment) It's like your own private version of the Museum Negeri Propinsi Bali: Gusti Ayu Made Mardiani is locally famous for her *endek* (traditional sarong) and *songket* (silver- or gold-threaded cloth) clothes woven using traditional techniques. You can visit her gracious home and workshop, in south Denpasar, and see the old machines in action, then ponder her beautiful polychromatic selections in silk and cotton.

Maju TEXTILES
(☎0361-224003; Jl Sulawesi 19; ⏰9am-6pm) Jammed into a string of fabric stores just east of Pasar Badung, this narrow shop stands out for its huge selection of genuine Balinese batik. The colours and patterns are bewildering, while the clearly marked reasonable prices are not.

Shopping Malls

Western-style shopping malls are jammed on Sundays with locals shopping and teens flirting; the brand-name goods are genuine.

Most malls have a food court with stalls serving fresh Asian fare, as well as fast-food joints.

Matahari MALL
(☎0361-237364; www.matahari.co.id; Jl Teuku Umar; ⏰10am-9pm) Main branch of the department store plus numerous other shops.

Mal Bali MALL
(☎0361-246180; www.ramayana.co.id; Jl Diponegoro 103; ⏰10am-10pm) This hive of consumerism has the Ramayana Department

Store, Bali's largest. It also houses a big supermarket, food court and many clothing shops.

Information

MEDICAL SERVICES

Denpasar has many medical providers that serve the entire island.

BaliMed Hospital (☎0361-484748; www.balimedhospital.co.id; Jl Mahendradatta 57) On the Kerobokan side of Denpasar, this private hospital has a range of medical services. A basic consultation is 250,000Rp.

RSUP Sanglah Hospital (Rumah Sakit Umum Propinsi Sanglah; ☎0361-227911; www.sanglahhospitalbali.com; Jl Diponegoro; ⏲24hr) The city's general hospital has English-speaking staff and an ER. It's the best hospital on the island, although standards are not the same as those in developed countries. It has a special wing for well-insured foreigners, **Paviliun Amerta Wing International** (☎0361-247250, 0361-232603; off Jl Pulau Bali).

Kimia Farma (☎0361-227811; Jl Diponegoro 125; ⏲24hr) The main outlet of the island-wide pharmacy chain has the largest selection of prescription medications in Bali.

POLICE

Police Station (☎0361-227711, 0361-424346; Jl Supratman) The place for any general problems.

POST

Main Post Office (☎0361-223565; Jl Raya Puptuan; ⏲8am-9pm Mon-Fri, to 8pm Sat) Your best option for unusual postal needs (such as surfboards and other large items). Has a photocopy centre and ATMs.

Getting There & Away

AIR

Sometimes called 'Denpasar' in airline schedules, Bali's Ngurah Rai International Airport is 12km south, closer to Kuta.

BEMO & MINIBUS

The city has several bemo and bus terminals – if you're travelling by bemo around Bali you'll often have to go via Denpasar and transfer from one terminal to another by bemo (7000Rp).

Note that the bemo network is sputtering and fares are approximate and at times completely subjective. Drivers often try to charge nonlocals at least 25% more.

Ubung

Well north of the town, on the road to Gilimanuk, the **Ubung Bus & Bemo Terminal** (Jl HOS Cokroaminoto) is the hub for northern and western Bali. It also has long-distance buses in addition to the ones serving the terminal 12km northwest in Mengwi.

DESTINATION	FARE
Gilimanuk (for the ferry to Java)	45,000Rp
Mengwi bus terminal	15,000Rp
Munduk	60,000Rp
Singaraja (via Pupuan or Bedugul)	70,000Rp

Batubulan

Located a very inconvenient 6km northeast of Denpasar on a road to Ubud, this terminal is for destinations in eastern and central Bali.

DESTINATION	FARE
Amlapura	25,000Rp
Padangbai (for the Lombok ferry)	20,000Rp
Sanur	10,000Rp
Ubud	20,000Rp

Tegal

On the western side of town, **Tegal Bemo Terminal** (Jl Imam Bonjol) is the terminal for Kuta and the Bukit Peninsula.

DESTINATION	FARE
Airport	15,000Rp
Jimbaran	20,000Rp
Kuta	15,000Rp

Kereneng

East of the town centre, Kereneng Bemo Terminal has bemos to Sanur (10,000Rp).

Wangaya

Near the centre of town, this small **terminal** (Jl Kartini) is the departure point for bemo services to northern Denpasar and the outlying Ubung bus terminal (8000Rp).

Gunung Agung

This **terminal** (Jl Gunung Agung) is at the northwestern corner of town (look for an orange sign) and has bemos to Kerobokan and Canggu (15,000Rp).

BUS

Long-distance bus services use the Ubung Bus & Bemo Terminal. Most long-distance services also stop at the **Mengwi terminal** (Jl Mengwi-Mengwitani). **Damri office** (☎0361-232793; Jl Diponegoro) sells tickets for long-distance buses.

TRAIN

Bali doesn't have trains but the state railway company does sell tickets via travel agents in Denpasar. Buses leave from the nearby Damri office and travel to eastern Java where they link with trains at Banyuwangi for Surabaya, Yogyakarta and Jakarta among others. Fares and times are comparable to the bus but the air-conditioned trains are more comfortable, even in economy class.

Getting Around

BEMO

Bemos take various circuitous routes from and between Denpasar's many bus/bemo terminals. They line up for various destinations at each terminal or you can try and hail them from anywhere along the main roads – look for the destination sign above the driver's window.

TAXI

As always, the cabs of **Blue Bird Taxi** (www.bluebirdgroup.com) are the most reliable choice.

SANUR

0361 / POP 38,453

Many consider Sanur 'just right', as it lacks most of the hassles found to the west while maintaining a good mix of restaurants and bars that aren't all owned by resorts.

The beach, while thin, is protected by a reef and breakwaters, so families appreciate the limpid waves. Sanur has a good range of places to stay and it's well placed for day trips. Really, it doesn't deserve its local moniker, 'Snore'.

Sanur stretches for about 5km along an east-facing coastline, with the lush and green landscaped grounds of resorts fronting right onto the sandy beach. West of the beachfront hotels is the busy main drag, Jl Danau Tamblingan, with hotel entrances and oodles of tourist shops, restaurants and cafes.

Noxious, traffic-choked Jl Ngurah Rai Bypass skirts the western side of the resort area, and is the main link to Kuta and the airport. Don't stay out here.

Sights

★ **Museum Le Mayeur** MUSEUM

(0361-286201; Jl Hang Tuah; adult/child 50,000/25,000Rp; 8am-3.30pm Sat-Thu, 8.30am-12.30pm Fri) Artist Adrien-Jean Le Mayeur de Merpres (1880–1958) arrived in Bali in 1932, and married the beautiful Legong dancer Ni Polok three years later, when she was just 15. They lived in this compound back when Sanur was still a quiet fishing village. After the artist's death, Ni Polok lived in the house until she died in 1985. Despite security (some of Le Mayeur's paintings have sold for US$150,000) and conservation problems, almost 90 of Le Mayeur's paintings are displayed.

The house is an interesting example of Balinese-style architecture – notice the beautifully carved window shutters that recount the story of Rama and Sita from the Ramayana. The museum has a naturalistic Balinese interior of woven fibres. Some of Le Mayeur's early works are impressionist paintings from his travels in Africa, India, the Mediterranean and the South Pacific. Paintings from his early period in Bali are romantic depictions of daily life and beautiful Balinese women – often Ni Polok. The works from the 1950s are in much better condition, displaying the vibrant colours that later became popular with young Balinese artists. Look for the haunting black-and-white photos of Ni Polok.

Taman Festival Bali AMUSEMENT PARK

(Jalan Padang Galak 3) One of the more unusual Bali attractions, Taman Festival Bali is an abandoned theme park about a 20-minute drive north of Sanur. Some say that the 8-hectare park closed its doors in 2000 after

PULAU SERANGAN

Otherwise known as Turtle Island, Pulau Serangan is an example of all that can go wrong with Bali's environment. Originally it was a small (100-hectare) island offshore of the mangroves to the south of Sanur. However, in the 1990s it was selected by Suharto's son Tommy as a site for new development. More than half of the original island was obliterated while a new landfill area over 300 hectares in size was grafted on. The Asian economic crisis pulled the plug on the scheme. Nothing has happened since.

Meanwhile, on the original part of the island, the two small and poor fishing villages, **Ponjok** and **Dukuh**, remain, as does one of Bali's holiest temples, **Pura Sakenan**, just east of the causeway. Architecturally it is insignificant, but major festivals attract huge crowds of devotees, especially during the Kuningan festival.

Some fast boats to the Gili Islands and Lombok leave from here.

DON'T MISS

SANUR'S BEACHFRONT WALK

Sanur's beachfront walk has been delighting locals and visitors alike from day one. Over 4km long, it curves past resorts, beachfront cafes, wooden fishing boats under repair and quite a few elegant old villas built decades ago by the wealthy expats who fell under Bali's spell. While you stroll, look out across the water to Nusa Penida.

Even if you're not staying in Sanur, the beach walk makes a good day trip or stop on the way to someplace else.

Grand Bali Beach Hotel (Jl Hang Tuah) Built in the Sukarno era, this vast hotel is now slowly fading away. Local leaders, properly horrified at its outsized bulk, imposed the famous rule that no building could be higher than a coconut palm.

Turtle Tanks (Beachfront Walk) An engaging display about Bali's endangered sea turtles that usually includes some young hatchlings.

Small Temple (Beachfront Walk) Amid the tourist bustle, this little shrine is shaded by huge trees.

Batu Jimbar (☎0361 737498; www.villabatujimbar.com; Beachfront Walk; villas from US$1400) Just north of the old Hyatt, this villa compound has a colourful history: it was redesigned by the famous Sri Lankan architect Geoffrey Bawa in 1975, Mick Jagger and Jerry Hall were unofficially married here in 1990, and it has accommodated celebrities from Yoko Ono to Sting to Fergie. If your income approaches theirs, you too can stay here.

Fishing Boats (Beachfront Walk) Just south of the old Hyatt is a long area where multi-hued fishing boats are pulled ashore and repaired under the trees.

its $5 million laser equipment was struck by lightning, but it is more likely that the park closed due to the Asian economic crisis.

Today, the park is home to a variety of overgrown structures, including a man-made volcano and a crocodile pit.

Sanur Beach BEACH

Sanur Beach curves in a southwesterly direction and stretches for more than 5km. It is mostly clean and overall quite serene – much like the town itself. Offshore reefs mean that the surf is reduced to tiny waves lapping the shore. With a couple of unfortunate exceptions, the resorts along the sand are low-key, leaving the beach uncrowded.

Bali Orchid Garden GARDENS

(☎0361-466010; www.baliorchidgardens.com; Coast Rd; 100,000Rp; ⏲8am-6pm) Orchids thrive in Bali's warm weather and rich volcanic soil. At this garden you can see thousands of orchids in a variety of settings. It's 3km north of Sanur along Jl Ngurah Rai just past the major intersection with the coast road and is an easy stop on the way to Ubud.

Stone Pillar MONUMENT

(off Jl Danau Poso) The pillar, down a narrow lane to the left as you face Pura Belangjong, is Bali's oldest dated artefact and has ancient inscriptions recounting military victories from more than a thousand years ago. These inscriptions are in Sanskrit and are evidence of Hindu influence 300 years before the arrival of the Majapahit court.

Activities

Water Sports

Sanur's calm water and steady breeze make it a natural centre for wind- and kitesurfing.

Sanur's fickle breaks (tide conditions often don't produce waves) are offshore along the reef. The best area is called **Sanur Reef**, a right break in front of the Grand Bali Beach Hotel. Another good spot is known as the **Hyatt Reef**, in front of, you guessed it, the old Bali Hyatt.

You can get a boat out to the breaks from Surya Water Sports (p127).

★ **Rip Curl School of Surf** KITESURFING

(☎0361-287749; www.ripcurlschoolofsurf.com; Beachfront Walk, Sanur Beach Hotel; kitesurfing lessons from 1,100,000Rp, rental per hour from 550,000Rp; ⏲8am-5pm) Sanur's reef-protected waters and regular offshore breezes make for good kitesurfing. The season runs from June to October. Rip Curl also rents boards for windsurfing and stand-up paddle boarding (including SUP yoga for 450,000Rp per hour) as well as kayaks.

Sanur

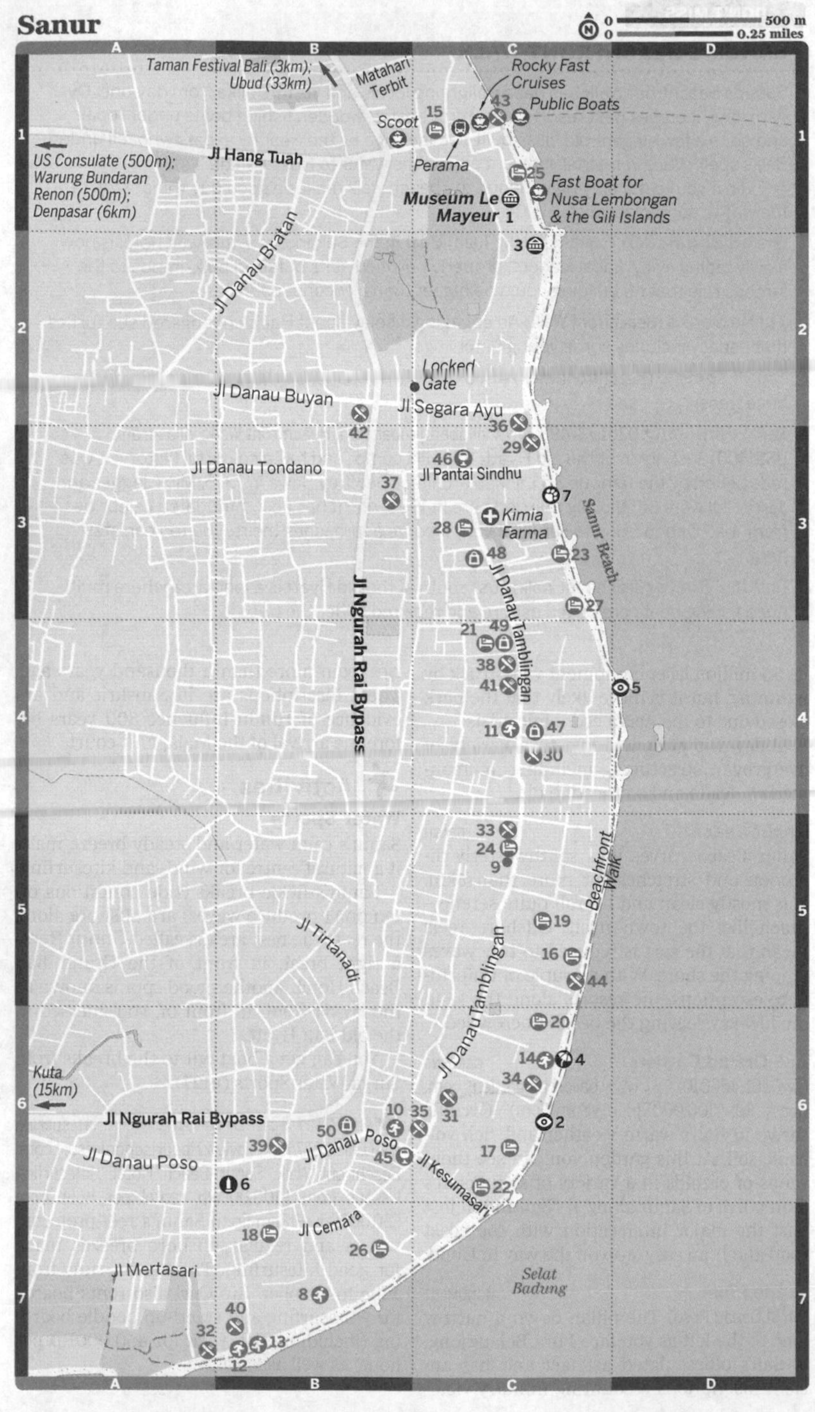

Taman Festival Bali (3km); Ubud (33km)
Matahari Terbit
Rocky Fast Cruises
Public Boats
Scoot
Perama
US Consulate (500m); Warung Bundaran Renon (500m); Denpasar (6km)
Jl Hang Tuah
Fast Boat for Nusa Lembongan & the Gili Islands
Museum Le Mayeur
Jl Danau Bratan
Locked Gate
Jl Danau Buyan
Jl Segara Ayu
Jl Danau Tondano
Jl Pantai Sindhu
Kimia Farma
Sanur Beach
Jl Danau Tamblingan
Jl Ngurah Rai Bypass
Beachfront Walk
Jl Tirtanadi
Kuta (15km)
Jl Danau Poso
Jl Kesumasari
Jl Cemara
Jl Mertasari
Selat Badung

Bali Stand Up Paddle WATER SPORTS
(0813 3823 5082; www.bali-standuppaddle.org; Jl Cemara 4B; rental per day 350,000Rp, lessons per 90min 350,000Rp) This specialist store offers great advice, gear sales and rental as well as lessons. It also offers windsurfing and kiteboarding.

Surya Water Sports WATER SPORTS
(0361-287956; www.balisuryadivecenter.com; Jl Duyung 10; 8am-8pm;) One of several water-sports operations along the beach, Surya is the largest. You can go parasailing (338,000Rp per person), windsurfing (473,000Rp per hour) or hire a canoe and paddle the smooth waters (203,000Rp per hour), among other things.

Spas & Yoga

★ Power of Now Oasis YOGA
(0878 6153 4535; www.powerofnowoasis.com; Beachfront Walk, Hotel Mercure; classes from 120,000Rp) Enjoy a yoga class in this atmospheric bamboo pavilion looking out to Sanur Beach. Several levels are offered. Sunrise yoga is a popular choice.

★ Jamu Wellness SPA
(0811 389 9930; www.jamuwellnessbali.com; Jl Danau Tamblingan 140; 1hr massage 195,000Rp; 9am-9pm) This gracious spa has classy digs and offers a range of treatments including a popular Earth and Flower Body Mask and a Kemiri Nut Scrub.

Glo Day Spa & Salon SPA
(0361-282826; https://glo-day-spa.business.site/; Jl Danau Poso 57, Gopa Town Centre; massage 1hr from 225,000Rp; 8am-6pm) An insider pick by the many local Sanur expats, Glo eschews a fancy setting for a clean-lined storefront. Services and treatments run the gamut, from skin and nail care to massages and spa therapies.

Courses

Balinese Cooking Class COOKING
(0361-288009; www.santrian.com; Puri Santrian, Beachfront Walk; 90min class from US$70; Wed & Fri) With a kitchen that's set on the beachfront, this is a memorable spot to learn to

Sanur

Top Sights
1 Museum Le Mayeur C1

Sights
2 Fishing Boats C6
3 Grand Bali Beach Hotel C2
4 Sanur Beach C6
5 Small Temple D4
6 Stone Pillar B6
7 Turtle Tanks C3

Activities, Courses & Tours
8 Bali Stand Up Paddle B7
Balinese Cooking Class .... (see 26)
9 Crystal Divers C5
10 Glo Day Spa & Salon B6
11 Jamu Wellness C4
12 Power of Now Oasis B7
13 Rip Curl School of Surf B7
14 Surya Water Sports C6

Sleeping
15 Agung & Sue Watering Hole I C1
16 Batu Jimbar C5
17 Fairmont Sanur Beach Bali C6
18 Gardenia B7
19 Hotel Peneeda View C5
20 Hyatt Regency Bali C6
21 Keke Homestay C4
22 Kesumasari C6
23 La Taverna Suites C3
24 Maison Aurelia Sanur C5
25 Pollok & Le Mayeur Inn C1
26 Puri Santrian B7
27 Tandjung Sari C3
28 Yulia 1 Homestay C3

Eating
29 Byrdhouse Beach Club C3
30 Café Smorgås C4
31 Char Ming C6
32 Genius Cafe A7
33 Hardy's Supermarket C5
34 La Playa Cafe C6
35 Massimo C6
Minami .... (see 29)
36 Nasi Bali Men Weti C2
37 Pasar Sindhu Night Market B3
38 Porch C4
Pregina Warung .... (see 49)
39 Sari Bundo B6
40 Sunday Market B7
41 Three Monkeys Cafe C4
42 Warung Babi Guling Sanur B2
43 Warung Mak Beng C1
44 Warung Pantai Indah C5

Drinking & Nightlife
45 Fire Station B6
46 Kalimantan C3

Shopping
47 A-Krea C4
48 Ganesha Bookshop C3
49 Nogo C4
50 To~ko B6

KITE-FLYING OVER SANUR

Travelling through south Bali you can't help but notice scores of kites overhead much of the year. These creations are often huge (10m or more wide, with tails stretching up to an astonishing 160m) and fly at altitudes that worry pilots. Many have noisemakers called *gaganguan* producing eerie humming and buzzing noises that are unique to each kite. Like many things in Bali, there are spiritual roots: the kites are meant to whisper figuratively into the ears of the gods suggestions that abundant harvests might be nice. But for many Balinese, these high-fliers are simply a really fun hobby (although it has its serious side as if one of these monsters crashes to earth it can kill and injure).

Each July, hundreds of Balinese and international teams descend – as it were – on open spaces north of Sanur for the **Bali Kite Festival**. They compete for an array of honours in categories such as original design and flight endurance. The action is centred around flat land behind the sand at **Pantai Padang Galak**, about 1km up the coast from Sanur. You can catch kite-flying Balinese-style here from May to September.

cook Balinese food. For a bit extra you can visit the market to source ingredients.

Crystal Divers DIVING
(☎0361-286737; www.crystal-divers.com; Jl Danau Tamblingan 168; dives from 890,000Rp) This slick diving operation has its own hotel (the Santai) and a large diving pool. The shop offers a long list of courses, including PADI open-water (7,450,000Rp) and options for beginners.

Sleeping

Beachfront

Amid the larger resorts you'll find some smaller beachfront hotels that are surprisingly affordable.

Pollok & Le Mayeur Inn HOMESTAY $
(☎0812 4637 5364; sulaiman.mei1980@gmail.com; Jl Hang Tuah, Museum Le Mayeur; r with fan/air-con from 250,000/350,000Rp; ❄📶) The grandchildren of the late artist Le Mayeur de Merpres and his wife Ni Polok run this small homestay. It's within the Museum Le Mayeur compound (p124) and offers a good budget option on the beachfront. The 17 rooms vary in size; ask to see a few.

Kesumasari GUESTHOUSE $$
(☎0361-287824; villa_kesumasari@yahoo.com; Jl Kesumasari 6; r from 500,000Rp; ❄📶🏊) The only thing between you and the beach is a small shrine. Beyond the lounging porches, the multihued carved Balinese doors don't prepare you for the riot of colour inside the 15 idiosyncratic rooms at this family-run homestay.

★**Tandjung Sari** HOTEL $$$
(☎0361-288441; www.tandjungsarihotel.com; Jl Danau Tamblingan 41; bungalows incl breakfast from 3,200,000Rp; ❄@📶🏊) One of Bali's first boutique hotels, Tandjung Sari has flourished since it opened in 1967 and continues to be lauded for its style. The 29 traditional-style bungalows are beautifully decorated with crafts and antiques. The gracious staff is a delight. Local children practise Balinese dance by the pool at 3pm Friday and Sunday.

La Taverna Suites HOTEL $$$
(☎0361-288497; http://latavernasuites.com; Jl Danau Tamblingan 29; r US$150-180; ❄@📶🏊) One of Sanur's first hotels, La Taverna has been reconstructed as an all-suites property while retaining its artful, simple charm. The pretty grounds and paths that link the buildings hum with a creative energy, infusing the 10 vintage bungalow-style units with an air of understated luxury.

Hotel Peneeda View HOTEL $$$
(☎0361-288425; www.peneedaviewhotel.com; Jl Danau Tamblingan 89; r from US$166; ❄@📶🏊) Another basic, small beachfront hotel, the Peneeda (which is *not* phonetically accurate for Penida) is a good choice for sun, sand and room service at a very affordable price. The 56 rooms are somewhat dated but you simply can't beat the (narrow) beach frontage and the price.

Fairmont Sanur Beach Bali RESORT $$$
(☎0361-3011888; www.fairmont.com; Jl Kesumasari 8; r from 3,530,000Rp; ❄@📶🏊) Looming over Sanur's beachfront, this massive hotel has 120 elegant suites and villas on a sprawling site that includes a 50m infinity pool. The design is strikingly modern and high-tech pleasures abound. There are also lavish spas and restaurants, and a state-of-the-art gym. Kids get their own pool and play area.

Hyatt Regency Bali RESORT $$$
(www.hyatt.com; Jl Danau Tamblingan) *The* landmark Sanur beachfront resort, the former Bali Hyatt now has a slightly grander name and has had a recent makeover.

Puri Santrian HUT, BUNGALOW $$$
(☎0361-288009; www.santrian.com; Jl Cemara 35; r US$130-300; ❄📶🏊) Lush gardens, three large pools with fountains, a tennis court and beach frontage, as well as 199 comfortable, well-equipped rooms, make this a popular choice. Many rooms are in older-style bungalows, others in two- and three-storey blocks. It offers a recommended Balinese cooking class (p127).

Off the Beach

Hotels near Jl Danau Tamblingan are a short walk from the beach, cafes and shopping. Lacking sand as a feature, many try a bit harder than their beachfront brethren (as well as being more affordable).

Keke Homestay GUESTHOUSE $
(☎0361-472 0614; www.keke-homestay.com; Jl Danau Tamblingan 100; r with fan/air-con from 350,000/400,000Rp; ❄📶) Set 150m down a *gang* (alley) from the noisy road, Keke welcomes backpackers into its genial family (who are often busy making offerings). The five quiet, clean rooms vary from fan-only to air-con cool.

Agung & Sue Watering Hole I GUESTHOUSE $
(☎0361-288289; www.wateringholesanurbali.com; Jl Hang Tuah 35; r 275,000-400,000Rp; ❄📶) Ideally located for an early fast boat to Nusa Lembongan or the Gilis, this long-running guesthouse has a veteran conviviality. Rooms are standard, but the beer is indeed cold and Sanur Beach is a five-minute walk away. Further south, Agung & Sue Watering Hole II is another lovely budget option, with a pool and rooms from 250,000Rp.

Yulia 1 Homestay GUESTHOUSE $
(☎0361-288089; yulia1homestay@gmail.com; Jl Danau Tamblingan 38; r incl breakfast with fan/air-con from 250,000/350,000Rp; ❄📶🏊) Run by a friendly family, this mellow guesthouse is set in a lovely bird-filled garden full of palms and flowers. Rooms vary in standards (some cold water, fan only), but all come with fridges. The plunge pool is a nice area for relaxing.

Gardenia GUESTHOUSE $$
(☎0361-286301; www.gardeniaguesthouse-bali.com; Jl Mertasari 2; r 650,000-755,000Rp; ❄📶🏊) Like its many-petalled namesake, the Gardenia has many facets. The seven rooms are visions in white and sit well back from the road. Nice verandahs face a plunge pool in a pretty courtyard. Up front there is a good cafe.

Maison Aurelia Sanur HOTEL $$$
(☎0361-472 1111; http://preferencehotels.com/maison-aurelia; Jl Danau Tamblingan 140; r US$100-160; ❄📶🏊) High-style on the far side from the beach, this four-storey hotel is a dramatic addition to Sanur's main drag. The 42 rooms are capacious, have balconies and boast a richly restful decor. Details are plush and comforts include fridges.

Eating

Along the beach path, you can catch a meal, a drink or just some sea breeze in one of the traditional open-air pavilions or in a laid-back bar. And although there are plenty of uninspired places on Jl Danau Tamblingan, there are also some gems.

Nasi Bali Men Weti BALINESE $
(Jl Segara Ayu; meals from 25,000Rp; ⏲7am-1pm) This simple stall prepares excellent *nasi campur*, the classic Balinese lunch plate of mixed dishes. Everything is very fresh and prepared while you wait in the inevitable queue. Enjoy your meal perched on a small plastic stool.

Sari Bundo INDONESIAN $
(☎0361-281389; Jl Danau Poso; mains from 20,000Rp; ⏲24hr) This spotless Padang-style shopfront is one of several at the south end of Sanur. Choose from an array of fresh and very spicy food. The curry chicken is a fiery treat that will have your tongue alternatively loving and hating you.

Warung Mak Beng BALINESE $
(☎0361-282633; Jl Hang Tuah 45; meals 35,000Rp; ⏲8am-9pm) You don't need a menu at this local favourite: all you can order is its legendary barbecued fish (*ikan laut goreng*), which comes with various sides and some tasty soup. Service is quick, the air fragrant and diners of all stripes are very happy.

Warung Babi Guling Sanur BALINESE $
(☎0361-287308; Jl Ngurah Rai Bypass; mains from 25,000Rp; ⏲10am-10pm) Unlike many of Bali's *babi guling* (spit-roast pig) places that buy their suckling pigs precooked from large suppliers, this small outlet does all its cooking right out back. The meat is succulent and shows the benefits of personal attention.

Porch CAFE $
(☎0361-281682; www.flashbacks-chb.com; Jl Danau Tamblingan 111, Flashbacks; mains from 50,000Rp; ⏰7am-10pm; ❄📶) Housed in a traditional wooden building, this cafe offers a tasty mix of comfort food like burgers and freshly baked goods such as ciabatta. Snuggle up to a table on the porch or shut it all out in the air-con inside. Popular for breakfast; there's a long list of fresh juices. High tea is popular too (150,000Rp for two).

Pasar Sindhu Night Market MARKET $
(off Jl Danau Tamblingan; ⏰5am-11pm) This market sells fresh vegetables, dried fish, pungent spices, various household goods and many tempting Balinese meals.

Sunday Market MARKET $
(☎0812 1888 3343; www.facebook.com/sundaymarketsanur; Jl Mertasari, Mercure Resort Sanur; ⏰10am-6pm last Sun of month) Organic produce, prepared foods, handicrafts and much more are sold by local vendors at this monthly market.

Hardy's Supermarket SUPERMARKET $
(☎0361-282705; Jl Danau Tamblingan 136; ⏰8am-10pm) For groceries and personal items, there's this large supermarket, which has all manner of local and imported food items, plus a range of souvenirs on its 2nd floor at very good prices.

★**Genius Cafe** CAFE $$
(☎0877 0047 7788; http://geniuscafebali.com; Mertasari Beach; mains from 65,000Rp; ⏰7am-10pm) This hub for entrepreneurship, which is part of a growing, membership-based network of beach clubs, also serves up delicious food and drinks from a stunning seafront perch. Yes to the ginger latte, yes to the fresh coconut water with lavender and dragon fruit, yes to the happiness bowl of raw salad, avocado, fresh herbs, nuts, seed and other goodness.

Although this is mainly a place to linger, snack and socialise, the space is regularly used for engaging talks on conservation and the environment.

★**Char Ming** ASIAN $$
(☎0361-288029; www.charming-bali.com; Jl Danau Tamblingan N97; mains from 95,000Rp; ⏰5-11pm) Asian fusion with a French accent. A daily menu board lists the fresh seafood available for grilling. Look for regional dishes, many with modern flair. The highly stylised location features lush plantings and carved-wood details from vintage Javanese and Balinese structures.

★**Three Monkeys Cafe** ASIAN $$
(☎0361-286002; www.threemonkeyscafebali.com; Jl Danau Tamblingan; mains 62,000-199,000Rp; ⏰11am-11pm; 📶) This branch of the Ubud original is no mere knock-off. It's spread over two floors, there's cool jazz playing in the background and live performances some nights. Set well back from the road, you can enjoy excellent coffee drinks on sofas or chairs. The creative menu mixes Western fare with pan-Asian creations.

Byrdhouse Beach Club INTERNATIONAL $$
(☎0361-288407; www.facebook.com/byrdhousebeachclubbali; Segara Village, Sanur Beach; mains from 60,000Rp; ⏰6am-midnight; 📶) With sun lounges, a swimming pool, a restaurant, bar and table tennis on-site, you could happily spend an entire day here by the beach. Check the club's Facebook page for upcoming events, including outdoor-cinema screenings and street-food stalls.

Pregina Warung BALINESE $$
(☎0361-283353; Jl Danau Tamblingan 106; mains 45,000-90,000Rp; ⏰11am-11pm) Classic Balinese duck dishes and crowd-pleasers such as *sate* (satay) are mainstays of the interesting menu here. It serves local foods several cuts above the all-too-common bland tourist versions (try anything with duck). The dining room has spare, stylish wooden decor and features vintage photos of Bali.

Minami JAPANESE $$
(☎0812 8613 4471; Beachfront Walk; mains from 60,000Rp; ⏰10am-11pm) With its minimalist white decor, bright open-air atmosphere and a vast range of uberfresh fish, this authentic Japanese place is a great find on Sanur Beach.

Warung Pantai Indah CAFE $$
(Beachfront Walk; mains 30,000-110,000Rp; ⏰9am-9pm) Sit at battered tables and chairs with your toes in the sand at this timeless beach cafe. It specialises in fresh barbecue-grilled seafood and cheap local dishes.

Café Smorgås CAFE $$
(☎0361-289361; www.cafesmorgas.com; Jl Danau Tamblingan; meals 58,000-135,000Rp; ⏰7am-10pm; ❄📶🖉) A nice place with wicker chairs on a large terrace and cool air-con inside. The menu has a healthy range of fresh detox juices and salads, plus comfort

food such as burgers and sandwiches. Good breakfasts and desserts as well.

Massimo ITALIAN $$
(☎0361-288942; www.massimobali.com; Jl Danau Tamblingan 206; meals 55,000-200,000Rp; ⏲11am-11pm) The interior is like an open-air Milan cafe; the outside is like a Balinese garden – it's a combo that goes together like spaghetti and meatballs. Pasta, pizza and more are prepared with authentic Italian flair. No time for a meal? Nab some excellent gelato from the counter up front.

La Playa Cafe SEAFOOD $$
(☎0821 4794 4514; Jl Duyung, Sanur Beach; meals 50,000-250,000Rp; ⏲8am-10pm) You can hear the surf and see the moonlight reflected on the water at this welcoming beachside seafood grill, set on the sand amid palm trees and fishing boats. The seafood platter is packed with garlic – yum!

Drinking & Nightlife

Fire Station PUB
(☎0361-285675; Jl Danau Poso 108; ⏲4pm-late) There's some old Hollywood style at this open-fronted pub. Vaguely 1960s Hollywood-esque portraits line walls; you almost expect to see a young Dennis Hopper lurking in the rear. Enjoy pitchers of sangria and other interesting drinks along with a varied menu of good pub food (mains from 99,000Rp) that features many specials. Order the fine Belgian beer, Duvel.

Kalimantan BAR
(Borneo Bob's; ☎0361-289291; Jl Pantai Sindhu 11; ⏲7.30am-11pm) This veteran boozer has an old *South Pacific* thatched charm and is one of several casual bars on this street. Enjoy cheap drinks under the palms in the large, shady garden. The Mexican-style food (mains from 47,000Rp) features homegrown chilli peppers.

Shopping

★ **Ganesha Bookshop** BOOKS
(☎0361-970320; www.ganeshabooksbali.com; Jl Danau Tamblingan 42; ⏲10am-6pm) A branch of Bali's best bookshop for serious readers.

To~ko CLOTHING
(☎0361-282477; Jl Danau Poso 51A; ⏲10am-10pm Mon-Sat) This fascinating store in a small complex of shared workspaces showcases local designers. Look for the ecologically designed clothing of Maya Nursari. Her goods are edgy and simple, black and white.

A-Krea CLOTHING
(☎0361-286101; Jl Danau Tamblingan 51; ⏲9am-9pm) An excellent spot for souvenirs, A-Krea has a range of items designed and made in Bali in its attractive store. Clothes, accessories, homewares and more are all handmade.

Nogo TEXTILES
(☎0361-288765; www.nogobali.com; Jl Danau Tamblingan 104; ⏲9am-8pm) Look for the wooden loom out front of this classy store, which bills itself as the 'Bali Ikat Centre'. The goods are gorgeous and easy to enjoy in the air-con comfort.

ℹ Information

MEDICAL SERVICES

Kimia Farma (☎0361-271611; Jl Danau Tamblingan 20; ⏲8am-10pm) Reliable local pharmacy chain.

MONEY

Money changers here have a dubious reputation. There are numerous ATMs along Jl Danau Tamblingan and several banks.

ℹ Getting There & Away

BOAT

Fast boats (prices vary by destination) The myriad fast boats to Nusa Lembongan, Nusa Penida, Lombok and the Gilis depart from a strip of beach south of Jl Hang Tuah. None of these services use a dock – be prepared to wade to the boat. Most companies have shady waiting areas facing the beach.

Public boats (one way 150,000Rp) Regular boats to Nusa Lembongan and Nusa Penida depart from the beach at the end of Jl Hang Tuah three times daily (50,000Rp one way, 40 minutes).

Rocky Fast Cruises (☎0821 4404 0928, 0361-283624; www.rockyfastcruise.com; Jl Hang Tuah 41; return 500,000Rp; ⏲8am-10pm) Has an office for its services to Nusa Lembongan (500,000Rp return, 9am, 11am, 1pm and 4.30pm).

Scoot (☎0361-285522; www.scootcruise.com; Jl Hang Tuah; return adult/child from 400,000/280,000Rp; ⏲8am-10pm) Has an office for its network of services to Nusa Lembongan, Lombok and the Gilis (adult/child from 400,000/280,000Rp return). Boats to Lembongan depart four times daily (9.30am, 11.45am, 1.30pm, 5.15pm).

TAXI

A cartel of taxis at the airport has a set price of 250,000Rp to Sanur.

ROYALTY & EXPATS

Sanur was one of the places favoured by Westerners during their pre-WWII discovery of Bali. Artists Miguel Covarrubias, Adrien-Jean Le Mayeur de Merpres and Walter Spies, anthropologist Jane Belo and choreographer Katharane Mershon all spent time here. The first tourist bungalows appeared in Sanur in the 1940s and '50s, and more artists, including Australian Donald Friend (whose antics earned him the nickname Lord Devil Donald), made their homes in Sanur.

During this period Sanur was ruled by insightful priests and scholars, who recognised both the opportunities and the threats presented by expanding tourism. They established village cooperatives that owned land and ran tourist businesses, ensuring that a good share of the economic benefits remained in the community.

The priestly influence remains strong, and Sanur is one of the few communities still ruled by members of the Brahmana caste. It is known as a home of sorcerers and healers, and a centre for both black and white magic. The black-and-white chequered cloth known as *kain poleng*, which symbolises the balance of good and evil, is emblematic of Sanur.

TOURIST SHUTTLE BUS

The Kura-Kura tourist bus (p453) has a route linking Sanur with Kuta and Ubud. Buses run every hour and cost 80,000Rp.

The **Perama office** (☎0361-751875; www.peramatour.com; Jl Hang Tuah 39; ⏰7am-10pm) is at Warung Pojok at the northern end of town. Its destinations include Ubud (50,000Rp, one hour), Padangbai (75,000Rp, two hours) and Lovina (125,000Rp, three hours).

BUKIT PENINSULA

Hot and arid, the southern peninsula is known as Bukit (meaning 'hill' in Bahasa Indonesia). It's popular with visitors, from the cloistered climes of Nusa Dua to the sybaritic retreats along the south coast.

The booming west coast (often generically called Pecatu) with its string-of-pearls beaches is a real hotspot. Accommodation sits precariously on the sand at Balangan Beach, while the cliffs are dotted with idiosyncratic lodges at Bingin and elsewhere. New places sprout daily and most have views of the turbulent waters here, which have world-famous surf breaks all the way south to the important temple of Ulu Watu.

The south coast to the east and west of Ungasan is the site of some huge cliff-side resorts, with serene views of the limitless ocean, while Nusa Dua and Tanjung Benoa cater to more traditional package-holiday-makers seeking a homogenised experience.

Getting There & Away

You'll need your own wheels – whether taxi, hire car or motorbike – to explore the Bukit. Expect to pay upwards of 5000Rp per vehicle to use the beach-access roads.

Jimbaran

☎0361 / POP 44,376

Teluk Jimbaran (Jimbaran Bay) is an appealing crescent of white-sand beach and blue sea fronted by a long string of seafood warungs and ending at the southern end in a bushy headland, home to the Four Seasons Jimbaran Bay.

Despite increased popularity, Jimbaran remains a relaxed alternative to Kuta and Seminyak to the north (and as it's just south of the airport, you can't beat the access!). Its markets offer a fascinating glimpse into local life.

Beaches

★Jimbaran Beach BEACH

One of Bali's best beaches, Jimbaran's 4km-long arc of sand is mostly clean and there is no shortage of places to get a snack, drink or seafood dinner, or to rent a sun lounge. The bay is protected by an unbroken coral reef, which keeps the surf more mellow than at popular Kuta further north, although you can still get breaks that are fun for bodysurfing.

Tegalwangi Beach BEACH

Folding around limestone bluffs some 4.5km southwest of Jimbaran, Tegalwangi is the first of cove after cove with patches of beautiful sand all the way down the west coast of the peninsula. A small parking area lies in front of Pura Segara Tegalwangi temple, a popular place for addressing the ocean gods.

There's usually a lone drinks vendor offering refreshment before (or after) you make the short but challenging trip over the rough paths down to the beach. Immediately south, the vast Ayana Resort sprawls over the cliffs. From Jimbaran, take Jl Bukit Permai for 3km until the gates of the Ayana, where it veers west 1.5km to the temple.

Sights

★ Jimbaran Fish Market MARKET

(Jimbaran Beach; ⏲6am-5pm) A popular morning stop on a Bukit peninsula amble, this fish market is smelly, lively and frenetic – watch where you step. Brightly painted boats bob along the shore while huge cases of everything from small sardines to fearsome langoustines are hawked. The action is fast and furious. Buy your seafood here and have one of the warungs cook it up or, for an even better price, buy direct from the boats between 6am and 7am.

There's also a street vendor selling delicious sugar-cane juice for 10,000Rp.

Morning Market MARKET

(Jl Ulu Watu; ⏲6am-noon) This is one of the best markets in Bali for a visit because it's compact, so you can see a lot without wandering forever. Local chefs swear by the quality of the fruit and vegetables – ever seen a cabbage that big?

Pura Ulun Siwi HINDU TEMPLE

(Jl Ulu Watu) Across from the morning market, this ebony-hued temple from the 18th century is a snoozy place until it explodes with life, offerings, incense and more on a holy day.

Sleeping

Sari Segara Resort SPA HOTEL $

(☎0361-703647; www.sarisegara.com; Jl Pantai Kedonganan; r from 190,000Rp;) A rare budget find amid the pricey resorts of Jimbaran, this former spa is older and slightly rundown, but in an aesthetically interesting way. The best features are the enormous pool surrounded by statues and abundant wild flowers (with a swim-up bar) and the kind owner, who is knowledgeable about the area and offers great advice regarding the fish market.

Keraton Jimbaran Resort HOTEL $$

(☎0361-701961; www.keratonjimbaranresort.com; Jl Mrajapati; r from 1,400,000Rp;) Sharing the same idyllic Jimbaran beach as the pricier neighbouring resorts, the low-key Keraton is great value for a beachfront resort. Its 102 rooms are scattered about one- and two-storey bungalow-style units. The grounds are spacious and typically Bali-lush.

Hotel Puri Bambu HOTEL $$

(☎0361-701468; www.hotelpuribambu.com; Jl Pengeracikan; r from 950,000Rp;) A mere 200m from the beach, the flash-free

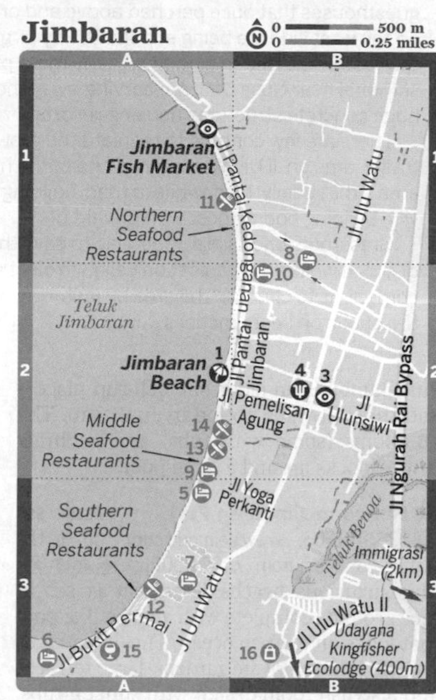

Jimbaran

Top Sights

1 Jimbaran Beach A2
2 Jimbaran Fish Market A1

Sights

3 Morning Market B2
4 Pura Ulun Siwi B2

Sleeping

5 Belmond Jimbaran Puri A3
6 Four Seasons Jimbaran Bay A3
7 Hotel Intercontinental Bali A3
8 Hotel Puri Bambu B1
9 Keraton Jimbaran Resort A2
10 Sari Segara Resort B2

Eating

11 Jimbaran Bay Seafood A1
12 Made Bagus Cafe A3
13 Warung Bamboo A2
14 Warung Ramayana A2

Drinking & Nightlife

15 Jimbaran Beach Club A3

Shopping

16 Jenggala Keramik Bali Ceramics B3

PILLAGING THE BUKIT PENINSULA

Many environmentalists consider the always-arid Bukit Peninsula a harbinger for the challenges that face the rest of Bali, as land use far outpaces water supply. The small guesthouses that once perched above and on the string of pearls that are the beaches on the west side are being supplanted by large, water-sucking developments. Besides the vast Pecatu Indah complex, many more projects, such as the controversial Kempinski Hotel near Nusa Dua, are carving away the beautiful limestone cliffs to make way for huge concrete structures housing resorts.

There are few controls to regulate the growth; many of the vehicles stuck with you in traffic jams on Jl Ulu Watu will be one of the hundreds of water trucks that service the area's thirst daily. Meanwhile, a road-building frenzy on the southern coast has sparked a villa building boom, most with private pools.

Grassroots efforts are underway to save the vast Benoa Bay mangroves at the base of Bukit, while an organisation called Project Clean Ulu Watu (www.projectcleanuluwatu.com) aims to clean up the area by installing waste-management systems and educating the public on best practices.

Puri Bambu is an older but well-run place – and the best-value option in Jimbaran. The 48 rooms (some with tubs) are in three-storey blocks around a large pool.

★Belmond Jimbaran Puri RESORT **$$$**
(☎0361-701605; www.belmond.com; off Jl Ulu Watu; cottages from 7,200,000Rp; ❄@🛜🏊) This luxurious beachside retreat is set in nice grounds complete with a maze-like pool that looks on to open ocean. The 64 cottages and villas have private gardens, large terraces and a stylish room design with sunken tubs. It's a lavish yet low-key escape.

Four Seasons Jimbaran Bay RESORT **$$$**
(☎0361-701010; www.fourseasons.com; Jl Bukit Permai; villas from US$700; ❄@🛜🏊) Each of the 147 villas here are designed in traditional Balinese manner, complete with a carved entrance way that opens on to an open-air living pavilion overlooking a plunge pool. The site is a hillside overlooking Jimbaran Beach, which is a short walk away; most villas have sweeping views across the bay.

Hotel Intercontinental Bali RESORT **$$$**
(☎0361-701888; www.bali.intercontinental.com; Jl Ulu Watu; r from US$260; ❄@🛜🏊) With 419 rooms, the Intercontinental is really a little city on the beach. Decorated with Balinese arts and handicrafts, it tries to meld local style to a huge resort. The plethora of pools feed each other and meander through the grounds. There is a good kids' club and the resort is on a prime swathe of beach.

Eating

Jimbaran's three groups of seafood restaurants cook fresh, barbecued seafood every evening (most serve lunch as well), drawing tourists from across the south. The open-sided affairs are right by the beach and perfect for enjoying sea breezes and sunsets. Tables and chairs are set up on the sand almost to the water's edge. Arrive before sunset so you can get a good table and enjoy the show over a couple of beers before you dine.

Fixed prices for seafood platters in a plethora of varieties have become common and allow you to avoid the sport of choosing your fish and then paying for it by weight on scales that cause locals to break out in laughter. However, should you go this route, be sure to agree on costs first. Generally, you can enjoy a seafood feast, sides and a couple of beers for less than US$20 per person. Lobster (from US$30) will bump that figure up considerably, but you can keep the price low by purchasing your own lobster beforehand at the seafood market.

The best kitchens marinate the fish in garlic and lime, then douse it with chilli and oil while grilling it over coconut husks. Thick clouds of smoke from the coals are part of the atmosphere, as are roaming bands, who perform cheery cover tunes (think the *Macarena*). Almost all take credit cards.

Expect mixed seafood grills to cost between 90,000Rp and 350,000Rp.

Northern Seafood Restaurants

The northern seafood restaurants run south from the fish market along Jl Kedonganan and Jl Pantai Jimbaran. This is the area you will likely be taken to by a taxi if you don't specify otherwise. Most of these places are restaurant-like, with tables inside and out on the raked sand. However, the area lacks the fun atmosphere of the two areas to the south.

Jimbaran Bay Seafood SEAFOOD $$
(JBS; ☎0851-0172 5367; www.jimbaranbayseafoods.com; Jl Pantai Kedonganan; fresh seafood from 20,000Rp/100gr; ⊙11am-10pm) The menu assures patrons that seeing the prices means 'Don't be worry!' Part of the rather staid northern group, JBS is especially welcoming with a huge variety of tables: inside under cover, on the concrete terrace or out where your toes can tickle the sand.

Middle Seafood Restaurants

The middle seafood restaurants are in a compact and atmospheric group just south of Jl Pantai Jimbaran and Jl Pemelisan Agung. These are the simplest affairs, with old-fashioned thatched roofs and wide-open sides. The beach is a little less manicured, with the fishing boats resting up on the sand. Huge piles of coconut husks await their turn on the fires.

Warung Bamboo SEAFOOD $$
(☎0361-702188; off Jl Pantai Jimbaran; meals 80,000-200,000Rp; ⊙10am-11pm) Warung Bamboo is slightly more appealing than its neighbours, all of which have a certain raffish charm. The menu is simple: choose your seafood and the sides and sauces are included.

Warung Ramayana SEAFOOD $$
(☎0361-702859; off Jl Pantai Jimbaran; mains from 80,000Rp; ⊙8am-11pm) Fishing boats dot the beach in front of this long-running favourite. The seafood marinates from the early morning and grills smoke all evening. The menu has useful fixed prices so you can avoid bargaining.

Southern Seafood Restaurants

The southern seafood restaurants (also called the Muaya group) are a compact and festive collection of about a dozen places at the south end of the beach. There's a parking area off Jl Bukit Permai, and the beach here is well groomed, with nice trees.

Made Bagus Cafe SEAFOOD $$
(☎0361-701858; off Jl Bukit Permai; meals 80,000-200,000Rp; ⊙8am-10.30pm) Tucked away at the north end of the southern group; the staff serving their narrow patch of tables on the beach here radiate charm. Go for one of the mixed platters and ask for extra sauce, it's that good.

Drinking & Nightlife

Nightlife entirely revolves around the seafood restaurants. They tend to close by 10pm, so after that head north to the bright lights of Kuta and beyond.

Jimbaran Beach Club CAFE
(☎0361-709959; www.jimbaranbeachclub.com; Jl Bukit Permai Muaya; minimum spend 200,000Rp; ⊙8am-11pm; 📶) Just in case Jimbaran Bay wasn't inviting enough, this beach bar has a long pool bordering the sand. It's rather upmarket: you can rent a comfy lounger and umbrella and enjoy ordering from a long drinks and food menu.

Rock Bar BAR
(☎0361-702222; www.ayanaresort.com/rockbarbali; Jl Karang Mas Sejahtera, Ayana Resort; ⊙4pm-midnight, to 1am Fri & Sat; 📶) Star of a thousand glossy articles written about Bali, this bar perched 14m above the crashing Indian Ocean is very popular. In fact, at sunset the wait to ride the lift down to the bar can top one hour. There's a no-backpacks, no-singlets dress code. The food is Med-flavoured bar snacks.

Shopping

Jenggala Keramik Bali Ceramics CERAMICS
(☎0361-703311; www.jenggala.com; Jl Ulu Watu II; ⊙8am-8pm) This modern warehouse showcases beautiful ceramic homewares that are a popular Balinese purchase. There's a viewing area where you can watch production, as well as a cafe. Ceramic courses are available for adults and children; a paint-a-pot scheme lets you create your own work of art (ready five days later after a trip through the kiln).

Getting There & Away

Plenty of taxis wait around the beachfront warungs in the evening to take diners home (about 150,000Rp to Seminyak in no traffic). Some of the seafood warungs provide free transport if you call first. Ask for a flat fee on your transport if you travel during high traffic times, from 4pm to 8pm. Sundays are remarkably traffic-free.

The Kura-Kura tourist bus (p453) has a route linking Jimbaran with its Kuta hub. Buses run every two hours and cost 50,000Rp.

Central Bukit

☎0361

Compared to its idyllic fringes, the hilly heart of the Bukit Peninsula is scant on sights – but a 200m ascent up its namesake slope (*bukit* means 'hill' in Bahasa Indonesia) affords views across southern Bali. The area is home to the currently developing Garuda Wisnu Kencana Cultural Park.

Sights

Garuda Wisnu Kencana Cultural Park HINDU MONUMENT
(GWK; ☎0361-700808; www.gwkbali.com; Jl Raya Ulu Watu; 100,000Rp; ⏰9am-10pm; 👪) After years of false starts, development of the gigantic Garuda Wisnu Kencana Cultural Park is well under way. The centrepiece, completed in August 2018, is an impressive 120m-tall monument that includes a 66m-high statue of Garuda and is the largest monument dedicated to Vishnu in the world. The Brobdingnagian dream is meant to be on top of a shopping and gallery complex, but for now, there's not much of a draw beyond the statue to justify the entrance fee.

Eating

Bali Buda CAFE $
(☎0361-701980; www.balibuda.com; Jl Ulu Watu 104; treats from 20,000Rp; ⏰7am-9pm) A small outlet of the excellent island-wide bakery/cafe chain.

Nirmala Supermarket SUPERMARKET $
(☎0361-705454; Jl Ulu Watu; ⏰7am-10pm) Useful for supplies and groceries; also a good landmark for an important crossroads.

Information

ATMs can be found by Nirmala Supermarket.

Getting There & Away

You'll need your own wheels to get around here and keep going. Daytime traffic can be awful. About 2km south of Garuda Wisnu Kencana Cultural Park is a vital crossroads with a useful landmark, the Nirmala Supermarket – you can reach all points on the Bukit from here.

Balangan Beach

☎0361

A bit of the Wild West not far from Bali's glitz, Balangan Beach is a long, low strand at the base of rocky cliffs. It's covered with palm trees and fronted by a ribbon of near-white sand, picturesquely dotted with sun umbrellas. Surfer bars, cafes in shacks and even slightly more permanent guesthouses precariously line the shore where buffed bods soak up rays.

Beaches

At the northern end of the beach is a small temple, **Pura Dalem Balangan**. Bamboo beach shacks line the southern end; visitors laze away with one eye cast on the action at the fast-left surf break Balangan. Though unsurfable at low tide, it's good at midtide with anything over a 4ft swell; with an 8ft swell, this is one of the classic waves.

You can access the beach via rough tracks from two parking areas: the north end is near the uncrowded temple, the south end is above and back from the beach bars.

Balangan Beach BEACH
A long, low strand at the base of rocky cliffs. It's covered with palm trees and fronted by a ribbon of near-white sand, picturesquely dotted with sun umbrellas.

Sleeping

Balangan Beach has some established guesthouses up on the bluff, five minutes from the surf. Down on the sand, things are much more ad hoc, but undeniably charming. With the latter you can negotiate for small, windowless thatched rooms in bars next to cases of Bintang. Don't pay more than 250,000Rp.

Numerous guesthouses have appeared on the access road from Jl Ulu Watu, but many are far from the beach.

Santai Bali Homestay BUNGALOW $
(☎0338-695942; r from 250,000Rp; 📶) Right on the sands of Balangan Beach, the 19 bare-bones rooms at this shack bungalow are perfect for surfers and beach bums wanting easy access to the water. Its restaurant has tables and chairs plonked on the beach. Wednesday and Saturday there's a BBQ on the beach here.

Balangan Sea View Bungalow GUESTHOUSE $
(☎0851 0080 0499; www.balanganseaviewbungalow.com; off Jl Pantai Balangan; r with fan/air-con 350,000/475,000Rp, bungalow 975,000Rp; ❄📶🏊) This cluster of thatched bungalows (some with multiple rooms) is the pick here. The 25 rooms surround a 14m pool in an attractive compound; some have sea views.

La Joya HOTEL $$
(☎0811 399 0048; www.la-joya.com; Jl Pantai Balangan; r US$100-130; ❄📶🏊) The pick of the Balangan bunch, these two luxe compounds have hotel rooms, bungalows and villas. There are 21 different units, but all enjoy a position on the lush grounds. Sinuous curves dominate from the lines of the rooms to the infinity pool. The beach is a short walk.

Flower Bud Bungalows GUESTHOUSE $$
(0816 472 2310, 0828 367 2772; www.flowerbudbalangan.com; off Jl Pantai Balangan; r incl breakfast from 570,000Rp;) On top of a knoll, 14 bamboo bungalows are set on spacious, pretty grounds near a classic kidney-shaped pool. There's a certain Crusoe-esque motif and a small spa.

Eating

Nerni Warung INDONESIAN $
(0813 5381 4090; mains from 30,000Rp) Down on the sand at the south end of the beach, this simple place has great views from its cafe. Nerni keeps a close watch on things; simple sleeping rooms (from 200,000Rp) are cleaner than the competition. She may seem dour but she is smiling on the inside. We think.

Nasa Café CAFE $
(meals from 30,000Rp; 8am-11pm) Inside the shady bamboo bar built on stilts above the sand, the wraparound view through the drooping thatched roof is of a vibrant azure ribbon of crashing surf. The simple Indo meals set the tone for the four very basic rooms (about 200,000Rp) off the bar. It's one of several similar choices.

Getting There & Away

Balangan Beach is 6.2km off Jl Ulu Watu on Jl Pantai Balangan. Turn west at the crossroads at Nirmala Supermarket.

Taxis from the Kuta area cost approximately 150,000Rp per hour for the round-trip and waiting time.

Bingin

0361

An ever-evolving scene, Bingin comprises scores of unconventionally stylish lodgings scattered across cliffs and on the strip of white-sand that is Bingin Beach below. Smooth Jl Pantai Bingin runs 1km off Jl Melasti (look for the thicket of accommodation signs) and then branches off into a tangle of lanes.

The scenery here is simply superb, with sylvan cliffs dropping down to surfer cafes and the foaming edge of the azure sea. The beach is a five-minute walk down fairly steep paths. The surf here is often savage but the boulder-strewn sands are serene and the roaring breakers mesmerising.

Beaches

Bingin Beach BEACH
One of Bukit's classic surf breaks, Bingin is also famous as a beach hang-out with spectacular views. You reach the beach down a long set of stairs from the bluff.

Given the walk down to Bingin Beach from the isolated parking area, you could be forgiven if you decide to leave your board up top, but don't. Waves here are best at mid-tide with a 6ft swell when short but perfect left-hand barrels form, and you'll do well to have somebody onshore recording your action.

Sleeping

This is one of the Bukit's coolest places to stay. Numerous individual places are scattered along and near the cliffs, well off the main road. You can also get basic accommodation down the cliff at a string of bamboo-and-thatch surfer crash pads near the water.

Olas Homestay HOMESTAY $
(0857 3859 5257; http://olashomestaybali.com; Jl Labuan Sait; r from 300,000Rp;) This family-run surfer crash pad is excellent value in Bingin, with lush landscaping and five private rooms offering air-con and hot water. The owners are super nice and can arrange airport pick ups, surf lessons, tours and rental vehicles.

Adi's Homestay BUNGALOW $
(0816 297 106, 0815 5838 8524; Jl Pantai Bingin; r with fan/air-con from 300,000/450,000Rp;) The nine bungalow-style rooms facing a nice garden are comfy. It's down a very small lane, near the beach parking. It has a small cafe.

Chocky's Place GUESTHOUSE $
(0818 0530 7105; www.chockysplace.com; Bingin Beach; r from 300,000Rp;) Down the bottom of the stairs and right on Bingin Beach, this classic surfer hang-out has cosy rooms varying from charming with awesome views to rudimentary with shared bathrooms. Its bamboo restaurant looks out to the beach; it's a great place to meet fellow travellers over a few cold ones.

Bingin Garden GUESTHOUSE $
(0816 472 2002; tommybarrell76@yahoo.com; off Jl Pantai Bingin; r with fan/air-con 320,000/460,000Rp;) There's a relaxed hacienda feel to Bingin Garden, where eight bungalow-style rooms are set among an arid garden and a large pool. It's back off the

Balangan Beach & Ulu Watu

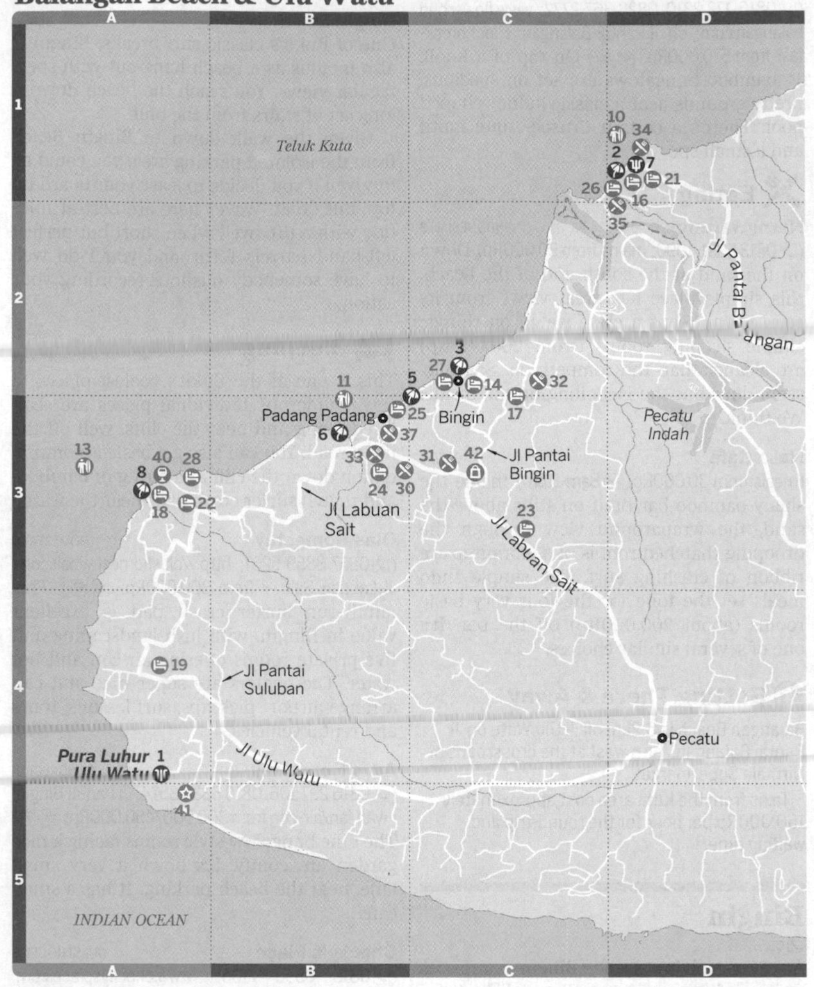

cliffs and about 300m from the path down to the beach. It's run by gun local surfer Tommy Barrell and his lovely wife.

★**Temple Lodge** BOUTIQUE HOTEL $$
(0857 3901 1572; www.thetemplelodge.com; off Jl Pantai Bingin; r incl breakfast US$90-230;) 'Artsy and beautiful' just begins to describe this collection of huts and cottages made from thatch, driftwood and other natural materials. Each sits on a jutting shelf on the cliffs above the surf breaks, and there are superb views from the infinity pool and some of the nine units. You can arrange for meals and there are morning yoga classes.

Mick's Place BOUTIQUE HOTEL $$
(0812 391 3337; www.micksplacebali.com; off Jl Pantai Bingin; r from US$100, villa from US$300;) A hippie-chic playground where you rough it in style, Mick's never has more than 16 guests. Seven artful bungalows and one luxe villa are set in lush grounds. The turquoise water in the postage-stamp-sized infinity pool matches the turquoise sea below. By day there's a 180-degree view of the world-famous surf breaks.

Kembang Kuning Bungalows GUESTHOUSE $$
(0361-743 4424; www.binginbungalows.com; off Jl Pantai Bingin; r from US$75;) The

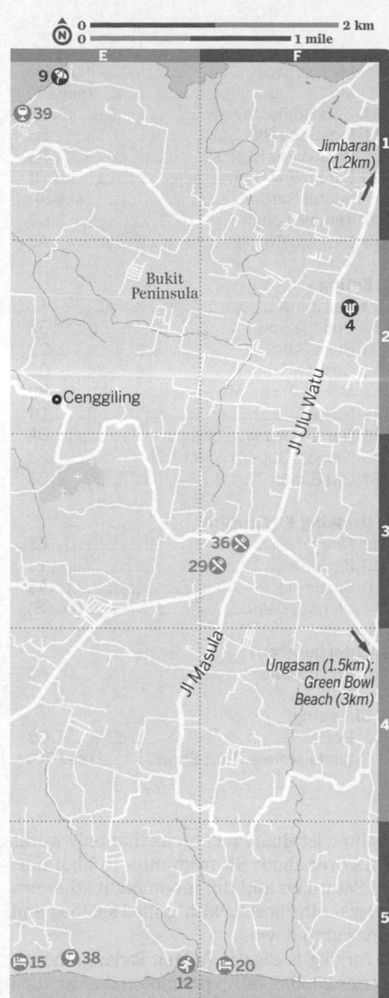

best-value cliff-side option has 12 rooms in modern, two-storey bungalow-style blocks. The grounds are thickly landscaped but the real appeal is the infinity swimming pool on the edge of the limestone and the various nearby loungers, all with sensational views.

Mu GUESTHOUSE $$

(☎0361-895 7442; www.mu-bali.com; off Jl Pantai Bingin; bungalows from US$90; ❄📶🏊) The 16 very individual bungalows with thatched roofs are scattered about a compound dominated by a cliff-side infinity pool. All have open-air living spaces and air-con bedrooms, some have hot tubs with a view. Some units have multiple bedrooms. There's an excellent cafe as well as a yoga studio.

Secret Garden GUESTHOUSE $$

(☎0816 474 7255; r from 750,000Rp; 📶) Tasteful and ultra laid-back, this guesthouse has open-plan bamboo bungalows with futon beds and a design that incorporates its natural environment. It's run by a Japanese surfer-photographer who has good knowledge of the local waves. It's at the top of the hill near the path leading down to the beach.

Eating

★Cashew Tree CAFE $

(☎0813 5321 8157; www.facebook.com/thecashewtreebingin; Jl Pantai Bingin; meals from 55,000Rp; ⏰8am-10pm; 📶🌿) *The* place to hang out in Bingin. Surfers and beachgoers gather in this large garden for tasty vegetarian meals. Expect the likes of burritos, salads, sandwiches and smoothies – it's also a good spot for a drink. Thursday nights especially go off, with live bands attracting folk from up and down the coast.

Shopping

Drifter FASHION & ACCESSORIES

(☎0817 557 111; http://driftersurf.com; Jl Labuan Sait; ⏰7.30am-9pm; 📶) Right at the turn to Bingin, this outlet of the awesome Seminyak surf shop is also a small cafe (mains from 55,000Rp) and gallery. All the Drifter surf goods are on offer, plus you can settle back at a table for some of the Bukit's best coffee, plus a range of snacks, healthy breakfasts and lunches and alluring cakes.

Getting There & Away

A metered taxi from Kuta will cost about 250,000Rp and take at least an hour, depending on traffic. An elderly resident collects 3000/5000Rp for a motorbike/car at a T-junction near where you park for the trail down to the beach.

Padang Padang

☎0361

Padang Padang Beach and Impossibles Beach are the stuff tropical surf dreams are made of. The backdrop of rocky cliff faces gives them an isolated feel you won't get in Kuta or Seminyak. A very cool scene has developed, with groovy cafes, oddball sleeps and iconoclastic surf shops.

The namesake beach here is near Jl Labuan Sait and is fairly easily reached.

Balangan Beach & Ulu Watu

Top Sights
1 Pura Luhur Ulu Watu A4

Sights
2 Balangan Beach D1
3 Bingin Beach C2
4 Garuda Wisnu Kencana Cultural Park F2
5 Impossibles Beach C3
6 Padang Padang Beach B3
7 Pura Dalem Balangan D1
Pura Mas Suka .... (see 20)
8 Suluban Beach A3
9 Tegalwangi Beach E1

Activities, Courses & Tours
10 Balangan D1
11 Padang Padang B3
12 Sundays Beach Club E5
13 Ulu Watu A3

Sleeping
14 Adi's Homestay C2
15 Alila Villas Uluwatu E5
16 Balangan Sea View Bungalow D1
17 Bingin Garden C3
Chocky's Place .... (see 14)
18 Delpi Uluwatu Beach Rooms A3
Flower Bud Bungalows .... (see 16)
19 Gong Accommodation A4
20 Karma Kandara F5
Kembang Kuning Bungalows .... (see 27)
21 La Joya D1
22 Mamo Hotel A3
Mick's Place .... (see 14)
Mu .... (see 27)
23 Olas Homestay C3
24 PinkCoco Bali B3
25 Rock'n Reef B3
26 Santai Bali Homestay D1
Secret Garden .... (see 14)
27 Temple Lodge C2
28 Uluwatu Cottages A3

Eating
29 Bali Buda F3
30 Buddha Soul B3
31 Bukit Cafe C3
32 Cashew Tree C2
33 Mango Tree Cafe B3
34 Nasa Café D1
35 Nerni Warung D2
36 Nirmala Supermarket F3
37 Om Burger B3

Drinking & Nightlife
38 Omnia E5
39 Rock Bar E1
40 Single Fin A3
Warung Delpi .... (see 8)

Entertainment
41 Kecak Dance A5

Shopping
42 Drifter C3
White Monkey Surf Shop .... (see 30)

Immediately east, Impossibles Beach is more of a challenge. Rocks and tide may prevent you from coming over from Padang Padang.

Beaches

There are two beaches here that are popular with experienced surfers.

About 100m west of Jl Pantai Bingin on Jl Melasti, you'll see a turn towards the ocean. Follow this paved road for 700m and look for a scrawled sign on a wall reading **Impossibles Beach**. Follow the treacherous path and you'll soon understand the name. It's a tortuous trek but you'll be rewarded with an empty cove with splotches of creamy sand between boulders. For surfers, it's a challenging outside reef break that has three shifting peaks with fast left-hand tube sections that can join up if the conditions are perfect.

Padang Padang (Padang for short), slight in size but not in perfection, is a cove near the main Ulu Watu road where a stream flows into the sea. Experienced surfers flock here for the tubes. It's a super-shallow, left-hand reef break that only works if it's over about 6ft from mid- to high tide. On Saturdays and full-moon nights there's a party on the beach, with grilled seafood and tunes until dawn.

Parking is easy at Padang Padang, though it costs 2000/5000Rp per motorbike/car. It's a short walk through a temple and down a well-paved trail where you'll be hit up for bananas by monkeys and 5000/10,000Rp per motorbike/car for entering the beach. There are patches of shade near the sand plus a couple of simple warungs (food stalls). The beach-bar scene of *Eat Pray Love* was filmed here.

If you're feeling adventurous, you can enjoy a much longer stretch of nearly deserted white sand that begins on the west side of the river. Ask locals how to get there or take the precipitous stairs by Thomas Homestay off the main road.

Sleeping

To get close to the waves, consider one of the cliff-side guesthouses that are reached by a steep path down from the bluff. The trail starts at the end of a twisting lane that runs for 200m from Jl Labuan Sait just west of Om Burger.

★Rock'n Reef BOUTIQUE HOTEL $$

(☎0813 5336 3507; www.rock-n-reef.com; Impossibles Beach; r incl breakfast US$105-125; ❄📶) Seven individualistic bungalows are built into the rocks on Impossibles Beach. All share the stunning views of the ocean directly in front. Each has a rustic, artful design with natural materials such as stucco and driftwood. There are private balconies and sunny decks. An all-day cafe offers simple Indonesian meals. During peak surf season, staying here is a fantasy.

PinkCoco Bali HOTEL $$

(☎0361-895 7371; http://pnkhotels.com; Jl Labuan Sait; r US$75-135; ❄📶🏊) One of the pools at this romantic hotel is suitably tiled pink. The 25 rooms have terraces and balconies, plus artistic touches. There is a lush Mexican motif throughout, with an appealing mix of white walls accented with bold, tropical colours. Surfers are catered to and you can rent bikes.

Eating

★Bukit Cafe AUSTRALIAN $

(☎0822 3620 8392; www.bukitcafe.com; Jl Labuan Sait; mains 40,000-75,000Rp; ⏲7am-10pm; 🌿) For heaping plates of Australian-style brunch composed of fresh, local ingredients, Bukit Cafe is unbeatable. Standout dishes include vegan pancakes, smoothie bowls and smashed avocado, and the open-air, convivial setting has loads of appeal.

Mango Tree Cafe CAFE $$

(☎0878 6246-6763; Jl Labuan Sait 17; mains 60,000-120,000Rp; ⏲7am-11pm) This two-level cafe has a long menu of healthy options. Sandwiches and the tasty burgers have amazing buns. The salads, soups, breakfast burritos and more are fresh and interesting. There are good juices and a decent drinks list. Try for a table under the namesake tree. The owner, Maria, is a generous delight.

Buddha Soul CAFE $$

(☎0821-1214 0470; www.facebook.com/buddhasoul; Jl Labuan Sait 99X; mains 50,000-150,000Rp; ⏲7.30am-10pm; 📶🌿) This chilled-out roadside cafe has an outdoor deck where you can enjoy healthy, organic meals such as grilled calamari, chicken salad and lentil burgers.

Om Burger BURGERS $$

(☎0819 9905 5232; Jl Labuan Sait; mains from 55,000Rp, burgers from 75,000Rp; ⏲7am-10pm; 📶) 'Superfood burgers' – that's the come-on at this joint with nice 2nd-floor views. The burgers are indeed super and supersized. The shaka burger (with Wagyu beef) is the speciality, but the nasi goreng veggie burger is unique. There are intimations of health across the menu: baked sweet-potato fries, vitamin-filled juices and more.

It's very popular; expect to wait for a table at night.

Shopping

White Monkey Surf Shop SPORTS & OUTDOORS

(☎0853 3816 7729; www.instagram.com/white monkey_surfshop; Jl Labuan Sait 63; surfboard rental 250,000Rp; ⏲10am-9pm) Great little surf shop offering board sales and rental, plus gear.

Getting There & Away

A metered taxi from Kuta will cost about 200,000Rp and take at least an hour, depending on traffic.

Ulu Watu

☎0361

Ulu Watu has become the generic name for the southwestern tip of the Bukit peninsula. It includes the much-revered temple and the fabled namesake surf breaks.

About 2km north of the temple there is a dramatic cliff with steps leading to the water and Suluban Beach. All manner of cafes and surf shops spill down the nearly sheer face to the water below. Views are stellar and it's quite the scene.

Sights & Activities

Ulu Watu has plenty of establishments that sell and rent out surfboards (100,000Rp to 150,000Rp per hour), and provide ding repairs and supplies.

★Pura Luhur Ulu Watu HINDU TEMPLE

(off Jl Ulu Watu; adult/child 30,000/20,000Rp, parking 2000Rp; ⏲7am-7pm) This important temple is perched precipitously on the southwestern tip of the peninsula, atop sheer cliffs that drop straight into the ceaseless surf. You enter through an unusual arched gateway flanked by statues of Ganesha. Inside, the walls of coral bricks are covered with intricate carvings of Bali's mythological menagerie.

Only Hindu worshippers can enter the small inner temple that is built on to the jutting tip of land. However, the views of the endless swells of the Indian Ocean from the cliffs are almost spiritual. At sunset, walk around the clifftop to the left (south) of the temple to lose some of the crowd.

Ulu Watu is one of several important temples to the spirits of the sea along the south coast of Bali. In the 11th century the Javanese priest Empu Kuturan first established a temple here. The complex was added to by Nirartha, another Javanese priest who is known for the seafront temples at Tanah Lot, Rambut Siwi and Pura Sakenan. Nirartha retreated to Ulu Watu for his final days when he attained *moksa* (freedom from earthly desires).

A popular Kecak dance is held in the temple grounds at sunset.

Suluban Beach BEACH

(Ulu Watu) While others paddle out to the Ulu Watu surf breaks, you can linger on this strip of sand in an uberdramatic setting: limestone cliffs and caves surround the beach. Check the tides before making the steep climb down.

Sleeping

The cliffs above the main Ulu Watu breaks are dotted with various accommodation options; since most people are here for the view, quality inside the rooms is not always assured.

BALI'S BIGGEST WAVE

On its day **Ulu Watu** is Bali's biggest and most powerful wave. It's the stuff of dreams and nightmares, and definitely not one for beginners! Since the early 1970s when it featured in the legendary surf flick *Morning of the Earth*, Ulu Watu has drawn surfers from around the world for left breaks that seem to go on forever.

Teluk Ulu Watu (Ulu Watu Bay) is a great set-up for surfers – locals will wax your board and get drinks for you. You'll have to carry your board down stairs through a cave to access the wave. There are seven different breaks and conditions change continuously.

Delpi Uluwatu Beach Rooms GUESTHOUSE $

(balibrook@juno.com; Ulu Watu; r US$45) Six basic cliff-side rooms rattle to the beat of the surf day and night. Set in the rocks amid the various bars, this is the place if all you want is a 24-hour view of the breaks. It's closed between surf seasons. Prices are negotiable for longer stays.

★**Uluwatu Cottages** BUNGALOW $$

(☎0857 9268 1715; www.uluwatucottages.com; off Jl Labuan Sait; r from US$79;) Fourteen bungalows are spread across a large site right on the cliff, just 400m east of the Ulu Watu cafes (about 200m off Jl Labuan Sait). The units are comfortable, have individual terraces and enjoy views that are simply stunning. The pool is large and a great place to lose a day.

Gong Accommodation GUESTHOUSE $$

(☎0361-769976; Jl Pantai Suluban; r 450,000-550,000Rp;) The 20 tidy rooms here have good ventilation and hot water, and face a small compound with a lovely pool. Some 2nd-floor units have distant ocean views, TVs and air-con. It's about 1km south of the Ulu Watu cliff-side cafes; the host family is lovely. Recent renovations have raised rates.

Mamo Hotel HOTEL $$

(☎0361-769882; www.mamohoteluluwatu.com; Jl Labuan Sait; r incl breakfast 700,000-800,000Rp;) Right at the entrance to the area above the Ulu Watu breaks, this modern 30-room hotel is a good mainstream choice. The three-storey main building surrounds a pool and there's a breezy basic cafe across the street.

Drinking & Nightlife

★**Single Fin** BAR

(☎0361-769941; www.singlefinbali.com; Jl Mamo; ⏱8am-9pm Mon-Sat, to 1am Sun;) From this triple-level cafe, you can watch never-ending swells march across the Indian Ocean from this cliff-side perch, and the surfers carve it up when the waves are big. Drinks here aren't cheap (or very good), but the food (mains 65,000Rp to 165,000Rp) is tasty, the sunsets are killer and the Sunday night party is the best on the peninsula.

An attached poke-bowl joint, Coco & Poke, is under the same ownership. The bowls start at 75,000Rp and are available from 11am to 7pm Monday through Saturday, and to 9pm Sunday. There's a tofu bowl for vegetarians.

★Omnia CLUB

(☎0361-848 2150; https://omniaclubs.com/bali; Jl Belimbing Sari; cover charge varies by day & event, check website for details; ⏱11am-10.30pm) Perched at the base of the Bukit peninsula, Bali's hottest new day club is home to seekers of sunshine-fuelled revelry and house and hip-hop beats. The imposing architecture of the modern Cube bar is a stunning focal point, but a peek over its patio's glass barriers yields an eyeful of jagged cliffs, lush oceanside canopy and hypnotic azure waves.

There's an impressive infinity pool that blends into a seamless panorama of the Indian Ocean, fringed with plush sun lounges. Cocktails are inventive and the food spans a broad range of cuisines and preparations. This playground is for adults only (21+). Reservations recommended.

Warung Delpi CAFE

(☎0819 9998 2724; ⏱7am-9pm) A relaxed cafe-bar sitting on a cliff away from other cafe spots, with stunning views. One area is perched on a gigantic mushroom of concrete atop a rock out above the surf. The food is basic (mains 55,000Rp to 85,000Rp); the most popular dish is the beef *rendang*, slow-cooked with local spices.

☆ Entertainment

★Kecak Dance DANCE

(off Jl Ulu Watu; 100,000Rp; ⏱sunset) Although the performance obviously caters for tourists, the gorgeous setting at Pura Luhur Ulu Watu in a small amphitheatre in a leafy part of the grounds makes it one of the more evocative on the island. The views out to sea are as inspiring as the dance. It's very popular in high season; expect crowds.

ℹ Getting There & Away

The best way to see the Ulu Watu region is with your own wheels. Note that the cops often set up checkpoints near Pecatu Indah for checks on motorcycle-riding Westerners. Be aware you may pay a fine for offences such as a 'loose' chin strap.

Coming to the Ulu Watu cliff-side cafes from the east on Jl Labuan Sait, you will first encounter an access road to parking near the cliffs. Continuing over a bridge, there is a side road that leads to another parking area, from where it is a pretty 200m walk north to the cliff-side cafes.

A taxi ride out here will cost at least 200,000Rp from Kuta and takes more than an hour in traffic.

ℹ MONKEY MARAUDERS

Pura Luhur Ulu Watu is home to scores of grey monkeys. Greedy little buggers, when they're not energetically fornicating, they snatch sunglasses, handbags, hats and anything else within reach – be careful. And if you want to start a riot, peel them a banana...

Ungasan

☎0361 / POP 14,221

If Ulu Watu is all about celebrating surf culture, Ungasan is all about celebrating yourself. From crossroads near this otherwise nondescript village, roads radiate to the south coast where some of Bali's most exclusive oceanside resorts can be found. With the infinite turquoise waters of the Indian Ocean rolling hypnotically in the distance, it's hard not to think you've reached the end of the world, albeit a very comfortable one.

The scalloped cliff faces hide many a tiny cove beach with white sand. Some are now crowded with top-end resorts, others await discovery down perilous cliff-side stairs.

Sights & Activities

Green Bowl Beach BEACH

(Jl Pura Batu Pageh; parking 5000Rp) One of the Bukit's southern-facing cove beaches, Green Bowl is reached by a pretty and strenuous walk down 300 concrete steps that begin near the Pura Batu Pageh temple and the failed Bali Cliff Resort. This splotch of sand is uncrowded during the week but draws many at weekends (including a few persistent vendors). There are caves, bats and monkeys. The water is deep turquoise.

Pura Mas Suka HINDU TEMPLE

This diminutive temple (one of seven devoted to the sea gods) is reached by a twisting narrow road through a mostly barren red-rock landscape that changes dramatically when you reach the Karma Kandara resort (p144), which surrounds the temple. It's a perfect example of a Balinese seaside temple. It is often closed, so consider that before setting off on the rough track to the temple.

Sundays Beach Club BEACH CLUB

(☎0811 942 1110; www.sundaysbeachclub.com; Jl Pantai Selatan Gau; day pass adult/child 450,000/200,000Rp; ⏱9am-10pm) Located

PANDAWA BEACH

An old quarry on the remote southern coast of the Bukit Peninsula has been transformed into a Hindu-shrine-cum-beach-attraction. Pay a steep admission price (10,000Rp) to guards and then descend on a road through dramatically cut limestone cliffs. Large statues of Hindu deities are carved into niches in the stone. At the base, you'll find a long swathe of sand known as Pandawa Beach, which is all but deserted weekdays except for a few village seaweed farmers. But come weekends this makes for a major day trip for the Balinese.

Some warungs (food stalls) provide refreshments and sun-lounger rental, and the reef-protected waters are good for swimming. Look for Pandawa Beach signs on the main road between Ungasan and Nusa Dua – Jl Dharmawangsa. It's 2km down to the village where you can park by the sand.

on a pocket of powdery white sand at the base of a cliff, this private beach club offers a full day's worth of activities and pampering. Admission includes a 250,000Rp food and drink credit (150,000Rp for kids), which will go quickly. There are weekend afternoon DJs, sunset bonfires and, crucially, an elevator up and down the cliff.

Sleeping

★Alila Villas Uluwatu RESORT $$$

(☎0361-848 2166; www.alilahotels.com/uluwatu; Jl Belimbing Sari; r incl breakfast from US$800; ❄@🛜≋) Visually stunning, this vast resort has an artful contemporary style that is at once light and airy while still conveying a sense of luxury. The 85-unit Alila offers gracious service in a setting where the blue of the ocean contrasts with the green of the surrounding (hotel-tended) rice fields. It's 2km off Jl Ulu Watu.

Karma Kandara RESORT $$$

(☎0361-848 2200; www.karmaresorts.com; Jl Villa Kandara Banjar; villa from US$450; ❄@🛜≋) This beautiful resort clings to the side of hills that roll down to the sea. Stone paths lead between walled villas draped in bougainvillea and punctuated by painted doors, creating the mood of a tropical hill town. The restaurant, Di Mare (meals US$15 to US$30), is linked to the bifurcated property by a little bridge; there's a beach elevator.

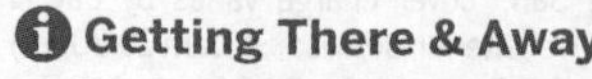

Getting There & Away

You'll be on your own for transport. Taxis from Seminyak can easily run 200,000Rp and take well over an hour.

Nusa Dua

☎0361

Nusa Dua translates literally as 'Two Islands' – although they are actually small raised headlands, each with a small temple. But Nusa Dua is much better known as Bali's gated compound of resort hotels. It's a vast and manicured place where you leave the chaos of the rest of the island behind as you pass the guards.

Built in the 1970s, Nusa Dua was designed to compete with international beach resorts the world over. Balinese 'culture', in the form of condensed cultural displays, is literally trucked in nightly in an effort to make it seem like less of a generic beach resort.

With more than 20 large resorts and thousands of hotel rooms, Nusa Dua can live up to some of its promise when full, but during slack times it's desolate.

Sights

★Pasifika Museum MUSEUM

(☎0361-774935; www.museum-pasifika.com; Bali Collection shopping centre, block P; 100,000Rp; ⏱10am-6pm) When groups from nearby resorts aren't around, you'll probably have this large museum to yourself. A collection of art from Pacific Ocean cultures spans several centuries and includes more than 600 paintings (don't miss the tikis). The influential wave of European artists who thrived in Bali in the early 20th century is well represented. Look for works by Arie Smit, Adrien-Jean Le Mayeur de Merpres and Theo Meier. There are also works by Matisse and Gauguin.

Pura Gegar HINDU TEMPLE

(road toll 2500Rp) Just south of Gegar Beach is a bluff with a good cafe and a path that leads up to Pura Gegar, a compact temple shaded by gnarled old trees. Views are great and you can spot swimmers who've come south in the shallow, placid waters around the bluff for a little frolic. There's a pleasant walkway up to the temple from the Nusa Dua beach promenade. It has a large shady parking area.

Nusa Dua

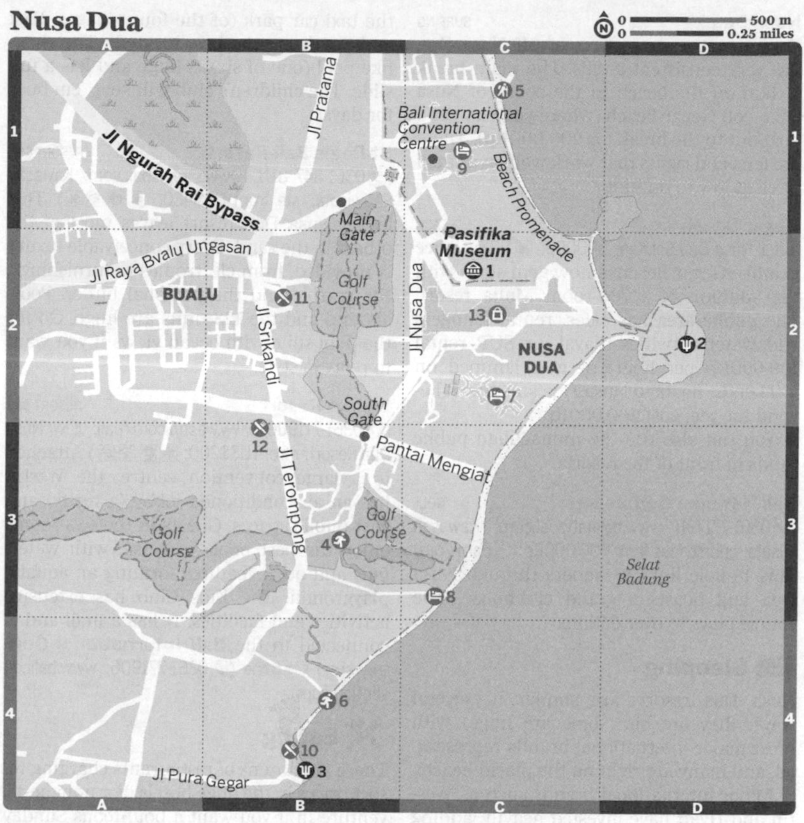

Pura Bias Tugal HINDU TEMPLE
(Jl Pantai Mengiat) Pretty seafront Balinese temple.

Activities

Nusa Dua's beaches are clean and raked; offshore reefs catch the swells, so the surf is almost nil.

All the resort hotels have pricey spas that provide a broad range of therapies, treatments and just plain, simple relaxation. The most lauded of the spas include those at the Westin (p146) and St Regis (p146) hotels. They are open to nonguests; expect fees for a massage to start at US$100.

★Beach Promenade WALKING
One of the nicest features of Nusa Dua is the 5km-long beach promenade that stretches the length of the resort from Pura Gegar in the south and north along much of the beach through Tanjung Benoa.

Nusa Dua

Top Sights
1 Pasifika Museum C2

Sights
2 Pura Bias Tugal D2
3 Pura Gegar B4

Activities, Courses & Tours
4 Bali National Golf Resort B3
5 Beach Promenade C1
6 Gegar Beach B4

Sleeping
7 Grand Hyatt Bali C2
8 St Regis Bali Resort C3
9 Westin Resort C1

Eating
10 Nusa Dua Beach Grill B4
11 Warung Dobiel B2
12 Warungs B3

Shopping
13 Bali Collection C2

Nusa Dua SURFING

During wet season, the reef off Nusa Dua has very consistent swells. The main break is 1km off the beach to the south of Nusa Dua – off Gegar Beach (where you can get a boat out to the break for 200,000Rp). There are lefts and rights that work well on a small swell at low to midtide.

Gegar Beach BEACH

(off Jl Nusa Dua Selatan; 3000Rp;) The once gemlike Gegar Beach is now gem-sized with the addition of a 700-room Mulia resort. The public area has cafes, rental loungers and water activities (kayak or SUP rental 100,000Rp per hour); it gets jammed on weekends. Boats to Nusa Dua surf break beyond the reef cost 200,000Rp.

You can also use the immaculate public sands in front of the resorts.

Bali National Golf Resort GOLF

(0361-771791; www.balinational.com; Kawasan Wisata; course fees from 900,000Rp; 6am-7pm) This 18-hole links meanders through Nusa Dua and boasts a grand clubhouse. The course plays to over 6500m.

Sleeping

Nusa Dua resorts are similar in several ways: they are big (some are huge) with most major international brands represented, and many are right on the placid beach.

Major international brands such as Westin and Hyatt have invested heavily, adding loads of amenities (such as elaborate pools and kids' day camps). Other hotels seem little changed from when they were built in the 1970s heyday of the Suharto era.

★ Sofitel Bali Nusa Dua Beach Resort RESORT $$$

(0361-849 2888; www.sofitelbalinusadua.com; Jl Nusa Dua; r from US$200;) Making up part of the resort strip, the Sofitel has a vast pool that meanders past the 415 rooms, some of which have terraces with direct pool access. The room blocks are huge; many rooms have at least a glimpse of the water. The Sofitel's lavish Sunday brunch (11am to 3pm) is one of Bali's best; it costs from 400,000Rp.

Grand Hyatt Bali RESORT $$$

(0361-771234; www.hyatt.com/en-US/hotel/indonesia/grand-hyatt-bali/balgh; r from US$200;) A little city, of sorts, the 636-room Hyatt has areas that are better than others. Some rooms in the West Village face the taxi car park (of the four villages, East and South are the best located). The river-like pool (one of six) is huge and has a fun slide. The children's club will keep 'em busy for days.

St Regis Bali Resort RESORT $$$

(0361-847 8111; www.stregisbali.com; Kawasan Pariwisata; ste from US$480;) This lavish Nusa Dua resort leaves most of the others in the sand. Every conceivable luxury is provided, from electronics to furnishings, the marble and the personal butler. Pools abound and the 123 units are huge. Go for the pool suite with ocean views if you want to relax in style.

Westin Resort RESORT $$$

(0361-771906; www.westin.com/bali; Jl Kw Nusa Dua Resort; r from US$200;) Attached to a large convention centre, the Westin has an air-conditioned lobby (a rarity) and vast public spaces. Guests in the 433 rooms enjoy the best pools in Nusa, with waterfalls and other features forming an aquatic playground. The Kids Club has extensive activities and facilities. It has a mall and is connected to the **Bali International Convention Centre** (0361-771906; www.baliconvention.com).

Eating

There are dozens of restaurants charging resort prices in the huge hotels. For nonguests, venture in if you want a bounteous Sunday brunch, such as the Sofitel's.

Good warungs cluster at the corner of Jl Srikandi and Jl Pantai Mengiat. Also along the latter street, just outside the central gate, open-air eateries offer an unpretentious dining alternative. None will win culinary awards, but most provide transport.

Warungs INDONESIAN $

(off Jl Terompong; meals from 20,000Rp; 8am-10pm) Your best bet for fresh and delicious local fare in the Nusa Dua area.

Warung Dobiel BALINESE $

(0361-771633; Jl Srikandi 9; meals from 40,000Rp; 9am-4pm) A bit of authentic food action amid the bland streets of Nusa, this is a good stop for *babi guling* (spit-roast pig). Pork soup is the perfect taste bud awakener, while the jackfruit is redolent with spices. Diners perch on stools and share tables; service can be slow and tours may mob the place. Watch out for 'foreigner' pricing.

Hardy's SUPERMARKET $
(0361-774639; www.hardysretail.com; Jl Ngurah Rai Bypass; 8am-10pm) This huge outlet of the local chain of supermarkets is about 1km west of the main gate. Besides groceries, it has most other goods you might need and at real (ie not inflated resort) prices.

Nusa Dua Beach Grill INTERNATIONAL $$
(0851 0043 4779; www.nusaduabeachgrill.com; Jl Pura Gegar; mains from 85,000Rp; 8am-10.30pm) A good spot for day trippers, this warm-hued cafe (hidden by the Mulia resort) is just south of Gegar Beach. The drinks menu is long, the seafood fresh and the relaxed beachy vibe intoxicating.

Shopping

Bali Collection MALL
(0361-771662; www.bali-collection.com; off Jl Nusa Dua; 10am-10pm) Often empty except for the dozens of assistants in the glacially air-conditioned Sogo Department Store, this security-conscious mall gamely soldiers on. Chains such as Starbucks and Bali brands such as Animale mix with humdrum outlets offering souvenirs.

Information

MONEY

ATMs can be found at the Bali Collection shopping centre, some hotel foyers and at the huge Hardy's department store out on the Jl Ngurah Rai Bypass.

Getting There & Away

The Bali Mandara Toll Rd (motorbike/car 4000/11,000Rp) greatly speeds journeys between Nusa Dua and the airport and Sanur.

BUS

The Kura-Kura tourist bus (p453) has two routes linking Nusa Dua with its Kuta hub. Buses run every two hours and cost 50,000Rp.

Bali's Trans-Sarbagita bus system (p453) serves Nusa Dua on a route that follows the Jl Ngurah Rai Bypass up and around past Sanur to Batabulan.

SHUTTLE

Find out what shuttle-bus services your hotel provides before you start hailing taxis. A free **shuttle bus** (0361-771662; www.bali-collection.com/shuttle-bus; 9am-10pm) connects all Nusa Dua and Tanjung Benoa resort hotels with the Bali Collection shopping centre about every hour. Better still, walk the delightful beach promenade.

TAXI

The taxi from the airport cartel is 150,000Rp; a metered taxi to the airport will be much less. Taxis to/from Seminyak average 150,000Rp for the 45-minute trip, although traffic can double this time.

Tanjung Benoa

0361

The peninsula of Tanjung Benoa extends about 4km north from Nusa Dua to Benoa village. It's flat and lined with family-friendly resort hotels, most of midrange calibre. By day the waters buzz with the roar of dozens of motorised water-sports craft. Group tours arrive by the busload for a day's aquatic excitement – straddling a banana boat among other thrills.

Overall, Tanjung Benoa is a fairly sedate place, although the Bali Mandara Toll Rd speeds access to the nightlife diversions of Kuta and Seminyak.

Sights

The village of Benoa is a fascinating little fishing settlement that makes for a good stroll. Amble the narrow lanes of the peninsula's tip for a multicultural feast. Within 100m of each other on Jl Segara Lor are a brightly coloured **Chinese Buddhist temple**, a domed **mosque** and a **Hindu temple** with a nicely carved triple entrance. Entry to all is free. Enjoy views of the busy channel to the port. On the dark side, Benoa's backstreets hide Bali's illegal trade in turtles, although police raids are helping to limit it.

Activities & Courses

★**Bumbu Bali Cooking School** COOKING
(0361-774502; www.balifoods.com; Jl Pratama; course with/without market visit US$95/85; 6am-3pm Mon, Wed & Fri) This much-lauded cooking school at the eponymous restaurant strives to get to the roots of Balinese cooking. Courses start with a 6am visit to Jimbaran's fish and morning markets, continue in the large kitchen and finish with lunch.

★**Jari Menari** SPA
(0361-778084; www.jarimenarinusadua.com; Jl Pratama; massage from 435,000Rp; 9am-10pm) This branch of the famed Seminyak original offers all the same exquisite massages by the expert all-male staff. Call for transport.

Benoa Marine Recreation WATER SPORTS
(BMR; ☎0361-772438; www.bmrbali.com; Jl Pratama; ⏰8am-4pm) This is the largest of the many water-sports vendors in Tanjung Benoa. It has a cafe area called Whacko Beach Club, which serves as a place to corral sales prospects.

Sleeping

Tanjung Benoa's east shore is lined with low-key midrange resorts aimed at groups. They are family-friendly, offer kids' programs and enjoy repeat business by holidaymakers who are greeted with banners such as 'Welcome Back Underhills!' There are also a couple of simple guesthouses.

Pondok Hasan Inn GUESTHOUSE $
(☎0361-772456; hasanhomestay@yahoo.com; Jl Pratama; r incl breakfast from 250,000Rp; ❄📶) Back 20m off the main road, this friendly family-run homestay has 11 immaculate hot-water rooms that include breakfast. The tiles on the outdoor verandah (shared by the rooms) gleam and there is a small garden.

Rumah Bali GUESTHOUSE $$
(☎0361-771256; www.bedandbreakfastbali.com; off Jl Pratama; r incl breakfast from US$90, villa from US$250; ❄@📶🏊) Rumah Bali is a luxurious interpretation of a Balinese village by cookbook author Heinz von Holzen, who also runs local restaurant Bumbu Bali. Guests choose from large family rooms or individual villas (some have three bedrooms) with their own plunge pool and kitchen. There's a large communal pool and a tennis court. The beach is a short walk away.

Conrad Bali RESORT $$$
(☎0361-778788; www.conradbali.com; Jl Pratama 168; r incl breakfast US$200; ❄@📶🏊) The top-end choice in Tanjung Benoa, the huge Conrad combines a modern Bali look with a refreshing, casual style. The 353 rooms are large and thoughtfully designed. Some units have patios with steps right down into the 33m pool. Bungalows have their own private lagoon and there is a large kids' club.

Eating & Drinking

★**Bumbu Bali 1** BALINESE $$
(☎0361-774502; www.balifoods.com; Jl Pratama; mains from 100,000Rp, set menus from 325,000Rp; ⏰noon-9pm) Long-time resident and cookbook author Heinz von Holzen, his wife Puji,

Tanjung Benoa 0 500 m / 0 0.25 miles

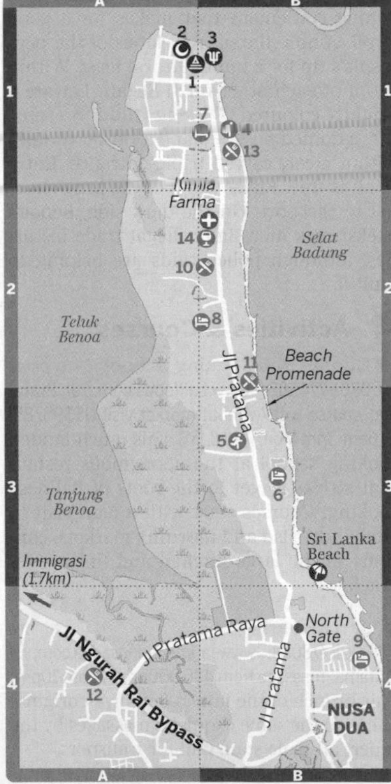

Tanjung Benoa

Sights
1 Caow Eng Bio A1
2 Mosque A1
3 Pura Dalem Ning Lan Taman Beji B1

Activities, Courses & Tours
4 Benoa Marine Recreation B1
Bumbu Bali Cooking School .... (see 11)
5 Jari Menari B3

Sleeping
6 Conrad Bali B3
7 Pondok Hasan Inn B1
8 Rumah Bali B2
9 Sofitel Bali Nusa Dua Beach Resort B4

Eating
10 Bali Cardamon B2
11 Bumbu Bali 1 .... B2
12 Hardy's A4
13 Tao B1

Drinking & Nightlife
14 Atlichnaya Bar B2

WATER SPORTS

Water-sports centres along Jl Pratama offer daytime diving, cruises, windsurfing and waterskiing. Each morning convoys of buses arrive with day trippers from all over south Bali, and by 10am parasailers float over the water.

All the centres feature unctuous salespeople whose job it is to sell you the banana-boat ride of your dreams while you sit glassy-eyed in a thatched-roof sales centre and cafe. Check equipment and credentials before you sign up, as a few tourists have died in accidents.

Among the established water-sports operators is Benoa Marine Recreation. As if by magic, all operators have similar prices. Note that 'official' price lists are just the starting point for bargaining. Activities here include the following (with average prices): .

Banana-boat rides Wild rides for two as you try to maintain your grasp on the inflatable fruit moving over the waves (US$25 per 15 minutes).

Glass-bottomed boat trips The dry way to see the denizens of the shallows (US$50 per hour).

Jet-skiing Go fast and belch smoke (US$30 per 15 minutes).

Parasailing Iconic; you float above the water while being towed by a speedboat (US$25 per 15-minute trip).

Snorkelling Trips include equipment and a boat ride to a reef (US$40 per hour).

One nice way to use the beach here is at Tao restaurant, where for the price of a drink you can enjoy resort-quality loungers and a pool.

and their well-trained and enthusiastic staff serve exquisitely flavoured dishes at this superb restaurant. Many diners opt for one of several lavish set menus. Cooking classes (p147) on Monday, Wednesday and Friday (from US$85) are highly recommended.

There's a second location (number two) 500m north on Jl Pratama.

Bali Cardamon ASIAN $$

(☎0361-773745; Jl Pratama 97; mains 55,000-120,000Rp; ⌚10am-10pm) A cut above most of the other restaurants on the Jl Pratama strip, this ambitious spot has a creative kitchen that takes influences from across Asia. It has some excellent dishes, including pork belly seasoned with star anise. Sit under the frangipani trees or in the dining room.

Tao ASIAN $$

(☎0361-772902; www.taobali.com; Jl Pratama 96; mains 85,000-210,000Rp; ⌚8am-10pm; 📶) On its own swathe of pure-white sand, Tao has a large curling pool that wends between the tables. The food is an eclectic mix of Asian (but a club sandwich awaits philistines).

Atlichnaya Bar BAR

(☎0813 3818 9675; www.atlichnaya.com; Jl Pratama 88; ⌚8am-late; 📶) A lively and convivial alternative to the stiff hotel bars, this rollicking place serves a long list of cheap mixed drinks and even offers massages (from 50,000Rp). There are cheap and cheery Indo and Western menu items as well.

Information

Kimia Farma (☎0361-916 6509; Jl Pratama 87; ⌚8am-10pm) Reliable chain of pharmacies.

Getting There & Away

Taxis from the airport cartel cost 200,000Rp. Occasional bemos (minibuses) shuttle up and down Jl Pratama (5000Rp) – although after about 3pm they become scarce.

A free **shuttle bus** (☎0361-771662; www.bali-collection.com/shuttle-bus; ⌚9am-10pm) connects Nusa Dua and Tanjung Benoa resort hotels with the Bali Collection shopping centre about every hour. Or stroll the Beach Promenade and enjoy the view in lieu of the bus. Many restaurants will provide transport from Nusa Dua and Tanjung Benoa hotels.

NUSA LEMBONGAN & ISLANDS

Look towards the open ocean southeast of Bali and the hazy bulk of Nusa Penida dominates the view. But for many visitors the real focus is Nusa Lembongan, which sits in the shadow of its vastly larger neighbour. Here, there's great surfing, amazing diving, languorous beaches and the kind of laid-back vibe travellers cherish.

Once ignored, Nusa Penida is now attracting visitors, but its dramatic vistas and unchanged village life are still yours to explore. Tiny Nusa Ceningan huddles between the larger islands. It's a quick and popular jaunt from Lembongan.

The islands have been a poor region for many years. Thin soils and a lack of fresh water do not permit the cultivation of rice, but other crops such as maize, cassava and beans are staples. The main cash crop has been seaweed, although the big harvest now comes on two legs.

Nusa Lembongan

☎0366 / POP 7529

Once the domain of shack-staying surfers, Nusa Lembongan has hit the big time. Yes, you can still get a simple room with a view of the surf breaks and the gorgeous sunsets, but now you can also stay in a boutique hotel and have a fabulous meal.

The new-found wealth is bringing changes, for instance, you'll see boys riding motorcycles 300m to school, temples being expensively renovated, multistorey hotels being built and time being marked by the arrival of tourist boats (which still lack any kind of dock). But even as Nusa Lembongan's popularity grows, it manages to keep a mellow vibe. You can still cock your ear to the crow of a rooster or the fall of a coconut, but you also need to be ready to get stuck in traffic.

Beaches

Jungutbatu Beach BEACH

The beach here, a mostly lovely arc of white sand with clear blue water, has views across to Gunung Agung in Bali. The pleasant seawall walkway is ideal for strolling, especially – as you'd guess – at sunset. Floating boats save the scene from being an idyllic cliché. The once redolent odour of drying farmed seaweed is fading away as all available land is turned over to tourism.

Pantai Tanjung Sanghyang BEACH

(Mushroom Bay) This beautiful bay, unofficially named Mushroom Bay after the mushroom corals offshore, has a crescent of bright white beach. By day, the tranquillity can be disturbed by banana-boat riders or parasailers. Otherwise, this is a dream beach.

The most interesting way to get here from Jungutbatu is to walk along the trail that starts from the southern end of the main beach and follows the coastline for a kilometre or so. Alternatively, take a boat or a motorbike from Jungutbatu.

Pantai Selegimpak BEACH

The long, straight beach is usually lapped by small waves at this remote-feeling spot where, unfortunately, some guesthouses have built seawalls below the low-tide line. This makes an easy traverse at high tide though. About 200m east along the shoreline path where it goes up and over a knoll is a minute cove with a nub of sand, good swimming and a tiny warung.

Dream Beach BEACH

Down a lane, on the southwestern side of the island, Dream Beach is a 150m-deep pocket of white sand with pounding surf and pretty azure waters. From the right angle it looks lovely – until you see the ugly hotel that's been built over one end. It also gets unpleasantly crowded with day trippers.

Sights

The main settlement on the island, **Lembongan**, looks across the seaweed-farm-filled channel to Nusa Ceningan. It's a beautiful scene of clear water and green hills. A few cafes have sprung up to take advantage of the view. The town also has an interesting market and a grand old banyan tree.

At the north end of town where the island's main road passes, you can ascend a long stone staircase to Pura Puseh, the village temple. It has great views from its hilltop location.

Heading north, **Jungutbatu** village is mellow, although its lanes buzz with motorcycles and the rumble of trucks. Pura Segara and its enormous sacred tree are the site of frequent ceremonies. The north end of town holds the metal-legged lighthouse. Follow the road around east for about 1km to another temple, Pura Sakenan.

Activities

Surfing

Surfing here is best in dry season (April to September), when the winds come from the southeast. It's not for beginners and can be dangerous even for experts.

There are three main breaks on the reef, all aptly named. From north to south are **Shipwrecks**, **Lacerations** and **Play-**

grounds. Depending on where you are staying, you can paddle directly out to whichever of the three is closest (although at lowest tide you may have to do some walking so booties are essential); for others it's better to hire a boat. Prices are negotiable, from about 70,000Rp for a one-way trip – you tell the owner when to return. A fourth break – **Racecourses** – sometimes emerges south of Shipwreck.

The surf can be crowded here even when the island isn't – charter boats from Bali sometimes bring groups of surfers for day trips from the mainland for a minimum of 1,000,000Rp.

Thabu Surf Lessons SURFING
(☎0812 4620 2766; http://thabusurflessons.webs.com; adult/child based on skill level & group size from 450,000/400,000Rp) Very professional surf instruction outfit that offers private and

Nusa Lembongan

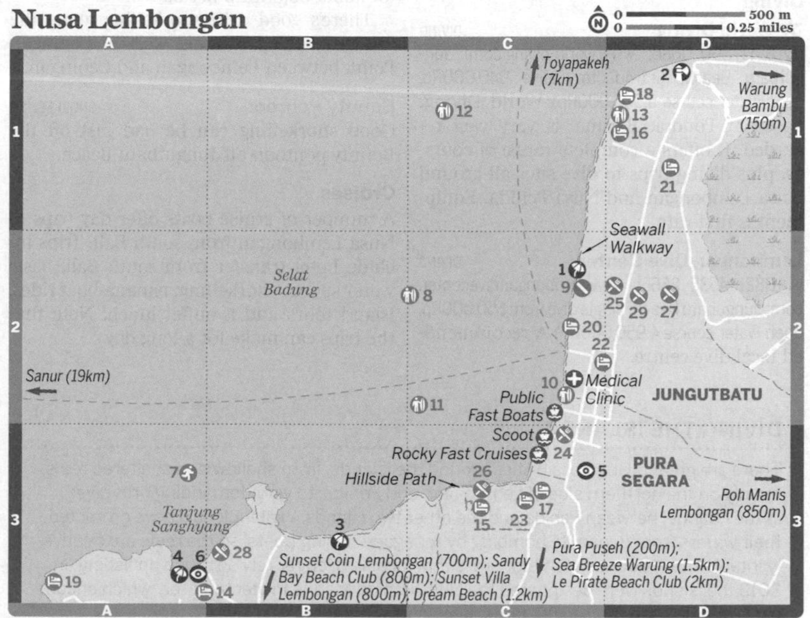

Nusa Lembongan

Sights
1 Jungutbatu Beach C2
2 Lighthouse D1
3 Pantai Selegimpak B3
4 Pantai Tanjung Sanghyang A3
5 Pura Segara C3
6 Sacred Tree A3

Activities, Courses & Tours
7 Bounty Cruise A3
Bounty Pontoon .... (see 7)
8 Lacerations C2
9 Lembongan Dive Center C2
10 Monkey Surfing C2
11 Playgrounds C2
12 Shipwrecks C1
13 Thabu Surf Lessons D1
World Diving .... (see 20)

Sleeping
14 Alam Nusa Huts A3
15 Batu Karang C3
16 Indiana Kenanga D1
17 Lembongan Island Beach Villas C3
18 Pemedal Beach D1
19 Point Resort Lembongan A3
20 Pondok Baruna C2
21 Pondok Baruna Frangipani D1
22 Secret Garden Bungalows C2
23 Ware Ware Surf Bungalows C3

Eating
24 99 Meals House C3
25 Bali Eco Deli D2
26 Deck Cafe & Bar C3
27 Green Garden Warung D2
28 Hai Bar & Grill B3
29 Pondok Baruna Warung D2

group lessons, with prices including return boat transfer to the surf break, booties and rash vests.

Monkey Surfing SURFING
(☎0821 4614 7683; www.monkeysurfing.com; Jungutbatu Beach; surfboard rental per day from 110,000Rp, lessons from 600,000Rp; ⏲8am-7pm) Rent surfboards and stand-up paddle boards from this shop on the beach, which offers guiding services.

Diving

★World Diving DIVING
(☎0812 390 0686; www.world-diving.com; Jungutbatu Beach; introductory dive 940,000Rp, open water course 5,500,000Rp) World Diving, based at Pondok Baruna, is very well regarded. It offers a complete range of courses, plus diving trips to dive sites all around Nusa Lembongan and Nusa Penida. Equipment is first-rate.

Lembongan Dive Center DIVING
(☎0821 4535 2666; www.lembongandivecenter.com; Jungubatu Beach; single dive from 550,000Rp, open-water course 4,950,000Rp) A recommended local dive centre.

Snorkelling

Good snorkelling can be had just off Tanjung Sanghyang and the Bounty Pontoon, as well as in areas off the north coast of the island. You can charter a boat for about 200,000Rp per hour, depending on demand, distance and the number of passengers. A trip to the challenging waters of Nusa Penida costs from 300,000Rp for three hours; to the nearby mangroves also costs about 300,000Rp. Snorkelling gear can be rented for about 50,000Rp per day.

There's good drift snorkelling along the mangrove-filled channel west of Ceningan Point, between Lembongan and Ceningan.

Bounty Pontoon SNORKELLING
Good snorkelling can be had just off the Bounty pontoon off Jungutbatu Beach.

Cruises

A number of cruise boats offer day trips to Nusa Lembongan from south Bali. Trips include hotel transfer from south Bali, basic water sports, snorkelling, banana-boat rides, island tours and a buffet lunch. Note that the trips can make for a long day.

DIVING THE ISLANDS

There are great diving possibilities around the islands, from shallow and sheltered reefs, mainly on the northern side of Lembongan and Penida, to very demanding drift dives in the channel between Penida and the other two islands. Vigilant locals have protected their waters from dynamite bombing by renegade fishing boats, so the reefs are relatively intact. And a side result of tourism is that locals no longer rely so much on fishing. In 2012 the islands were designated the Nusa Penida Marine Protected Area, which encompasses more than 20,000 hectares of the surrounding waters.

If you arrange a dive trip from Padangbai or south Bali, stick with the most reputable operators as conditions here can be tricky and local knowledge is essential. Note that the open waters around Penida are challenging, even for experienced divers. Diving accidents regularly happen and people die diving in the waters around the islands every year.

Using one of the recommended operators on Nusa Lembongan puts you close to the action from the start. The large marine animals are a particular attraction, including turtles, sharks and manta rays. The large (3m fin-to-fin) and unusual *mola mola* (sunfish) is sometimes seen around the islands between mid-July and October, while manta rays are often seen south of Nusa Penida from June to October.

The best dive sites include **Blue Corner** and **Jackfish Point** off Nusa Lembongan and **Ceningan Point** at its tip. The channel between Ceningan and Penida is renowned for drift diving, but it is essential you have a good operator who can judge fast-changing currents and other conditions. Upswells can bring cold water from the open ocean to sites such as **Ceningan Wall**. This is one of the world's deepest natural channels and attracts all manner and sizes of fish.

Sites close to Nusa Penida include **Crystal Bay**, **SD**, **Pura Ped**, **Manta Point** and **Batu Aba**. Of these, Crystal Bay, SD and Pura Ped are suitable for novice divers and are good for snorkelling.

Island Explorer Cruise CRUISE
(☎0361-728088; http://islandexplorercruises.com; adult/child from 1,400,000/740,000Rp) This operator's large boat doubles as the base for day-trip aquatic fun. It also has a sailing ship and fast boats for transfers. Boats leave from Benoa Harbour. It's affiliated with Coconuts Beach Resort.

Bounty Cruise CRUISE
(☎0361-726666; www.balibountycruises.com; Jl Wahana Tirta 1, Denpasar; adult/child US$119/59; ⏲7am-11pm) Boats dock at the garish yellow offshore Bounty pontoon with water slides and other amusements. The boat departs from Benoa Harbour.

Hiking & Biking

You can circumnavigate the island in a day on foot, or less on a bike. It's a fascinating journey into the small island's surprisingly diverse scenery. Start along the hillside path from Jungutbatu and overcome whatever obstacles developers have put on the path to Tanjung Sanghyang; with a little Tarzan spirit you can stay with the faint trail (you can't do this segment by bike: use the roads inland).

Next head to Lembongan village and cross the narrow bridge to Nusa Ceningan. Alternatively, from Lembongan village you take a gentle uphill walk along the sealed road to the killer hill that leads *down* to Jungutbatu, which cuts the circuit to about half a day.

To fully explore the island by foot, stick to the paved road that follows the channel between Nusa Lembongan and Nusa Ceningan. After a rugged uphill detour, curve back down and go north along the mangroves all the way to the lighthouse.

Bikes are easily rented for about 40,000Rp per day.

Sleeping

Rooms and amenities generally become increasingly posh as you head south and west along the water to Mushroom Bay.

Jungutbatu

Many lodgings in Jungutbatu have shed the surfer-shack cliché and are moving upmarket. But you can still find inland cheapies with cold water and fans.

★**Pondok Baruna** GUESTHOUSE $
(☎0812 394 0992; www.pondokbaruna.com; Jungutbatu Beach; r from 400,000Rp; ❄📶🏊) Associated with World Diving, a local dive operator, this place offers fantastic rooms with terraces facing the ocean. Six plusher rooms surround a dive pool behind the beach. There are another eight rooms at sister site Pondok Baruna Frangipani, set back in the palm trees around a large pool. Staff members, led by Putu, are charmers.

Secret Garden Bungalows GUESTHOUSE $
(☎0813 5313 6861; www.bigfishdiving.com; Jungutbatu Beach; r with fan/air-con 250,000/450,000Rp; ❄📶🏊) 🍃 Affiliated with Big Fish Diving, there are nine bungalow-style, cold-water and fan rooms in this palm-shaded compound back off the beach. Nearby there are also some newer air-con bungalows. It has on-site yoga classes for 100,000Rp. Marine Mega Fauna (p154) gives regular talks here about the amazing marine ecology around the islands.

★**Pemedal Beach** GUESTHOUSE $$
(☎0822 4477 2888; www.pemedalbeach.com; Jungutbatu Beach; r from 975,000Rp; ❄📶🏊) A lovely affordable option if you want to be near a sandy beach; the 20 bungalows are set back a bit from the infinity pool.

Pondok Baruna Frangipani GUESTHOUSE $$
(☎0823 3953 6271; www.pondokbarunafrangipani.com; Jungutbatu; r incl breakfast from 1,000,000Rp; ❄📶🏊) The more upmarket sister guesthouse to Pondok Baruna on the waterfront, Frangipani has eight spacious, luxurious bungalow-style rooms and a good-sized pool. It's a perfectly lovely property, but management staff isn't the friendliest.

★**Indiana Kenanga** BOUTIQUE HOTEL $$$
(☎0366-559 6371; www.indiana-kenanga-villas.com; Jungutbatu Beach; r US$240-400; ❄📶🏊) Two posh villas and 18 stylish suites shelter near a pool behind the beach at Lembongan's most upscale digs. The French designer-owner has decorated the place with Buddhist statues, purple armchairs and other whimsical touches. The restaurant has an all-day menu of seafood and various surprises cooked up by the skilled chef, plus there's a poolside creperie!

Hillside

The steep hillside just south of Jungutbatu offers great views and an ever-increasing number of luxurious rooms. The uppermost rooms at some places have gorgeous views across the water to Bali (on a clear day say hello to Gunung Agung), but such

AQUATIC ALLIANCE

The waters around Nusa Lembongan, Ceningan and Penida are filled with some truly spectacular creatures: huge manta rays, the ponderous *mola mola* and more. Yet while they are regularly spotted by flocks of divers who explore these rich waters, little is known about the actual ecology of the area – except that it's remarkable.

A group called **Marine Mega Fauna** (www.marinemegafauna.org) is working to change that. Through extensive field studies they are beginning to understand just what's swimming around out there. One early discovery: like whales, manta rays have markings that make it easy to identify individuals. The group's website is filled with fascinating information and you can learn more at their regular public talks on Tuesday and Thursday evenings at the Secret Garden Bungalows (p153).

thrills come at a cost: upwards of 120 steep concrete steps. A motorcycle-friendly path runs along the top of the hill, good for leg-saving drop-offs.

Ware Waro Surf Bungalows GUESTHOUSE $$
(☎0812 397 0572, 0812 380 3321; www.waresurfbungalows.com; r incl breakfast from 750,000Rp; ❄📶🏊) The nine units at this hillside place are a mix of square and circular numbers with thatched roofs and balconies. The large rooms (some with fan only) have rattan couches and big bathrooms. The cafe scores with its spectacular, breezy location on a large cliff-side wooden deck.

Batu Karang HOTEL $$$
(☎0366-559 6376; www.batukaranglembongan.com; r incl breakfast from 3,250,000Rp; ❄@📶🏊) This upmarket resort perched on a terraced hillside has a large infinity pool. Some of its 25 luxury units are villa-style and have multiple rooms and private plunge pools. All have open-air bathrooms and wooden terraces with sweeping views. Right on the hillside path, the hotel's Deck Cafe & Bar is a good pause for a gourmet snack or a drink.

Lembongan Island Beach Villas VILLA $$$
(☎0813 3856 1208; www.lembonganresort.com; villa from 3,800,000Rp; ❄📶🏊) Eleven luxe villas climb the hillside from a lobby right by the corner of Jungutbatu Beach. Units have comfy wicker loungers and hammocks as well as large kitchens. The covered balconies have great views across to Bali.

Tanjung Sanghyang

It's your own treasure island. Also known as Mushroom Bay, there is a nice beach, plenty of overhanging trees and some of the most atmospheric lodging on Lembongan. Get here from Jungutbatu by foot or with a ride (25,000Rp) or boat (80,000Rp).

Alam Nusa Huts GUESTHOUSE $$
(☎0819 1662 6336; r from 475,000Rp; ❄📶) This small property is less than 100m from the beach. Four bungalows sit in a lush garden; each has an open-air bathroom and a terrace. The interiors feature a lot of rich wood and bamboo. The staff is especially welcoming.

Elsewhere on Lembongan

Poh Manis Lembongan GUESTHOUSE $
(☎0821 4746 2726; r from US$43; ❄📶🏊) If Nusa Lembongan is a getaway, this is the getaway from Nusa Lembongan. Perched on a bluff on the southeast corner of the island, there are sweeping views of the other two Nusas. The pool area is lovely and the 10 rooms are light and airy with a woodsy charm.

Sunset Coin Lembongan GUESTHOUSE $$
(☎0812 364 0799; www.sunsetcoinlembongan.com; Sunset Bay; r incl breakfast from 1,100,000Rp; ❄📶🏊) Run by an awesome family, this collection of 10 cottages is everything an island escape should be. It's near the little spot of sand called Sunset Bay. The *lumbung*-style (thatched rice barn) units have terraces and fridges.

Sunset Villa Lembongan GUESTHOUSE $$
(☎0812 381 9023; www.sunsetvillaslembongan.com; Sunset Bay; r US$56-77; ❄📶🏊) Twelve modern-style bungalows surround a large pool in a serene compound with fast-growing vegetation. The units have terraces and sitting areas; some have fridges and flat-screen TVs. The large open-air bathrooms have natural stone details.

Point Resort Lembongan INN $$$
(www.thepointlembongan.com; ste from US$150, villa US$290; ❄📶🏊) About 500m west of Tanjung Sanghyang is this eponymously named property with four plush suites and a two-bedroom villa. The views are sweeping, and should pirates sail in you can watch them get dashed on the rocks below the

infinity pool. The units are bright and airy, with lovely sitting areas.

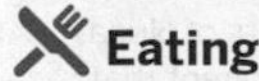

Eating

Almost every place to stay has a cafe serving – unless noted – Indonesian and Western dishes from about 50,000Rp. There are also many good stand-alone options.

Markets can be found near the bank, but unless you're on a diet of bottled water and Ritz crackers, the selection is small.

Jungutbatu

★Green Garden Warung INDONESIAN **$**
(0813 374 1928; mains 20,000-50,000Rp; 7am-10pm;) Tucked into a garden on a side street off Jungutbatu Beach, this locally owned warung serves up tasty smoothie bowls and creative Indonesian dishes, many of which are vegetarian friendly. The owners donate a portion of their proceeds to local schools and are in the process of adding five guest rooms.

Bali Eco Deli CAFE **$**
(0812 3704 9234; www.baliecodeli.net; mains from 40,000Rp; 7am-10pm) This irresistible cafe has great green cred and is noted for giving back to the community. But what it gives customers is also good: fresh and creative breakfasts, healthy snacks, delicious baked goods, good coffees and juices plus an array of salads, all served in a garden setting.

Pondok Baruna Warung INDONESIAN **$**
(mains from 50,000Rp; 8am-10pm) The dining part of the Baruna empire boasts some of the best food on the island. Look for excellent Balinese dishes as well as a range of fine curries. Many order not one but two chocolate brownies.

99 Meals House INDONESIAN, CHINESE **$**
(Jungutbatu Beach; mains from 20,000Rp; 8am-10pm) An absolute bargain. Fried rice, omelettes, Chinese stir-fries and more prepared by a family at this great open-air spot overlooking the beach.

★Warung Bambu SEAFOOD **$$**
(0813 3867 5451; mains 35,000-90,000Rp; 9am-10pm) On the road to the mangroves, past the lighthouse, this family-run restaurant serves excellent seafood meals. The menu depends on what's caught offshore. Tables are on a large covered terrace with a sandy floor. By day you may luck out with Gunung Agung views, by night the lights of Bali twinkle.

Hillside

★Deck Cafe & Bar CAFE **$$**
(0855 390 4830; http://thedecklembongan.com; mains from 60,000Rp; 7.30am-11pm;) Straddling the main hillside walkway, the stylish bar and cafe of the Batu Karang hotel offers creative drinks from a long list, gorgeous views and interesting snacks (it has a good bakery) plus upscale pub fare. On Sunday there's a DJ.

Tanjung Sanghyang

★Hai Bar & Grill INTERNATIONAL **$$**
(0361-720331; www.haitidebeachresort.com/hai-bar-and-grill; Hai Tide Beach Resort; mains 59,000-160,000Rp; 7am-10pm;) This wide-open bar with wide-open views of the bay and sunsets is the most stylish restaurant bar along Tanjung Sanghyang. The menu mixes Asian and Western dishes, and there are comforts such as fresh-baked muffins. You can use the pool if you eat here and open-air movies screen some nights. Call for pick up from Jungutbatu.

Elsewhere on Lembongan

Sandy Bay Beach Club INTERNATIONAL **$$**
(0828 9700 5656; www.sandybaylembongan.com; Sunset Bay; mains from 60,000Rp; 8.30am-10.30pm;) Pushing the distressed bleached-wood look for all it's worth, this appealing beach club occupies a fine position on a sweet pocket of sand most call Sunset Beach (unless you're this place and call it Sandy Bay...). The menu spans Asia and Europe, with a detour to Burgerville. The evening seafood barbecues are popular.

Information

The **Medical Clinic** (consultation from 250,000Rp; 8am-6pm), in a modern building in the village, is well versed in treating minor surfing and diving injuries and ear ailments.

It's best that you bring sufficient cash in rupiah for your stay. There are four ATMs on the island but sometimes they run out of cash or refuse foreign cards.

Getting There & Away

Getting to/from Nusa Lembongan offers numerous choices, some quite fast. Note: anyone with money for a speedboat is getting into the fast-boat act; be wary of fly-by-night operators with fly-by-night safety.

Boats anchor offshore, so be prepared to get your feet wet. And travel light – wheeled bags

FORSAKING SEAWEED

Few ice-cream fans know this but they owe big thanks to the seaweed growers of Nusa Lembongan, Nusa Ceningan and Nusa Penida. Carrageenan, an emulsifying agent that is used to thicken ice cream as well as cheese and many other products, is derived from the seaweed grown here.

As you walk around the villages, you'll see – and smell – vast areas used for drying seaweed. Looking down into the water, you'll see the patchwork of cultivated seaweed plots. The islands are especially good for production as the waters are shallow and rich in nutrients. The dried red and green seaweed is exported around the world for final processing.

But for how much longer is the real question. Farming seaweed is back-breaking work with tiny returns. Where just a decade ago 85% of Lembongan's people farmed seaweed, today that number is quickly diminishing as the population gets caught up in the tourist boom, with its comparatively better wages and much easier work.

And Nusa Penida is just a little way behind. We asked one former seaweed farmer who now works as a guide if he missed the work. His response was comically unprintable.

are comically inappropriate in the water and on the beach and dirt tracks. Porters will shoulder your steamer trunk for 20,000Rp (and don't be like some low-lifes we've seen who have stiffed them for their service). They'll also try to lead you to a particular hotel where they can collect a commission on your stay.

Public Fast Boats (Jungutbatu Beach; one way 200,000Rp) Leave from the northern end of Sanur Beach for Nusa Lembongan 10 times daily, between 8.30am and 5.30pm, and take 30 minutes.

Rocky Fast Cruises (☎0361-283624; www.rockyfastcruise.com; Jungutbatu Beach; one way/return 300,000/500,000Rp) Runs several large boats daily that take 30 minutes.

Scoot (☎0361-285522, 0812 3767 4932; www.scootcruise.com; Jungutbatu Beach; adult/child one way 400,000/280,000Rp) Makes a few trips daily; each takes 30 minutes.

Getting Around

The island is fairly small and you can walk to most places. Cars, small motorcycles (60,000Rp per day) and bicycles (40,000Rp per day) are widely available for hire. One-way rides on motorcycles or trucks cost 15,000Rp and up. One unwelcome development is the SUV-sized golf carts that seem to be mostly rented by tourists who find a big cigar to be the perfect driving companion.

Nusa Ceningan

☎0361

Tiny Nusa Ceningan is connected to Nusa Lembongan by an atmospheric, narrow yellow suspension bridge crossing the lagoon, making it quite easy to explore the island. Besides the lagoon filled with frames for seaweed farming, you'll see several small agricultural plots and a fishing village. Nusa Ceningan is quite hilly and, if you're up for it, you can get glimpses of great scenery while wandering or cycling around. Key roads have been paved, which is opening up the island, although it is still very rural.

There's a **surf break**, named for its location at Ceningan Point, in the southwest; it's an exposed left-hander.

Sights

Blue Lagoon LAGOON

Surges of stunning turquoise waves tumble into jagged black rock formations at this cliffside cove overlooking the Bandung Strait. Posted signs point to cliff jumping for the ultra brave (if you opt in, check tide conditions and know your limits). Look for the wooden sign at the end of Jl Sarang Burung and follow the trail through the palm trees.

Tours

To really savour Nusa Ceningan, take an overnight tour of the island with JED (p449), a cultural organisation that gives people an in-depth look at village and cultural life. Trips include family accommodation in a village, local meals, a fascinating tour with seaweed workers and transport to/from mainland Bali.

Sleeping & Eating

Le Pirate Beach Club GUESTHOUSE $$

(☎0811 388 3701, reservations 0361-733493; https://lepirate.com/nusa-ceningan/; Jl Nusa Ceningan; r incl breakfast from 700,000Rp; ❄📶🏊) With a sprightly white and blue colour scheme, the theme here is retro-chic island kitsch. The accommodation consists of air-conditioned beach boxes, which range from bunk beds that sleep four to doubles. The popular restaurant looks over the small kidney-shaped pool and has broad views of the channel. Two-night minimum.

Secret Point Huts GUESTHOUSE $$
(0819 9937 0826; www.secretpointhuts.com; r from US$80;) In the southwest corner of the island overlooking the Ceningan Point surf break, this cute little resort has a tiny beach and clifftop bar. The rooms are in *lumbung* (rice barn) style bungalows with open-air bathrooms.

Getting There & Away

To reach Nusa Ceningan you first travel to Nusa Lembongan, then walk or take a motorbike over the short bridge.

Nusa Penida

0366 / POP 37,581

Just beginning to appear on visitor itineraries, Nusa Penida still awaits proper discovery. It's an untrammelled place that answers the question: what would Bali be like if tourists never came? There are just a handful of formal activities and sights; instead, you go to Nusa Penida to explore and relax, to adapt to the slow rhythm of life here.

The population of around 37,000 is predominantly Hindu, although there is a Muslim community in Toyapakeh. It's an unforgiving area: Nusa Penida was once used as a place of banishment for criminals and other undesirables from the kingdom of Klungkung (now Semarapura), and still has a somewhat sinister reputation. Yet, it's also a centre of rebirth: the iconic Bali starling is being reintroduced here after being thought nearly extinct in the wild. And there's a growing visitor scene near Ped.

Sights

The island is a limestone plateau with a strip of sand on its north coast and views over the water to the volcanoes in Bali. The south coast has 300m-high limestone cliffs dropping straight down to the sea and a row of offshore islets – it's rugged and spectacular scenery. The interior is hilly, with sparse-looking crops and old-fashioned villages. Rainfall is low and parts of the island are arid, although you can see traces of ancient rice terraces.

Beaches are very few although some are spectacular.

Activities

Nusa Penida has world-class diving; most people make arrangements through a dive shop on Nusa Lembongan. Between Toyapakeh and Sampalan there is excellent cycling on the beautiful, flat coastal road. The roads elsewhere are good for mountain bikes. Ask around to rent a bike, which should cost about 40,000Rp per day.

Quicksilver WATER SPORTS
(0361-721521; www.quicksilver-bali.com; adult/child US$110/55) Has day trips from Bali (that leave from Benoa Harbour). A large barge anchored off Toyapakeh is the base for all sorts of water sports. There are also village tours.

Information

DANGERS & ANNOYANCES

There have been accidents involving boats between Bali and the surrounding islands. These services are unregulated and there is no safety authority should trouble arise. Take precautions (see p452).

MONEY

The two ATMs are occasionally out of order or cash. Bring plenty of rupiah just in case.

TOURIST INFORMATION

Penida Tours (p159) is an excellent contact for island-wide info.

VOLUNTEERING

Various environmental and aid groups are active on Nusa Penida, with volunteers needed for a variety of projects. They normally collect a fee (US$10 to US$20 per day, depending on the length of your stay) that includes accommodation and contributes to the cause. The following organisations have programs you can join.

Friends of the National Parks Foundation (FNPF; 0361-479 2286; www.fnpf.org) This group has a centre near Ped on the island's north coast. Volunteer work includes aid in the

PENIDA'S DEMON

Nusa Penida is the legendary home of Jero Gede Macaling, the demon who inspired the Barong Landung dance. Many Balinese believe the island is a place of enchantment and *angker* (evil power) – paradoxically, this is an attraction. Thousands of Balinese come every year for religious observances aimed at placating the evil spirits.

conservation of the critically endangered native Bali starling and teaching in local schools. Accommodation is in simple but comfortable rooms with fans and cold water.

Green Lion Bali (☎0812 4643 4964; http://new.greenlionbali.com; Jl Penestanan, Ubud) Has an award-winning program to breed and protect turtles along Penida's north shore. Volunteers sign on for at least two weeks and work in the turtle compound as well as teaching in local schools. There is a nearby guesthouse.

Getting There & Away

The strait between Nusa Penida and southern Bali is deep and subject to heavy swells – if there is a strong tide, boats often have to wait. Charter boats to/from Kusamba are not recommended due to their small size and the potential for heavy seas.

NUSA LEMBONGAN

Nusa Penida public boats run between Lembongan town by the bridge and Toyapakeh (50,000Rp, 20 minutes). Boats depart from 6am, waiting for a crowd of at least six passengers. Chartering a boat costs a negotiable 300,000Rp to 400,000Rp each way.

PADANGBAI

Fast boats run across the strait from Padangbai to Buyuk, 1km west of Sampalan on Nusa Penida (110,000Rp, 45 minutes, four daily). The boats run between 7am and noon.

A large public car ferry also operates daily (adult/child/motorbike/car) 31,000/26,000/52,000/380,000Rp) leaving at 11am each morning. It takes 40 minutes to two hours, depending on the sea.

SANUR

Various speedboats leave from the same part of the beach as the fast boats to Nusa Lembongan and make the run in less than an hour.

Maruti Express (☎0361-465086, 0811 397 901; http://lembonganfastboats.com/maruti_express.php; one way adult/child from 362,500/290,000Rp) One of several fast boats making the Penida run.

Getting Around

Bemos are rare after 10am. There are often people who can set you up with transport where boats arrive. Options for getting around are as follows.

Car & driver From 350,000Rp for a half day.

Motorcycle Easily hired for 80,000Rp per day.

Ojek Not common, but if you find a ride on the back of a motorcycle, expect to pay about 50,000Rp per hour.

Sampalan

POP 4635

Sampalan, the main town on Penida, is quiet and pleasant and strung out along the curving coast road. The interesting market is in the middle of town. It's a good place to absorb village life.

Nusa Garden Bungalows GUESTHOUSE $
(☎0812 3990 1421, 0813 3812 0660; r from 200,000Rp; 📶) Crushed-coral pathways running between animal statuary link the 10 very basic rooms here. Turn on Jl Nusa Indah just east of the centre.

MaeMae Beach House GUESTHOUSE $
(☎0857 4383 60225; maemaebeachhouse2015@gmail.com; Kutampi; r from 370,000Rp; ❄📶) In the town of Kutampi just outside Sampalan, this guesthouse is convenient for the main harbour. The manager Agus speaks excellent English and is a wealth of knowledge about everything Penida. Rooms are modern, but with a few rough edges. The chilled-out warung does decent food and is close to the water.

Getting There & Away

Sampalan is on the main coastal road. Transport is easily arranged if you get here by boat.

Ped

POP 3787

Ped is home to a very important Balinese temple. Just 600m west, the tiny subvillage of Bodong is the appealing centre of Penida's nascent tourist scene.

Sights & Activities

★Pura Dalem Penetaran Ped HINDU TEMPLE
FREE This important temple is near the beach at Ped, 3.5km east of Toyapakeh. It houses a shrine for the demon Jero Gede Macaling that is a source of power for practitioners of black magic, and a place of pilgrimage for those seeking protection from sickness and evil. The temple structure is sprawling and you will see people making offerings for safe sea voyages from Nusa Penida; you may wish to join them.

Octopus Dive DIVING
(☎0878 6268 0888, 0819 77677677; www.octopusdiveindonesia.com; Bodong; 2-tank dives from 1,100,000Rp) A small and enthusiastic local dive operator.

★ **Penida Tours** TOUR
(☎0852 0587 1291; www.penidatours.com; Jl Raya Bodong; tours from 750,000Rp; ⏰9am-6pm) A great local operation that arranges cultural tours around Penida, covering anything from black magic to diving to camping trips. The office is located next door to Gallery cafe.

Sleeping

Full Moon Bungalows BUNGALOW $
(☎0813 3874 5817; www.fullmoon-bungalows.com; Bodong; dm/r from 125,000/300,000Rp; ❄📶) A well-run compound with 15 bungalows. Each is basic but comfortable with thatched walls. You're mere steps from Ped's small but delightful nightlife.

Jero Rawa HOMESTAY $
(☎0852 0586 6886; www.jerorawahomestay.com; Jl Raya Ped; r incl breakfast with fan/air-con from 200,000/300,000Rp) Run by a delightful family, this laid-back guesthouse has clean bungalow-style rooms just across the street from the beach.

Ring Sameton Inn GUESTHOUSE $
(☎0813 798 5141; www.ringsameton-nusapenida.com; Bodong; r incl breakfast 400,000-500,000Rp; ❄📶🏊) If you're seeking comfort, this is easily the best place to stay on Penida. As well as spiffy business-style rooms, there's a pool, an atmospheric restaurant and quick beach access.

Eating

★ **Gallery** CAFE $
(☎0819 9988 7205; Bodong; mains from 30,000Rp; ⏰7.30am-9pm) A popular spot for volunteers at the NGOs, this small cafe and shop is run by the ever-charming Mike, a Brit who is a fount of Penida knowledge. There's art on the walls, hand-roasted filter coffee, house-made Rosella tea and a Western menu of breakfast items and sandwiches.

★ **Penida Colada** CAFE $
(☎0821 4676 3627; www.facebook.com/penidacolada; Bodong; mains 45,000-70,000Rp; ⏰9am-late; 📶) The cocktails at this charming seaside-shack cafe, run by an Indo–Aussie couple, are a must. Fresh, creative concoctions include mojitos and daiquiris to go with a menu of grilled fish, BLTs and chips with aioli. There's often a seafood barbecue in the evenings. Enjoy the soothing sound of the ocean lapping at the narrow beach. *This* is Penida's nightlife.

Warung Pondok Nusa Penida INDONESIAN $
(Bodong; mains from 30,000Rp; ⏰9am-9pm) A cute little breezy place right on the beach. Enjoy well-prepared Indo classics and seafood (plus the odd international item) while taking in the views to Bali. Try the 'seaweed mocktail' dessert.

Made's Warung INDONESIAN $
(Ped; mains 8000-18,000Rp; ⏰8am-10pm) Right across from the temple, this very clean warung is one of several and has tasty *nasi campur* (rice with a choice of side dishes).

Getting There & Away

Ped and Bodong are right on the coastal road. Motorbike or private car are the only way to get around.

Crystal Bay Beach

This idyllic beach fronts the popular dive spot Crystal Bay. The sand here is pale, and palm trees add a *South Pacific* motif. The beach is popular with Bali day trippers who arrive in boats (one operator is Bali Hai Cruises; www.balihaicruises.com), but mostly the beach remains blessedly rural. At busy times, however, up to 60 boats might arrive at once, so conditions can get very crowded. Come after 3pm to avoid the crowds. A couple of warungs (food stalls) and beach cafes rent snorkelling gear. The temple, **Segara Sakti**, adds the perfect touch.

Namaste GUESTHOUSE $$
(☎0813 3727 1615; www.namaste-bungalows.com; r with fan/air-con from 500,000/650,000Rp; ❄📶🏊) A very steep 1km back from the beach, on the road to Toyapakeh, expat-owned Namaste is a high-concept guesthouse with 10 rustic-style bungalows made with recycled materials and set around a large pool. It has a good cafe.

Getting There & Away

South of Toyapakeh, a paved 10km road through the village of Sakti leads you here. You'll need your own wheels, which you can arrange through your accommodation or when you arrive on Nusa Penida. Given the hills, trying to bike here is unimaginable.

Ubud Region

Includes ➡

Best Places to Eat

- ➡ Hujon Locale (p184)
- ➡ Dumbo (p188)
- ➡ Mozaic (p189)
- ➡ Pica (p187)
- ➡ Moksa (p188)
- ➡ Locavore (p187)

Best Places to Stay

- ➡ Mandapa (p181)
- ➡ Swasti Eco Cottages (p180)
- ➡ Bambu Indah (p181)
- ➡ Como Uma Ubud (p181)
- ➡ Komaneka at Monkey Forest (p179)
- ➡ Three Win Homestay (p177)

Why Go?

Though Ubud will always claim the limelight in this region, there are some minor players well worthy of attention. A day spent visiting the temples of Tampaksiring, pausing en route to indulge in a photographic frenzy at the famed Ceking rice terraces, is time well spent, and the same can be said for a visit to the many traditional artisans' villages south of Ubud, which are deservedly famous for the quality of their craftsmanship. Basing yourself in Ubud, which is replete with alluring sleeping and eating options, is a no-brainer, but so too is hopping on a motorcycle or organising a car and driver to see the rest that this part of Bali has to offer. There may be few top-drawer sights, but there are many scenic side roads that amply reward exploration.

When to Go

➡ From October to April the weather is slightly cooler but much wetter than in the south; expect it to rain at any time. At night, mountain breezes make air-con unnecessary.

➡ Temperatures during the day average 30°C and at night 20°C, although extremes are possible. Seasonal variation is muted.

➡ Peak season (July, August and the Christmas holidays) bring a huge influx of visitors, and lodgings and restaurants are booked.

➡ In October, the Ubud Writers & Readers Festival is hugely popular.

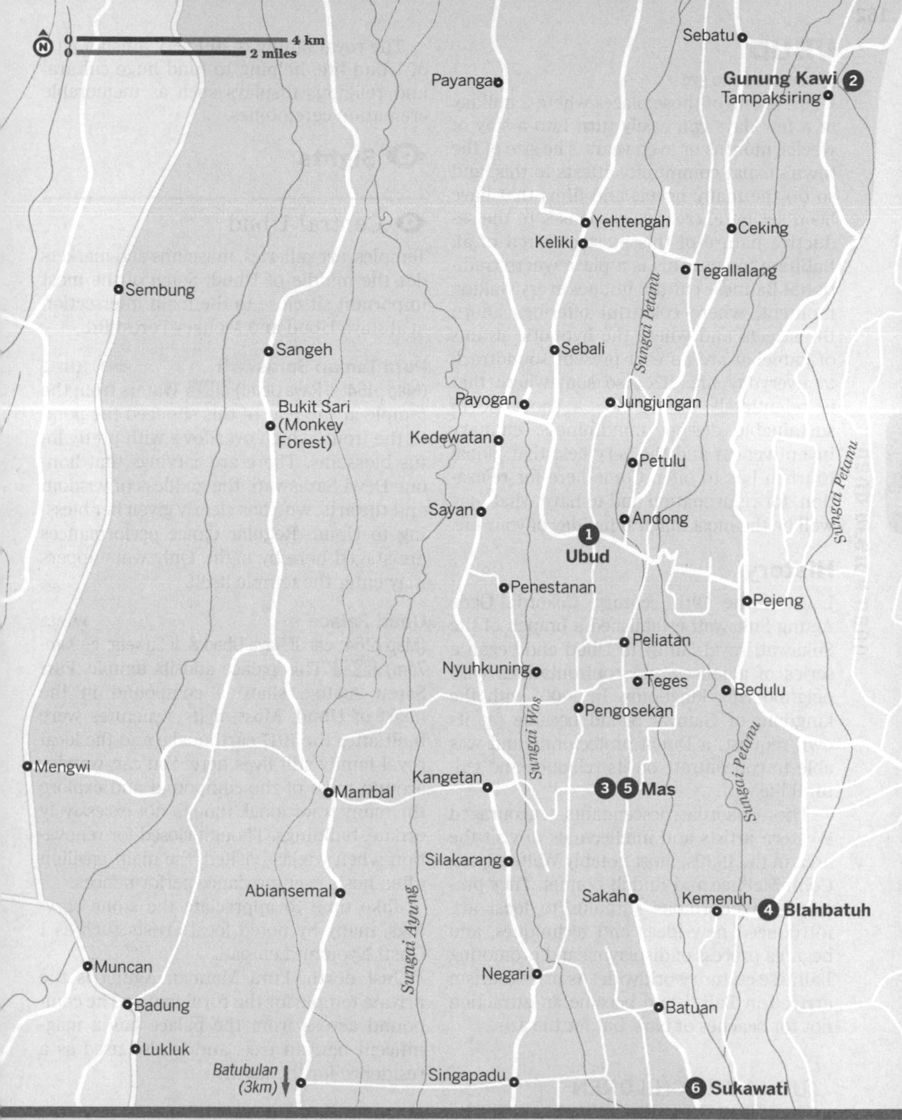

Ubud Region Highlights

1 Ubud (p162) Enjoying the temples, museums, cafe culture and focus on wellness in Bali's cultural capital.

2 Gunung Kawi (p197) Making like Indiana Jones at these ancient *candi* (shrines), cut out of rock faces.

3 Traditional Villages (p199) Exploring artisan villages, such as Mas, to source artworks, crafts, ceremonial objects and other treasures.

4 Pertenunan Putri Ayu (p201) Hearing the click-klack of looms at this traditional textile workshop in Blahbatuh.

5 Setia Darma House of Mask and Puppets (p199) Marvelling at the thousands of ceremonial masks and puppets exhibited at this labour-of-love museum in Mas.

6 Sukawati Market (p201) Watching locals bargain for the flowers, baskets, fruits, knick-knacks and other items used in temple offerings.

UBUD

☎ 0361 / POP 10,870

Ubud is one of those places where a holiday of a few days can easily turn into a stay of weeks, months or even years. The size of the town's expat community attests to this, and so do the many novels and films that have been set here, creative responses to the seductive nature of this most cultured of all Balinese towns. This is a place where traditional Balinese culture imbues every waking moment, where colourful offerings adorn the streets and where the hypnotic strains of gamelan are an ever-present soundtrack to everyday life. It's also somewhere that is relentlessly on trend – a showcase of sustainable design, mindfulness, culinary inventiveness and the very best that global tourism has to offer. Come here for relaxation, for rejuvenation and to have what may well be the most magical holiday of your life.

History

Late in the 19th century, Cokorda Gede Agung Sukawati established a branch of the Sukawati royal family in Ubud and began a series of alliances and confrontations with neighbouring kingdoms. In 1900, with the kingdom of Gianyar, Ubud became (at its own request) a Dutch protectorate and was able to concentrate on its religious and cultural life.

The Cokorda descendants encouraged Western artists and intellectuals to visit the area in the 1930s, most notably Walter Spies, Colin McPhee and Rudolf Bonnet. They provided an enormous stimulus to local art, introduced new ideas and techniques, and began a process of displaying and promoting Balinese culture worldwide. As mass tourism arrived in Bali, Ubud became an attraction not for beaches or bars, but for the arts.

> **UBUD FOR CHILDREN**
>
> Ubud is an excellent destination for children. There are often resident children at homestays, providing play companions, and many of the resorts have kids clubs or activity programmes.
>
> If bribery is necessary to ensure good behaviour, the multiple branches of Gelato Secrets and Gaya Gelato can oblige, as can the many eateries serving pizza. On Sundays, Uma Cucina (p188) offers a popular brunch with family-friendly food and entertainment.

The royal family is still very much a part of Ubud life, helping to fund huge cultural and religious displays such as memorable cremation ceremonies.

Sights

Central Ubud

Temples, art galleries, museums and markets dot the middle of Ubud. Some of the most important sit close to the main intersection at Jl Raya Ubud and Monkey Forest Rd.

Pura Taman Saraswati HINDU TEMPLE

(Map p164; Jl Raya Ubud) FREE Waters from the temple at the rear of this site feed the pond in the front, which overflows with pretty lotus blossoms. There are carvings that honour Dewi Saraswati, the goddess of wisdom and the arts, who has clearly given her blessing to Ubud. Regular dance performances are staged here by night. Only worshippers may enter the temple itself.

Ubud Palace PALACE

(Map p164; cnr Jl Raya Ubud & Jl Suweta; ⏲ 9am-7pm) FREE This palace and its temple, Puri Saren Agung, share a compound in the heart of Ubud. Most of its structures were built after the 1917 earthquake and the local royal family still lives here. You can wander around most of the compound and explore the many traditional, though not excessively ornate, buildings. Though closed for renovation when we last visited, the main pavilion often hosts evening dance performances.

Take time to appreciate the stone carvings, many by noted local artists such as I Gusti Nyoman Lempad.

Just north, Pura Marajan Agung is the private temple for the royal family. The compound across from the palace has a magnificent banyan tree, and is also used as a residence for the family.

Museum Puri Lukisan MUSEUM

(Museum of Fine Arts; Map p164; ☎ 0361-975136; www.museumpurilukisan.com; off Jl Raya Ubud; adult/child under 11yr 85,000Rp/free; ⏲ 9am-5pm) It was in Ubud that the modern Balinese art movement started, when artists first began to abandon purely religious themes and court subjects for scenes of everyday life. This museum set in a lovely formal garden has four buildings displaying works from all schools and periods of Balinese art, with a focus on modern masters such as I Gusti Nyoman Lempad (1862–1978), Ida

Bagus Made (1915–1999) and I Gusti Made Kwandji (1936–2013). All works are labelled in English.

The **East Building**, to the right upon entry, has a collection of early works from Ubud and surrounding villages. These include examples of classical *wayang*-style paintings (art influenced by shadow puppetry) from the 10th to 15th centuries, and impressive 20th-century works such as *The Death of Karna* (1935) by I Wayan Tutur.

The **North Building** features fine ink drawings by I Gusti Nyoman Lempad and paintings by artists of the Pita Maha school. Don't miss *Temple Festival* (1938) by I Gusti Ketut Kobot (1917–1999).

In the **West Building** is detailed art by 20th-century Balinese painters. Look for *Barong Dance* (1970) by I Gusti Made Kwandji (1936–2013). The **South Building** is used for special exhibitions and contains some museum history.

The museum ticket includes a drink in the garden cafe.

Pura Desa Ubud HINDU TEMPLE

(Map p164; Jl Raya Ubud) FREE The main temple for the Ubud community. It is often closed but comes alive for ceremonies.

Neka Gallery GALLERY

(Map p164; ☎0361-975034; Jl Raya Ubud; ⏱8am-5pm) FREE Operated by Suteja Neka since 1966, this low-key gallery is a separate entity from the other gallery bearing Neka's name, Neka Art Museum. It has a somewhat motley selection of works from all the schools of Balinese art, as well as works by past European residents, including Arie Smit.

Komaneka Art Gallery GALLERY

(Map p164; ☎0361-401 2217; www.gallery.komaneka.com; Monkey Forest Rd; ⏱8am-8pm) FREE Stages exhibitions by established Balinese artists.

South Ubud

You can reach some of Ubud's best sights via walks along Jl Hanoman and Monkey Forest Rd, which are both lined with interesting shops and cafes. Duck down narrow paths to find hidden rice fields.

★Agung Rai Museum of Art GALLERY

(ARMA; Map p168; ☎0361-976659; www.armabali.com/museum; Jl Raya Pengosekan; adult/child under 10yr 100,000Rp/free; ⏱9am-6pm) If you only visit one museum in Ubud, make it this one. Founder Agung Rai built his fortune selling Balinese artwork to foreigners in the 1970s, and during his time as a dealer he also built one of Indonesia's most impressive private collections of art. This cultural compound opened in 1996 and displays his collection in two purpose-built gallery buildings – highlights include the wonderful 19th-century *Portrait of a Javanese Nobleman and his Wife* by Javanese artist Raden Saleh (1807–1880).

Exhibits include classical Kamasan paintings and Batuan-style work from the 1930s and '40s and among the artists represented are I Gusti Nyoman Lempad, Ida Bagus Made, Anak Agung Gede Sobrat (1912–1992) and I Gusti Made Deblog (1906–1986). Stand-out works to seek out in the modern art gallery are *Green Rice Paddies* (1987) by Nasjah Djamin (1924–1999) and *Wild Orchids* (1988) by Widaya (1923–2002). In the traditional art gallery, look for *The Dance Drama Arja* (1945) by I Ketut Kasta (b 1945), *Cremation Cememony* (1994) by I Ketut Sepi (b 1941) and the extraordinarily detailed *Wali 'Ekadesa Rudra'* (2015) by I Wayan Mardiana (b 1970). The traditional art gallery is also home to a collection of works by expat artist Walter Spies (1895–1942), who played a significant role in the development of the Ubud painting school.

THE HERONS OF PETALU

Every evening after 5pm, up to 20,000 big herons fly in to Petulu, a village about 2.5km north of Jl Raya Ubud, squabbling over the prime perching places before settling into the trees beside the road and becoming a tourist attraction.

The herons, mainly the striped Java pond species, started their visits to Petulu in 1965 for no apparent reason. Villagers believe they bring good luck (as well as tourists), despite the smell and the mess. A few warung (food stalls) have been set up in the paddy fields, where you can have a drink while enjoying the spectacle; entry to the village costs 20,000Rp. Walk quickly under the trees if the herons are already roosting. Nesting and egg-laying begins in November, with the fledglings taking flight in March.

Petulu is a pleasant walk or bicycle ride on any of several routes north of Ubud, but if you stay for the birds, you'll be heading back in the dark.

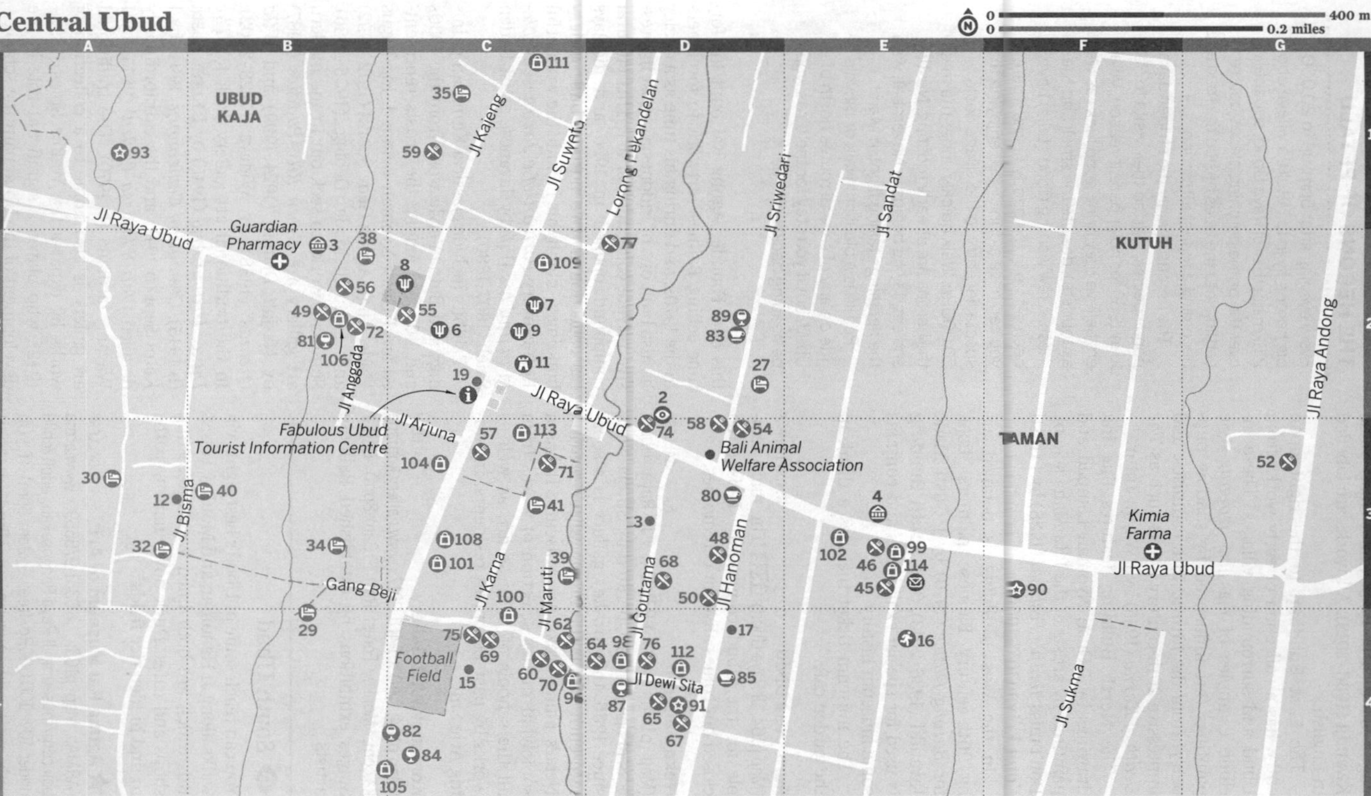
Central Ubud
0 400 m
0 0.2 miles
A
B
C
D
E
F
G
1
2
3
4
UBUD KAJA
KUTUH
TAMAN
Jl Raya Ubud
Jl Raya Andong
Jl Kajeng
Jl Suweta
Lorong Pekandelan
Jl Sriwedari
Jl Sandat
Jl Anggada
Jl Arjuna
Jl Bisma
Gang Beji
Jl Karna
Jl Maruti
Jl Goutama
Jl Hanoman
Jl Dewi Sita
Jl Sukma
Guardian Pharmacy
Fabulous Ubud Tourist Information Centre
Bali Animal Welfare Association
Kimia Farma
Football Field
93
35
59
111
38
3
8
56
55
49
72
81
106
6
7
9
11
109
77
19
2
74
58
54
89
83
27
57
113
104
71
41
30
12
40
32
34
29
108
101
100
39
62
75
69
15
60
70
96
64
98
76
112
87
65
91
67
68
48
50
17
85
80
4
102
99
46
114
45
16
90
52
82
84
105

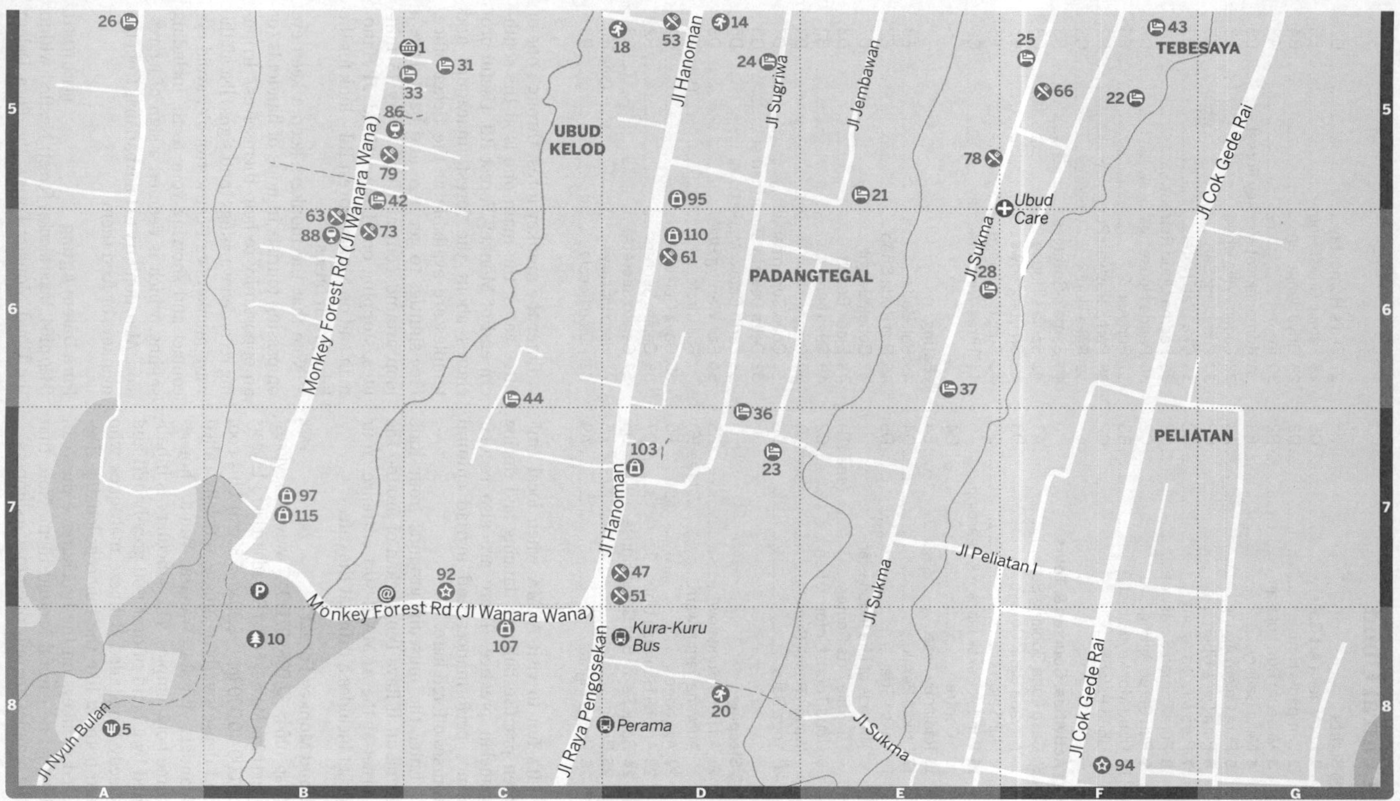

TEBESAYA
UBUD KELOD
PADANGTEGAL
PELIATAN
Jl Hanoman
Jl Sugriwa
Jl Jembawan
Jl Cok Gede Rai
Jl Sukma
Jl Peliatan I
Monkey Forest Rd (Jl Wanara Wana)
Jl Raya Pengosekan
Jl Nyuh Bulan
Ubud Care
Kura-Kuru Bus
Perama

Central Ubud

Sights
1 Komaneka Art Gallery ... C5
2 Lempad's House ... D2
3 Museum Puri Lukisan ... B2
4 Neka Gallery ... E3
5 Pura Dalem Agung ... A8
6 Pura Desa Ubud ... C2
7 Pura Mrajan Agung ... C2
8 Pura Taman Saraswati ... C2
9 Puri Saren Agung ... C2
10 Ubud Monkey Forest ... B8
11 Ubud Palace ... C2

Activities, Courses & Tours
12 Casa Luna Cooking School ... A3
13 Nirvana Batik Course ... D3
14 Nur Salon ... D5
15 Pondok Pekak Library & Learning Centre ... C4
16 Radiantly Alive ... E4
17 Studio Perak ... D4
18 Taksu Spa ... D5
Threads of Life Indonesian Textile Arts Center ... (see 111)
19 Ubud Tourist Information ... C2
Wayan Pasek Sucipta ... (see 27)
20 Yoga Barn ... D8

Sleeping
21 Adipana Bungalow ... E5
Adiwana Jembawan ... (see 16)
22 Aji Lodge ... F5
23 Artotel Haniman Ubud ... D7
24 Batik Sekar Bali Guest House ... D5
25 Biangs ... F5
26 Bisma Eight ... A5
27 Eka's Homestay ... D2
28 Family Guest House ... E6
29 Griya Jungutan ... B4
30 Ina Inn ... A3
31 Komaneka at Monkey Forest ... C5
32 Ladera Villa Ubud ... A3
33 Lumbung Sari ... C5
34 Oka Wati Hotel ... B3
35 Padma Ubud Retreat ... C1
36 Pande House ... D7
37 Puri Asri 2 ... E6
38 Puri Saraswati Bungalows ... B2
39 Raka House ... C3
40 Sama's Cottages ... B3
41 Sania's House ... C3
42 Sri Bungalows ... B5
43 Suastika Lodge ... F5
44 Three Win Homestay ... C6

Eating
45 Bali Buda ... E3
46 Bali Buda Shop ... E3
47 Bebek Bengil ... D7
48 Black Beach ... D3
49 Casa Luna ... B2
50 Clear ... D3
51 Coco Supermarket ... D7
52 Delta Dewata Supermarket ... G3
53 Earth Cafe & Market ... D5
54 Fair Warung Balé ... D3
Full Circle ... (see 23)
55 Gaya Gelato ... C2
56 Gelato Secrets ... D2
57 Gelato Secrets ... C3
Herb Library ... (see 16)
58 Hujon Locale ... D3

It's fun to visit ARMA when local children practise Balinese dancing and during gamelan practice. There are also regular dance performances and myriad cultural courses offered here.

Enter the museum grounds from Kafe Arma on Jl Raya Pengosekan or around the corner at the ARMA Resort entrance. Your ticket includes a drink at the cafe.

Ubud Monkey Forest PARK

(Map p164; 0361-971304; www.monkeyforestubud.com; Monkey Forest Rd; adult/child 3-12 years 50,000/40,000Rp; 8.30am-5.30pm) This cool and dense swath of jungle, officially called Mandala Wisata Wanara Wana, houses three holy temples. The sanctuary is inhabited by a band of over 600 grey-haired and greedy long-tailed Balinese macaques who are nothing like the innocent-looking doe-eyed monkeys on the brochures – they can bite, so be careful around them. Note that the temples are only open to worshippers.

Enter the monkey forest through one of three gates: the main one is at the southern end of Monkey Forest Rd. Useful brochures about the forest, macaques and temples are available at the ticket office. Free shuttles to get here and back drive a loop around central Ubud every 15 minutes, stopping on JI Raya Ubud, JI Hanoman and on Money Forest Rd – look for the lime-green buses.

Note that the monkeys keep a keen eye on passing tourists in hope of handouts (or an opportunity to help themselves). Irritating recorded warnings (and signs) list all the ways monkeys can cause trouble: avoid eye contact and showing your teeth, including smiling, which is deemed a sign of aggression. Also, don't try to take bananas from the monkeys or feed them.

Pura Dalem Agung HINDU TEMPLE

(Map p164; Ubud Monkey Forest) Nestled within the Ubud Monkey Forest, the Pura Dalem

Agung has a real *Indiana Jones* feel to it; the entrance to the inner temple features Rangda figures devouring children. Entrance is limited to worshippers.

West Ubud

Strolling Jl Raya Campuan down to the bridge (note the older historic wooden bridge just south) over the Sungai Wos (Wos River) and then up the busy and interesting Jl Raya Sanggingan takes you past a range of interesting sights. Venture up the steep steps to Penestanan for walks among small guesthouses and rice fields coursing with water.

★Neka Art Museum GALLERY

(Map p168; ☎0361-975074; www.museumneka.com; Jl Raya Sanggingan; adult/child under 12yr 75,000Rp/free; ⏲9am-5pm) Offering an excellent introduction to Balinese art, this impressive museum displays its top-notch collection of works in a series of pavilions and halls. Don't miss the multi-room **Balinese Painting Hall**, which showcases *wayang* (puppet) style as well as the European-influenced Ubud and Batuan styles introduced in the 1920s and 1930s. Also notable is the **Lempad Pavilion**, with works by the master I Gusti Nyoman Lempad, and the **East-West Art Annexe**, where works by Affandi (1907–1990) and Widayat (1919–2002) impress.

The museum is the creation of Suteja Neka, a private collector and dealer in Balinese art, and his collection is huge. As well as works by Balinese and Indonesian artists, there are plenty of works by foreign artists who have called the island home, including Arie Smit, Johan Rudolf Bonnet, Theo Meier, Louise Garrett Koke, Donald Friend and Tay Moh-Leong.

There's also a gift shop (p194) where quality local handicrafts can be purchased.

Ubud Area

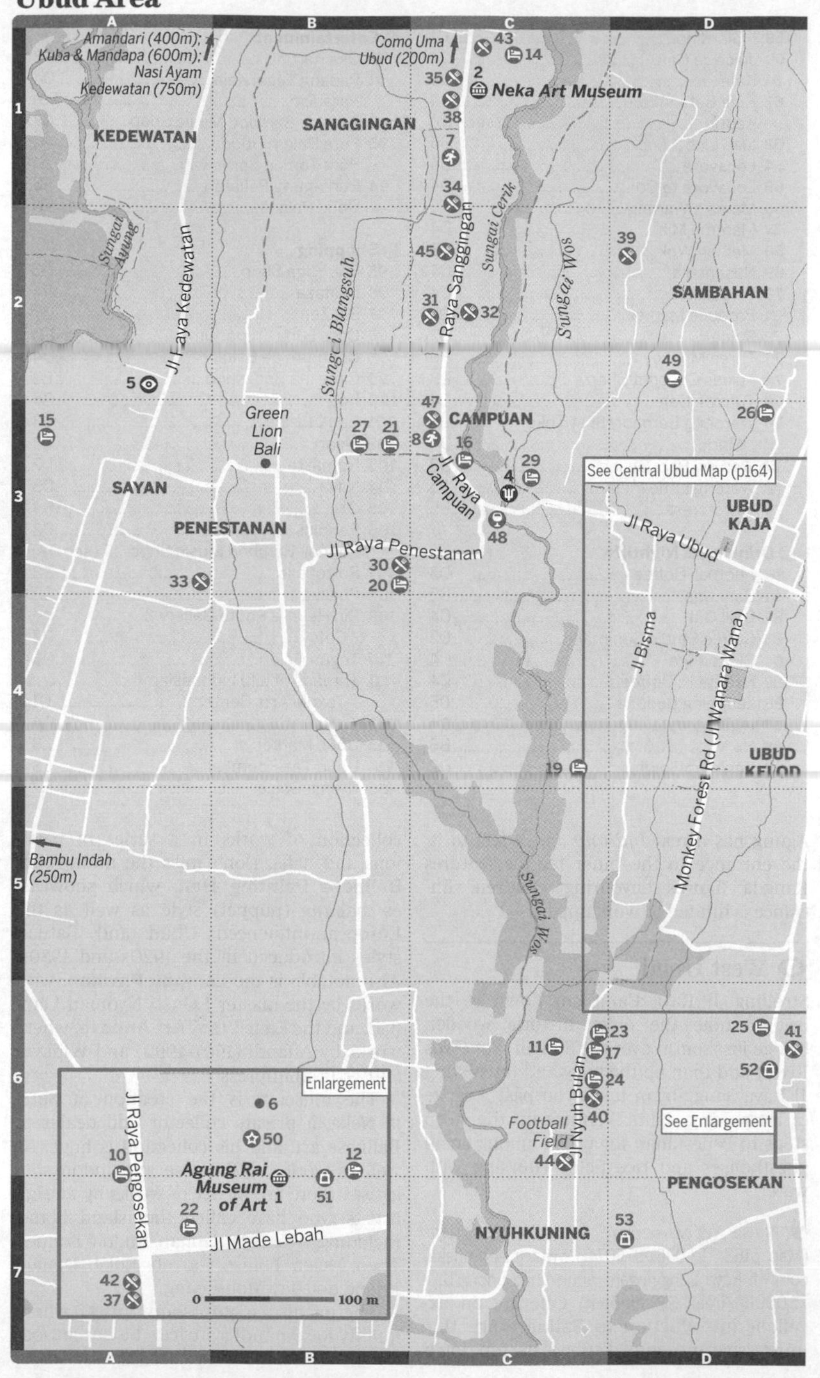

Amandari (400m); Kuba & Mandapa (600m); Nasi Ayam Kedewatan (750m)
Como Uma Ubud (200m)
Neka Art Museum
KEDEWATAN
SANGGINGAN
Sungai Ayung
Jl Raya Kedewatan
Sungai Blangsuh
Raya Sanggingan
Sungai Cerik
Sungai Wos
SAMBAHAN
Green Lion Bali
CAMPUAN
Jl Raya Campuan
SAYAN
PENESTANAN
Jl Raya Penestanan
See Central Ubud Map (p164)
UBUD KAJA
Jl Raya Ubud
Jl Bisma
Monkey Forest Rd (Jl Wanara Wana)
UBUD KELOD
Bambu Indah (250m)
Enlargement
Jl Raya Pengosekan
Agung Rai Museum of Art
Jl Made Lebah
0 100 m
Football Field
Jl Nyuh Bulan
See Enlargement
PENGOSEKAN
NYUHKUNING

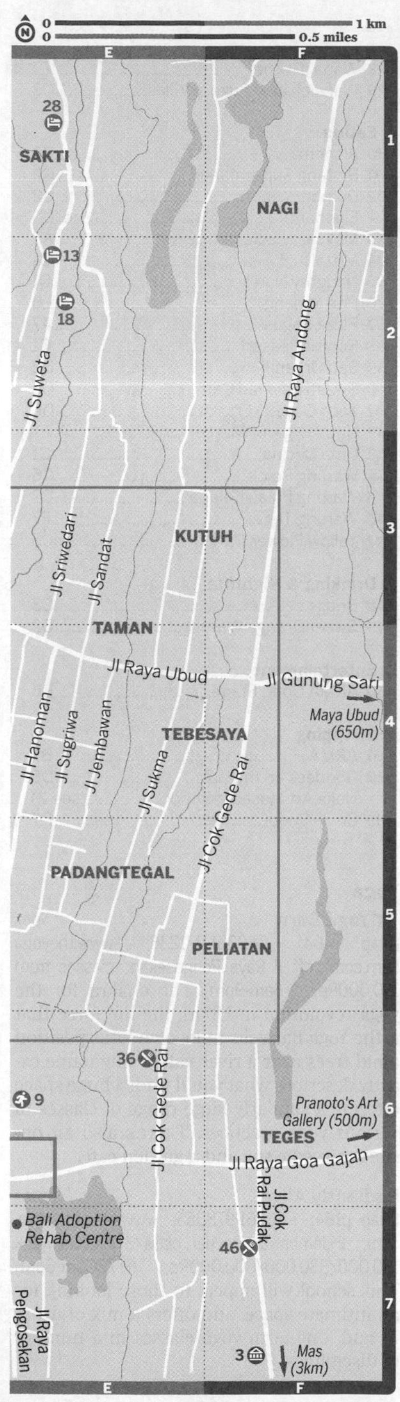

Pura Gunung Lebah HINDU TEMPLE

(Map p168; off Jl Raya Campuan) This old temple, which sits on a jutting rock at the confluence of two tributaries of Sungai Cerik (*campuan* means 'two rivers'), has recently benefited from a huge building campaign. The setting is magical; listen to the rushing waters while admiring the impressive *meru* (multi-tiered shrine) and a wealth of elaborate carvings.

Activities

Yoga and meditation are popular activities here, as are spa sessions. Walks through local rice fields are popular, and easily achieved without guides. Cycling is possible, but local traffic conditions mean that it's not particularly enjoyable.

Massages & Spas

★Taksu Spa SPA

(Map p164; ☎0361-479 2525; www.taksuspa.com; Jl Goutama; massage from 450,000Rp; ⏲9am-10pm) One of Ubud's most popular spas, Taksu has a long and rather lavish menu of massages and beauty treatments, as well as a strong focus on yoga. There are private rooms for couples massages and a healthy garden cafe.

Mandapa Spa SPA

(☎0361-4792777; www.ritzcarlton.com/en/hotels/indonesia/mandapa/spa; Mandapa Resort, Kedewatan; massages 1,600-000-2,100,000Rp, facials 1,700,000-2,500,000Rp; ⏲9am-9pm) The sybaritic riverside spa and wellness centre at the Mandapa resort offers massage and beauty treatments, a yoga pavilion, a meditation temple, a vitality pool, a 24-hour fitness centre and saunas.

Made Surya HEALTH & FITNESS

(www.balihealers.com; per hr/day US$35/200) One of Bali's top *balian* (traditional healers). He is an excellent resource if you'd like to try Balinese therapies.

Ubud Wellness Spa SPA

(Map p168; ☎0361-970493; www.ubudwellnessbalispa.com; off Jl Pengosekan; treatments from 95,000Rp; ⏲9am-10pm) A spa that concentrates on what counts, not the fru-fru. A favourite among Ubud's creative community. Try the 3½ hour Royal Kumkuman Body Wellness spa package (500,000Rp).

Bali Botanica Day Spa SPA

(Map p168; ☎0361-976739; www.balibotanica.com; Jl Raya Sanggingan; massage from 190,000Rp; ⏲9am-9pm) This little spa offers a range of

Ubud Area

Top Sights
1 Agung Rai Museum of Art ... B7
2 Neka Art Museum ... C1

Sights
3 Museum Rudana ... F7
4 Pura Gunung Lebah ... C3
5 Sayan Terrace ... A2

Activities, Courses & Tours
6 ARMA ... B6
7 Bali Botanica Day Spa ... C1
8 Intuitive Flow ... C3
Mozaic Cooking Classes ... (see 34)
Ubud Sari Health Resort ... (see 26)
9 Ubud Wellness Spa ... E6
Wayan Karja Painting ... (see 21)

Sleeping
10 Agung Raka ... A6
11 Alam Indah ... C6
12 ARMA Resort ... B6
13 Bali Asli Lodge ... E2
14 Como Uma Ubud ... C1
15 Four Seasons Resort ... A3
16 Hotel Tjampuhan ... C3
17 Kertiyasa Bungalows ... C6
18 Ketut's Place ... E2
19 Komaneka at Bisma ... C4
20 Roam ... B3
21 Santra Putra ... B3
22 Sapodilla ... A7
23 Saren Indah Hotel ... C6
24 Swasti Eco Cottages ... C6
25 Tegal Sari ... D6
26 Ubud Sari Health Resort ... D3
27 Villa Nirvana ... B3
28 Wapa di Ume ... E1
29 Warwick Ibah Luxury Villas ... C3

Eating
30 Alchemy ... B3
31 Bintang Supermarket ... C2
32 Dumbo ... C2
Elephant ... (see 32)
33 Moksa ... A3
34 Mozaic ... C1
35 Naughty Nuri's ... C1
36 Pitri Minang ... E6
37 Pizza Bagus ... A7
38 Room4Dessert ... C1
39 Sari Organik ... D2
40 Swasti Beloved Cafe ... C6
41 Taco Casa ... D6
42 Ubud Organic Market ... A7
43 Uma Cucina ... C1
44 Warung Pojok ... C6
45 Warung Pulau Kelapa ... C2
46 Warung Teges ... F7
47 Yellow Flower Cafe ... C3

Drinking & Nightlife
48 Bridges ... C3
49 Sweet Orange Warung ... D2

Entertainment
50 ARMA Open Stage ... B6

Shopping
51 ARMA ... B7
52 Goddess on the Go! ... D6
Neka Art Museum Shop ... (see 2)
53 Smile Shop ... D7

treatments, including Ayurvedic. The herbal massage is popular. Transport is provided if needed (two or more treatments only).

Ubud Sari Health Resort SPA
(Map p168; ☎0361-974393; www.ubudsari.com; Jl Kajeng 35; 1hr massage from 240,000Rp; ⏲9am-8pm) This wellness centre in the hotel of the same name is a serious place offering an extensive menu of treatments, including massage, detox programmes, reflexology and beauty treatments.

Nur Salon SPA
(Map p164; ☎0361-975352; www.nursalonubud.com; Jl Hanoman 28; 1hr massage 175,000Rp; ⏲noon-8pm Aug-Oct, 9am-9pm Nov-Jul) Set in a traditional Balinese compound filled with labelled medicinal plants, Nur offers a long menu of straightforward spa and salon services.

Yoga

★ **Yoga Barn** YOGA
(Map p164; ☎0361-971236; www.theyogabarn.com; off Jl Raya Pengosekan; classes from 130,000Rp; ⏲6am-9pm) The chakra for the yoga revolution in Ubud, the life force that is the Yoga Barn sits in its own lotus position amid trees near a river valley. The name exactly describes what you'll find: a huge space offering a similarly large range of classes in various yoga practices. There's also an on-site Ayurvedic spa and a garden cafe.

Radiantly Alive YOGA
(Map p164; ☎0361-978055; www.radiantlyalive.com; Jl Jembawan 3; per class/3 classes/week 130,000/330,000/800,000Rp; ⏲7.30am-6pm) This school will appeal to those looking for an intimate space, and offers a mix of drop-in and long-term yoga classes in a number of disciplines.

Intuitive Flow YOGA

(Map p168; ☎0361-977824; www.intuitiveflow.com; Penestanan; yoga from 120,000Rp; ⊙classes daily) A lovely yoga studio up amid the rice fields – although climbing the concrete stairs to get here from Campuan may well leave you too spent for a round of asanas. Wide range of workshops in healing arts. Cash payments only.

Cycling

Many shops and hotels in central Ubud display mountain bikes for hire. The price is usually a negotiable 35,000Rp per day. If in doubt about where to rent, ask at your hotel and someone with a bike is soon likely to appear.

In general, the land is dissected by rivers running south, so any east–west route will involve a lot of ups and downs as you cross the river valleys. North–south routes run between the rivers, and are much easier going, but can have heavy traffic. Most of the sites within Ubud are reachable by bike, but the traffic-choked streets and total lack of bike paths makes walking or driving preferable.

Rafting

The Sungai Ayung (Ayung River) is the most popular river in Bali for white-water rafting. You start north of Ubud and end near the Amandari hotel in the west. Note that depending on rainfall the run can range from sedate to thrilling.

Courses

Ubud is the perfect place to develop your artistic or language skills, or learn about Balinese culture and cuisine. The range of courses offered could keep you busy for a year. With most classes you must book in advance.

★ARMA CULTURAL TOUR

(Map p168; ☎0361-976659; www.armabali.com/museum/cultural-workshops; Jl Raya Pengosekan; classes from US$25; ⊙9am-6pm) A cultural powerhouse offering classes in painting, woodcarving, gamelan and batik. Other courses include Balinese dance, Hinduism and architecture.

Threads of Life Indonesian Textile Arts Center TEXTILE

(Map p164; ☎0361-972187; www.threadsoflife.com; Jl Kajeng 24; 2hr class 200,000-400,000Rp; ⊙10am-7pm) Textile-appreciation courses in the gallery and educational studio last from one to eight days. Some classes involve extensive travel around Bali and should be considered graduate level.

Pondok Pekak Library & Learning Centre LANGUAGE

(Map p164; ☎0361-976194; www.facebook.com/pg/pondokpekak; off Monkey Forest Rd; classes per hr from 150,000Rp; ⊙9am-9pm) On the far side of the football field, this centre offers a huge range of courses and workshops. Try a

WALKING WISELY IN UBUD

Walking in and around the Ubud region with its endless beauty, myriad fascinations and delightful discoveries is a great pleasure and a superb reason to visit the area.

There are lots of interesting walks in the area to surrounding villages and through the rice fields. You'll frequently see artists at work in open rooms and on verandas, and the timeless tasks of rice cultivation continue alongside luxury villas.

Consider the following to better enjoy your walk:

Bring your own water In most places there are plenty of warung (food stalls) or small shops selling snack foods and drinks but don't risk dehydration between stops.

Gear up Bring a good hat, decent shoes and wet-weather gear for the afternoon showers; long trousers are better for walking through thick vegetation.

Start early Try to begin at daybreak, before it gets too hot. The air also feels crisper and you'll catch birds and other wildlife before they spend the day in shadows. It's also much quieter before the day's buzz begins.

Avoid tolls Some entrepreneurial rice farmers have erected little toll gates across their fields. You can either simply detour around them, or pay a fee (never accede to more than 10,000Rp).

Quit while ahead Should you tire, don't worry about reaching some goal – the point is to enjoy your walk. Locals on motorbikes will invariably give you a ride home for around 30,000Rp.

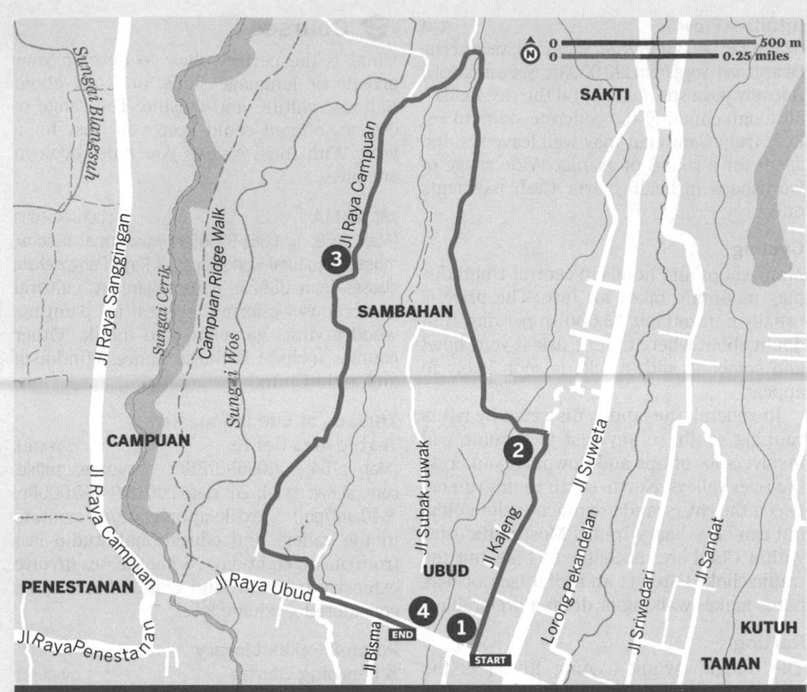

Walking Tour
Ubud's Urban Rice Fields

START PURA TAMAN SARASWATI
END MUSEUM PURI LUKISAN
LENGTH 3.5KM; ONE HOUR

Start at ❶ **Pura Taman Saraswati** (p162), where you can pose for a photograph or two in front of the temple's carved entrance gate and gorgeous lotus-filled pond. Then head north up Jl Kajeng, following the 'To Rice Field' signs. Pass the ❷ **Pura Catur Bhuana**, one of hundreds of small neighbourhood temples in Ubud, and then head uphill as the road becomes a path. You'll soon see a lush green vista of rice fields on your left and come to a small shrine, where you should veer right. Continue north, passing a few villas, and turn left when you come to a path before a simple warung. This path soon joins another footpath, where you should turn left, looping back towards the town centre (if you veer right, the path will take you to the village of Tegallalang, passing many studio shacks used by local artists on the way).

Having taken the left turn, you will pass two organic farms where some of the produce used in Ubud's restaurants is grown; one is home to the ❸ **Sari Organik** (p188) cafe, where you could pause for a drink or organic meal. Continuing south, you'll soon enjoy wonderful views over to the Campuan Ridge. This area was among the first to attract Western painters in the 1920s and 1930s and you'll understand why from the still-lush foliage and the sound of the river swiftly flowing that can be heard when the wind is in the right quarter. The path becomes serpentine at this point, and you'll be sharing it with darting lizards, scraggy chickens and the occasional pedestrian or motorbike rider. Birds sing, and the hilltop breezes can be blissful on hot days.

Continue walking until you come to a T-intersection and then veer left, passing the Abangan Bungalows and emerging on Jl Raya Ubud, close to ❹ **Museum Puri Lukisan** (p162).

dance, music or woodcarving workshop, or sign up for a private course of 10 Indonesian language classes (1,200,000Rp). Some workshops are geared to kids.

Wayan Karja Painting ART
(Map p168; ☎0361-977810; Jl Pacekan 18, Penestanan; 2hr class 350,000Rp) Intensive painting and drawing classes are run by abstract artist Karja, whose studio is behind his guesthouse, the Santra Putra (p181).

Wayan Pasek Sucipta MUSIC
(Map p164; ☎0361-970550; Eka's Homestay, Jl Sriwedari 8; classes per hr 100,000Rp) Learn the gamelan from a master.

Nirvana Batik Course ART
(Map p164; ☎0361-975415; www.nirvanaku.com; Nirvana Pension, Jl Goutama 10; classes per day 450,000-485,000Rp; ⏲10am-2pm Mon-Sat) Nyoman Suradnya teaches these highly regarded batik courses.

Studio Perak JEWELLERY
(Map p164; ☎081 2365 1809; www.studioperak.com; Jl Hanoman 15; lessons per 3hr 430,000Rp) Specialises in Balinese-style silversmithing courses. In one three-hour lesson you'll make at least one finished piece. Classes can be geared to children aged eight years or older.

Cooking

A cooking class is one of the most popular activities for visitors to Ubud. Classes often start at one of the local markets, where you can learn about the huge range of fruits, vegetables and other foods that are part of the Balinese diet.

★Casa Luna Cooking School COOKING
(Map p164; ☎0361-973282; www.casalunabali.com/casa-luna-cooking-school; Honeymoon Guesthouse, Jl Bisma; classes from 400,000Rp) A different cooking class or food tour is offered every day of the week at this well-regarded cooking school associated with the Casa Luna (p186) restaurant. Half-day courses cover a range of dishes; some include a market visit. A three-hour tour to the famous Gianyar night market is offered on Thursday and Friday, and a 'Food as Medicine' class on Saturday.

Mozaic Cooking Classes COOKING
(Map p168; ☎0361-975768; www.mozaic-bali.com; Jl Raya Sanggingan; half-/full-day class 900,000/1,300,000Rp) Learn cooking techniques at one of Bali's best restaurants. A full menu of classes is taught, from casual to professional. Classes include tastings.

Cafe Wayan Cooking Class COOKING
(☎0361-975447; www.alamindahbali.com/cafe_wayan.htm; classes 350,000Rp; ⏲10am & 4pm) Held at two locations in town, this beginner's class is held over two hours. Afterwards, you'll get to eat your work.

☞ Tours

Fabulous Ubud Tourist Information Centre CULTURAL
(Fabulous Ubud; Map p164; ☎0361-973285; www.fabulousubud.com; Jl Raya Ubud; tours 185,000-300,000Rp; ⏲8am-9pm) Owned and operated by members of Ubud's royal family, this travel and events agency runs interesting and affordable half- and full-day trips to a huge range of places, including Besakih and Kintamani.

Dhyana Putri Adventures CULTURAL
(www.balispirit.com/tours/bali_tour_dhyana.html; half-/full-day tours US$120/185) Bicultural and trilingual, author and Balinese dance expert Rucina Ballinger offers custom tours, with an emphasis on Balinese performing arts and in-depth cultural experiences.

Bali Nature Walk WALKING
(☎0817 973 5914; www.balinaturewalks.net; tour US$25) Dewa Rai conducts a three-to-four-hour nature walk through jungle and rice field landscapes in the Ubud region. The cost includes hotel pick up.

Banyan Tree Cycling Tours CYCLING
(☎0813 3879 8516; www.banyantreebiketours.com; tours adult/child from US$55/35) Enjoy day-long tours of remote villages in the hills north of Ubud. The tours are very popular, and emphasise interaction with villagers. Hiking and rafting trips are also available.

Bali Bird Walks BIRDWATCHING
(☎0361-975009; www.balibirdwalk.com; tour incl lunch US$37; ⏲9am-12.30pm Tue, Fri, Sat & Sun) Started by Victor Mason more than three decades ago, this tour, ideal for keen birders, is still going strong. On a gentle morning's walk (from the long-closed Beggar's Bush Bar) you may see up to 30 of the 100-odd local species.

Bali Nature Herbal Walks WALKING
(☎0812 381 6020, 0812 381 6024; www.baliherbalwalk.com; tour 200,000Rp; ⏲8.30am) Three-hour walks through lush Bali landscape. Medicinal and cooking herbs and plants are identified and explained in their natural environment. Includes herbal drinks.

LONGJON/SHUTTERSTOCK ©

1. Pura Desa Ubud (p163)
Explore the intricate architecture of this Hindu temple.

2. Gunung Kawi (p107)
One of Bali's oldest and most important monuments, with huge shrines cut out of the rock faces.

3. Ubud Monkey Forest (p166)
This sprawling sanctuary is inhabited by more than 600 macaques.

PUTYATO PAVEL/SHUTTERSTOCK ©

CAMPUAN RIDGE WALK

Following this paved trail along a ridge between two rivers is a popular sunrise and sunset activity, but can be enjoyed at any time of the day. Start at the driveway of the Warwick Ibah Luxury Villas and then take the path to the left, where a walkway crosses the Sungai Wos (Wos River) and passes the tranquil Pura Gunung Lebah (p169) with its impressive multi-stepped *meru* (multi-tiered shrine). Continue north on the concrete path, climbing up onto the Campuan Ridge between the two rivers (Campuan means 'Where Two Rivers Meet', referring to the confluence of the Wos and Cerik). Fields of elephant grass, traditionally used for thatched roofs, slope away on either side of the path and you'll be able to see the rice fields above Ubud in all of their lush green majesty. Continue uphill past rice fields to the village of Bangkiang Sidem, where you should turn around and return the way you came, as the road connecting the village with Payegan and central Ubud has no footpaths and is dangerous for pedestrians.

Festivals & Events

The Ubud area is one of the best places to see the many religious and cultural events celebrated in Bali each year. The Fabulous Ubud Tourist Information Centre (p195) is unmatched for its comprehensive information on local events.

★Ubud Writers & Readers Festival LITERATURE
(www.ubudwritersfestival.com; 1-day pass 1,200,000Rp; ⏲late Oct/early Nov) Southeast Asia's major literary event brings together writers and readers from around the world in a five-day celebration of writing – especially writing that touches on Bali.

★Bali Spirit Festival DANCE, MUSIC
(www.balispiritfestival.com; ⏲late Mar/early Apr) A popular yoga, dance and music festival from the people behind the Yoga Barn, a local yoga hub. There are hundreds of workshops and concerts, plus a market and more.

Ubud Village Jazz Festival MUSIC
(⏲Aug) First staged in 2013, this annual two-day jazz festival is staged at the Agung Rai Museum of Art (ARMA; p163) and features an international line-up of performers.

Ubud Food Festival FOOD & DRINK
(☎0361-977408; www.ubudfoodfestival.com; ⏲Apr) Diverse and delicious Indonesian cuisine takes centre stage at this three-day foodie festival. Events include cooking demonstrations, workshops, forums, markets, food tours and film screenings.

Bali Vegan Festival FOOD & DRINK
(www.baliveganfestival.com; ⏲Oct) Aiming to inspire converts to the vegan lifestyle, this three-day festival includes talks, cooking demonstrations, workshops and films staged at the Paradiso cinema (p192) and in the events pavilion of the Taksu Spa (p169). A second festival is staged in Canggu.

Sleeping

Simple accommodation within a family home compound is a cultural experience and can cost as little as US$15 per night. Ubud enjoys cool mountain air at night, so air-con isn't necessary.

Guesthouses may be a bit larger and have amenities such as swimming pools but are still likely to be fairly intimate, often nestled amid rice fields and rivers. The best hotels and resorts are often perched on the edges of the deep river valleys, with superb views (although even some budget places have amazing views). Some provide shuttle service around the area.

Addresses in Ubud can be imprecise – but signage at the end of a road will often list the names of all the places to stay. Away from the main thoroughfares there are few streetlights and it can be challenging to find your way after dark. If walking, you'll want a torch.

Due to its popularity and the lack (so far) of an invasion of chain hotels, Ubud is one place on the island where accommodation prices are on the rise.

Central Ubud

This original heart of Ubud has a vast range of places to rest your weary head and you'll enjoy a location that will cut down on the need for long walks or 'transport'. If you're near Jl Raya Ubud, don't settle for a room with noise from the main drag. Small and quiet streets to the east of the main crossroads, including Jl Karna, Jl Maruti and Jl Goutama, have numerous family-style homestays. Immediately north of Jl Raya

Ubud, streets such as Jl Kajeng and Jl Suweta offer a timeless tableau, with kids playing in the streets and many fine homestays. Monkey Forest Rd has a high concentration of lodgings; go for one well off the traffic-choked road. Jl Bisma runs into a plateau of rice fields but these are shrinking in size as new hotels open here, especially down at the south end where a path links to Monkey Forest Rd.

★Three Win Homestay HOMESTAY $
(Map p164; ☎0819 9945 3319, 0812 3819 7835; www.threewinhomestay.com; Anila Ln, off Jl Hanoman; r 350,000-450,000Rp; ❄📶) Putu, her husband Sampo and her father Nyoman are understandably proud of the five modern guest rooms in their family compound off JI Hanoman. These have tiled floors, comfortable beds and sparkling bathrooms; request one upstairs, as these have spacious balconies overlooking the rooftops.

Batik Sekar Bali Guest House GUESTHOUSE $
(Map p164; ☎0361-975351; Jl Sugriwa 32; ⊙r 250,000-310,000Rp; ❄📶) In a primo location, this family homestay offers the timeless Ubud experience. Come and go past Made, Putu and their family as they make offerings and go about daily tasks. The four rooms have terraces and cold-water bathrooms.

Pande House HOMESTAY $
(Map p164; ☎0361-970421; www.pandehomestayubud.wordpress.com; Jl Sugriwa 59; r with fan/air-con from 250,000/400,000Rp; 📶) Yet another one of Ubud's delightful family-compound homestays, old-fashioned Pande is but one of many clustered on this residential street. Each room has a terrace; the deluxe version has air-con. The frills are few and far between, but the welcome is warm.

Puri Asri 2 GUESTHOUSE $
(Map p164; ☎0361-973210; Jl Sukma 59; s 400,000Rp, d 450,000-500,000Rp; ❄📶🏊) Work your way through a classic family compound and you'll come to this homestay with eight extremely well-maintained bungalow-style rooms. Three have air-con, but the best are those upstairs, which are light and airy. Cool off in the small but pretty infinity pool.

Griya Jungutan HOMESTAY $
(Map p164; ☎0361-975752; www.griyajungutan.com; Gang Beji, off Monkey Forest Rd; r with fan 270,000Rp, r with air-con from 310,000Rp, f 1,020,000Rp; ❄📶🏊) In a tranquil location overlooking a small river valley in the very heart of Ubud, Griya and family offer well-priced rooms that are simple but comfortable enough. Rooms come in several flavours: the cheapest are fan-only, the best have terraces with lush views. Guests love the made-to-order breakfasts.

Aji Lodge HOMESTAY $
(Map p164; ☎0361-973255; ajilodge11@yahoo.com; off Jl Sukma; s 200,000-250,000Rp, d 250,000-300,000Rp; ❄📶) Run by local painter Aji, who will be pleased to show you his work, this homestay next to the river has four guest rooms with wooden ceilings and large beds draped in mosquito nets; two have air-con and all have terraces. Prices are 50,000Rp cheaper without breakfast.

Family Guest House HOMESTAY $
(Map p164; ☎0361-974054; www.familyubud.com; Banjar Tebesaya 39; s 250,000-300,000Rp, d 350,000-400,000Rp; ❄📶) There's a bit of bustle from the busy family at this well-maintained homestay. The eight rooms are simple but clean; three have air-con. Opt for one upstairs, as these are light and airy.

Suastika Lodge HOMESTAY $
(Map p164; ☎0361-970215; suastika09@hotmail.com; off Jl Sukma; r 150,000-250,000Rp; 📶) On the little lane just east of Jl Sukma, you'll find four tidy rooms in a classic family compound. It's bungalow-style and you'll enjoy privacy and serenity. Rooms in Ubud don't come much cheaper.

Sania's House GUESTHOUSE $
(Darma Yogi Guest House; Map p164; ☎0361-975535; sania_house@yahoo.com; Jl Karna 7; r with fan 300,000-350,000Rp, r with air-con 450,000-500,000Rp; @📶🏊) A large pool and garden setting are the main attractions at this

ℹ REFILL YOUR WATER BOTTLE

The number of plastic water bottles emptied in Bali's tropical heat daily and then tossed in the trash is colossal. In Ubud there are a few places where you can refill your water bottle (plastic or reusable) for a small fee, usually 3000Rp for a large bottle, 2000Rp for a small bottle. The water is the same Aqua brand that is preferred locally and you'll be helping to preserve Bali's beauty, one plastic bottle at a time. A good central location is Pondok Pekak Library & Learning Centre (p171).

compound off the Ubud Market. The 27 rooms are simple but pleasant; some have air-con and all are closely spaced. There's an on-site restaurant and a clutch of souvenir stalls at the compound entrance.

Eka's Homestay HOMESTAY **$**
(Map p164; 0813 3957 1134; Jl Sriwedari 8; s 150,000-180,000Rp, d 200,000-250,000Rp;) Eka's is the home of Wayan Pasek Sucipta, a teacher of Balinese music, and the melodious tones of gamelan can often be heard in his family compound. Accommodation is in seven simple bungalows. A one-hour gamelan lesson with Wayan costs 100,000Rp.

Raka House GUESTHOUSE **$**
(Map p164; 0361-976081; Jl Maruti; r 350,000-450,000Rp;) Eight simple bungalow-style rooms cluster at the back of a compact family compound in the very centre of town. You can soak your toes in a small trapezoidal plunge pool. Excellent value

Ina Inn GUESTHOUSE **$**
(Map p164; 0361-971093; http://inainnubud.com; Jl Bisma; r 300,000-400,000Rp;) Stroll the thickly planted grounds and enjoy views across Ubud and the rice fields from the elevated pool. The 12 rooms (some fan-cooled) are basic but clean and comfy.

Biangs HOMESTAY **$**
(Map p164; 0361 976520; wah_oebued@yahoo.com; Jl Sukma 28; s 100,000-200,000Rp, d 200,00-300,000Rp, d with air-con 300,000Rp;) In a little garden, this homestay has six worn but clean rooms with simple bathrooms; only one has air-con. The best are at the rear of the compound, overlooking the forest. Three generations of the family live here ('Biangs' means 'mama'), and they make guests feel welcome.

Artotel Haniman Ubud HOTEL **$$**
(Map p164; 0361-9083470; www.artotelindonesia.com/haniman-ubud; Jl Jatayu Ubud; r from 1,050,000Rp;) The latest offering from Indonesia's hip Artotel chain, this place offers 22 good-size studios (20, 30 and 40 sq m) with amenities including a coffee machine. There's a small pool, a spa and a complimentary shuttle into central Ubud. Breakfast is served in the Full Circle (p184) cafe at the front of the hotel – you'll enjoy the best coffee in town here.

Ladera Villa Ubud HOTEL **$$**
(Map p164; 0361-978127; Jl Bisma 25; r from 950,000Rp, villa from 1,400,000Rp;) Close to the central Ubud action but far enough removed to offer a tranquil retreat, this hotel offers an array of well-equipped rooms and more-luxurious villas; the villas have private pools and basic kitchens. Attentive service; excellent value.

Sama's Cottages GUESTHOUSE **$$**
(Map p164; 0361-973481; www.samascottagesubud.com; Jl Bisma; bungalow with fan/air-con from 495,000/585,000Rp, villa from 2,200,000Rp;) Terraced down a hill, this lovely little hideaway has a mix of rooms, cottages and pool villas, all with a pleasing veneer of Balinese style. The property feels like a jungle oasis, particularly around the pool and meditation *bale* (pavilion).

Puri Saraswati Bungalows HOTEL **$$**
(Map p164; 0361-975164; www.purisaraswatiubud.com; Jl Raya Ubud; r 700,000-1,000,000Rp;) This midrange choice is centrally located and has lovely gardens that open onto the Ubud Water Palace. Its bungalow-style rooms are simply furnished but quite attractive; beds could be better. Its quiet at most times of the day, but in the early evening the dance performance next door is noisy.

Sri Bungalows GUESTHOUSE **$$**
(Map p164; 0361-975394; www.sribungalowsubud.com; Monkey Forest Rd; r 620,000-950,000Rp, ste 1,400,000Rp, f 1,900,000Rp;) Surprisingly tranquil considering its central location, this friendly place has 49 rooms in five categories – the super deluxe and suite rooms look over rice fields and are the best choices, although the suites are slightly overpriced. Wi-fi in communal areas only.

Padma Ubud Retreat GUESTHOUSE **$$**
(Map p164; 0821 4419 5910, 0361-977247; www.padmaubud.com; Jl Kajeng 13; r 350,000-600,000Rp;) Located at the rear of the family home and workplace of local artist Nyoman Sudiarsa, this guesthouse in a modern three-storey building offers 12 rooms in two categories – superior rooms have fans, Padma rooms have air-con. Some of the rooms are up six flights of stairs. The emerald-green pool in the garden is directly in front of the ground-floor rooms.

Oka Wati Hotel GUESTHOUSE **$$**
(Map p164; 0361-973386; www.okawatihotel.com; off Monkey Forest Rd; r US$49-100, f US$60-79;) Owner Oka Wati is a lovely lady and guests inevitably enjoy her hospitality. The 20 rooms have terraces or balconies, where there's always a thermos of tea available; those in the modern building are more comfortable, but the older bunga-

OFF THE BEATEN TRACK

PEJENG

Located 5km east of central Ubud, the village of Pejeng was the capital of the Balinese Pejeng kingdom for a short period between Javanese invasions. It collapsed in 1343, when the Majapahits defeated King Dalem Bedaulu.

Pura Penataran Sasih (Jl Raya Tampaksiring; 20,000Rp; ⏲7am-5pm) This was once the state temple of the Pejeng kingdom. In the inner courtyard, high up in a pavilion and difficult to see, is the huge bronze drum known as the Fallen Moon of Pejeng. The hourglass-shaped drum is 186cm long, the largest single-piece cast drum in the world. Estimates of its age vary from 1000 to 2000 years.

Pura Pusering Jagad (Jl Raya Tampaksiring; by donation) Dating from 1329, this temple is visited by young couples who pray at the stone lingam and yoni. Also in the compound is a large stone urn, with elaborate but worn carvings of gods and demons searching for the elixir of life in a depiction of the Mahabharata tale 'Churning the Sea of Milk'. The temple is located on a small paved lane running west of the main road.

Pura Kebo Edan (Jl Raya Tampaksiring; donation requested) Who can resist a sight called Crazy Buffalo Temple? Although not an imposing structure, it's famous for its much-weathered 3m-high statue, known as the Giant of Pejeng, thought to be approximately 700 years old. Details are sketchy, but it may represent Bima, a hero of the Mahabharata, dancing on a dead body, as in a myth related to the Hindu Shiva cult.

Museum Gedung Arca (Museum Arkelogi Gedung Arca; I Raya Tampaksiring; ⏲8am-4pm Mon-Thu, to 4.30pm Fri) FREE This archaeological museum has a reasonable collection of Balinese artefacts. The exhibits in several small buildings include some of Bali's first pottery from near Gilimanuk, and sarcophagi dating from as early as 300 BC. The museum is about 500m north of the Bedulu junction, and is easy to reach by bemo or bicycle. It's a sleepy place and you'll get the most out of it if you come with a knowledgeable guide.

lows are more atmospheric. A tasty breakfast is served in a pavilion next to the pool. Overpriced.

Adipana Bungalow GUESTHOUSE $$
(Map p164; ☎0817 978 8934; www.adipanabungalow.com; Jl Jembawan 27; r incl breakfast 600,000Rp; ❄📶🏊) Each of the six slightly grubby rooms here have a terrace with direct access to the pool or a balcony with views of the guesthouse's bamboo-bedecked backdrop. The kitchen facilities in each unit are handy, but guests report that electricity and wi-fi access can be sporadic.

Lumbung Sari GUESTHOUSE $$
(Map p164; ☎0361-976396; www.lumbungsari.com; Monkey Forest Rd; r 650,000-1,700,000Rp; P❄📶🏊) A nice breakfast *bale* (traditional pavilion) by the pool is the major draw here. The 14 rooms are divided between standard, superior and deluxe categories – the deluxe are next to the pool and are slightly more spacious. It's overpriced.

★**Komaneka at Monkey Forest** BOUTIQUE HOTEL $$$
(Map p164; ☎361-4792518; www.komaneka.com; Monkey Forest Rd; ste 2,300,000-3,100,000Rp, villa 3,800,000-4,200,000Rp; P❄📶🏊) It calls itself a resort, but this place has a boutique feel. The Monkey Forest Rd location may seem strange, but the hotel is hidden in lush gardens overlooking a rice field behind the Komaneka Art Gallery and is remarkably tranquil. Ultra-comfortable suites and villas have an elegant decor and abundant amenities; facilities include a restaurant (mains 79,000Rp to 129,000Rp) and spa.

Adiwana Jembawan RESORT $$$
(Map p164; ☎0361-9083289; www.adiwanahotels.com/adiwanaresortjembawan; Jl Jembawan; r 2,200,000-5,000,000Rp, ste 5,000,000-7,000,000Rp; P❄📶🏊) A tranquil pocket in the midst of central Ubud's bustle, this resort opened in 2016 and has settled seamlessly into its riverside location. Rooms are large, with excellent amenities. Facilities include a yoga shala (one-hour meditation or yoga class 100,000Rp), two infinity pools, a spa (massages from 450,000Rp) and the stylish Herb Library (p185) restaurant.

Warwick Ibah Luxury Villas HOTEL $$$
(Map p168; ☎0361-974466; www.warwickibah.com; off Jl Raya Campuan; ste/villa from US$190/350; ❄📶🏊) Overlooking the rushing waters and rice-clad hills of the Wos Valley, the Ibah offers refined luxury in 17 spacious, stylish,

FINDING LONG-TERM ACCOMMODATION

There are many houses and flats you can rent or share in the Ubud area. For local information about options, check the noticeboards at Pondok Pekak Library (p171). Also look in the free *Bali Advertiser* (www.baliadvertiser.biz) newspaper and the local website www.banjartamu.org. Prices start at about US$300 a month and climb rapidly as you add amenities.

individual suites and villas that combine ancient and modern details. Each could be a feature in an interior-design magazine. The swimming pool is set into the hillside amid gardens and lavish stone carvings.

Komaneka at Bisma BOUTIQUE HOTEL **$$$**
(Map p168; ☎0361-971933; www.bisma.komaneka.com; Jl Bisma; ste from 2,800,000Rp, f from 4,100,000Rp, villas from 5,500,000Rp; ❄@🛜🏊) Set well back in the rice fields near the river valley, this resort has a heavy overlay of Bali style. Accommodation ranges from suites to large three-bedroom villas. The compound itself is quite beautiful, with a long lap pool as the focal point. Facilities include a spa, restaurant, bar, gym and jogging track.

Bisma Eight DESIGN HOTEL **$$$**
(Bisma 8, Map p164; ☎0361-4792888; www.bisma-eight.com; Jl Bisma 8; ste 3,000,000-9,000,000Rp; P❄🛜🏊) Sleek Singapore style has arrived in Ubud courtesy of this 2018 hotel opening. There's loads to like, including a spectacular infinity pool, a hip restaurant (mains 140,000Rp to 350,000Rp) and a complimentary activity programme (cooking classes, yoga, cycling). Guest suites have ultra-comfortable beds, good reading lights and swish bathrooms featuring a Japanese tub and separate shower. Book directly to enjoy perks such as afternoon tea.

South Ubud

★Swasti Eco Cottages GUESTHOUSE **$$**
(Map p168; ☎0361-974079; www.baliswasti.com; Jl Nyuh Bulan; r with fan/air-con from 770,000/880,000Rp; ❄@🛜🏊) 🍃 A five-minute walk from the south entrance to the Monkey Forest, this compound has large grounds that feature an organic garden (produce is used in the cafe), a pool, spa and yoga shala. Some rooms are in simple two-storey blocks; others are in traditionally styled houses. Yoga and meditation classes are available.

Alam Indah HOTEL **$$**
(Map p168; ☎0361-974629; www.alamindahbali.com; Jl Nyuh Bulan; r 1,000,000-1,600,000Rp; ❄🛜🏊) Just south of the Monkey Forest, this spacious and tranquil resort has 16 rooms that are beautifully finished in natural materials to traditional designs. The Wos Valley views are entrancing, especially from the multilevel pool area. There's a free shuttle into central Ubud.

Sapodilla HOTEL **$$**
(Map p168; ☎0361-981596; https://sapodillaubud.com; Jl Raya Pengosekan; r/ste 1,200,000/1,700,000Rp) One of Ubud's new crop of boutique-style guesthouses, Sapodilla is notable for its large, stylishly presented rooms and its high levels of service – expect free on-demand shuttle rides to the centre, afternoon tea and plenty of fluffy towels to lay on the sun lounges arranged alongside the emerald-green pool. Request a suite or upstairs room, as these offer more privacy.

Kertiyasa Bungalows HOTEL **$$**
(Map p168; ☎0361-971377; www.kertiyasabungalow.com; Jl Nyuh Bulan 10; r 430,000-950,000Rp; P❄🛜🏊) Set in a quiet location, this well-maintained hotel offers well-sized rooms with excellent amenities (kettle, satellite TV, free minibar). Facilities include a large pool and a restaurant. Room rates can vary dramatically, so shop around.

Agung Raka BOUTIQUE HOTEL **$$**
(Map p168; ☎0361-975757; www.baliagungrakaresort.com; Jl Raya Pengosekan; r from US$70, villa from US$140; P❄🛜🏊) This 43-room slightly worn hotel sprawls out across picture-perfect rice fields just south of the centre of Ubud. Rooms are large and suitably Balinese in motif but the real stars are the bungalow-style villas set back on a rice terrace amid palm trees. You'll enjoy a night-time symphony of bugs and birds. Services include a shuttle to the town centre.

Tegal Sari HOTEL **$$**
(Map p168; ☎0361-973318; www.tegalsari-ubud.com; Jl Raya Pengosekan; r from 350,000Rp, ste from 1,350,000Rp, villa 1,550,000Rp; ❄@🛜🏊) Though literally a stone's throw from the hectic main road, here rice fields (complete with ducks) miraculously materialise. Huge rooms and suites with a chic contemporary decor are in new brick buildings, and there

are also two particularly attractive villas. All are well-equipped. Facilities include a yoga space, and there's a complimentary shuttle into the town centre.

Saren Indah Hotel HOTEL $$
(Map p168; ☎0361-971471; Jl Nyuh Bulan; r from 650,000Rp;) South of the Monkey Forest (you may be joined by a monkey visitor on your balcony), this small hotel sits in the middle of rice fields – be sure to get a 2nd-floor room to enjoy the views. Rooms have classic Balinese charm; some are small, so it's worth upgrading.

ARMA Resort HOTEL $$$
(Map p168; ☎0361-976659; www.armabali.com; Jl Raya Pengosekan; r from US$90, villas from US$185;) Get full Balinese cultural immersion at the hotel enclave of the ARMA cultural compound. Accommodation is provided in modern, well-equipped rooms and in elegant villas that have their own pool.

West Ubud

Santra Putra HOMESTAY $
(Map p168; ☎0361-977810, 0812 8109 9940; www.santraputra.com; Jl Pacekan 18, Penestanan; r 350,000-500,000Rp;) Owned by artist I Wayan Karja – whose studio-gallery (p173) is also on-site – this homestay in the village of Penestanan has 19 rooms that are slowly undergoing renovation. The newly renovated versions have queen-sized beds, outdoor bathrooms and terraces with small outdoor kitchen. Breakfast is enjoyed at a large communal table.

Roam DESIGN HOTEL $$
(Map p168; ☎0800 853 7626, 0361-479 2884; www.roam.co/places/ubud; Jl Raya Penestanan; r per night/week US$98/550;) This hipster haunt behind the Alchemy cafe (p188) has a classic motel configuration overlaid with rock-and-roll panache. The 24 rooms are set up for global nomads, offering stylish decor, good beds, small fridges and fast wi-fi. Facilities include a communal kitchen and laundry, central pool, rooftop co-working space and yoga studio. Minimum three-night stay.

Hotel Tjampuhan HOTEL $$
(Map p168; ☎0361-975368; www.tjampuhan-bali.com; Jl Raya Campuan, Campuan; r 1,100,000-1,950,000Rp;) This venerable 67-room place overlooks the confluence of Sungai Wos and Campuan. The influential German artist Walter Spies lived here in the 1930s, and his former home, which sleeps four people, is part of the hotel. Bungalow-style units spill down the hill and enjoy mesmerising valley and temple views. Facilities include two pools, a spa and restaurant.

★Mandapa RESORT $$$
(☎0361-4792777; www.ritzcarlton.com; Jl Kedewatan, Kedewatan; ste US$600-900, villa US$1000-5000Rp;) Set in a spectacular river valley enclosed by rice fields, this stunning Ritz Carlton resort is the size of a small village. It's replete with facilities – the luxe spa (p169) and Kubu (p189) restaurant are particularly impressive. Guests are offered a programme of 17 complimentary daily activities including yoga, aqua aerobics and a kids club. Suites and villas are large and gorgeous.

★Bambu Indah RESORT $$$
(☎0361-977922; www.bambuindah.com; Jl Banjar Baung; r US$95-495, 2-bedroom house US$645-695;) A labour of love by expat entrepreneurs John and Cynthia Hardy, this eco-resort on a ridge near the Sungai Ayung offers accommodation in 100-year-old Javanese wooden houses and new, quite extraordinary, structures made from natural materials. Some are simple, others luxurious; all are super stylish. Facilities include tiers of natural swimming pools, an organic restaurant and massage pods.

Guests are offered a free twice-daily shuttle service into central Ubud. The resort recycles and composts waste, filters water rather than using plastic bottles, and uses lava stones and a vegetation regeneration zone to naturally cleanse, filter and oxygenate the water in the hotel's swimming pools.

★Como Uma Ubud BOUTIQUE HOTEL $$$
(Map p168; ☎0361-972448; www.comohotels.com; Jl Raya Sanggingan; r US$290-320, villa US$580-610;) A celebration of contemporary Balinese style, this Australian-owned property is one of the few accommodation options in Ubud that can rightfully claim a boutique tag. The 46 rooms come in a variety of sizes but all are attractive and have good amenities; bathrooms are particularly nice. Facilities include an infinity pool, pool bar, spa, yoga pavilion and excellent Italian restaurant (p188).

Amandari HOTEL $$$
(☎0361-975333; www.amanresorts.com; Jl Raya Kedewatan; ste US$700-2400, villa US$4200-4500;) Luxurious Amandari does everything with the charm and grace of a classical Balinese dancer. Superb views

BALI'S TRADITIONAL HEALERS

Bali's traditional healers, known as *balian* (*dukun* on Lombok), play an important part in Bali's culture by treating physical and mental illness, removing spells and channelling information from the ancestors. Numbering about 8000, *balian* are the ultimate in community medicine, making a commitment to serve their communities and turning no one away.

In the past decade, this system has come under stress in some areas due to the attention brought by the book and film phenomenon *Eat, Pray, Love*. Curious tourists are turning up in village compounds, taking the *balian's* time and attention from the ill. However, that doesn't mean you shouldn't visit a *balian* if you're geniunely curious. Just do so in a manner that befits the experience: gently.

Consider the following before a visit.

- Make an appointment before visiting a *balian*.
- Know that English is rarely spoken.
- Dress respectfully (long trousers and a shirt, better yet a sarong and sash).
- Women should not be menstruating.
- Never point your feet at the healer.
- Bring an offering into which you have tucked the consulting fee, which will average about 250,000Rp per person.
- Understand what you're getting into: your treatment will be very public and probably painful. It may include deep-tissue massage, being poked with sharp sticks or having chewed herbs spat on you.

Finding a *balian* can take some work. Ask at your hotel, which can probably help with making an appointment and providing a suitable offering for stashing your fee. Or consider getting a referral from Made Surya (p169), who is an authority on Bali's traditional healers and offers one- and two-day intensive workshops on healing, magic, traditional systems and history, which include visits to authentic *balian*. His website is an excellent resource on visiting healers in Bali and he can also select an appropriate *balian* for you to visit and accompany you there as liaison and translator.

Some Western medical professionals question whether serious medical issues can be resolved by this type of healing, and patients should see a traditional healer in conjunction with a Western doctor if their ailment is serious.

over the green river valley – the 30m green-tiled swimming pool seems to drop right over the edge – are just some of the inducements. The 30 private pavilions (some with their own pools) are extremely comfortable and complimentary activities include yoga classes and afternoon tea. Facilities include a restaurant (mains 180,000Rp to 390,000Rp), spa, gym and tennis court.

Four Seasons Resort HOTEL **$$$**
(Map p168; ☎0361-977577; www.fourseasons.com; Sayan; ste from US$500, villas from US$850; ❄@🛜≋) Set below the valley rim, the curved open-air reception area looks like a Cinerama screen of Ubud beauty. Many villas have private pools and all share the same amazing views and striking modern design. At night you hear just the water rushing below from any of the 60 units (each of which is very sizeable).

Villa Nirvana HOTEL **$$$**
(Map p168; ☎0361-979419; www.villanirvanabali.com; Jl Raya Penestanan Kaja, Penestanan; villas 1,200,000-2,500,000Rp; P❄🛜≋) Designed by local architect Awan Sukhro Edhi, this 12-villa compound is a serene retreat. Modern villas set in garden surrounds have either one or two bedrooms; six have private pools. Facilities include a spa and restaurant. The location is a reasonable distance from central Ubud, but can be walked.

East Ubud

Omah Apik HOTEL **$$**
(☎0361-944324; www.omah-apik.com; Jl Kenyem Bulan, Pejeng; r 700,000-1,100,000Rp, ste 1,100,000-1,400,000Rp; P❄🛜≋) The name means 'Beautiful Home', and this tranquil family-run hotel secreted in rice fields east of Ubud does indeed have a beautiful set-

ting. The place is looking a bit faded, but the rooms have a simple but stylish decor and are very comfortable. Breakfast is fine, but our advice is to eat other meals elsewhere.

Maya Ubud HOTEL $$$
(☎0361-977888; www.mayaubud.com; Jl Gunung Sari, Peliatan; r/villa from US$200/250; P ❄ @ 📶 🏊) Located in a river valley amidst the rice fields of Peliatan, 2km from the centre of town, this huge resort was built in 2001 and is looking a bit dated; it will benefit from a planned renovation. The riverside spa, cafe and swimming pool are major draws, but are a reasonable distance from most rooms and villas. Other facilities include a gym, yoga studio and tennis court.

North Ubud

Bali Asli Lodge HOMESTAY $
(Map p168; ☎0361-970537; www.baliaslilodge.com; Jl Suweta; r 250,000-300,000Rp; 📶) Escape the central Ubud hubbub here. Made and Ketut are your friendly hosts, and their five rooms are in traditional Balinese stone-and-brick houses set in verdant gardens; interiors are clean and comfy. There are terraces where you can let the hours pass, and Made will cook meals on request. Town is a 15-minute walk away. Fabulous value.

Ubud Sari Health Resort SPA HOTEL $$
(Map p168; ☎0361-974393; www.ubudsari.com; Jl Kajeng; r US$75-90; ❄ 📶 🏊) Overlooking a bubbling stream and surrounded by forest, the 21 rooms at this alternative health treatment centre are popular – book well ahead of your visit. The on-site cafe serves organic vegetarian fare and there's an on-site wellness centre offering a big menu of services.

Ketut's Place HOMESTAY $$
(Map p168; ☎0361-975304; Jl Suweta 40; r with fan/air-con from 500,000/700,000Rp; ❄ 📶 🏊) A step up from the usual homestay, the 16 rooms here are well-equipped and have river-valley and garden views. They range from basic with fans to deluxe versions with air-con and bathtubs.

Wapa di Ume RESORT $$$
(Map p168; ☎0361-973178; www.wapadiume.com; Jl Suweta; r from 2,000,000Rp, ste from 2,700,000Rp, villas from 3,400,000Rp; ❄ @ 📶 🏊) Located a gentle 2.5km uphill from the centre, this elegant compound enjoys engrossing verdant views across rice fields. New and old styles mix in the 33 large units; go for a villa with a view. Service is assured yet relaxed. Listening to gamelan practice echoing across the fields at night is quite magical.

Eating

Ubud's cafes and restaurants are some of the best in Bali. Local and expat chefs produce a bounty of authentic Balinese dishes, plus inventive Asian and other international cuisines. Healthy menus abound. Cafes with good coffee seem as common as frangipani blossoms. Be sure to be seated by 9pm or your options will narrow rapidly. Book dinner tables in high season.

Central Ubud

★ **Kafe** CAFE $
(Map p164; ☎0361-479 2078; www.kafe-bali.com; Jl Hanoman 44; sandwiches & wraps 65,000-89,000Rp, mains 39,000-97,000Rp; ⏰7am-11pm; 📶 ✍) 🌿 This is the type of place that Ubud does particularly well. Attractive decor, laid-back vibe, friendly staff and healthy food are the hallmarks, and together they form a tempting package. The huge organic menu has something for most tastes, with a huge range of vegan, veggie and raw offerings with Balinese, Indonesian, Indian and Mexican accents. Good value.

Liap Liap INDONESIAN $
(Map p164; ☎0361-9080800; www.liapliap.com; Monkey Forest Rd; satays 35,000-65,000Rp; ⏰10am-11pm) The name references the sound that charcoal embers make as they heat up, paying tribute to the technique that chef Mandif Warokka uses when grilling the spicy Indonesian dishes that dominate the menu at this contemporary warung. Watch the grilling action in the front window while sipping a cocktail drawn from a long list of classics and house signatures.

Mamma Mia PIZZA $
(Map p164; ☎0361-976397; www.facebook.com/MammaMiaBali; Jl Hanoman 36; pizzas 28,000-85,000Rp, pastas 50,000-75,000Rp; ⏰9am-11pm) It can be difficult to source a decent pizza in Ubud (there are plenty of sub-par versions on offer), so the existence of Mamma Mia is something to celebrate. The Roman-style thin-base pizzas are cooked in a wood-fired oven and given the full range of classic toppings. Enjoy one with a beer, as they do in Rome. Free delivery, too.

Warung Little India INDIAN $
(Map p164; ☎0819 9962 4555; www.facebook.com/Warung-Little-India-1388656398032001; Jl Sukma 36; mains 35,000-75,000Rp, thalis

55,000-85,000Rp; ⌚10am-10pm) Run by the delightful Siti, this spice-scented Indian restaurant is decked out in vintage Bollywood posters and diners are serenaded by a soundtrack of Hindi pop. Its Punjabi-style thalis, samosas and biriyanis are all delicious. Lunch specials are as cheap as 30,000Rp.

Waroeng Bernadette at Toko Madu INDONESIAN $

(Map p164; ☎0821 4742 4779; Jl Goutama; mains 35,000-75,000Rp; ⌚11am-11pm; 📶) It's not called the 'Home of Rendang' for nothing. The west Sumatran classic dish of long-marinated meats (beef is the true classic, but here there's also a veggie jackfruit variety) is pulled off with colour and flair. Other dishes have a zesty zing missing from lacklustre versions served elsewhere. The elevated dining room is a vision of kitsch.

Mama's Warung INDONESIAN $

(Map p164; ☎0361-977047; www.facebook.com/Mamaswarung; Jl Sukma; mains 30,000-40,000Rp; ⌚8am-10pm; 📝) Ultra-friendly Mama and her retinue cook up Indo classics that are spicy and redolent with garlic. The freshly made peanut sauce for the satay is silky smooth, the fried sambal superb. Many guests enjoy their meals so much they opt to stay in one of the upstairs rooms (single/double 250,000/300,000Rp) on their next visit to Ubud.

Tutmak Cafe CAFE $

(Map p164; ☎0361-975754; www.facebook.com/tutmakubud; Jl Dewi Sita; sandwiches 48,000-65,000Rp, mains 35,000-100,000Rp; ⌚8am-11pm; 📶) This smart, breezy multilevel terrace cafe is a popular choice for a coffee or simple meal. It roasts its own coffee beans, and also serves house-baked bread.

Bali Buda CAFE $

(Map p164; ☎0361-976324; www.balibuda.com; Jl Jembawan 1; mains 38,000-67,000Rp, pizzas 63,000-81,000Rp; ⌚7am-10pm; 📝) This breezy upper-floor place offers a full range of vegetarian *jamu* (health tonics), all-day breakfasts, salads, sandwiches, thin-crust pizzas and gelato. The bulletin board downstairs is packed with idiosyncratic Ubud notices. No alcohol

★Hujon Locale INDONESIAN $$

(Map p164; ☎0813 3972 0306; www.hujanlocale.com; Jl Sriwedari 5; mains 120,000-200,000Rp; ⌚noon-10pm; 📶📝) Chef Will Meyrick is the culinary genius behind Mama San in Seminyak, and his Ubud outpost is just as impressive. The menu delivers traditional Indonesian with modern, creative flair and the results are delicious. The setting within a chic colonial-style two-storey bungalow is casually stylish and cleverly flexible – enjoy cocktails and snacks in the downstairs lounge; lunch and dinner upstairs.

★Watercress CAFE $$

(Map p164; ☎0361-976127; www.watercressubud.com; Monkey Forest Rd; breakfast dishes 45,000-90,000Rp, sandwiches 65,000-75,000Rp, mains 90,000-290,000Rp; ⌚7.30am-11pm; 📶) A young and fashionable crowd flocks to this Aussie-style contemporary cafe to nosh on all-day breakfasts, burgers, sourdough sandwiches, homemade cakes, gourmet salads and more. Drink good coffee during the day and cocktails at night (happy hour daily 5pm to 7pm, live music Friday).

★Full Circle CAFE $$

(Map p164; ☎0361-982638; www.fullcirclebyexpatroasters.com; Jl Jatayu; breakfast dishes 35,000-100,000Rp, mains 65,000-130,000Rp; ⌚7am-11pm; ❄📶📝) Australian-style cafe society is represented by a few popular businesses here in Ubud, and this is its most recent – and sleek – incarnation. Though it's in a slightly out-of-the-way location, it's worth making the trek to enjoy Ubud's best coffee (Expat Roasters beans), all-day brekkies featuring sourdough from Starter Lab bakery and cafe favourites including smashed avocado, sushi bowls and burgers. Love it.

Nusantara BALINESE $$

(Map p164; ☎0361-972973; www.locavore.co.id/nusantara; 9C Jl Dewi Sita; small plates 60,000-95,000Rp, large plates 80,000-225,000Rp; ⌚6-9.30pm Mon, noon-2.30pm & 6-9.30pm Tue-Sun; 📶) Can't score a table at acclaimed Locavore? You might have more luck here at the same team's stylish Indonesian restaurant. Nusantara means 'archipelago', and the menu draws inspiration from the country's multiple islands in its fresh, highly spiced offerings. The complimentary starter platter is a nice touch, and the daily changing six-dish tasting menu (215,000Rp) is a convenient ordering option.

Earth Cafe & Market VEGETARIAN $$

(Map p164; ☎0361-976546; www.earthcafebali.com; Jl Gotama Selatan; mains 79,000-98,000Rp; ⌚7am-10pm; 📶📝) 🍃 'Eliminate free radicals' is but one of many healthy drinks at this hard-core outpost for organic and macrobiotic vegan dining and drinking. The

ICE CREAM & GELATO

Ubud has been undergoing a gelato and ice cream craze in recent years, which is to everyone's benefit. Top choices for a cone or cup include:

Tukies Coconut Shop (Map p164; ☎0361-9083562; Jl Raya Ubud 14; 1/2 scoops ice cream 28,000/54,000Rp; ⏱9am-10.30pm; ✍) Home to Ubud's best coconut ice cream, which is served topped with shaved coconut and coconut brittle. It's vegan, too. Also sells dried coconut, coconut granola and other coconut-y delights.

Gelato Secrets (www.gelatosecrets.com; gelato 33,000-66,000Rp; ⏱9am-11.30pm) Local fruits and spices (think dragonfruit cinnamon or cashew black sesame) are used to make the delicious gelato sold by this popular chain. There are branches on Monkey Forest Road (Map p164) and Jl Raya Ubud (Map p164).

Gaya Gelato (Map p164; ☎0361-979252; www.facebook.com/gayagelato; Jl Raya Ubud; small gelato 30,000Rp; ⏱10am-10pm) International chain selling fresh flavours including lemongrass, passion fruit, durian and tamarillo, as well as classics such as pistachio and chocolate.

huge menu has a plethora of soups, salads and platters that are heavy on Med flavours, and there are loads of raw options in it. There's a market on the main floor, and a handy delivery service.

Herb Library BALINESE $$
(Map p164; ☎0361-9083289; www.facebook.com/herblibrarybali; Jl Jembawan; mains 80,000-105,000Rp; ⏱7.30am-10.30pm; 📶✍) This *bale* (open-sided pavilion) in front of the Adiwana Resort Jembawan is an exemplar of Bali chic, with an attractive colour scheme, well-spaced tables, slowly revolving ceiling fans and comfortable seating. The menu is predominantly plant based and dishes are notable for their freshness. Service is excellent, too.

Spice INDONESIAN $$
(Map p164; ☎0361-479 2420; www.spicebali.com; Jl Raya Ubud 23; small plates 70,000-110,000Rp, mains 70,000-140,000Rp; ⏱11am-11pm; ❄📶👪) Well-known Ubud restaurateur Chris Salans is the brains behind this air-conditioned gastrobar on the town's main street. It's a good choice for a late afternoon drink and snack (sliders, dumplings, crab cake, carpaccio), but also serves a crowd-pleasing array of Indonesian and Asian dishes, including laksa and pork ribs. The kids menu (99,000Rp) is a winner.

Fair Warung Balé INTERNATIONAL $$
(Map p164; ☎0361-975370; www.fairfuturefoundation.org; Jl Sriwedari 6; mains 50,000-110,000Rp; ⏱11am-10pm; ✍) 🍃 Run by the Swiss-based NGO, Fair Future Foundation, this eatery donates 100% of its profit towards healthcare in the local community. Food ranges from local curries to freshly baked baguettes with tuna tartare.

Il Giardino ITALIAN $$
(Map p164; ☎0823 3988 3511; www.ilgiardinobali.com; Jl Kajeng 3, Siti Bungalows; pizzas 60,000-150,000Rp, pastas 69,000-135,000Rp; ⏱4-10.30pm; 📶) Located in the grounds of the studio/residence of the late Dutch painter Han Snel, this romantic outdoor Italian restaurant has a beautiful setting overlooking a lily pond. Head here for wood-fired pizzas, homemade pastas and rustic Italian mains.

Black Beach ITALIAN $$
(Map p164; ☎0361-971353; www.blackbeach.asia; Jl Hanoman 5; pizzas 48,000-90,000Rp, pastas 26,000-91,000Rp; ⏱8am-10.30pm; 📶✍) The thin-crust pizzas bubble as they emerge from the busy oven here. If that doesn't draw your attention, the tasty pasta might. Views from the upstairs dining area are nice but what really draws in the intelligentsia are the regular Wednesday and Thursday night screenings of documentary art-house movies on the terrace. Happy hour applies between 5pm and 7pm.

Melting Wok ASIAN $$
(Map p164; ☎0821 4417 4906; meltingwokwarung@gmail.com; Jl Goutama 13; mains 50,000-72,000Rp; ⏱10am-10pm Tue-Sun) Pan-Asian fare pleases the masses at this very popular open-air restaurant on the Goutama strip. Curries, noodle dishes, tempe and a lot more fill a menu that makes decisions tough. Desserts take on a bit of colonial flavour: French accents abound. Booking advised; cash only.

GROCERY & PRODUCE SHOPPING

There's a good range of local produce markets, organic food stores and Western-style supermarkets in Ubud, making self-catering here an easy proposition. Good choices include the following:

Produce Market (Map p164; Jl Raya Ubud; ⏲6am-1pm) Ubud's traditional produce market is a multilevel carnival of tropical foods and worth exploring despite the clamouring tourist hordes. It's in the back corner of the Pasar Seni.

Bali Buda Shop (Map p164; www.balibuda.com; Jl Raya Ubud; ⏲7am-10pm) Great source for organic produce and groceries; its baked goods are excellent.

Earth Cafe & Market (Map p164; ☎0361-976546; Jl Gotama Selatan; ⏲7am-10pm) Organic and macrobiotic vegan produce. There's a handy delivery service.

Bintang Supermarket (Map p168; ☎0361-972972; www.bintangsupermarket.com; Jl Raya Sanggingan; ⏲8am-10pm) In west Ubud. Sells fresh produce and alcohol as well as usual supermarket items.

Delta Dewata (Map p164; ☎0361-973049; Jl Raya Andong 14; ⏲8am-10pm) Supermarket in east Ubud; stocks a large range of food and other essentials.

Coco Supermarket (Map p164; Jl Raya Pengosekan; ⏲7am-10pm) In south Ubud; stocks a good range of grocery items, fresh produce and alcohol.

Ubud Organic Market (Ubud Pasar Organik; Map p168; www.ubudorganicmarket.com; ⏲9am-2pm Sat) Farmers market operating on Saturdays on the front porch of Pizza Bagus on Jl Raya Pengosekan.

Bebek Bengil INDONESIAN $$
(Dirty Duck Diner; Map p164; ☎0361-975489; www.bebekbengil.co.id/en; Jl Hanoman; half duck 130,000Rp; ⏲10am-11pm; 📶) This famous place is hugely popular for one reason: its crispy Balinese duck, which is marinated for 36 hours in spices, steamed and then fried. Those who don't enjoy fried food can enjoy a duck salad, duck spring rolls or duck satay. You'll eat in a huge open-air dining pavilion.

Locavore to Go CAFE $$
(Map p164; ☎0361-9080757; www.locavore.co.id/togo; Jl Dewi Sita 108; breakfast dishes 30,000-79,000Rp, sandwiches 79,000-129,000Rp; ⏲8.30am-7pm Mon-Sat; 📶) From the team behind foodie favourite Locavore, this cafe attached to a butcher shop offers creative breakfast choices (order the waffle with fried duck egg, hollandaise, bacon and chervil for an indulgent start to the day) and an array of sandwiches and wraps – think banh mi, falafel, pulled-pork and burgers – for lunch. It's tiny, so you may need to queue.

Kebun MEDITERRANEAN $$
(Map p164; ☎0361-972490; www.kebunbistro.com; Jl Hanoman 44; mains 65,000-155,000Rp; ⏲11am-11pm Mon-Fri, from 9am Sat & Sun; 📶) Paris meets Ubud at this charming bistro and it's a good match. Your choice from the substantial cocktail and wine lists can be paired with French- and Italian-accented dishes large and small. Dine or sip a drink in the bar area, or claim a table on the greenery-screened terrace.

Clear FUSION $$
(Map p164; ☎0878 6219 7585, 0361-889 4437; www.clearcafebali.com; Jl Hanoman 8; meals US$4-15; ⏲8am-10pm; 📶🖉) Known for its theatrical decor and crowd pleasing menu, Clear is one of Ubud's most popular eateries. The relentlessly healthy dishes feature local produce and have artful presentation; menu influences range from Japan (sushi) to Mexico (tacos, quesadillas), with loads of veggie and vegan options. No alcohol, but the huge choice of fruit smoothies, tonic, juices and milkshakes compensates. Cash only.

Juice Ja Café CAFE $$
(Map p164; ☎0361-971056; www.facebook.com/juicejacafe; Jl Dewi Sita; mains 55,000-95,000Rp; ⏲7am-11pm; 📶) 🍃 Superfoods and organic fruits and vegetables from the cafe's own farm are used to excellent effect here. The menu holds lots of joy for vegans, vegetarians and those who are gluten-free, and all of the dishes, shakes and fresh juices are beautifully presented. The home-made gelato in a charcoal cone is a popular finale. Indoor and balcony seating.

Casa Luna INDONESIAN $$
(Map p164; ☎0361-977409; www.casalunabali.com; Jl Raya Ubud; mains 50,000-125,000Rp; ⏲8am-11pm; 🅿📶) One of the first contemporary-

chic eateries to open in Ubud, Casa Luna has sadly become a victim of its own success. The interior is still stylish, but our recent visits have featured disappointing meals and abrupt service. Its cooking school remains well-regarded, and the energy of owner Janet DeNeefe, a force behind the Ubud writers and food festivals, is admirable.

Warung Babi Guling BALINESE $$
(Ibu Oka 3; Map p164; 0361-976345; Jl Tegal Sari; set meal 70,000Rp; 11am-6pm;) Once a resolutely local warung with few frills, this joint was 'discovered' by both Rick Stein and Anthony Bourdain, and has now moved to larger premises with river valley views so as to cater to tourists. It's famous for one dish: Balinese-style roast *babi guling* (suckling pig). The set meal comes with pork, rice and soup.

Three Monkeys INTERNATIONAL $$
(Map p164; 0361-975554; www.threemonkeyscafebali.com; Monkey Forest Rd; mains 59,000-125,000Rp; 7am-11pm;) The setting here is quite magical, with an ornamental koi pond and a rear dining area overlooking a little rice field. The food isn't as impressive, alas – you might do better to visit for a coffee during the day or a cocktail in the evening.

Kafe Batan Waru INDONESIAN $$
(Map p164; 0361-977528; www.batanwaru.com; Jl Dewi Sita; small plates 35,000-65,000Rp, mains 55,000-175,000Rp; 8am-11pm;) This cafe serves consistently good Indonesian food. Tired of *mie goreng* made from instant noodles? With noodles made fresh daily, this version celebrates a lost art. Western dishes include sandwiches and salads. *Bebek betutu* (smoked duck) and *babi guling* can be ordered in advance.

★Pica SOUTH AMERICAN $$$
(Map p164; 0361-971660; www.facebook.com/PicaSouthAmericanKitchen; Jl Dewi Sita; mains 170,000-330,000Rp; 6-10pm Tue-Sun;) Much-acclaimed, the contemporary South American cuisine served at this small restaurant is one of Ubud's culinary highlights. From the open kitchen, dishes making creative use of meat and fish issue forth – be sure to ask about daily specials. Ordering the delectable tre leche dessert should be mandatory. Bookings advisable.

★Locavore FUSION $$$
(Map p164; 0361-977733; www.restaurantlocavore.com; Jl Dewi Sita; 5-course menu 675,000-775,000Rp, 7-course menu 775,000-875,000Rp; 6.30-9pm Mon, noon-2pm & 6.30-9pm Tue-Sat;) Foodies book months in advance to sample the tasting menus at this temple to modern gastronomy. Flavours are fresh, bold and often unorthodox; presentation is exquisite. However, the noisy theatre of the open kitchen ('Yes chef!') can be annoying, and service sometimes oversteps from attentive to obtrusive.

South Ubud

Swasti Beloved Cafe INTERNATIONAL $
(Map p168; 0361-974079; www.baliswasti.com; Jl Nyuh Bulan; mains 40,000-65,000Rp; 8am-10pm;) This cafe attached to Swasti Eco Cottages (p180) is reason enough to take a stroll through the Monkey Forest. Indonesian and Western dishes prepared from the large in-house organic garden are fresh and tasty. Have a smoothie or glass of fresh juice with the beloved fondant au chocolat or raw mango cheesecake. Plenty of vegan options, but no alcohol.

Pitri Minang INDONESIAN $
(Map p168; 0812 3690 5732; Jl Cok Gede Rai; meals from 15,000Rp; 7am-late) In the heart of the unadorned neighbourhood of Peliatan, this open-fronted warung serves up fresh and tasty Padang-style meals. Choose from the variety of prepared mains and settle down for a fine local meal in view of a historic old banyan tree.

Warung Pojok INDONESIAN $
(Map p168; 0361-749 4535; Jl Nyuh Bulan; mains 20,000-40,000Rp; 8am-10pm;) This buzzing corner cafe has a serene spot overlooking a football field. Besides plenty of rice and noodle dishes, there are lots of veggie options, lassies and juices.

Taco Casa MEXICAN $$
(Map p168; 0812 2422 2357; www.tacocasabali.com; Jl Raya Pengosekan; tacos 62,000-84,000Rp; 11am-10pm) Sure, Mexico is almost exactly on the opposite side of the globe, but its culinary delights are popular here in Bali. Tasty versions of burritos, tacos and more have just the right mix of heat and spice. It delivers.

Pizza Bagus PIZZA $$
(Map p168; 0361-978520; www.pizzabagus.com; Jl Raya Pengosekan; pizzas 28,000-74,000Rp, pastas 40,000-85,000Rp; 9am-10pm;) Thin-crust pizzas, bowls of pasta and sandwiches are served in this characterless place attached to an organic grocery store. Delivery is available; cash payments only.

West Ubud

Nasi Ayam Kedewatan BALINESE $

(0361-974795; Jl Raya Kedewatan, Kedewatan; mains 25,000-35,000Rp; 8am-6pm) Few locals making the trek up the hill through Sayan pass this Bali version of a roadhouse without stopping. The star is *sate lilit:* chicken is minced, combined with a selection of spices including lemongrass, then moulded onto bamboo skewers and grilled. It's served as part of the *nasi ayam campur* (25,000Rp) or *nasi ayam pisah* (35,000Rp) set meals.

Yellow Flower Cafe INDONESIAN $

(Map p168; 0812 3889 9695; www.facebook.com/Yellow-Flower-Cafe-Ubud-Bali-274160762626728; mains from 59,000Rp; 7.30am-9pm;) A New Age ambience reigns at this cute cafe in Penestanan, just up the stairs and along a greenery-edged path from Jl Raya Campuan. Organic mains include *nasi campur* and there's a good range of health drinks (turmeric, kombucha, chia water) as well as decent coffees. Great views.

Warung Pulau Kelapa INDONESIAN $

(Map p168; 0361-971872; www.facebook.com/warungpulaukelapa; Jl Raya Sanggingan; mains 40,000-85,000Rp; 10am-10pm;) Kelapa serves Indonesian classics plus more unusual dishes from around the archipelago; its vegetarian Rijstafel is made with produce grown in the on-site organic garden and is particularly delicious.

★**Dumbo** VEGETARIAN $$

(Map p168; 0812 3838 9993; www.dumbobali.com; Jl Raya Sanggingan; pizza 80,000-95,000Rp, small plates 55,000-80,000Rp, large plates 85,000-180,000Rp; 9am-11pm;) Music, mixology and Italian food are a particularly good trio, so you'd need to be a dumbo not to eat here, especially as pizzas cooked in a wood-fired oven are also on offer (after 4pm only). Trained bar staff and baristas ensure that the cocktails and coffee are as good as the food, and the DJ's playlist is a winner.

★**Moksa** VEGETARIAN $$

(Map p168; 0813 3977 4787; www.moksaubud.com; Gang Damai, Sayan; mains 40,000-80,000Rp; 10am-8.30pm;) Based at its own permaculture farm, Moksa shows that extraordinary meals can be created with vegetables prepared simply. Half the dishes are raw, half cooked; many are vegan. The setting is bucolic, but the kitchen is state of the art – a fab mix. The approach is via a path through fields: follow the signs from Jl Raya Sayan.

Uma Cucina ITALIAN $$

(Map p168; 0361-972448; www.comohotels.com/en/umaubud/dining/uma-cucina; Como Uma Ubud, Jl Raya Sanggingan; pizzas 100,000-180,000Rp, mains 110,000-240,000Rp; noon-10.30pm Mon-Sat, from 11.30am Sun;) There's lots to like about this Italian restaurant. Its flexible kitchen serves an antipasto set menu at lunch (eight antipasti, 299,000Rp), a filling afternoon tea (200,000Rp) and dinners featuring pizza cooked in a wood-fired oven, handmade pasta, classic Italian mains and delectable desserts. On Sunday the brunch buffet (from 399,000Rp) with its child-friendly entertainment is particularly popular with families.

Alchemy VEGAN $$

(Map p168; 0361-971981; www.facebook.com/AlchemyBali; Jl Raya Penestanan 75; salads 60,000-65,000Rp, mains 55,000-69,000Rp; 7am-9pm;) A prototypical 100% vegan Ubud restaurant, Alchemy offers create-your-own salad and smoothie bowl opportunities, as well as pizzas, Mexican and Japanese dishes, raw vegan ice creams and desserts, cold-pressed juices and a lot more.

There's also an on-site boutique selling herbal toiletries, herbals teas and more.

Elephant VEGETARIAN $$

(Map p168; 0851 0016 1907; www.elephantbali.com; Hotel Taman Indrakila, Jl Raya Sanggingan; mains 70,000-80,000Rp; 8am-9.30pm;) Globally influenced vegetarian dining and gorgeous views across the Sungai Cerik valley are on offer here. Dishes are well seasoned, interesting and attractively plated. The chef strives to use 100% organic and ethically sourced produce. Weekend brunch (8am to 5pm) is particularly popular.

Sari Organik HEALTH FOOD $$

(Map p168; Jl Raya Campuan; mains 55,000-80,000Rp; 8am-8pm) In a beautiful location on a plateau overlooking rice terraces, this cafe in the middle of a big organic farm serves a large menu of healthy food and drink, including raw options. The walk through the rice fields means that at least half the fun is getting here.

Naughty Nuri's BARBECUE $$

(Map p168; 0361-977547; Jl Raya Sanggingan; mains 30,000-180,000Rp; 10.30am-9.30pm) Meats are cooked on a streetside BBQ here, and the pork spare ribs have many fans. Enjoy them with a fresh juice, beer or cocktail.

★Room4Dessert DESSERTS $$$
(R4D; Map p168; ☎0821 4429 3452; www.room4dessert.asia; Jl Raya Sanggingan; tasting dessert & cocktail menu 1,000,000Rp; ⊙5-11pm Tue-Sun) Celebrity chef Will Goldfarb, who hails from the States and gained fame via Netflix's *Chef's Table*, runs what could be a nightclub but is in fact a dessert bar where patrons who book far enough in advance (you'll need to do so at least a month before your visit) can enjoy a decadent nine-course tasting menu matched with cocktails/mocktails/wine. Those who wish to limit themselves to one dessert and a drink are relegated to the rear garden; bookings aren't always required for this option.

★Mozaic FUSION $$$
(Map p168; ☎0361-975768; www.mozaic-bali.com; Jl Raya Sanggingan; lunch tasting menu 500,000-700,000Rp, dinner tasting menu 700,000-1,600,000Rp; ⊙6-9.45pm Mon-Wed, noon-2pm & 6-9.45pm Thu-Sun;) Chef Chris Salans oversees this much-lauded top-end restaurant. Fine French fusion cuisine features on a constantly changing seasonal menu that takes its influences from tropical Asia. Dine in an elegant garden twinkling with romantic lights or an ornate pavilion. Tasting menus are obligatory, unless you wish to limit yourself to tapas in the lounge (from 5pm). Lunch in high season only.

Kubu MEDITERRANEAN $$$
(☎0361-4792777; www.ritzcarlton.com/en/hotels/indonesia/mandapa/dining; Mandapa Resort, Jl Kedewatan, Kedewatan; mains 280,000-500,000Rp, degustation menus 750,000-1,150,000Rp; ⊙6.30-11pm) Resembling a posh version of the Balinese bamboo hut that it is named for, Mandapa's premier restaurant offers a memorable and romantic dining experience. Reserve a table in the main dining area or opt for a private cabana overlooking the Sungai Ayung. Chef Maurizio Bombini's Mediterranean-European cuisine is as excellent as the surrounds and service. Book well in advance.

Drinking & Nightlife

No one comes to Ubud for wild nightlife, although that may slowly be changing. A few bars get lively around sunset and later in the night; still, the venues don't aspire to the extremes of boozy debauchery and clubbing found in Kuta and Seminyak. Most bars close early in Ubud, often by 11pm.

The quality of the coffee served in Ubud's growing number of cafes is good, with many places roasting their own beans and employing expert baristas.

Central Ubud

★Night Rooster COCKTAIL BAR
(Map p164; ☎0361-977733; www.locavore.co.id/nightrooster; Jl Dewi Sita 10B; ⊙4pm-midnight Mon-Sat) From the same folks at Locavore (p187), this neighbouring, second-storey cocktail bar boasts a talented mixologist and some fascinating flavour combos. Inventive cocktails include things such as jackfruit-infused dry gin, homemade bitters and flaming cassia bark. The selection of appetisers and cheese and charcuterie platters make for satisfying pairings.

No Màs BAR
(Map p164; ☎0361-9080800; www.nomasubud.com; Monkey Forest Rd; ⊙5pm-1am) DJs and Latin bands crank the volume up every night at this small bar on one of the town's main strips, and there are occasional theme nights too. It can get hot when the dancing starts, but the pool bar in the rear garden provides a welcome relief.

Food is supplied by next-door Liap Liap (p183).

Seniman Spirits BAR
(Bar Seniman; Map p164; www.senimancoffee.com; Jl Sriwedari; ⊙6pm-midnight) The highly caffeinated masterminds behind the Seniman coffee brand recently opened this bar next to their coffee studio, and it has become one of Ubud's most fashionable drinking dens. Unsurprisingly, espresso martinis are the cocktail of choice.

F.R.E.A.K. Coffee COFFEE
(Map p164; ☎0361-975927; www.facebook.com/freakcoffee; Jl Hanoman 19; ⊙8am-8pm) The name is appropriate here as these people are coffee fanatics. The best Bali beans are hand-selected and then roasted with precision before being brewed with great attention to detail. Enjoy the results at this simple, open-fronted shop, which has a few indoor and streetside tables. Food options include sandwiches (30,000Rp to 40,000Rp).

Coffee Studio Seniman CAFE
(Map p164; ☎0361-972085; www.senimancoffee.com; Jl Sriwedari 5; ⊙8am-10pm;) That 'coffee studio' moniker isn't for show; the baristas here make a point of experimenting with different styles of single-origin coffee. Take a seat on the designer rocker chairs and choose from a menu of pourovers,

syphon, cold brew, Aeropress or espresso using house-roasted Indonesian beans. It's also popular for food (mains 43,000Rp to 111,000Rp). If you enjoy your coffee, consider signing up for a two-hour barista workshop (450,000Rp).

Bar Luna LOUNGE
(Map p164; ☎0361-977409; www.facebook.com/barlunaubud; Jl Raya Ubud; ⏰3-11pm; 📶) The basement bar at Casa Luna hosts a popular jazz club on Sunday evenings from 7.30pm – bookings recommended. On other days, the 5pm happy hour and tasty tapas menu are lures. It's a hive of activity and literary chatter during the Ubud Writers & Readers Festival.

Anomali Coffee COFFEE
(Map p164; Jl Raya Ubud; snacks from 20,000Rp; ⏰7am-11pm; 📶) Local hipsters get their java from this place which is, well, from Java. Indonesia's answer to Starbucks takes its (excellent) coffee seriously and so does the young crowd that gathers here. A relaxed place filled with chatter.

Laughing Buddha LOUNGE
(Map p164; ☎0361-970928; www.facebook.com/laughingbuddhabali; Monkey Forest Rd; ⏰11am-1am; 📶) Head to this popular bar between 8pm and 11pm, when musicians (rock, blues, latin, acoustic and more) entertain the crowd. The kitchen serves Asian bites.

CP Lounge BAR, CLUB
(Map p164; ☎0361-978954; www.cp-lounge.com; Monkey Forest Rd; ⏰8pm-3am) Open til early morning, CP is the place to kick on once everything else has closed. It has garden seating, a tapas menu, live bands and a club with a DJ.

OFF THE BEATEN TRACK

SWEET ORANGE WARUNG

An idyllic location in the midst of a rice field a short walk from the centre of town makes this **warung** (Map p168; ☎0813 3877 8689; www.sweetorangewarung.com; Jl Subak Juwak; ⏰9am-8.30pm) a wonderful spot for a drink or simple meal. You'll be serenaded by water running through the farming channels, birds singing and local children playing. Drinks include French-press coffee, beer and fresh juice.

To get here, take the narrow path to the left of the Museum Puri Lukisan.

Chill Out BAR
(Map p164; ☎0361-741343; Monkey Forest Rd 25; ⏰11am-midnight) This whitewashed space stays open at least until midnight, with live reggae and rock often staged.

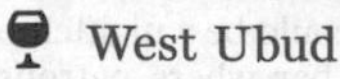

West Ubud

★**Bridges** LOUNGE
(Map p168; ☎0361-970095; www.bridgesbali.com; Jl Raya Campuan, Bridges Bali; ⏰4-11.30pm daily, happy hour 4-6.30pm Sat-Thu) The namesake bridges are right outside the Divine Wine & Cocktail Bar on the lower level of this bar/restaurant complex, which has sweeping views of the river gorge. You'll hear the rush of the water far below while you indulge in a top-end cocktail. There are gourmet bites for sharing and a long wine list for exploring. Upstairs, there's a formal restaurant and another bar.

✩ Entertainment

Few travel experiences are more magical than watching Balinese dance, especially in Ubud. It's the perfect base for nightly cultural entertainment and for events in surrounding villages. You can see Kecak, Legong and Barong dances, Mahabharata and Ramayana ballets, *wayang kulit* (shadow-puppet plays) and gamelan (traditional Javanese and Balinese orchestras). There are eight or more performances each night.

Dance

Dances performed for visitors are usually adapted and abbreviated to some extent to make them more enjoyable, but usually have appreciative locals in the audience (or peering around the screen!). It's also common to combine the features of more than one traditional dance in a single performance.

Fabulous Ubud Tourist Information Centre (p195) can supply a performance schedule and also sells tickets (usually between 75,000Rp and 100,000Rp). For performances outside Ubud, transport is often included in the price. Tickets are also sold at many hotels, at the venues and by street vendors – all charge the same price.

Vendors often sell drinks at the performances, which typically last about 1½ hours. Before the show, you might notice the musicians checking out the size of the crowd – ticket sales fund the troupes.

One note about your phone: nobody wants to hear it; nor do the performers want flash in their eyes. And don't be rude and walk out loudly in the middle.

DANCE TROUPES: GOOD & BAD

All dance groups on Ubud's stages are not created equal. You have true artists with international reputations and then you have some who really shouldn't quit their day jobs. If you're a Balinese dance novice, you shouldn't worry too much about this; just pick a venue and go. But after a few performances, you'll start to appreciate the differences in talent, and that's part of the enjoyment. Clue: if the costumes are dirty, the orchestra seems particularly uninterested, performers break character to tell stale jokes (really!) and you find yourself watching a dancer and saying 'I could do that', then the group is B-level.

Excellent troupes who regularly perform in Ubud include:

Semara Ratih High-energy, creative Legong interpretations. The best local troupe musically.

Gunung Sari Legong dance; one of Bali's oldest and most respected troupes.

Semara Madya Kekac dance; especially good for the hypnotic chants. A mystical experience for some.

Tirta Sari Legong dance.

Cudamani One of Bali's best gamelan troupes. It rehearses in Pengosekan, runs a school for children and tours internationally. You have to seek them out, though, as they no longer perform in tourist venues.

Finally, watch for temple ceremonies (which are frequent). Go around 8pm and you'll see Balinese dance and music in its full cultural context. You'll need to be appropriately dressed – your hotel or a local can tell you what to do.

The website Ubud Now & Then (www.ubudnowandthen.com) has schedules of special events and performances. Also check with Fabulous Ubud Tourist Information Centre (p195).

★Pura Dalem Ubud DANCE

(Map p164; Jl Raya Ubud; adult/child under 10yr 80,000/40,000Rp; ⏲Mon-Sat) This open-air venue in a temple compound has a flame-lit, carved-stone backdrop and is an evocative place to see a dance performance. Different companies perform Legong (7.30pm Tuesday and Saturday), Jegog (7.30pm Wednesday), Barong (7pm Thursday) and the Kecak fire dance (7.30pm Monday and Friday).

★Pura Taman Saraswati DANCE

(Ubud Water Palace; Map p164; Jl Raya Ubud; tickets 80,000Rp; ⏲7.30pm) The beauty of the setting may distract you from the dancers, although at night you can't see the lily pads and lotus flowers that are such an attraction by day. Janger dance is performed on Sunday and Monday, the Ramayana ballet on Wednesday and Legong on Saturday. On Tuesday and Thursday, women play the gamelan and children dance.

ARMA Open Stage DANCE

(Map p168; ☎0361-976659; info@armabali.com; Jl Raya Pengosekan; dance performances 80,000-100,000Rp) Hosts some of the best troupes performing Barong and Legong dance; performances are held on Tuesday and Sunday at 7.30pm, Wednesday at 7pm and Friday at 6pm. On nights when there is a new or full moon, the Cak Rina trance and fire dance is held at 7.30pm.

Puri Agung Peliatan DANCE

(Map p164; Jl Peliatan; tickets 75,000Rp; ⏲7.30pm Thu & Sat) A simple setting backed by a large carved wall where excellent performances of Legong and the Kecak fire dance are staged. A free shuttle leaves the Ubud Tourist Information office at 6.45pm.

Ubud Palace DANCE

(Map p164; Jl Raya Ubud) Performances are held here against a beautiful backdrop, but were suspended in 2018 while a renovation of the palace compound was underway. Check in to see if performances have resumed.

Padang Tegal Kaja DANCE

(Map p164; Jl Hanoman; tickets 75,000Rp; ⏲7.30pm) A simple, open terrace in a convenient location. In many ways this location hints at what dance performances have looked like in Ubud for generations. Enjoy the Kecak fire dance on Saturday and Sunday or Barong and Keris on Tuesday.

Shadow Puppets

Shadow-puppet shows are greatly attenuated from traditional performances, which often last the entire night.

Pondok Bamboo Music Shop PUPPET THEATRE
(Map p164; ☎0361-974807; Monkey Forest Rd; tickets 75,000Rp; ⏰performances 8pm Mon & Thu) Short shadow-puppet shows are performed here by noted experts.

Oka Kartini PERFORMING ARTS
(Map p164; ☎0361-975193; Jl Raya Ubud; adult/child 100,000/50,000Rp; ⏰8pm Wed, Fri & Sun) Regular shadow-puppet shows are held at Oka Kartini, which also has a boutique.

Cinema

★Paradiso CINEMA
(Map p164; ☎0361-976546; www.paradisoubud.com; Jl Gautama Selatan; incl food or drinks 50,000Rp; ⏰films from 5pm) Sharing a building with the vegan Earth Cafe & Market (p184), this surprisingly plush 150-seat cinema screens two films daily. The price of admission is redeemable against items from the cafe menu – so a great deal. Mondays are half-price; on Tuesday and Thursday a community choir sings here. Check the website for a schedule.

Shopping

You can spend days in and around Ubud shopping. Jl Dewi Sita, Monkey Forest Rd and the northern stretch of Jl Hanoman have the most interesting local shops. Look for jewellery, homewares and clothing. Arts and crafts and yoga goods are found everywhere and at every price point and quality.

Ubud is the best place in Bali for books. Selections are wide and varied, especially for tomes on Balinese art and culture.

Central Ubud

★Threads of Life Indonesian Textile Arts Center TEXTILES
(Map p164; ☎0361-972187; www.threadsoflife.com; Jl Kajeng 24; ⏰10am-7pm) This textile gallery and shop sponsors the production of naturally dyed, handmade ritual textiles from around Indonesia. It exists to help recover skills in danger of being lost to modern dyeing and weaving methods. Commissioned pieces are displayed in the gallery, which has good explanatory material, and other textiles are available for purchase. It also runs regular textile-appreciation courses (p171).

★Kou COSMETICS
(Map p164; ☎0361-971905, 0821 4556 9663; www.facebook.com/koubali.naturalsoap; Jl Dewi Sita; ⏰9am-8pm) Concocted from pure coconut oil, the handmade soaps sold here will bring the evocative scents of frangipani, tuberose, jasmine, orange and lemon tea-tree to your bathroom. The attractive packaging makes products suitable for gifts. It also operates Kou Cuisine.

BaliZen TEXTILES
(Map p164; ☎0361-976022; www.tokobalizen.com; Monkey Forest Rd; ⏰9am-8pm) Locally made cushions, bed and home linens, kimonos and kids clothing are sold at this stylish boutique, all made with fabrics featuring designs drawn from nature or utilising traditional Balinese motifs. It also sells natural bath products and traditional Balinese umbrellas.

Kou Cuisine HOMEWARES
(Map p164; ☎0361-972319; www.facebook.com/koucuisine.jam; Monkey Forest Rd; ⏰10am-8pm) A repository of small and exquisite culinary gifts, including beautiful jars of jam made with Balinese fruit and jam jar–sized carved wooden spoons. It also sells containers of sea salt harvested from along Bali's shores.

Utama Spice COSMETICS
(Map p164; ☎0361-975051; www.utamaspicebali.com; Monkey Forest Rd; ⏰9am-8.30pm) The scent of Utama's Balinese-made natural skincare products wafts out into the street, luring shoppers inside to investigate the pricey but nice essential oils, cosmetics and toiletries sold here. All are made without parabens, mineral oils, synthetic fragrances and artificial colourants.

Casa Luna Emporium HOMEWARES
(Map p164; ☎0361-971605; www.casalunabali.com/the-emporium; Jl Raya Ubud 23; ⏰8.30am-10pm) Yet another enterprise started by local entrepreneur Janet DeNeefe, this shop sells its own brand of cotton bedlinen, cushion covers and napery, as well as handwoven textiles, batik, furniture and art made by Balinese artisans. It's accessed via a staircase next to the Casa Luna restaurant.

OH DESIGN
(Map p164; ☎0812 3945 0402; ohdecobali@gmail.com; Monkey Forest Rd; ⏰9am-9pm) Stocking everything from textiles to beaded boxes to *kris* (traditional Balinese daggers), this French-owned store has been designed to

please those with an inclination for designer homewares and clothing.

Balitaza SPICES
(Map p164; ☎0811 393 9499; www.balitaza.com; Jl Dewi Sita; ⏰9.30am-9.30pm) Coconut sugar, traditional Balinese coffee, herbal teas and Indonesian herbs and spices make great gifts to take home, especially with their attractive packaging.

Nava HOMEWARES
(Map p164; Monkey Forest Rd; ⏰9am-9pm) Chic wooden and ceramic homewares line the shelves of this tiny shop, alongside a range of hand-carved wooden spoons.

Pusaka CLOTHING
(Map p164; ☎0821 4649 8865; Monkey Forest Rd 71; 9am-9pm) Stylish Balinese-made clothing, toys, jewellery, textiles and shoes are sold at this branch of Denpasar's popular Ethnologi boutique.

Ubud Tea Room FOOD & DRINKS
(Map p164; Jl Jembawan; ⏰7am-9pm) This hole-in-the-wall shop is lined with glass jars of teas grown in Bali, including fragrant herbal infusions. It shares premises with Bali Buda (p184).

Confiture de Bali FOOD
(Map p164; ☎0852 3884 1684; www.confituredebali.net; Jl Goutama 26; ⏰9am-10pm) Jams made from local fruits, butters (cashew, lemon and peanut) and kombucha are sold at this sweet boutique.

Bali Yoga Shop CLOTHING
(Map p164; ☎0361-4792077; Jl Hanoman 44B; ⏰8am-9pm) Huge range of quality yoga gear and clothing.

Namaste GIFTS & SOUVENIRS
(Map p164; ☎0361-970528; www.facebook.com/namastethespiritualshop; Jl Hanoman 64; ⏰9am-7pm) Just the place to buy a crystal to get your spiritual house in order, Namaste stocks a top range of New Age supplies. Incense, yoga mats, moody instrumental music – it's all here.

Pondok Bamboo Music Shop MUSICAL INSTRUMENTS
(Map p164; ☎0361-974807; Monkey Forest Rd; ⏰9am-8pm) Hear the music of a thousand bamboo wind chimes at this store owned by noted gamelan musician Nyoman Warsa, who also offers music lessons (per hour 150,000Rp to 200,000Rp).

WOODCARVING

On Bali, woodcarving has been a traditional art of the priestly Brahmana caste, with the skills being said to be a gift of the gods. Historically, carving was limited to temple decorations, dance masks and musical instruments, but in the 1930s carvers began to depict people and animals in a naturalistic way. Today, local woodcarvers turn their skills to furniture making as well as traditional handicrafts.

Periplus BOOKS
(Map p164; ☎0877 8286 6087; www.periplus.com; Jl Raya Ubud 23; ⏰8am-10pm) A centrally located outlet of the popular Indonesian bookshop chain.

Ganesha Bookshop BOOKS
(Map p164; ☎0361-970320; www.ganeshabooksbali.com; Jl Raya Ubud; ⏰9am-6pm) Bookshop with a selection of titles on Indonesian-related subjects as well as a large selection of second-hand books, with a particular focus on crime fiction. Also operates as a (charged) book exchange.

Tegun Galeri HOMEWARES
(Map p164; Jl Hanoman 44; ⏰10am-8pm) It's everything the souvenir stores are not, with beautiful handmade items from around the island.

Tn Parrot CLOTHING
(Map p164; www.tnparrot.com; Jl Dewi Sita; ⏰9am-9pm Mon-Fri, 10.30am-8.30pm Sat & Sun) The trademark parrot of this T-shirt shop is a characterful bird and he (she?) appears in many guises on this shop's line of custom T-shirts. Designs range from cool to groovy to offbeat. Everything is made from high-quality cotton that's been pre-shrunk.

Ubud Market GIFTS & SOUVENIRS
(Pasar Seni; Map p164; Jl Raya Ubud; ⏰7am-8pm) The large Ubud Market is your one-stop shop for kitschy souvenirs, clothing and presents for back home. It's inside a large complex; stallholders set up across several buildings, and also along Jl Karna. Push to the far southeast corner for the produce market (p186), which still serves the daily needs of locals.

SAVING BALI'S DOGS

Mangy curs. That's the only label you can apply to many of Bali's dogs. As you travel the island – especially by foot – you can't help but notice dogs that are sick, ill-tempered, uncared for and victims to a litany of other maladies.

How has this situation developed? The answers are complex, but benign neglect has a lot to do with it. Dogs are at the bottom of the social strata: few have owners and local interest in them is next to nil.

Some nonprofits in Ubud are hoping to change the fortunes of Bali's maligned best friends through rabies vaccinations, spaying and neutering, and public education. Donations are always greatly needed.

Bali Adoption Rehab Centre (BARC; Map p168; ☎0361-971208; https://barc4balidogs.org.au; Jl Raya Pengosekan; ⊙10am-5pm) Rehabilitation facility for injured and abused dogs. Organises dog adoptions.

Bali Animal Welfare Association (BAWA; Map p164; ☎0361-981490; www.bawabali.com; Jl Ubud Raya 10; ⊙9am-8pm Mon-Fri, to 5pm Sat & Sun) Runs lauded mobile rabies vaccination teams, organises adoption and promotes population control.

Rio Helmi's Photo Gallery & Cafe PHOTOGRAPHY
(Map p164; ☎0361-972304; www.riohelmi.com; Jl Suweta 06B; ⊙7am-7pm) Noted photographer and Ubud resident Rio Helmi has a small commercial gallery and cafe where you can admire or purchase his journalistic and artistic work.

Moari MUSIC
(Map p164; ☎0361-977367; moari_bali@yahoo.com; Jl Raya Ubud 4; ⊙9am-6pm) New and restored Balinese musical instruments are sold alongside souvenirs at this tiny shop.

South Ubud

Goddess on the Go! CLOTHING
(Map p168; ☎0361-976084; www.goddessonthego.net; Jl Raya Pengosekan; ⊙9am-5pm) A large selection of women's clothes designed for adventure, made to be super-comfortable, easy to pack and ecofriendly.

Portobello CLOTHING
(Map p164; ☎0361-976246; Monkey Forest Rd; ⊙9am-9pm) Locally made kimonos, kaftans and wrap-around dresses in bright fabrics are the speciality of this boutique near the Ubud Monkey Forest.

ARMA BOOKS
(Map p168; ☎0361-976659; www.armabali.com/arma-bookshop; Jl Raya Pengosekan; ⊙9am-6pm) Large selection of cultural titles.

Smile Shop ARTS & CRAFTS
(Map p168; www.senyumbali.org; Jl Nyuh Kuning; ⊙10am-5pm) All manner of second hand, donated goods are for sale in this charity shop to benefit the Smile Foundation of Bali.

West Ubud

★**Neka Art Museum Shop** BOOKS
(Map p168; ☎0361-975074; www.museumneka.com; Jl Raya Sanggingan; ⊙9am-5pm) One of the best places in Ubud to source top-quality traditional Balinese handicrafts. Also stocks books.

Information

DANGERS & ANNOYANCES

➡ Traffic in the heart of Ubud can be noisy, smelly and dangerous for pedestrians, especially around lunch time.

➡ Skimming scams have been reported at ATM kiosks; try to use ones attached to banks, as security is better at these.

INTERNET ACCESS

Wi-fi access is near universal in places to stay as well as at most cafes and restaurants. Mobile data speeds are fast.

Hubud (Map p164; ☎0361-978073; www.hubud.org; Monkey Forest Rd; per day/month US$17/60; ⊙24hr Mon-Fri, 9am-midnight Sat & Sun; 📶) is for the digital nomads; this cowork space and digital hub has ultrafast web connections, developer seminars and much more. Take in rice-field views as you create a billion-dollar app.

MEDICAL SERVICES

Guardian Pharmacy (Map p164; ☎0361-8493682; www.guardianindonesia.co.id; cnr Jl Raya Ubud & Cok Sudarsana; ⊙8am-10pm) One of numerous branches around town.

Kimia Farma (Map p164; ☎0361-9080997; jfubudraya@gmail.com; Jl Raya Ubud 88; ⏱8am-11pm) Branch of a respected pharmacy chain.

Ubud Care (Map p164; ☎0811 397 7911; www.ubudcare.com; Jl Sukma 37; ⏱office 7am-10pm Mon-Sat) A modern clinic that provides examinations and consultations, prescriptions, and house and hotel calls.

MONEY

Ubud has numerous banks and ATMs. Be aware that the skimming of cards at kiosk ATMs has been reported; try to use ATMs attached to banks as these have better security.

POST

Main Post Office (Map p164; Jl Jembawan; ⏱8am-5pm) Handles parcels.

TOURIST INFORMATION

Fabulous Ubud Tourist Information Centre (Map p164; ☎0361-973285; www.fabulousubud.com; Jl Raya Ubud; ⏱8am-9pm; 📶) Operated by the Ubud royal family and is the closest thing that the town has to an official tourist office. It offers both transport information and up-to-date details on events, ceremonies and traditional dances held in the area; dance tickets and tours are sold here, as are tickets for the Kura-Kura Bus.

ℹ Getting There & Away

Most guesthouses and hotels can organise transport to/from other destinations around the island on request.

TOURIST SHUTTLE BUS

Kura-Kura Bus (www.kura2bus.com; one way 80,000Rp) Runs from near the Ubud Palace to its hub in Kuta five times daily (80,000Rp, two hours).

Perama (Map p164; ☎0361-973316; www.peramatour.com; Jl Raya Pengosekan; ⏱7am-9pm) The major tourist-shuttle operator. Destinations include Sanur (50,000Rp, one hour), Kuta and the airport (60,000Rp, two hours) and Padangbai (75,000Rp, two hours). Its terminal is located in Padangtegal, south of the town centre; to get to/from your destination in Ubud will cost another 15,000Rp.

ℹ Getting Around

Many high-end spas, hotels and restaurants located outside the town centre offer free shuttles for guests and customers. Ask about this before booking accommodation.

TO/FROM THE AIRPORT

A taxi or hired car with driver from the airport to Ubud will cost 350,000Rp (400,000Rp between midnight and 6am). A hired car with driver to the airport will cost about the same.

CAR & MOTORCYCLE

With numerous attractions nearby and no public transport, renting a car or motorcycle is sensible. Ask at your accommodation or hire a car and driver.

Expect to pay around 50,000Rp per day for a late model motorbike in good condition, considerably more for a car.

Most drivers are very fair; a few – often from out of the area – not so much. If you find a driver you like, get their number and call to organise rides during your stay. From central Ubud to, say, Sanggingan should cost about 40,000Rp. A ride from the palace to the end of Jl Hanoman should cost about 20,000Rp.

It's easy to get a ride on an *ojek* (motorbike taxi); rates are half those of cars.

TAXI

There are no metered taxis based in Ubud – those that honk their horns at you have usually dropped off passengers from southern Bali and are hoping for a fare back. There are plenty of drivers with private vehicles on the streets hectoring passers-by, in contrast some quietly hold up 'transport' signs.

BEDULU

☎0361 / POP 10,300

Bedulu was once the capital of a great kingdom. The legendary Dalem Bedaulu ruled the Pejeng dynasty from here, and was the last Balinese king to withstand the onslaught of the powerful Majapahit from Java. He was defeated by Gajah Mada in 1343. The capital shifted several times after this, to Gelgel and then later to Klungkung (Semarapura). Today Bedulu is absorbed into the greater Ubud sprawl, and is worth visiting for its temples.

👁 Sights

Yeh Pulu HISTORIC SITE

(adult/child 15,000/7500Rp; ⏱8am-5.30pm) Set amid rice terraces, this 25m-long carved cliff face next to the Sungai Petanu (Petanu River) is believed to be the remnants of a 14th-century hermitage. Even if your interest in carved Hindu art is minor, the site is attractive and you're likely to have it all to yourself. Apart from the figure of Ganesha, elephant-headed son of Shiva, most scenes depict scenes of everyday life. From the site entrance, a 300m walk on a gently inclined path goes to the carvings.

You can walk between Yeh Pulu and Goa Gajah, following small paths through the paddy fields, but you might need to pay a local to guide you. By car or bicycle, look for the signs to 'Relief Yeh Pulu' or 'Villa Yeh Pulu', east of Goa Gajah.

Pura Samuan Tiga HINDU TEMPLE

(Jl Pura Samuan Tiga; 10,000Rp; ⌚7am-5pm) The majestic and tranquil Pura Samuan Tiga (Temple of the Meeting of the Three) is on a small lane about 200m east of the Bedulu junction. The name is possibly a reference to the Hindu trinity, or it may refer to meetings held here in the early 11th century. Despite these early associations, all the temple buildings have been rebuilt since being destroyed in the 1917 earthquake.

Pranoto's Art Gallery GALLERY

(☎0361-970827; www.facebook.com/Pranotos-Art-Gallery-10150148979210532; Jl Raya Goa Gajah, Teges; ⌚9am-5pm) Pranoto, a long-time Ubud artist, displays his works at this gallery/studio/home which backs up to beautiful rice fields between Bedulu and Ubud. Ask about an atmospheric walking path you can take back to central Ubud. There are figure modelling sessions (30,000Rp) Wednesday and Saturday at 10am.

Goa Gajah CAVE

(Elephant Cave; Jl Raya Goa Gajah; adult/child 15,000/7500Rp, parking car/motorcycle 5000/2000Rp; ⌚7.30am-7pm) Visitors enter this rock-hewn cave through the cavernous mouth of a demon. Inside, there are fragmentary remains of a lingam, the phallic symbol of the Hindu god Shiva, and its female counterpart the yoni, as well as a statue of Shiva's son, the elephant-headed god Ganesha. Outside, two square bathing pools have waterspouts held by six female figures. Located 2km southeast of Ubud on the road to Bedulu, the compound has a sideshow atmosphere and is inevitably crammed with foreign tourists.

There were never any elephants in Bali (until tourist attractions changed that); ancient Goa Gajah probably takes its name from the nearby Sungai Petanu, which at one time was known as Elephant River, or perhaps because the face over the cave entrance might resemble an elephant.

The origins of the cave are uncertain; one tale relates that it was created by the fingernail of the legendary giant Kebo Iwa. It probably dates to the 11th century, and was certainly in existence during the Majapahit takeover of Bali. The cave was rediscovered by Dutch archaeologists in 1923, but the fountains and pool were not found until 1954.

From Goa Gajah you can clamber down through the rice paddies to Sungai Petanu, where there are crumbling rock carvings of stupas (domes for housing Buddhist relics) on a cliff face, and a small cave.

As it's a popular stop for tour buses, try to get here before 10am to avoid the crowds.

THE LEGEND OF DALEM BEDAULU

As the legend goes, Pejeng dynasty ruler Dalem Bedaulu possessed magical powers that allowed him to have his head chopped off and then put right back on ('Bedaulu' means 'he who changed heads'). On one occasion, the king attempted to perform this unique party trick but a servant botched it, lopping off the head and mistakenly dropping it in a river. As it floated away, the servant panicked and grabbed a pig, cut off its head and popped it on the king's shoulders. Thereafter, the king sat on a high throne and forbade his subjects to look up at him.

Getting There & Away

The road from Ubud is reasonably flat, so coming to Bedulu by bicycle or on foot is a reasonable option.

NORTH OF UBUD

North of Ubud, Bali becomes cooler and more lush. Ancient sites and natural beauty abound. A popular route from Ubud northeast towards Gunung Batur passes through Tegallalang, home to the photogenic Ceking rice terraces, and then continues via Tampaksiring, passing Gunung Kawi Sebatu, Pura Gunung Kawi and Tirta Empul en route. The scenery on this route is green and extremely picturesque – you'll see farmers working in their fields, colourful flags fluttering in the wind and plenty of rice terraces and roadside shrines.

Getting There & Away

You'll need your own transport to explore this part of the island.

Sebatu

The western approach to **Gunung Kawi Sebatu** (adult/child 15,000/7500Rp, parking 5000Rp) offers wonderful views down on to the complex – many visitors are content to admire these from the side of the road rather than entering the actual temple. Inside, spring-fed pools are set against a lush green backdrop. The temple is dedicated to Vishnu and is used locally for purification rituals.

Tegallalang

☎0361 / POP 9940

Heading north from Ubud, it's worth stopping to enjoy the stupendous views of the Ceking rice-field terraces from Tagallalang's main road. If lucky, you may also hear one of the town's noted gamelan orchestras practising. Shoppers may wish to investigate the many handicraft stalls here, which sell products carved from albesia wood.

Ceking Terraces VIEWPOINT

(Ceking; 10,000Rp) This is one of the best views of rice-field terraces in Bali, so it's not surprising that tourists flock here from Ubud to indulge in a frenzy of photography. The canny locals now charge visitors to park their cars (look for the 'Sentral Parkir Ceking Terrace' sign) and to wander down the staircases looking for good vantage points. Purchase tickets at one of the two booths on the main road or wait for a ticket seller to find you.

Kampung Resort RESORT $$

(☎0361-901201; www.thekampungresortubud.com; Ceking; r 900,000-1,300,000Rp; [P] [wi-fi] [pool]) Staying in one of the nine rooms here is like having your own tree house – you're surrounded by soaring palms and rice terraces. Rooms have a stylish decor, featuring traditional furniture and fabrics; some are huge. The on-site restaurant is a plus and Ubud is only a 20-minute ride away.

Kampung Cafe CAFE $$

(☎0361-901201; www.thekampungresortubud.com; Ceking; sandwiches 55,000-65,000Rp, mains 62,000-120,000Rp; ⌚8am-9pm; [wi-fi]) Jaw-dropping rice terrace views are enjoyed alongside a menu of Indonesian and Western dishes in this *bale* (open-sided pavilion) in Ceking's Kampung Hotel. A good lunch spot.

Getting There & Away

Parking in the central car park in Ceking is included in the entrance ticket; look for the 'Sentral Parkir Ceking Terrace' sign. Scooters and motorbikes can be parked on the roadside for free.

> **BALINESE FARM COOKING SCHOOL**
>
> This highly recommended **cooking course** (☎0812 3953 4446; www.balinesecooking.net; Banjar Patas; 1-day course adult/child 400,000/250,000Rp) is held in the village of Taro, set in untrammelled countryside 18km north of Ubud. Run by villagers passionate about organic farming, the course is an excellent introduction to Balinese cooking – you'll learn lots about local produce and foods. Morning courses include a visit to a local produce market. Vegan, vegetarian and omnivore courses are available.

Tampaksiring

☎0361 / POP 10,480

Located in the Pakerisan Valley, 18km northeast of Ubud, Tampaksiring was the base of one the major kingdoms during Bali's pre-colonial period. It's home to both Pura Tirta Empul, an ancient and important water temple, and Gunung Kawi, one of the most impressive ancient sites in Bali. The area is replete with terraced rice fields running down to the river and streams – wonderful subject matter for photographers.

Sights

There are groups of *candi* and monks' cells in the area once encompassed by the ancient Pejeng kingdom, notably **Pura Krobokan** and **Goa Garba**, but none so grand as Gunung Kawi. Between Gunung Kawi and Tirta Empul, **Pura Mengening** temple has a freestanding *candi* (shrine), similar in design to those at Gunung Kawi and much less visited. The road running north to Penelokan is lined with gift shops and cafes that are predominantly visited by tour groups.

Gunung Kawi MONUMENT

(adult/child 15,000/7500Rp, parking 2000Rp; ⌚7am-5pm) One of Bali's oldest and most important monuments, this river-valley complex consists of 10 huge *candi* cut out of rock faces. Each is believed to be a memorial to a member of 11th-century Balinese royalty. Legends relate that the whole group was carved out of the rock in one hard-working night by the mighty fingernails of Kebo Iwa.

You'll need to be fit to explore here, as access to the valley and shrines is via a steep 250-step staircase.

The five monuments on the eastern riverbank are probably dedicated to King Udayana, Queen Mahendradatta and their sons Airlangga, Anak Wungsu and Marakata. While Airlangga ruled eastern Java, Anak Wungsu ruled Bali. The four monuments on the western side are, by this theory, to Anak Wungsu's chief concubines. Another theory is that the whole complex is dedicated to Anak Wungsu, his wives, concubines and, in the case of the remote 10th *candi,* to a royal minister.

Get to Gunung Kawi as early as possible. If you start down the steps by 7.30am, you'll avoid some of the vendors and see residents going about morning business. You can hear the birds, the flowing water and your own voice going 'ooh' and 'aah' without the distractions that come later when large groups arrive. In addition, you'll still have cool air when you start back up the endless steps. Sarong hire is included in the ticket cost, but it's best to bring your own in case there is nobody yet offering them for use. If the ticket office is closed, pay on your way out.

Pura Tirta Empul HINDU TEMPLE

(Holy Spring Temple; Tampaksiring; adult/child 15,000/7500Rp, parking 5000Rp; ⏲7am-6pm) Discovered in AD 962 and believed to have magical powers, the holy springs at this water temple close to the ancient site of Gunung Kawi bubble up into a large pool and gush out through waterspouts into a *petirtaan* (bathing area) used for ritual purification. The water can be polluted, so bathing isn't recommended. The ticket price includes sarong hire.

SOUTH OF UBUD

The roads between Ubud and south Bali are lined with little shops making and selling handicrafts. Many visitors shop along the route as they head to and from Ubud, but as much of the craftwork is done in small

South of Ubud

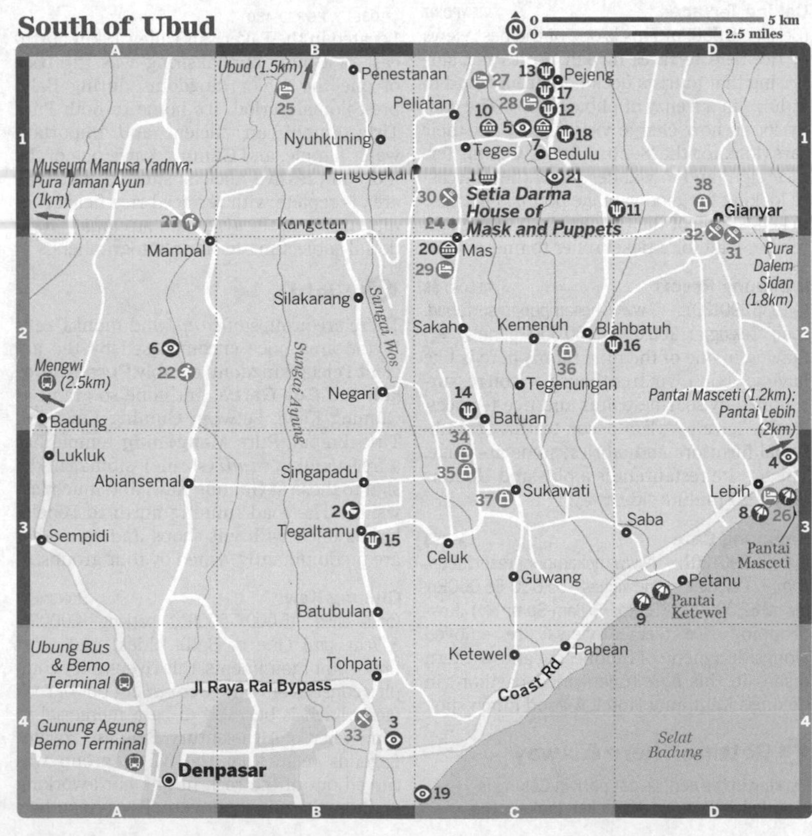

workshops and family compounds on quiet back roads, it's worth veering off the major roads. If you do this, you'll likely discover temples and atmospheric villages, too.

Getting There & Away

South of Ubud, the roads are mostly flat, so good for cyclists. However, note that the main roads are busy with traffic heading to and from the coast. There's no regular public transport, so you'll need your own.

If you plan to hire a car and driver to explore here, note that your driver may receive a commission from any place you spend your money – this can add 10% or more to the cost of purchases (think of it as his tip). Also, a driver may try to steer you to workshops or artisans that he favours, rather than those of most interest to you.

Mas

0361 / POP 13,120

Mas means 'gold' in Bahasa Indonesia, but woodcarving is the principal craft in this artisans' village just south of Ubud. Stores and galleries line the main road, Jl Raya Mas, and workshops are located both here and in side streets.

Sights

★Setia Darma House of Mask and Puppets MUSEUM

(0361-898 7493; www.maskandpuppets.com; Jl Tegal Bingin; admission by donation; 8am-6pm) This is one of the best museums in the Ubud area, home to more than 7000 ceremonial masks and puppets from Bali, other parts of Indonesia, Asia and beyond. All are beautifully displayed in a series of renovated historic buildings. Among the many treasures, look for the amazing Barong Landung puppets and the Kamasan paintings. There's also a large collection of puppets from other countries. The museum is about 2km northeast of the main Mas crossroads.

Tonyraka Art Lounge GALLERY

(0812 3600 8035; www.tonyrakaartgallery.com; Jl Raya Mas 86; 10am-5pm) One of the premier galleries in the Ubud area, showing top-notch Balinese tribal and contemporary art. Come to browse, buy and to enjoy lunch or a coffee at the chic cafe, which is one of the best in the Ubud area.

Museum Rudana GALLERY

(Map p168; 0361-975779; www.museumrudana.com; Jl Raya Mas; 50,000Rp; 9.30am-5pm) This imposing museum overlooking rice fields is

South of Ubud

Top Sights

1 Setia Darma House of Mask and Puppets C1

Sights

2 Bali Bird Park B3
3 Bali Orchid Garden B4
Bali Reptile Park .... (see 2)
4 Bali Safari Park D3
5 Goa Gajah C1
6 Green School A2
7 Museum Gedung Arca C1
8 Pantai Keramas D3
9 Pantai Purnama D3
10 Pranoto's Art Gallery C1
11 Pura Kahyangan Jagat D1
12 Pura Kebo Edan C1
13 Pura Penataran Sasih C1
14 Pura Puseh Batuan & Pura Dasar Batuan C2
15 Pura Puseh Desa Batubulan B3
16 Pura Puseh Desa Blahbatuh C2
17 Pura Pusering Jagad C1
18 Pura Samuan Tiga C1
19 Taman Festival Bali C4
20 Tonyraka Art Lounge C2
21 Yeh Pulu C1

Activities, Courses & Tours

22 Big Tree Farms A2
23 Fivelements A1
24 Ida Bagus Anom C1

Sleeping

25 Bambu Indah B1
26 Hotel Komune D3
27 Maya Ubud C1
28 Omah Apik C1
29 Taman Harum C2

Eating

Art Lounge Cafe .... (see 20)
30 Bebek Semar Warung C1
31 Gianyar Night Market D1
Hotel Komune Beach Club .... (see 26)
32 Produce Market D1
33 Warung Satria B4

Shopping

34 Baruna Art Shop C3
35 Nyoman Ruka C3
36 Pertenunan Putri Ayu C2
37 Sukawati Market C3
38 Tenun Ikat Setia Cili D1

the creation of local politician and art lover Nyoman Rudana and his wife, Ni Wayan Olasthini. The three floors contain more than 400 traditional paintings, including a calendar dated to the 1840s, some Lempad drawings and more modern pieces. It's next to the Rudana's commercial gallery.

Courses

Ida Bagus Anom ART
(☎0812 380 1924, 0898 914 2606; www.balimask making.com; Jl Raya Mas; 4hr class 250,000Rp; ⏰hours vary) Three generations of some of Bali's best mask carvers will show you their secrets in a family compound opposite the football field; a mask usually takes 10 days to make.

Sleeping

Taman Harum HOTEL $$
(☎0361-975567; www.tamanharumcottages.com; Jl Raya Mas; r 500,000-800,000Rp, ste 800,000-1,100,000Rp, villas 1,200,000-1,500,000Rp; P❄📶🏊) On the busy main road in Mas, this hotel offers rooms, suites and villas – the suites are much nicer than the ugly rooms and villas. It's behind a gallery and a restaurant serving wood-fired pizzas (35,000Rp to 80,000Rp) and beer. The hotel offers its guests a free shuttle to/from Ubud.

Eating

Warung Teges BALINESE $
(Map p168; ☎0361-975251; Jl Cok Rai Pudak; nasi campur 25,000Rp; ⏰8am-6pm) This ultra-simple warung serves only one dish – *nasi campur* – and it's one of the better versions available in the Ubud area. The restaurant gets just about everything right, from the pork sausage to the chicken satay, the *babi guling* to the tempe. The sambal is delicious: fresh and tangy, with a perfect amount of heat.

★**Art Lounge Cafe** CAFE $$
(☎0361-908 2435; www.facebook.com/Tonyraka ArtLounge; Jl Raya Mas 86; panini 73,000-88,000Rp, mains 45,000-135,000Rp; ⏰8am-10pm; 📶🌿) An outpost of Bali chic on one of the main roads between Ubud and the coast, this fashionable cafe in the Tonyraka Art Lounge is an excellent lunch, dinner or coffee spot. Staff know how to make a good coffee, and the food is good – we particularly recommend the cakes.

Bebek Semar Warung BALINESE $$
(☎0361-974677; Jl Raya Mas 165; mains 85,000-135,000Rp; ⏰8am-9pm) It doesn't look promising from the street but step through to the breezy dining area and you'll be confronted with a green vista of rice fields stretching off to palm trees. The Balinese duck dishes that are the house specialty are unusual and delicious. Find it 1km south of where Jl Raya Mas meets Jl Raya Pengosekan.

BALI'S VILLAGE ARTISTS

In small villages throughout the Ubud region, from Sebatu to Mas and beyond across Bali, you'll see small signs for artists and craftspeople, often near the local temple. As one local told us, 'we are only as rich of a village as our art', so the people who create the ceremonial costumes, masks, *kris* (traditional dagger), musical instruments and all the other beautiful aspects of Balinese life and religion are accorded great honour. It's a symbiotic relationship, with the artist never charging the village for the work and the village in turn seeing to the welfare of the artist. Often there are many artists in residence because few events would bring more shame to a village than having to go to another village to procure a needed sacred object.

Shopping

Mas is a good place to come if you want something custom-made in sandalwood – just be prepared to pay well (and be sure to check the wood's authenticity carefully). The village is also a big player in Bali's furniture industry, producing chairs, tables and antiques ('made to order!'), mainly from teak imported from other Indonesian islands.

Blahbatuh

☎0361 / POP 9010

This village is known for its association with Kebo Iwa, the legendary strongman and minister to the last king of the Bedulu kingdom. An 11th-century carved head of the warrior can be admired in the village's major temple, the Pura Puseh Desa Blahbatuh, and a massive modern statue depicting him in full warrior mode adorns a roundabout on the main road between Blahbatuh and Gianyar.

Pura Kahyangan Jagat HINDU TEMPLE
(Pura Bukit Dharma – Durga Kutri; Jl Raya Buruan; by donation) Located 1.4km north of Blahbatuh's massive Kebo Iwa statue, this road-

side temple compound has Bukit Dharma (Dharma Hill) as a backdrop. Climb up the hill to reach a hilltop shrine featuring a stone statue of the six-armed goddess of death and destruction, Durga, killing a demon-possessed water buffalo. Temple minders will usually meet you at the gate to take a donation and provide you with a sash to wear during your visit.

Pura Puseh Desa Blahbatuh HINDU TEMPLE
(Pura Kebo Iwa; Jl Kebo Iwa) A carved stone head inside this temple compound is believed to be a portrait of Kebo Iwa, the legendary strongman and minister to the last king of the Bedulu kingdom. The carving is thought to predate the Javanese 11th-century influence in Bali. Foreign visitors aren't always welcome at the temple complex, which was reconstructed after being destroyed in the 1917 earthquake.

★ **Pertenunan Putri Ayu** TEXTILES
(☎0361-942658; Jl Lapangan Astina 3, off Jl Wisma Gajah Mada; ⏲8am-5pm) A symphony of click-klacking looms greets visitors to this large workshop in Blahbatuh, which produces colourful ikat and batik fabrics. The friendly staff will show you through the workshop and explain the process; fabric and clothes can be purchased in an adjoining showroom.

Batuan

☎0361 / POP 8650

Batuan's recorded history goes back 1000 years, and in the 17th century its royal family controlled most of southern Bali. The decline of its power is attributed to a priest's curse, which scattered the royal family to different parts of the island. These days, the only reason to come here is to visit the twin Puseh Batuan and Dasar Batuan temples.

Pura Puseh Batuan & Pura Dasar Batuan HINDU TEMPLE
(Jl Raya Batuan; 10,000Rp; ⏲9am-5.30pm) Just west of the centre, these twin temples are among Bali's oldest. They're accessible studies in classic Balinese temple architecture, with elaborate carvings. Visitors are given the use of sarongs.

Sukawati

☎0361 / POP 12,570

Once a royal capital, Sukawati is now known for its vibrant produce market and for its specialised artisans, who busily work in small shops along the roads.

CELUK

Located on Sukawati's western edge, the artisans' enclave of Celuk is the silver and gold centre of Bali. The flashier showrooms are on the main road, and have marked prices that are quite high, although you can always bargain.

Hundreds of silversmiths and goldsmiths work in their homes on the backstreets north and east of the main road. Most of these artisans are from pande families, members of a sub-caste of blacksmiths whose knowledge of fire and metal has traditionally put them outside the usual caste hierarchy. Their small workshops are interesting to visit, and have the lowest prices, but they don't keep a large stock of finished work. They will make something to order if you bring a sample or sketch.

Shopping

In Sukawati look for shops of the *tukang prada,* who make temple umbrellas that are beautifully decorated with stencilled gold paint. The area known as Puaya, west of Jl Raya Sukawati, specialises in high-quality leather shadow puppets and masks for Topeng and Barong dances. On its main street, Jl Lettu Nengah Duaji I, look for a row of workshops where local artisans both make and sell ceremonial items for dance performances.

Most workshops welcome visitors.

★ **Sukawati Market** MARKET
(Pasar Umum Sukawati; Jl Raya Sukawati; ⏲6am-8pm) Always lively, this sprawling market is a major source of the flowers, baskets, fruits, knick-knacks and other items used in temple offerings, and also sells fresh produce. Across the road, the so-called Sukawati Art Market sells clothes and souvenirs.

Nyoman Ruka ARTS & CRAFTS
(Jl Lettu Nengah Duaji I; ⏲10am-6pm) A workshop producing and selling Barong masks.

Baruna Art Shop ARTS & CRAFTS
(☎0361-299490; cnr Jl Lettu Nengah Duaji I & Gang Subali; ⏲9am-6pm) Has many Barong masks in stock for you to admire.

FIVELEMENTS

Located around 11km southwest of central Ubud, next to the Sungai Ayung, this luxe **health retreat** (☎0361-469206; www.fivelements.org; Puri Ahimsa Banjar Baturning, Mambal; r from 5,000,000Rp, 3-night wellness package 39,000,000Rp) utilises therapies including mindfulness, yoga, meditation and massage and is serious about offering a healthy experience – everything on the menu is vegan and raw and there's no alcohol. Facilities include a lovely spring-water pool and three yoga studios. The sybaritic guest rooms are stylish and well equipped, with outdoor bathrooms.

Batubulan

☎0361 / POP 8450

Stone carving is the main craft of Batubulan, and the start of the main road to Ubud from south Bali is lined with outlets for stone sculptures. Workshops are found right along the road to Tegaltamu, with another batch further north around Silakarang. The village is also the source of the stunning temple-gate guardians seen all over Bali. The stone used for these sculptures is a porous grey volcanic rock called *paras*, which resembles pumice; it's soft and surprisingly light. It also ages quickly, so that 'ancient' work may be years rather than centuries old.

Sights

Pura Puseh Desa Batubulan HINDU TEMPLE

(Jl Raya Batuan; by donation; 8am-noon) The temples around Batubulan are noted for their fine stonework. Just 200m to the east of the busy main road, Pura Puseh Desa Batubulan is worth a visit for its perfectly balanced overall composition. Statues draw on ancient Hindu and Buddhist iconography and Balinese mythology; however, they are not old – many are copied from books on archaeology.

Bali Bird Park BIRD SANCTUARY

(☎0361-299352; www.balibirdpark.com; Jl Serma Cok Ngurah Gambir; adult/child 2-12yr 385,000/192,500Rp; 9am-5.30pm; P) More than 1000 birds from 250 species and seven regions of the world flit about here, including rare cendrawasih (bird of paradise) from Papua and the all-but-vanished Bali starlings. Many are housed in special walk-through aviaries. Daily free-flight bird and bird of prey shows are staged, along with pelican and lory feedings. The park is popular with kids; allow at least two hours.

Bali Reptile Park ANIMAL SANCTUARY

(Jl Serma Cok Ngurah Gambir; adult/child 2-12yr 100,000/50,000Rp; 9am-5pm) This sanctuary claims to have the most complete collection of reptiles in Southeast Asia. There are snakes and lizards galore. Try to time your visit with the daily feedings of the park's huge prehistoric Komodo dragons (11am and 2.30pm).

Abiansemal

☎0361 / POP 6060

This area 14km south of central Ubud has a reputation for innovation courtesy of two businesses established by expat residents: the internationally renowned Green School built on the banks of the Sungai Ayung and the Big Tree Farms cocoa and palm-tree sugar processing factory in the small village enclave of Sibang. Both businesses are notable for their focus on environmental sustainability.

Green School SCHOOL

(www.greenschool.org; Jl Raya Sibang Kaja, Banjar Saren) Just south of Mambal, this school has enjoyed a lot of hype as much for its unorthodox curriculum as its flamboyant and innovative bamboo architecture by PT Bambu. It is not open to the public.

Big Tree Farms FOOD & DRINK

(☎0361-846 3327; www.bigtreefarms.com; Br Piakan, Sibang Kaja; 8am-noon & 1-5pm Mon-Fri) Processing coconut-palm sugar and cocoa, this factory is more notable for its architecture than its product – it's one of the world's largest commercial buildings constructed from bamboo, and has been designed to be a showcase of sustainable building practice. American architect Pete Celovsky specified bamboo and dried native alang-alang grass as the materials for the three-storey structure, which is a cross between a *lumbung* (Balinese rice barn) and a cathedral.

East Bali

Includes ➡

Best Places to Eat

➡ Bali Asli (p225)

➡ Gianyar Night Market (p206)

➡ Gusto (p233)

➡ Vincent's (p223)

➡ Warung Enak (p233)

Best Places to Stay

➡ Hotel Komune (p215)

➡ Pondok Batur Indah (p226)

➡ Darmada Eco Resort (p210)

➡ Ocean Prana Hostel (p230)

➡ Melasti Beach Bungalows (p230)

Why Go?

Exploring east Bali is one of the island's great pleasures. Rice terraces spill down hillsides, wild volcanic beaches are pounded by surf and traditional villages are barely touched by modernity. Watching over this region is Gunung Agung, the 3142m active volcano known as the 'Navel of the World' and 'Mother Mountain'.

Temples, palaces and whimsically designed water gardens are dotted throughout the landscape. Two of the temples – Pura Besakih and Pura Lempuyang – are among Bali's most important pilgrimage sites, and evocative reminders of the island's royal dynasties can be found in Klungkung (Semarapura), in Amlapura and at Tirta Gangga.

Up on the northeast coast, Amed and Tulamben are laid-back beach destinations for those keen to escape the crowds on the south coast. Diving, snorkelling, enjoying yoga and lazing by swimming pools are the priorities up here, and can be enjoyed by travellers on every budget.

When to Go

➡ The best time to visit east Bali is during the dry season – April to September – although recent weather patterns have made the dry season wetter and the wet season drier.

➡ Along the coast there's little reason to pick one month over another; it's almost always tropical and perfect for swimming, snorkelling and diving.

➡ Top-end resorts and coastal accommodation may book up in peak season (July, August and Christmas), but it's never jammed like south Bali.

➡ To surf the breaks off the beaches northeast of Sanur, aim for October to March.

East Bali Highlights

1 Pura Lempuyang (p226) Visiting important temples and marvelling at panoramic views on a magical uphill trek.

2 Sidemen (p209) Trekking through green rice fields in this picture-perfect river valley.

3 Amed Coast (p227) Chilling out in one of the little villages along this beautiful stretch of coast.

4 Tulamben (p234) Diving into the blue waters to explore a shipwreck right off the beach.

5 Gianyar Night Market (p206) Sampling aromatic and tasty local specialities at one of Bali's best night markets.

6 Puri Agung Semarapura (p207) Visiting the imposing palace compound of the Dewa Agung rajas.

7 Taman Tirta Gangga (p225) Wandering through the gardens of a water palace built for the last raja of Karangasem.

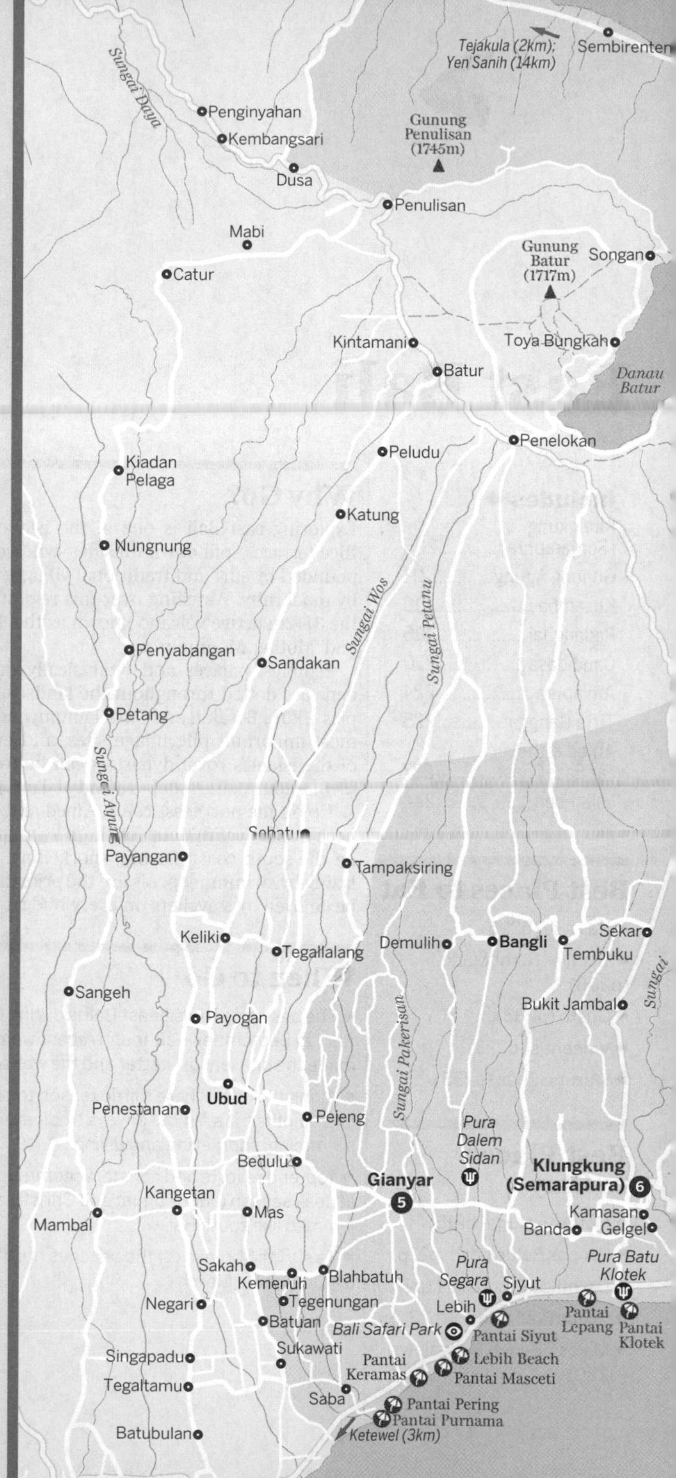

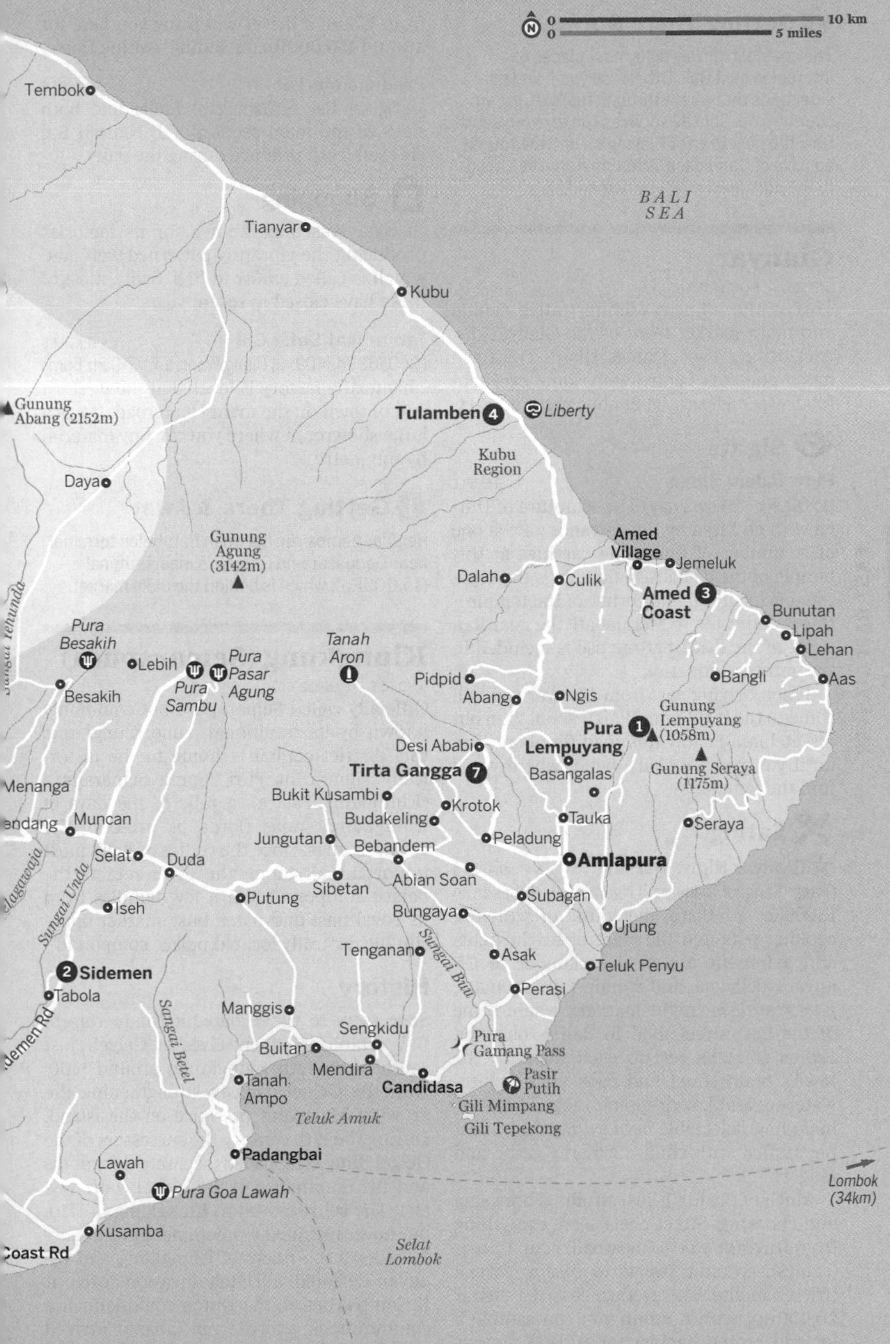

0
10 km
0
5 miles
BALI SEA
Tembok
Tianyar
Kubu
Gunung Abang (2152m)
Tulamben 4
Liberty
Kubu Region
Daya
Gunung Agung (3142m)
Amed Village
Jemeluk
Dalah
Culik
Amed Coast 3
Bunutan
Lipah
Lehan
Aas
Bangli
Pura Besakih
Lebih
Pura Pasar Agung
Pura Sambu
Tanah Aron
Pidpid
Abang
Ngis
Besakih
Pura 1 Lempuyang
Gunung Lempuyang (1058m)
Gunung Seraya (1175m)
Desi Ababi
Tirta Gangga 7
Basangalas
Menanga
Bukit Kusambi
Krotok
Budakeling
Tauka
Seraya
Muncan
Jungutan
Peladung
Selat
Bebandem
Amlapura
Duda
Abian Soan
Sibetan
Putung
Subagan
Iseh
Bungaya
Ujung
Sungai Unda
Tenganan
Asak
Sungai Buu
2 Sidemen
Teluk Penyu
Tabola
Perasi
Sangai Betel
Manggis
Sidemen Rd
Sengkidu
Pura Gamang Pass
Buitan
Mendira
Tanah Ampo
Candidasa
Pasir Putih
Gili Mimpang
Teluk Amuk
Gili Tepekong
Padangbai
Lawah
Pura Goa Lawah
Lombok (34km)
Kusamba
Coast Rd
Selat Lombok
Nusa Penida (4km)

Getting There & Away

The coastal highway links most places of interest in east Bali. Otherwise you'll find hillside roads that weave through the lush, green countryside. Shuttle services run to/from south Bali, the port town of Padangbai and the tourist enclave of Candidasa. Additional shuttles head to the northeast coast by demand.

Gianyar

0361 / POP 13,380

This is the affluent administrative capital and main market town of the Gianyar district, which also includes Ubud. The town has a compact centre with some excellent food, especially at the famous night market.

Sights

Pura Dalem Sidan TEMPLE

(15,000Rp; hours vary) The sculpture of Durga with children by the entrance gate is one of a number of fine stone carvings at this temple of the dead. Also notable is the separate enclosure in one corner of the temple – this is dedicated to Merajapati, the guardian spirit of the dead. Sarong use is included in the entrance donation.

When driving east from Gianyar you will come to the turn-off to Bangli about 2km out of Peteluan. Follow this road for about 1km until you reach a sharp bend, where you'll find the temple.

Eating

★Gianyar Night Market MARKET $

(Pasar Senggol Gianyar; Jl Ngurah Rai; dishes from 15,000Rp; 5-11pm) The sound of scores of cooking pots and the glare of bright lights add a frenetic and festive clamour to Gianyar's delicious and wonderfully aromatic *pasar malam* (night market), where some of the best street food in Bali is on offer. Scores of stalls set up each night in the town's main street and cook up a mouthwatering and jaw-dropping range of dishes, including delectable *babi guling* (spit-roast pig stuffed with chilli, turmeric, garlic and ginger).

Much of the fun is just strolling, browsing and choosing. Street chefs serve everything from fragrant *bakso* (meatball) soup to *sate* (satays), coconut sweets to *piseng goreng* (fried banana). The average cost of a dish is 20,000Rp; with a group you can sample a lot and be the happier for it. Peak time is the two hours after sunset. Best of all, the night market is only a 20-minute drive from Ubud: a driver will bring you here for around 150,000Rp, including waiting time.

Produce Market MARKET $

(Jl Ngurah Rai; 11am-2pm) Stalls line both sides of the main section of Jl Ngurah Rai and sell fresh produce during the day.

Shopping

Gianyar was once known for its factories producing the vibrantly patterned weft ikat, which is called *endek* in Bali. Sadly, most of these have closed in recent years.

Tenun Ikat Setia Cili TEXTILES

(0361-943409; Jl Ciung Wanara 7; 9am-5pm) This textile factory is located at the western end of town on the main Ubud road. It has a large showroom where you can buy material by the metre.

Getting There & Away

Regular bemos run between Batubulan terminal near Denpasar and Gianyar's main terminal (15,000Rp), which is behind the main market.

Klungkung (Semarapura)

0366 / POP 22,610

Officially called Semarapura but commonly known by its traditional name Klungkung, this district capital is home to the historically significant Puri Agung Semarapura (Klungkung Palace), a relic of the days of Klungkung's rajas (lords or princes), the Dewa Agungs. Once the centre of Bali's most important kingdom, the town retains the palace compound and a few temples from its royal past and has a busy market opposite the centrally located palace compound.

History

Successors to the Majapahit conquerors of Bali established themselves at Gelgel (just south of modern Klungkung) around 1400, with the Gelgel dynasty strengthening the growing Majapahit presence on the island. During the 17th century the successors of the Gelgel line established separate kingdoms and the dominance of the Gelgel court was lost. The court moved to Klungkung in 1710, but never regained a preeminent position.

In 1849 the rulers of Klungkung and Gianyar defeated a Dutch invasion force at Kusamba. Before the Dutch could launch a counterattack, a force from Tabanan arrived and the trader Mads Lange was able to broker a peace settlement.

Klungkung (Semarapura)

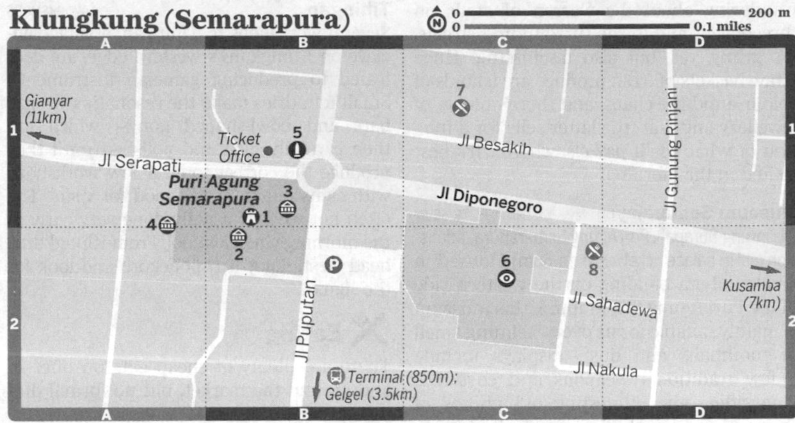

The south Bali kingdoms jostled between themselves for supremacy for the next 50 years, until the raja of Gianyar petitioned the Dutch for support. When the Dutch finally invaded the south, the king of Klungkung was forced to choose between a suicidal *puputan,* like the raja of Denpasar, or an ignominious surrender, such as that made by Tabanan's raja (or cutting a deal as the raja did up the road in Bangli). He chose the first option. In April 1908, as the Dutch surrounded his palace, the Dewa Agung and hundreds of his relatives and followers marched out to certain death from Dutch gunfire or the blades of their own *kris* (traditional daggers). The sacrifice is commemorated in the towering Puputan Monument.

Klungkung (Semarapura)

Top Sights

Sights

Eating

Sights

★Puri Agung Semarapura PALACE

(Klungkung Palace; Jl Untung Surapati; adult/child 12,000/6000Rp; ⏲8am-6pm) Built when the Dewa Agung dynasty moved here in 1710, this palace compound was laid out as a large square, believed to be in the form of a mandala, with courtyards, gardens, pavilions and moats. Most of the original palace and grounds were destroyed by the 1908 Dutch attacks; all that remain are the carved **Pemedal Agung**, the gateway on the south side of the square, the Kertha Gosa and the Bale Kambang. The ticket office is on the opposite side of Jl Untung Surapati, next to the Puputan Monument.

➡ Bale Kambang

Located within the palace compound, the ceiling of this beautiful floating *bale* (open-sided pavilion) showcases rows of paintings dealing with various subjects. The first row is based on the astrological calendar, the second on the folk tale of Pan and Men Brayut and their 18 children, and the upper rows on the adventures of the hero Sutasona.

➡ Kertha Gosa

(Hall of Justice) This open-sided pavilion in the northeastern corner of Puri Agung Semarapura was effectively the supreme court of the Klungkung kingdom, where disputes and cases that could not be settled at village level were eventually brought. A superb example of Klungkung architecture, it features a ceiling covered with fine 20th-century paintings in Kamasan (aka Wayang) style. These replaced the original 19th-century cloth paintings, which had deteriorated over time, and depict the Garuda story among other scenes.

Semarapura Market MARKET

(cnr Jl Diponegoro & Jl Puputan; ⏲6am-5pm) Klunkgkung's market is a vibrant hub of commerce and a meeting place for people of the region. You can easily spend an hour wandering about the warren of stalls on three levels, and in the surrounding streets. It's grimy, yes, but also fascinating. Huge straw baskets of fresh produce are islands of colour amid the chaos, and there's plenty of jewellery and ikat (the latter sells for a fraction of what you'll pay elsewhere). It's best visited in the morning.

Museum Semarajaya MUSEUM
(Jl Untung Surapati, Puri Agung Semarapura; admission incl in palace ticket; ⏲8am-6pm) Housed in a colonial-era building on the western side of the Puri Agung Semarapura, this museum is mainly notable for its overwhelming smell of mothballs and dust; displays include a few traditional weapons and costumes alongside some interesting old photos of the royal court, including a portrait of Dewa Agung Gede Jambe, the five-year-old crown prince who died in the 1908 *puputan* (mass ritual suicide).

Puputan Monument MONUMENT
(Jl Untung Surapati) Klungkung was the last Balinese kingdom to succumb to the Dutch (1908) and the sacrifice of its royal family, who committed *puputan* rather than surrender, is commemorated in the towering Puputan Monument, just across Jl Serapati from the Klungkung Palace.

WORTH A TRIP

NYOMAN GUNARSA MUSEUM

For an introduction to the work of the internationally renowned Balinese painter Nyoman Gunarsa (1944–2017), head to Klungkung's western outskirts to visit this vast three-storey **museum** (☎0366-22256; crn Jl Raya Takmung & Jl Raya Banda, Takmung; adult/child 75,000Rp/free; ⏲9am-4pm Mon-Sat).

Built and opened by the artist himself, it is home to many of his colourful and expressionistic depictions of traditional life, a number of which reference local folklore. As well as Gunarsa's works, there is an impressive variety of older pieces from his personal collection, including stone carvings, woodcarvings, architectural antiques, masks, puppets and textiles.

The museum is about 4km west from Klungkung, near a bend on the Gianyar road – look for the dummy policemen at the base of a large statue nearby.

Tihingan WORKSHOPS
Several workshops in Tihingan, a village enclave on Klungkung's western edge, are dedicated to producing gamelan instruments. Small foundries make the resonating bronze bars and bowl-shaped gongs, which are then carefully filed and polished until they produce the correct tone. A few workshops with signs out front are good for visits. The often hot work is usually done very early in the morning when it's cool. From Klungkung, head west along Jl Diponegoro and look for the signs.

Eating

There are plenty of cheap eats on offer in and around the market, but no formal dining options.

Pasar Senggol MARKET $
(crn Jl Besakih & Jl Gunung Rinjani; ⏲5pm-midnight) A night market, this is by far the best spot to eat if you're in town late. It's the usual flurry of woks, customers and noise.

Sumber Rasa CHINESE $
(☎0366-25097; Jl Nakula 5; dishes 20,000-30,000Rp; ⏲7am-10pm) A veteran and an affable Chinese sit-down place offering simple meals.

Getting There & Away

The best way to visit Klungkung is with your own transport and as part of a circuit taking in other sites up the mountains and along the coast.

This is one of the few towns in east Bali with a functioning *terminal bis* (bus station). Located south of the palace compound, just off Jl Puputan, it has bemo and bus services to/from Denpasar's Batubulan terminal (25,000Rp), Amlapura (20,000Rp), Padangbai (25,000Rp), Sideman (15,000Rp) and Gianyar (20,000Rp).

Bangli

☎0366 / POP KAWAN 8390, CEMPAGA 7520

Halfway up the slope to Penelokan, Bangli, once the capital of a kingdom, is a humble market town noteworthy for its sprawling temple, Pura Kehen, which is on a beautiful jungle road that runs east past rice terraces and connects at Sekar with roads to Rendang and Sideman.

History

Bangli dates from the early 13th century. In the Majapahit era, it broke away from Gelgel to become a separate kingdom, even though it was landlocked, poor and involved in long-running conflicts with neighbouring states.

In 1849, Bangli made a treaty with the Dutch that gave it control over the defeated north-coast kingdom of Buleleng, but Buleleng then rebelled and the Dutch imposed direct rule there. In 1909 the raja of Bangli chose for it to become a Dutch protectorate rather than face suicidal *puputan* (a warrior's fight to the death) or complete conquest by the neighbouring kingdoms or the colonial power.

Sights

★Pura Kehen HINDU TEMPLE

(Jl Sriwijaya, Cempaga; adult/child incl sarong 30,000Rp/free, parking 2000Rp; 9am-5pm) The state temple of the Bangli kingdom, Pura Kehen is a miniature version of Pura Besakih, Bali's most important temple. It's terraced up the hillside, with a flight of steps leading to the beautifully decorated entrance. The first courtyard has a huge banyan tree with a *kulkul* (hollow tree-trunk drum used to sound warnings) entwined in its branches and the inner courtyard has an 11-roof *meru* (multitiered shrine). Other shrines have thrones for the Hindu trinity: Brahma, Shiva and Vishnu.

Pura Kehen is located in Cempaga, 2km north of Bangli's town centre.

Pura Dalem Penunggekan HINDU TEMPLE

(Jl Merdeka, Kawan) FREE The exterior wall of this fascinating temple of the dead features vivid relief carvings of evil-doers getting their just desserts in the afterlife. One panel addresses the lurid fate of adulterers (men in particular may find the viewing uncomfortable). Other panels portray sinners as monkeys, while another is a good representation of sinners begging to be spared the fires of hell. It's in Kawan, 3km south of the Bangli's town centre.

Eating

The *pasar malam,* on Jl Merdeka beside the bemo terminal, has traditional warungs (food stalls) and you'll also find fresh and tasty food stalls in the shambolic **day market**. Temple-offering supplies are sold here 24 hours a day.

Getting There & Away

Most people visit Bangli under their own steam or on organised tours to Pura Besakih.

OFF THE BEATEN TRACK

GELGEL

Situated about 4km south of central Klungkung, on the way to the coast, Gelgel was once the seat of Bali's most powerful dynasty. The town's decline started in 1710, when the court moved to present-day Klungkung, and finished when the Dutch bombarded the place in 1908. Today, few traces of its past grandeur remain. The main temple, **Pura Dasar Bhuana**, has vast courtyards that point to its past as a royal place of worship.

About 500m east of Pura Dasar Bhuana, the **Masjid Nurul Huda Gelgel** is Bali's oldest mosque. Although modern-looking, it was established in the late 16th century for the benefit of Muslim missionaries from Java who were unwilling to return home after failing to make any converts.

Sidemen

0366 / POP 3780

In Sidemen (pronounced Si-da-men), a walk in any direction is a communion with nature. Winding through one of Bali's most beautiful river valleys, the road to this hilltop village offers marvellous paddy-field scenery, a delightful rural character and extraordinary views of Gunung Agung (when the clouds permit).

German artist Walter Spies lived in this part of Bali for some time from 1932 in order to escape the perpetual party of his own making in Ubud. Later the Swiss painter Theo Meier, nearly as famous as Spies for his influence on Balinese art, lived in the same house. These days, tourists head here to get away from the bustle of the island's larger towns and hike the scenic countryside.

Activities

There are many **walks** through the rice and chilli fields in the multihued green valley. One involves a spectacular three-hour, round-trip climb up to **Pura Bukit Tageh**, a small temple with big views. No matter where you stay, you'll be able to arrange guides for in-depth hiking (about 75,000Rp per person for a two-hour hike) or just set out on your own exploration. Many of the resorts offer their guests guided walks as part of activities programmes, too.

Nyoman Trekking HIKING
(0852 3999 5789; nyomansidemen@gmail.com; 2hr trek 75,000Rp) Nyoman Subrata can guide you through the local countryside; he also guides on Gunug Agung when it's safe.

Sleeping

There is a decent range of resorts, hotels and guesthouses at various budget levels in Sidemen; most are located on Jl Raya Tebola. It can get cool and misty at night, so pack an extra layer or two of clothing.

Khrisna Home Stay HOMESTAY $
(0815 5832 1543; pinpinaryadi@yahoo.com; Jl Raya Tebola; s 250,000-350,000Rp, d 350,000-700,000Rp, f 900,000-1,000,000Rp;) This friendly nine-room homestay is surrounded by organic fruit trees and has a cute pool area. The rooms are comfortable, although the singles are very small; all have fans. One deluxe double has a lovely view over the rice fields. The little restaurant serves excellent breakfasts and vegetable-dominated dinners (mains 35,000Rp to 50,000Rp).

★ **Darmada Eco Resort** RESORT $$
(0853 3803 2100; www.darmadabali.com; Jl Raya Luah; r 500,000-700,000Rp, f 900,000-1,100,000Rp;) Rooms at this well-priced resort set in a lush river valley are simple affairs, but this isn't a problem as most guests spend their time in the lovely spring-water swimming pool or taking advantage of the extensive programme of paid activities (meditation, yoga, massage, trekking, cooking classes). The resort's riverside restaurant is excellent. Wi-fi in common areas only.

★ **Samanvaya** BOUTIQUE HOTEL $$
(0821 4710 3884; www.samanvaya-bali.com; Jl Raya Tebola; r US$90-142, ste US$124-170;) Sidemen's original boutique choice, the Samanvaya commands sweeping views over rice fields to the ocean and has a textbook 'Bali chic' decor. Every room is comfortable and has a view, but the best are in the superior and deluxe categories. Facilities include a bamboo yoga space, infinity pool, hot tub, spa pavilion (massages from 120,000Rp) and restaurant (mains 75,000Rp to 120,000Rp).

★ **Alamdhari Resort and Spa** HOTEL $$
(0812 3700 6290; www.alamdhari.com; Jl Raya Tebola; d/tw 680,000-850,000Rp, f 1,000,000-1,250,000Rp; P) Recently opened, this boutique choice is pleasing to both the eye and the wallet. The 14 rooms are light and airy, with comfortable beds, fans, excellent bathrooms and good-sized balconies. The view from the pool – best appreciated from one of the comfy sun lounges provided – is spectacular, and facilities include a restaurant (mains 50,000Rp to 120,000Rp) and a small spa. Love it.

Giri Carik GUESTHOUSE $$
(0819 3666 5821, 0813 3955 4604; www.facebook.com/GiriCarik; Jl Raya Tebola; r 450,000-550,000Rp;) The key to Sidemen's charm lies in its simplicity, and this place is a good example. Five basic rooms (some with wonderful views from small terraces), a restaurant (mains 40,000Rp to 55,000Rp) and a small pool are all that's on offer, but in our minds that's enough for a recommendation.

Nirarta Centre RESORT $$
(0812 465 2123; www.awareness-bali.com; off Jl Raya Tebola; s €55-65, d €55-75; P) Guests here partake in serious programs for personal and spiritual development, including free daily meditation sessions. The comfortable rooms are split among six bungalows, some right on the river; the restaurant serves a good range of Thai, Indian and Indonesian veggie and organic dishes (mains 45,000Rp to 125,000Rp). Sadly, there's no pool.

Subak Tabola RESORT $$
(0811 389 3444, 0811 386 6197; www.subaktabolavilla.com; Jl Raya Tebola; r US$90-135, ste US$135-150, f US$200-250; P) Set in an amphitheatre of rice terraces, this slightly faded but well-maintained resort has spacious grounds and is a great choice for families as there's a free daily activities programme (yoga, trekking) and dedicated children's activities can be organised (paid by donation). Facilities include a bar, Thai/Indonesian restaurant (mains 45,000Rp to 125,000Rp) and pool. Wi-fi is available in common areas only.

Wapa di Ume RESORT $$$
(0366-543 7600; www.wapadiumesidemen.com; Jl Raya Tebola; r US$300-350, ste US$380-430, pool villa US$530-580.; P@) Associated with the Ubud hotel of the same name, this is the first luxury resort in the Sidemen area. Villas (some with private pool) are scattered across the 1.2-hectare site, which has a riverfront location and enjoys wonderful views of the rice terraces. Facilities include two pools, a gym, yoga pavilion, spa, panoramic rooftop bar and swish restaurant (mains 65,000Rp to 198,000Rp). Complimentary daily activities and offerings include trekking, sightseeing, yoga and afternoon tea.

Eating

Most accommodation options have restaurants and there are warungs along Jl Raya Tebola. The restaurants at Darmada Eco Resort, Samanvaya and Wapa di Ume welcome non-guests.

★Warung Melita INTERNATIONAL $
(☎0853 3803 2100; www.darmadabali.com/warung.html; Jl Raya Luah, Darmada Eco Resort; mains 30,000-100,000Rp; ⏲7.30am-9pm; P) Head to this riverside *bale* (open-air pavilion) in the Darmada Eco Resort to dine on tasty Balinese and Western dishes, including pizza and home-made ice cream. The chefs grow their own veggies in an organic kitchen garden, and drinks include beer, wine, home-made chai and fresh juice. It's also a good place for afternoon tea (cake 400,000Rp).

★Dapur Kapulaga BALINESE $
(☎0852 3861 5775; Jl Raya Tebola; mains 32,000-50,000Rp; ⏲1-10pm;) Serving a predominantly organic menu of Western and Balinese staples, this friendly and clean warung with its distinctive checkerboard-tiled floor is a great choice. You'll find it in front of the Alamdhari Resort & Spa. No alcohol, but the house-concocted Sidemen Cooler steps into the breach nicely.

Joglo D'Uma BALINESE $
(☎0819 1566 6456; Jl Raya Tebola; mains 38,000-50,000Rp; ⏲11am-9pm;) The food at this pavilion restaurant is of average quality but the view is anything but – the panorama of rice fields and verdant hills is absolutely stunning. It also accepts credit cards and is licensed.

Shopping

Pelangi Traditional Weaving ARTS & CRAFTS
(☎0812 392 3483; Jl Soka 67; ⏲8am-6pm) Sidemen is a centre for culture and arts, particularly *endek* cloth (vibrantly patterned weft ikat) and *songket* (silver- or gold-threaded cloth). Here, employees man the looms downstairs and customers can admire their work and enjoy the Sideman views from the upstairs showroom.

Getting There & Away

The Sideman road can be a beautiful part of any day trip from south Bali or Ubud. It connects in the north with the Rendang–Amlapura road just west of Duda. Unfortunately the road is busy due to huge trucks hauling rocks for Bali's incessant construction.

A less-travelled route to Pura Besakih goes northeast from Klungkung (Semarapura), via Sideman and Iseh, to another scenic treat: the Rendang–Amlapura road.

Near the centre of Sideman, a small road heads west for 500m to a fork where signs will direct you to various guesthouses.

Gunung Agung

Bali's highest and most revered mountain, Gunung Agung is an imposing volcano that can be seen from most of south and east Bali when clear of cloud and mist. Most sources say it's 3142m high. The summit is an oval crater, about 700m across, with its highest point on the western edge above Pura Besakih.

As it's the spiritual centre of Bali, traditional houses are laid out on an axis in line with Agung and many locals always

GUNUNG AGUNG: READY TO BLOW?

In September 2017, an increase in seismic activity within the bowels of Gunung Agung (Mt Agung) prompted Indonesian officials to announce that an eruption was 'imminent'. More than 130,000 people fled their homes near the flanks of the rumbling giant, clearing out a 12km radius and pouring into temporary shelters as the volcano approached its 'critical' phase.

The officials were right: the volcano erupted five times in November 2017, and four times in 2018. None of these eruptions claimed lives or caused significant damage, but the 2017 incidents involved major evacuations from local villages and led to the temporary closure of both Ngurah Rai International Airport on Bali and Lombok International Airport. At the time of writing, there was an official Level 3 (standby) alert current, with an exclusion zone of 4km around the volcano's crater; deep volcanic tremors were being reported. Many Balinese fear that another, possibly devastating, eruption is inevitable. The Mount Agung Daily Report Facebook page (www.facebook.com/groups/415222448896889/) posts regular updates.

Gunung Agung previously erupted in 1963, killing approximately 1600 people and sending ash as far as the capital Jakarta.

know where they are in relation to the peak, which is thought to house ancestral spirits.

Sights

★Pura Besakih HINDU TEMPLE

(60,000Rp, parking 5000Rp) Perched nearly 1000m up the side of Gunung Agung, this is Bali's most important Hindu temple. The site encompasses 23 separate but related temples, with the largest and most important being **Pura Penataran Agung**, built on six levels terraced up the slope. It has an imposing *candi bentar* (split gateway); note that tourists are not allowed inside. The Pura Besakih complex hosts frequent ceremonies, but the recent eruptions of the volcano have kept both worshipper and visitor numbers down.

The precise origins of the temple complex are not totally clear, but it almost certainly dates from prehistoric times. The stone bases of Pura Penataran Agung and several other temples resemble megalithic stepped pyramids and date back at least 2000 years. It was certainly used as a Hindu place of worship from 1284, when the first Javanese conquerors settled in Bali. By the 15th century Besakih had become a state temple of the Gelgel dynasty.

When you reach the site there are two parking areas: Parkir Bawa and Parking Atas. The former is the main parking area and the first you'll encounter coming from the south; all tourists must park here. There is a ticket office close by. Sarongs and sashes are available next to the office, and must be worn; rental is included in your ticket. Many visitors bring their own.

Activities

Hiking

Climbing Gunung Agung takes you through verdant forest in the clouds and rewards with sweeping (dawn) views. It's best to climb during the dry season (April to September); July to September are the most reliable months. At other times the paths can be slippery and dangerous and the views are clouded over (especially true in January and February). Climbing is not permitted when major religious events are being held at Pura Besakih, which generally includes most of April.

Points to consider for a climb:

- Always check official warnings before planning or setting out on a climb.
- Use a guide.
- Respect your guide's pauses at shrines for prayers on the sacred mountain.
- Get to the top before 8am – the clouds that often obscure the view of Agung also obscure the view *from* Agung.
- Take a strong torch (flashlight), extra batteries, plenty of water (2L per person), snack food, waterproof clothing and a warm jumper (sweater).
- Wear strong shoes or boots and have manicured toes – the trail is very steep and the descent is especially hard on your feet.
- This is a hard climb, don't fool yourself.
- Take frequent rests and don't be afraid to ask your guide to slow down.

Pura Besakih Complex

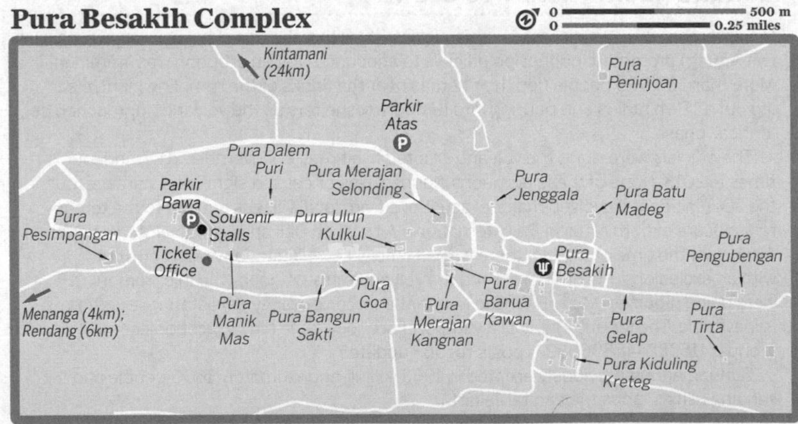

AN UNHOLY EXPERIENCE?

Some visitors to Pura Besakih report being hassled by touts and scammed by locals; others have an enjoyable, hassle-free experience. What follows are some of the possible ploys you should be aware of before a visit:

➡ Unofficial and official guides hang around looking for visitors. They may emphatically tell you that guide services are compulsory, tell you that temples are 'closed for a ceremony' and quote a ridiculously high price for a short visit. None of this is true: you may always walk among the temples and no 'guide' can get you into a closed temple. Only hire a guide if you want one, and always agree on a fee before you start.

➡ Once inside the complex, you may receive offers to 'come pray with me'. Visitors who seize on this chance to gain entry to a forbidden temple can face demands of 100,000Rp or more.

➡ Never allow anyone to keep the ticket you are issued with. It's just an excuse for someone else to sell you another.

➡ Local women may try to give you offerings – if you accept them, they will then demand 10,000Rp or so. It is not necessary to make offerings in the temples.

➡ Sarong and sash hire is included in the ticket price – get one when you pay for your ticket. Alternatively, bring your own.

➡ A scooter ride up the hill from the ticket office is also included in the ticket price. Drivers will ask for a tip but this is at your discretion.

Routes

It's possible to climb Agung from various directions. The two most popular routes are from the following places:

Pura Pasar Agung (on the southern slopes; about four hours to ascend) This route involves the least walking because Pura Pasar Agung (Agung Market Temple) is high on the southern slopes of the mountain (around 1500m) and can be reached by a good road north from Selat.

Pura Besakih (on the southwest side of the mountain; about six hours to ascend) This climb is much tougher than the already demanding southern approach and is only for the very physically fit; for the best chance of a clear view before the clouds close in, you should start at midnight.

Either route can take you to the summit, although most people on the shorter route go to the crater rim (2866m).

Practicalities

Trips with guides on either of the routes up Gunung Agung generally include breakfast and other meals as well as a place to stay, but be sure to confirm all details in advance. Guides are also able to arrange transport.

Most of the places to stay in the region, including those at Selat, along the Sidemen road and at Tirta Gangga, will recommend guides for Gunung Agung climbs.

Most guides charge between 600,000Rp and 900,000Rp per person for the climb from Pura Besikah and 450,000Rp to 600,000Rp per person from Pura Pasar Agung.

Wayan Tegteg HIKING
(☎0813 3852 5677; www.facebook.com/wayan.tegteg.7) A recommended Gunung Agung guide who wins plaudits from hikers.

I Ketut Uriada HIKING
(☎0812 364 6426; ketut.uriada@gmail.com) This knowledgeable guide in Muncan can arrange treks throughout the region. He also operates a small guesthouse (rooms 125,000Rp to 160,000Rp) and can organise transport to/from the area.

Getting There & Away

Usually you'll make arrangements with your guide to get to the trailheads for a climb. There is no public transport.

Coast Road to Kusamba

☎0361

The coastal highway between Sanur and Kusamba runs alongside a swathe of black-sand beaches and past two of the island's best surf breaks (at Keramas and Ketewel). There aren't many compelling reasons to pause on your journey, as most beaches are dirty and many aren't safe to swim at. The highway is lined with stores, factories and warungs used by truckers.

Sights

Bali Safari Park AMUSEMENT PARK

(☎0361-950000; www.balisafarimarinepark.com; off Prof Dr Ida Bagus Mantra Bypass Km19.8; adult/child from 513,000/411,000Rp; ⏰9am-5pm, Bali Agung show 2.30pm Tue-Sun) This theme park is filled with critters whose species never set foot in Bali until their cage door opened (tigers, lions, elephants, hippos, rhinos etc). Entry is by package tickets that can be tailored to interests – opt for safaris, a Bali Agung show, waterpark access, animal shows, meals, night safaris and more. Note that animal shows and rides are offered here despite there being overwhelming evidence that shows and rides are harmful for animals such as elephants.

The park is near Pantai Lebih; free shuttles run to tourist centres across south Bali. Tickets are cheapest when purchased online.

Beaches

As you head east on the coast road from Sanur, pretty much any road or lane heading south will end up at a beach.

The shoreline is striking, with beaches in volcanic shades of grey pounded by waves. The entire coast has great religious significance and there are oodles of temples scattered along it. At the many small coastal-village beaches, cremation formalities reach their conclusion when the ashes are consigned to the sea. Ritual purification ceremonies for temple artefacts are also held on these beaches.

Some key points:

- Ketewel and Keramas are top spots for surfing.
- Swimming in the often pounding surf is dangerous.
- Most beaches have no shade.
- Many beaches have a food or drinks vendor or two.
- You'll need your own transport to reach these beaches.
- Locals will sometimes charge you an access fee – about 5000Rp.
- Rubbish is a depressing fact at most of the beaches.

Pantai Lebih BEACH

Just off the coastal highway, Lebih Beach has glittering mica-infused sand. Fishing boats line the shore and the air is redolent with the smell of BBQ fish emanating from a strip of beachside warungs; this is an excellent stop for lunch.

North, just across the coast road, impressive **Pura Segara** looks across the strait to Nusa Penida, home of Jero Gede Macaling (king of the demons) – the temple helps protect Bali from his evil influence.

Pantai Purnama BEACH

(Purnama) A small beach with black sand reflecting billions of sparkles in the sunlight. Religion is big here: the temple close to the coastal highway, **Pura Erjeruk**, hosts elaborate full-moon purification ceremonies.

Pantai Keramas BEACH

(Keramas) Villa and hotel projects are sprouting here. The surf is consistent and world-class.

Pantai Masceti BEACH

Masceti beach is a study in contrasts. Some 15km east of Sanur, it has a few drinks vendors and one of Bali's nine sacred directional temples, **Pura Masceti**. Right on the beach, the temple is built in the shape of a *garuda* (a large mythical bird) and enlivened with gaudy statuary. There's a certain irony to the bird-shape as both the temple grounds and a huge building nearby are used for cockfights.

Pantai Klotok BEACH

Sacred statues from Pura Besakih are brought to the temple at this beach for ritual cleansing. Admire the pale blue flowers – they're sacred – on the wild midori shrubs here.

Pantai Ketewel BEACH

Ketewel is known for its surfing, which demands advanced skills; it's a tricky reef-rocky right.

Sleeping

Wyndham Tamansari Jivva Resort RESORT $$

(☎0366-543 7988; www.wyndhamjivvabali.com; Pantai Lepang; r from 800,000Rp; P❄📶🏊) Popular with Chinese tour groups, this 222-room resort next to unappealing Pantai Lepang offers a mix of comfortable room types; decor is bland but amenities are good (kettle, iron, work desk). When we last visited, one of the two pools had been badly damaged by a king tide and was closed. Facilities include a spa, gym and two restaurants.

★Hotel Komune RESORT $$$

(☎0361-301 8888; www.komuneresorts.com; Jl Pantai Keramas, Keramas; r from US$99, ste from US$130, villas from US$250; P❄☎≋) A resort in the true sense of the word, Komune offers everything needed for an active and enjoyable holiday. The surf here is among Bali's best, although not suitable for beginners. Other activities include yoga, meditation and kids movie nights. Rooms are stylish and comfortable, and the beachfront Beach Club (restaurant/bar/pool) has a party vibe at every time of the day.

Light towers make it possible for surfers to take their boards out at night; board and wetsuit hire is available. The kids club has a trampoline, swing and skate park.

Eating

Most beaches have a food or drinks vendor or two, at least. Pantai Lebih has a dozen good warung with grilled seafood and more.

★Hotel Komune Beach Club INTERNATIONAL $$

(☎0361-301 8888; www.komuneresorts.com/keramasbali/beach-club; sandwiches & burgers 65,000-95,000Rp, mains 58,000-250,000Rp; ⏲6.30am-11pm; ☎) Enjoying the restaurant, bar, pool and outdoor cinema at Hotel Komune's beach club isn't limited to the resort's in-house guests, which is good news for those travelling along the coastal highway in east Bali. The menu includes something for every taste, with burgers, sandwiches, pizza, pasta and Indonesian dishes on offer. We applaud the dedicated vegan and kids menus.

Getting There & Away

There's no public transport, so you'll need your own wheels. Cyclists will enjoy the beach access roads, but the truck-dominated traffic on the main road can be harrowing.

Kusamba

☎0366 / POP 5910

At the fishing and salt-making village of Kusamba you will see rows of colourful *jukung* (outrigger fishing boats) lined up all along the grey-sand beach. The fishing is usually done at night and the 'eyes' on the front of the boats help navigate through the darkness. The fish market in Kusamba displays the night's catch. Both east and west of Kusamba there are small salt-making huts lined up in rows along the beach.

Pura Goa Lawah CAVE

(Bat Cave Temple; Jl Raya Goa Lawah; adult/child 30,000/15,000Rp, car parking 5000Rp; ⏲8am-7pm) One of nine directional temples in Bali, this cave in a cliff face 3km east of Kusamba is full of bats and the complex is equally overcrowded with tour groups, both foreign and local. You'll probably want to exclaim 'Holy Bat Guano, Batman!' when you get a whiff of the odours emanating from the cave – Alfred Pennyworth definitely wouldn't approve. Superficially, the temple is small and unimpressive, but it is very old and of great significance to the Balinese.

Legend says the cave leads all the way to Pura Besakih, some 19km away, but it's unlikely that you'd want to try this route. The bats provide sustenance for the legendary giant snake, the deity Naga Basuki, which is also believed to live in the cave. Ignore touts offering guiding services (unnecessary) and if someone asks your name, don't give it or when you exit the cave you'll be presented with a 'gift' with your name on it and told you have to buy it. Bring a sarong or hire one at the ticket office (5000Rp).

Merta Sari BALINESE $

(☎0366-30406; Jl Kresna, Pesinggahan; meals 25,000Rp; ⏲10am-6pm) Popular traditional eatery in the village of Pesinggahan, two kilometres southeast of Kusamba. The set menu comprises juicy fish satay, fragrant fish soup, vegetables, rice and a super-spicy sambal.

Warung Lesehan Sari Baruna BALINESE $

(☎0813 3952 5459; Jl Raya Goa Lawah; meals 30,000Rp; ⏲6am-7pm) Follow the crowds of Balinese to this open-air pavilion near Pura Goa Lawah. There's only one meal option: a *paket pesinggahan* (set meal) comprising spicy fish satay, fragrant fishball broth, fish steamed in banana leaves, rice, snake beans, peanuts and a fiery red sambal.

Sari Baruna is on the coast road 1km east of Kusamba, just before Pura Goa Lawah.

Getting There & Away

The coast road from Sanur crosses the traditional route to the east at Kusamba before joining the road near Pura Goa Lawah. The main coast road is busy with traffic and allows easy access to the region of east Bali if you have your own transport.

Small local boats travel to Nusa Penida and Nusa Lembongan, which are clearly visible from Kusamba (boats from Padangbai are generally faster and safer).

Padangbai

0363 / POP 3090

This little beach town is the port for public ferries connecting Bali with Lombok and Nusa Penida; there are also fast boats to Lombok and the Gilis. When not inundated by travellers in transit, it has a laid-back vibe and its accommodation, eating and drinking options are solidly geared towards the backpacker and diving markets. Though its location on a small bay with a curve of beach is attractive, the town itself is quite ugly and dirty – don't come here seeking a sybaritic sojourn.

Beaches

Blue Lagoon Beach BEACH

On the far side of Padangbai's eastern headland, about a 500m walk from the town centre, is this small sandy beach. It has a couple of warungs and gentle, family-friendly surf.

Bias Tugal BEACH

Walk southwest from the ferry terminal and follow the trail up the hill for about 1.3km to Bias Tugal, also known as Pantai Kecil (Little Beach), on the exposed coast outside the bay. Be careful in the water as it is subject to strong currents. There are a couple of daytime warung here.

Sights

Pura Silayukti TEMPLE

(Jl Silayukti) See the place where Empu Kuturan – who introduced the caste system to Bali in the 11th century – is said to have lived by following a path up to this headland at the northeast corner of Padangbai's bay. From the three temples here, you'll have good views.

Activities

The main activities are diving and snorkelling; there are a number of dive centres and shops on Jl Silayukti, opposite the main beach.

Padangbai

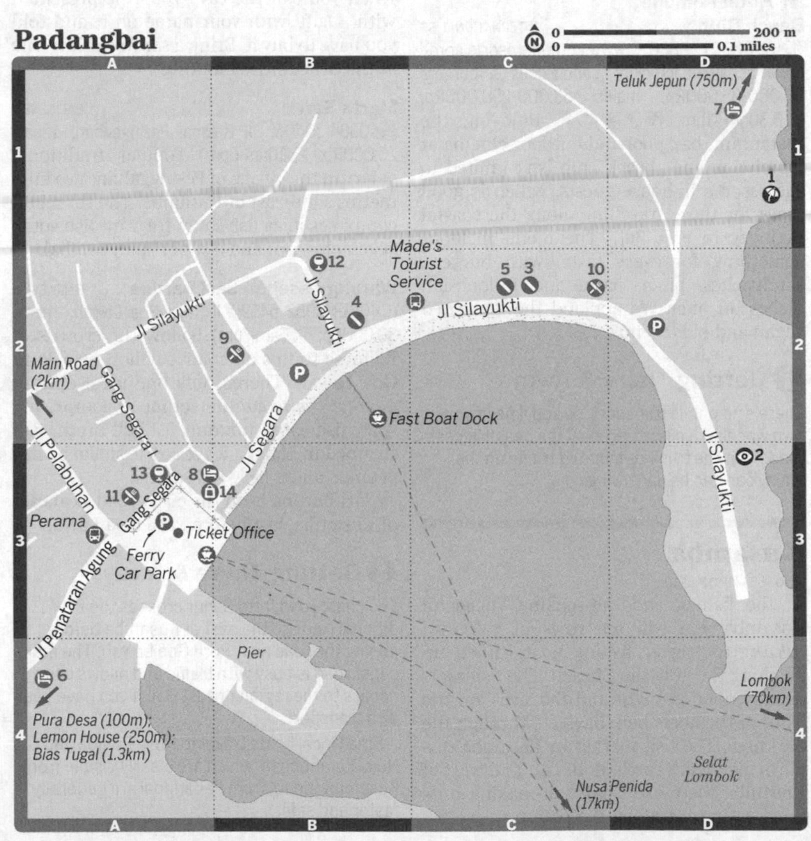

Diving

There is good diving on the coral reefs around Padangbai, but the water can be a bit cold and visibility is not always ideal. The most popular local dives are **Blue Lagoon** and **Teluk Jepun** (Jepun Bay), both in Teluk Amuk, the bay just east of Padangbai. There's a good range of soft and hard corals and varied marine life, including sharks, turtles and wrasse, and a 23m wall at Blue Lagoon.

Many local outfits offer diving trips in the area, including to Gili Tepekong and Gili Biaha and on to Tulamben and Nusa Penida.

Snorkelling

One of the best and most accessible walk-in snorkel sites is off **Blue Lagoon Beach**. Note that it is subject to strong currents when the tide is out. Other sites such as **Teluk Jepun** can be reached by local boat (or check with the dive operators to see if they have any room on their boats; the cost will be around 130,000Rp). Snorkel-set hire costs around 50,000Rp per day.

The local dive shops can organise snorkelling trips for beginners and experienced snorkellers (450,000Rp to 750,000Rp per person) and will also hire snorkel gear by the half- or full day.

OK Divers DIVING
(☎0811 385 8830; www.okdiversbali.com; Jl Silayukti 6, OK Divers Resort; 2 dives 1,080,000Rp) Offers a range of PADI diving courses and diving safaris around the island, as well as local dives and snorkelling opportunities. The associated resort offers good accommodation.

Water Worxx DIVING
(☎0363-41220; www.waterworxbali.com; Jl Silayukti; 2 dives US$80-125) A well-regarded dive operator offering trips to surrounding areas, plus PADI and SSI courses. Can also arrange dives for travellers with disabilities.

Geko Dive DIVING
(☎0363-41516; www.gekodivebali.com; Jl Silayukti; dives from 650,000Rp) With a base just across from the beach, this long-established PADI-accredited operator offers equipment hire, dives and snorkelling trips.

Sleeping

Decent accommodation options are thin on the ground, with dark, dirty and depressing homestays and guesthouses well represented. Fortunately, there are a couple of decent hostels and at least two resorts worthy of the appellation. Most accommodation choices sit in the budget category.

Bamboo Paradise HOSTEL $
(☎0822 6630 4330, 0363-438 1765; www.facebook.com/bambooparadisebali/; Jl Penataran Agung; dm 120,000Rp, s 200,000-350,000Rp, d 250,000-400,000Rp; ❄📶) In a leafy street close to the port, this is Padangbai's best budget accommodation. A full makeover with a new architect-designed building was due to be revealed in 2019, but the laid-back vibe, bar, lounge, dorm accommodation and good breakfast will be retained.

Fat Barracuda HOSTEL $
(☎0822 6630 4330; www.facebook.com/fatbarracuda; Jl Segara; dm 115,000Rp, s/d without bathroom 200,000/280,000Rp; ❄📶) Right next to the harbour, this backpacker joint offers 10 beds in a clean, air-conditioned dorm; beds are curtained for privacy. There are lockers (BYO padlock) but no common areas; breakfast is served in the next-door office. The one private room is upstairs but shares the dorm's hot-water bathroom.

Padangbai

Sights
1 Blue Lagoon Beach ... D1
2 Pura Silayukti ... D3

Activities, Courses & Tours
3 Geko Dive ... C2
4 OK Divers ... B2
5 Water Worxx ... C2

Sleeping
6 Bamboo Paradise ... A4
7 Bloo Lagoon Eco Village ... D1
8 Fat Barracuda ... A3
OK Divers Resort & Spa ... (see 4)

Eating
Colonial Restaurant ... (see 4)
9 Ozone Café ... B2
10 Topi Inn ... C2
11 Zen Inn ... A3

Drinking & Nightlife
12 Omang Omang ... B2
13 Shelter Bay ... A3

Shopping
14 Ryan Book Shop ... A3

Lemon House GUESTHOUSE $
(☎0812 4637 1575; www.lemonhousebali.com; Gang Melanting 5; dm 120,000Rp, r without bathroom 210,000Rp, r 300,000Rp; 📶) On a clear day you can see Lombok from this hillside guesthouse. The downside of the elevated location is a steep walk up 70 steps to get here from the port. One room has views and its own bathroom; others (including a cramped mixed dorm sleeping four in bunks) share bathrooms. Wi-fi access can be patchy, and plumbing temperamental.

OK Divers Resort & Spa RESORT $$
(☎0811 385 8830; www.okdiversbali.com; Jl Silayukti 6; r from 990,000Rp; P❄📶🏊) 🍃 Facilities here are the best the town has to offer, with a spa, two pools, a dive centre and a pavilion cafe. Rooms are well set up, with satellite TV and tea- and coffee-making facilities. One room has been designed to accommodate guests in wheelchairs. The only negative is the wi-fi access – guests report that it is consistently unreliable.

★**Bloo Lagoon Eco Village** RESORT $$$
(☎0363-41211; www.bloolagoon.com; Jl Silayukti; 1-/2-/3-bed bungalow from US$124/181/202; P❄@📶🏊) 🍃 Crowning a clifftop at the town's eastern edge, this place is notable for its sea-facing yoga deck (free classes daily), well-priced spa (massages 210,000Rp to 600,000Rp) and kid-friendly pool with water slide. The 25 guest bungalows come with one, two or three bedrooms. All overlook Blue Lagoon Beach and have large outdoor living terraces, kitchens and open-air bathrooms; some have air-con.

The resort's panoramic restaurant, **Helix 64**, offers a varied menu (mains 50,000Rp to 170,000Rp) that makes the most of local organic vegetables and includes plenty of vegan options.

Eating

Beach fare and backpacker staples dominate menus in Padangbai – lots of fresh seafood, Indonesian classics, pizza, burgers and, yes, banana pancakes. You can easily laze away a few hours soaking up the scene at the places along Jl Segara and Jl Silayukti, which have harbour views during the day and cool breezes in the evening.

Topi Inn CAFE $
(☎0363-41424; Jl Silayukti; mains 39,000-176,000Rp; ⏰7.30am-10pm; 📶✎) A laid-back vibe (sometimes a bit *too* laid back in terms of its service) and a huge menu of Western and Indonesian food await at this beach shack bar/eatery below the guesthouse of the same name. It offers a particularly good breakfast (eggs, jaffles or pancakes) and a decent nasi goreng at other times.

Zen Inn INTERNATIONAL $
(☎0363-41418; www.zeninn.com; Gang Segara; breakfast dishes 30,000-95,000Rp, mains 40,000-110,000Rp; ⏰7am-11pm; 📶) Burgers, pastas and barbecue mains are served in this clean and airy portside cafe that stays open late by local standards – often until 11pm.

Ozone Café INTERNATIONAL $
(☎0817 470 8597; off Jl Silayukti; mains from 20,000Rp; ⏰8am-11pm) Close to the port, this beach shack–style place serves burgers, jaffles, sandwiches and Indonesian staples.

★**Colonial Restaurant** CAFE $$
(☎0811 397 8837; www.facebook.com/thecolonialpadangbai; Jl Silayukti 6, OK Divers Resort & Spa; mains 50,000-150,000Rp; ⏰7am-11pm; 📶✎) The most stylish eatery in town, this pavilion cafe overlooking the pool at the OK Divers resort is a great place to while away a few hours. Food is much better than the Padangbai norm, with an eclectic range of both Western and Indonesian choices on offer. Drinks include fresh juices, milkshakes and Bintang on tap. Patrons can use the pool.

Drinking & Nightlife

Most of Padangbai's bars and cafes are clustered in the town centre, east of the port; many of the bars offer live music a few nights a week. The town's best coffee is available at the Double Barrel Cafe, which is attached to the Omang Omang bar and eatery.

★**Omang Omang** BAR
(☎0363-438 1251; www.facebook.com/OmangOmang999; Jl Silayukti 12) A loyal crew of Omangsters (regulars) join a constant stream of blow-ins at this friendly eatery, bar and live-music venue. Nosh on toasties, tacos, burgers and Indonesian favourites, down an ice-cold Bintang or two and rock along with the house blues band on Monday nights. Decent coffee, too.

Shelter Bay BAR
(☎0877 6153 5735; www.facebook.com/Shelter-Bay-204686660172027; Gang Segara; ⏰3.30-11pm) Opposite the port, this bar tries to mask its lack of atmosphere with the loudest music in town – it's definitely not the place for a quiet tipple. That said, it screens sport

on a big TV, has a dart board and is conveniently located for those waiting for their boat to depart.

Shopping

Ryan Book Shop BOOKS
(☎0363-41215; Jl Segara 38; ⊙8am-8pm) Source a used paperback or postcard at this shop near the port.

Information

There are several ATMs around town, including one on Jl Pelabuhan near the port and another on Jl Segara opposite the main beach.

Getting There & Away

BOAT

Anyone who carries your luggage on or off the ferries or fast boats will expect to be paid, so agree on the price first or carry your own stuff. Also, watch out for scams where the porter may try to sell you a ticket you've already bought.

Ignore touts who meet all arriving boats and departing passengers. Only buy public ferry tickets from the official window in the ferry building.

Lombok & Gili Islands

You can travel to/from Lombok on fast boat or public ferry, and head to/from the Gilis by fast boat. Be sure to consider important safety information.

Fast Boats Several companies link Padangbai to the Gilis and Lombok; they have offices on the waterfront. Fares are negotiable and start at 250,000Rp one-way. Travel times will be more than the 90 minutes advertised.

Public Ferries (off Jl Segara) Car ferries travel between Padangbai and Lembar on Lombok (adult/child/motorbike/car 46,000/29,000/129,000/917,000Rp, four to six hours). Passenger tickets are sold at an office at the port. Boats supposedly run 24 hours and leave about every 90 minutes, but the service can be unreliable.

Nusa Penida

Public ferries (adult/child/motorbike/car 31,000/26,000/50,000/295,000Rp) leave most days; the trip takes one hour. Large car ferries leave from the main wharf at the port; smaller passenger-only ferries usually leave from the jetty to the left of the main wharf. Passenger tickets for the car ferries are sold at an office at the port; buy tickets for the smaller ferries on board.

TAXI

Local taxis charge 300,000Rp to travel to Ubud and Sanur; it costs 350,000Rp to Kuta, Legian, Seminyak, Jimbaran or Denpasar airport.

TOURIST BUSES

Perama (☎0361-751875; www.peramatour.com; Jl Pelabuhan) Shuttles connect Padangbai with other parts of Bali. Destinations include Kuta, Denpasar airport, Sanur and Ubud (all 75,000Rp, three daily); Amed and Tulamben (100,000Rp, one daily); Lovina (175,000Rp, one daily); Candidasa (35,000Rp, three daily) and Tirta Gangga (75,000Rp, one daily). Buses leave from outside the Perama office, near the port.

Made's Tourist Service (☎0877 0145 0700, 0363-41441; ⊙vary) Sells tickets for shuttles. It can organise for you to get to Ubud (75,000Rp), Sanur (75,000Rp), Kuta (75,000Rp), Denpasar airport (75,000Rp), Tirta Gangaa (95,000Rp, three passenger minimum), Candidasa (65,000Rp, two passenger minimum), Tulamben (125,000Rp, three passenger minimum) and Lovina (250,000Rp, three passenger minimum).

Manggis

☎0363 / POP 5030

Inland from the coast, the village of Manggis is the jumping off point for a rewarding detour up to the hilltop village of Putung. The section of coast to its immediate south, which runs east to Candidasa and west to Padangbai, has some tourist development, including several luxury resorts (these are hidden along the water off the main road).

★ **Alila Manggis** RESORT $$$
(☎0363-41011; www.alilahotels.com; Desa Buitan; r US$135-210, ste US$35-425; P ❄ 🛜 ≈) A huge swimming pool fringed with palms is the centrepiece of this family-friendly resort on the coast. The 55 good-sized rooms have a simple but stylish decor and good amenities. There's a restaurant (mains 85,000Rp to 285,000Rp), a beach bar and a small spa. We award top marks for the complimentary afternoon tea, free bicycle use and daily yoga and tai chi classes. Check online for deals.

Amankila RESORT $$$
(☎0363-41333; www.amankila.com; ste from US$700; P ❄ @ 🛜 ≈) Perched on jutting cliffs, this luxury resort has three infinity pools that step down to the sea in a cascade of aqua blue – a magnificent sight. The 33 free-standing bungalow-style suites are among the most luxurious on the island, with comfortable furnishings and huge terraces; some have private pools. Facilities include three restaurants, private beach, spa and a children's playroom.

Amankila Restaurant INTERNATIONAL $$$
(☎0363-41333; www.amankila.com; Amankila, Manggis; mains 280,000-580,000Rp; ⏰noon-10.30pm) Sadly, the food served at the open-air restaurant at the Amankila resort is nowhere near as impressive as its wonderful view over a multi-tiered infinity pool to the sea. The menu includes pasta dishes, noodles and salads but their execution leaves much to be desired. There's an excellent choice of cocktails and wine by the glass and bottle, though.

Getting There & Away

If you're staying in the Manggis resorts, you'll either have to stay put or have your own wheels. Alila Manggis offers its guests free use of bicycles.

Candidasa

☎0363 / POP 2190

Officially known as Segkidu Village but called Candidasa for tourism purposes, this east coast settlement is heavily developed with hotels. The beach here was pretty well destroyed in the 1970s, when its offshore reef was mined for lime to make cement and other construction materials, so those seeking to swim, snorkel or dive in the sea should steer clear. However, the hinterland is attractive, the picturesque lagoon in the centre of town is full of water lillies that bloom in the morning and many of the local hotels have gorgeous beachside infinity pools where guests can laze their days away.

History

Until the 1970s, Candidasa was a quiet little fishing village. From the end of that decade, beachside losmen (small Balinese hotels) and restaurants sprang up and suddenly this stretch of coast became a tourism hotspot. As the facilities developed, the beach eroded – unthinkingly, offshore barrier-reef corals were harvested to produce lime for cement in the orgy of construction that took place – and by the late 1980s Candidasa was a beach resort with no beach. Mining stopped in 1991 and concrete sea walls and breakwaters have limited the erosion and provided some tiny pockets of sand.

Sights

Pantai Pasir Putih BEACH
(Virgin Beach) The most popular 'secret' beach on Bali, Pantai Pasir Putih (White Sand Beach) lives up to its name. Once a mooring spot for local fishing boats, this long crescent of white sand backed by coconut palms is now a popular tourist attraction, with thatched beach warungs and cafes lining the sand and souvenir stalls clustered around the car park. Sun lounges await bikini-clad bottoms. The water is safe for swimming and you can rent snorkelling gear to explore the sparkling aquamarine water.

From Jl Raya Perasi (the main highway), look for the large 'White Sand Beach' sign and then turn off the main road and follow a paved track for 1.2km to a large dirt parking area; other tracks are signed 'Virgin Beach'. Locals will collect an access fee (10,000Rp per person including parking).

Cars and motorbikes are barred from driving close to the beach. There's a track down to the sand from the parking area.

Pura Candidasa HINDU TEMPLE
(Jl Raya Candidasa; admission by donation) Candidasa's temple is on the hillside across from the lagoon at the eastern end of the village strip. It has twin temples devoted to the male-female gods Shiva and Hariti.

Activities & Tours

There are a few options for diving and offshore snorkelling here, but you'll be much happier heading northeast to Amed to enjoy these activities. Instead, consider taking a hike in the attractive hinterland. If you walk along the coastline from Candidasa towards Amlapura, a trail climbs up over the headland, with fine views over the rocky islets off the coast and a good swathe of the region. Beyond this headland there's a long sweep of wide, exposed black-sand beach.

Ocean Spa SPA
(☎0363-41234; www.candibeachbali.com; Candi Beach Resort & Spa, Jl Raya Mendira, Sengkidu Village; treatments 257,000-1,200,000Rp; ⏰by appointment) The most popular massage and Jacuzzi room at this resort spa has a huge window framing an ocean view – it's a wonderful place to indulge in a treatment or package. Choose from a large menu of options, including massages, flower baths and facials.

★**Trekking Candidasa** WALKING
(☎0878 6145 2001; www.trekkingcandidasa.com; treks 250,000-350,000Rp) The delightful Somat leads walks through the verdant rice fields and hills behind Candidasa. There are two routes: an easy trek through the rice

fields to the village of Tenganan and a more difficult trek to a nearby waterfall. Prices include transport and drinks.

Sleeping

Candidasa's busy main drag is well supplied with seaside accommodation, with most options on the beach side of the highway. Tranquil pockets can be found east of the centre along Jl Pantai Indah and also at Mendira Beach, at the western entrance to the town. To get to the Mendira Beach hotels, turn off the main road at the school and huge banyan tree (there's also a sign listing places to stay here).

Sleepy Croc HOSTEL $
(☎0363-4381003, 0877 6256 3736; Jl Raya Candidasa; dm 100,000Rp, breakfast 50,000Rp; P❄📶) Opened in 2018, this small backpacker-style hostel offers two dorms (one mixed, one female only); each sleeps eight and fronts onto the pool. Most action unfolds in the bar/restaurant fronting the street (mains 50,000Rp to 110,000Rp), and live music is staged there every Friday and Saturday night. Dorms have bunk beds, under-bed lockers, air-con and a bathroom.

Puri Oka Beach Bungalows GUESTHOUSE $
(☎0363-41092; www.purioka.com; Jl Pantai Indah; r 400,000-450,000Rp, bungalow 550,000-650,000Rp; P❄📶🏊) Resembling a homestay compound, this well-priced guesthouse is hidden behind a banana grove east of town. Cramped standard rooms have air-con, simple bathrooms and a small terrace; bungalows are larger and also have a TV and kettle. The small beachside pool is set next to a pavilion cafe (mains 45,000Rp to 70,000Rp); at low tide there's a little beach out front.

Ari Homestay HOMESTAY $
(☎0817 970 7339; www.arihomestaycandidasa.com; Jl Raya Candidasa; r with fan & cold water 180,000Rp, r with air-con & hot water 260,000-330,000Rp; P❄📶) Run by ebullient Aussie expat Gary and his family, this dead-simple place has 12 rooms that range from cold-water with fans to air-con with hot water; a few have cooking facilities. Its position on the main road across from the water isn't ideal, but very cold beer is always available and there's a cheap and cheerful hot dog stand downstairs.

Ashram Gandhi Chandi GUESTHOUSE $
(☎0363-41108, 0812 360 4733; www.ashramgandhi.com; Jl Raya Candidasa; s/d from

Candidasa

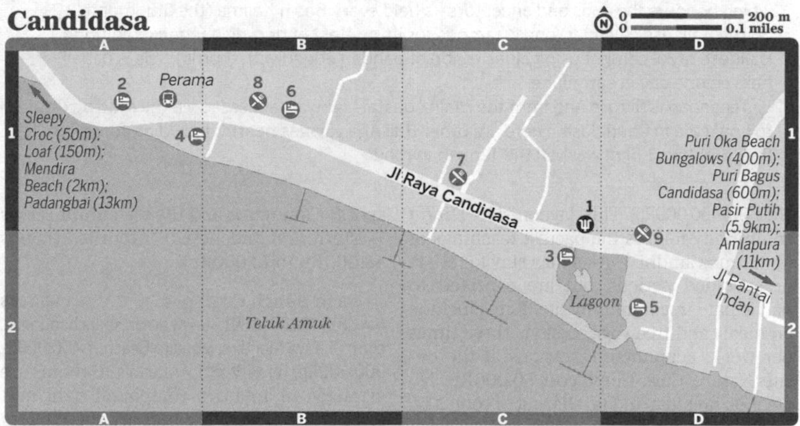

Candidasa

Sights
1 Pura Candidasa....C1

Sleeping
2 Ari Homestay....A1
3 Ashram Gandhi Chandi....C2
4 Ashyana Candidasa....A1
5 Rama Shinta Hotel....D2
6 Watergarden....B1

Eating
7 Crazy Kangaroo....C1
Hot Dog Shop....(see 2)
8 R@Fresh Family Restaurant....B1
9 Vincent's....D2

WORTH A TRIP

TENGANAN

A popular side trip from Candidasa, the village of Tenganan is home to Bali Aga people – the descendants of the original Balinese who inhabited Bali before the Majapahit arrival in the 11th century. A visit here offers a chance to visit many traditional homes, as these double as workshops and retail outlets for handicrafts made here and around the region.

The Bali Aga have a reputation as being conservative and resistant to change, but this is only partially true: TVs and other modern conveniences are hidden away in the traditional houses here in Tenganan, and many locals carry mobile phones. But it is fair to say that the village has a much more traditional feel than most other villages in Bali. Cars and motorcycles are forbidden from entering; there's a carpark near the village entrance.

The compact 500m by 250m village is surrounded by a wall and consists basically of two rows of identical houses stretching up the gentle slope of a hill. As you enter past the ticket office you'll be asked to make a 10,000Rp donation and you may be greeted by a guide who will take you on a tour – and generally lead you back to his family compound to look at textiles and other handicrafts for sale. However, there's no pressure to buy anything.

If you are interested in shopping, look for the cloth known as *kamben gringsing,* which has traditionally been woven in Tenganan – a person wearing it is said to be protected against black magic. Sadly, though, there are few looms producing it in the village today. The cloth is made using the 'double ikat' technique, in which both the warp and weft threads are 'resist dyed' before being woven.

Many baskets and bags made from ata palm are on sale in the village, but are made elsewhere. One craft that continues to be based here is traditional Balinese calligraphy, with the script inscribed onto *lontar* (a palm-leaf manuscript).

A peculiar, old-fashioned version of the gamelan known as the gamelan selunding is played here and girls dance an equally ancient dance known as the Rejang; a good time to see this is during the month-long, mid-year **Usaba Sambah Festival**. This festival, which honours the gods and ancestors, is held every Sasih Kalima (the fifth month on the Balinese calendar) and is famous for its contest of *perang pandan* (traditional Balinese ritual combat using clubs made of pandan edged with thorns); this is usually held on one day in early June.

Tenganan is 5km inland from the main coastal highway, accessed via the road next to Loaf cafe in Candidasa. There are other Bali Aga villages nearby, including Tenganan Dauh Tenkad, 1.5km west off the Tenganan road.

350,000/450,000Rp) This lagoon-side Hindu community follows the pacifist teachings of Mahatma Gandhi. Guests may stay for short or extended periods, but are expected to participate in community life. Rates include all meals and free yoga sessions three times per week; acupuncture sessions at the on-site Nature Cure Clinic cost 50,000Rp. No alcohol, no meat and no sharing of rooms by unmarried couples.

Rama Shinta Hotel HOTEL **$$**
(☎0363-41778; www.ramashintahotel.com; off Jl Raya Candidasa; r 650,000-1,100,000Rp; ❄📶🏊) Set next to Candidasa's pretty lagoon, Rama Shinta's 15 rooms are split between a two-storey stone structure and bungalows. All have terraces and have been nicely updated with open-air bathrooms – request number 101 or 102, which have ocean and lagoon views. The pool area is an inviting spot for lounging, and the restaurant serves Western and Indonesian favourites (mains 48,000Rp to 73,000Rp).

Amarta Beach Cottages HOTEL **$$**
(☎0819 3650 6891; www.amartabeachcottages.com; Jl Raya Mendira, Mendira Beach; r 450,0000-900,000Rp; P❄📶🏊) Amarta's 16 rooms are arranged in a garden compound right next to Mendira Beach; the best are the modern suites at the rear of the compound, which have air-con, kettle, minifridge, balconies and good bathrooms with open-air showers. Bungalow rooms are older and more-basic; there's no air-con in the standard variety. Facilities include a small pool and pavilion restaurant.

Ashyana Candidasa HOTEL **$$**
(☎0363-41539; www.ashyanacandidasa.com; Jl Raya Candidasa; r from 1,100,000Rp; P❄📶🏊)

With a guesthouse feel, this hotel offers 12 small, simple and well-maintained bungalow-style units. Most are far enough from the main road to escape traffic noise. There's an on-site spa and a restaurant with a seafront terrace.

Watergarden HOTEL $$

(☎0363-41540; www.watergardenhotel.com; Jl Raya Candidasa; r US$75-285; P❄📶🏊) Lushly planted surrounds featuring plenty of lily-planted ponds are the main draws at this tranquil hotel on the mountain side of the main road. Though overpriced and in need of refurbishment, the bungalow accommodation is comfortable enough; deluxe rooms have showers rather than the shower-over-bath set-up in standard rooms. There's a streetside restaurant (mains 46,000Rp to 149,000Rp) and a small spa.

★Candi Beach Resort and Spa RESORT $$$

(☎0363-41234; www.candibeachbali.com; Jl Raya Mendira, Mendira Beach; r $US100-170, ste US$300-340, villa US$350-405; P❄📶🏊) 🍃 Stylish, environmentally conscious and lavishly endowed with facilities, this is undisputedly Candidasa's best accommodation option. Rooms come in six categories – luxury ocean view suites and villas are particularly swish, but all are impressive. There's a huge palm-fringed pool, a luxe spa (p220) and two restaurants (one Asian and Western, the other Indonesian; mains 63,000Rp to 183,000Rp). The resort's private beach offers good snorkelling opportunities.

The hotel uses eco-friendly cleaning products, harvests rain water to use in the garden and contributes to local programmes for coral regeneration.

★Nirwana Resort & Spa RESORT $$$

(☎0363-41136; www.thenirwana.com; off Jl Raya Sengkidu; r 1,250,000-1,750,000Rp; P❄📶🏊) A dramatic walk across a lotus pond sets the atmospheric tone at this classy and tranquil resort. The 18 well-spaced units are arranged around a gorgeous infinity pool by the ocean; four have oceanfront positions and all sport an attractive decor, big four-poster bed, satellite TV, kettle and good-sized terrace. Facilities include a pavilion spa and a restaurant (mains 55,000Rp to 150,000Rp).

Puri Bagus Candidasa HOTEL $$$

(☎0363-41131; www.puribaguscandidasa.com; Jl Pantai Indah; r US$140-220; P❄📶🏊) Though it is both friendly and well-maintained, this hotel has a worn appearance and its accommodations are old-fashioned. Bungalows are dotted among the palm trees, and both the pavilion bar/restaurant (mains 54,000Rp to 110,000Rp) and large pool have good sea views; the beach is illusory (and often missing). The rack rates are overpriced – seek out deals.

Eating

Loaf CAFE $

(☎0363-438 1130; apit@outlook.co.id; Jl Raya Candidasa; breakfast & lunch dishes 30,000-55,000Rp; ⏰8am-6pm; 📶✍) DiMattina espresso coffee, home-made bread and a tempting all-day breakfast menu are three of the inducements at this contemporary-chic cafe on the main road. The menu includes global treats such as banh mi, smashed avocado, veggie lasagne and lentil burgers.

Refresh Family Restaurant HEALTH FOOD $

(☎0812 3751 6001; www.facebook.com/refresh4family; Jl Raya Candidasa; breakfast dishes 25,000-50,000, mains 30,000-50,000; ⏰8am-10pm; 📶✍👪) Surfing the vegan, raw, organic and gluten-free culinary wave that has deluged Bali in recent years, this simple place has an exclusively vegetarian menu that is chock-full of favourites such as laksa, falafel, spicy wraps and nut curries. Breakfast choices include scrambled tofu, smoothie bowls and granola. The children's play area is a popular feature.

Hot Dog Shop FAST FOOD $

(www.arihomestaycandidasa.com; Jl Raya Candidasa; dishes 35,000-60,000Rp; ⏰11am-8pm; 📶) When he set this place up, owner Gary vowed that it would never serve nasi goreng, and he has remained true to his word. Head here for dogs, burritos and burgers, washed down with cheap ice-cold Bintang.

★Vincent's INTERNATIONAL $$

(☎0363-41368; www.vincentsbali.com; Jl Raya Candidasa; mains 75,000-295,000Rp; ⏰11am-10pm; 📶✍) One of east Bali's better restaurants, Vincent's has several distinct open-air rooms and a large rear garden. The comfy front bar area hosts live jazz on both Monday (high season only) and Thursday (all year), kicking off around 7pm. The menu offers sandwiches, salads, Balinese staples and various Western dishes – the 'coconut texture' dessert is justly popular.

Crazy Kangaroo INTERNATIONAL $$

(☎0363-41996; www.crazy-kangaroo.com; Jl Raya Candidasa; mains 80,000-165,000Rp; ⏰noon-11pm; 📶) Wild by local standards, this open-air and pavilion pub is full of characters shooting pool or propping at the long bar to watch sports. The open kitchen cooks Western and local dishes; tasty seafood specials include sushi and sashimi. There are usually live performances on Tuesday, Thursday, Saturday and Sunday evening, everything from fire shows and traditional dance to live bands.

Shopping

Alam Zempol COSMETICS
(☎0363-41283; www.alamzempol.com; Jl Mendira, Mendira Beach; ⏱8am-6pm Mon-Wed, Fri & Sat, from 10am Sun) Located on the road to Mendira Beach, this sweet-smelling boutique sells locally made essential oils, incense, soaps and toiletries.

Getting There & Away

Candidasa is on the main road between Amlapura and south Bali, but there is no regular public transport. **Perama** (☎0363-41114/5; Jl Raya Candidasa; ⏱7am-7pm) has an office on the main road and runs shuttle services to destinations including Kuta (75,000Rp, three hours, three daily) via Ubud (75,000Rp, two hours) and Sanur (75,000Rp, 2½ hours); Padangbai (35,000Rp, 30 minutes, three daily); Tirta Gangga (75,000Rp, 45 minutes, one daily); and Amed (100,000Rp, 75 minutes, one daily). A pick up from your hotel will cost an extra 15,000Rp.

Amlapura

☎0363 / POP 15,960

The capital of Karangasem is the smallest of Bali's district capitals and is notable for its multicultural population, with both Muslim and Chinese residents. This gives its night market a slightly different flavour to others on the island. The town's palaces – two in the centre and one in Ujung, south of the city – are reminders of Karangasem's grand period as a kingdom supported by Dutch colonial power in the late 19th and early 20th centuries. Two of the three palaces can be visited.

Sights

Taman Ujung GARDENS
(Ujung Park, Sukasada Park; Ujung; 50,000Rp, car/scooter parking 5000/2000Rp) A hugely popular location for wedding photographs and romantic saunters, this complex five kilometres south of Amlapura dates to 1921, when the last king of Karangasem completed the construction of a grand water palace here. Largely destroyed by a 1979 earthquake, it has recently been restored courtesy of World Bank funding. It attracts fewer foreign visitors than Tirta Gangga, which predates it by approximately three decades.

Puri Agung Karangasem PALACE
(http://purikarangasem.com; Jl Teuku Umar; adult/child under 5yr 10,000/5000Rp; ⏱8am-5pm) The main residence in this palace compound is known as the Maskerdam (Amsterdam) because it was built by the Dutch as a reward for the Karangasem kingdom's acquiescence to Dutch rule. Looking considerably worse for wear these days (the Maskerdam has been uninhabited since 1966, when the last raja died), the compound also has an ornately decorated pavilion once used for royal tooth-filing ceremonies, and a large pond with a floating pavilion.

JASRI BAY

Just south of Amlapura, Jasri Bay has earned the nickname **Teluk Penyu**, or Turtle Bay. The shelled critters do indeed come here to nest and there have been some efforts made to protect them. If you see a turtle or nest, be sure to keep your distance; never attempt to touch or pick up a wild sea turtle.

To stay in this area overnight, make a booking at **Jasri Bay Hideaway** (☎0363-23611; www.jasribay.com; Jl Raya Pura Mascima, Jasri Bay; r US$180-195, 1-bed villa US$210-230, 2-bed villa US$295-350; ❄📶🏊). Accommodation is in three old wooden tribal houses – couples should opt for the lovely one-bedroom option, which has its own pool. The other houses can be rented by room or entire villa – these share a pool. Room service meals (mains 55,000Rp to 105,000Rp) are available.

Close to the Hideaway, the **Sorga Chocolate Factory** (☎0363-21687; www.sorgachocolate.com; Jl Pura Mastima, Jasri Bay; tours 25,000Rp, workshops 350,000Rp; ⏱8am-5pm, production tours 9am-2pm) offers tours with tastings, as well as chocolate-making workshops.

OFF THE BEATEN TRACK

GELUMPANG & BALI ASLI

Located in the fertile green foothills of Gunung Agung, the farming village of Gelumpang may seem a strange place to find a world-class restaurant and cooking school. However, this is where much-travelled Australian chef Penelope Williams has established the renowned **Bali Asli** (☎0822 3690 9215; www.baliasli.com.au; Jl Raya Gelumpang, Gelumpang; nasi campur 165,000-228,000Rp; ⏰10am-3pm; 📶), which offers visitors to Bali a truly unique culinary experience. Asli is the Balinese term used for something that is created in the traditional way, and there is much that is traditional here – the Balinese menu changes daily, dictated by what is fresh at the local *pasar* (market) or has been harvested in the restaurant's own garden. Dishes are cooked on wood-fired, mud-brick stoves by local chefs – many female – and the results are enjoyed in a magnificent open-sided dining room overlooking rice terraces and the famous but often mist-shrouded volcano. The food is authentically village style – diners choose between an array of small dishes to make up a personalised and extremely flavoursome version of *nasi campur*.

The daily cooking classes include a hike into the surrounding countryside to visit locals farmers – maybe to see rice being planted or palm wine being made – or to a local market before heading back to the kitchen for a 2½-hour cooking class followed by lunch.

You'll need your own transport to get here. From the south coast, drive towards Amlapura via Jl Achmad Yani, turn right at the first traffic light and then left at the second traffic light onto the main road to Amed and Tirta Gangga. Soon you'll pass a football ground and big school on the left and should then turn right at the next traffic light. Follow this smaller road to the T-intersection then turn left and head up the hill, taking a sharp right turn to arrive at Bali Asli.

Pantai Ujung BEACH

(Edge Beach) This rocky beach southeast of Amlapura is home to one of the more unusual sights in east Bali – a 2m-long penis-shaped rock (lingga). Locals attribute great power to the rock and it's the scene of regular ceremonies. Experts have speculated that the stone is an ancient fertility symbol and this has in turn led to additional speculation that a nearby large stone that somewhat resembles a yoni (the female counterpart of a lingga) may be a companion piece.

Getting There & Away

The bus terminal recently closed, and public transport is pretty well non-existent.

Tirta Gangga

☎0363 / POP 7300

Tirta Gangga (Water of the Ganges) is the site of a *taman* (garden) built for the enjoyment of the last raja of Karangasem; it also boasts some of the best rice-terrace vistas in east Bali. Capping a sweep of green flowing down to the distant sea, it's an excellent place to overnight if you are heading to or from Pura Lempuyang. Its also a popular base for those wanting to hike the surrounding terraced countryside, which ripples with coursing water and is dotted with temples.

Sights

★Taman Tirta Gangga GARDENS

(www.tirtagangga.nl; Jl Abang-Amlapura; adult/child 30,000/15,000Rp, swimming 5000Rp, parking car/scooter 5000/1000Rp; ⏰7am-7pm) This 1.2-hectare water palace serves as a fascinating reminder of the old Bali. Built for the last raja of Karangasem in 1946, it was almost fully destroyed by the eruption of nearby Gunung Agung in 1963, but has subsequently been rebuilt. Admire the 11-tiered Nawa Sanga fountain and the ponds filled with huge koi and lotus blossoms, and jump between the round stepping stones in the water. It's also possible to take a swim in the huge stone spring-water pool.

Activities & Tours

Hiking in the surrounding hills transports you far from your memories of frenetic south Bali. This far east corner of Bali is alive with coursing streams through rice fields and tropical forests that suddenly open to reveal vistas taking in Lombok, Nusa Penida and the lush green surrounding lands stretching down to the sea. The rice terraces around Tirta Gangga are some of the most beautiful in Bali. Back roads and walking paths take you to many picturesque traditional villages.

WORTH A TRIP

PURA LEMPUYANG

One of the eight temple complexes in the Pura Kahyangan Padma Bhuwana group, which mark the island's cardinal directions, **Pura Lempuyang** (Gunung Lempuyang; donation requested, car/scooter parking 2000Rp/free; ⌚24hr) is perched on a hilltop on the side of 1058m Gunung Lempuyang, a twin of neighbouring 1175m Gunung Seraya. Together, the pair of mountains form the distinctive double peaks of basalt that loom over Amlapura to the south and Amed to the north. The complex, which comprises seven temples on the steep mountain slope, is one of the most important religious sites in east Bali.

The largest and most easily accessed temple here is Penataran Tempuyang, which has a wonderfully photogenic *candi bentar* (split temple gateway). The highest and most important temple is Pura Lempuyang Luhur, which also has a *candi bentar*. To visit all seven temples in the complex takes at least four hours and involves 2900 steps – only those who are fit should attempt it. Reaching Penataran Tempuyang is relatively easy, as it's only a five-minute uphill walk from the security entrance. Many visitors queue for hours to have their chance to be photographed in front of the *candi bentar* here.

From Penataran Tempuyang, the second temple is 2km uphill and after that the calf-punishing stair climb begin; it's 1700 steps from the second temple to Pura Lempuyang Luhur.

From the car park, jeeps transport visitors up the steep road and to the security entrance for 20,000Rp per person; the same charge applies for the return trip. You'll be asked for a donation at the entrance (10,000Rp per person is appropriate) and will need to pay another 10,000Rp to hire a sarong, unless you have your own. Local guides congregate near the security check and charge 150,000/200,000/300,000/400,000Rp to the 1st/2nd/4th/top temple.

From the complex, the mottled green patchwork that is east Bali unfolds to the eye. The temple's significance means there are always faithful Balinese in meditative contemplation at the temples; be warned that temples sometimes close to visitors during ceremonies.

Sights that make a perfect excuse for a day trek are scattered in the surrounding hills. Among the possible treks is a six-hour loop to Tenganan village, plus shorter ones across the local hills, which include visits to remote temples and plenty of stunning vistas.

Guides for the more complex hikes are a good idea as they can help you plan routes and see things you simply would never find otherwise. Ask at any of the various accommodation options. Rates average about 100,000Rp per hour for one or two people.

Komang Gede Sutama HIKING
(☎0813 3877 0893; ⌚2/4/6hr guided hike for 2 people 150,000/350,000/550,000Rp) Local resident Komang Gede Sutama speaks basic English and has a good reputation as a guide to the countryside around Tirta Gangga and up to Gunung Agung.

Bung Bung Adventure Biking CYCLING
(☎0813 3840 2132, 0363-21873; bungbungbikeadventure@gmail.com; Homestay Rijasa, Jl Abang-Amlapura; 2hr tour 300,000Rp) Ride downhill through the picture-perfect rice fields, terraces and river valleys around Tirta Gangga with this grassroots tour company. The price includes a guide and use of a mountain bike and helmet. The office is at Homestay Rijasa, across from the Taman Tirta Gangga entrance. Book in advance.

Sleeping

There are a number of accommodation options in and around the water palace; the best are on the ridge in Ababi.

★**Pondok Batur Indah** HOMESTAY $
(☎0363-22342, 0812 398 9060; pondokbaturindah@yahoo.com; Ababi; d 350,000-400,000Rp, tr 500,000Rp; P 📶) Jaw-dropping is the only word to use when describing the rice-terrace views enjoyed from the terrace of this homestay on the ridge above Tirta Gangga. The five rooms are simple but clean, with fans and basic bathrooms. There's an on-site restaurant serving home-style dishes (25,000Rp to 55,000Rp) and the water palace is a 10- to 15-minute walk away, down a steep set of steps.

★Pondok Alam Bukit HOMESTAY $
(☎0812 365 6338; kutaketut@hotmail.com; Ababi; r 350,000-400,000Rp) One of a number of tranquil homestays perched on the edge of a ridge overlooking the water palace, this *pondok* (guesthouse) currently offers two attractive and comfortable rooms with outdoor bathrooms, panoramic windows overlooking the rice terraces and private terraces; two extra rooms are planned. Owner Ketut also works as a hiking guide. Cash only.

Side by Side Organic Garden & Homestay HOMESTAY $
(☎0812 3623 3427; www.facebook.com/Side-by-Side-Organic-Farm-331639733544054; Dausa; dm 150,000Rp, minimum 2 nights; P) Set amid lush rice fields near Tirta Gangga in the tiny village of Dausa, this non-profit endeavour was set up to give work to locals and improve their economic futures. It offers dorm accommodation in two *bale* (open-sided pavilions) and serves bounteous and delicious buffet lunches (150,000Rp). Meals use organic foods grown and raised in the garden and around the village. To stay or eat here, call at least one day ahead of your arrival.

Pondok Lembah Dukuh GUESTHOUSE $
(☎0813 3829 5142; dukuhstay@gmail.com; Ababi; r 250,000-270,000Rp, q 350,000Rp; P wi-fi) On the edge of a ridge commanding spectacular views over the rice fields, this guesthouse offers four charming bungalows with individual terraces. Rooms are small and basic, but a stay here is a good chance to get close to local life. The water palace is a 10- to 15-minute walk away, via a steep set of steps.

Good Karma Bungalows HOMESTAY $
(☎0363-22445; goodkarma.tirtagangga@gmail.com; Jl Abang-Amlapura; s/d/tw 200,000/250,000/300,000Rp; wi-fi) This classic homestay right next to the water palace has a good vibe derived from the surrounding pastoral rice field. Four simple and musty bungalows have fans, uncomfortable beds and basic bathrooms. There's also a cafe where meat and veggie satays are grilled over coconut-shell charcoal (mains 40,000Rp to 60,000Rp; open 7am to 9pm).

Tirta Ayu Hotel HOTEL $$$
(☎0363-22503; www.hoteltirtagangga.com; Pura Tirta Gangga; r 1,500,000-1,800,000Rp, ste 1,800,000-2,000,000Rp; air-con wi-fi pool) We're disappointed to report that the idea of spending the night inside the royal water palace is far more glamorous than the reality. Rooms are attractive (and the villa suites are huge), but noise is a problem and on our last visit the breakfast that was served was appalling.

Eating

Food vendors and warungs are located on the pedestrianised road leading to the water palace, around the parking area and on the main road. Most accommodation options offer meals.

Genta Bali INDONESIAN $
(☎0812 4629 6509; Jl Abang-Amlapura; mains 35,000-60,000Rp; ⏲7am-10pm) You can order a homemade yoghurt lassi to accompany your satay at this warung across the road from Tirta Gangga's parking area, or live dangerously and instead try the potent house-made black-rice arak wine.

Information

There is an ATM next to the car park near the water palace.

Getting There & Away

You'll need your own transport to get here.

Amed & the Far East Coast

☎0363 / POP 3180

Stretching from Amed village to Bali's far eastern tip, this semi-arid coast has long drawn visitors with its succession of small, scalloped, grey-sand beaches (some more rocks than sand), relaxed atmosphere and excellent diving and snorkelling.

'Amed' is actually a misnomer for the area, as the coast is a series of seaside *dusun* (small villages) that starts with Amed village in the north and then runs southeast to Aas. Amed village, Jemeluk, Lipah and Selang are popular destinations for scuba divers, freedivers and snorkellers, and the entire coastline is dotted with resorts boasting yoga shalas, infinity pools and pavilion restaurants.

Sights

Lookout VIEWPOINT
(Jemeluk; parking 10,000Rp) To appreciate the narrow band of the coast, stop at the lookout and cafes on the hillside at Jemeluk. The deep-blue water sparkles, dotted with polychromatic fishing boats.

Activities

Snorkelling is excellent along the coast. Jemeluk is a protected area where you can admire live coral and plentiful fish within 100m of the beach. The coral gardens and colourful marine life at Selang are highlights. Snorkelling equipment rents for about 35,000Rp per day.

Diving is also good, with dive sites off Jemeluk, Lipah and Selang featuring coral slopes and drop-offs with soft and hard corals and abundant fish. Some are accessible from the beach, while others require a short boat ride. The *Liberty* wreck at Tulamben is only a 20-minute drive away.

Several dive operators have shown a commitment to the communities by organising regular beach clean-ups and educating locals on the need for conservation. All have similar prices for a long list of offerings (eg local two-dive packages start from around US$70).

Ocean Prana DIVING
(WhatsApp 061 435 441 414; www.oceanprana.com; Jl I Ketut Natih, Jemeluk; introductory course US$150, level 1-3 US$290-490) Courses at this self-styled 'freediving village' are led by Yoram Zekri, a former world freediving vice-champion and French national multirecord holder. The village has its own practice pool, an organic cafe and excellent hostel-style accommodation (p230). It also offers daily one-hour **yoga classes** at 6.30pm (100,000Rp).

Apneista DIVING
(0812 3826 7356; www.apneista.com; Green Leaf Cafe, Jl I Ketut Natih, Jemeluk; 2-day courses US$200; 8.30am-10pm) Based at Jemeluk's laid-back Green Leaf Cafe (p233), this outfit offers freediving classes, courses and workshops; its freediving technique uses tools from yoga and meditation.

Euro Dive DIVING
(0363-23605; www.eurodivebali.com; Lipah; 1/2 introductory dives €50/70, 2/4 open-water dives €210/295) Has a large facility and offers dive and accommodation packages with local hotels.

Ecodive Bali DIVING
(0363-23482; www.ecodivebali.com; Jl Raya Amed, Jemeluk; 2 dives US$75-85) Well-regarded full-service dive operator.

Jukung Dive DIVING
(0363-23469; www.jukungdivebali.com; Amed Village; 2-dive packages US$60-75) Chinese owned and operated, this company has a dive pool and offers dive and accommodation packages. Its nine-dive safari package (US$270) includes one night dive and represents good value.

Hiking

Before the Gunung Agung volcano started rumbling, visitors regularly hiked on a few trails heading inland from the coast, up the slopes of **Gunung Seraya** (1175m) and to some little-visited villages. The countryside is sparsely vegetated and most trails are well defined, so guides aren't usually required for shorter walks. Ask your hotel if it's safe to walk (staff are sure to be monitoring volcano warnings) and if it's OK to set off, allow a good three hours to get to the top of Seraya, starting from the rocky ridge just east of Jemeluk Bay. Sunrises from here are spectacular but to enjoy one you'll need to climb in the dark; ask at your hotel about a guide to help you with this.

Yoga

Yoga is a popular activity in this corner of the island and many hotels and resorts have yoga studios or shalas.

Blue Earth Village YOGA
(0821 4554 3699; www.blueearthvillage.com; Jemeluk Lookout; 90-minute class 100,000Rp; noon-10pm) Enjoy magnificent views of Gunung Agung and Jemeluk Bay while you exercise and meditate at Blue Earth Village's elevated bamboo shala (yoga studio) at the Jemeluk Lookout. Hatha yoga classes for all levels are offered daily, and there's also pilates once per week.

Festivals & Events

Deepweek Festival SPORTS
(www.adamfreediver.com/deep-week; Jemeluk) Organised by champion freediver Adam Stern and involving world-record holder Alexey Molchanov, this hybrid course and festival is the world's largest freediving get-together. Hosted by Apneista, it is run a few times per year.

Sleeping

The Amed region offers overnight options at most price points and for many tastes and interests. There are dive resorts, health and meditation retreats and lots of hotels and guesthouses offering their guests bungalows, pools and restaurants. The only accommodation type lacking is the luxury resort – you'll need to head to Tulamben and

Amed & the Far East Coast

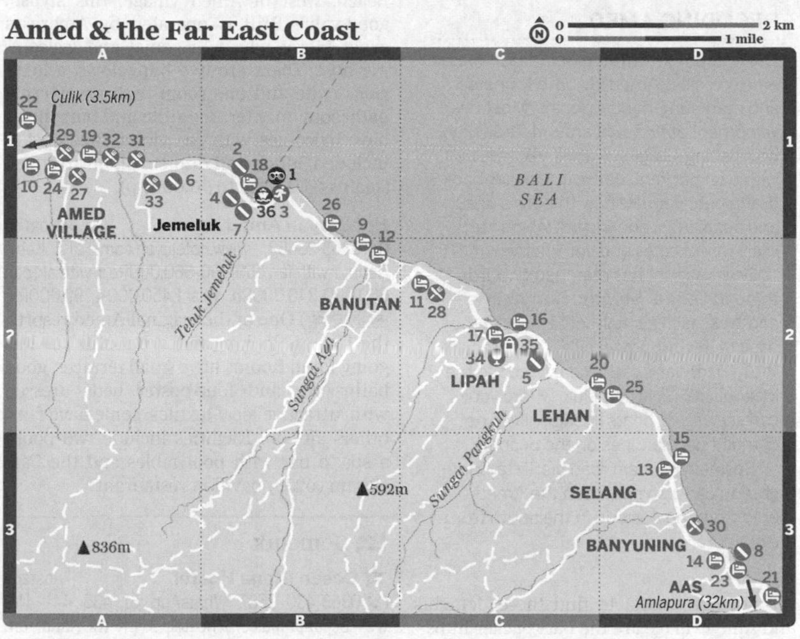

Amed & the Far East Coast

Sights
1 Lookout ... B1

Activities, Courses & Tours
2 Apneista ... B1
3 Blue Earth Village ... B1
4 Ecodive Bali ... B1
5 Euro Dive ... C2
6 Jukung Dive ... A1
7 Ocean Prana ... B1
8 Sunken Japanese Fishing Boat ... D3

Sleeping
9 Aiona Garden of Health ... B2
10 Amed Stop Inn ... A1
11 Anda Amed Resort ... C2
12 Apa Kabar Villas ... B2
13 Aquaterrace ... D3
14 Baliku Dive Resort ... D3
15 Blue Moon Villas ... D3
16 Coral View Villas ... C2
17 Double One Villas ... C2
18 Galang Kangin Bungalows ... B1
19 Hotel Uyah Amed ... A1
20 Life in Amed ... C2
Lumbung Sari Homestay ... (see 10)
21 Meditasi ... D3
22 Melasti Beach Bungalows ... A1
23 Nalini Resort ... D3
24 Narayana Homestay ... A1
Ocean Prana Hostel ... (see 7)
25 Palm Garden Amed ... D2
26 Santai Hotel ... B1

Eating
Blue Earth Village Restaurant ... (see 3)
Cafe Garam ... (see 19)
27 Dread Light Bar ... A1
Green Leaf Cafe ... (see 2)
28 Gusto ... C2
29 Meeting Point ... A1
Sama-Sama Cafe ... (see 18)
Smiling Buddha Restaurant ... (see 21)
Sunset Point Warung ... (see 3)
30 Trattoria Cucina Italia ... D3
31 Tropikal Cafe ... A1
32 Warung Amsha ... A1
33 Warung Enak ... A1

Drinking & Nightlife
34 Wawa-Wewe I ... C2

Shopping
35 Peduli Alam Bali ... C2

Transport
36 Amed Sea Express ... B1
Kuda Hitam Express ... (see 36)

DECODING AMED

The entire 10km stretch of far east coast is often called 'Amed' by both tourists and marketing-minded locals. Most development at first was around three bays with fishing villages: **Amed village**, big with backpackers; **Jemeluk**, a laid-back diving hub; **Banutan**, with both a beach and headlands; and **Lipah**, which has a lively mix of cafes and commerce.

Development has marched onwards through **Lehan**, **Selang**, **Banyuning** and **Aas**, each a small settlement at the base of the dry, brown hills. To appreciate the narrow band of the coast, stop at the lookout (p227) at Jemeluk, where you can see fishing boats lined up like a riot of multihued sardines on the beach.

Besides the main road via Tirta Gangga, you can also approach the Amed area from the Aas end in the south from Amlapura.

the northeast coast to find these. Jemeluk and Amed village are the backpacker hubs.

Amed Village

★Narayana Homestay HOMESTAY $
(☎0819 3623 2767; Jl Celuk Amed; r 400,000-500,000Rp; 📶) Secreted at the rear of a family compound on the mountain side of the main road, this friendly place has an authentic village flavour. Five rooms are set side-by-side around a pool and have a contemporary all-white decor, fans, modern bathrooms and small terraces with bean bags; two have outdoor kitchenettes. There's also a washing machine and dining pavilion.

Amed Stop Inn HOSTEL $
(☎0812 4657 7272; amedstopin@gmail.com; Jl I Ketut Natih; dm 95,000Rp, r 175,000-250,000Rp; 📶) This place at the western entrance to the village has two single-sex dorms with single beds, small lockers and fans; shared bathrooms are cold-water only. There are also six private rooms; four have hot-water bathrooms and small terraces overlooking the fields. There's a warung at the front of the compound (mains 25,000Rp to 35,000Rp).

★Melasti Beach Bungalows HOMESTAY $$
(☎0877 6018 8093; www.melastibeachamed.com; Jl Melasti; r without bathroom 400,000Rp, ste 700,000-800,000Rp, bungalows 900,000-1,000,000Rp; P❄📶) Located at Melasti Beach, west of Amed village, this stylish, good-value B&B is operated by American expat Missy, who is a genial and welcoming host. There are two bungalows, a luxurious suite and one room with an external bathroom on offer; the suite and bungalows have balconies with sea views. Breakfast is included, lunch and dinner can be arranged (mains 35,000Rp to 90,000Rp).

Hotel Uyah Amed RESORT $$
(☎0363-23462; www.hoteluyah.com; Jl I Ketut Natih; r with fan 550,000-660,000Rp, r with air-con 660,000-840,000Rp, villa 1,450,000-1,199,000Rp; P❄📶🏊) One of the original Amed resorts, the Uyah is looking faded but still has lots going for it. Rooms have small terraces, good bathrooms and four-poster beds dressed with attractive local textiles; some have fans, others air-con. Facilities include two pools, a spa, a bar with pool tables and the Cafe Garam (p233) pavilion restaurant.

Jemeluk

★Ocean Prana Hostel HOSTEL $
(☎0363-430 1587, WhatsApp 61 435 441 414; www.oceanprana.com/hostel; Jl I Ketut Natih; dm 150,000Rp; P❄📶🏊) Attached to the freediving school of the same name, this hostel has two new thatched bungalows in a large compound. Each has four bunk beds downstairs, two single beds upstairs, powerpoints, small lockers and an outdoor bathroom with hot water. There's also a pool (often used for freediving training) and an organic cafe with table, beanbag and hammock seating. Breakfast costs 20,000Rp.

Galang Kangin Bungalows GUESTHOUSE $
(☎0363-23480; Jl Raya Amed; r from 400,000Rp; P❄📶) Basic choice that offers cheap-ish accommodation and a warung. Its biggest drawcard is the beachfront location.

Banutan Beach

Aiona Garden of Health RESORT $$
(☎0813 3816 1730; www.aionabali.com; s/d €28/32) Those seeking inner transformation may well achieve it at this beachside spiritual retreat. Guests partake in yoga sessions, tarot readings, energy-wave healing, fire ceremonies, sound baths and consciousness-sharing circles. The cafe serves super-healthy offerings (Ayervedic 'Golden Aura' drinks, veggies galore) and rooms range from cold-water bungalows with squat toilets to seafront rooms with hot-water showers. No wi-fi, no alcohol.

Santai Hotel HOTEL $$$

(☎0363-23487; www.santaibali.com; bungalow 1,300,000-2,800,000Rp; P❄📶≋) The name of this lovely clifftop option means 're-lax', and its facilities make this easy, with a bougainvillea-fringed pool, plenty of sun lounges, a spa, beach bar and cafe. There's also a complimentary shuttle service to Lipah and Jemeluk beaches. Traditional thatched bungalows gathered from around the archipelago host 10 rooms with four-poster beds, open-air bathrooms and big balcony sofas. The best accommodation is in the bungalows with sea views; economy rooms at the rear of the property (800,000Rp to 1,900,000Rp) are nowhere near as nice.

Banutan

Apa Kabar Villas HOTEL $$

(☎0363-23492; www.apakabarvillas.com; cottage 350,000-700,000Rp, 2-/4-/6-person villa from 850,000/1,400,000/1,700,000Rp; P📶≋) Villas in this compact compound are in a variety of sizes and have kitchen facilities, so are ideal for families; cottages are smaller but have sea views. Facilities include a pool and cafe/bar, and there's a terrace right on the rocky shore where you can relax and read to sounds of the lapping water. Wi-fi access in the bar only.

Anda Amed Resort HOTEL $$$

(☎0363-23498; www.andaamedresort.com; Jl Raya Lipah; villa from 1,600,000Rp; P❄📶≋) This whitewashed hillside hotel complex contrasts with its lushly green grounds. The infinity pool is an ahhh-inducing classic of the genre and has sweeping views of the sea from well above the road. Well-maintained one- or two-bedroom villas are set on a hillside terrace and have sea views.

Lipah

Double One Villas HOTEL $$

(☎0813 3726 6856, 0877 8171 2083; www.doubleonevillasamed.com; Jl Raya Lipah; r 400,000-560,000Rp, villa 720,000Rp; P❄📶≋) Offering good value, this place is split in two: simple but comfortable rooms and villas are on the hill side of the road, and there's a larger villa with its own pool on the ocean side next to the pebbly shore; the latter is accessed by steep stairs. There's a restaurant and another pool on the hillside.

Coral View Villas HOTEL $$$

(☎0363-23493; www.coralviewvillas.com; Jl Raya Amed; r US$90-99, ste US$100-110, villa US$170-200; ❄📶≋) Lush grounds incorporating a naturalistic pool and plenty of palm trees are the main draw at this well-run hotel. The bungalows may be set too close together for some tastes, but they all have pleasant terraces and stone-lined, open-air bathrooms. Families appreciate the ocean-view villa, which sleeps four. The restaurant (mains 60,000Rp to 100,000Rp) is right on the beach.

Lehan

Palm Garden Amed RESORT $$

(☎0363-4301058; www.palmgardenamed.com; Jl Raya Amed; r 750,000-2,000,000Rp, bungalow 1,200,000-1,800,000Rp, villa 1,800,000-2,200,000Rp; P❄📶≋) Swiss owned, this small resort has a garden setting and a good stretch of beach. There are three standard rooms with cramped bathrooms, five larger garden bungalows with terraces, a beachfront villa with private room and two deluxe beachfront rooms (one with its own pool). Facilities include a pool, small spa and pavilion restaurant with espresso machine.

OFF THE BEATEN TRACK

AMED, THE LONG WAY

Typically, travellers bound for the coast of Amed travel the inland route through Tirta Gangga. However, there is a longer, twistier and more adventurous road much less travelled that runs from **Ujung** right around the coast to the Amed area. The road climbs up the side of the twin peaks of Seraya and Lempuyang, and the views out to sea are breathtaking. Along the way it passes through numerous small villages where people are carving fishing boats, bathing in streams or simply standing a bit slack-jawed at the appearance of *tamu* (visitors or foreigners). Don't be surprised to see a pig, goat or boulder on the road. After the lush east, it's noticeably drier here and the people's existence thinner; corn replaces rice as the staple. The road is narrow but paved and covering the 35km to Aas will take about one hour without stops. Combine this with the inland road through Tirta Gangga for a good circular visit to Amed from the west.

Life in Amed HOTEL $$$

(☎0363-23152, 0813 3850 1555; www.lifebali.com; cottage US$75-95, villa d US$125-145, villa q US$280-340; P❄📶🏊) Six bungalow-style garden units and rooms in a beachside villa with private pool are on offer in this cramped compound next to the river. Facilities include a small restaurant and a yoga shala.

Selang

Aquaterrace HOTEL $$

(☎0813 3791 1096; www.aquaterrace-amed.com; Jl Raya Amed; r 680,000-1,200,000Rp; ❄📶🏊) Perched on the headland right above the blue water of the Bali Sea, this hotel has a distinctive white and aquamarine colour scheme that complements its setting. Rooms are on either side of the road; some are directly on the beach and others have panoramic balconies. The restaurant serves Japanese, Italian and Balinese food (mains 42,000Rp to 75,000Rp) and there are two pools.

Blue Moon Villas HOTEL $$$

(☎0363-21428, 0817 4738 100; www.bluemoonvilla.com; Jl Raya Amed; hillside r €75-95, beachside r €125-160; ❄📶🏊) Arranged on both sides of the road, this overpriced place has standard and sea-view rooms on the hillside and a mix of rooms and villas next to the sea; they're comfortable enough but could do with a facelift. Villas come in one-, two- and three-bedroom configurations. There are four pools and a restaurant serving Indonesian and Chinese dishes (mains 75,000Rp to 135,000Rp).

Banyuning

Baliku Dive Resort RESORT $$

(☎0363-4301871, 0828 372 2601; www.amedbaliresort.com; r from 640,000Rp; P❄📶🏊) Nine large freestanding villa-style units with spacious sea-facing verandahs and romantic four-poster beds sheathed in mosquito nets are among the attractions at this hillside resort overlooking one of the best snorkelling spots on the Amed coast. Facilities include a panoramic pool terrace, dive centre, small library and restaurant (mains 30,000Rp to 138,000Rp). Guests love the complimentary afternoon tea.

Nalini Resort RESORT $$

(☎0821 4592 3608, 0363-430 1946; www.naliniresort.com; r from 780,000-2,000,000Rp; P❄📶🏊) Though the stony beach in front of this boutique hotel isn't ideal for swimming or sunbathing, a small jade-green pool compensates. The eight rooms are modern, comfortable and attractive and the restaurant on the water's edge serves global dishes (mains 60,000Rp to 90,000Rp); breakfast is varied and generous. Daily yoga classes (150,000Rp) are available. Children over 11 years only.

Aas

Meditasi RESORT $$

(☎0363-430 1793; www.facebook.com/meditasibungalows; standard r 350,000-500,000Rp, luxury r 800,000-1,000,000Rp; P❄📶) Get off the grid at this chilled-out hideaway. Meditation, healing and yoga classes help you relax and the rooms are well situated for good swimming and snorkelling (lucky, because there's no pool). By far the best bet are the luxury rooms, complete with private gardens, air-con and sea-facing balconies; some standard rooms are limited to fans and cold-water bathrooms. The on-site Smiling Buddha Restaurant (p234) serves some of the best food in Amed. Yoga classes (100,000Rp) are held each day.

Eating

Almost every guesthouse and hotel has a restaurant or cafe, some are noteworthy. Amed village and Jemeluk are the restaurant and cafe hotspots. Gusto restaurant offers complimentary transport to/from hotels along the coast for its diners, and Smiling Buddha Restaurant (p234) does the same for those who sign up for one of its cooking classes.

Amed Village

★ **Warung Amsha** BALINESE $

(☎0819 1650 6063; Amed Beach; mains 25,000-65,000Rp; ⏰11.30am-10pm; 📶) Tables at this popular beach warung are arranged on the sand and are hotly sought after – it's a good idea to make a booking or arrive early. The menu is resolutely local, featuring freshly caught fish (try the *pepes ikan* –spiced fish cooked in banana leaves) as well as chicken, veggies and spices grown and raised nearby. Juices, cocktails, lassies and beer are on offer.

Dread Light Bar CAFE $

(☎0819 1567 7046; www.facebook.com/MadeInAmed; Jl I Ketut Natih; sandwiches 40,000-45,000Rp, mains 35,000-50,000Rp; ⏰9am-10pm; 📶🍸) 🌿 During the day, the atmosphere at this recently opened cafe is so laid-back it's almost comatose; at night, cocktails and reggae on the sound system pick up the pace. The food is good (Gusto sourdough bread, organic produce, no MSG) and the beanbag seating and book exchange deserve kudos. You can also get tattoos and dreads here.

Tropikal Cafe CAFE $

(0819 1629 6520; Jl I Ketut Natih; breakfast dishes 32,000-60,000Rp, panini 42,000-45,000Rp, cakes 32,000-62,000Rp; 8am-6.30pm) Known for its homemade cakes and ice cream (we can vouch for the decadently rich banoffee pie and the 'Tropical fresh' ice cream sundae), this cute cafe on the main road is a popular breakfast and lunch stop.

Meeting Point CAFE $

(0859 6591 2020; Jl I Ketut Natih; breakfast dishes 35,000-45,000Rp, sandwiches 40,000-60,000Rp, mains 40,000-75,000Rp; 7am-10pm;) Modestly hip, this on-trend cafe at the western entrance to Amed village is a popular pit stop for granola, smashed avocado and egg Benedict breakfasts, lunches of cafe standards such as shakshuka (eggs poached in a spiced tomato sauce) and Balinese fish cakes, and coffee and juices throughout the day.

Cafe Garam INDONESIAN $

(0363-23462; www.hoteluyah.com; Hotel Uyah Amed, Jl I Ketut Natih; mains 29,000-65,000Rp; 7.30am-9.30pm;) There's a relaxed feel here, with pool tables and Balinese food plus the lyrical and haunting melodies of live *genjek* (traditional Balinese with percussion instruments) music at 8pm on Wednesday and Saturday. *Garam* means 'salt' and the cafe honours the local salt-making industry. Try the *salada ayam*, an addictive mix of cabbage, grilled chicken, shallots and tiny peppers.

★ **Warung Enak** BALINESE $$

(0819 1567 9019; Jl I Ketut Natih; mains 55,000-80,000Rp; 7am-10.30pm;) Owners Komang and Wayan have their own organic vegetable garden, and use the produce in the tasty dishes created in their busy kitchen. Balinese dishes include a tasty *ikan kare* (fish curry), satays and gado-gado; Western alternatives include pizzas and pastas. Black-rice pudding is a popular finale. Drinks include juices, beer and wine by both the glass and bottle.

Jemeluk

★ **Green Leaf Cafe** CAFE $

(0812 3826 7356; www.facebook.com/GreenLeafCafeAmed; Jl I Ketut Natih; breakfast dishes 36,000-60,000Rp, lunch mains 43,000-70,000Rp; 8am-6pm;) This excellent cafe right on the beach serves good, fresh food, with many vegetarian, vegan and gluten-free options. There's a wide range of coffees, teas and medicinal juices. Sit at a table inside or on loungers outside. This is also a hub for yoga and freediving – Apneista (p228) is associated with the cafe.

Sama-Sama Cafe INDONESIAN $

(0363-430 1004; www.samasamaamed.com; Jl I Ketut Natih; sandwiches 35,000-40,000Rp, mains 28,000-70,000Rp; 7.30am-10pm;) *Junkungs* (outrigger canoes used for fishing) lined up on the sand provide a picturesque backdrop when enjoying a casual meal or drink at this beachside cafe. Claim a seat next to the water or in the airy pavilion and enjoy a sandwich, meal or drink while watching the waves gently break. Menu choices include sandwiches, jaffles and seafood mains. The cafe also has simple bungalows on the opposite side of the road.

Blue Earth Village Restaurant INDONESIAN $

(0821 4554 3699; www.blueearthvillage.com/restaurant; Jemeluk Lookout; tapas 35,000-40,000Rp, mains 45,000-70,000Rp; noon-10pm) Spectacular views and a wide array of menu choices lure diners away from the action in Jemeluk's main strip and up to this restaurant overlooking the blue waters of the bay. There are plenty of vegetarian and vegan options on offer, and the menu includes tapas, pasta, pizza, Thai noodles and Indonesian mains. It's an excellent spot for a sundowner.

Sunset Point Warung BALINESE $

(0363-4301569; Jemeluk Lookout; mains 35,000-95,000Rp; 10am-9pm;) Here, you have a bird's eye perspective over the activity of the freedivers, snorkellers and *jukungs* in Jemeluk Bay. Tables are outdoors on the cliff's edge; claim one to enjoy a drink or simple meal.

Banutan

★ **Gusto** INTERNATIONAL $$

(0813 3898 1394; www.facebook.com/Gusto-Amed-553633071346005; Jl Raya Amed; pizzas 70,000-85,000Rp, pastas 65,000-85,000Rp, mains 55,000-120,000Rp; 2-10pm) Don't be put off by the unusual mix of cuisines on Gusto's menu (Indonesian, Italian and Hungarian) – the chefs have mastered them all. Serving the best pizzas on the east coast, homemade pasta dishes, schnitzels and Indonesian seafood dishes, it is a particularly good choice in daylight hours, when the sea view charms. It's small, so bookings are essential.

Banyuning

Trattoria Cucina Italia ITALIAN $$
(☎0363-4501848; www.trattoriaasia.com; Jl Karangasem Seraya; pizzas 69,000-99,000Rp, pastas 64,000-180,000Rp, mains 99,000-270,000Rp; ⏲10am-10pm; Ⓟ✎) The Amed branch of a multinational chain, this pavilion restaurant at Ibus Beach is perched on a cliffside and offers its diners wonderful sea views to savour alongside antipasti, good pizzas, pastas and grills. Head here between 3pm and 6pm to enjoy a happy-hour beer or cocktail.

Aas

Smiling Buddha Restaurant BALINESE $
(☎0828 372 2738; Meditasi Resort; mains 40,000-75,000Rp; ⏲8am-10pm; ✎) The restaurant at Meditasi (p232) offers tasty organic fare, much of it sourced from its own garden. The Balinese and Western dishes (mainly pastas) are enjoyed in a pavilion right on the beach, and it's possible to sign up for a two-hour cooking class (300,000Rp) to re-create them at home.

Drinking & Nightlife

Wawa-Wewe I BAR
(☎0812 3973 7662; Lipah; ⏲10am-11pm; 📶) You won't know your wawas from your wewes if you spend an evening downing Bintangs here. This old-fashioned backpackers dive is the coast's most raucous bar – which by local standards means that sometimes it gets sorta loud. Local bands jam from 8pm on Wednesday, Friday and Sunday nights. Balinese food is served (mains 35,000Rp to 50,000Rp).

Information

There are ATMs in Amed village and Lipah.

ECO ENTREPRENEURS

A non-profit outfit encouraging recycling and raising eco-consciousness in Amed, **Peduli Alam Bali** (☎0877 6156 2511; www.pedulialam.org; Jl Raya Lipah, Lipah; ⏲9am-5pm Mon-Fri, to noon Sat) collects 50 tonnes of rubbish from this part of the island each month, much of which is then used to make the bags and other items that are sold in this shop. The project gives employment to four truck drivers and 14 local women.

The shop also sells bamboo straws and water bottles; the latter can be refilled with filtered water here at no charge.

Getting There & Away

Public transport to and around Amed is nonexistent. Most people drive here via the main highway from Amlapura and Culik. The spectacular road, going all the way around the twin peaks from Aas to Ujung, makes a good circle.

You can arrange for a driver and car to/from south Bali and the airport for about 500,000Rp.

Amed Sea Express (☎0853 3925 3944; www.gili-sea-express.com; Jemeluk Beach; one-way from US$29) Makes crossings to Gili Trawangan on an 80-person speedboat in under an hour.

Kuda Hitam Express (☎0363-23482; www.kudahitamexpress.com; Jemeluk Beach; adult/child one-way from 650,000/450,000Rp) Serves Gili Trawangan and Gili Air.

Tulamben

☎0363 / POP 8050

Tulamben's big attraction sunk over 60 years ago. The wreck of the US cargo ship *Liberty* is among the best and most popular dive sites in Bali and has transformed what was a tiny fishing village into an entire town based on diving. Even snorkellers can easily swim out and enjoy exploring the wreck and the coral reefs that are strung along the coastline. Swimming is a different story – the shore is made up of rather beautiful, large washed stones that are difficult to walk on, so visitors tend to swim in hotel pools.

For non-aquatic delights, check out the **morning market** in Tulamben village, 1.5km north of the dive site.

Activities

The **shipwreck** USAT *Liberty* is about 50m directly offshore from Puri Madha Dive Resort; look for the schools of black snorkels. Swim straight out and you'll see the stern rearing up from the depths, heavily encrusted with coral and swarming with dozens of species of colourful fish – and with scuba divers most of the day. The ship is more than 100m long, but the hull is broken into sections and it's easy for divers to get inside. The bow is in quite good shape, the midship's region is badly mangled and the stern is almost intact – the best parts are between 15m and 30m deep. You will want at least two dives to really explore the wreck.

Many divers commute to Tulamben from Amed or Lovina, and in busy times it can get quite crowded between 11am and 4pm, with 50 or more divers at a time around the wreck. Stay the night in Tulamben to get an early start. Most hotels have their own dive centre and some offer good-value dive and accommodation packages for guests.

Expect to pay around 1,200,000Rp for two dives at Tulamben and a little more for night dives around Amed. Snorkelling gear is rented everywhere for 100,000Rp or so.

Note the privately run parking area (10,000Rp) behind Tauch Terminal where there are gear-rental stands, vendors, porters and more ready to get your attention. There are also pay-showers and toilets.

Puri Madha Dive Centre DIVING
(☎0363-22921; www.purimadhadiveresort.com; ⏲6am-6.30pm) This place hires snorkelling gear (200,000Rp) and offers off-shore dives (one/two dives 700,000/1,200,000Rp) and PADI open water courses (two to three days 5,400,000Rp). It also offers dive and accommodation packages at its resort.

Tauch Terminal DIVING
(☎0363-774504; www.tauch-terminal.com; 2/4 dives €55/109) Long-established dive operator offering a range of diving packages and equipment rental (one-day scuba/snorkel €15/6). A four-day SSI open-water certificate course costs €450. It also runs its own **dive resort** (s/d bungalow €69/79, deluxe r €89/109; ❄📶🏊).

Apnea Bali DIVING
(☎WhatsApp 0822 3739 8854, WhatsApp 0822 6612 5814; www.apneabali.com; Jl Kubu-Abang; courses from 800,000Rp) This polished operator on Tulamben's main strip specialises in freediving courses and trips for all skill levels, including down to the *Liberty* wreck. Choose from an introductory half-day course (800,000Rp), a 2-day course (3,200,000Rp) and a 3-day course (4,600,000Rp).

Sleeping

Tulamben is a quiet place and is essentially built around the wreck – its hotels, all with a cafe or restaurant and most with dive centres, are spread along a 4km stretch either side of the main road. You can choose between roadside (cheaper) options or those by the water (nicer). At high tide even the rocky shore vanishes.

Matahari Tulumben Resort, Dive & Spa HOTEL $
(Matahari 1; ☎0813 3863 6670, 0363-22916; www.divetulamben.com; r 280,000-520,000Rp, bungalow 600,000Rp; ❄📶🏊) This modest 34-room hotel has a loyal following of divers, many of whom stay for weeks at a time. Rooms have air-con, fridge and better-than-average bathrooms. There's a dive shop, pool, bar and small restaurant with ocean views (mains 25,000Rp to 80,000Rp).

THE WRECK OF THE LIBERTY

In January 1942, the small US Navy cargo ship USAT *Liberty* was torpedoed by a Japanese submarine near Lombok. Taken in tow, it was beached at Tulamben so that its cargo of rubber and railway parts could be saved. The Japanese invasion prevented this and the ship sat on the beach until the 1963 eruption of Gunung Agung broke it in two and left it just off the shoreline, much to the delight of divers ever since. (And just for the record, it was *not* a Liberty-class WWII freighter.)

Liberty Dive Resort RESORT $$
(☎0812 3684 5440; www.libertydiveresort.com; r US$50-60, fm US$80, cottages US$65-120; ❄📶🏊) Just 100m up the hill from the rocky shore in front of the eponymous wreck, this old-fashioned place has simple rooms and cottages set in a well-maintained garden; facilities include a restaurant and two swimming pools. The onsite dive centre offers day/night dives for US$30/35 as well as a one-day PADI dive course (US$85).

Puri Madha Dive Resort RESORT $$
(☎0363-22921; www.purimadhadiveresort.com; r 550,000Rp, cottage 650,000Rp; ❄📶🏊) Close to the *Liberty* wreck dive site, this place offers basic rooms and cottages that are arranged cheek by jowl on terraces. It's popular with divers, who arrange dives and equipment hire through the on-site dive centre. Facilities include two pools, one of which is used for dive lessons, and a waterside cafeteria.

Siddhartha RESORT $$$
(☎0363-23034; www.siddhartha-bali.com; Kubu; s €69-188, d €146-240, villas €210-370; P❄🏊) The oceanside pool and yoga pavilion at this swish German-owned resort are major drawcards, as is the extensive range of facilities and amenities (restaurant, bar, dive centre, gym, billiard and table-tennis tables, TV room, spa). Well-spaced rooms and villas are located in garden surrounds, and feature comfortable beds and outdoor bathrooms; villas have plunge pools. Spa treatments include massages (€38 for one hour). The ocean in front of the resort is home to a reef that can be explored using equipment hired from the in-house dive centre; the *Liberty* wreck dive site isn't far away.

TEJAKULA

Located on the coastal road to Yeh Sanih, the small town of Tejakula is home to a stream-fed public bathing area called **Pemandian Kuda Desa** (Horse Village Bath) that is said to have been built for washing horses. The renovated bathing areas (separate for men and women) are behind walls topped by rows of elaborately decorated arches; they are regarded as a sacred area. The baths are 100m inland on a narrow road with lots of small shops and some finely carved *kulkul* (alarm drum) towers.

Getting There & Away

If you are driving to Lovina for the night, be sure to leave by about 3pm so you'll still have a little light when you get there. The car park in front of the Puri Madha Dive Resort is often full of vans dropping off organised groups of divers to the *Liberty* wreck, so you may have trouble sourcing a park there. There is paid parking near the Tauch Terminal Resort.

Northeast Coast

Say hello to small villages, volcanic landscapes, lush jungle and rocky seascapes on this 50km section of coast between Tulamben and Yeh Sanih.

Sights

Air Terjun Yeh Mampeh WATERFALL
(Yeh Mampeh Waterfall, Les Waterfall; Les; adult/child 20,000/10,000Rp, car/scooter parking 5000/1000Rp; from 7am) One of Bali's highest waterfalls (40m), Yeh Mampeh is in the hinterland at Les, near Tejakula. The entrance is about 2.5km off the main road, look for the 'Welcome to Waterfalls' sign. The best time to visit is between December and February, during the peak rainy season. Landslides here are common, so it's worth paying the extra 100,000Rp for a guide.

Sleeping

★ **Segara Lestari Villa** GUESTHOUSE $
(0815 5806 8811; www.facebook.com/lesvillagevilla; Jl Segara Lestari 99, Les; dm 150,000Rp, s/d without view 180,000/230,000Rp, seafront r 350,000Rp;) Associated with the Sea Communities social enterprise (www.seacommunities.com), Gede and Made's oceanside guesthouse has simple garden bungalows and four dorm rooms. Dorms have single beds, fans and basic outdoor bathroom; most bungalows have air-con and sea views. Snorkelling and diving equipment hire allows you to explore the coral reef directly in front of the hotel. The on-site restaurant is a plus.

Bali Sandat Guest House GUESTHOUSE $$
(0813 3755 5792; www.bali-sandat.com; Bondalem; s/d 460,000/650,000Rp;) You'll feel like you're staying with friends at this family-run guesthouse located deep in a waterfront palm forest in a remote part of East Bali. The five rooms have beds with mosquito nets, basic bathrooms and a fan; all share deep and shady verandahs. Balinese dinners are available (85,000Rp to 110,000Rp). The village of Bondalem is a 1km walk away.

Alam Anda HOTEL $$
(0812 465 6485; www.alam-anda.com; Sambirenteng; s €37-95, d €54-170, villa from €152;) German-owned, this oceanside resort is dated but well maintained. A reef just offshore keeps the on-site dive centre busy (dives €23 to €60, snorkel rental €8 per day). Accommodation ranges from simple losmen rooms to bungalows and villas, and facilities include a small gym, library, pool, restaurant and Ayurvedic spa. Wi-fi is charged (19,000Rp per day).

★ **Spa Village Resort Tembok** HOTEL $$$
(0362-32033; Tembok; full board r/cottage/villa from US$250/350/420;) In need of rejuvenation? If so, the packages at this tranquil oceanfront resort northeast of Tembok will appeal. These include comfortable accommodation as well as three meals (vegetarian and vegan options available), a daily spa treatment and plenty of activities (yoga, star-gazing, drawing). W-fi is only available in the lobby.

Eating

Segara Lestari Restaurant INTERNATIONAL $
(0815 5806 8811; Segara Lestari Villa, Les; pizzas 40,000-50,000Rp, burgers 40,000-50,000Rp, mains 25,000-65,000Rp; 7am-9pm;) At laid-back Segara Lestari Villa, this light and breezy restaurant right next to the ocean serves fresh and tasty food, with an emphasis on vegetarian and vegan dishes.

Getting There & Away

You'll need a car or scooter to access this part of the coast. Getting here from the airport or south Bali can take three hours or more via two routes: one up and over the mountains via Kintamani and then down a rustic, scenic road to the sea near Tejakula; the other going right round east Bali on the coast road via Candidasa and Amed.

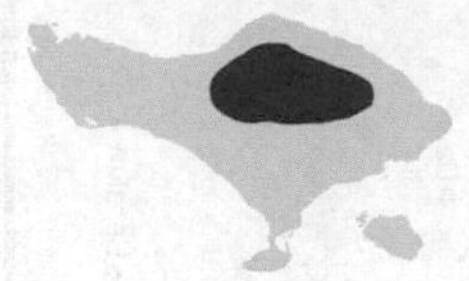

Central Mountains

Includes ➡

Best Places to Eat

- ➡ Pulu Mujung Warung (p241)
- ➡ Strawberry Hill (p245)
- ➡ Terrasse du Lac (p247)
- ➡ Puri Lumbung Cottages (p249)

Best Places to Stay

- ➡ Munduk Moding Plantation (p249)
- ➡ Puri Lumbung Cottages (p249)
- ➡ Sarinbuana Eco Lodge (p251)
- ➡ Bali Mountain Retreat (p251)
- ➡ Sanda Boutique Villas (p252)

Why Go?

Bali has a hot soul. The volcanoes stretching along the island's spine are seemingly cones of silence but their active spirits are just below the surface, eager for expression.

Gunung Batur (1717m) is constantly letting off steam; this place has an other-worldly beauty that may overwhelm the attendant hassles of a visit. At Danau Bratan there are sacred Hindu temples, while the village of Candikuning has an engrossing botanic garden.

The old colonial village of Munduk, a hiking centre, has views down the hills to the coast of north Bali, which match the beauty of the many nearby waterfalls, and the lakes of Tamblingan and Buyan. In the shadow of Gunung Batukau (2276m) you'll find one of Bali's most mystic temples. And, just south, the Unesco-listed ancient rice terraces around Jatiluwih bedazzle.

Amid it all, little roads lead to untouched villages. Start driving north from Antasari for one surprise after another.

When to Go

➡ Bali's central mountains can be cool and misty throughout the year. They also get a lot of rain and this is the starting point for the water that courses through rice terraces and fields all the way south. Temperatures show few seasonal variations but can drop to 10°C at night at high elevations.

➡ It rains most from October through April, but can pour at any time during the year.

➡ There's no peak tourist season, except when the group-tour hordes hit the Kintamani area during the peak visitor months of July and August. It's a good idea to book ahead for Munduk too at this time.

Central Mountains Highlights

❶ **Munduk** (p248) Admiring waterfalls while trekking around this mountain idyll.

❷ **Pura Luhur Batukau** (p250) Hearing the chant of priests at one of Bali's holiest temples.

❸ **Danau Tamblingan** (p247) Hiking past old temples on the banks of this ancient volcanic lake.

❹ **Gunung Batur** (p239) Beholding the other-worldly, lava-strewn side of a still-active volcano.

❺ **Danau Batur** (p241) Driving through stunning landscapes on the road to Trunyan via Buahan and Abang.

❻ **Antosari Road** (p251) Passing jade-green rice terraces on this rural drive.

❼ **Jatiluwih** (p250) Gazing in awe at these magnificent Unesco-recognised terraces.

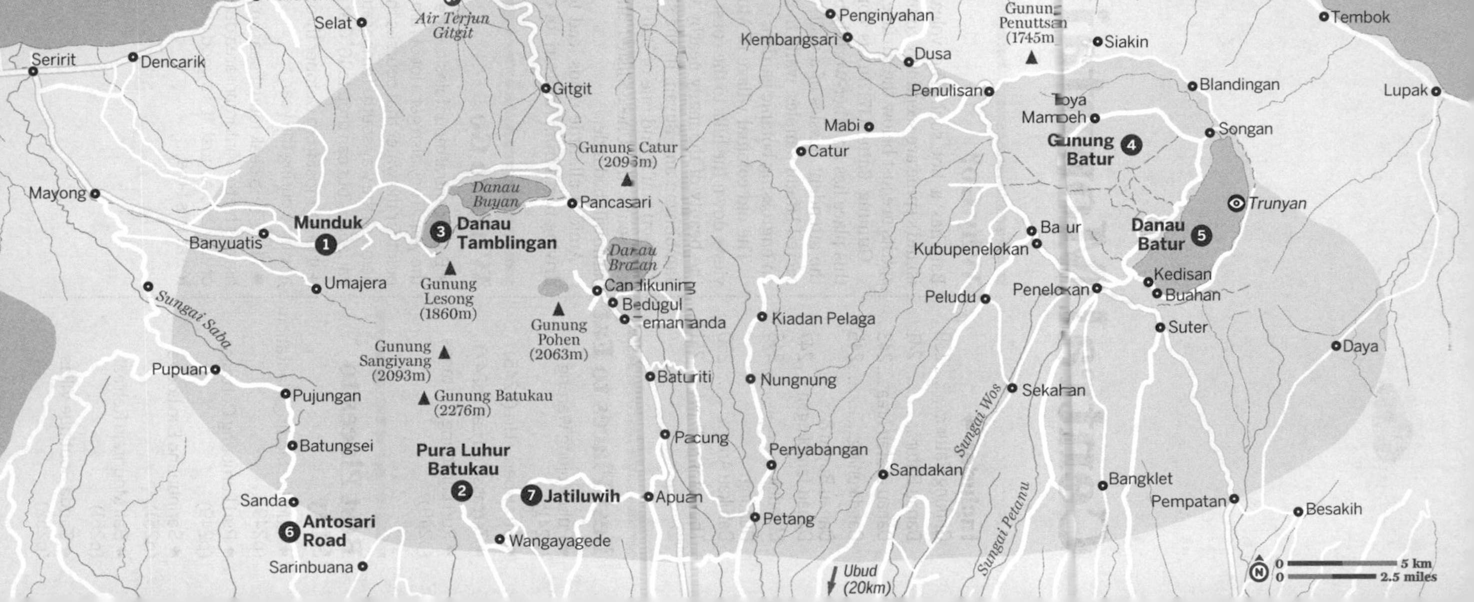

Getting There & Away

To fully explore the mountains at the heart of Bali, you will want your own vehicle. A car with hired driver will keep you from getting lost on the tangle of back roads, although that may be the very point of your day out.

GUNUNG BATUR AREA

☎0366

The Gunung Batur area is like a giant bowl, with its bottom half covered by water and a set of volcanic cones jutting out of the middle. Sound a bit spectacular? It is. On clear days – vital to appreciating the spectacle – the turquoise waters wrap around the newer volcanoes, which have paths of old lava flows snaking down their sides.

Information

DANGERS & ANNOYANCES

Be wary of touts on motorcycles, who will attempt to steer you to a tour or hotel of *their* choice as you descend into the Danau Batur area from the village of Penelokan. Very persistent, they offer no service of value and you should ignore them. Vendors in the area can be aggressive.

MONEY

Services are limited in the Gunung Batur area, but there are a few ATMs along Jl Raya Penelokan.

Getting There & Away

Buses on the Denpasar–Singaraja route (via Batubulan, where you may need to change) will stop in Penelokan and Kintamani (about 40,000Rp). Alternatively, you can hire a car or use a driver but be sure to rebuff buffet-lunch entreaties.

If you arrive by private vehicle, you will be stopped at Penelokan or Kubupenelokan to buy an entry ticket (40,000/5000Rp per vehicle/person, beware of scams demanding even more) for the entire Gunung Batur area. You shouldn't be charged again – save your receipt.

Getting Around

It's best to arrange private transport to get around this area; bemos are rare and roads are small, winding and crowded.

Gunung Batur

Vulcanologists describe Gunung Batur as a 'double caldera', with one crater inside another. The outer crater is an oval about 14km long, with its western rim about 1500m above sea level. The inner is a classic volcano-shaped peak that reaches 1717m. Geological activity occurs regularly, and activity over the last decade has spawned several smaller cones on its western flank. There were major eruptions in 1917, 1926 and 1963.

One look at this other-worldly spectacle and you'll understand why people want to go through the many hassles and expenses of a trek. Note that the odds of clouds obscuring your reason for coming are greater from July to December, but at any time of year you should check conditions before committing to a trip, or even coming up the mountain.

Activities

The cartel of local guides known as PPPGB (formerly HPPGB) has a monopoly on guided climbs up Gunung Batur. It requires all trekking agencies to hire at least one of its guides for trips up the mountain, and has

WORTH A TRIP

PENULISAN

The road north from Kintamani gradually climbs along the crater rim and is often shrouded in clouds, mist or rain. Penulisan is where the road bends sharply and splits: the main branch runs down towards the north coast while the other leads to the remote scenic drive to Bedugul. A **viewpoint** about 400m south of here offers an amazing panorama over three mountains: Gunung Batur, Gunung Abang and Gunung Agung.

Near the Penilusan road junction, several steep flights of steps lead to Bali's highest temple, the 1745m **Pura Puncak Penulisan** (admission free). Inside the highest courtyard are rows of old statues and fragments of sculptures in the open *bale* (pavilion with steeply pitched thatch roof). Some of the sculptures date to the 11th century. The temple views are superb on clear days: facing north you can see over the rice terraces clear to the Singaraja coast.

a reputation for tough tactics in requiring climbers to use its guides and in negotiations for its services.

That said, many people use the services of PPPGB guides without incident, and some of the guides win plaudits from visitors due to their ideas for customising trips.

The following strategies should help you have a good climb:

- Be absolutely clear in your agreement with PPPGB about the terms you're agreeing to, such as whether fees are per person or per group, whether they include breakfast, and exactly where you will go.
- Deal with one of the trekking agencies. There will still be a PPPGB guide along, but all arrangements will be done through the agency.

PPPGB rates and times are posted at its main Toya Bungkah office and its second access road office. Treks on offer include:

Mt Batur Sunrise A simple ascent and return; from 4am to 8am, 400,000Rp per person.

Mt Batur Main Crater Includes sunrise from the summit and time around the rim; from 4am to 9.30am, 500,000Rp per person.

Mt Batur Exploration Sunrise, caldera and some of the volcanic cones; from 4am to 10am, 650,000Rp per person.

Getting There & Away

Aside from hiking and trekking, you need your own wheels here.

Around Gunung Batur Crater

The extraordinary geology of the Gunung Batur area is explained in fascinating detail at **Batur Geopark Museum** (☎0366-91537, What'sApp 0818-0551-5504; www.baturglobalgeo

Gunung Batur Area

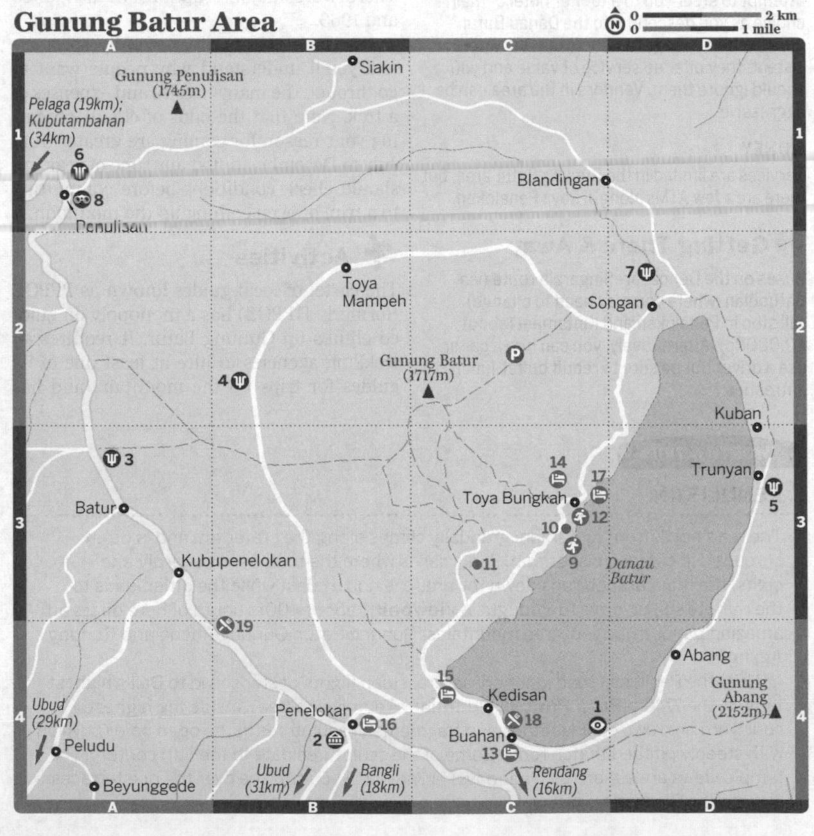

park.com; Penelokan; 9am-4pm Mon, from 8am Tue-Fri, 8am-2pm Sat & Sun) FREE right near the crater rim. Using interactive displays, models and rock samples, the enormous forces that continue to shape this area are made real. Expect to spend about an hour here and thank the Unesco Geopark designation for funding this complex. Note that you have to pay the region's access fees before you reach the museum.

Spiritually, Gunung Batur is the second-most-important mountain in Bali (only Gunung Agung outranks it), so this temple, the ever-more-flamboyant **Pura Batur** (15,000Rp, sarong & sash rental 20,000Rp), is of considerable importance. It's a great stop for the architectural spectacle. Within the complex is a Taoist shrine.

Sleeping & Eating

Lakeview Hotel HOTEL $$
(0366-52525; www.lakeviewbali.com; Penelokan; r incl breakfast from 750,000Rp; cafe 7.30am-3.30pm;) This venerable hotel complex was recently revitalised by the family who've owned it for three generations. Twelve comfortable rooms have amazing views and access to a private lounge with snacks and meals until 10pm. The terrace cafe here has sweeping views.

Gunung Batur Area

Sights

1 Banyan Tree C4
2 Batur Geopark Museum B4
3 Pura Batur A3
4 Pura Bukit Mentik B2
5 Pura Pancering Jagat D3
6 Pura Puncak Penulisan A1
7 Pura Ulun Danu Batur D2
8 Viewpoint A1

Activities, Courses & Tours

9 Batur Natural Hot Spring C3
C.Bali .... (see 15)
10 PPPGB C3
11 PPPGB C3
12 Toya Devasya C3

Sleeping

13 Baruna Cottages C4
14 Black Lava Hostel C3
15 Hotel Segara C4
16 Lakeview Hotel B4
17 Under the Volcano III C3

Eating

18 Kedisan Floating Hotel C4
19 Pulu Mujung Warung B4

★ **Pulu Mujung Warung** INDONESIAN $
(0853 3842 8993; Penelokan; mains 45,000-70,000Rp; 9am-5pm) Easily the best option for a meal in the area, this fantastic cafe has epic volcano views. Soups are enjoyable in the cool mountain air, and you can also choose from salads, pizzas, Indo specials, homemade dragon-fruit wine, juices, smoothies and more.

Accommodation is available in three simple rooms (from 250,000Rp) but book ahead.

Danau Batur

The little villages around Danau Batur have a crisp lakeside setting and views up to the surrounding peaks. There's a lot of fish farming, and the air is pungent with the smell of onions from the myriad tiny vegetable farms. Don't miss the trip along the east coast to Trunyan.

A road hairpins its way down from Penelokan to the shore of Danau Batur. At the lakeside you can go left along the road that twists through lava fields to Toya Bungkah. Watch out for huge sand trucks battering the road into dust as they haul materials for construction across Bali.

Sights

You can spend a day exploring the villages around Danau Batur. It's a pleasant 15-minute stroll between the villages of Buahan and Kedisan; market gardens grow right down to the lakeshore.

Pura Pancering Jagat HINDU TEMPLE
The village of Trunyan is known for the Pura Pancering Jagat, which is very impressive with its seven-roofed *meru*. Inside the temple is a 4m-high statue of the village's guardian spirit, although tourists are not usually allowed in. Ignore the touts and guides lurking about and know that 5000Rp is the absolute maximum you should pay to park here.

Pura Bukit Mentik HINDU TEMPLE
Although completely surrounded by molten lava from the 1974 eruption, the temple itself and its impressive banyan tree were quite untouched – it's called the 'Lucky Temple'.

Pura Ulun Danu Batur HINDU TEMPLE
(Songan) At the lakeside road end is Pura Ulun Danu Batur, under the edge of the crater rim.

Activities

Hot springs bubble in a couple of spots, and have long been used for bathing pools. Cycling around the lake is an ideal way to explore the villages.

Cycling

The tiny lakeside villages have built bicycle paths that make it easy to enjoy the incredible views across to Gunung Batur from along the lake's east side.

From the T-junction of the access road down from Penelokan near Kedisan, it's 9km to Trunyan via Abang. Whether walking, cycling or riding a motorbike, this is a very rewarding adventure. Cyclists will need to dismount for a few short and steep stretches north of Abang. Besides the views, there is a magnificent banyan tree east of Buahan and some good Geopark-sponsored information panels on the area's wild geology at the Abang pier.

Hot Springs

Batur Natural Hot Spring HOT SPRINGS
(☎0366-51194; www.baturhotspring.com; adult/child from 190,000/100,000Rp; ⏰7am-7pm) This ever-expanding complex is on the edge of Danau Batur. The three pools have different temperatures, so you can simmer yourself successively. The overall feel of the hot springs matches the slightly shabby feel of the entire region. The simple cafe has good views.

Toya Devasya HOT SPRINGS
(☎0366-51204; www.toyadevasya.com; Toya Bungkah; adult/child 200,000/160,000Rp; ⏰7am-7pm) This glossy retreat is built around springs. One huge hot pool is 38°C, while a comparatively brisk lake-fed pool is 20°C. There is a cafe with illusions of grandeur as well as lodging options (from 3,000,000Rp per night); 200,000Rp gets you a towel and a locker. It also offers good bike tours (650,000Rp) and canoe trips (1,000,000Rp).

Tours

★C.Bali ADVENTURE
(☎info only 0813 5342 0541; www.c-bali.com; Hotel Segara, Kedisan; tours adult/child from 500,000/400,000Rp) Operated by an Australian-Dutch couple, C.Bali offers cultural bike tours around the region and canoe tours on Danau Batur. Prices include pick up across south Bali. Packages also include multiday trips. Note: these tours often fill up far in advance, so book ahead through the website.

GUNUNG BATUR TREKKING ROUTES

The climb to see the sunrise from Gunung Batur is still the most popular trek. In high season 100 or more people will arrive at the top for dawn. Guides will provide breakfast on the summit for a fee (50,000Rp), which often includes the novelty of cooking an egg or banana in the steaming holes at the top of the volcano. There are pricey refreshment stops along the way.

Most travellers use one of two trails that start near Toya Bungkah. The shorter one is straight up (three to four hours return), while a longer trek (five to six hours return) links the summit climb with the other craters. Climbers have reported that they have easily made this journey without a PPPGB guide, although it shouldn't be tried while it's dark because people have fallen to their deaths. The major obstacle is actually avoiding any hassle from the guides.

There are a few separate paths at first, but they all rejoin sooner or later and after about 30 minutes you'll be on a ridge with quite a well-defined track. It gets pretty steep towards the top and it can be hard walking over the loose volcanic sand – you'll climb up three steps only to slide back two. Allow about two hours to get to the top.

There's also a track that enables you to use private transport to within about 45 minutes' walk of the top. From Toya Bungkah, take the road northeast towards Songan and take the left fork after about 3.5km at Serongga, just before Songan. Follow this inner-rim road for another 1.7km to a well-signposted track on the left, which climbs another 1km or so to a car park. From here, the walking track is easy to follow to the top.

If you're climbing before sunrise, take a torch (flashlight) or be absolutely sure that your guide provides you with one. You'll need good strong footwear, a hat, a jumper (sweater) and drinking water.

BATUR CALDERA GEOPARK

In 2012 Unesco honoured the area by adding it to a list of more than 90 geologic wonders worldwide (www.globalgeopark.org) and naming it the Batur Caldera Geopark (www.baturglobalgeopark.com). Some interesting signs detailing the unique geology of the area are posted along roads in the region; the Batur Geopark Museum (p240) has full details.

The road around the southwestern rim of the Gunung Batur crater offers stunning vistas, though the villages around the crater rim have grown into one continuous, untidy strip. Kintamani is the main village, though the whole area is often referred to by that name. Coming from the south, the first village is Penelokan, where tour groups first stop to gasp at the view.

Day trippers should bring some sort of wrap in case the mist closes in and the temperature drops (it can get to 16°C).

Sleeping & Eating

A few guesthouses with lake views dot the shore.

Beware of the motorcycle touts, who will follow you down the hill from Penelokan trying to nab a hotel commission. Local hotels ask that you call ahead and reserve so that they have your name on record and thus can avoid paying the touts.

★Black Lava Hostel HOSTEL $
(0813 3755 8998; www.facebook.com/blacklavahostel123; Jl Raya Pendakian Gunung; dm 150,000Rp, r from 400,000Rp) Tucked in the hills of Toya Bungkah, this friendly hostel offers basic, affordable dorm accommodation and a toasty dipping pool filled with mineral water from the nearby hot springs. The views of the nearby lake and Mount Abang are breathtaking, and management can organise (somewhat pricey) early-morning hikes up Gunung Batur.

Baruna Cottages GUESTHOUSE $
(0813 5322 2896; www.barunacottage.com; Buahan; r/bungalow from 400,000/550,000Rp) The 10 rooms at this small and tidy compound vary greatly in design and size; the middle grade have the best views. It's right across the Trunyan road from the lake, and there's a cute cafe.

Under the Volcano III GUESTHOUSE $
(0813 3860 0081; Toya Bungkah; s/d incl breakfast from 200,000/250,000Rp) Featuring a lovely, quiet lakeside location opposite chilli plots, this inn has six clean and simple rooms; go for room 1 right on the water. There are two other nearby inns in the Volcano empire, all run by the same lovely family.

Hotel Segara GUESTHOUSE $
(0366-51136; www.segara-id.book.direct; Kedisan; r incl breakfast 250,000-600,000Rp) The popular Segara has bungalows set around a cafe and courtyard. The cheaper of the 32 rooms have cold water; the best rooms have hot water and bathtubs – perfect for soaking after an early trek.

Kedisan Floating Hotel BALINESE $
(0366-51627, 0813 3775 5411; Kedisan; meals from 27,000Rp; 8am-8pm) This hotel on the shores of Danau Batur is hugely popular for its daily lunches. On weekends tourists vie with day-trippers from Denpasar for tables out on the piers over the lake. The Balinese food, which features fresh lake fish, is excellent. You can also stay here: the best rooms are cottages at the water's edge (from 500,000Rp).

Getting There & Away

Aside from hiking and trekking, you'll be happiest with your own wheels here.

DANAU BRATAN AREA

Approaching from south Bali, you gradually leave the rice terraces behind and ascend into the cool mountain country around Danau Bratan. Candikuning is the main village in the area, and has the important and picturesque temple Pura Ulun Danu Bratan. Munduk anchors the region with fine trekking to waterfalls and cloud-cloaked forests and nearby Danau Tamblingan. Wherever you go, you are likely to see tasty local strawberries on offer. Note that it is often misty and can get chilly up here.

Danau Bratan Area

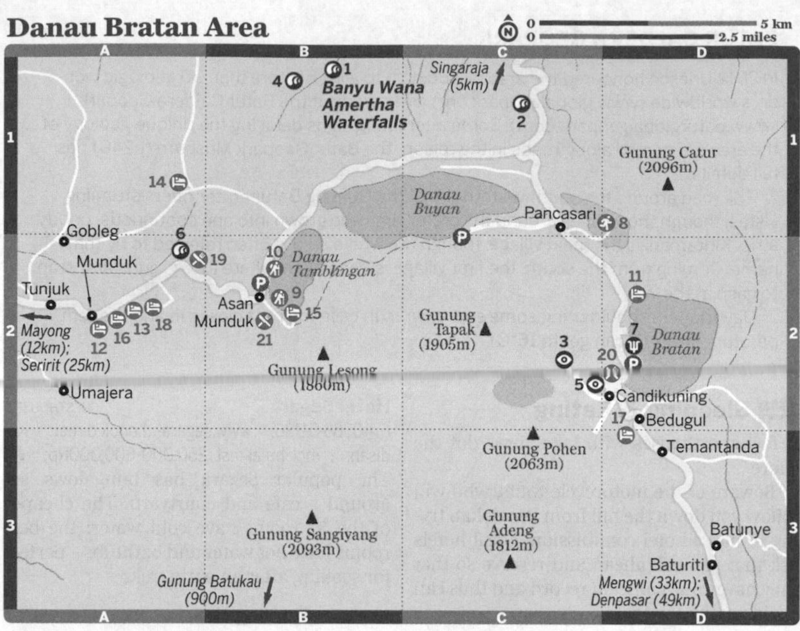

Danau Bratan Area

Top Sights

1 Banyu Wana Amertha Waterfalls B1

Sights

2 Air Terjun Gitgit C1
3 Bali Botanic Garden C2
4 Banyumala Twin Waterfalls B1
5 Candikuning Market C2
6 Munduk Waterfall A2
7 Pura Ulun Danu Bratan D2

Activities, Courses & Tours

Bali Treetop Adventure Park ......(see 3)
8 Handara Golf & Country Club Resort D1
9 Organisasi Pramuwisata Bangkit Bersama B2
10 Pramuwisata Amerta Jati B2

Sleeping

11 Enjung Beji Resort D2
12 Guru Ratna A2
Kebun Raya Bali ......(see 3)
13 Manah Liang Cottages A2
Meme Surung Homestay ......(see 12)
14 Munduk Moding Plantation A1
15 Pondok Kesuma Wisata B2
16 Puri Alam Bali A2
Puri Lumbung Cottages ......(see 13)
17 Strawberry Hill D3
18 Villa Dua Bintang A2

Eating

Don Biyu ......(see 12)
19 Ngiring Ngewedang A2
20 Roti Bedugul D2
21 Terrasse du Lac B2

Sleeping

The choice of accommodation near the lake is limited because much of the area is geared towards domestic, not foreign, tourists. On Sundays and public holidays the lakeside can be crowded with courting couples and Toyotas bursting with day-tripping families. Munduk, with its many excellent inns, has the best selection of places to stay.

Eating

Good eating choices bookend this region: Bedugal and Munduk. Day trippers can bring a picnic from the south.

Getting There & Away

Danau Bratan is along the main north–south road between south Bali and Singaraja. Bemos (minibuses) have largely gone the way of the dinosaur and operate very infrequent services here, stopping along the road in Bedugul and Candikuning on runs between Denpasar's Ubung terminal and Singaraja's Sangket terminal a couple of times a week, at best, for around 100,000Rp. To get around the scattered attractions of this region, you'll want your own transport.

Bedugul

☎0368

'Bedugul' is sometimes used to refer to the whole lakeside area, but strictly speaking it's just the first place you reach at the top of the hill when coming from south Bali, and even then you might not pause long because it's small.

Sleeping

Avoid the string of rundown places up at the ridge around Bedugul.

★Strawberry Hill GUESTHOUSE $$
(☎0368-21265; www.strawberryhillbali.com; Jl Raya Denpasar-Singaraja; r incl breakfast from 450,000Rp;) Just outside Candikuning you'll find 17 small conical woodsy cottages arrayed on a hill. Each has a deep soaking tub and nice views down to south Bali (some have better views than others, so compare).

The cafe's Indo menu (mains from 40,000Rp) includes soul-healing *soto ayam* (chicken soup) and *gudeg yogya* (jackfruit stew). Pick your own strawberries for free from the hotel's patch.

Bali Ecovillage BOUTIQUE HOTEL $$
(☎0819 9988 6035, reservations 0813 5338 2797; www.baliecovillage.com; Dinas Lawak; r/bungalow from US$47/95) A vision in bamboo and set in a remote corner of Bali near coffee plantations, this idiosyncratic lodge is so green that just about the only other colour you'll see is the blue sky. The restaurant serves organic local and Western fare and there are numerous cultural activities plus a spa and yoga.

It's located in a hidden valley near the village of Kiadan Pelaga, about 25km from Bedugul.

Getting There & Away

Any bemo or minibus between south Bali and Singaraja will stop at Bedugul on request.

Candikuning

☎0368

Often misty, Candikuning is home to a good botanic garden as well as one of Bali's most photographed temples. There's also the simple beauty of Danau Bratan amid the bowl of lushly forested mountains.

Sights

Pura Ulun Danu Bratan HINDU TEMPLE
(off Jl Raya Denpasar-Singaraja; adult/child 50,000/25,000Rp, parking 5000Rp; 7am-4pm) An iconic image of Bali, depicted on the 50,000Rp note, this important Hindu-Buddhist temple was founded in the 17th century. It is dedicated to Dewi Danu, the goddess of the waters, and is built on small islands. Pilgrimages and ceremonies are held here to ensure that there is a supply of water for farmers all over Bali as part of the Unesco-recognised *subak* system. Incredibly popular, you'll need to dodge selfie sticks unless you set out early.

The tableau includes classical Hindu thatch-roofed *meru* (multi-tiered shrines) reflected in the water and silhouetted against the often cloudy mountain backdrop.

Unfortunately, there's a bit of a sideshow atmosphere here: animals, including some very sad-eyed deer, are apparently being held here before ritual sacrifices, and the car park is lined with souvenir stalls. You can escape the masses by renting a pedal boat shaped like a deformed swan (100,000Rp) or taking a guided canoe tour (200,000Rp).

Bali Botanic Garden GARDENS
(☎0368-203 3211; www.krbali.lipi.go.id; Jl Kebun Raya Eka Karya Bali; 20,000Rp, parking 6000Rp; 7am-6pm) This garden is a showplace. Established in 1959 as a branch of the national botanic gardens at Bogor, near Jakarta, it covers more than 154 hectares on the lower slopes of Gunung Pohen. Don't miss

SUNRISE JOY

For an almost surreal experience, take a quiet paddle across Danau Bratan and see Pura Ulun Danu Bratan at sunrise – arrange it with a boatman at the temple the night before. The mobs see it by day, but you'll see something entirely different – and magical – in the mists of dawn.

OFF THE BEATEN TRACK

SCENIC SIDE ROADS

A series of narrow roads links the Danau Bratan area and the Gunung Batur region. Few locals outside this area even know that the roads exist, and your driver (if you have one) may need some convincing. Over a 30km route you not only step back to a simpler time, but also leave Bali altogether for something resembling less-developed islands such as Timor. The scenery is beautiful and may make you forget you had a destination.

South of Bedugul, turn east at Temantanda and take a small and winding road down the hillside into some lush ravines cut by rivers. After about 6km you'll come to a T-junction: turn north and travel about 5km to reach the pretty village of **Kiadan Pelaga**. This area is known for its organic coffee and cinnamon plantations, which you'll both see and smell. Consider a tour and homestay in Pelaga organised by JED (p449), a nonprofit group that offers rural tourism experiences.

From Pelaga, ascend the mountain, following terrain that alternates between jungle and rice fields. Continue north to Catur, then veer east to the junction with the road down to north Bali and drive east again for 1km to Penulisan.

A fun detour on *this* detour is the **Tukad Bangkung Bridge** at Petang: at 71m it is reputed to be the tallest bridge in Asia. It is a local tourist attraction and the roads are lined with vendors on weekends.

the **Panca Yadnya Garden** (Garden of Five Offerings), which preserves plants used in ancient Hindu ceremonies. For an extra 12,000Rp you can drive your own car (no motorbikes) about the gardens.

Some plants are labelled with their botanical names, and a booklet of self-guided walks (20,000Rp) is helpful. The gorgeous orchid area is often locked to foil flower filchers, you can ask for it to be unlocked. Look for the 'roton' or rattan bush to see the unlikely source of so much furniture.

Within the park, you can cavort like an ape or a squirrel at the Bali Treetop Adventure Park.

Candikuning Market MARKET
(Jl Raya Denpasar-Singaraja; parking 2000Rp) This roadside market is very touristy, but among the eager vendors of tat, you'll find locals shopping for fruit, veg, herbs, spices and potted plants.

Activities

Handara Golf & Country Club Resort GOLF
(☎0362-342 3048; www.handaragolfresort.com; greens fees from 1,000,000Rp, club rental from 450,000Rp) Just south of Pancasari, you will see the entrance to this well-situated, 18-hole golf course (compared with south Bali courses, there's plenty of water here). It also offers comfortable accommodation (rooms from US$100) in the sterile atmosphere of a 1970s resort (that could pass for Drax's lair in the Bond movie *Moonraker*).

The property's iconic gate draws more visitors to the area than the resort itself – pay 30,000Rp and get 10 minutes of selfie time in front of it. Your Instagram followers will eat it up.

Bali Treetop Adventure Park OUTDOORS
(☎0361-934 0009; www.balitreetop.com; Jl Kebun Raya Eka Karya Bali, Bali Botanic Garden; adult/child from US$25/10, ⏰9.30am-6pm) Within the Bali Botanic Garden (p245), you can cavort like a bird or a squirrel at the Bali Treetop Adventure Park. Winches, ropes, nets and more let you explore the forest well above the ground. And it's not passive: you hoist, jump, balance and otherwise circumnavigate the park. Special programs are geared to different ages.

Sleeping

Kebun Raya Bali GUESTHOUSE $$
(☎0368-2033211; www.kebunrayabali.com; Jl Kebun Raya Eka Karya Bali, Bali Botanic Garden; r incl breakfast from 450,000Rp) Wake up and smell the roses. The Bali Botanic Garden (p245) has 14 comfortable hotel-style rooms and a four-cottage guesthouse in the heart of the botanic gardens.

Enjung Beji Resort HOTEL $$
(☎0852 8521; www.enjungbejiresort.com; Candikuning; cottages incl breakfast 400,000-750,000Rp) Just north of the temple and overlooking Danau Bratan is this peaceful, pleasant option. The 23 cottages are modern

and clean, the nicest with outdoor showers and sunken baths.

Eating

For an excellent bowl of *bakso ayam* (chicken soup), stop at one of the roadside stands where the road from Candikuning reaches Danau Bratan and turns north. Otherwise there are numerous mediocre restaurants with car parks suitable for tour buses along the main road near the temple.

Roti Bedugul BAKERY $
(☎0368-203-3102; Jl Raya Denpasar-Singaraja; snacks from 5000Rp; ⊙8am-4pm) Just north of the market, this bakery produces fine versions of its namesake, as well as croissants and other baked goods.

Getting There & Away

Any minibus or bemo between south Bali and Singaraja will stop in Candikuning on request.

Danau Buyan & Danau Tamblingan

Northwest of Danau Bratan are two less-visited lakes, Danau Buyan and Danau Tamblingan, where some excellent guided hikes are on offer. The Munduk road on the hill above the lakes has sweeping views. There are several tiny villages and old temples along the shores of both lakes that reward those who take the time to explore. You'll leave crowded Bali behind and enjoy a tropical hike in nature, with few of the hassles so prevalent elsewhere.

Activities

★Pramuwisata Amerta Jati HIKING
(☎0857 3715 4849; Munduk Rd; guided hikes 250,000-750,000Rp; ⊙8am-5pm) Located in a hut along the road above Danau Tamblingan, this group of excellent guides offers several different trips down and around the lakes. A popular two-hour trip includes ancient temples and a canoe trip on the lake (per person 250,000Rp). Trips can be as short as an hour or last all day.

★Organisasi Pramuwisata Bangkit Bersama HIKING
(Guides Organization Standing Together; ☎0852 3867 8092; Danau Tambligan, Asan Munduk; guided hikes from 200,000Rp; ⊙8.30am-4pm) This great group is based in a hut near the car park for Danau Tamblingan. Like the guiding group along the Munduk road, it offers a range of trips around the lakes, temples and mountains. You can ascend nearby Gunung Lesong for 600,000Rp (there are walking sticks for you to use).

Sleeping

Pondok Kesuma Wisata GUESTHOUSE $
(☎0812 3791 5865; Asan Munduk; r from 350,000Rp) This useful 12-room guesthouse features clean rooms with hot water and a pleasant cafe (meals 15,000Rp to 30,000Rp, confirm in advance). It's just up from the Danau Tamblingan car park. Note at times there will be very little service beyond getting you checked in or out.

Eating

There are good and simple cafes and picnic spots with views along the Munduk road that runs along the ridge north of the lakes.

★Terrasse du Lac CAFE $$
(☎0819 0330 1917; Jl Danau Tamblingan; mains 60,000-75,000Rp; ⊙9am-8pm; 🔲) There's a French accent and excellent food at this cafe, which has lovely lake views. Breakfast features pancakes, while later in the day there are meaty mains, pasta and veggie specials. Excellent fresh juices, plus beer, coffee etc. Try the turmeric tea. You can rent two modern, tidy rooms that have sunset views from the balconies (from 600,000Rp).

PANCASARI TO MUNDUK

Heading to Munduk from Pancasari, the main road climbs steeply up the rim of the old volcanic crater. It's worth stopping to enjoy the views back over the valley and lakes – show a banana and the swarms of monkeys will get so excited they'll start spanking themselves with joy. Turning right (east) at the top will take you on a scenic descent to Singaraja. Taking a sharp left turn (west), you follow a ridgetop road with Danau Buyan on one side and a slope to the sea on the other.

At Asan Munduk, you'll find another T-junction. The left turn will take you down a road leading to Danau Tamblingan. Turning right takes you along beautiful winding roads to the main village of Munduk. Watch for superb panoramas of north Bali and the ocean.

Getting There & Away

You will need your own wheels to explore the region around these two lakes. Danau Buyan has parking right at the lake, a pretty 1.5km drive off the main road. Danau Tamblingan has parking at the end of the road from the village of Asan Munduk.

Munduk

0362

The simple village of Munduk is one of Bali's most appealing mountain retreats. It has a cool misty ambience set among lush hillsides covered with jungle, rice fields, fruit trees and pretty much anything else that grows on the island. Waterfalls tumble off precipices by the dozen. There are hikes and treks galore and a number of really nice places to stay, from old Dutch colonial summer homes to retreats where you can plunge full-on into local culture. Many people come for a day and stay for a week.

Archaeological evidence suggests there was a developed community in the Munduk region between the 10th and 14th centuries. When the Dutch took control of north Bali in the 1890s, they experimented with commercial crops, establishing plantations for coffee, vanilla, cloves and cocoa.

Activities

Wherever you stay, staff will fill you in on walking and hiking options. There are numerous trails suitable for hikes of varying lengths to destinations as diverse as coffee plantations, rice paddies, waterfalls or villages. You could even hike around both Danau Tamblingan and Danau Buyan. Most trails are easy to do on your own, but guides will take you far off the beaten path to waterfalls and other delights that are hard to find.

Ask about the walking path linking Munduk's guesthouses, which saves you from traversing the perilous road.

Sleeping

Puri Alam Bali GUESTHOUSE $
(0812 465 9815; www.purialambali.com; r 400,000-800,000Rp;) Perched on a precipice at the east end of the village, the 15 rooms (all with hot water and balconies) have better views the higher you go. The rooftop cafe is worth a visit for its huge views. Think of the long concrete stairs down from the road as trekking practice.

WORTH A TRIP

MUNDUK'S WATERFALLS

Munduk's many waterfalls include the following three, which you can visit on a hike of four to six hours (note that the myriad local maps given out by guesthouses and hotels can be vague on details and it's easy to take a wrong turn). Fortunately, even unplanned detours are scenic; but if you'd prefer more guidance, wonderful local expert guides like Bayu Sunrise (p262) can provide car pick-up from anywhere on Bali and accompany you on the trails down to the falls. Clouds of mist from the water add to the already misty air; drips come off every leaf. There are a lot of often slippery and steep paths; rest up at tiny cafes perched above some of the falls.

Banyu Wana Amertha Waterfalls (0857 3943 9299; www.facebook.com/banyu wanaamertha; Jl Bhuana Sari, Wanagiri; 20,000Rp, parking 2000Rp; 8am-5pm) Newly developed for tourism, the four separate waterfalls here range in size, from a petite pair of serene cascades to a broad, 40m behemoth pouring over into an atmospheric pool. From the road running north along Lake Buyan, Jl Raya Wanagiri, head north on Jl Bhuana Sari for 1.8km and look for the signs for the parking area on the left. It's about a 500m walk from the car park to the path leading to the different falls.

Banyumala Twin Waterfalls (0819 1648 5556; Wanagiri Village; 20,000Rp, parking 2000Rp) Located in Wanagiri village, the only thing giving these secluded falls away is the sign off the bumpy road. From Jl Raya Wanagiri, the road running north of Lake Buyan, follow the signs posted near the west end of the lake and take that road north 2.3km to the parking area. From there, the walk to the falls is about 20 minutes downhill.

Munduk Waterfall (Tanah Braak; 20,000Rp, parking 2000Rp) From the western edge of Lake Tamblingan, continue along the main road, Jl Munduk–Wanagiri, 4.6km to the Munduk Waterfall car park signs. From there, its a 700m walk to the falls.

Guru Ratna GUESTHOUSE $
(☎0813 3719 4398; www.guru-ratna.com; r 300,000-330,000Rp; 📶) The cheapest place in the village has seven comfortable hot-water rooms (some share bathrooms). The best rooms have some style, carved wood details and nice porches, and are in a colonial Dutch house.

Meme Surung Homestay GUESTHOUSE $
(☎0812 387 3986; www.memesurung.com; r incl breakfast from 400,000Rp; 📶) Two atmospheric old Dutch houses adjoin to form a compound of six rooms, immersed amid an English-style garden. The decor is traditional and simple; the view from the long wooden veranda is both the focus and joy here. It's located along the main strip of Munduk's township.

★**Puri Lumbung Cottages** GUESTHOUSE $$
(☎0812 387 4042; www.purilumbung.com; cottages incl breakfast US$80-175; @📶) 🍃 Founded by Nyoman Bagiarta to develop sustainable tourism, this lovely hotel has 43 bright two-storey thatched cottages and rooms set among rice fields. Enjoy intoxicating views (units 32 to 35 have the best) from the upstairs balconies. Dozens of trekking options and courses are offered.

The hotel's restaurant is very good, with dishes created and presented with attention to detail (mains 50,000Rp to 120,000Rp). The hotel is on the right-hand side of the road coming from Bedugul, 700m before Munduk. Ask about the remote forest rooms. The name 'Sunset Bar' says everything you need to know.

Manah Liang Cottages INN $$
(☎0362-700 5211; www.manahliang.com; r from 450,000Rp; 📶) About 800m east of Munduk, this country inn (whose name means 'feeling good') has traditional cottages overlooking the lush local terrain. The open-air bathrooms (with tubs) are as refreshing as the porches are relaxing. A short trail leads to a small waterfall. There are cooking classes and guided walks.

Villa Dua Bintang GUESTHOUSE $$
(☎0812 3700 5593, 0812 3709 3463; www.villaduabintang.com; Jl Batu Galih; r incl breakfast 800,000Rp; 📶🏊) Hidden 500m down a tree-shaded lane that's off the main road, 1km east of Munduk. Eight gorgeous rooms are elaborately built amid fruit trees and forest (two rooms are family-size). The scent of cloves and nutmeg hangs in the air from the porch. There's a cafe, and the family who owns it is lovely.

★**Munduk Moding Plantation** RESORT $$$
(☎0811 381 0123; www.mundukmodingplantation.com; Jl Raya Asah Gobleg; ste/villa from US$189/$367; ❄📶🏊) 🍃 Set among a coffee plantation, the modern Balinese-designed villas and suites of this intimate eco-resort offer luxurious respite. But the real relaxation happens in the award-winning 18m infinity pool, where water blends seamlessly with sky; with such panoramic views of mountains and sea, which extend to Java on a clear day, it may very well be the best in all of Bali.

Munduk Moding Plantation's sustainability practices extend beyond environmental efforts. In addition to on-site water filtration, renewable energy production, a kitchen garden and ecological waste management initiatives, the coffee plantation provides social and economic development opportunities to support the local community.

Eating

There are a couple of cute warungs (food stalls) in the village and a few stores with very basic supplies (including insect spray). Guesthouses have cafes: the restaurant at Puri Lumbung Cottages is the best option for nonguests.

Don Biyu CAFE $
(☎0812 3709 3949; www.donbiyu.com; mains 22,000-87,000Rp; ⏰7.30am-10pm; 📶) Catch up on your blog, enjoy good coffee or zone out before the sublime views, while choosing from a mix of Western and interesting Asian fare. Dishes are served in mellow open-air pavilions. It also has five double rooms (600,000Rp to 750,000Rp), all with balconies and views. It's on the main road leading into Munduk.

Ngiring Ngewedang CAFE $
(☎0812 380 7010; www.ngiringngewedang.com; snacks 15,000-40,000Rp; ⏰10am-5pm) Stop in at this coffeehouse, 5km east of Munduk, and savour sweeping views of the surrounding slopes – where they grow their own coffee – and mountain village below.

ℹ Getting There & Away

Minibuses leave Ubung terminal in Denpasar for Munduk (60,000Rp) a few times a day. Driving to the north coast, the main road west of Munduk goes through a number of picturesque villages to Mayong (where you can head south to west Bali). The road then goes down to the sea at Seririt in north Bali.

GUNUNG BATUKAU AREA

☎0361

Gunung Batukau is Bali's second-highest mountain (2276m), the third of Bali's three major mountains and the holy peak of the island's western end. It's often overlooked, which is probably a good thing given what the vendor hordes have done to Gunung Agung.

You can climb its slippery slopes from one of the island's holiest and most underrated temples, Pura Luhur Batukau, or just revel in the ancient rice-terrace greenery around Jatiluwih.

Sights

★Pura Luhur Batukau HINDU TEMPLE
(adult/child 20,000/10,000Rp; ⏲8am-6.30pm)
On the slopes of Gunung Batukau, Pura Luhur Batukau was the state temple when Tabanan was an independent kingdom. It has a seven-roofed *meru* dedicated to Maha Dewa, the mountain's guardian spirit, as well as shrines for Bratan, Buyan and Tamblingan lakes. This is certainly the most spiritual temple you can easily visit in Bali.

The main *meru* in the inner courtyard have little doors shielding small ceremonial items. Outside the compound, the temple is surrounded by forest and the atmosphere is cool and misty; the chants of priests are backed by birds singing.

Facing the temple, take a short walk around to the left to see a small white-water stream where the air resonates with tumbling water. Note the unusual fertility shrine.

There's a general lack of touts and other characters here – including hordes of tourists. Respect traditions and act appropriately while visiting temples. Sarong rental is included in the entrance price. Guides at the entrance offer worthwhile **two-hour jungle hikes** for 250,000Rp.

Activities

Gunung Batukau HIKING
At Pura Luhur Batukau you are fairly well up the side of Gunung Batukau. For the trek to the top of the 2276m peak, you'll need a

DON'T MISS

JATILUWIH RICE TERRACES

At **Jatiluwih** (adult/child 40,000/30,000Rp, car 5000Rp), which means 'truly marvellous' (or 'real beautiful' depending on the translation), you will be rewarded with vistas of centuries-old rice terraces that exhaust your ability to describe green. Emerald ribbons curve around the hillsides, stepping back as they climb to the blue sky.

The terraces are part of Bali's emblematic – and Unesco-recognised – ancient rice-growing culture. You'll understand the nomination just viewing the panorama from the narrow, twisting 18km road, but getting out for a rice-field walk is even more rewarding, following the water as it runs through channels and bamboo pipes from one plot to the next. Much of the rice you'll see is traditional, rather than the hybrid versions grown elsewhere on the island. Look for heavy short husks of red rice.

Take some time, leave your driver behind and just find a place to sit and enjoy the views. It sounds like a cliché, but the longer you look the more you'll see. What at first seems like a vast palette of greens reveals itself to be rice at various stages of growth.

Note, however, that the terraces have become very popular and the road can be less than tranquil. Worse, tour companies now operate ATV tours through the heart of the rice fields. Under threat by Unesco to have the site's status rescinded, the government has proclaimed a freeze on development, which is not a moment too soon after developers announced plans to bulldoze terraces for hotels.

There are cafes for refreshments along the route, including a rather garish collection about mid-drive. Your best bet is to browse a couple.

Because the road is sharply curved, vehicles are forced to drive slowly, which makes the Jatiluwih route a good one for bikes. There are toll booths for visitors (adult/child 40,000/30,000Rp per person, plus 5000Rp per car), which does *not* seem to be going to road maintenance – it's rough. Still the drive won't take more than an hour.

You can access the road in the west off the road to Pura Luhur Batukau from Tabanan, and in the east off the main road to Bedugul near Pacung. Drivers all know this road well and locals offer directions.

guide, which can be arranged at the temple ticket booth. Expect to pay more than 1,000,000Rp for a muddy and arduous journey that will take at least seven hours in one direction. Be sure to negotiate.

The rewards are potentially amazing views (depending on mist) alternating with thick dripping jungle, and the knowledge that you've taken a trail that is much less travelled than the ones on the eastern peaks. You can get a taste of the adventure on a two-hour mini-jaunt (300,000Rp for two).

Staying the night up the mountain might be possible but the assumption is that you will go up and back the same day. Talk to the guides ahead of time to see if you can make special arrangements to camp on the mountain.

Sleeping

A couple of lodges are hidden away on the slopes of Gunung Batukau. You reach them via a spectacular small and twisting road that makes a long inverted V far up the mountain from Bajera and Pucuk on the main Tabanan–Gilimanuk road in west Bali.

★Sarinbuana Eco Lodge LODGE $$
(0361-743 5198; www.baliecolodge.com; Sarinbuana; bungalows 900,000-2,000,000Rp;) These beautiful two-level bungalows are built on the side of a hill just a 10-minute walk from a protected rainforest preserve. Notable amenities include fridges, marble bathrooms and handmade soap. Think rustic luxe – there's even a treehouse. The organic Balinese restaurant is excellent (mains 60,000Rp to 150,000Rp). There are cultural workshops, yoga classes and guided treks.

The lodge has top-notch green cred – sustainability practices include water and energy consumption measures, green waste management, chemical-free products and social and economic empowerment of local community members.

Bali Mountain Retreat LODGE $$
(0828 360 2645; www.balimountainretreat.com; r 550,000-1,260,000Rp;) Luxurious rooms set in refined cottages are arrayed artistically at this hillside location. Lush gardens mix with mannered architecture that combines new and old influences. Some rooms have large verandahs perfect for contemplating the views. Budget options include a bed in a vintage rice-storage barn. There are excellent treks.

OFF THE BEATEN TRACK

RICE, SPICE & COFFEE TRAIL

Starting from Antosari, head north through the rice paddies. After 8km the road runs alongside a beautiful valley of rice terraces. Gorgeous gardens line the bluff and only enhance the already remarkable vistas.

Once you're deep in the foothills of Gunung Batukau, 20km north of Antosari, you'll smell the fragrant spice-growing village of **Sanda** before you see it. Look for the old wooden elevated rice barns that still feature in every house.

After another 8km north through coffee plantations, you'll reach **Pupuan**. A further 6km and you'll reach a highlight of the trip: the gorgeous **rice-growing valley** near Subuk. From here it is 6km or so to Mayong, where you can turn east to Munduk and on to Danau Bratan, or go straight to Seririt.

Getting There & Away

The only realistic way to explore the Gunung Batukau area is with your own transport.

There are two main approaches to the Gunung Batukau area. The easiest is via Tabanan: take the Pura Luhur Batukau road north 9km to a fork in the road, then take the left-hand turn (towards the temple) and go a further 5km to a junction near a school in Wangayagede village. Here you can continue straight to the temple or turn right (east) for the rice fields of Jatiluwih.

The other way is to approach from the east. On the main Denpasar–Singaraja road, look for a small road to the west, just south of the Pacung Indah hotel. Here you follow a series of small paved roads west until you reach the Jatiluwih rice fields. You'll get lost, but locals will quickly set you right and the scenery is superb anyway.

THE ANTOSARI ROAD

0361

Although most people cross the mountains via Candikuning or Kintamani, there is a very scenic third alternative that links Bali's south and north coasts. From the Denpasar–Gilimanuk road in west Bali, a road goes north from Antosari through the village of Pupuan and then drops to Seririt, west of Lovina in north Bali.

OFF THE BEATEN TRACK

THE OTHER ROAD TO PUPUAN

You can reach the mountain village of Pupuan on the road from Antosari but there is another route, one that wanders the back roads of deepest mountain Bali. Start at Pulukan, which is on the Denpasar–Gilimanuk road in west Bali. A small road climbs steeply from the coast, providing fine views back down to west Bali and the sea. It runs through spice-growing country – you'll see (and smell) spices laid out to dry on mats by the road. After about 10km and just before Manggissari, the narrow and winding road actually runs right through **Bunut Bolong** – a tunnel formed by two enormous trees (the *bunut* is a type of ficus; *bolong* means 'hole').

Further on, the road spirals down to Pupuan through some of Bali's most beautiful rice terraces. It's worth stopping for a walk to the magnificent **waterfalls** near Pujungan, a few kilometres south of Pupuan. Follow signs down a narrow rough road and then walk 1.5km to the first waterfall – it's nice, but before you say 'Is that all there is?' follow your ears to a second one that's 50m high.

Sleeping

Sanda Boutique Villas LODGE $$

(☎0828 372 0055; www.sandavillas.com; bungalows incl breakfast from US$85; ❄📶🏊) This boutique hotel offers a serene escape. Its large infinity pool seems to disappear into the rice terraces, while its eight bungalows are really quite luxe (not all have wi-fi). It's well run and the fusion cafe is excellent. The engaging owners will recommend walks among the coffee plantations and rice fields. It is just north of the village of Sanda.

Kebun Villas LODGE $$

(☎0361-780 6068; www.kebunvilla.com; r from US$45; 🏊) Eight antique-filled cottages scattered down a hillside make the most of the sweeping views over rice fields in the valley. Getting to the pool area requires a hike down to the valley floor, but the pool is huge, and once there you may just linger all day.

Getting There & Away

This entire area requires you to supply your own wheels.

North Bali

Includes ➡

Best Places to Eat

- ➡ Damai (p265)
- ➡ Jasmine Kitchen (p264)
- ➡ Buda Bakery (p265)
- ➡ Global Village Kafe (p264)
- ➡ Santai Warung (p270)

Best Places to Stay

- ➡ Matahari Beach Resort (p269)
- ➡ Damai (p264)
- ➡ Taman Selini Beach Bungalows (p269)
- ➡ Taman Sari Bali Resort (p269)
- ➡ Funky Place (p263)

Why Go?

The land on the other side of the map, that's north Bali. Although one-sixth of the island's population lives here, this vast region is overlooked by many visitors who stay cocooned in the south Bali–Ubud axis.

The big draw here is the incredible diving and snorkelling at nearby Pulau Menjangan. Arcing around a nearby bay, booming Pemuteran may be Bali's best beach escape. To the east is Lovina, a sleepy beach strip with cheap hotels and even cheaper sunset beer specials. All along the north coast are interesting little boutique hotels, while inland you'll find quiet treks to waterfalls.

Getting to north Bali for once lives up to the cliché: it's half the fun.

When to Go

- ➡ Most of north Bali doesn't have a high season in terms of visitors.
- ➡ The exceptions are Pemuteran, which is busy July, August and around Christmas and New Year; as are the diving and snorkelling sites around Menjangan, which can get overcrowded with schools of swimming visitors.
- ➡ Weather-wise north Bali is drier than the south. Days of perpetual sun are the norm year-round (most visitors get accommodation with air-con). The only real variation is when you venture back into the hills; mornings can be cool.

North Bali Highlights

1. **Pulau Menjangan** (p267) Plunging into the depths at Bali's best dive spot.
2. **Pemuteran** (p266) Exploring underwater marvels while staying at this idyllic beach town.
3. **Sekumpul Waterfall** (p257) Getting a glimpse of local village life on the way to this set of narrow cascades.
4. **Lovina** (p258) Losing track of time, but not of your budget, at this laid-back, beachside town.
5. **Air Terjun Singsing** (p258) Hiking to this plunging waterfall in verdant hills.
6. **Singaraja** (p255) Savouring Buleleng's rich culture at the museums of this historic royal city.
7. **Bali Barat National Park** (p271) Wildlife-spotting amid mangroves and savannah in Bali's only national park.

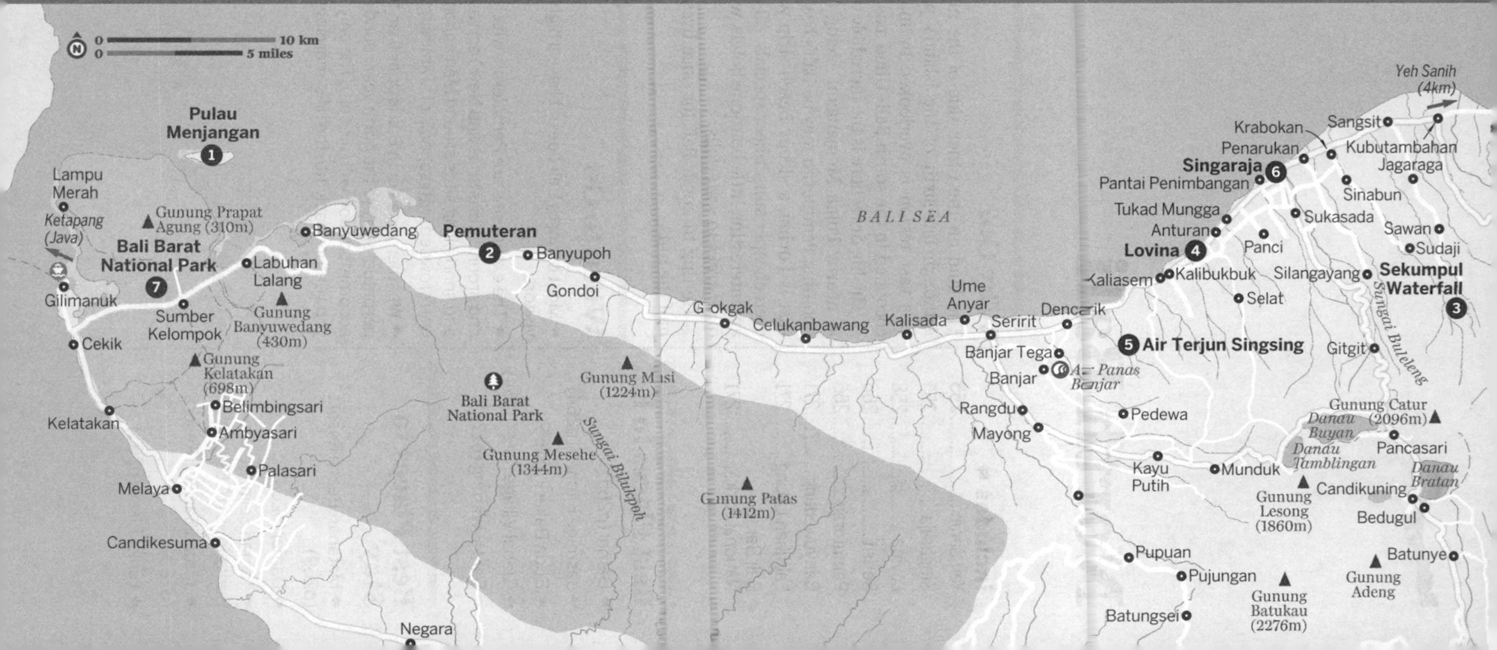

Getting There & Away

Routes here follow the thinly populated coastlines east and west, or you can go up and over the mountains by any number of routes, marvelling at crater lakes and maybe stopping for a misty trek on the way. Singaraja is the main hub for bus services. Buses from south Bali come here and there is service along the main coast roads east and west. Otherwise, note that heavy traffic can make journeys to the north from south Bali last three hours or more.

Yeh Sanih

0362

Known for its famous hot springs, the Yeh Sanih area sits along a secluded stretch of north Bali coastal road. Sights and services may be few, but it's a great drive towards the beach and diving towns of east Bali.

Sights & Activities

Pura Maduwe Karang HINDU TEMPLE

(Temple of the Land Owner; Kubutambahan) One of the most intriguing temples in north Bali, Pura Maduwe Karang is particularly notable for its sculptured panels, including the famous stone-carved bicycle relief that depicts a gentleman riding a bicycle with a lotus flower serving as the back wheel. It's on the base of the main plinth in the inner enclosure. The cyclist may be WOJ Nieuwenkamp, a Dutch artist who, in 1904, brought what was probably the first bicycle to Bali.

Like Pura Beji at Sangsit, this temple of dark stone is dedicated to agricultural spirits, but this one looks after nonirrigated land. The temple is easy to find in the village of Kubutambahan – seek the 34 carved figures from the Ramayana outside the walls. Kubutambahan is on the road between Singaraja and Amlapura, about 1km east of the turn-off to Kintamani.

Symon Studios GALLERY

(0819 1643 7718; www.symonstudios.com; Jl Airsanih-Tejakula; 8am-6pm) Completely out of character for the Yeh Sanih area is a place run by Symon, the irrepressible American artist. It's bursting with a creativity that is, at times, vibrant, exotic and erotic. It's 5.7km east of Yeh Sanih on the Singaraja road.

Pura Ponjok Batu HINDU TEMPLE

Boasting a commanding location between the sea and the road, Pura Ponjok Batu is some 7km east of Yeh Sanih. It has some very fine limestone carvings in the central temple area. Legend holds that it was built to provide some spiritual balance for Bali, what with all the temples in the south.

Air Sanih SWIMMING

(Jl Airsanih-Tejakula; adult/child 20,000/10,000Rp; 8am-6pm) The freshwater springs of Air Sanih are channelled into large swimming pools before flowing into the sea. The pools are particularly picturesque at sunset, when throngs of locals bathe under blooming frangipani trees – most of the time they're alive with frolicking kids. It's about 15km east of Singaraja.

Sleeping

Cilik's Beach Garden GUESTHOUSE $$

(0878 6055 1888; www.ciliksbeachgarden.com; Jl Airsanih-Tejakula; r incl breakfast from €90, villas from €140; @) Coming here is like visiting your rich friends, albeit ones with good taste. These custom-built villas, 3km east of Yeh Sanih, are large and have extensive private gardens. Other accommodation is in stylish *lumbung* (rice barns with round roofs) set in a garden facing the ocean. The owners have even more remote villas further south on the coast. Good cafe.

Getting There & Away

Yeh Sanih is on the main road along the north coast. Occasional bemos (minibuses) and buses from Singaraja stop outside the springs (12,000Rp).

If heading to Tulamben or Amed, make certain you're on your way south from here by 4pm in order to arrive while there's still some light to avoid road hazards.

Singaraja

0362 / POP 120,000

Singaraja (which means 'lion king') is Bali's second-largest city and the capital of Buleleng Regency, which covers much of the north. With its tree-lined streets, surviving Dutch colonial buildings and charmingly sleepy waterfront area north of Jl Erlangga, it's worth exploring for a couple of hours. Most people stay in nearby Lovina.

Singaraja was the centre of Dutch power in Bali and remained the administrative centre for the Lesser Sunda Islands (Bali through to Timor) until 1953. It is one of the few places in Bali where there are visible traces of the Dutch period, as well as

Chinese and Islamic influences. Today, Singaraja is a major educational and cultural centre, with several university campuses.

Sights

At the old harbour and waterfront, you can get a whisper of when Singaraja was Bali's main port before WWII. At the north end of Jl Hasanudin, you'll find a modern **pier** out over the water with a couple of simple cafes and some vendors.

Across the car park, look for some old Dutch warehouses. Nearby are the conspicuous Yudha Mandala Tama Monument and the colourful Chinese temple, Ling Gwan Kiong. There are a few old canals here as well.

Walk up Jl Imam Bonjol and you'll see the art deco lines of late-colonial Dutch buildings. Just 2km west of the centre, **Pantai Penimbangan** is a popular beach area. The sand may be a narrow ribbon but there are dozens of seafood cafes that draw throngs of locals, especially on weekend evenings.

Sangsit VILLAGE

About 6km northeast of Singaraja is an excellent example of the colourful architectural style of north Bali. Sangsit's **Pura Beji** is a temple for the *subak* (village association of rice-growers), dedicated to the goddess Dewi Sri, who looks after irrigated rice fields. The over-the-top sculptured panels along the front wall feature cartoonlike demons and amazing *naga* (mythical snakelike creatures). The inside also has a variety of sculptures covering every available space. It's 500m off the main road towards the coast.

The **Pura Dalem** (Temple of the Dead) shows scenes of punishment in the afterlife, and other humorous, sometimes erotic, pictures. You'll find it in the rice fields, about 500m northeast of Pura Beji.

Pura Dalem Jagaraga HINDU TEMPLE

(Jagaraga) In the village of Jagaraga, Pura Dalem is a small, interesting temple with delightful sculptured panels along its front wall. On the outer wall, look for a vintage car driving sedately past, a steamer at sea and even an aerial dogfight between early aircraft. It's about 8km east of Singaraja.

Air Terjun Gitgit WATERFALL

(Gitgit; adult/child 20,000/10,000Rp) Around 11km south of Singaraja, a well-signposted path goes 800m west from the main road to the touristy waterfall, Air Terjun Gitgit. The path is lined with souvenir stalls and guides to nowhere. The 40m waterfalls pound away and the mists are more refreshing than any air-con. Approximately 2km further up the hill, there's a multitiered waterfall about 600m off the western side of the main road. The path crosses a narrow bridge and follows the river through verdant jungle past several small sets of waterfalls.

Gedong Kirtya Library LIBRARY

(☎0362-22645; Jl Veteran 23; 5000Rp; ⏲8am-4pm Mon-Thu, 8am-1pm Fri) This small historical library was established in 1928 by Dutch colonialists and named after the Sanskrit for 'to try'. It has a collection of *lontar* (dried palm leaf) books, as well as some even older written works in the form of inscribed copper plates called *prasasti*. Dutch publications, dating back to 1901, may interest students of the colonial period. It's on the same grounds as Museum Buleleng.

Museum Buleleng MUSEUM

(Jl Veteran 23; ⏲9am-4pm Mon-Fri) **FREE** Museum Buleleng recalls the life of the last *radja* (rajah; prince) of Buleleng, Pandji Tisna, who is credited with developing tourism in Lovina to the west. Among the items here is the Royal (brand) typewriter he used during his unlucrative career as a travel writer before his death in 1978. It also traces the history of the region back to when there was no history.

LONTAR BOOKS

Lontar is made from the fan-shaped leaves of the *rontal* palm. The leaf is dried, soaked in water, cleaned, steamed, dried again, then flattened, dyed and eventually cut into strips. The strips are inscribed with words and pictures using a very sharp blade or point, then coated with a black stain which is wiped off – the black colour stays in the inscription. A hole in the middle of each *lontar* strip is threaded onto a string, with a carved bamboo 'cover' at each end to protect the 'pages', and the string is secured with a couple of *kepeng* (Chinese coins with a hole in the centre).

The Gedong Kirtya Library in Singaraja has the world's largest collection of *lontar* works.

WORTH A TRIP

SEKUMPUL WATERFALL

Sitting 18km southeast of Singaraja, some six or seven separate waterfalls – all fed by upland streams – pour up to 80m over cliffs in a verdant bamboo-forested valley. Collectively known as **Sekumpul Waterfall** (Sekumpul Village; 20,000Rp, parking 2000Rp), they're a hilly 45-minute 1km walk from the car park through tiny Sekumpul village, where trees of clove, cacao, jackfruit, mangosteen and more lead the way to steep stairs. Trails wind through the valley from one cascade to the other and its easy to while the day away in their splendor.

Given its remote location, hiring a driver to get you to Sekumpul is ideal. Bayu Sunrise (p262) in Lovina goes the extra mile by providing transport from anywhere on Bali, in addition to accompanying you through the village and hiking to the falls.

From the car park, take a left and walk up the road. From here, it's 10 minutes to the official waterfall entrance. Beware of stalls marked 'Registration Station' in the area – they are not officially affiliated with the falls and have been known to trick tourists into paying up. When you see the 'Sekumpul Waterfall' sign, take another left and continue along the brick road past village residences and small shops – at the end of this path you'll find the official hut where you'll pay the admission fee. From here, continue down the trail to a steep hill where the stairs begin. You'll eventually make your way down to a stream (prepare to get your feet wet as you cross it); and the falls are shortly ahead.

Heading back to Singaraja, consider stopping at the village of **Sawan**, known as a centre for the manufacturing of gamelan gongs and instruments. You can see the gongs being cast and the intricately carved gamelan frames being fashioned. **Pura Batu Bolong** (Temple of the Hollow Stone) and its baths are also worth a look. Around Sawan there are cold-water springs believed to cure all sorts of illnesses. Nearby **Villa Manuk** (0362-27080; www.villa-manuk.com; near Sawan; r incl breakfast from 850,000Rp; @), a three-villa complex with rice-field views, has its own large natural-spring-fed pool and is a tranquil choice if you choose to overnight here.

Pura Jagat Natha HINDU TEMPLE
(Jl Pramuka) Singaraja's main temple, the largest in northern Bali, is not usually open to foreigners. You can appreciate its size and admire the carved stone decorations from the outside.

Eating

Cozy Resto INDONESIAN $
(0362-28214; Jl Pantai Penimbangan; mains 25,000-90,000Rp; 10am-10pm) One of the more established cafes at Pantai Penimbangan, Cozy has a long menu of Balinese, Indonesian and seafood dishes. Celebrating locals fill the open-air dining areas. Nearby, along the waterfront road, you'll find dozens more vendors and stalls with cheap and cheerful local fare.

Dapur Ibu INDONESIAN $
(0362-24474; Jl Jen Achmed Yani; mains 10,000-20,000Rp; 8am-4pm) A nice local cafe with a small garden off the street. The nasi goreng (fried rice) is fresh and excellent; wash it down with a fresh juice or bubble tea.

Istana Cake & Bakery BAKERY $
(0362-21983; Jl Jen Achmed Yani; snacks from 3000Rp; 8am-6pm) Fallen in love in Lovina? Get your wedding cake here. For lesser life moments like the munchies, choose from an array of tasty baked goods. There is a freezer full of ice-cream cakes and treats.

Information

Buleleng Tourism Office (Diparda; 0362-21342; Jl Kartini 6; 8am-3.30pm Mon-Fri) Has some OK maps and good information if you ask specifically about dance and other cultural events. It's 550m southeast of the Banyuasri bus station.

Singaraja Public Hospital (0362-22046, 0362-22573; Jl Ngurah Rai 30; 24hr) The largest hospital in northern Bali.

Getting There & Away

Singaraja is the main transport hub for the northern coast, with three bemo/bus terminals. From the Sangket terminal, 10km south of town on the main road, minibuses go sporadically to Denpasar (Ubung terminal; 40,000Rp) via Bedugul/Pancasari.

The **Banyuasri terminal**, on the western side of town, has buses heading to Gilimanuk (60,000Rp, two hours) and bemos to Lovina (20,000Rp). For Java, several companies have services, which include the ferry trip across the Bali Strait.

The **Penarukan terminal** (off Jl Surapati), 2km east of town, has bemos to Yeh Sanih (20,000Rp) and Amlapura (about 30,000Rp, three hours) via the coastal road; and also minibuses to Denpasar (Batubulan terminal; 100,000Rp, three hours) via Kintamani.

Getting Around

Bemos link the three main bemo/bus terminals and cost about 10,000Rp.

Lovina

0362 / POP 20,550

'Relaxed' is how people most often describe Lovina, and aside from the pushy touts, thcy arc correct. This low-key, low-rise, low-priced beach resort town is a far cry from Kuta. The waves are calm, the beach thin and overamped attractions nil.

Lovina is sun-drenched, with patches of shade from palm trees. A highlight every afternoon at fishing villages such as Anturan is watching *prahu* (traditional outrigger canoes) being prepared for the night's fishing; as sunset reddens the sky, the lights of the fishing boats appear as bright dots across the horizon.

The Lovina tourist area stretches over 8km, and consists of a string of coastal villages – Kaliasem, Kalibukbuk, Anturan and Tukad Mungga – collectively known as Lovina. The main focus is Kalibukbuk, 10.5km west of Singaraja and the heart of Lovina. Daytime traffic on the main road is loud and fairly constant.

Beaches

The beaches are made up of washed-out grey and black volcanic sand, and while they're mostly clean near the hotel areas, they're not spectacular. Reefs protect the shore, calming the waves and keeping the water clear.

A paved beach footpath runs along the sand in Kalibukbuk and extends in a circuitous route along the seashore; it ranges from clean to grubby. Enjoy the postcard view to the east of the mountainous north Bali coast. Sunsets can be breathtaking.

The best beach areas include the main beach east of Kalibukbuk's elaborate Dolphin Monument, as well as the curving stretch a bit west. There's a pier popular for sunset watching at the end of Jl Mawar.

For a glitzy beach experience, walk west to Spice Beach Club (p265).

Sights

There are no notable sights in town, but you'll find waterfalls and village temples relatively short distances away.

Air Terjun Singsing WATERFALL

About 5km west of Lovina, a sign points to Air Terjun Singsing (Daybreak Waterfall); about 1km from the main road there's a warung (food stall) on the left and a car park on the right. Walk past the warung and along the path for about 200m to the lower falls. The waterfall isn't huge, but the pool underneath is ideal for swimming, though not crystal-clear. The water, cooler than the sea, is very refreshing.

Clamber further up the hill to another, slightly bigger fall, **Singsing Dua**. It has a mud bath that is supposedly good for the skin (we'll let you decide about this). These falls also cascade into a deep swimming pool.

The area is thick with tropical forest and makes a nice day trip from Lovina. The falls are more spectacular in the wet season (October to March), and may be just a trickle at other times.

Brahma Vihara Arama BUDDHIST MONASTERY

(0362-92954; www.brahmaviharaarama.com) Bali's single Buddhist monastery is only vaguely Buddhist in appearance, with colourful decorations, a bright orange roof and statues of Buddha – it also has very Balinese decorative carvings and door guardians plus elaborately carved dark stones. It is quite a handsome structure in a commanding location, with views that reach down into the valley and across rice fields to the sea. You should wear long pants or a sarong, which can be hired for a small donation.

The monastery does not advertise any regular courses or programs, but visitors are more than welcome to meditate in special rooms.

The temple is 3.3km off the main road west of Lovina – take the obvious turn-off in Dencarik.

Activities

Dolphin Watching

Sunrise boat trips to see dolphins are Lovina's much-hyped tourist attraction, so much so that they have a monument in their honour.

Some days no dolphins are sighted, but most of the time at least a few surface.

Expect pressure from your hotel and touts selling dolphin trips. The price is fixed at 150,000/75,000Rp per adult/child by the boat-owners' cartel. Trips start at a nonholiday-like 5.30am and last about two hours. Note that the ocean can get pretty crowded with roaring powerboats.

There's great debate about what all this means to the dolphins. Do they like being chased by boats? If not, why do they keep coming back? Maybe it's the fish, of which there are plenty off Lovina.

Diving & Surfing

Diving on the local reef is better at lower depths and night diving is popular. Many people stay here and dive Pulau Menjangan, a 1½-hour drive west.

Generally, the water is clear and some parts of the reef are quite good for snorkelling, though the coral has been damaged by bleaching and, in places, by dynamite fishing. The best place is to the west, a few hundred metres offshore from Billibo Beach Cottages. A two-hour boat trip will cost about 450,000Rp per person, including equipment.

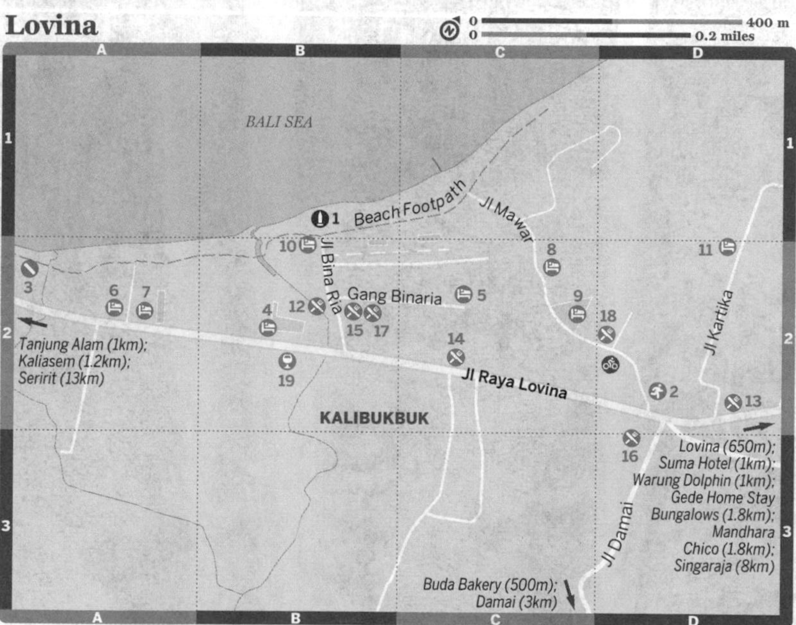

Lovina

Sights

1 Dolphin Monument B1

Activities, Courses & Tours

2 Araminth Spa D2
3 Spice Dive A2

Sleeping

4 Funky Place B2
5 Harris Homestay C2
6 Homestay Purnama A2
7 Lovina Beach Hotel A2
8 Puri Bali Hotel C2
9 Rambutan Boutique Hotel C2
10 Sea Breeze Lovina B2
11 Villa Taman Ganesha D2

Eating

12 Akar B2
13 Bakery Lovina D2
14 Global Village Kafe C2
15 Jasmine Kitchen B2
16 Night Market D3
Sea Breeze Café .... (see 10)
17 Seyu B2
Spice Beach Club .... (see 3)
18 Warung Barclona D2

Drinking & Nightlife

19 Pashaa B2

1

2

JASOMTOMO/SHUTTERSTOCK ©

3

FEATHERCOLLECTOR/SHUTTERSTOCK ©

Sekumpul Waterfall (p257)
'k through a valley of clove, cacao,
‹fruit and mangosteen trees to this
ection of waterfalls.

2. Lovina (p258)
Soak up the relaxed atmosphere of this low-key beach town.

3. Bali Barat National Park (p271)
Birds are prolific in the park, and include species such as the Javan banded pitta.

COOKING SINGARAJA STYLE

Sign up for one of the excellent cooking classes offered by **Warung Bambu Pemaron** (☎0362-31455; www.warung-bambu.mahanara.com; Pemaron; classes from 405,000Rp; ⏰8am-1pm) and you'll kick off with a trip to a large Singaraja food market before retreating to a breezy setting amid rice fields east of Lovina to learn to cook up to nine classic Balinese dishes. Levels range from beginner to advanced, and there are vegetarian options. The staff are charming, and the fee includes transport within the area. Best of all, when you're done you'll get to feast on your labours.

Spice Dive DIVING

(☎0813 3724 2221; www.balispicedive.com; off Jl Raya Lovina, Kalibukbuk; 2-tank dives from €80; ⏰8am-9pm) Spice Dive is a large operation. It offers snorkelling trips (€55) and night dives (€45), plus popular Pulau Menjangan trips (snorkel/dive €70/80). It's based at the west end of the beach path, with Spice Beach Club. It also has an office on Jl Bina Ria.

Cycling

The roads south and west of Jl Raya Lovina are excellent for biking, with limited traffic and enjoyable rides amid the rice fields and into the hills for views. It's easy to rent a bike from 30,000Rp per day.

Spas

Araminth Spa SPA

(☎0362-343 5759; Jl Mawar; massage per hr from 200,000Rp; ⏰10am-9pm) Araminth Spa offers many types of therapies and massages, including Balinese and Ayurvedic, in a simple but soothing setting.

Ciego Massage MASSAGE

(☎0877 6256 1660; Jl Raya Lovina, Anturan; 1hr massage from 100,000Rp; ⏰8am-5pm) Highly skilled blind massage therapists provide no-nonsense muscle relief in a simple setting.

Tours

★**Bayu Sunrise** TRAVEL AGENCY

(☎0877 6206 6287, WhatsApp 0877 6206 6063; www.bayusunriseunpackbalitour.wordpress.com; waterfall excursions per car from Lovina/Ubud/south Bali 700,000/850,000/950,000Rp) Wonderfully kind, knowledgeable and humble, Lovina local Bayu customises everything from private driving services to volcano trekking and adventure trips all over Bali. He's the go-to guy for excursions to the best waterfalls in the Central Mountains, including Banyu Wana Amertha (p248), Banyumala (p248) and Sekumpul (p257); ask him about the ones that are still so secret that they don't yet have names.

After a day of chasing waterfalls, catch the multi-talented Bayu jamming out on the guitar and wailing rock and roll covers during one of his gigs at various bars and restaurants around Lovina. His hustle never ends.

Sleeping

Hotels are spread along Jl Raya Lovina and on the side roads going to the beach. Overall, choices tend to be more budget-focused; don't come here for a luxe experience. Be wary of hotels right on the main road due to traffic noise, or those near the late-night Kalibukbuk bars.

During slow periods, room prices are negotiable; beware of touts who'll lead you astray and quote prices that include a large kickback.

Anturan

A few tiny side tracks and one proper sealed road, Jl Kubu Gembong, lead to this lively little fishing village, which is a real travellers' hang-out. But it's a long way from Lovina's nightlife – expect to pay around 40,000Rp for transport the 3km back to Anturan from Kalibukbuk.

Mandhara Chico GUESTHOUSE $

(☎0812 360 3268; www.mandhara-chico-bali.com; off Jl Kubu Gembong; r with fan/air-con from 140,000/175,000Rp; ❄📶🏊) This spiffy family-run guesthouse is right on a small strip of charcoal-sand beach. The 12 rooms are basic but tidy.

Gede Home Stay Bungalows HOMESTAY $

(☎0362-41526; www.gede-homestay.com; Jl Kubu Gembong; r incl breakfast 150,000-300,000Rp; ❄📶) Don't forget to shake the sand off your feet as you enter this beachside eight-room homestay owned by a local fisherman. Cheap rooms have cold water while better ones have hot water and air-con.

Anturan to Kalibukbuk

Jl Pantai Banyualit has many modest hotels, although the beach is not very inspiring. There is a little park-like area by the water and the walk along the shore to Kalibukbuk is quick and scenic.

★Villa Taman Ganesha GUESTHOUSE **$$**
(☎0812 377 1381; www.taman-ganesha-lovina.com; Jl Kartika 45; r 550,000-700,000Rp; ❄📶🏊) This lovely guesthouse is down a quiet lane lined with family compounds. The grounds are lush and fragrant with frangipani from around the world that have been collected by the owner, a landscape architect from Germany. The three units are private and comfortable. The beach is 400m away and it's a 10-minute walk along the sand to Kalibukbuk.

Suma Hotel GUESTHOUSE **$$**
(☎0362-41566; www.sumahotel.com; Jl Pantai Banyualit; r incl breakfast 435,000-950,000Rp; ❄@📶🏊) Enjoy views of the sea from the upstairs rooms; the best of the 26 have aircon and hot water; large bungalows are quite nice as is the pool and cafe. An elaborate temple is nearby. Balconies and terraces have comfy wicker furniture for lounging.

Lovina BOUTIQUE HOTEL **$$$**
(☎0362-343 5800; www.thelovinabali.com; Jl Mas Lovina; ste from US$165; ❄📶🏊) Clean, modern lines are the hallmark of this luxe beach resort, which is walkably close to the centre of Kalibukbuk. The 66 rooms are large, all with sitting areas and terraces or balconies. The furnishings are all in light colours, which adds to the contemporary feel. The pool is huge; guests can use bikes, kayaks and more.

Kalibukbuk

The 'centre' of Lovina is the village of Kalibukbuk. Mellow Jl Mawar is quieter and more pleasant than Jl Bina Ria. Small *gang* (alleys) lined with cheap accommodation lead off both streets.

★Funky Place HOSTEL **$**
(☎0878 6325 3156; Jl Seririt-Singaraja; tent 130,000Rp, tree house 170,000Rp, dm 150,000-170,000Rp, r from 230,000Rp) From the unicycle bar stools to the affordable tree house to the free foot massage (and with heaps of reclaimed wood, clever signage and weird antiques scattered throughout), this compound is basically a backpacker's dream. There's a path directly to the beach, and it also holds BBQs, Balinese dancing events and beer-pong competitions. Live music happens every weekend.

The staff is very knowledgeable, and the hostel can arrange trips to a bunch of the area's attractions including parks, temples, waterfalls and hot springs.

Harris Homestay HOMESTAY **$**
(☎0362-41152; Gang Binaria; s/d incl breakfast from 130,000/150,000Rp; 📶) Sprightly, tidy and white, Harris avoids the weary look of some neighbouring cheapies. The charming owner lives in the back; guests enjoy four bright, modern rooms up the front.

Sea Breeze Lovina GUESTHOUSE **$**
(☎0362-41138; off Jl Bina Ria; r/bungalow incl breakfast 450,000/550,000Rp; ❄📶🏊) One of the best choices in the heart of Kalibukbuk, the Sea Breeze has five bungalows and two rooms by the pool and the beach, some with sensational views from their verandas. The only downside is that it can get noisy from nearby bars at night.

Puri Bali Hotel HOTEL **$**
(☎0362-41485; www.puribalihotel.wixsite.com/lovina; Jl Mawar; r incl breakfast from 250,000Rp; ❄📶🏊) The pool area is set deep in a lush garden – you could easily hang out here all day and let any cares wander off to the ether. The 25 rooms are simple but comfortable.

Homestay Purnama HOMESTAY **$**
(☎0362-41043; Jl Raya Lovina; r from 150,000Rp; 📶) One of the best deals on this stretch, Homestay Purnama has seven clean cold-water rooms, and the beach is only a two-minute walk away. This is a family compound, and a friendly one at that.

Lovina Beach Hotel HOTEL **$**
(☎0362-41005; www.lovinabeachhotel.com; Jl Raya Lovina; r incl breakfast 350,000-800,000Rp; ❄📶🏊) This older, well-run beach hotel hasn't changed in years and neither have its prices. The 30 rooms, in a two-storey block, are clean if a bit frayed. Bungalows feature carving and Balinese details, the ones on the beach are a bargain. The grounds feel like a park.

Rambutan Boutique Hotel HOTEL **$$**
(☎0362-41388; www.rambutan.org; Jl Mawar; r from 400,000Rp, villa from 1,100,000Rp; ❄@📶🏊) The hotel, on 1 hectare of lush gardens, features two pools and a

playground. The 30 rooms are decorated in Balinese style. Villas are good deals; the largest are good for families and have kitchens.

Outside Town

★Damai HOTEL $$$
(0813 3843 7703; www.thedamai.com; Jl Damai; villas US$220-500;) Set on a hillside behind Lovina, Damai has the kind of sweeping views you'd expect. Its 14 luxury villas mix antiques and a modern style accented by beautiful Balinese fabrics. The infinity pool seemingly spills onto a landscape of peanut fields, rice paddies and coconut palms. The spa is quite posh.

Larger villas have private pools and multiple rooms that flow from one to another. The restaurant is lauded for its organic fusion cuisine. Call for transport, or at the main junction in Kalibukbuk, go south on Jl Damai and follow the road for about 3km.

Eating

Just about every hotel has a cafe or restaurant. Walk along the beach footpath to choose from a selection of basic places with cold beer, standard food and sunsets.

Anturan to Kalibukbuk

Warung Dolphin SEAFOOD $
(0813 5327 6985; Jl Pantai Banyualit; mains from 40,000Rp; 10am-10pm) Near the beach, this small cafe serves a fine grilled-seafood platter (which was probably caught by the guy next to you). There's live acoustic music many nights; a few other tasty cafes are nearby.

Bakery Lovina CAFE $$
(0362-42225; Jl Raya Lovina; mains 58,000-175,000Rp; 7am-7pm;) Enjoy Lovina's best cup of coffee amid groceries at this upmarket deli a short walk from the centre. The croissants and German breads are baked fresh daily, and there are good fresh meals, including European-style breakfasts. The lunch menu is long.

Kalibukbuk

★Global Village Kafe CAFE $
(0362-41928; Jl Raya Lovina; mains from 32,000Rp; 8am-10pm;) Che Guevara, Mikhail Gorbachev and Nelson Mandela are just some of the figures depicted in the paintings lining the walls of this artsy cafe. The baked goods, fruit drinks, pizzas, breakfasts, Indo classics and much more are excellent. There are free book and DVD exchanges, plus a selection of local handicrafts. Profits go to a foundation that funds local healthcare.

★Jasmine Kitchen THAI $
(0362-41565; Gang Binaria; mains 45,000-80,000Rp; 11am-10pm;) The Thai fare at this elegant two-level restaurant is excellent. The menu is long and authentic, and the staff are gracious. Try the homemade ice cream for dessert and enjoy it while listening to the sounds of soft jazz. You can refill water bottles here for 2000Rp. The ground-floor coffee bar brews excellent drinks.

Akar VEGETARIAN $
(0362-343 5636; Jl Bina Ria; mains 55,000-70,000Rp; 7am-10pm;) The many shades of green at this vegetarian cafe aren't just for show. They reflect the earth-friendly ethics of the owners. Enjoy organic smoothies, house-made gelato, and fresh and tasty international dishes, such as chargrilled aubergine filled with feta and chilli.

Warung Barclona BALINESE $
(0362-41894; Jl Mawar; mains from 40,000Rp; 8am-9pm;) Despite the vaguely Catalan name, this family-run restaurant has an ambitious and good Balinese menu. Choose a table on the open-air terrace and order *babi guling* (suckling pig). There are usually several seafood specials.

Night Market BALINESE $
(Jl Raya Lovina; mains from 20,000Rp; 5-11pm) Lovina's night market is a good choice for fresh and cheap local food. Each year it adds a few more interesting stands. Try the *piseng goreng* (fried bananas).

Seyu JAPANESE $$
(0362-41050; www.seyulovina.com; Gang Binaria; dishes from 50,000Rp; 11am-10pm;) This authentic Japanese place has a skilled sushi chef and a solid list of fresh nigiri and sashimi choices. The dining room is suitably spare and uncomplicated.

Sea Breeze Café INDONESIAN $$
(0362-41138; off Jl Bina Ria; mains from 55,000Rp; 8am-10pm;) Right by the beach, this breezy cafe is the best – and most intimate – of the beachside choices, especially after a recent stylish makeover. The Indonesian and Western dishes are well-presented, as are the excellent breakfasts.

The 'royal seafood platter' is like an entire fish market on a plate. The peanuts served with drinks are among Bali's best.

Outside Town

Tanjung Alam SEAFOOD $

(☎0362-41223; Jl Raya Lovina; meals 40,000-80,000Rp; ⏰9am-10pm; 📶) You'll see the fragrant column of smoke rising through the palms before you find this entirely open-air waterfront restaurant where grilled seafood is king. Settle back at one of the tables in the long shady pavilions, let the gentle lapping of the nearby waves soothe you, and enjoy an affordable feast. It's 1.2km west of the centre.

★**Buda Bakery** BAKERY, CAFE $$

(☎0812 469 1779; off Jl Damai; mains 50,000-150,000Rp; ⏰8am-9pm) North Bali's best bakery has a huge array of breads, cakes and other treats produced fresh daily. However, the real reason to make the 10-minute walk here from Jl Raya Lovina is for the upstairs cafe, which does simple yet superlative Indonesian and Western fare. Note that the baked goods often sell out fast.

Spice Beach Club INTERNATIONAL $$

(☎0851 0001 2666; www.spicebeachclubbali.com; off Jl Raya Lovina; mains 75,000-240,000Rp; ⏰kitchen 9am-11pm, bar to 12.30am; 📶) Mirrored shades are de rigueur at this stylish hang-out on a nice patch of beach. There's a whiff of Cannes about the rows of beach loungers backed by a pool. The menu ranges from burgers to seafood, while the bar list is long. Amenities include house music, lockers and showers.

★**Damai** FUSION $$$

(☎0362-41008; www.thedamai.com; Jl Damai; 3-course meals from 485,000Rp; ⏰7-11am, noon-4pm & 7-11pm; 📶) Enjoy the renowned organic restaurant at this boutique hotel in the hills behind Lovina. Tables enjoy views across the north coast. The changing menu draws its fresh ingredients from the hotel's organic farm and the local fishing fleet. Dishes are artful and the wine list one of the best in Bali. Sunday brunch is popular. Call for pick up.

Drinking & Nightlife

Many of Lovina's eateries are also fine for a drink, especially those on the beach. There's a clutch of similar cafes good for a sunset Bintang at the end of Jl Mawar. There's a compact nightlife zone in Kalibukbuk.

Pashaa CLUB

(☎0877 8701 7149; Jl Raya Lovina, Kalibukbuk; ⏰7pm-3am) A small but high-concept club near the centre; DJs from around the island mix it up while bands play on and on.

Getting There & Away

BUS & BEMO

To reach Lovina from south Bali by public transport, take a bus from Denpasar's Ubung Bus & Bemo Terminal to the Sangket terminal in Singaraja. Once there take a bemo to Singaraja's Banyuasri terminal. Finally, get another bemo to the Lovina area. This will take much of a day.

Regular bemos go from Singaraja's Banyuasri terminal to Kalibukbuk (about 15,000Rp) – you can flag them down anywhere on the main road and may need to wait a while.

OFF THE BEATEN TRACK

AIR PANAS BANJAR

These hot springs percolate amid lush tropical plants. Eight fierce-faced carved stone *naga* pour water from a natural hot spring into the first bath, which then overflows (via the mouths of five more *naga*), into a second, larger pool. In a third pool, water pours from 3m-high spouts to give you a pummelling massage. The water is slightly sulphurous and pleasantly steamy (about 38°C).

You must wear a swimsuit and you shouldn't use soap in the pools, but you can use an adjacent outdoor shower. You can relax here for a few hours and have lunch at the cafe, or even stay the night.

West of Lovina, you can take an *ojek* (motorcycle that takes passengers) from the bemo stop on the main road to the hot springs; going back is a 2.4km downhill stroll. Those who feel so relaxed after their soak that they don't feel like travelling far can overnight at **Pondok Wisata Grya Sari** (☎0362-92903; Jl Air Panas Banjar; r incl breakfast 300,000-400,000Rp), an old-fashioned but welcoming guesthouse in a verdant setting on a hillside 100m from the springs.

If you're coming by long-distance bus from the west, you can ask to be dropped off anywhere along the main road.

TOURIST SHUTTLE BUS

Perama (☎0362-41161; www.peramatour.com; Jl Raya Lovina, Anturan) buses stop in Anturan. Passengers are then ferried to other points on the Lovina strip (15,000Rp). There's a daily bus to/from the south, including Kuta, Sanur and Ubud (all 125,000Rp).

Getting Around

The Lovina strip is *very* spread out, but you can travel back and forth on bemos to Singaraja (10,000Rp). Note that these are often infrequent.

Given its small size, Lovina is a nice town to see by bike. Hire one from **Sovina Shop** (☎0362-41402; Jl Mawar; ⏲10am-10pm).

Seririt

☎0362

Seririt is a junction for roads that run south through the central mountains to Munduk or Pupuan and west Bali via the beautiful Antosari road or an equally scenic road to Pulukan.

The **market** in the centre of town is renowned for its many stalls selling supplies for offerings.

Some 10km west of Seririt at Celukan bawang you won't be able to miss a shockingly huge power plant being built as a joint venture with China. Public details have been few, but it's designed to burn Chinese coal arriving on large ships at the port.

Sleeping

Some 2km west of Seririt on Jl Singaraja-Gilimanuk, a smaller road, Jl Ume Anyar, runs north towards the narrow beaches and passes several secluded small resorts.

Mayo Resort RESORT **$$$**
(☎0811 380 0500; www.mayoresort.com; Jl Ume Anyar; r from 2,000,000Rp; ❄📶🏊) Rare for Bali, this small waterfront resort has a refreshing light-blue-and-white colour scheme. There are seven large units in a two-storey main building, each with a big terrace. And should you need it, there's a massage pavilion near the narrow beach. It is about 200m past Zen Resort Bali, 3km northwest of Seririt.

Zen Resort Bali BOUTIQUE HOTEL **$$$**
(☎0362-93578; www.zenresortbali.com; Jl Ume Anyar; r incl breakfast from US$155; ❄📶🏊) The name says it all, albeit very calmly. Yoga and a lavish spa figure prominently in the lifestyle at this resort devoted to your internal and mental well-being. The 26 villas in bungalow-style units have a minimalist look designed to not tax the synapses, gardens are dotted with water features and the beach is 200m away. It's 600m off the main road.

Getting There & Away

Buses to west Bali pass through Seririt. More importantly, this is where the Antosari road from south Bali reaches the coast.

Pemuteran

☎0362 / POP 8620

This popular oasis in the northwest corner of Bali has a number of artful resorts set on a little dogbone-shaped bay that's incredibly calm, thanks to its location within an extinct volcano crater protected by flourishing coral reefs. The beach is decent, but most people come to view the undersea wonders just offshore and at nearby Pulau Menjangan.

The busy Singaraja–Gilimanuk road is the town's spine and ever more businesses aimed at visitors can be found along it. Despite its popularity, Pemuteran's community and tourism businesses have forged a sustainable vision for development that should be a model for the rest of Bali.

Sights

Pemuteran Beach BEACH
The grey-brown sand is a little thin and definitely not powdery but you can't beat the setting. The blue waters and surrounding green hills make for a beautiful scene, especially when crimson and orange join the colour palette at sunset. Strolling the beach is popular, as you'd expect. The little fishing village is interesting; walk around to the eastern end of the dogbone to escape a lot of the development. Look for various traditional-style boats being built on the shore.

Proyek Penyu HATCHERY
(Project Turtle; ☎0362-93001; www.reefseenbali.com/turtle-hatchery; Reef Seen; adult/child 25,000Rp/free; ⏲8am-5pm) 🍃 Pemuteran is home to the nonprofit Proyek Penyu, run by Reef Seen Divers' Resort. Turtle eggs and small turtles purchased from locals are looked after here until they're ready for ocean release. Thousands of turtles have been released since 1994. You can visit the

small hatchery and make a donation to sponsor and release a tiny turtle. It's just off the main road, along the beach just east of Taman Selini Beach Bungalows.

Pulaki VILLAGE

Pulaki is famous for its grape vines (Bali's Hattan Wines owns many), watermelons and for Pura Pulaki, a coastal temple that was completely rebuilt in the early 1980s, and is home to a large troop of monkeys. The area is also known for troops at a nearby army base. It's an easy walk from Pemuteran.

Activities

Extensive coral reefs are about 3km offshore. Closer coral is being restored as part of the Bio Rocks project. Diving and snorkelling are universally popular and are offered by dive shops and hotels. You can rent snorkelling gear from 50,000Rp. The bay has a depth of less than 15m closer to the shore, so shore diving is popular, especially at night.

★Reef Seen Divers' Resort DIVING

(☎0362-93001; www.reefseenbali.com; 2-tank dives from 1,200,000Rp) Right on the beach in a large compound, Reef Seen is a PADI dive centre and has a full complement of classes. It also offers pony rides on the beach for kids and some dive packages include accommodation at the dive complex (rooms from 525,000Rp). The company is active in local preservation efforts.

Garden of the Gods DIVING

Out in Pemuteran Bay, you can make like Indiana Jones underwater at this intriguing dive site. More than 30 statues and sculptures have been erected on the sea floor about 400m offshore. Shiva is at the centre and various Balinese gods and icons surround him.

Bali Diving Academy DIVING

(☎0813 3391 76652; www.scubali.com; Beachfront, Taman Sari Bali Resort; Pulau Menjangan dives from 1,275,000Rp) The well-respected Bali-wide dive company has a shop right on the sand on the bay. It's near the Bio Rocks info booth. Ask about some of the lesser-known dive sites.

Easy Divers DIVING

(☎0813 5319 8766; www.easy-divers.eu; Jl Singaraja-Gilimanuk; introductory dive from €55) Easy Divers' founder, Dusan Repic, has befriended many a diver new to Bali, and this shop is well recommended. It's on the main road near Taman Selini and Pondok Sari hotels.

EXPLORING PULAU MENJANGAN UNDERWATER

With its great selection of lodgings, Pemuteran is the ideal base for diving and snorkelling Pulau Menjangan. Banyuwedang's harbour is just 7km west of town, so you have only a short ride before you're on a boat for the relaxing and pretty 30-minute journey to Menjangan. Dive shops and local hotels run snorkelling trips that cost US$65 to US$85; two-tank dive trips cost from US$95. That includes a 250,000Rp park entrance fee, but note that on Sundays and other national holidays, the price for entering the park increases to 350,000Rp.

Some tours to Menjangan leave by boat right from Pemuteran Beach; this is best. Other trips involve a car ride and transfer at Banyuwedang.

Sleeping

Pemuteran has one of the nicest selections of beachside hotels in Bali, plus a growing number of budget guesthouses. Many have a sense of style and all are low-key and relaxed, with easy access to the beach.

Some of the hotels are accessed directly off the main road, while others are off small roads that run either to the bay or south towards the mountains.

Pande Guest House GUESTHOUSE $

(☎0818 822 088; Jl Singaraja-Gilimanuk; r from 250,000Rp; ❄📶) This guesthouse is well-run and charming, with immaculate, comfy rooms featuring open-air bathrooms with lovely garden showers. It's by far the best budget option in town.

Double You Homestay GUESTHOUSE $

(☎0813 3842 7000; www.doubleyoupemuteran.com; off Jl Singaraja-Gilimanuk; r incl breakfast from 360,000Rp; ❄📶) On a small lane south of the main road, this stylish guesthouse has nine immaculate units set in a flower-filled garden, with hot water and other comforts.

Bali Gecko Homestay GUESTHOUSE $

(☎0852 3808 2285; bali.gecko@ymail.com; Desa Pemuteran; r 400,000-500,000Rp; ❄📶) About 500m west of Pemuteran's main strip and

DIVING & SNORKELLING PULAU MENJANGAN

Bali's best-known underwater attraction, Pulau Menjangan is ringed by over a dozen superb dive sites. The experience is excellent – iconic tropical fish, soft corals, great visibility (usually), caves and spectacular drop-offs.

Lacy sea fans and various sponges provide both texture and hiding spots for small fish that together form a colour chart for the sea. Few can resist the silly charms of parrotfish and clownfish. Among larger creatures, you may see whales, whale sharks and manta rays.

Of the named sites here, most are close to shore and suitable for snorkellers or diving novices. But you can also venture out to where the depths turn black as the shallows drop off in dramatic cliffs, a magnet for experienced divers, who can choose from eight walls here.

This uninhabited island boasts what is thought to be Bali's oldest temple, **Pura Gili Kencana**, dating from the 14th century and about 300m from the pier. It has a huge Ganesha (elephant-headed Hindu deity) at the entrance. You can walk around the island in about an hour; unfortunately, the beaches often have garbage problems.

Practicalities

Tips to maximise what will likely be a highlight of your Bali trip:

➡ Boats often tie up to the jetty at Pulau Menjangan. The wall here – which rewards both divers and snorkellers – is directly out from the shore. Currents tend to flow gently southwest (the shore is on your right) so you can just literally go with the flow and enjoy the underwater spectacle. The richly rewarding north side of the island is another place where boats stop.

➡ For jetty stops, your guide may try to get you to swim back to the boat along the less-interesting bleached coral near the shore; this turns out to be for their convenience. Instead, suggest that the boat come down and pick you up when you're ready, thus avoiding the swim against the current followed by downtime at the jetty. The jetty wall extends far to the southwest and gets more pristine and spectacular as you go.

➡ North of the jetty, you can snorkel from shore and cover the sites in a big circle.

➡ Although the jetty area on the south side of the island is spectacular, most boat operators will take you there simply because it's the closest to the harbours and saves them fuel. The north side is also spectacular and is the best place to go midday. The coral is more varied here and there are turtles. **Mangrove Point** is an excellent snorkelling area.

➡ In the west, **Coral Gardens** is a fine spot. The **Anker Wreck**, a mysterious sunken boat, challenges even experts.

➡ Try to hover over some divers along the walls. Watching their bubbles sinuously rise in all their multihued silvery glory from the inky depths is just plain spectacular.

➡ Park fees add up: 250,000Rp per person, plus a diving/snorkelling fee 25,000/15,000Rp.

➡ If your guide really adds to your experience, tip accordingly.

➡ Friends of Menjangan (www.friendsofmenjangan.blogspot.com) has info. For updates, check its Facebook page.

Getting There & Away

The closest and most convenient dive operators are found at Pemuteran, where the hotels also arrange diving and snorkelling trips. Independent snorkellers can arrange trips from Banyuwedang and Labuhan Lalang. If you are day tripping from elsewhere on Bali, carefully find out how much time you'll be travelling each way. From Seminyak, congestion woes can make for seven or more hours on the road.

another 200m north off the main road, this family-run guesthouse is isolated. You can walk to a quiet part of the beach along a short trail or ascend a nearby hill for great views. The four rooms are very simple.

Taruna GUESTHOUSE $

(☎0813 3853 6318; www.tarunapemuteran.com; Jl Singaraja-Gilimanuk; r incl breakfast fan/air-con 450,000/700,000Rp; ❄📶🏊) On the beach side of the main road and just a short walk from the sand, this professionally run place has nine well-designed rooms on a long, narrow site.

Rare Angon Homestay HOMESTAY $

(☎0362-94747; Jl Singaraja-Gilimanuk; r 350,000-600,000Rp; ❄) Four good basic rooms (some with air-con) in a homestay located on the mountain side of the main road at the east end of the strip. Patios overlook the gardens.

Kubuku Ecolodge GUESTHOUSE $$

(☎0362-343 7302; www.kubukubali.com; Jl Singaraja-Gilimanuk; r incl breakfast from 765,000Rp; ❄📶) A slice of modern style in Pemuteran, Kubuku has a smallish pool with a bar and an inviting patch of lawn. The 17 comfortable rooms are decent value, and the restaurant serves tasty organic meals. The compound is down a lane on the mountain side of the main road.

Jubawa Homestay GUESTHOUSE $$

(☎0362-94745; www.jubawa-pemuteran.com; r incl breakfast 500,000-600,000Rp; ❄📶🏊) One of Pemuteran's originals, Jubawa is a rather plush midrange choice. The 24 rooms are set in expansive gardens around a pool. The popular cafe-bar serves Balinese and Thai food. It's on the south side of the main road, near the large Matahari Beach Resort.

★Matahari Beach Resort RESORT $$$

(☎0362-92312; www.matahari-beach-resort.com; Jl Singaraja-Gilimanuk; r from US$370; ❄📶🏊) This lovely beachside resort, on the quieter east end of the bay, is set in spacious and verdant grounds. Widely spaced bungalows are works of traditional art. Common areas include a library and other luxuries. The spa is elegant and the beachside bar a good place for a pause as you explore the bay.

★Taman Sari Bali Resort HOTEL $$$

(☎0362-93264; www.tamansaribali.com; r incl breakfast from 1,755,000Rp, villas from 4,235,000Rp; ❄@📶🏊) Off a small lane, traditional-style rooms are set in gorgeous bungalows that feature intricate carvings and traditional artwork inside and out – some are extra roomy and have views of the bay; a nearby compound holds large and lavish villas. Book ahead for beachside dinners. The resort is located on a long stretch of quiet beach on the bay, and is part of the reef restoration project.

★Taman Selini Beach Bungalows BOUTIQUE HOTEL $$$

(☎0362-94746; www.tamanselini.com; Jl Singaraja-Gilimanuk; r incl breakfast from 1,500,000Rp; ❄📶🏊) The 11 bungalows here recall an older, refined Bali, from the quaint thatched roofs down to the antique carved doors and detailed stonework. Rooms, which open on to a large garden running down to the beach, have four-poster beds and large outdoor bathrooms. The outdoor daybeds can be addictive, and the beachfront restaurant – with Indonesian and Greek dishes – is fantastic.

Puri Ganesha Villas BOUTIQUE HOTEL $$$

(☎0362-94766; www.puriganesha.com; villas from US$550; ❄@🏊) These four two-storey villas are on sweeping grounds; each has a unique style that mixes antiques with silks and relaxed comfort. Outside the air-con bedrooms, life is in the open air, including at your private pool. Dine in the small restaurant (it is a member of Slow Food Bali) or in your villa. It's located on the western point of the bay.

Pondok Sari HOTEL $$$

(☎0362-94738; www.pondoksari.com; Jl Singaraja-Gilimanuk; r incl breakfast €70-210; ❄🏊) There are 36 rooms here set in densely planted gardens that assure privacy. The pool is down by the beach; the cafe has sweet water views through the trees. Traditional Balinese details abound; bathrooms are open-air and a calling card for the stone-carvers. Deluxe units have elaborate stone tubs among other details. The resort is just off the main road.

Amertha Bali Villas HOTEL $$$

(☎0362-94831; www.amerthabalivillas.com; Jl Singaraja-Gilimanuk; incl breakfast r 1,200,000-7,000,000Rp; ❄📶🏊) A slightly older resort with spacious grounds, the beachfront Amertha benefits from having big mature trees that give it that timeless tropical feel. Rooms are large; the 14 villas are sizeable, with a lot of natural wood and spacious covered patios. All have plunge pools.

BIO ROCKS: GROWING A NEW REEF

Pemuteran is set among a fairly arid part of Bali where people have always had a hard-scrabble existence. In the early 1990s, tourist operators began to take advantage of the excellent diving in the area. Locals who'd previously been scrambling to grow or catch something to eat began getting language and other training to welcome people to what would become a collection of resorts.

But there was one big problem: dynamite and cyanide fishing plus El Niño warming had bleached and damaged large parts of the reef.

A group of local hotels, dive-shop owners and community leaders hit upon a novel solution: grow a new reef using electricity. The idea had already been floated by scientists internationally, but Pemuteran was the first place to implement it on a wide – and hugely successful – scale.

Using local materials, the community built dozens of large metal cages that were placed out along the threatened reef. These were then hooked to *very* low-wattage generators on land (you can see the cables running ashore near the Taman Sari hotel). What had been a theory became a reality. The low current stimulated limestone formation on the cages, which in turn quickly grew new coral. All told, Pemuteran's small bay is getting new coral (aka Bio Rocks) at five to six times the rate it would take to grow naturally.

The results are win-win. Locals and visitors are happy and so are the reefs; the project has gained international attention and awards. The collaborative local group, the Pemuteran Foundation (www.pemuteranfoundation.com), has an info booth with a sign reading 'Bio Rocks Reef Gardeners' on the beach by Pondok Sari. Info on their work is in most local resort lobbies. Note their list of rules for swimming in the bay, including not standing on coral, not taking coral and shells and not feeding the fish.

Eating

Cafes and restaurants are found along the main drag. Otherwise the beachside hotels and resorts have good midrange restaurants. You can wander along the beach debating which one to choose.

★Santai Warung INDONESIAN $
(☎0852 3737 0220; Jl Hotel Taman Sari; mains from 35,000Rp; ⊙11am-9pm; ☑) Follow the glowing lanterns off Pemuteran's main road to this adorable Indonesian restaurant, which serves up spicy, authentic dishes – including lots of great vegetarian options – in a wonderful garden setting. The restaurant also features rice tables (banquets involving dozens of Balinese dishes that must be ordered 24 hours in advance), along with a traditional Javanese *joglo* house and cooking classes.

Joe's INDONESIAN $
(☎0852 3739 0151; Jl Singaraja-Gilimanuk; mains from 40,000Rp; ⊙11am-midnight) The closest thing Pemuteran has to a party bar, Joe's has a dash of vintage style. Enjoy a seafood meal sitting around an old boat in the open-air dining room. Later, listen to diving tales great and small at the genial bar. It's in the middle of the main strip. A sign reads: 'Drinker of the month wins a bottle of whiskey'.

Bali Balance Café & Bistro CAFE $
(☎0853 3745 5454; www.bali-balance.com; Jl Singaraja-Gilimanuk; mains from 30,000Rp; ⊙7.30am-7pm; 📶) Excellent coffee, plus juices and tasty cakes, make this spotless cafe a good place for a pause any time. There's a short menu of sandwiches and salads, which can be enjoyed in the leafy back garden. It's on the hillside, roughly in the middle of the main strip.

La Casa Kita PIZZA $
(☎0852 3889 0253; Jl Gilimanuk-Seririk; mains 40,000-75,000Rp; ⊙10am-10pm) Grab a table and a cold Bintang on the outdoor lawn and choose from a menu with a classic holiday mix of thin-crust wood-fired pizzas plus Western and Indonesian dishes. It's on the main road across from Easy Divers.

Getting There & Away

Pemuteran is served by buses on the Gilimanuk–Lovina–Singaraja run. To Pemuteran from Gilimanuk or Lovina, you should be able to negotiate a fare of around 20,000Rp. There's no stop, so just flag one down. It's a four-hour drive from south Bali, either over the hills or around the west coast. A private car and driver costs around 850,000Rp to either Ubud or Seminyak, among other destinations.

Banyuwedang

This mangrove-fringed cove just east of the national park is the main hub for boat trips to Pulau Menjangan.

Activities

If you are visiting Menjangan to dive or snorkel as part of a group, it's highly likely that you'll catch your boat at this bustling little harbour, which is 1.2km off Jl Singaraja-Gilimanuk.

You can also arrange your own snorkelling trips here; they typically take three hours, with one hour of that transit time. You can leave from 8am to 3pm daily. Prices are fixed, reward groups and quickly add up: a boat (for one to 10 people) 600,000Rp; mandatory guide (for the group, many do little actual 'guiding') 250,000Rp; snorkel-set rental per person 40,000Rp; park-entrance fee per person 250,000Rp; diving/snorkelling fees 25,000/15,000Rp and insurance per person 10,000Rp.

Sleeping

Mimpi Resort Menjangan RESORT $$
(☎0362-94497, 0361-415020; www.mimpi.com; Pejarakan; incl breakfast r from US$110, villas from US$160; ❄@📶🏊) Near the docks for boats to Menjangan, this 54-unit resort extends down to a small, mangrove-fringed, white-sand beach. The rooms have an unadorned monochromatic motif with open-air bathrooms. Hot springs feed communal pools and private tubs in the villas. The grand villas, with a private pool and lagoon views, are a great tropical fantasy escape.

Menjangan RESORT $$$
(☎0362-94700; www.themenjangan.com; Jl Raya Gilimanuk-Singaraja, Km 17; r/ste/villas incl breakfast from US$180/350/500; ❄📶🏊) Set on Bali Barat National Park land, this luxe resort is the perfect spot for those wanting to fully experience the national park. Spread over 382 hectares, it has two entities: the Monsoon Lodge has rooms set in the bush section; the Beach Villas overlook the mangroves and Pulau Menjangan. Activities include the resort's beach, horse riding, kayaking, hiking and more.

Getting There & Away

You'll need your own wheels to get here.

Labuhan Lalang

To catch a boat to visit or snorkel Pulau Menjangan, head to the jetty at this small harbour inside Bali Barat National Park. Prices should be the same as those at Banyuwedang. There are warungs and a pleasant beach 200m to the east.

Makam Jayaprana HINDU TEMPLE
A 20-minute walk up some stone stairs from the southern side of the road, a little west of Labuhan Lalang, will bring you to Jayaprana's grave. There are fine views to the north at the top.

Jayaprana, the foster son of a 17th-century king, planned to marry Leyonsari, a beautiful girl of humble origins. The king, however, also fell in love with Leyonsari and had Jayaprana killed. Leyonsari learned the truth of Jayaprana's death in a dream, and killed herself rather than marry the king. This Romeo and Juliet story is a common theme in Balinese folklore, and the grave is regarded as sacred, even though the ill-fated couple were not gods.

Information

Labuhan Lalang Information Office (Jl Singaraja-Gilimanuk; ⏲7am-7pm) Labuhan Lalang information office.

Getting There & Away

Buses making the run between Gilimanuk and Singaraja can occasionally be flagged down here, but it's easiest to arrange your own transport.

Bali Barat National Park

☎0365

Most visitors to Bali's only national park, Bali Barat National Park (Taman Nasional Bali Barat), are struck by the mellifluous sounds emanating from the birds darting among the rustling trees.

The park covers 190 sq km of the western tip of Bali, including almost 70 sq km of coral reef and coastal waters. Together this represents a significant commitment to conservation on an island as densely populated as Bali.

It's a place where you can enjoy Bali's best diving at Pulau Menjangan, hike through forests and explore coastal mangroves.

Activities

By land, by boat or underwater, the park awaits exploration. You'll pay 250,000Rp to 350,000Rp to enter the park, depending on the day, plus another few thousand rupees for your activity within the park. You'll also need a guide and negotiating this fee can be confounding. Virtually all costs are variable. You can arrange things at the park offices in Cekik or Labuhan Lalang. **Iwan Melali** (☎0819 3167 5011; iwan.melali@gmail.com) is a knowledgeable, English-speaking guide who excels at tracking down wildlife.

Boat Trips

The best way to explore the mangroves of Teluk Gilimanuk (Gilimanuk Bay) or the west side of Prapat Agung is by chartering a boat. Let the fixed prices at nearby Banyuwedang be your guide to negotiating your price: a boat (for one to 10 people) is 600,000Rp and a mandatory guide (for the group, many do little actual 'guiding') 235,000Rp. Additionally, there is snorkel-set rental per person 40,000Rp; and park-entrance fees per person 250,000Rp to 350,000Rp, plus diving/snorkelling fees 25,000/15,000Rp.

Hiking

All hikers must be accompanied by an authorised guide. It's best to arrive the day before you want to hike and make arrangements at the park offices.

The set rates for guides in the park depend on the size of the group and the length of the hike – about 350,000Rp per hour for two people for up to two hours is the starting price. Transport costs and the price is negotiable. Early morning, say 6am, is the best time to start – it's cooler and you're more likely to see some wildlife.

If, once you're out, you have a good rapport with your guide, you might consider getting creative. Although you can try to customise your hike, the guides prefer to set itineraries, including some of the following sites.

From Sumber Kelompok, hikes head up **Gunung Kelatakan** (Mt Kelatakan; 698m), then down to the main road near Kelatakan village (six to seven hours). You may be able to get permission from park headquarters to stay overnight in the forest – if you don't have a tent, your guide can make a shelter from branches and leaves, which will be an adventure in itself. Clear streams abound in the dense woods.

Bali Barat National Park

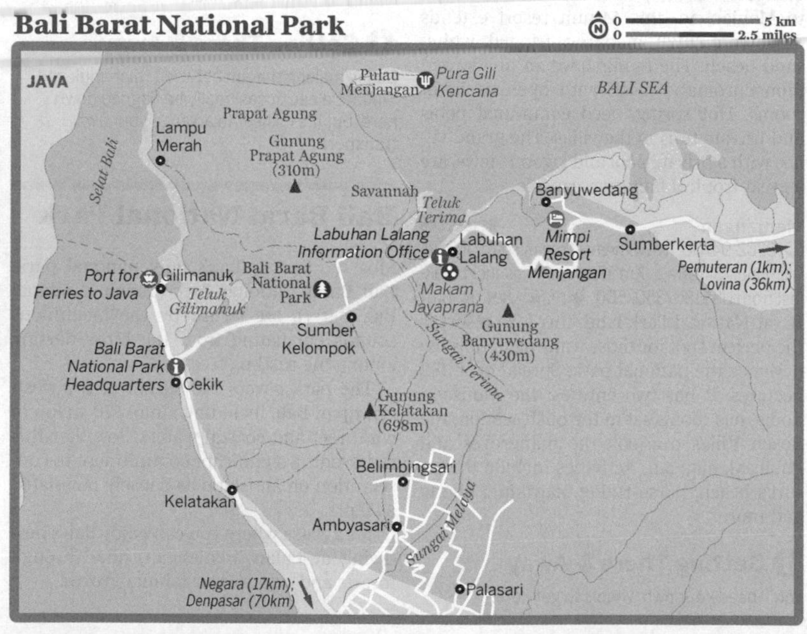

FLORA & FAUNA IN THE PARK

Most of the natural vegetation in the park is not tropical rainforest, which requires year-round rain, but rather coastal savannah, with deciduous trees that become bare in the dry season. The southern slopes receive more rainfall, and so have more tropical vegetation, while the coastal lowlands have extensive mangroves.

There are more than 200 species of plants growing in the park. Local fauna includes leaf monkeys and macaques (seen in the afternoon along the main road near Sumber Kelompok); rusa and barking deer; and some wild pigs, squirrels, buffalo, iguanas, pythons and green snakes. There were once tigers, but the last confirmed sighting was in 1937 – and that one was shot. The birdlife is prolific, with many of Bali's some 300 species found here, including the very rare Bali starling.

Just getting off the road a bit on one of the many trails transports you into the heart of nature.

A three- to four-hour hike will allow you to explore the savannah area along the coast northwest of Teluk Terima. You have a chance of seeing monitor lizards, barking deer and leaf monkeys – you may even spot a Bali starling, part of a release project in the park. The trek includes a ride to and from the trailhead.

From a trail west of Labuhan Lalang, a three-hour hike exploring **Teluk Terima** (Terima Bay) can begin at the mangroves. You then partially follow Sungai Terima (Terima River) into the hills and walk back down to the road. If you're lucky, you might see grey macaques, deer and leaf monkeys.

Sleeping

The closest options are top end and although there is camping, you must pay the park fee each day plus another 10,000Rp for a campsite. However, there's a large variety of options in Pemuteran, which is 12km east, and one decent budget hotel about 500m from Cekik. You'll need to head to Gilimanuk or Pemuteran to find eateries.

Information

DANGERS & ANNOYANCES

People claiming to be guides hang around the park offices. Their legitimacy can be as hard to discern as their fees. Proffered plastic-laminated rate guides are often works of fiction. Negotiate hard. For hiking, the prices start at around 350,000Rp for two people for up to two hours. A boat ride through the mangroves starts at 700,000Rp for two people for up to three hours.

TOURIST INFORMATION

The park headquarters (p281) at Cekik displays a map of the park area, and has a little information about plants and wildlife. The Labuhan Lalang Information Office (p271) is in a hut located in the parking area where boats leave for Pulau Menjangan.

You can arrange trekking guides and permits at either office; however, there are always a few characters hanging around, and determining who is an actual park official can be like spotting a Bali starling: difficult.

The main roads to Gilimanuk go through the national park, but you don't have to pay an entrance fee just to drive through. However, any activities in the park, such as hiking or diving Menjangan, require paying the 250,000Rp to 350,000Rp park fee plus any activity fees.

Getting There & Away

If you don't have transport, any Gilimanuk-bound bus or bemo from north or west Bali can drop you at park headquarters at Cekik (those from north Bali can drop you at Labuhan Lalang).

West Bali

Includes ➡

Why Go?

Even as development from south Bali creeps ever further west (via hot spots such as Canggu), Bali's true west, which is off the busy main road from Tabanan to Gilimanuk, remains infrequently visited. It's easy to find serenity amid its wild beaches, jungle and rice fields.

On the coast, surfers hit the breaks at Balian and Medewi. Some of Bali's most sacred sites are here, from the ever-thronged Pura Tanah Lot to the lily-pad-dappled beauty of Pura Taman Ayun and on to the wonderful isolation of Pura Rambut Siwi.

The tidy town of Tabanan is at the hub of Bali's Unesco-listed *subak,* the system of irrigation that ensures everybody gets a fair share of the water. On narrow back roads you can cruise beside rushing streams with bamboo arching overhead and fruit piling up below.

Best Places to Eat

- ➡ Bali Silent Retreat (p278)
- ➡ Sushi Surf (p279)
- ➡ Ten Pandan (p281)

Best Places to Stay

- ➡ Bali Silent Retreat (p278)
- ➡ Soori Villas (p277)
- ➡ Gajah Mina (p279)
- ➡ Taman Wana Villas & Spa (p282)
- ➡ Puri Dajuma Cottages (p281)

When to Go

➡ The best time to visit west Bali is during the dry season from April to September, although recent weather patterns have made the dry season wetter and the wet season drier. Hiking and trekking in Bali Barat National Park is much easier when it isn't muddy, and the waters of Pulau Menjangan are at their world-class best for diving on clear days.

➡ Along the coast, the west has yet to develop a peak season – although surfing is best June to August. Yet even in busy months you'll still find the waves less crowded than you will further south.

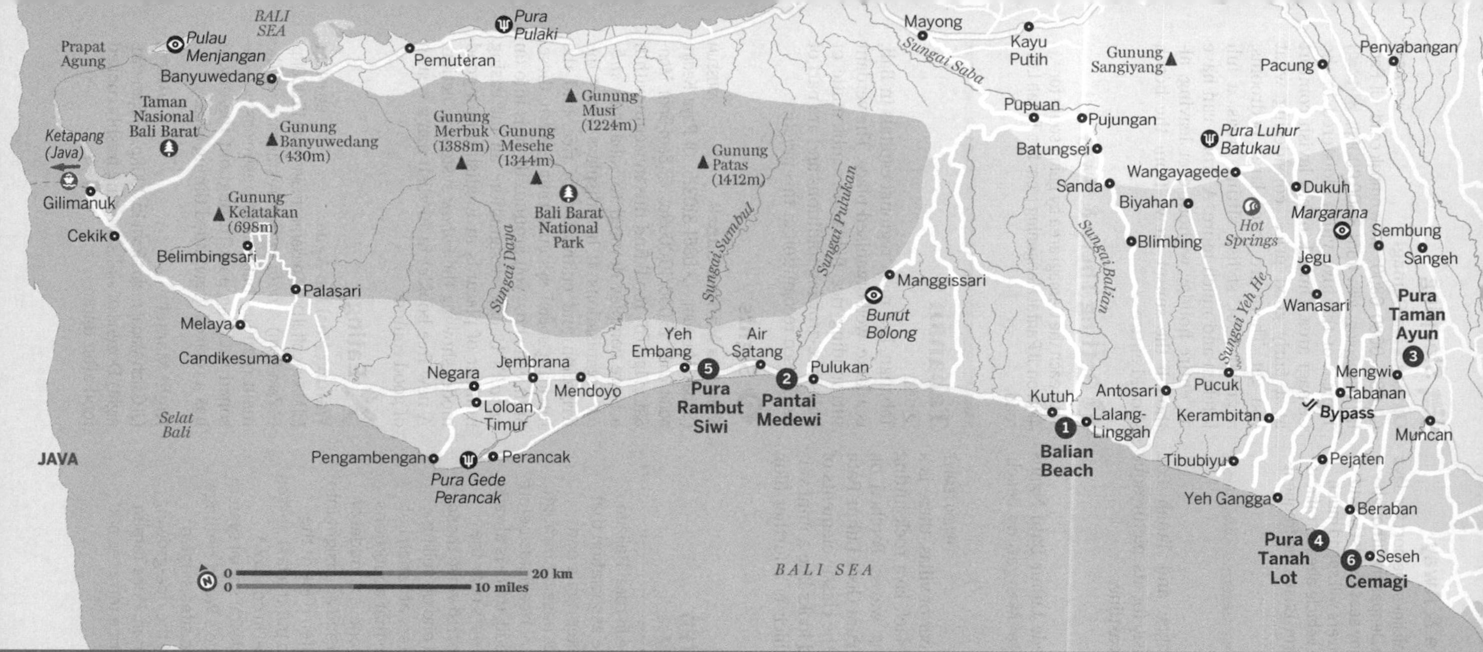

West Bali Highlights

1 Balian Beach (p278)
Revelling in the cool beach vibe and pounding surf visuals in a place where surfer hang-outs and stylish digs rub shoulders.

2 Pantai Medewi (p280)
Nailing the long left break at this low-key, quietly expanding haven.

3 Pura Taman Ayun (p279)
Finding your own tranquil corner at one of Bali's most evocative temples.

4 Pura Tanah Lot (p277)
Enjoying the morning spirituality of this tourist-filled temple before it gives way to the chaos of the afternoon.

5 Pura Rambut Siwi (p280)
Feeling the serenity at this historic and important seaside temple.

6 Cemagi (p276)
Substituting the seaside temple of Pura Gede Luhur Batu Ngaus for the Tanah Lot crowds.

Getting There & Away

The main road in west Bali links the port for Java ferries in Gilimanuk with Denpasar. Although portions of the route enjoy seaside vistas and rice-field views, most drivers will spend much of their time viewing the vehicle ahead; traffic is heavy and delays the norm. Buses run frequently on this route.

Cemagi

Nestled between Canggu and Tanah Lot, Cemagi is worth a visit for its picturesque temple and striking coastline.

Sights

Just north of Pura Gede Luhur Batu Ngaus is the black-sand **Pantai Mengening** beach.

Pura Gede Luhur Batu Ngaus HINDU TEMPLE

Amid a growing number of villas, there is a dramatic outcrop of black lava rock jutting out into the pounding waves. Perched on top is the photogenic Pura Gede Luhur Batu Ngaus, which has all the classic elements of a Balinese temple and looks like a mini version of Tanah Lot, which is a further 3km northwest.

A UNESCO-LISTED SOCIAL SYSTEM

Playing a critical role in rural Bali life, the *subak* is a village association that deals with water, water rights and irrigation. With water passing through many, many scores of rice fields before it drains away for good, there is always the chance that growers near the source will be water-rich while those at the bottom could end up selling carved wooden critters at Tanah Lot. Regulating a system that apportions a fair share to everyone is a model of mutual cooperation and an insight into the Balinese character. (One of the strategies used is to put the last person on the water channel in control.)

This complex and vital social system was added to Unesco's World Heritage List in 2012. Specific sites singled out include much of the rice-growing region around Tabanan, Pura Taman Ayun, the Jatiluwih rice terraces and Danau Batur.

Sleeping

Ombak Villa Cemagi VILLA $$$

(0851 0080 0800; www.ombak.co.id; Jl Pantai Mengening; villa from 3,600,000Rp;) Typical of the luxe villas cloistered in the Cemagi area, Ombak offers lavish comfort at a fairly good price, considering what you get. There are three large bedrooms, a grand pool, stylish sitting areas, a full kitchen and much more. A group can have an entire holiday without ever leaving, although the sunset views from the beach should entice.

Getting There & Away

You reach the Cemagi area by going south for 4km on Jl Pantai Mengening from the Tanah Lot road.

Tabanan

0361

Tabanan, like most regional capitals in Bali, is a large, well-organised place. The verdant surrounding rice fields are emblematic of Bali's rice-growing traditions and are part of its Unesco recognition of this practice.

Sights

Mandala Mathika Subak MUSEUM

(Subak Museum; 0361-810315; Jl Raya Kediri; adult/child 15,000/10,000Rp; 8am-5pm Mon-Sat, to 1pm Fri) You'll find this museum within a large complex devoted to Tabanan's *subak* organisations. It has displays about the irrigation and cultivation of rice, and the intricate social systems that govern these. Staff will show you around; there is info on *subak*'s Unesco designation, an increasing number of placards in English and a good model showing the *subak* system in action. A new free booklet in English has a wealth of good content.

Eating

Warung Nasi Ibu Agus BALINESE $

(Jl Mawar, off Jl Dr Ir Soekarno; mains from 15,000Rp; 7am-9pm) A *babi guling* restaurant off the main road has batches of fresh-roasted seasoned suckling pork throughout the day. It has a relaxed green-hued dining area.

Night Market MARKET $

(Jl Gajah Mada; mains from 15,000Rp; 5pm-midnight) Dozens of stalls offering freshly cooked food after dark.

Hardy's SUPERMARKET $

(☎0361-819841; ⏰7am-10pm) Hardy's is a huge, modern supermarket with groceries and sundries. Stock up for your villa here or get a fresh meal in the food court.

Getting There & Away

Some bemo (minivans) and buses between Denpasar (Ubung terminal) and Gilimanuk stop at the terminal at the western end of Tabanan (10,000Rp).

The road to Pura Luhur Batukau and the beautiful rice terraces of Jatiluwih heads north from the centre of town.

South of Tabanan

Driving in the southern part of Tabanan district takes you though many charming villages and past a lot of vigorously growing rice. The fields are revered by many as the most productive in Bali.

Sights

Joshua District CULTURAL CENTRE

(☎0811 388 121; www.joshuadistrict.com; Pangkung Tibah, Kediri, Tabanan Regency; ⏰8am-10pm) FREE Set amid rice fields near the iconic temple of Tanah Lot, Joshua District is a creative complex – coffee shop, gallery, fashion concept store and a number of villas – made out of shipping containers. With the motto 'recycle or die', the community space promotes environmental awareness and sustainable lifestyles. Cash only.

Pura Tanah Lot HINDU TEMPLE

(Beraban; adult/child 60,000/30,000Rp, parking cars/motorbikes 5000/2000Rp; ⏰7am-7pm) Pura Tanah Lot is a hugely popular tourist destination. It does have cultural significance to the Balinese, but this can be hard to discern amid the crowds, clamour and chaos – especially for the overhyped sunsets. It's the most visited and photographed temple in Bali; however, it has all the authenticity of a stage set – even the tower of rock that the temple sits upon is an artful reconstruction (the entire structure was crumbling) and more than one-third of the rock is artificial.

For the Balinese, Pura Tanah Lot is one of the most important and venerated sea temples. Like Pura Luhur Ulu Watu, at the tip of the southern Bukit Peninsula, and Pura Rambut Siwi to the west, it is closely associated with the Majapahit priest Nirartha.

> **ENJOYING TANAH LOT**
>
> When visiting this important temple, try to arrive before noon: you'll beat the crowds and the vendors may still be asleep. You'll actually hear birds chirping rather than buses idling and be able to focus on the temple buildings rather than tourists taking selfies.

It's said that each of the sea temples was intended to be within sight of the next, so they formed a chain along Bali's southwestern coast – from Pura Tanah Lot you can usually see the clifftop site of Pura Ulu Watu far to the south, and the long sweep of sea shore west to Perancak, near Negara.

But at Tanah Lot itself you may just see from one vendor to the next. To reach the temple, take the walkways that run from the vast car parks through a mind-boggling sideshow of tatty souvenir shops down to the sea. Clamorous announcements screech from loudspeakers.

You can walk over to the temple itself at low tide, but non-Balinese people are not allowed to enter.

You won't be able to miss the looming Pan Pacific Nirwana resort with its water-sucking golf course. It has been controversial since the day it was built, because many feel its greater height shows the temple disrespect.

If coming from south Bali, take the coastal road west from Kerobokan and follow the signs. From other parts of Bali, turn off the Denpasar–Gilimanuk road near Kediri and follow the signs. During the pre- and post-sunset rush, traffic is awful with backups stretching for many kilometres.

Sleeping

★**Soori Villas** VILLA $$$

(☎0361-894 6388; www.sooribali.com; Kelating; villas from 7,500,000Rp; ❄📶🏊) This luxury villa compound on a (still) remote stretch of Bali's west coast has 48 very private villas, each with its own plunge pool. The accommodation has a modern minimalism and the setting is very secluded. Canggu and Seminyak are 45 minutes to an hour away; the resort offers transport.

Getting There & Away

This is a place for your own wheels. The back roads reward cyclists.

OFF THE BEATEN TRACK

TABANAN TO THE COAST

About 10km south of Tabanan is **Pejaten**, a centre for the production of traditional pottery, including elaborate ornamental roof tiles. Porcelain clay objects, which are made purely for decorative use, can be seen in a few workshops in the village. Check out the small showroom of **Pejaten Ceramic Art** (081 657 7073; 9am-4pm Mon-Sat), one of several local producers. Its trademark pale-green pieces are quite lovely and the shop is close to the daily **village market**.

A little west of Tabanan, a road goes 8km south via Gubug to the secluded coast at **Yeh Gangga**, where there's a good, usually quiet beach.

Further west of Tabanan on the main road, a road turns south to the coast via **Kerambitan**, a village noted for its dance troupe and musicians who perform across the south and in Ubud. Banyan trees shade beautiful old buildings, including the 17th-century palace **Puri Anyar Kerambitan** (0812 392 6720; Jl Raya Kerambitan; donation requested; 9am-6pm)

About 4km from southern Kerambitan is the small beachside village of **Tibubiyu**. For a lovely drive through huge bamboo, fruit trees, rice paddies and more, take the scenic road, Jl Meliling Kangin, northwest from Kerambitan to the main Tabanan–Gilimanuk road.

North of Tabanan

The area north of Tabanan is a good spot to travel around with your own transport. There are some strictly B-grade attractions; the real appeal is just driving the fecund back roads where the bamboo arches temple-like over the road. Rice-field vistas await around almost every turn.

Sleeping & Eating

★Bali Silent Retreat BOUTIQUE HOTEL $
(0813 5348 6517; www.balisilentretreat.com; Penatahan; dm US$25, r US$40-120) Set amid gorgeous scenery, this place is just what its name says: somewhere to meditate, practise yoga, go on nature walks and more – all in total silence. The minimalist ethos stops at the food, however, which is organic and fabulous (included in the US$37 day pass). It's 18km northwest of Tabanan.

Bali Homestay Program HOMESTAY $
(0851 0488 9996; www.bali-homestay.com; Jegu; 2 nights all-inclusive s/d from US$185/330) You can sample village life as part of this innovative program that places travellers in the homes of residents of the rice-growing village of Jegu, 9km north of Tabanan. The recommended full two-night package includes activities such as making offerings, village visits and cultural tours plus all meals. Book at least two weeks in advance.

Getting There & Away

The bamboo-shaded back roads north of Tabanan require your own wheels. Cyclists ready for hills will enjoy rewarding rides.

Balian Beach

0361

Ever more popular, Balian Beach is a rolling area of dunes and knolls overlooking pounding surf. It attracts both surfers and those looking to escape the bustle of south Bali.

You can wander between cafes and join other travellers for a beer, to watch the sunset and to talk surf. There are simple places to rent boards along the black-sand beach, while nonsurfers can enjoy yoga or bodysurfing.

Balian Beach is right at the mouth of the wide Sungai Balian (Balian River). It is 800m south of the town of Lalang-Linggah, which is on the main road 10km west of Antosari.

Sleeping

Much of the accommodation is fairly close together and near the beach, but there are also some comfortable homestays set back from the water.

★Surya Homestay GUESTHOUSE $
(0813 3868 5643; wayan.suratni@gmail.com; r incl breakfast 200,000-350,000Rp;) There are eight rooms in bungalow-style units at this sweet little family-run place (Wayan and

Putu are charmers), which is about 200m along a small lane from the main road. It's spotless, and rooms have cold water and fans or air-con. Ask about long-term rates.

Made's Homestay HOMESTAY $
(☎0812 396 3335; r 150,000-200,000Rp) Three basic bungalow-style units are surrounded by banana trees back from the beach. The rooms are basic, clean, large enough to hold numerous surfboards and they have cold-water showers.

Ayu Balian HOMESTAY $
(☎0812 399 353; Jl Pantai Balian; r incl breakfast 100,000-300,000Rp; ❄) The seven rooms in this slightly shambolic two-storey block look down the road to the surf. Some have hot water and air conditioning; the friendly owner Ayu is a genuine character.

★**Gajah Mina** BOUTIQUE HOTEL $$
(☎0812 381 1630; www.gajahminaresort.com; villas incl breakfast US$115-250; ❄📶🏊) Designed by the French architect-owner, this 11-unit boutique hotel is close to the ocean. The private, walled bungalows march out to a dramatic outcrop of stone surrounded by surf. The grounds are vast and there are little trails for wandering and pavilions for relaxing. The on-site seafood restaurant, **Naga** (mains from 70,000Rp), overlooks a picture-perfect private black-sand beach.

Pondok Pitaya GUESTHOUSE $$
(☎0819 9984 9054; www.pondokpitaya.com; Jl Pantai Balian; r incl breakfast US$60-155; 📶🏊) Right on wave-tossed Balian Beach and fresh with the scent of ocean spray, this complex features an eclectic range of rooms: from vintage Indonesian buildings (including a 1950 Javanese house and an 1860 Balinese alligator hunter's shack) to more modest accommodation. It's a great place for families as it has a popular pool. The **cafe** (mains 40,000Rp to 85,000Rp) serves juices, organic fare and pizzas.

Pondok Pisces GUESTHOUSE $$
(☎0361-831 1220, 0813 3879 7722; www.pondokpiscesbali.com; Jl Pantai Balian; r 460,000-1,300,000Rp; 📶) You can certainly hear the sea at this tropical fantasy of thatched cottages and flower-filled gardens. There are 12 rooms; those on the upper floor have large terraces with surf views. In-house **Tom's Garden Cafe** (mains 52,000Rp to 120,000Rp) has grilled seafood and surf views.

Gubug Balian Beach GUESTHOUSE $$
(☎0812 3963 0605; gubugbalian@gmail.com; Jl Pantai Balian; r 380,000-700,000Rp; ❄📶) On a spacious site close to the beach are 14 rooms, some of which have views down the lane to the surf. The cheapest rooms are fan and cold water only.

Eating

★**Sushi Surf** JAPANESE $
(☎0812 3870 8446; Jl Pantai Balian; rolls from 20,000Rp, mains from 55,000Rp; ⏲10am-10pm) *The* place for a sunset cocktail and bite of sushi. The surf action is arrayed out right in front of the quirky multilevel seating area. There are specials and a broad menu that goes beyond California rolls. It's run by the Pondok Pitaya people.

WORTH A TRIP

PURA TAMAN AYUN

A place of enveloping calm, this huge royal water **temple** (Mengwi; adult/child 20,000/10,000Rp; ⏲8am-6.15pm) northeast of Tabanan is surrounded by a wide, elegant moat. It was the main temple of the Mengwi kingdom, which survived until 1891, when it was conquered by the neighbouring kingdoms of Tabanan and Badung. The complex was built in 1634 and extensively renovated in 1937. It's a spacious place to wander around, away from crowds.

The first courtyard is a large, open, grassy expanse and the inner courtyard has a multitude of *meru* (multitiered shrines). Lotus-blossoms fill the pools; the temple is part of the *subak* (complex rice-field irrigation system) sites recognised by Unesco in 2012. The market area immediately east of the temple has many good warungs for a simple lunch.

Inside the temple complex is the **Museum Manusa Yadnya** (Jl Ayodya; ⏲8.30am-5pm) FREE, which documents the numerous Hindu rituals involved during a Balinese person's life, starting from six months after conception to death.

PURA RAMBUT SIWI

Picturesquely situated on a clifftop overlooking a long, wide stretch of black-sand beach, the superb Pura Rambut Siwi is shaded by flowering frangipani trees is one of the important sea temples of west Bali. Like Pura Tanah Lot and Pura Luhur Ulu Watu, it was established in the 16th century by the priest Nirartha, who had a good eye for ocean scenery. Unlike Tanah Lot, it remains a peaceful and little-visited place: on non-ceremony days you'll just find a couple of lonely drink vendors.

Legend has it that when Nirartha first came here, he donated some of his hair to the local villagers. The hair is now kept in a box buried in a three-tiered *meru* (multitiered shrine), the name of which means 'Worship of the Hair'. Although the main *meru* is inaccessible, you can view it easily through the gate. The entire temple is reached by an imposing set of stone stairs from the parking area.

The caretaker rents sarongs for 2000Rp and is happy to show you around the temple and down to the beach. He will then open the guestbook and request a donation – a suitable sum is about 10,000Rp (regardless of the much higher amounts attributed to previous visitors). A path along the cliff leads to a staircase down to a small and even older temple, **Pura Penataran**.

The temple is located between Air Satang and Yeh Embang, 7km west of Medewi and 48km east of Gilimanuk. The broad 500m road to the site through lovely rice fields is well signposted; look for the turn-off near a cluster of warung on the Tabanan–Gilimanuk main road.

Tékor Bali INTERNATIONAL **$**
(☎0815 5832 3330; tekorbali@hotmail.com; off Jl Pantai Balian; mains from 30,000Rp; ⏰7.30am-10pm; 📶) Down a small lane 100m back from the beach, this inviting restaurant with a grassy lawn feels a bit like you've come to a mate's backyard for a barbecue. The menu is broad, with all the usual local and surfer favourites, and the burgers are excellent. Cocktails are well made and there's cheap Bintang on tap. Accommodation is available in two simple rooms (350,000Rp).

ℹ Getting There & Away

Because the main west Bali road is usually jammed with traffic, Balian Beach is often at least a two-hour drive from Seminyak or the airport (55km). A car and driver will cost 900,000Rp or more for a day trip. You can also get a bus (60,000Rp) going to Gilimanuk from Denpasar's Ubung terminal and be dropped off at the road entrance, which is 800m from the beach places.

Jembrana Coast

Jembrana, Bali's most sparsely populated district, offers beautiful scenery and little tourism development, with the exception of the surfing action at Medewi. The main road follows the south coast most of the way to Negara, and at Pulukan you can turn north to enjoy a remote and scenic drive to north Bali.

Once capital of the region, Jembrana is the centre of the gamelan *jegog*, a gamelan using huge bamboo instruments that produces a low-pitched, resonant sound. Performances often feature gamelan groups engaging in a musical contest. Your best bet to hear this music is at a local festival. Have your driver or another local ask around to see if one is on while you're there.

ℹ Getting There & Away

It's a good thing the scenery is superb as the main road is frequently clogged with slow-moving trucks.

Medewi

☎0365

This is the home of the surfing mecca of **Pantai Medewi** and its much-vaunted *long* left-hand wave. Rides of 200m to 400m are common.

The beach is a stretch of huge, smooth grey rocks interspersed among round black pebbles – think of it as free reflexology. Cattle and goats graze by the shore as spectators view the action out on the water. There are a few guesthouses plus a couple of surf shops (board rental is from 100,000Rp per day).

Medewi proper is a classic market town with shops selling all the essentials of west Bali life.

Sleeping

You'll find accommodation along short little Jl Pantai Medewi, which runs down to the surf break. Other lanes, about 2km in either direction of the main surf break, have isolated guesthouses and surf camps. You'll want at least a motorbike for these.

Anara Surf Camp GUESTHOUSE $
(0817 0323 6684; www.facebook.com/anarasurfcamp/; r from 250,000Rp;) This surf camp and modern guesthouse is on the shores of Pantai Medewi, with the sea on one side and rice paddies on the other. There are different levels of accommodation, but all are newly constructed with attractive hardwoods, comfy four-poster beds and mosquito nets. A couple of bungalows near the water offer large glass windows and open-air bathrooms.

Surfboard rental costs just 70,000Rp per day, and instruction is also available. Be mindful of rip tides, as they're common in the stretch of ocean in front of the surf camp.

Surf Villa Mukks GUESTHOUSE $
(0812 397 3431; www.surfvillamukks.com; Pulukan; r incl breakfast with fan/air-con 250,000/400,000Rp;) About 900m east of the Medewi surf break at Pulukan, this Japanese-owned guesthouse has modern rooms overlooking rice fields and distant surf. It's a chilled spot where some rooms have large bamboo blinds instead of doors. It rents boards and offers surf lessons.

★ **Puri Dajuma Cottages** HOTEL $$
(0361-813230, 0811 388 709; www.dajuma.com; cottages from 1,600,000Rp;) Coming from the east on the main road, you won't be able to miss this seaside resort, thanks to its prolific signage. Happily, the 35 rooms – either in suites, cottages or villas – actually live up to the billing. Each has private garden, hammock and walled outdoor bathroom; most have ocean views. The Medewi surf break is 2km west.

Eating

★ **Ten Pandan** INDONESIAN $
(mains 20,000-40,000Rp; 9am-9pm) This charming beachfront restaurant serves cheap and tasty Indonesian dishes in traditional *joglos* perched on stilts by the sea. The gado gado (a favourite Indonesian dish made with boiled vegetables, tofu, egg and peanut sauce) is top-notch, and the service is super friendly. The owner plans to build a sports bar and dance club beside the restaurant.

Warung Gede & Homestay INDONESIAN $
(0812 397 6668; meals from 20,000Rp; 6am-10pm) From the simple open-air cafe of this guesthouse, you can watch the breaks and enjoy basic Indonesian fare as well as good breakfasts. Rooms (from 150,000Rp) are surfer-simple: cold water and fans.

Mai Malu CAFE $
(0819 1617 1045; maimalu.medewi@yahoo.com; off Tabanan-Gilimanuk Rd; mains from 35,000Rp;) Near the highway on the Medewi side road, guesthouse Mai Malu is a popular (and almost the only) hang-out. The modern, breezy upstairs cafe serves crowd-pleasing pizza, burgers and Indonesian meals. Rooms (from 150,000Rp) have the basics plus fans.

CEKIK

More a junction than a proper town, Cekik is the gateway to Bali Barat National Park from the south. Archaeological excavations here during the 1960s yielded the oldest evidence of human life in Bali. Finds include burial mounds with funerary offerings, bronze jewellery, axes, adzes and earthenware vessels from around 1000 BC, give or take a few centuries. Look for some of these at the **Museum Manusia Purbakala Gilimanuk** (Prehistoric People Museum; 0365-61328; Jl Rajawali; suggested donation 10,000Rp; hours vary) in Gilimanuk.

On the southern side of the junction, the pagoda-like structure with a spiral stairway around the outside is a **war memorial**. It commemorates the landing of independence forces in Bali to oppose the Dutch, who were trying to reassert control of Indonesia after WWII. The park headquarters of the **Bali Barat National Park** (0365-61060; Jl Raya Cekik; 6am-6pm) is also here – you'll find it just off the main road.

At the junction, one road continues 3km west to the Gilimanuk ferry port and another heads northeast towards north Bali. Buses from Gilimanuk to both Denpasar and Singaraja can be flagged down here; all buses and bemo to and from Gilimanuk pass through Cekik.

Getting There & Away

Medewi Beach is 75km from the airport. A car and driver will cost from 850,000Rp for a day trip. You can also get a bus (45,000Rp) going to Gilimanuk from Denpasar's Ubung terminal and be dropped off at the road entrance. On the main road, a large sign points down the short paved road (200m) to Pantai Medewi.

Palasari & Belimbingsari

Christian evangelism in Bali was discouraged by the secular Dutch, but sporadic missionary activity resulted in a number of converts, many of whom were rejected by their own communities. In 1939 they were encouraged to resettle here in the wilds of west Bali. The two communities they established are worthy of a detour off west Bali's main road when heading toward Gilimanuk and the island's only national park.

Palasari is home to a Catholic community, which boasts the huge Sacred Heart Catholic Church, largely made from white stone and set on a large town square. It is really rather peaceful, and with the gently waving palms, it feels like old missionary Hawaii rather than Hindu Bali. The church does show Balinese touches in the spires, which resemble the *meru* in a Hindu temple, and features a facade with the same shape as a temple gate.

Nearby Belimbingsari was established as a Protestant community, and now has the largest Protestant church, Pura Gereja, in Bali, although it doesn't reach for the heavens the way the Palasari church does. Still, it's an amazing structure, with features rendered in a distinctly Balinese style – in place of a church bell there's a *kulkul* (hollow tree-trunk drum used to sound a warning) like those in a Hindu temple. The entrance is through a gate in the style of an *aling aling* (guard wall), and the attractive carved angels look very Balinese. Go on Sunday to see inside.

★**Taman Wana Villas & Spa** BOUTIQUE HOTEL **$$$**
(0828 9712 3456, 0361-727770; www.bali-tamanwana-villas.com; Palasari; r US$80-280;) For a near-religious experience you might consider staying at this remote boutique resort, a striking 2km drive through a jungle past the Palasari church. An architectural stunner, it has 27 rooms in unusual round structures. 'Posh' only begins to describe the luxuries available at this cloistered refuge. Views are panoramic; get a room overlooking the rice fields.

Getting There & Away

The two villages are north of the main road, and the best way to see them is on a loop with your own transport. On the main road about 17km west from Negara, look for signs for the Taman Wana Villas. Follow these for 6.1km to Palasari. From the west, look for a turn for Belimbingsari, some 20km southeast of Cekik. A good road leads to the village. Between the two towns, only divine intervention will allow you to tackle the thicket of narrow but passable lanes unaided. Fortunately directional help is readily at hand.

Gilimanuk

0365

Gilimanuk is the terminus for ferries that shuttle back and forth across the narrow strait to Java. Most travellers to or from Java can get an onward ferry or bus straightaway, and won't hang around.

Warung Ment Tempeh BALINESE **$**
(Terminal Lama; meals from 25,000Rp; 8am-10pm) An extended family runs several neighbouring iterations of this cafe, which serves a local dish Gilimanuk is known for: *betutu* chicken, a spicy form of steamed chicken that is redolent with herbs. It is located in the former bus terminal, about 500m south of the ferry port, 50m off the main road.

Information

On Jl Raya Gilimanuk, there is a **police station** (0365-61101), BRI ATM and **post office** (0365-61525; www.posindonesia.co.id).

Getting There & Away

BOAT

Car ferries to and from Ketapang on Java (30 minutes, adult/child 7000/5000Rp, motorbike/car 25,000/225,000Rp) run around the clock. Their safety record has been fair at best. The pedestrian terminal is 300m north of the large bus station.

BUS

Frequent buses run between Gilimanuk's large depot and Denpasar's Ubung terminal (45,000Rp, three hours), or along the north-coast road to Singaraja (40,000Rp). Smaller, slightly more comfortable minibuses serve both routes for 5000Rp more.

Lombok

Includes ➡

Best Places to Eat

- El Bazar (p307)
- Nugget's Corner (p307)
- Taliwang Irama 3 (p289)
- Milk Espresso (p307)
- Coco Beach (p294)

Best Places to Stay

- Rinjani Beach Eco Resort (p300)
- Qunci Villas (p294)
- Livingroom Hostel (p306)
- Kuta Cabana Lodge (p306)
- Heaven on the Planet (p310)

Why Go?

Long overshadowed by its superstar neighbour across the Lombok Strait, Lombok has a steady hum about it that catches the ear of travellers looking for something different from Bali. Blessed with exquisite white-sand beaches, epic surf, a lush forested interior and hiking trails through tobacco and rice fields, Lombok is fully loaded with equatorial allure. Oh, and you'll probably notice mighty Gunung Rinjani, Indonesia's second-highest volcano, its summit complete with hot springs and a dazzling crater lake.

And there's much more. Lombok's southern coastline is nature on a very grand scale: breathtaking turquoise bays, world-class surf breaks and massive headlands.

Transport options are good in Lombok and the mood could not be more laid back. If you're planning to head further east in Nusa Tenggara, you can pass through Lombok overland to Sumbawa, or catch a boat to Flores.

When to Go

- July and August are the peak tourist seasons; it's best to prebook your accommodation.
- The weather stays generally dry from May to June and also in September, and tourist numbers are relatively low.
- From October to April, rains make the paths up Gunung Rinjani unsafe (they're closed from January to April) but surfing is at its best and many festivals take place: Perang Topat, Peresean stick-fighting competitions and Narmada buffalo races.
- Christmas and the New Year bring a revival of high-season prices (and crowds).

Lombok Highlights

1 Gunung Rinjani (p299) Tackling Lombok's incomparable sacred peak, which lures trekkers with a challenging climb and magnificent views of Rinjani's sacred crater lake and the smoking mini-cone of Gunung Baru below. (See p287 and p299 for post-earthquake information.)

2 Tanjung Desert (p296) Taking the ride of your life on the temperamental break at Desert Point, Bangko Bangko.

3 Pantai Selong Blanak (p311) Swimming in the clear, turquoise-tinged water off this pristine beach with its perfect swath of powdery white sand.

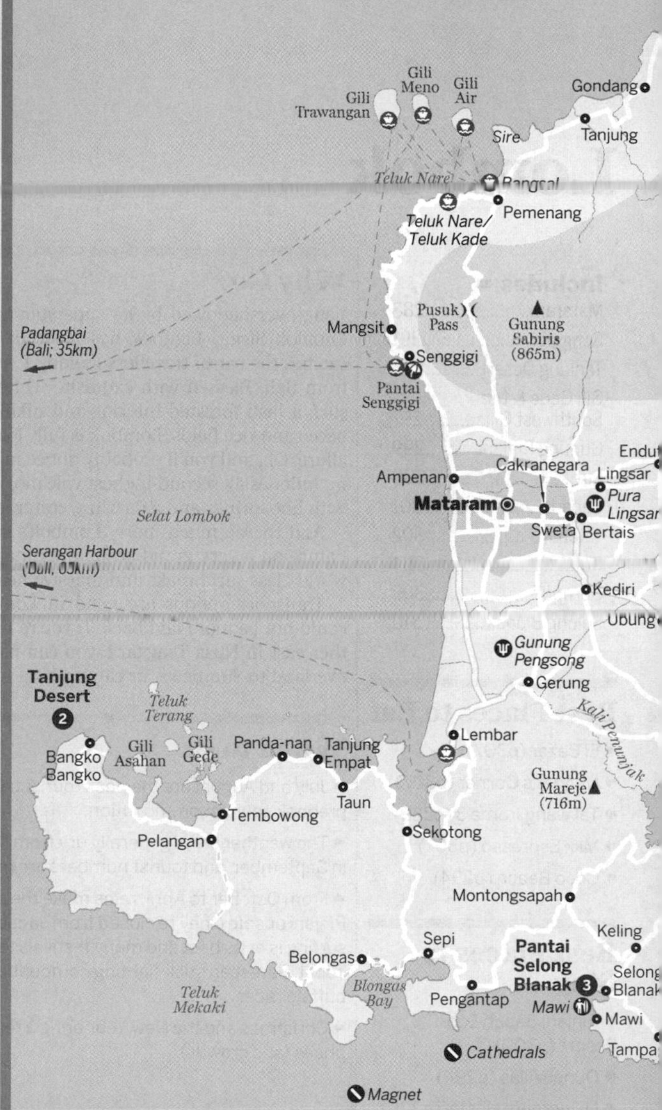

0
10 km
0
5 miles
Akar Akar
Selengan
Anyar
Kayangan
Beleq
Kokok
Putek
Obel Obel
Bayan
Batu Koq
Kali Putih
Protected
Forest
Gili
Lawang
Blantung
Senaru
Air Terjun
Sindang
Gila
Sajang
Gili
Sulat
Air Terjun
Tiu Pupas
Air Terjun
Gangga
Sembalun
Lawang
Gunung
Rinjani
(3726m)
Sembalun
Bumbung
Labuhan
Pandan
Danau
Segara
Anak
Gunung
Nangi
(2330m)
Mayung
Putih
Taman Nasional
Gunung Rinjani
Kali Menimting
Sapit
Labuhan
Lombok
Sumbawa
Aik
Berik
Timbanuh
Swela
Pengadangan
Pringgabaya
Tetebatu
Aikmel
Suranadi
Lendang
Nangka
Pringgasela
Narmada
Pancordao
Kotaraja
Surulaga
Anjani
Mantang
Masabagik Timur
Kali Babak
Pomotong
Masbagik
Kopang
Selat
Alas
Pancor
Selong
Kali Runtak
Puyung
Langko
Sakra
Sukarara
Janapria
Labuhan
Haji
Praya
Lombok
International
Airport
Beleka
Penujak
Mujur
Ganti
Keruak
Tanjung
Luar
Sukaraja
Mangkung
Jerowaru
Sengkol
Kateng
Rembitan
Sade
Batu
Nampar
Tanjung
Ringgit
Teluk Ekas
Awang
Ekas
Ekas
Mawan
Kuta
Kaliantan
Pantai
Seger
Tanjung
Aan
Gerupuk
Mawan
Pantai
Dagong
Gili Melayu
Gili Saya
INDIAN OCEAN

History

In the early 17th century, Balinese warriors overthrew Lombok's Sasak royalty in the west, while the Makassarese invaded from the east. By 1750, the whole island was dominated by Bali's Hindu monarchy. In western Lombok, relations between the Balinese and the Sasaks were relatively harmonious, but in eastern Lombok peasant rebellions were common.

The Dutch intervened in the late 19th century and, after an initial defeat that cost 100 lives, they took control of Cakranegara. Here the last raja families were made martyrs during a grizzly *puputan* suicide ritual in which men, women and children in white robes threw themselves upon perplexed Dutch soldiers, who shot to kill. Afterwards, the Dutch galvanised the support of the surviving Balinese and the Sasak aristocracy and soon controlled more than 500,000 people with 250 troops.

Even after Indonesian independence, Lombok continued to be dominated by its Balinese and Sasak elite. In 1958, Lombok was declared part of the new province of Nusa Tenggara Barat (West Nusa Tenggara) and Mataram became its administrative capital. Following the attempted coup in Jakarta in 1965, Lombok experienced mass killings of communists and ethnic Chinese.

Under president Suharto's 'New Order', there was stability and some growth, but crop failures led to famine in 1966 and to severe food shortages in 1973. Many moved away from Lombok under the government-sponsored *transmigrasi* program, a scheme that encouraged settlers to move from overcrowded regions to sparsely populated ones.

Tourism picked up in the 1980s but was mostly developed by outside investors and speculators. Indonesia descended into economic crisis and political turmoil in the late 1990s and, on 17 January 2000, serious riots engulfed Mataram. Christians and Chinese were the primary victims, but the agitators were from outside Lombok. Ultimately all Lombok suffered, and the faint pulse of tourism was muted further by the Bali bombings of 2002 and 2005.

Then something miraculous happened: Lombok took off. Bali's booming tourism spilled over, big time. The island became a hot travel destination and development boomed.

These boom times slowed ever so slightly in the wake of three powerful earthquakes that rocked Lombok in July and August of 2018. The first forced a mass evacuation of Gunung Rinjani, while the second saw more than a thousand tourists scrambling for boats off the Gili Islands. When all was said and done, an estimated 80% of all structures in North Lombok were damaged and some 563 people killed. Recovery on the Gili Islands and Senggigi was relatively swift, but the hard-hit towns at the base of Rinjani were left to pick up the pieces and build anew.

ℹ Getting There & Away

AIR

Lombok is very accessible by air, with daily flights to/from major Indonesian destinations such as Jakarta and Denpasar, plenty more to lesser Indonesian hubs, and international connections with Singapore and Kuala Lumpur.

Surrounded by rice fields and 5km south of Praya proper is the modern **Lombok International Airport** (LOP; www.lombok-airport.co.id; Jl Bypass Bil Praya). The airport is not huge, but has a full range of services such as ATMs, convenience stores and coffee shops.

BOAT

Public ferries connect Lembar on Lombok's west coast with Bali, and Labuhan Lombok on its east coast with Sumbawa. Fast-boat companies link Lombok with the Gili Islands and Bali. These are centred on Senggigi, Bangsal and Gili Gede.

PUBLIC BUS

Mandalika Terminal (Jl Pasar Bertais B8) in Mataram is the departure point for major cities in Bali, Sumbawa and Flores, via interisland ferries. For long-distance services, book tickets a day or two ahead at the terminal, or from a travel agent.

If you get to the terminal before 8am without a reservation, there may indeed be a spare seat on a bus going in your direction, but don't count on it, especially during holidays.

There are direct buses from Denpasar on Bali that connect to the Padangbai–Lembar ferry and then continue on to the Mandalika Terminal in Mataram (225,000Rp). Buses also connect to Bima via the Lombok–Sumbawa ferry (225,000Rp).

TOURIST SHUTTLE BUS

There are tourist shuttle-bus services between the main tourist centres in Lombok (Senggigi and Kuta) and most tourist centres in south Bali and the Gilis. Typically these combine a minibus with public ferries. Tickets can be booked directly or through a travel agent.

Getting Around

Moving around Lombok is easy, with a good – though often traffic-clogged – road across the middle of the island between Mataram and Labuhan Lombok.

TO/FROM THE AIRPORT

Thanks to multilane roads, Lombok International Airport is less than a 45-minute drive from both Mataram and Kuta and is well linked to the rest of the island.

Damri operates regular tourist buses, timed to meet flights; buy tickets in the arrivals area. Destinations include Mataram's Mandalika Terminal (30,000Rp), Senggigi (40,000Rp) and east to Selong (35,000Rp).

Taxi counters outside arrivals offer fixed-price rides to destinations that include Kuta (150,000Rp, 30 minutes), Mataram (180,000Rp, 40 minutes), Senggigi (300,000Rp, 75 minutes) and Bangsal (350,000Rp, 1¾ hours), where you can access the Gili Islands.

BEMO

Small, cheap, public bemos (minibuses) operate around population centres, often radiating out along predetermined routes from dedicated terminals.

BOAT

Ferries both public (slow and often overloaded) and private (faster and appreciably more expensive) can take you to Lombok's offshore attractions.

BUS

Almost every corner of Lombok can be reached by bus, mostly with private operators connecting transport and tourist hubs.

CAR & MOTORCYCLE

It's easy to hire a car in all the tourist areas (with/without driver per day from 600,000/350,000Rp). Motorbikes are also widely available from about 70,000Rp per day. Check your insurance arrangements carefully. Some agencies do not offer any coverage at all; others offer only basic coverage. Even insured Balinese vehicles are often not covered in Lombok.

There's little reason to bring a car or motorbike from Bali when you can avoid the ferry charges and easily rent your own wheels on Lombok.

TAXI

Metered taxis operate from the airport and other transport hubs.

WEST LOMBOK

As the economy of West Nusa Tenggara grows, west Lombok's biggest city, Mataram, grows along with it. Meanwhile the famed beach resort Senggigi continues in a 1990s time warp. The greatest allure is southwest of Lembar port, where the peninsula bends forward and back, the seas are placid and bucolic offshore islands beckon.

THE 2018 EARTHQUAKES

Some 1090 trekkers, guides and support staff were on the slopes of Gunung Rinjani (p299) on 29 July, 2018, when a shallow earthquake measuring 6.4 on the Richter scale struck the Sembalun Valley, triggering landslides that trapped them on the volcano. The trekkers were evacuated the following day, but the worst was yet to come.

Two larger earthquakes, each measuring 6.9 on the Richter scale, rocked the island over the next three weeks, damaging an estimated 80% of all structures in North Lombok, killing some 563 people and lifting the island by as much as 25cm by the time it all ended. The first of these larger quakes caused widespread panic on the Gili Islands, where tourists scrambled to catch rescue boats after a sleepless night in fear of a tsunami (which never actually materialised).

The final quake, located on a separate thrust fault to the prior two, convinced many in North Lombok to put off rebuilding for several weeks. With thousands of homeless earthquake refugees living in makeshift tent villages, the conditions were ripe for the consequent malaria outbreak. The government declared a health emergency in West Lombok in mid-September to bring it under control.

The hard-hit towns to the north of Rinjani (including Sire, Senaru, Sembalun Lawang and Sembalun Bumbung) were ostensibly closed to visitors at the time of research and face a very long road to recovery. Gunung Rinjani was similarly closed to trekkers. Senggigi and the Gili Islands were badly bruised, but are well into recovery mode and once again receiving tourists. Damage in Mataram was less severe and the city was operating as usual. The resort towns of South Lombok were largely unaffected by the quakes, with only minor cosmetic damages.

Getting There & Away

Public ferries (child/adult/motorcycle/car 29,000/46,000/125,000/917,000Rp, five to six hours) travel between Lembar's large ferry port and Padangbai in Bali. Passenger tickets are sold near the pier. Boats supposedly run 24 hours and leave about every 90 minutes, but the service can be unreliable – boats have even caught fire and run aground.

Bemo and bus connections are abundant and bemos run regularly to the Mandalika Terminal (p286) for 25,000Rp, so there's no reason to linger. Taxis cost around 100,000Rp to Mataram and 200,000Rp to Senggigi.

Mataram

☎0370 / POP 402,843

Lombok's capital is a sprawling amalgam of several once-separate towns with fuzzy borders: Ampenan (the port), Mataram (the administrative centre), Cakranegara (the business centre, often called simply 'Cakra') and Sweta to the east, where you'll find the Mandalika bus terminal. Mataram stretches for 12km from east to west.

There aren't many tourist attractions, yet Mataram's broad tree-lined avenues buzz with traffic, thrum with motorbikes and teem with classic markets and malls. If you're hungry for a blast of Indo realism, you'll find it here. Sights around Mataram include the old port town of Ampenan – if you pause you'll discover a still-tangible sense of the Dutch colonial era in the leafy main street and the older buildings.

Sights

★Pura Lingsar TEMPLE

(off Jl Gora II; grounds free, temple entry by donation; 8am-6pm) This large temple compound is the holiest in Lombok. It was built in 1714 by King Anak Agung Ngurah and is nestled beautifully in lush rice fields. It is multidenominational, with a temple for Balinese Hindus (Pura Gaduh) and one for followers of Lombok's mystical take on Islam, the Wektu Telu religion.

It's just 6km east of Mataram in the village of Lingsar. Take a bemo from the Mandalika Terminal to Narmada, another to Lingsar and ask to be dropped off at the temple.

Islamic Center Nusa Tenggara Barat MOSQUE

(☎0819 1732 5666; http://islamiccenter.ntbprov.go.id; cnr Jl Udayana & Jl Pejanggik; 5000Rp; casual visits 10am-5pm) Opened in 2016, and superficially damaged in the 2018 quakes, this towering green-and-gold mosque is the most striking building in Lombok, with fabulous views from the top of its tallest minaret (it rises 114m above Mataram). Foreigners in shorts will be provided with more modest clothing before entering.

Pura Meru HINDU TEMPLE

(Jl Selaparang; 8am-5pm) FREE Pura Meru is the largest and second-most important Hindu temple on Lombok. Built in 1720, it's dedicated to the Hindu trinity of Brahma, Vishnu and Shiva. The inner court has 33 small shrines and three thatched teak-wood *meru* (multi-tiered shrines). The central *meru*, with 11 tiers, is Shiva's house; the *meru* to the north, with nine tiers, is Vishnu's; and the nine-tiered *meru* to the south is Brahma's.

Mayura Water Palace PARK

(cnr Jl Selaparang & Jl Purba Sari; 25,000Rp; 7am-10pm) Built in 1744, this palace includes the former king's family temple, which is a pilgrimage site for Lombok's Hindus on 24 December. In 1894 it was the site of bloody battles between the Dutch and Balinese. You can get a slight sense of history here, but it's mostly just a public park these days with a polluted artificial lake.

Sleeping

Homestays and budget hotels are augmented by a few flashier hotels aimed at businesspeople. Staying in central Mataram is a good way to fully engage with the nontourist side of Lombok life.

Hotel Melati Viktor GUESTHOUSE $

(☎0370-633830; Jl Abimanyu 1; r 120,000Rp, with air-con & breakfast 200,000Rp) The high ceilings, 37 clean rooms and Balinese-style courtyards, complete with Hindu statues, make this one of the best-value places in town. It's forever growing and is now spread across three buildings on either side of Jl Abimanyu.

Hotel Lombok Raya HOTEL $$

(☎0370-632305; www.lombokrayahotel.com; Jl Panca Usaha 11; r incl breakfast 600,000-750,000Rp; P) Lombok Raya took more of a beating than most Mataram hotels in the 2018 quakes, but renovations were under way at the time of research. It's a well-located favourite of old-school business travellers, with 134 spacious, comfortable rooms with balconies. A glistening pool, well-equipped gym and bountiful breakfast buffet add to the appeal.

Mataram

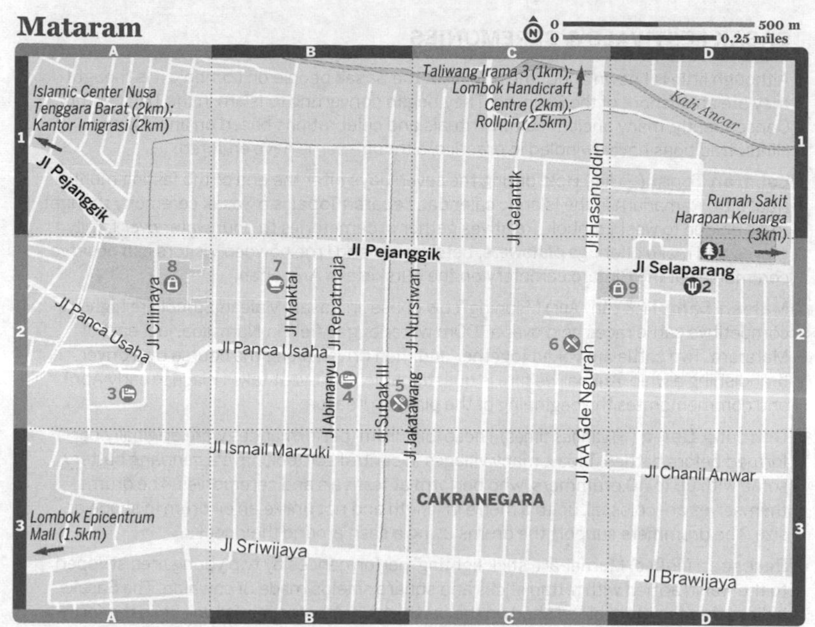

Eating & Drinking

The streets around the faded Mataram Mall are lined with Western-style fast-food outlets, Indonesian noodle bars and warungs (food shacks).

Ikan Bakar 99 SEAFOOD $

(☎0819 3313 8188; Jl Subak III 10; mains 30,000-55,000Rp; ⊙11am-10pm) Think squid, prawns, fish and crab, brushed with chilli sauce, perfectly grilled or fried, and drenched in spicy Padang or sticky sweet-and-sour sauce. You will eat among the Mataram families who fill the long tables in the arched, tiled dining room. It's in a Balinese neighbourhood.

Taliwang Irama 3 INDONESIAN $

(☎0370-629354; Jl Ade Irma Suryani 10; mains 20,000-50,000Rp; ⊙11am-10pm) Excellent spicy Indonesian dishes lure in diners day in and day out. Eat in the plant-shaded courtyard or inside. As testament to the popularity, there are vendors out front. The chicken here seems even more tender and spicy than the average bird on Lombok.

Mirasa BAKERY $

(☎0370-633096; Jl AA Gde Ngurah 88; snacks from 4000Rp; ⊙6am-10pm) Cakra's middle-class families adore this modern bakery. It does doughnuts, cookies and cakes as well as local wonton stuffed with chicken.

Mataram

Sights
1 Mayura Water Palace D2
2 Pura Meru D2

Sleeping
3 Hotel Lombok Raya A2
4 Hotel Melati Viktor B2

Eating
5 Ikan Bakar 99 .... B2
6 Mirasa C2

Drinking & Nightlife
7 Maktal Coffee Bar B2

Shopping
8 Mataram Mall A2
9 Pasar Cakranegara D2

★ Rollpin INTERNATIONAL $$

(www.rollpin.id; Jl Ahmad Yani; mains 50,000-100,000Rp; ⊙noon-10pm Tue-Sun; ☎) Fine dining, Mataram-style, in a leafy creekside setting northeast of the centre. Dig into grilled whole snapper, Lombok duck or steamed mahi-mahi and wash it down with creative mocktails like Pin Pure (mint, ginger, lime and honey). Excellent service and a lengthy kids menu add to the appeal.

SASAK FESTIVALS & CEREMONIES

Although little is known about the origins of the Sasak people on Lombok, it is thought they are an offshoot of the Balinese. They began converting to Islam in the 17th century. Consequently, many ancient cultural rituals and celebrations based on animist and Hindu traditions have dwindled in practice, although some have endured.

Lebaran Topat (Jun) Held during the seven days after the end of the fasting month (Idul Fitri; Ramadan) in the Islamic calendar, Lebaran Topat is a Sasak ceremony thought to be unique to west Lombok. Relatives gather in cemeteries to pour water over family graves and make offerings of flowers, betel leaves and lime powder. Visitors can observe ceremonies at the Bintaro cemetery on the outskirts of Ampenan.

Malean Sampi (early Apr) Meaning 'cow chase' in Sasak, Malean Sampi are highly competitive cattle races held over a 100m waterlogged field in Narmada, just east of Mataram. Two cattle are yoked together and then driven along the course by a driver brandishing a whip. Animal welfare is questionable. The event takes place in early April and commemorates the beginning of the planting season.

Gendang Beleq (various times) These 'big drum' performances were originally performed before battles. Today, many villages in central Lombok have a *gendang* battery, some with up to 40 drummers, who perform at festivals and ceremonies. The drums themselves are colossal, up to a metre in length and not unlike an oil drum in shape or size. The drummers support the drums using a sash around their necks.

Peresean (Dec) Martial-art 'stick fighting' performances by two young men stripped to the waist, armed with rattan sticks and square shields made of cowhide. The Sasaks believe that the more blood shed on the earth, the better the rainfall will be in the forthcoming wet season. In late July, demonstrations can be seen in Senggigi, and in late December there's a championship in Mataram.

Maktal Coffee Bar COFFEE
(www.facebook.com/maktalcoffeebar; Jl Maktal; 9am-11pm;) This hipstery little coffee bar does everything from cold drips to caramel lattes. The brews are local, strong, and you can buy the beans afterwards. Also does pancakes, dumplings and Indo staples (20,000Rp to 30,000Rp).

Shopping

Good-quality pearls, farmed in Lombok and Sumbawa, are a notable commodity here, particularly in Cakranegara.

★**Lombok Handicraft Centre** ARTS & CRAFTS
(Jl Kerajinan, off Jl Diponegoro; 8am-6pm) At Sayang Sayang (2km north of Cakra), this centre offers a wide range of small shops; look for the arched sign over the narrow road that reads 'Handy Craft'. Browse crafts, including masks, textiles and ceramics from across Nusa Tenggara. This is a great place to stroll around.

★**Pasar Mandalika** MARKET
(Bertais; 6am-6pm) There are no tourists at this vast market near the Mandalika bus terminal in Bertais, but it has everything else: fruit and veggies, fish (fresh and dried), baskets full of colourful, aromatic spices and grains, freshly butchered beef, palm sugar, pungent bricks of shrimp paste and cheaper handicrafts than you will find anywhere else in west Lombok.

It's a great place to get localised after you've overdosed on the *bule* (slang for foreigner) circuit.

Lombok Epicentrum Mall MALL
(0370-617 2999; www.lombokepicentrum.com; Jl Sriwijaya 333; 10am-10pm) With a cinema, food courts and the full spread of consumer pleasures, this four-floor mall is Lombok's biggest and fanciest.

Pasar Cakranegara MARKET
(cnr Jl AA Gede Ngurah & Jl Selaparang; 9am-6pm) Collection of quirky stalls, some of which sell good-quality ikat (traditional cloth), as well as an interesting food market. Think of it as a modern variation on a traditional market.

Mataram Mall MALL
(Jl Cilinaya; 9am-10pm) A multistorey shopping mall with a supermarket, department stores, electronics and clothes shops, and some international restaurants.

Information

MEDICAL SERVICES

Rumah Sakit Harapan Keluarga (☎0370-617 7009; www.harapankeluarga.co.id; Jl Ahmad Yani 9; ⏰24hr) The best private hospital on Lombok is just east of central Mataram and has English-speaking doctors.

MONEY

ATM machines are ubiquitous near malls. Most banks are found on or around Jl Pejanggik.

VISA RENEWAL

You can renew your Indonesian visa at the **Kantor Imigrasi** (Immigration Office; ☎0370-632520; Jl Udayana 2; ⏰8am-noon & 1-4pm Mon-Fri). The process takes three to four days.

Getting There & Away

BOAT

Should you want to sail to a far-flung Indonesian island from Lombok, you can make schedule enquiries and purchase tickets at the local **Pelni Office** (☎0370-637212; www.pelni.co.id; Jl Industri 1; ⏰8am-noon & 1-3.30pm Mon-Thu & Sat, 8-11am Fri), the national shipping line.

BUS

The Mandalika Terminal (p286), 3km from the centre and surrounded by the city's main market, is Lombok's biggest bus and bemo hub. Use the official ticket office to avoid touts and take yellow bemos to the city centre (5000Rp).

Long-distance buses for Sumbawa and Flores depart from here twice daily at 9am and 3pm. If you're travelling to Labuan Bajo on Flores (375,000Rp, 24 hours), you'll have to overnight in Bima (225,000Rp, 12 hours) if you take the morning bus; the afternoon one is direct. Damri buses over to Maluk and the Sumbawa surf towns leave at 9am and 9pm (90,000Rp, six hours).

A direct shuttle bus to Kuta departs at 11am daily (1½ hours, 60,000Rp). Buses and bemos departing hourly from the Mandalika Terminal include the following:

DESTINATION	FARE (RP)	DURATION
Airport (Damri Bus)	30,000	45min
Kuta (via Praya & Sengkol)	60,000	2-3hr
Labuhan Lombok	35,000	2½hr
Lembar	20,000	45min
Senggigi (via Ampenan)	15,000	1hr
Senggigi (direct Damri Bus)	40,000	45min

Getting Around

For a reliable metered taxi, use **Blue Bird Lombok Taksi** (☎0370-645000; www.bluebirdgroup.com). Solo travellers should download **Go-Jek** (www.go-jek.com), an app for cheap and reliable *ojeks* (motorbike taxis).

Senggigi

☎0370 / POP 52,000

Lombok's original tourist resort, Senggigi enjoys a fine location along a series of sweeping bays, with light-sand beaches below a backdrop of jungle-clad mountains and coconut palms. In the evening a setting blood-red sun sinks into the surf next to the giant triangular cone of Bali's Gunung Agung.

Less trendy these days than the Gilis or Kuta, and with an older crowd, Senggigi offers some excellent-value hotels and restaurants, many of which were hit hard by the 2018 earthquakes. While it remains somewhat tacky along its fringe, big strides were made both before the quakes and during the rebuilding phase to rein in some of the more salacious elements and return this family-friendly resort town to its 1990s heyday.

The greater Senggigi area spans 10km of coastal road; the upscale neighbourhood of **Mangsit** is 3km north of central Senggigi, while just beyond lie the picturesque beaches of **Malimbu** and **Nipah**.

Sights

Pura Batu Bolong HINDU TEMPLE

(off Jl Raya Senggigi; admission by donation; ⏰7am-7pm) It's not the grandest, but Pura Batu Bolong is Lombok's most appealing Hindu temple and is particularly lovely at sunset. Join ever-welcoming members of the Balinese community as they leave offerings at the 14 altars and pagodas that tumble down a rocky volcanic outcrop into the foaming sea about 2km south of central Senggigi. The rock underneath the temple has a natural hole, hence the name (*batu bolong* literally means 'rock with hole').

Activities

Snorkelling & Diving

There's reasonable snorkelling off the point in Senggigi, 3km north of the town. You can rent gear (per day 50,000Rp) from several spots on the beach. Diving trips from Senggigi usually visit the Gili Islands.

Senggigi

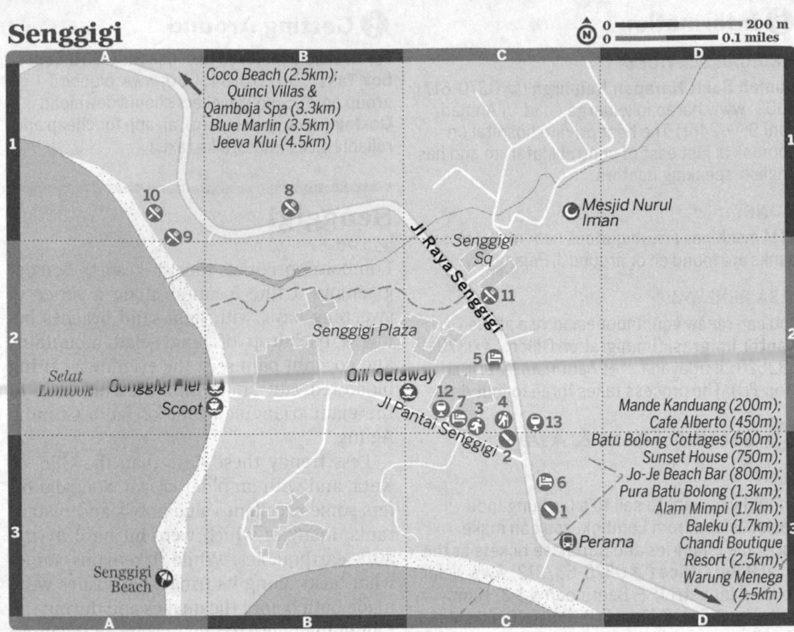

Senggigi

Activities, Courses & Tours

1 Blue Coral C3
2 Dream Divers C3
3 Hallo Lombok Spa C2
4 Rinjani Trekking Club C2

Sleeping

BC Inn .... (see 1)
5 Central Inn C2
6 Sendok Hotel C3
7 Tempatku C2

Eating

8 Asmara B1
9 Office A1
10 Spice A1
11 Square C2

Drinking & Nightlife

12 Honky Tonks Blues Bar & Grill C2
13 Papaya Café C2

Shopping

Asmara Collection .... (see 8)

Blue Coral DIVING

(☎0370-693441; Jl Raya Senggigi; 2 dives 850,000Rp, open-water course 4,950,000Rp; ⏲8am-9pm) This locally run dive shop in the heart of Senggigi offers no-decompression dives at between 18m and 22m deep in the waters off western Lombok and the Gili Islands. It also offers PADI certification courses and accommodation packages at the neat, modern guesthouse behind the shop.

Dream Divers DIVING

(☎0812 3754 583; www.dreamdivers.com; Jl Raya Senggigi; intro dives from 910,000Rp) The Senggigi office of the Gili diving original. Runs snorkelling trips out to the Gilis for 400,000Rp. It also runs dive courses and organises activities such as Rinjani treks.

Blue Marlin DIVING

(☎0370-69444 ext 115; www.bluemarlindive.com; Holiday Resort Lombok, Jl Raya Senggigi; 2-tank dive 1,100,000Rp, open-water course 5,750,000Rp) This local branch of a well-regarded Gili Trawangan dive shop offers dive courses and trips to the Gili Islands. It's about 3km north of Senggigi in an upmarket resort.

Massages & Spas

Very determined local masseurs, armed with mats, oils and attitude, hunt for business on Senggigi's beaches. Expect to pay about 80,000Rp for one hour after bargaining.

Most hotels can arrange a masseur to visit your room; rates start at about 100,000Rp. Be warned, some of the streetside 'salons' you'll find are fronts for more salacious services.

★ Qamboja Spa SPA
(☎0370-693800; www.quncivillas.com; Qunci Villas, Mangsit; massages from US$30; ⏰8am-10pm) Gorgeous hotel spa where you select your choice of oil depending on the effect and mood you require from your massage (uplifting, harmony...); types available include Thai, Balinese and shiatsu. It also offers yoga classes at 8am daily.

Hallo Lombok Spa SPA
(☎0819 0797 6902; Jl Pantai Senggigi; 1hr massage from 70,000Rp; ⏰10am-9pm) An inexpensive spa with a range of scrubs, massages and treatments. The *lulur* (scrub) massage is a real treat and includes a body mask.

Hiking

Rinjani Trekking Club TREKKING
(☎0370-693202, 0817 573 0415; www.info2lombok.com; Jl Raya Senggigi; 3-day/2-night trek US$245; ⏰9am-8pm) Responsible, knowledgeable and run by the friendly Ronnie, the well-established RTC is the best of the many outfits along Senggigi's main strip hawking Rinjani treks. There is a wide choice of guided hikes available; all include entrance fees, three meals a day, camping equipment and a donation towards Rinjani clean-up efforts.

Sleeping

Senggigi's accommodation is very spread out, but even if you're located a few kilometres away (say, in Mangsit), you won't be isolated as taxis are inexpensive. Travellers with a bigger budget will find an excellent spread of options; backpackers fewer.

Many businesses in Senggigi were closed at the time of research due to the high-magnitude earthquakes between July and August 2018.

Tempatku GUESTHOUSE $
(☎0812 4612 9504; tempatkulombok@gmail.com; Jl Pantai Senggigi, Senggigi Plaza; r 200,000-240,000Rp; ❄📶) A spotless, centrally located budget option above a tasty Indonesian restaurant of the same name. The large, tiled rooms have some nice local touches and share two common bathrooms with hot water. There's also a helpful tour-booking desk onsite.

BC Inn GUESTHOUSE $
(☎0370-619 7880, 0876 595 0549; http://bcinnsenggigi.com; Jl Raya Senggigi; r from 200,000Rp; 📶) Spick and span, comfortable and right in the heart of Senggigi, BC is named for the Blue Coral dive shop, which it sits behind. All rooms have satellite TV, wi-fi, decent beds, walk-in showers and wooden decor. Two people buying a dive package get a night free.

Baleku GUESTHOUSE $
(☎0818 0360 0009; Jl Raya Senggigi; r 225,000-300,000Rp; ❄📶🏊) Set 300m south of Pura Batu Bolong, this thatched brick compound is compact, but there's a range of 15 good-value rooms, the most expensive of which have hot water and air-con. It's a little out of the way but it offers free transport to and from Senggigi town. The pool seems to fill all available space.

Sendok Hotel HOTEL $
(☎0813 3743 5453; Jl Raya Senggigi; dm 135,000Rp, r with fan/air-con from 200,000/400,000Rp; ❄📶🏊) Fronted by a friendly bar-restaurant, this hotel offers 17 rooms amid lovingly tended gardens nibbled by sunburnt rabbits and embellished with Hindu shrines and statues. The cheaper rooms are basic and don't have hot water. There's a huge jump in quality if you spend a few more rupiahs. All have private front porches.

Central Inn HOTEL $
(☎0370-692006; http://centralinnsenggigi.com; Jl Raya Senggigi; r from 250,000Rp; ❄📶🏊) The 52 rooms in motel-style blocks have high ceilings, shiny tiles and small seating areas out front. It's on the beach side of the main drag, though not on the sand. The street-facing

WORTH A TRIP

TAMAN WISATA ALAM KERANDANGAN

This pleasant, little-visited nature reserve is ideal for escaping the tourist bustle of Senggigi and indulging in a few hours of strolling in the rainforest. The Princess Twin and Swallow Cave waterfalls lie on the marked trail (which can get a little indistinct in parts) and there's the chance of seeing rare butterflies and black monkeys (alongside the common kind). To get here, head north of town to Mangsit, then take Jalan Wisata Alam inland through the Kerandangan Valley.

block was badly damaged in the 2018 earthquakes and closed at the time of research.

Sunset House HOTEL $$

(0370-692020; www.sunsethouse-lombok.com; Jl Raya Senggigi 66; r incl breakfast 800,000-1,100,000Rp;) Offers 20 rooms, all with a tasteful, well-equipped simplicity, in a quiet ocean-front location towards Pura Batu Bolong. Rooms on the upper floors have sweeping ocean views towards Bali. Wi-fi is only available in public areas. Good pool area and deck.

Alam Mimpi HOTEL $$

(0370-617 0645; http://alammimpilombok.com; Jl Vincent van Gogh; r incl breakfast 550,000Rp;) South of the centre and inland, this modern compound makes the most of its quiet location. The 14 rooms surround a large pool and have balconies and terraces. The design is refreshingly modern and the upper-floor cafe has wide views. There's a shuttle to town and the beach.

Batu Bolong Cottages HOTEL $$

(0370-693198, 0370-693065; bbcresort_lombok@yahoo.com; Jl Raya Senggigi; r 450,000-800,000Rp;) Charming two-level bungalow-style rooms by the sand are the best bets at this well-run hotel, which straddles both sides of the road south of the centre. The beachfront rooms have quaint touches such as carved doors, and there's a low-key pool area. The rest of the rooms are in a more standard block at the back. Good breakfast.

★ **Qunci Villas** RESORT $$$

(0370-693800; www.quncivillas.com; Jl Raya Mangsit, Mangsit; r US$150-250;) A spectacular, lovingly imagined property that comes close to a luxe experience. Everything, from the food to the pool area to the spa, and especially the sea views (160m of beachfront), is magical. It has 78 rooms (including many villas) that, together with the other diversions here, give you little reason to leave.

Chandi Boutique Resort RESORT $$$

(0370-692198; www.the-chandi.com; Jl Raya Senggigi, Batu Layar; r from US$150;) A stylish boutique hotel amid the palms about 1km south of Pura Batu Bolong. Each of the 15 luxe bungalows has an outdoor living room and a hip modern interior with high ceilings and groovy outdoor bathrooms. The ample oceanfront perch is likely to absorb your daylight hours.

Jeeva Klui RESORT $$$

(0370-693035; www.jeevaklui.com; Jl Raya Klui Beach; r from US$200, villas from US$265;) This is why you came to the tropics: a palm-shaded, shimmering infinity pool and a lovely, almost private beach, sheltered by a rocky outcrop. The 35 rooms and villas are evocatively thatched, and have bamboo columns and private porches. Villas are luxurious, private and have their own pools. It's one bay north of Mangsit.

Eating

Senggigi's dining scene ranges from fancy international eating to simple warungs. At sunset, locals head to hilltop lookouts alongside Jl Raya Senggigi where vendors sell grilled corn and fresh coconuts – a great experience for a sober sundowner. Many of the more tourist-oriented places offer free transport for evening diners – phone for a ride.

Warung Cak Poer INDONESIAN $

(www.facebook.com/warungcakpoer; Jl Raya Senggigi; mains 20,000-30,000Rp; 10am-11pm) This roadside warung south of town feeds the locals with hot-outta-the-wok Indo classics. Grab a plastic stool at a battered metal table, open a pack of *krupuk* (Indonesian crackers) and order the nasi goreng, made extra hot *(ekstra pedas)* and with extra garlic *(bawang putih ekstra)*. You'll be smiling (and sweating) through tears

Mande Kanduang INDONESIAN $

(Jl Raya Senggigi; mains 20,000Rp; 8am-11pm) The name means 'biological mother' and that's just who's doing the work at this barely there, open-air roadside cafe. No-compromises Indonesian cooking is the order of the day here; the *kepalaq ikan kakap* (fish head stew) is much revered. Duck into the cooking area to see what else is bubbling away.

★ **Coco Beach** INDONESIAN $$

(0817 578 0055; off Jl Raya Senggigi, Pantai Kerandangan; mains 55,000-70,000Rp; 11am-9pm;) This wonderful beachside restaurant 2km north of Senggigi has a blissfully secluded setting off the main road. Dining is at individual thatch-covered tables, with many choices for vegetarians. The nasi goreng and madras curry are locally renowned, and the seafood is the best in the area. It has a full bar and blends its own authentic *jamu* tonics (herbal medicines).

Square INTERNATIONAL $$
(☎0370-693688; www.squarelombok.com; Jl Raya Senggigi; mains 100,000-200,000Rp; ⏲11am-11pm; 📶) An upscale restaurant with beautifully crafted seating and a menu that features Western and Indonesian fusion fare. The cooking is a cut above the local norm in terms of ambition. Many newcomers to Indonesia have been introduced to the cuisine by the tourist-friendly tasting menu. Get a table away from the road noise.

Cafe Alberto ITALIAN $$
(☎0370-693039; www.cafealberto.com; Jl Raya Senggigi; mains 55,000-115,000Rp; ⏲8am-11pm; 📶) This long-standing, beachside Italian kitchen serves a variety of pasta dishes, but is known for its pizza. It offers free transport to and from your hotel, as well as generous surprises (like nibbles or digestifs). Best bit: wiggling your toes in the sand while sipping a cold one under the moonlight.

Spice INTERNATIONAL $$
(☎0370-619 7373; www.spice-lombok.com; Jl Raya Senggigi, Pasar Seni; mains 60,000-120,000Rp; ⏲noon-11pm) Spice has airy quarters in the back of the euphemistically named Art Market. Tables on the sand are perfect for sunset drinks chosen from the long list. There are upscale pub snacks. Later, the stylish upstairs dining room catches the breezes. The cuisine features global, island and beach flavours.

Asmara INTERNATIONAL $$
(☎0370-693619; www.asmara-group.com; Jl Raya Senggigi; mains 45,000-150,000Rp; ⏲8am-11pm; 📶👪) An ideal family choice, this place spans the culinary globe from tuna carpaccio to burgers to Lombok's own *Sate pusut* (minced-meat or fish sate). It also has a sizable kids menu. Service and presentation are smooth.

Warung Menega SEAFOOD $$
(☎0853 3865 3044; Jl Raya Senggigi, Pantai Batu Layar; meals 80,000-120,000Rp; ⏲11am-11pm; 📶) If you fled Bali before experiencing the Jimbaran fish grills, you can make up for it at this beachside seafood barbecue. Choose from a daily catch of barracuda, squid, snapper, grouper, lobster, tuna and prawns – all of which are grilled over smouldering coconut husks and served on candlelit tables on the sand. Good sambal selection.

Office INTERNATIONAL $$
(☎0370-693162; Jl Raya Senggigi, Pasar Seni; mains 55,000-70,000Rp; ⏲9am-10pm; 📶) This pub near the so-called 'art market' (which mostly offers cheap souvenirs) has typical Indonesian and Western choices along with pool tables, ball games and barflies. It also offers a Thai menu, which is the choice of those in the know. Tables overlooking the bay and its bobbing fishing boats and pleasurecraft are among Senggigi's best places for a sundowner.

Drinking & Nightlife

Not too long ago, Senggigi's bar scene was pretty vanilla, with most cafes and restaurants doing double duty. However, like something out of a Pattaya fever dream, huge cinderblock buildings went up on the centre's outskirts in the 2010s, featuring karaoke joints and massage parlours.

Few miss the chance to enjoy a sunset beverage at one of the many low-key places along the beach.

Jo-Je Beach Bar BAR
(☎0878-6388-1436; off Jl Raya Senggigi; ⏲8am-11pm) A classic beach bar with multicolour beanbags and happy-hour prices that coincide with the sunset. The cocktails are exceptionally strong and there's also OK Indonesian and Western food.

Papaya Café BAR
(☎0370-693161; Jl Raya Senggigi; ⏲11am-midnight) The decor here is slick, with exposed stone walls, sturdy wooden furniture and evocative tribal art. There's a wide selection of imported liquor. By day the road noise intrudes, but it dies down at night, especially when live bands drown it out.

Honky Tonks Blues Bar & Grill BAR
(☎0370-619 7717; off Jl Pantai Senggigi, Senggigi Plaza; ⏲2pm-midnight Wed-Mon) We won't even try to make sense of this British-owned, New Orleans–inspired jazz bar with great Aussie meat pies and rugby league playing on the TVs. Oh, and the decor pays homage to the Rolling Stones (the owner's seen them live a mere 72 times!). Come for live jazz Thursdays to Saturdays and return Sundays for evening roasts.

Shopping

Asmara Collection ARTS & CRAFTS
(☎0370-693109; Jl Raya Senggigi; ⏲9.30am-9.30pm) A cut above the rest, this store, next to the namesake restaurant, has well-selected tribal art, including richly detailed carvings and textiles from Sumba and Flores.

Getting There & Away

BEMO

Regular bemos travel between Senggigi and Ampenan's Kebon Roek terminal (5000Rp, 30 minutes), where you can connect to Mataram (10,000Rp, 20 minutes). Wave them down on the main drag. Bemos make the coast road run north towards Bangsal Harbour in the morning, less often later (20,000Rp, one hour). Note that you'll have to get off in Pemenang, from where it's a 1.2km walk to the harbour.

BOAT

Fast boats to Bali leave from the large pier right in the centre of the beach. Some companies sell tickets from an office out on the pier; others sell from the shore nearby.

Gili Getaway (☎0823 3918 8281; http://giligetaway.com; Jl Pantai Senggigi; ⏲8am-4pm) Useful services to Gili T and Gili Air (both 200,000Rp) as well as to Gili Gede (250,000Rp).

Perama (☎0370-693008; www.peramatour.com; Jl Raya Senggigi; ⏲7am-10pm) An economical shuttle-bus service that connects with the public ferry from Lembar to Padangbai in Bali (125,000Rp, 9am), from where there are onward shuttle-bus connections to Sanur, Kuta and Ubud (all 175,000Rp). These trips can take eight or more hours. It also offers a bus-and-boat connection to the Gilis for a reasonable 150,000Rp (two hours, 8am). It saves some hassle at Bangsal Harbour.

Scoot (☎0828 9701 5565; www.scootcruise.com; Senggigi Pier) Daily fast boats to Nusa Lembongan (675,000Rp) and Sanur (750,000Rp) on Bali, leaving at 12.30pm.

Kencana Adventure (☎0812 2206 6066; www.kencanaadventure.com; Jl Raya Senggigi; one-way deck/shared cabin 1,650,000/2,000,000Rp; ⏲9am-5pm Mon-Sat) For those going on adventures further into Nusa Tenggara, this operator has an office where you can get info about heading east to Labuan Bajo.

TAXI

A metered taxi to Lembar costs around 170,000Rp; to Praya around 200,000Rp; and to Bangsal Harbour, not served by public bemo, about 100,000Rp.

Getting Around

Senggigi's central area is easy to negotiate on foot. If you're staying further from the centre, note that many restaurants offer a free lift for diners.

Motorcycles can be rented from 60,000Rp per day. Vehicle rental is competitive and ranges from 200,000Rp to 350,000Rp per day. A car and driver costs from 500,000Rp per day.

SOUTHWESTERN PENINSULA

The sweeping coastline that stretches west of Lembar is blessed with boutique sleeps on deserted beaches and tranquil offshore islands. You can while away weeks here among the famous surf breaks, salty old mosques, friendly locals and relatively pristine islands. In fact, the buzz has started and the beautiful offshore islands are now touted as 'the next Gilis'.

The only off-note on the landscape is the dull town of Sekotong, which you have to pass through on your way west. Otherwise, you follow the narrow coastal road along the contours of the peninsula, skirting white-sand beach after white-sand beach on your way to the village of Bangko Bangko and one of Asia's legendary surf breaks, Tanjung Desert (Desert Point), which has one of the world's longest left-hand barrels and a thin beach.

Information

The only ATM in the Southwestern Peninsula is in Sekotong.

Getting There & Away

BEMO

Infrequent bemos run between Lembar and Pelangan (30,000Rp, 1½ hours) via Sekotong and Tembowong. West of Pelangan transport is highly irregular.

BOAT

You can take the slow public ferry from Bali to Lembar and then arrange ground transport to the Southwestern Peninsula.

CAR & MOTORCYCLE

Although winding, the road is in good shape almost until the end, when suddenly it switches to deeply rutted gravel and dirt. You can traverse it with a car or motorbike, but you'll have to drive at a walking pace. After 2km you'll reach a fork; turn right for the fishing village of Bangko Bangko. Turn left for another 1km of road misery that ends at the oceanic wonders of Tanjung Desert. Your reward for enduring the horrible last 3km of road to Tanjung Desert? An entrance fee of 10,000Rp per person and 5000Rp per vehicle.

Tanjung Desert

Tanjung Desert (Desert Point/Bangko Bangko; access per person/vehicle 10,000/5000Rp) is legendary and even nonexpert surfers will find much to enjoy. As you make the drive along the coast, you'll see various water-sports vendors offering boat rides to the Southwest Gilis. Feel free to stop and negotiate a day out at the beaches at the offshore islands for a fee beginning at 500,000Rp. These trips can include snorkelling stops and other fun.

Often called 'the world's best wave', this famous break draws skilled surfers from around the world. Patience is a virtue: the conditions sometimes go calm for a time. But when the swells are coming in, you get very long, hollow waves that usually end in a barrel. Peak season is May to October.

Sleeping

There are a few hotels and resorts sprinkled along the northern coast of the peninsula, though the most atmospheric beaches and lodging are on the offshore islands. Top-end places have dive operations. Note that Tanjung Desert gets crowded during peak surfing season (May to October), when you may not find room at the extremely basic huts. Several beachfront warungs there serve simple meals and cold beer and will let you crash for about 120,000Rp a night.

Desert Point Bungalows BUNGALOW $
(☎0878 6585 5310; nurbaya_sari@yahoo.com; Tanjung Desert; bungalow 200,000Rp) The most 'upscale' place to stay right at Tanjung Desert (that's because there's a phone number you can try calling) has 10 rather shack-like bungalows. A generator provides power at certain times and there's a two-level surf-viewing platform.

Cocotino's RESORT $$$
(☎0819 0797 2401; www.cocotinos-sekotong.com; Jl Sekotong Raya, Tanjung Empat; r/villa from US$200/410; ❄📶🏊) This walled compound along the main road 20km west of Lembar has an oceanfront location, a private beach and 36 high-quality bungalows (some with lovely outdoor bathrooms, some with sea views). It offers deals via its website. The setting is a sublime tropical idyll.

Gili Gede & the Southwest Gilis

☎0370

This chain of small sandy isles promises the peace and tranquility that were once hallmarks of those *other* Gili Islands to the north. On each island, soft white sands give way to turquoise waters and prismatic undersea realms that are ripe for exploration. To island-hop these 'secret gilis' on a local fishing boat is to float back to a simpler time.

The largest and most developed of the islands, **Gili Gede** (pronounced the way an Aussie might say g'day) has a few bungalows, some paved motorbike paths, friendly fishing villages and little else.

Gili Asahan is an idyllic spot: soothing winds gust, birds flutter and gather in the grass just before sunset, muted calls to prayer rumble and the stars and moon light up the sky. Though not as suited for snorkelling as nearby islands, it makes up for it with some of the sandiest beaches in the Southwest Gilis. **Gili Layar** is so laid back that it's almost comatose.

Sleeping & Eating

Gili Gede is the most natural base for exploring the Southwest Gilis, with the largest selection of accommodation. Refreshingly, there is no real tourist ghetto here as small bungalow complexes are found on a variety of beaches across the island. You can also find more isolated accommodation on Gili Asahan and Gili Layar.

Most visitors eat where they sleep, through there are a few stand-alone restaurants on Gili Gede serving both Indonesian and European fare.

Marina del Ray BUNGALOW $
(☎0823 2372 4873; www.lombokmarinadelray.com; Gili Gede; r/bungalow from 370,000/550,000Rp; @) Formerly known as Madak Belo, this is a fun beach-bum island paradise with ooh-la-la views and three basic rooms upstairs in the main wood-and-bamboo lodge. They share a bathroom and a lounge area. It also has two nicer bungalows with queen beds and private bathrooms.

Via Vacare BUNGALOW $
(☎0812 3732 4565; www.viavacare.com; Gili Gede; all-inclusive dm 300,000Rp, s/d bungalow 500,000/750,000Rp) This all-inclusive resort for the backpacker set envisions itself as a place to practise the art of doing nothing. Rates include three daily meals, snorkelling gear, yoga (in high season) and transport to/from the main harbour. The 'dorm' is just a mattress on an open-air platform, but the bungalows are spacious and have sea views. Expect cold bucket showers as there's no running water.

OFF THE BEATEN TRACK

SNORKELLING THE SOUTHWEST GILIS

With untouched corals and a wealth of marine life (including lionfish, scorpionfish, moray eels and large schools of fusiliers), snorkelling the shallow reefs around the Southwest Gilis is a highlight of any trip to Lombok.

The northwestern coast of Gili Gede provides the best shore snorkelling for those sleeping on the island, but you'll probably want to hire a boatman to take you to the southeastern coasts of **Gili Layar** and **Gili Rengit**, both of which have extremely healthy coral and massive schools of fish. You can also tack on tiny **Gili Goleng**, where seahorses amble around in the offshore seagrass. The entire trip should cost around 500,000Rp for the boat and gear.

Closer to Lembar are the smaller islands of the Gita Nada group (**Gili Nanggu**, **Gili Kedis**, **Gili Tangkong** and **Gili Sudak**), all of which are fantastic for snorkelling. Boatmen can take you here from Gili Gede for about 600,000Rp, or you can visit on a day trip from Kuta with Scuba Froggy (p305) or Mimpi Manis (p306).

★**Hula Hoop** BUNGALOW **$$**
(www.hulagili.com; Gili Gede; r/bungalow 650,000/950,000Rp;) This fantastically bohemian getaway is tucked away on a quiet west-coast hill with four stylish *lumbung* (rice-barn) rooms and four bigger and better-appointed bungalows. All get a great breeze and offer spectacular sea and sunset views. There are also seaside hammocks and funky chill zones with hanging shell art.

★**Pearl Beach Resort** BUNGALOW **$$**
(0819 0724 7696; www.pearlbeach-resort.com; Gili Asahan; cottage/bungalow from 790,000/1,190,000Rp;) One of the few places to sleep on Gili Asahan, cottages are simple, bamboo affairs with outdoor bathrooms and a hammock on the porch. The 10 bungalows are chic, with polished concrete floors, soaring ceilings, gorgeous outdoor bathrooms and fabulous daybed swings on the wooden porches. There's great diving, kayaks and more.

Kokomo Gili Gede RESORT **$$$**
(0819 0732 5135; http://kokomogiligede.com; Gili Gede; villas incl breakfast from 2,750,000Rp;) The poshest resort in the Southwest Gilis, Kokomo has 15 large villas in a beautiful position right by the ocean. Units have fridges and other kitchen appliances. The decor picks up the stark white beauty of the sand. A stay here will be a long study in white, backed by the blue of the water.

Tanjungan Bukit INDONESIAN **$$**
(0818 0529 0314; https://tanjungan-bukit-id.book.direct; Gili Gede; mains 40,000-90,000Rp) This is easily the island's most stylish bar and restaurant. Dine on fresh seafood and refined Sumatran fare at the bougainvillea-shaded tables, or down some cocktails (or wine by the glass!) on the beanbag-filled deck.

There are six beautifully designed bungalows surrounding a pool on the hill behind the restaurant (500,000Rp to 600,000Rp).

ℹ Getting There & Around

Taxi boats (per person from 25,000Rp) shuttle from Tembowong on the mainland to Gili Gede, Gili Asahan or Gili Layar. You'll see them near the old Pertamina gas station. There is no fixed price or schedule, but there are always boatmen waiting in the daylight hours. When you're done negotiating the price, they'll take you directly to your accommodation.

Gili Getaway (0813 3707 4147; http://giligetaway.com; Kokomo Gili Gede) has daily fast boat services from Gili Gede to Gili T and Gili Air (450,000Rp), as well as Senggigi (250,000Rp) and Serangan Harbour on Bali (710,000Rp).

There are no cars or taxis on the island (though a few residents have motorbikes). Unless you hire a fisher to drop you at a distant beach, walking around the perimeter – or along interior paths – is the only way to get around.

NORTH & CENTRAL LOMBOK

Lush and fertile, Lombok's scenic interior is stitched together with rice terraces, tropical forests, undulating tobacco fields and fruit and nut orchards, and is crowned by sacred Gunung Rinjani. Entwined in all this big nature are traditional Sasak settlements, many of which were hard hit by the earthquakes in 2018. With your own wheels you can explore black-sand fishing beaches, inland villages and waterfalls.

Gunung Rinjani

Lording it over the northern half of Lombok, Gunung Rinjani (3726m) is Indonesia's second-tallest volcano. It's an astonishing peak, sacred to Hindus and Sasaks who make pilgrimages to the summit and lake to leave offerings for the gods and spirits. To the Balinese, Rinjani is one of three sacred mountains, along with Bali's Agung and Java's Bromo. Sasaks ascend throughout the year around the full moon.

The mountain has climatic significance. Its peak attracts a steady stream of swirling rain clouds, while its ash emissions bring fertility to the island's rice fields and tobacco crops, feeding a tapestry of paddies, fields, and cashew and mango orchards.

Rinjani also attracts many trekkers who thrill to the otherworldly vistas. The volcano has become so popular that there were more than a thousand climbers on it during the first of the 2018 earthquakes, after which its slopes were evacuated. It remained closed for several months.

Inside Gunung Rinjani's immense caldera, sitting 600m below the rim, is the stunning, 6km-wide, turquoise crescent lake Danau Segara Anak (Child of the Sea). The Balinese toss gold and jewellery into the lake in a ceremony called *pekelan*, before they slog their way towards the sacred summit.

The mountain's newest cone, the minor peak of Gunung Baru (2351m), only emerged a couple of hundred years ago, its scarred, smouldering profile rising above the lake as an ominous reminder of the apocalyptic power of nature. This peak has been erupting fitfully for the last decade, periodically belching plumes of smoke and ash over the entire Rinjani caldera. Also in the crater are natural hot springs known as Aiq Kalak. Locals suffering from skin diseases trek here with a satchel of medicinal herbs to bathe and scrub in the bubbling mineral water.

The official website of **Gunung Rinjani National Park** (Taman Nasional Gunung Rinjani;

A BIG SHAKE-UP ON RINJANI

An estimated 1090 trekkers, guides and support staff were on the slopes of Gunung Rinjani on 29 July 2018, when an earthquake measuring 6.4 on the Richter scale struck the Sembalun Valley, triggering numerous landslides. Trapped on the volcano overnight, most tourists were rescued the following day in a large-scale evacuation operation that captured headlines around the world. Rinjani was subsequently closed to trekkers. Two additional earthquakes over the next three weeks, both measuring 6.9, further complicated plans for reopening Rinjani, as many area hotels and travel agencies were shaken to pieces.

Some local imams blamed the ballooning number of tourists climbing the sacred peak for causing the earthquakes, so there was some initial resistance to reopening it. However, the economic importance of the trekking industry in northern Lombok was hard to negate, and exploratory trips up Rinjani began in October to assess the viability of the original routes. The popular Senaru and Sembalun hiking trails had 14 landslide points apiece, with severe damage to many shelters, guard posts, park offices and water sources. Repair work was expected to begin in May 2019, with hopes of reopening these routes in late 2019 or early 2020. The new two-day, one-night Benang Stokel route to the crater rim from Aik Berik (about 30km east of Mataram on Rinjan's south side) was the only trek open at the time of research, as it did not have any landslide damage. However, there was a quota of only 150 people per day, and trekking down to the crater lake remained off limits. Trekking agencies in Senaru and the Sembalun Valley were operating alternative overnight treks up Gunung Nangi (2330m) and Bukit Pergasingan (1700m), as well as day trips to local waterfalls and villages, until paths up Rinjani reopened.

The following tour operators were up and running at the time of research and are your best sources for the latest information on routes and conditions:

- Rudy Trekker (p301)
- Rinjani Information Centre (p302)
- John's Adventures (p301)
- Senaru Trekking (p301)

(☎0370-660 8874; www.rinjaninationalpark.com) has good maps, info and a useful section on reported scams by dodgy hiking operators.

Sire

A hidden upmarket enclave, the Sire (or Sira) peninsula points out towards the three Gilis. It's blessed with gorgeous, broad white-sand beaches and good snorkelling offshore. Opulent resorts are now established here alongside a couple of fishing villages. Look out for the small **Hindu temple**, just beyond the Oberoi resort, which has shrines built into the coastal rocks and sublime ocean views.

Sire is a very short drive off the main road just north of Bangsal. The resorts can arrange any needed transport.

★Rinjani Beach Eco Resort BOUTIQUE HOTEL **$$**
(☎0819 3677 5960; www.rinjanibeach.com; Karang Atas; bungalows 350,000-1,350,000Rp; ❄ ≋) This gem has bamboo bungalows, each with its own theme; hammocks on private porches; and access to a pool on the black-sand beach. Two cheaper, smaller cold-water bungalows cater to budget travellers. It also has a restaurant, plus sea kayaks and mountain bikes. Waste water is treated and used to water the lush grounds. It's just along the coast from Sire.

Tugu Lombok RESORT **$$$**
(☎0370-612 0111; www.tuguhotels.com; bungalows/villas incl breakfast from US$220/330; ❄ ≈ ≋) An astonishing hotel, this larger-than-life amalgamation of luxury accommodation, eclectic design and spiritual Indonesian heritage sits on a wonderful white-sand beach. Room decor is a fantasy of Indonesian artistic heritage, while the exquisite spa is modelled on Java's Buddhist Borobudur. Smart green practices abound.

Oberoi Lombok RESORT **$$$**
(☎0370-613 8444; www.oberoihotels.com; r from US$280, villas from US$500; ❄ ≈ ≋) For sheer get-away-from-it-all bliss the Oberoi simply excels. The hotel's core is a triple-level pool, which leads the eye to a lovely private beach. Indonesian rajah-style luxury is the look: sunken marble bathtubs, teak floors, antique furniture and oriental rugs. The 50 rooms and villas took a hard hit in the 2018 quakes, but a planned reopening was set for mid 2019.

Northwest Coast

Market towns and glimpses of coast are the norm on the run around the northwest coast of Lombok. The green slopes of Gunung Rinjani increasingly dominate the inland view and traffic blissfully fades away.

Just northeast of Gondang village, which is on the main Bangsal–Bayan road, a 6km trail heads inland to **Air Terjun Tiu Pupas** (entry 30,000Rp), a 30m waterfall that's only worth seeing in the wet season. Trails continue from here to other wet-season waterfalls, including **Air Terjun Gangga**, the most beautiful of all. A guide (about 80,000Rp) is useful to navigate the confusing trails in these parts.

Wektu Telu, Lombok's animist-tinted form of Islam, was born in humble thatched mosques nestled in these Rinjani foothills. The best example is **Masjid Kuno Bayan Beleq**, next to the village of Beleq. Its low-slung roof, dirt floors and bamboo walls reportedly date from 1634, making this

WEKTU TELU

Wektu Telu is a complex mixture of Hindu, Islamic and animist beliefs, though it's now officially classified as a sect of Islam. At its forefront is a physical concept of the Holy Trinity. The sun, moon and stars represent heaven, earth and water, while the head, body and limbs represent creativity, sensitivity and control.

As recently as 1965, the vast majority of Sasaks in northern Lombok were Wektu Telu, but under Suharto's 'New Order' government, indigenous religious beliefs were discouraged and enormous pressure was placed on Wektu Telu to become Wektu Lima (Muslims who pray five times a day). But in the Wektu Telu heartland around Bayan, locals have been able to maintain their unique beliefs by differentiating their cultural traditions (Wektu Telu) from religion (Islam). Most do not fast for the full month of Ramadan and only attend the mosque for special occasions, and there's also widespread consumption of *brem* (alcoholic rice wine).

mosque the oldest on Lombok. Inside is a huge old drum that served as the call to prayer before PA systems.

Getting There & Away

Public transport north from Bangsal is infrequent. Several bemos a day go from Mataram's Mandalika Terminal (p286) to Bayan, but you'll have to get connections in Pemenang and/or Anyar, which can be difficult to navigate. Simplify things and get your own wheels.

Senaru

The scenic villages that make up Senaru merge into one along a steep road with sweeping volcano and sea views. Most visitors here are Gunung Rinjani–bound, but beautiful walking trails and spectacular waterfalls beckon to those who aren't.

Senaru derives its name from *sinaru*, which means light. As you ascend the hill towards the sky and clouds, you'll see just why this makes sense.

Senaru was hit particularly hard by the 2018 earthquakes. The recuperation process was expected to last several years and returning tourists will be a vital part of it, putting trekking guides back to work and funnelling much-needed cash into the rebuilding of area homes.

Sights

Air Terjun Sindang Gila WATERFALL

(10,000Rp) This spectacular set of falls is a 20-minute walk from Senaru via a lovely forest and hillside trail. The hardy make for the creek, edge close and then get pounded by the hard, foaming cascade that explodes over black volcanic stone 40m above. You do not need a guide to reach Air Terjun Sindang Gila; it is on a well-marked path.

Air Terjun Tiu Kelep WATERFALL

A further 50 minutes or so uphill from the popular Air Terjun Sindang Gila is this waterfall with a swimming hole. The track is steep and guides are recommended (100,000Rp each; negotiable). Long-tailed macaques (locals call them *kera*) and the much rarer silvered leaf monkey sometimes appear.

Activities

The main reason that people come to Senaru is for the trek up Gunung Rinjani. But if you have extra time, or aren't heading up the volcano, there are other worthy hikes here.

Guided walks and community tourism activities can be arranged at most guesthouses – they include a **rice-terrace and waterfalls walk** (per person 200,000Rp), which takes in Air Terjun Sindang Gila, rice paddies and an old bamboo mosque, and the **Senaru Panorama Walk** (350,000Rp per person), which incorporates the former plus stunning views and insights into local traditions.

Rudy Trekker HIKING

(☎0812 3929 9896, 0822 3531 4474; www.rudytrekker.com) Rudy Trekker is a conscientious organisation based in Senaru with a wide variety of itineraries for regional treks and a great list of what to pack displayed on the wall. The office is near the entrance to Air Terjun Sindang Gila falls and connected to Rudy's trekking lodge (rooms from 500,000Rp).

John's Adventures HIKING

(☎0817 578 8018; www.rinjanimaster.com) John's Adventures is a very experienced outfitter that has toilet tents, thick sleeping mats and multiple Rinjani itineraries that start from either Senaru or Sembalun. The Senaru office is 2km below the Gunung Rinjani Park Office.

Senaru Trekking HIKING

(☎0818 540 673; www.senarutrekking.com; Jl Pariwisata) Staffed by knowledgeable local guides and porters, including Rinjani expert Jul, Senaru Trekking offers a 5% discount to trekkers who carry a full bag of trash down from the mountain.

Sleeping

Note that many hotels were flattened in the earthquakes of July and August 2018, and all were closed at the time of research.

Getting There & Away

From Mandalika Terminal in Bertais (Mataram), catch a bus to Anyar (25,000Rp to 30,000Rp, 2½ hours). Bemos don't run from Anyar to Senaru, so you'll have to charter an *ojek* (per person from 30,000Rp, depending on your luggage). Due to the hassle, most visitors arrive in private transport arranged by a trekking agency.

Sembalun Valley

☎0376

High on the eastern side of Gunung Rinjani is what could be the mythical Shangri-La: the beautiful Sembalun Valley. This high plateau (about 1200m) is ringed by volcanoes and peaks. It's a rich farming region where the golden foothills turn vivid green in the wet season. When the high clouds part, Rinjani takes front stage.

The valley has two main settlements, Sembalun Lawang and Sembalun Bumbung, tranquil bread baskets primarily concerned with growing cabbage, potatoes, strawberries and, above all, garlic – though trekking tourism brings in a little income, too. Both villages were severely damaged during the 2018 earthquakes.

Rinjani Information Centre (RIC; ☎0818 540 673; www.rinjaniinformationcentre.com; Sembalun Lawang; ⏰6am-6pm) is a useful resource that organises Rinjani treks. It has well-informed English-speaking staff and lots of fascinating panels on the local flora, fauna, geology and history. Camping and trekking gear is available for hire. The office is right by a huge garlic statue on the main road and across from a very large mosque.

The centre also offers a four-hour Village Walk and a half-day rambling Panorama Walk in the foothills around the volcano.

Sembalun Lawang village is rustic; most guesthouses will heat *mandi* (bath) water for a fee. The Rinjani Information Centre can direct you to small homestays where rooms cost between 150,000Rp and 500,000Rp.

All hotels were closed at the time of research due to the 2018 earthquakes.

ℹ FERRIES TO SUMBAWA

The town of Labuhan Lombok on the east coast (also known as Labuhan Kayangan or Tanjung Kayangan) is the port for ferries and boats to Sumbawa. The ferry terminal is 3km east of the scruffy town centre.

Ferries run almost hourly, 24 hours a day, to/from Poto Tano on Sumbawa (passengers 17,000Rp, cars 431,000Rp, motorcycles 49,500Rp, 1½ hours). Through buses to points east from Bali and Lombok include the ferry fare.

Regular buses and bemos buzz between Mandalika Terminal in Mataram and Labuhan Lombok; the journey takes 2½ hours (35,000Rp). Some buses will only drop you off at the port entrance road, from where you can catch another bemo to the ferry terminal (5000Rp, 10 minutes). Don't walk – it's too far.

From Mataram's Mandalika Terminal, take a bus to Aikmel (20,000Rp) and change there for a bemo to Sembalun Lawang (20,000Rp).

There's no public transport between Sembalun Lawang and Senaru, so you'll have to charter an *ojek* for a potentially uncomfortable ride costing about 200,000Rp.

Tetebatu

☎0376

Laced with spring-fed streams emanating from the slopes of Rinjani and blessed with rich volcanic soil, Tetebatu is a Sasak breadbasket. The surrounding countryside is quilted with tobacco and rice fields, fruit orchards and cow pastures that fade into remnant monkey forest gushing with waterfalls. Tetebatu's sweet climate is ideal for long country walks (at 650m it's high enough to mute that hot, sticky coastal mercury). Dark nights come saturated with sound courtesy of a frog orchestra accompanied by countless gurgling brooks. Even insomniacs snore here.

Sights

Taman Wisata Tetebatu FOREST

(Monkey Forest) A shady 4km track leading from the main road, just north of the Tetebatu mosque, heads into this forest, where you'll find black monkeys – you'll want a guide, which you can arrange at your accommodation for around 500,000Rp, including stops at the nearby waterfalls.

Air Terjun Jukut WATERFALL

(150,000Rp) A steep 2km hike from the car park at the end of the access road to Gunung Rinjani National Park leads to beautiful Air Terjun Jukut, an impressive 20m drop to a deep pool surrounded by lush forest.

Air Terjun Kelelawar WATERFALL

(entry by donation) On the southern slopes of Rinjani, the Kelelawar waterfall is accessible by a spectacular 1½km walk (one way) through rice fields from Tetebatu. Walk 1km further and you'll reach **Koko Duren**, tucked into a steep ravine. The path is not easy to follow so you'll need to hire a guide, who can take you to both waterfalls for 300,000Rp.

Tours

A typical walking tour of greater Tetebatu takes in the rice fields, spice shops, Air Terjun Jukut, Air Terjun Kelelawar and the Monkey Forest. Alternatively, you can take a cultural tour to visit nearby artisan towns, including the bamboo-basket village of **Loyok**, the potters' village of **Masbagik Timur** and the weavers' village of **Pringgasela**. Each has several shops, often with live demonstrations.

Sandi Tour Guide OUTDOORS

(☎0823 4077 2008; sandiraga83@gmail.com) Knowledgable English-speaking guide for walking tours to rice fields, waterfalls and the Monkey Forest. Can also arrange guided treks up Rinjani, trips to Gili Kondo and cultural tours to nearby artist villages.

Sleeping & Eating

There is a mix of quality bungalows and guesthouses nestled in the lush countryside. The places where you can stay also provide meals, though there are a few nice standalone restaurants, too.

★ **Edriyan Bungalow** BUNGALOW $

(☎0853 3908 0120; http://edriyanbungalowtetebatu.blogspot.com; Jl Pariwisata Tetebatu; d from 400,000Rp, bungalow for 4 500,000Rp;) Three two-storey bamboo bungalows, each with intricate designs, offer astounding views over the glistening rice fields. Also on offer are an inviting pool, plant-filled gardens and Sasak cooking classes (200,000Rp, two hours) in the restaurant where you can learn how to make dishes such as jackfruit curry.

Pondok Indah Bungalows Tetebatu BUNGALOW $

(☎0877 6172 2576; Jl Pariwisata Tetebatu; bungalow from 250,000Rp) Three bi-level thatched bungalows are set amid beautiful rice fields. Although appearing romantically rustic, conditions are not: each has a bathroom, hardwood floors, outdoor seating areas with fabulous views and more. The grounds are a floral mix of colours.

Hakiki Bungalows & Cafe BUNGALOW $

(☎0818 0373 7407; www.hakiki-inn.com; Jl Kembang Kuning; r 175,000-450,000Rp;) A collection of seven bungalows in a blooming garden at the edge of the rice fields. You'll find it perched over the family rice plot about 600m from the intersection. There's even a honeymoon suite. Wi-fi is available in the cafe, which serves Indo classics, some nicely spicy.

Cendrawasih Cottages BUNGALOW $

(☎0878 6418 7063; Jl Kembang Kuning; r from 250,000Rp; ⏲restaurant 8am-9pm) Slightly neglected since the original owners moved away, these sweet little *lumbung* (rice-barn) brick cottages nestled in the rice fields are nevertheless a decent pick. Sit on floor cushions in the stunning stilted restaurant (mains 20,000Rp to 45,000Rp, only open high season) and take in 360-degree rice-field views. It's about 500m east of the intersection.

Tetebatu Mountain Resort BUNGALOW $$

(☎0853 3754 0777; www.mountainresorttetebatu.com; Jl Kembang Kuning; bungalows from 500,000Rp;) These Sasak bungalows with 23 rooms in total are some of the best digs in town. Four of them have separate bedrooms across two floors – perfect for travelling buddies – and a top-floor balcony with magical rice-field views.

Warung Monkey Forest INDONESIAN $

(☎0853 3702 0691; Jl Pariwisata Tetebatu; mains 30,000-40,000Rp; ⏲8am-11pm) A fantastic little thatch-roofed restaurant with lots of veggie options, fresh fruit juices and helpful English-speaking owners. Find it on the way up to the Monkey Forest.

Getting There & Away

All cross-island buses pass Pomotong (35,000Rp from Mandalika Terminal) on the main east–west highway. Get off here and you can hop an *ojek* (from 25,000Rp) to Tetebatu.

Most accommodation can arrange private transport from anywhere in Lombok. It's often easier and, if you have a group, just as cheap.

ALTERNATIVE HIKING BASE

Tetebatu makes a great alternative hiking base to Senaru and the Sembalun Valley for the climb up Gunung Rinjani, particularly for those short on time. You won't be able to dip into the lakes on the express two-day, one-night climbs from this side of the volcano with **Jaya Trekker** (☎0853 3792 0005; https://jayatrekker.com; Jl Pariwisata Tetebatu) and other local agencies, but you're guaranteed to see less rubbish and a fraction of the tourists. Expect to pay about 1,750,000Rp for the trip, including a guide, porters, equipment, food and entrance to the park.

Note that this route was closed at the time of research, but was expected to reopen in late 2019 or early 2020.

SOUTH LOMBOK

Beaches just don't get much better: the water is warm, striped turquoise and curls into barrels, and the sand is silky and snow white, framed by massive headlands and sheer cliffs. The south is noticeably drier than the rest of Lombok and more sparsely populated, with limited roads and public transport.

Southern Lombok's incredible coastline of giant bite-shaped bays is startling, its beauty immediate, undeniable and arresting. Yet this region has historically been the island's poorest; its sun-blasted soil is parched and unproductive. That will all change over the coming decade as high-end development projects drastically alter this once-virgin terrain.

Kuta

☎0370 / POP 5000

What could be a better gateway to the wonderful beaches of south Lombok? Imagine a crescent bay, turquoise in the shallows and deep blue further out. It licks a huge, white-sand beach, as wide as a football pitch and framed by headlands. Now imagine a coastline of nearly a dozen such bays, all backed by a rugged range of coastal hills spotted with lush patches of banana trees and tobacco fields, and you'll have a notion of Kuta's immediate appeal.

Kuta's original attraction was the limitless world-class breaks, and now even as developers lick their chops, the sets keep rolling in. Meanwhile, the town itself is an appealing mix of guesthouses, cafes, restaurants and low-key places for a beer.

Beaches

Kuta's main beach can easily snare you and keep you from looking elsewhere. It's got ideal white sand and all those views. Plus the surf is just right for swimming. The waterfront is a slowly gentrifying place as landscaped areas gradually replace expanses that used to be covered by bamboo huts. For now it's a slightly bleak strip, albeit one with a flashy new Kuta Mandalika sign and ostentatious bathing facilities (a local controversy).

West of Kuta is a series of awesome beaches and ideal surf breaks. Developers are nosing around here, and land has changed hands, but for now it remains almost pristine and the region maintains its raw beauty. In anticipation of future developments, the road has been much improved. It meanders inland, skirting tobacco, sweet potato and rice fields in between turn-offs to the sand and glimpses of the gorgeous coast.

Just east of Kuta there are also several excellent beaches.

★Pantai Mawan BEACH
(car/motorbike 10,000/5000Rp) How's this for a vision of sandy paradise? Some 8km west of Kuta and 600m off the main road, this half-moon cove is framed by soaring headlands with azure water and a swath of sand that's empty save for a fishing village of a dozen thatched homes. The beach is terrific for swimming. It has paved parking, some modest cafes and large trees for shade. An upscale vendor rents loungers for a pricey 150,000Rp for all day.

Tanjung Aan BEACH
(car/motorbike 20,000/10,000Rp) Some 5km east of Kuta, Tanjung Aan (aka A'an, Ann) is a spectacular sight: a giant horseshoe bay with two sweeping arcs of fine sand with the ends punctuated by waves crashing on the rocks. Swimming is good here and there are trees and shelters for shade, plus safe parking (for a small charge). **Warung Turtle**, at the east end of the beach, has cheery service and cheap beer, while the western headland **Bukit Merese** is worth climbing for spectacular sunsets.

Pantai Areguling BEACH
(car/motorbike 10,000/5000Rp) Look for a steep track off the main coast road 6km west of Kuta. A rough 2km ride brings you to this broad bay with a wide beach of beige sand. It's a little scruffy, but you can't beat the sense of space. Construction on the headland foreshadows changes to come.

Pantai Seger BEACH
(car/motorbike 10,000/5000Rp) Pantai Seger, a lovely beach about 2km east of Kuta around the first headland, has unbelievably turquoise water, decent swimming (though no shade) and a break 200m offshore. There are two more beaches nearby, a decent cafe and vendors renting snorkelling gear.

Activities

There's a whole row of activity sales agents along Jl Pariwisata and the main road leading to the waterfront. They can set you up on anything from surf tours to snorkelling in obscure locations. Don't be afraid to haggle.

Kuta

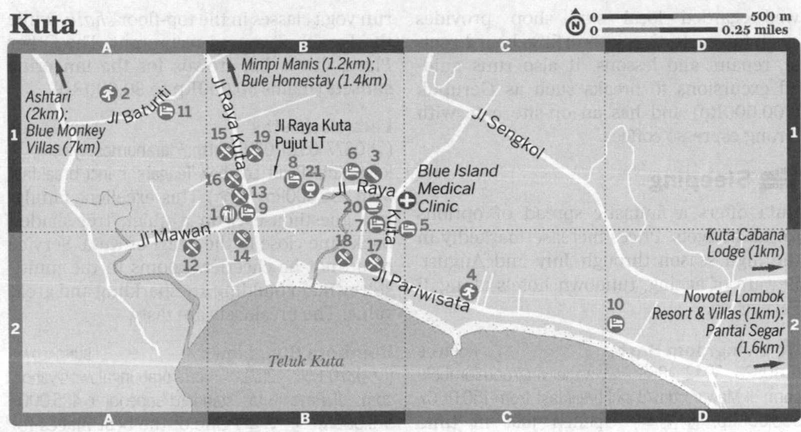

Kuta

Activities, Courses & Tours

1 Kimen Surf ... B1
2 Mana Yoga Studio ... A1
3 Scuba Froggy ... B1
4 Whatsup? Lombok ... C2

Sleeping

5 Bombora Bungalows ... C1
6 Kuta Baru Hotel ... B1
7 Lamancha Homestay ... B1
8 Lara Homestay ... B1
9 Livingroom Hostel ... B1
10 Puri Rinjani Bungalows ... D2
11 Yuli's Homestay ... A1

Eating

12 Dwiki's ... A2
13 El Bazar ... B1
14 Market ... B2
15 Milk Espresso ... B1
16 Nugget's Corner ... B1
17 Sea Salt ... B2
18 Warung Bule ... B2
19 Warung Flora ... B1

Drinking & Nightlife

20 DJ Coffee Corner ... B1
21 The Bus ... B1

Mimpi Manis (p306) can organise snorkelling trips to the Southwest Gilis from 350,000Rp per person, and six-hour fishing trips for 600,000Rp (minimum two people).

Ashtari restaurant (p308) on the road to Mawan offers a variety of yoga classes (100,000Rp) in a peaceful spot below the restaurant; these are held from 7am to 6.30pm.

★ Mana Retreat Lombok YOGA
(☎0853 38628 659; http://manalombok.com; Jl Baturiti; class 100,000Rp; ⏲8am-6.30pm) An open thatched pavilion in a serene jungly setting with vinyasa, yin/yang, surfer yoga and more. Yogis can also sleep onsite in rooms and bungalows (dm/d from 300,000/900,000Rp).

★ Scuba Froggy DIVING
(☎0878 6454 1402; www.scubafroggy.com; Jl Raya Kuta; single dive 600,000Rp, open-water course 5,500,000Rp; ⏲9am-7pm) Runs local trips to two-dozen dive sites, most no deeper than 18m. From June to November, staff also run trips to the spectacular and challenging ocean pinnacles in Belongas Bay, famous for schooling hammerheads and mobula rays. Snorkelling trips to the Southwest Gilis are 750,000Rp. It also rents out kayaks (80,000Rp per hour).

Whatsup? Lombok WATER SPORTS
(☎0878 6597 8701; http://whatsuplombok.com; Jl Pariwisata; SUP/kayak/kitesurfing rentals per hr 200,000/150,000/400,000Rp; ⏲8am-8pm) South Kuta's bays are known for being excellent places for kitesurfing, stand-up paddleboarding (SUP) and kayaking. At this shop you can rent gear, take lessons and join tours.

Kimen Surf SURFING
(☎0878 6590 0017; www.kuta-lombok.net; Jl Mawan; board rental per day 60,000Rp, lessons per person from 400,000Rp; ⏲8am-9pm) This

well-regarded local surf shop provides swell forecasts, tips, kitesurfing, board rental, repairs and lessons. It also runs guided excursions to breaks such as Gerupuk (700,000Rp) and has an on-site cafe with strong espresso coffees.

Sleeping

Kuta offers a fantastic spread of options for all budgets. Prices increase markedly in the high season through July and August. Beware of ageing, rundown hotels along Jl Pariwisata.

★Livingroom Hostel HOSTEL $
(0823 3942 1868; www.thelivingroomlombok.com; Jl Mawan; dm/d incl breakfast from 150,000/350,000Rp;) Opened just in time for the 2018 earthquakes to scare potential visitors away, the Livingroom is everything you'd want in a hostel. It's got an eclectic bar with swings for seats, home-baked bread for breakfast, clean and well-equipped dorm rooms and even a small pool. One of the Hungarian owners is a woodworker and this place is his magnum opus.

★Kuta Cabana Lodge LODGE $
(www.facebook.com/kutacabanalodge; off Jl Sengkol; r incl breakfast from 400,000Rp;) This eclectic thatch-roofed lodge spills down a hill just east of town, offering sweeping views over the bay from each artfully designed room. Teachers from Ashtari (p308) run yoga classes in the top-floor *shala*, while the French-flavoured restaurant, The Other Place, draws big crowds for the tangerine sunsets (mains 50,000Rp to 80,000Rp).

Lara Homestay GUESTHOUSE $
(0877 6310 0315; http://larahomestay.com; Jl Raya Kuta Pujut Lombok Tengah; r incl breakfast from 300,000Rp;) This excellent family-run guesthouse is on a quiet, tree-shaded back lane close to the heart of Kuta. Service could not be cheerier. Rooms in the multistorey main building are sparkling and great value. The breakfasts are tasty.

Bombora Bungalows BUNGALOW $
(0370-650 2571; bomborabungalows@yahoo.com; Jl Raya Kuta; standard/superior r 425,000/575,000Rp;) One of the best places for a low-cost stay in Kuta, these eight bungalows (some fan-cooled, all with bathrooms) are built around a lovely pool area. Coconut palms shade loungers, pink-flamingo inflatables stand ready and the entire place feels like an escape from the hubbub of town. The staff understand the needs of surfers and pretty much everyone else.

Mimpi Manis B&B $
(081 836 9950; www.mimpimanis.com; Jl Raya Kuta; dm/d 100,000/150,000-250,000Rp;) Run by Made and Gemma, a friendly Balinese/British couple, 'Sweet Dreams' is an inviting B&B offering spotless dorm and private rooms, some with air-con and showers. Located 1km inland, it's more peaceful than central Kuta options, with plenty of good books to borrow. It also offers a free drop-off service to the beach and town, plus bike and motorbike rental.

Bule Homestay GUESTHOUSE $
(0819 1799 6256; Jl Raya Bypass; r 250,000-320,000Rp;) About 2km back from the beach, near the junction of Jl Raya Kuta and Jl Raya Bypass, this nine-bungalow complex is worth considering for the quiet surrounds and snappy way it's run. Shoes are left on the front steps and dirt doesn't dare enter the small compound, where rooms gleam with a hospital white.

Lamancha Homestay HOMESTAY $
(0819 3313 0156, 0370-615 5186; zamroni293@yahoo.com; Jl Raya Kuta; r incl breakfast 175,000-300,000Rp;) A charming and expanding 10-room homestay offering spacious rooms with concrete floors, colourful tapestries and canopied beds. The management is endearing.

SURFING THE SOUTH COAST

Stellar lefts and rights break on the reefs off Kuta Bay (Telek Kuta) and east of Tanjung Aan (p304). Around 7km east of Kuta is the fishing village of Gerupuk (p309), where there's a series of reef breaks, both close to the shore and further out, but they require a boat, at a negotiable 200,000Rp per two-hour session. Wise surfers buzz past Gerupuk and take the road to Ekas (p310), where crowds are thin and two breaks, Inside Ekas and Outside Ekas, keep wave hunters happy. These also require a boat for about 400,000Rp. West of Kuta, you'll find Mawan (p304), a stunning swimming beach; Mawi (p311), a popular surf paradise with world-class swells and a strong rip tide; and lastly, the long white sands of Selong Blanak (p311), a great spot for beginners.

★ Yuli's Homestay

HOMESTAY $$

(☎0819 1710 0983; www.yulishomestay.com; Jl Baturiti; r incl breakfast 425,000-700,000Rp; ❄📶🏊) The 32 rooms at this ever-expanding place are immaculately clean, spacious and nicely furnished with huge beds and wardrobes. It also has big front terraces and cold-water bathrooms, not to mention a guest kitchen, a garden and three pools to enjoy.

Blue Monkey Villas

BUNGALOW $$

(☎0853 3775 6416; bluemonkeyvillas@gmail.com; Pantai Areguling; r 500,000-1,000,000Rp; 📶🏊) Set on a knoll above Pantai Areguling, 8km west of Kuta, this collection of traditional-style bungalows has sweeping views of the bay. The beach is a 500m walk down the hill. A simple cafe serves meals, where the view will compete with your food for your attention.

Puri Rinjani Bungalows

BUNGALOW $$

(☎0370-615 4849; Jl Pariwisata; r from 700,000Rp; ❄📶🏊) A solid beachfront option that gets everything right: it's sparklingly clean, well-managed and has a lovely pool area, with statues decorating the grounds. The 19 rooms are bright and airy and have nice, firm beds.

Kuta Baru Hotel

HOTEL $$

(☎0821 4538 8418; Jl Raya Kuta; r incl breakfast 400,000-1,000,000Rp; ❄📶🏊) One of Kuta's best hotels with 23 rooms surrounding an inviting pool, a grassy lawn and a thatch-roofed restaurant. It's 110m east of the main intersection.

Novotel Lombok Resort & Villas

RESORT $$$

(☎0370-615 3333; www.novotellombok.com; Pantai Putri Nyale; r/villa from US$180/310; ❄📶🏊) This appealing, Sasak-themed four-star resort spills onto a superb beach less than 3km east of the junction. The 102 rooms have high sloping roofs and modern interiors. There are three pools, a spa, resort-style restaurants, a swanky bar and a plethora of activities on offer.

Eating

Kuta's dining scene is getting more creative each day. There's a wide variety of choices – all casual – at great prices.

★ Nugget's Corner

INDONESIAN $

(☎0878 9131 7431; Jl Raya Kuta; mains 35,000-100,000Rp; ⏲7am-10.30pm) For a restaurant that seems cool and casual, this one has real drive. The vegan, veggie and meaty mains are all prepared with attitude and authority. Flavours are bold and presentation is lovely. It's BYOB; the juices, smoothies and iced teas are superb. The dining room is open-air.

Warung Flora

INDONESIAN $

(☎0878 6530 0009; Jl Raya Kuta; mains 20,000-80,000Rp; ⏲11am-10pm) A total tropical fantasy in bamboo and thatch. Sit under a palm tree while you dine on fresh fish caught by a local fisher. The chef is the owner's wife, and together they create beautiful meals.

Dwiki's

PIZZA $

(☎0853 3316 3443; Jl Mawan; mains 35,000-70,000Rp; ⏲10am-11pm; 📶🖉) A choice, relaxed spot for wood-fired thin-crust pizza in tiki-bar environs. And it delivers! Has lots of Indo standards, grilled seafood and an above-average list of veggie options. Live music Wednesday nights.

Market

MARKET $

(off Jl Raya Kuta; ⏲6.30-10.30am Sun & Wed) The market sells an ever-changing variety of foodstuffs and necessities.

★ Milk Espresso

CAFE $$

(www.facebook.com/milkespresso; Jl Raya Kuta; mains 55,000-130,000Rp; ⏲7am-midnight; 📶) Hopping all day long, this trendy bi-level cafe breathlessly segues from bountiful breakfasts to midday nibbles, healthy dinners and classy evening cocktails. Oh, and the strong coffee is sure to rev your engine any time of day!

★ El Bazar

MEDITERRANEAN $$

(☎0819 9911 3026; www.elbazarlombok.com; Jl Raya Kuta; mains 75,000-185,000Rp; ⏲8am-11pm) Kuta's trendiest and most popular restaurant lives up to its stellar reputation with authentic tastes from around the Mediterranean. Kick things off with a mezze platter and then move on to excellent kebabs, falafels or Moroccan tagines. You'll likely linger long after the meal as the vibe here is electric.

Sea Salt

SEAFOOD $$

(☎0813 8198 7104; Jl Pariwisata; mains 60,000-90,000Rp; ⏲11am-10pm) That a Scottish-owned, vaguely Greek seafood restaurant is one

> **BAU NYALE FESTIVAL**
>
> On the 19th day of the 10th month in the Sasak calendar (generally February or March), hundreds of Sasaks gather on Pantai Seger (p304) for big ceremonies and feasts involving stick fighting, live bands and the odd, worm-like nyale fish.

SASAK LIFE

Lombok's indigenous Sasak people comprise about 90% of the island's population. Virtually all are now orthodox Muslims, though before 1965 many Sasaks in remote areas were Wektu Telu (p300).

Traditional Sasak houses are made of bamboo and sit on a base of compacted mud and cow dung; they have a steeply angled and rather low-slung thatched roof, which forces guests to bow humbly before their hosts. Husbands and wives share a home, but not a bed (ie bamboo mat). They only spend the night together when they are trying to get pregnant. Once the job is done, the men sleep outside and the women and children huddle indoors. Villages in northern Lombok still maintain a caste system, which heavily influences courtship. Marriages between the highest castes – *Datu* (men) and *Denek Bini* (women) – and lower castes are quite rare.

Each village will have *lumbung*, stilted rice-storage barns, to keep rodents at bay. They look like little thatched cottages and have been mimicked by bungalow resorts throughout Lombok. There are several examples of traditional villages, including Sade and Rembitan near Kuta.

of Kuta's best speaks volumes for where the dining scene is at. At this small, arched dining room, open to the beach and hung with bird cages and shrimp traps, let super-enthusiastic, barefoot staff fuss over you as you tuck into the day's catch.

Warung Bule SEAFOOD **$$**
(☎0370-615 8625; Jl Pariwisata; mains 60,000-85,000Rp; ⏲10am-11pm; 📶) Tucked away from the main thoroughfares, on a quiet stretch of Kuta Beach, this friendly, tiled warung is one of the best in town. The grilled barracuda with Sasak spices is fantastic, while the trio of lobster, prawns and mahi-mahi (385,000Rp, expensive by local standards) is a full seafood fix. It can get very busy in high season.

Ashtari INTERNATIONAL **$$**
(☎0812 3608 0862; www.ashtarilombok.com; Jl Mawan; mains 40,000-100,000Rp; ⏲8am-9pm) Perched on a mountaintop 2km west of town on the road to Mawan, this breezy, Mediterranean-themed lounge-restaurant has spectacular vistas of pristine bays and rocky peninsulas that take turns spilling further out to sea. It's a slick yoga-luxe sort of place with several options for vegans.

Drinking & Nightlife

There are a couple of raucous beachfront bars where there are often well-advertised parties. Impromptu beer bashes set up on the sand right near the centre of town.

★The Bus BAR
(www.facebook.com/thebuslombok; Jl Raya Kuta; ⏲6pm-midnight) Great tunes, colourful graffiti art and the best pizzas in Lombok make this a must-visit come nightfall. Sit on pallet furniture in a rocky patch of central Kuta and let the wizards inside the namesake 1974 VW bus craft you some of the cheapest, tastiest cocktails in town. Live DJs spin Wednesdays and Saturdays.

DJ Coffee Corner CAFE
(Jl Raya Kuta; ⏲8am-5.30pm; 📶) A switch from the thatch-and-bamboo cliche that dominates the local design palette, this sleek air-con coffee bar has a nice back garden and satisfies with a real espresso fix. Also does juices, light bites and baked goods.

Information

DANGERS & ANNOYANCES

- If you decide to rent a bicycle or motorbike, take care with whom you deal – arrangements are informal and rental contracts are hardly ever exchanged. There are reports of some visitors having motorbikes stolen (often at late-night beach parties) and then having to pay substantial sums of money as compensation to the owner. Renting a motorbike from your guesthouse is the safest option.
- As you drive up the coastal road west and east of Kuta, keep an eye out – especially after dark. There have been rare reports of muggings in the area.
- The throngs of vendors, many of them children selling friendship bands, are relentless.

MEDICAL SERVICES

Blue Island Medical Clinic (☎0819 9970 5700; http://blueislandclinic.com; Jl Raya Kuta; ⏲24hr) Your best bet for minor issues in southern Lombok. For anything major, head to Mataram.

MONEY

Kuta has a half-dozen ATMs and is a good place to stock up on rupiahs before travelling further afield in south Lombok.

Getting There & Away

Outside the daily 11am shuttle bus to Kuta from Mataram's Mandalika Terminal (p286) (1½ hours, 60,000Rp), there is no real public transport linking the two cities. You could try to bemo-hop via Praya and Sengkol, but these bemos have become increasingly obsolete.

Simpler are the daily ride-share cars serving Mataram, plus Senggigi and Lembar (all 100,000Rp). Shared cars to the airport cost 60,000Rp, though a taxi may be simpler if you fly out at an odd hour (150,000Rp). Other ride-share destinations include Bangsal for Gili Islands public boats (110,000Rp), Seminyak (Bali) via the public ferry (180,000Rp) and Senaru (250,000Rp). All are advertised widely on sandwich boards across Kuta.

Getting Around

Guesthouses rent out motorbikes for about 70,000Rp per day. *Ojeks* are less frequent here than elsewhere in Lombok (most visitors rent their own wheels) but can often be hailed from the junction in the centre of town. Good paved roads run east to the various beaches. It's a terrific motorbike ride. Your own wheels are essential for exploring the beaches in the west. Cyclists will need to be ready for hills and narrow, curving roads.

Gerupuk

0370

Just 1.6km past Tanjung Aan beach, Gerupuk is a fascinating little ramshackle coastal village where the thousand or so local souls earn their keep from fishing, seaweed harvesting and lobster exports. Oh, and guiding and ferrying surfers to the five exceptional surf breaks in its huge bay.

As you'll see from the nascent grand boulevards and vast earthworks between Tanjung Aan and Gerupuk, construction on the gigantic Mandalika resort complex is under way in fits and starts. Expect the area to change greatly in the next few years. Judging by the way the existing mangroves have been destroyed, concerns about environmental damage are well placed.

Activities

To surf in the bay you'll need to hire a boat to ferry you from the fishing harbour, skirting the netted lobster farms, to the break (200,000Rp). The boat operator will help you find the right wave and wait patiently. There are four waves inside and a left break outside on the point. All can get head high or bigger when the swell hits.

Sleeping & Eating

★Bumbangku Beach Cottages BUNGALOW $
(0821 4715 3876; www.bumbangkulombok.com; Jl Raya Awang, Bumbangku; r 250,000-750,000Rp;) Bumbangku Beach is across the bay from Gerupuk and is wonderfully remote. This relaxed resort has 25 rooms ranging from simple bamboo huts on stilts with outdoor bathrooms and cold water to much nicer concrete rooms with hot water and air-con. It's 2km along a narrow lane off the main road.

Edo Homestay GUESTHOUSE $
(0818 0371 0521; Gerupuk; r incl breakfast 200,000-600,000Rp;) Right in the village, this place offers 18 clean rooms spread across three buildings. Most have colourful drapes and double beds; top-end rooms are in a villa. It has a decent restaurant and a surf shop too (boards per day 50,000Rp).

Surf Camp Lombok RESORT $$
(0852 3744 5949; www.surfcampindonesia.com; 1 week from €690) Lodging at this fun surf resort at the eastern end of Gerupuk village is in a bamboo Borneo-style longhouse, albeit with lots of high-tech diversions. The beach setting feels lush and remote. All meals are included plus surf lessons, yoga and more. Rooms sleep five, except for three doubles.

Inlight Lombok Resort BOUTIQUE HOTEL $$$
(0853 3803 8280; www.inlightlombok.com; r from 1,400,000Rp;) Curvaceously designed by the Russian architect-owner, this stunning hotel on a secluded beach just south of Gerupuk was built for detoxing. Wi-fi is only available in common areas, there is no alcohol and the health-food restaurant has an energising pescetarian menu. The four rooms, while not quite as show-stopping as the grounds, are spacious and comfortable with astonishing views.

Fin CAFE $
(0823 3956 4781; www.facebook.com/fingerupuk; mains 45,000-60,000Rp; 7.30am-4.30pm) This airy turquoise-and-white cafe with

OFF THE BEATEN TRACK

BUMBANGKU

Gerupuk's beach is narrow; much nicer is the powdery sand across the bay at Bumbangku. Follow a narrow track off the main road for 2.5km and you'll find this often deserted beach. The structures you see out in the bay are pearl farms.

distressed wood furnishings and birdcages for light fixtures is the kind of place you might expect to find in Gili T, not Gerupuk. But it's a welcome addition, with espresso coffees, yoghurt bowls, wheatgrass shots and veggie sandwiches.

Getting There & Away

You'll need your own wheels to get here. The road from Kuta to Gerupuk is anything but user friendly.

Ekas

0370

Ekas is an uncrowded find, where the breaks and soaring cliffs recall Bali's Ulu Watu – an almost deserted Ulu Watu.

Ekas itself is a sleepy little village, but head south into the peninsula and you'll soon make the sorts of jaw-dropping discoveries that will have you Instagramming like mad.

Beaches

Heaven Beach BEACH

Ask for directions to Heaven Beach for a real bit of sandy wonder. It's a stunning little pocket of white sand and surf about 4km from Ekas. Despite the omnipresent resort, you're free to access the shore: all Indonesian beaches are public.

Pantai Dagong BEACH

What a sight! An utterly empty and seemingly endless white beach backed by azure breakers. To get here, drive south 6.5km from Ekas over the rough but passable road.

Sleeping

There are posh boutique resorts hidden on the beautiful coves south of Ekas. Also look out for new and simple guesthouses along the rural roads.

Ekas Breaks GUESTHOUSE $$

(0822 3791 6767; www.ekasbreaks.com; r incl breakfast 600,000-900,000Rp;) Some 2km from Ekas' surf breaks and beaches amid rolling land is this sun-kissed compound. Some rooms are in a traditional *lumbung* style with thatched walls; others are in a modern style, with whitewashed walls and open bathrooms (we prefer those). The cafe makes a good mix of Western and Indo meals.

★**Heaven on the Planet** BOUTIQUE HOTEL $$$

(0812 375 1103; www.heavenontheplanet.com; Ekas Bay; per person all-inclusive US$120-240;) The aptly named Heaven on the Planet has units scattered along a cliff's edge, from where you'll have spectacular bird's-eye views of the sea. Others are down at the idyllic beach. Each is utterly different. Heaven is primarily a posh and idiosyncratic surf resort, but kitesurfing, scuba diving, yoga and snorkelling are also possible. Meals are bountiful and creative.

Getting There & Away

A good paved road runs along the coast from Kuta to Ekas, passing a seemingly endless series of beautiful bays punctuated by headlands. It's a terrific motorbike ride.

Selong Blanak

0370

Just when you think you've seen the most beautiful sands Kuta has to offer, you reach this popular curving bay and beach. And it gets stiff competition in the fabulous sweep-

A GRIM CATCH

Everyday fishing boats sail in and out of Tanjung Luar, a long-running fish market in southeast Lombok that has a bad reputation with environmental groups for the fishing of large species such as sharks, manta rays and dolphins.

While the meat is sold locally, the shark fins and manta gills are auctioned to buyers who ship their bounty to Hong Kong, where the items are considered delicacies.

Shark-fin buyers in Tanjung Luar confirm that few sharks remain in the sea around Lombok. In the 1990s fishermen didn't have to go far to hunt their take, but these days they travel all the way to the Sumba Strait between Australia and Indonesia, an important shark-migration channel.

Surveys by Project Aware (www.projectaware.org), a diving environmental group, found that mandatory government signs prohibiting dolphin catch as well as that of some shark species and sea turtles had been torn down.

Any real effect of Indonesia's declaration in 2014 of their waters being a protection zone for manta rays has yet to be seen.

WORTH A TRIP

BELONGAS BAY

Save a big 'Wow!' for this curving double bay with a sinuous strand of white ribbon that provides a brilliant line between the blue water and green hills. Nearby Bali has nothing even remotely like this beach and it's still yours to explore, as development has barely touched this area. The bay is located on the south coast, approximately 40km west of Kuta. From Pengantap, the main coast road climbs across a headland then descends to a superb bay; follow this around for 1km then look out for the turn-off west to Belongas – a steep and winding road with beautiful scenery. There's no public transport.

There are two famed dive sites here: **Magnet** and **Cathedrals**. Spotting conditions peak in mid-September when you may see schooling mobula rays in addition to hammerheads, which school around the pinnacle (a towering rock that breaks the surface of the ocean and is the heart of the dive sites) from June to November. It's not an easy dive, so you must be experienced and prepared for strong currents.

Belongas Bay is a focus area for Senggigi-based **Dive Zone** (0819 0785 2073; www.divezone-lombok.com; 2 local boat dives 1,650,000Rp), which runs trips out of the **Belongas Bay Lodge** (0370-645974; www.thelodge-lombok.com; bungalows 850,000-950,000Rp, meals 75,000Rp). This lodge offers spacious wooden bungalows with tiled roofs in a lovely coconut grove. It's fairly simple, which goes with the serene setting right on the water. Access is via a thin, severely rutted and challenging dirt road that's ill suited to novice motorbikers. Advanced bookings are essential.

stakes from nearby Pantai Mawi, a quiet cove for in-the-know surfers.

Beaches

Pantai Mawi BEACH

(car/motorbike 20,000/10,000Rp) This is a surf paradise: a stunning scene, with legendary barrels and several more beaches scattered around the great bay. Watch out for the strong rip tide. There's parking and vendors; surfboard rental is 50,000Rp for two hours. The turn for the beach is 16km west of Kuta; it's then a 3km drive down a rough road to the beach.

Pantai Selong Blanak BEACH

(parking 10,000Rp) Behold the wide, sugar-white beach with water streaked a thousand shades of blue, ideal for swimming. You can rent surfboards (per day 50,000Rp) and arrange for a boat out to area breaks (from 100,000Rp). The parking lot is just 400m off the main drag on a good road, the turn is 18km west of Kuta. The beach is popular with locals, loungers rent for 50,000Rp per day and there are lots of bamboo warungs.

Sleeping & Eating

Lodgings here skew upmarket, though you'll find the odd homestay or budget bungalow in the mix. Dining options from budget to top end can be found here, mostly near the beach in Selong Blanak.

Tiki Lodge RESORT $$

(0822 4744 7274; www.tikilombok.com; Jl Selong Belanak; r from 650,000Rp;) Comfortable thatch-roofed villas with bamboo beds and luxurious outdoor bathrooms surround an emerald-green pool in these jungly grounds. Breakfast and afternoon tea are included in the rate.

Sempiak Villas RESORT $$

(0821 4430 3337; www.sempiakvillas.com; villas from 960,000Rp;) Tucked away on the cliffs, this fabulous boutique resort is one of the Kuta area's most upscale properties. Seven villas are built into the hillside above the beach and feature antique wood; some have covered decks with stupendous views. Another five cheaper villas lie down below. It has a beach club for daytime frolics and dinners on the sand.

Laut Biru Bar & Restaurant SEAFOOD $$

(0821 4430 3339; mains 45,000-90,000Rp; 8am-10pm;) This seaside cafe at Sempiak Villas keeps it simple with Indo classics for lunch and dinner, though the setting is anything but. You'll dine in a fancy white-washed building with high ceilings, hanging shell art and remixed world music floating out toward the sandy patio.

Getting There & Away

It's an easy coastal drive from Kuta. Good roads lead west to beaches and north to Praya and Mataram. There's no public transport.

Gili Islands

Includes ➡

Best Places to Eat

➡ Pituq Waroeng (p323)

➡ Ruby's (p332)

➡ Pachamama (p333)

➡ Jali Kitchen (p322)

➡ Sasak Cafe (p328)

Best Places to Stay

➡ Gili Treehouses (p322)

➡ Gili Meno Eco Hostel (p327)

➡ Eden Cottages (p321)

➡ Wilson's Retreat (p322)

➡ Rabbit Tree (p327)

Why Go?

Floating in a turquoise sea and fringed by white sand and coconut palms, the Gilis are a vision of paradise. And they're booming like nowhere else in Indonesia – speedboats zip visitors directly from Bali and hip new hotels are rising like autumnal mushrooms.

The lure of big tourist dollars tugs against the traditionally laid-back culture of the islands, the alternative spirit imported by Western partygoers and a buoyant green sensibility. While the outcome is uncertain, for now the Gilis retain their languorous charm (partly due to local efforts to exclude dogs and motorbikes from the islands).

Each island has its own unique appeal. Gili Trawangan (aka Gili T) is the most cosmopolitan, with a raucous party scene and plenty of upscale dining and accommodation. Gili Air has an appealing mix of buzz and bliss, while little Gili Meno has the strongest local character.

When to Go

➡ The wet season is approximately late October until late March. But even in the height of the rainy season, when it's lashing it down on Lombok or Bali, the Gilis can be dry and sunny.

➡ High season is between June and late August (and again at Christmas), when rooms are very hard to find and prices surge. It can be quite windy, but sunny days are almost guaranteed.

➡ The perfect months to visit are May and September. It's fairly dry, the crowds have abated and there's no cyclone season to worry about.

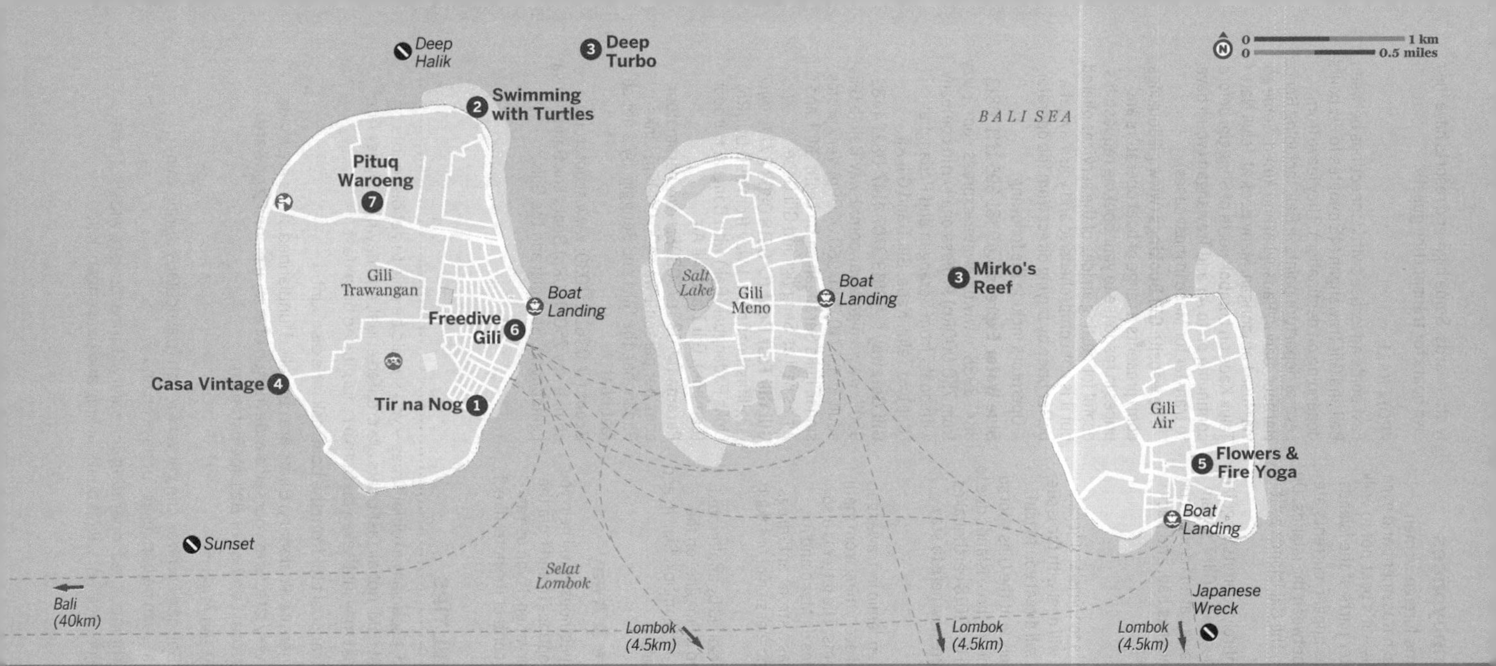

Gili Islands Highlights

1. **Partying till Dawn** (p325) Flying your freak flag at Gili T's legendary parties, held at venues like Tir na Nog.
2. **Swimming with Turtles** (p329) Cruising with green-sea and hawksbill turtles in 'The Turtle Capital of the World'.
3. **Diving** (p318) Getting up close to white-tip sharks at Deep Turbo and Shark Point, or marvelling at Mirko's Reef.
4. **Sunset over Gunung Agung** (p324) Nursing a drink at Casa Vintage as the sun slips behind Bali's active volcano.
5. **Yoga** (p331) Zenning out at one of Gili Air's tranquil yoga retreats, such as Flowers & Fire Yoga.
6. **Freediving** (p317) Plumbing the depths on a single breath, after taking lessons at one of Asia's best schools, Freedive Gili.
7. **Great Eats** (p323) Enjoying Gili Trawangan's food scene at creative eateries such as Pituq Waroeng.

Dangers & Annoyances

- Although it's rare, some foreign women have experienced sexual harassment and even assault while on the Gilis – it's best not to walk home alone to the quieter parts of the islands.
- As tranquil as the seas appear, currents are strong in the channels between the islands. Do not try to swim between the Gili Islands as it can be deadly.
- Bike riders (almost entirely tourists) regularly plough into and injure people on Gili T's main drag. *Cidomo* (horse-drawn carts) hauling construction goods are almost as bad, and pack considerably more punch.

THEFT

Immediately report thefts to the island *kepala desa* (village head), who will deal with the issue; staff at the dive schools will direct you to him.

While police used to only visit the Gilis sporadically, they set up shop on all three islands due to the looting that followed the 2018 earthquakes. Many predict that they are now here to stay.

INTOXICANTS

The drug trade remains endemic in Trawangan where you'll get offers of everything from meth to ecstasy and mushrooms. The latter is also openly advertised in cafes on Meno and Air. Remember, Indonesia has a strong anti-drugs policy; those caught in possession of or taking drugs risk jail or worse.

Tourists have been poisoned by adulterated *arak* (colourless, distilled palm wine) on the Gilis, as happens in Bali and Lombok. Skip it, and beware cut-price cocktails.

Getting There & Away

Most hotels and many guesthouses will help you sort out your transport options to and from the Gilis as part of your reservation. If you use an online booking website, contact the hotel directly afterwards. Some high-end resorts have their own boats for transporting guests.

FROM BALI

Fast boats advertise swift connections between Bali and Gili Trawangan (45 minutes to 2½ hours, depending on destination). They leave from several departure points in Bali, including Benoa Harbour, Sanur, Padangbai and Amed. Some go via Nusa Lembongan. Many dock at Teluk Nare/Teluk Kade on Lombok north of Senggigi before continuing on to Air and Trawangan (you'll have to transfer for Meno in most cases).

The website **Gili Bookings** (www.gilibookings.com) presents a range of boat operators and prices in response to your booking request. It's useful for getting an idea of the services offered but it is not comprehensive and you may get a better price by buying direct from the operator.

Operators include the following:

Blue Water Express (☎0361-895 1111, 0813 3841 8988; www.bluewater-express.com; 1-way from 750,000Rp) Professionally run company with boats from Serangan and Padangbai (Bali), to Teluk Kade, Gili T and Gili Air.

Gili Getaway (☎0813 3707 4147, 0821 4489 9502; www.giligetaway.com; 1-way Bali to Gilis adult/child 710,000/560,000Rp) Very professional; links Serangan on Bali with Gili T and Gili Air as well as Senggigi and Gili Gede.

Gili Gili Fast Boat (☎0818 0858 8777; www.giligilifastboat.com; 1-way from 690,000Rp) Links Padangbai (Bali) with Bangsal Harbour (Lombok), Gili T and Gili Air.

Perama (☎0361-750808; www.peramatour.com; per person 1 way 400,000Rp) Links Padangbai, the Gilis and Senggigi by a not-so-fast boat.

Scoot (☎0361-271030; www.scootcruise.com; 1-way 750,000Rp) Boats link Sanur, Nusa Lembongan, Senggigi and the Gilis.

BOAT TRAVEL TIPS

- Fares are not fixed, especially in quiet times – you should be able to get discounts on published fares. That said, not all fast boats are created equal, and paying a higher fare for a more sturdy boat may just save you from a regurgitated breakfast.
- If you don't need transport to/from the boat, ask for a discount.
- The advertised times are illusionary. Boats are cancelled, unplanned stops are made or boats simply run very late. Give yourself a wide margin of error if planning onward connections (flights from Lombok or Bali, for instance).
- Book ahead in July and August.
- The sea between Bali and Lombok can get very rough (particularly during rainy season) and fast boats can be cancelled for days on end.
- The fast boats are unregulated; operating and safety standards vary widely. There have been some major accidents, with boats sinking and passengers killed.

GILI STRONG: REBUILDING PARADISE

When a 6.4 magnitude earthquake rattled mainland Lombok on 29 July 2018, most on the Gili Islands simply shrugged their shoulders. Little did they know that it was a 'foreshock' for a larger 6.9 earthquake the following Sunday, August 5, that would topple resorts and restaurants across this mini-archipelago.

A tsunami warning prompted the majority of those staying on Trawangan to spend the night on the Gilis' lone hill. Many on the flatter islands of Air and Meno huddled together on interior fields. Thankfully, the tsunami waves never materialised, but the prolonged and chaotic rescue operation the following day captured global headlines.

There were widespread reports of looting on the Gili Islands in the immediate aftermath, forcing the police to set up posts on each island. Many businesses were shaken up beyond repair, particularly on the southeastern corner of Meno, in the main village of Trawangan and along Trawangan's western coastline. In general, businesses built of bamboo or wood fared far better than those made of concrete.

Residents rallied around the motto 'Gili Strong' in the weeks after the quake and used it as a marketing pitch to lure tourists back. By September, a few fast boats had resumed services from Bali, carrying intrepid visitors to these battered isles. Rebuilding was hampered slightly by a lack of workers (many were busy caring for families back on mainland Lombok). Yet the islands have shown incredible resilience and, at the time of writing, were well on their way to recovery.

FROM LOMBOK

Coming from Lombok, you can travel by fast boat from Teluk Nare/Teluk Kade north of Senggigi. Many of these services are operated by hotels and dive outfits based in the Gilis (making prearranged diving/accommodation and transfer options appealing), but private charters with local owners are also possible. Most people still use the public boats that leave from Bangsal Harbour.

Boat tickets at Bangsal Harbour are sold at the port's large ticket office, which is where you can also charter a boat. Buy a ticket elsewhere and you're getting played.

Schedules & Fares

Public boats to the Gilis run most frequently before noon; after that you shouldn't wait much more than an hour for boats to Gili T or Gili Air, while special boats depart for Gili Meno at 2pm and 5pm. With the exception of these afternoon transfers to Gili Meno, all boats leave, in both directions, only when full – about 45 people. If the seas are high and the boat (over)loaded, riding these battered outriggers can be a hair-raising experience. When no public boat is running to your Gili, you may have to charter a boat (350,000Rp to 500,000Rp, for up to 10 people), or decide this is the safer option in any case.

One-way public fares are 14,000Rp to Gili Air, 15,000Rp to Gili Meno (25,000Rp for the special afternoon boats) and 20,000Rp to Gili Trawangan. Boats often pull up on the beaches; be prepared to wade ashore.

Public fast boats now run almost hourly in daytime on a route linking Gili T, Gili Meno, Gili Air and Bangsal; they cost 85,000Rp.

Scams

Although Bangsal Harbour has had a bad reputation for years, hassles here are much reduced. One still-common rort is for shuttle buses to drop passengers just short of the harbour, where *cidomo* drivers, claiming there's some distance to go, ask 60,000Rp to complete the journey. Ignore them and walk the last 300m. Other touts may claim the public boats aren't running, or that you need to buy mosquito repellent and sunblock before getting to the Gilis. Ignore them too, but note that anyone who helps you with bags deserves a tip (10,000Rp per bag is appropriate). There are ATMs.

Getting to Bangsal Harbour

Coming by public transport via Mataram and Senggigi, catch a bus or bemo to Pemenang, from where it's a 1.2km walk to Bangsal Harbour – or 5000Rp by *ojek* (motorcycle taxi). A metered taxi to the port will take you to the harbour. From Senggigi, Perama (p296) offers a bus and boat connection to the Gilis for a reasonable 150,000Rp (two hours).

Arriving in Bangsal, you'll be offered rides in shared vehicles at the port. To Senggigi, 100,000Rp is a fair price. Otherwise, walk 500m down the access road past the huge tsunami shelter to the Blue Bird Lombok Taksi stand (p456), always the best taxi choice, for metered rides to Senggigi (around 100,000Rp), the airport (220,000Rp) and Kuta (250,000Rp).

Getting Around

There's no motorised transport on the Gilis – one of their greatest charms.

BOAT

Public fast boats run almost hourly in daytime on a route linking Gili T, Gili Meno, Gili Air and Bangsal; they cost 85,000Rp. This makes it easy to hop from one Gili to another.

There's also a slow island-hopping boat service that loops between all three islands (25,000Rp to 35,000Rp). There is typically a morning boat and an afternoon one, but it's best to check the latest timetable at the islands' docks. You can always charter boats between the islands (300,000Rp to 400,000Rp).

CIDOMO

We cannot recommend using *cidomo* (horse-drawn carts) due to the significant concerns about the treatment of the horses.

WALKING & CYCLING

The Gilis are flat and easy enough to get around by foot. Bicycles, available for hire on all three islands (40,000Rp to 60,000Rp per day), can be a fun way to get around, but sandy stretches of path mean that you will spend time pushing your bike in the hot sun.

GILI TRAWANGAN

☎0370 / POP 1500

Gili Trawangan is a tropical playground of global renown, ranking alongside Bali and Borobudur as one of Indonesia's top destinations. Trawangan's heaving main drag, busy with bikes, *cidomos* and mobs of scantily clad visitors, can surprise those expecting a languid island retreat. Instead, a bustling string of lounge bars, hip guesthouses, ambitious restaurants, convenience stores and dive schools clamours for attention.

And yet behind this glitzy facade, a bohemian character endures, with rickety warungs (cheap eating houses) and reggae joints surviving between the cocktail tables, and quiet retreats dotting the much-less-busy north coast. Even as massive 200-plus-room hotels begin to colonise the gentrifying west coast, you can head just inland to a village laced with sandy lanes roamed by free-range roosters, fussing *ibu* (mothers) and wild-haired kids playing hopscotch. Here the call of the muezzin, not happy hour, defines the time of day.

Beaches

Gili T is ringed by the sort of powdery white sand people expect to find on Bali, but don't. It can be crowded along the bar-lined main part of the strip, but walk just a bit north or south and west and you'll find some of Gili T's nicest swimming and snorkelling beaches. You can discover more solitude in parts of the west and north coasts, where it will be you and your towel on the sand – although water and Bintang vendors are never far away.

Note that at low tide large portions of the west and north coasts have rocks and coral near the surface, which makes trying to get off the shore deeply unpleasant.

Many people simply enjoy the sensational views of Lombok and Gunung Rinjani (from the east coast) as well as Bali and Gunung Agung (west).

Sights

Lookout — VIEWPOINT

See the spectacular sights from the only hill in the Gilis. During the August 2018 Lombok earthquake, more than a thousand tourists and locals slept atop this hill fearing an imminent tsunami (which, thankfully, never came).

Activities

Almost everything to do on Gili T will involve the water at some point, though yoga, spas and culinary classes all vie for attention.

Diving & Snorkelling

There's fun snorkelling off the beach 200m north of the boat landing – the coral isn't in the best shape here, but there are tons of fish and turtles. The reef is in slightly better shape off the northwest coast, but at low tide you'll have to scramble over some sharp dead coral (bring rubber booties) to access it. Snorkel-gear rental averages 50,000Rp per day.

Trawangan is a major diving hot spot, with two-dozen professional scuba and free-diving schools. Most dive schools and shops have good accommodation for clients who want to book a package.

Safety standards are reasonably high, but with the proliferation of new dive schools on Gili T, several have formed the Gili Island Divers Association (GIDA). We highly recommend diving with GIDA-associated shops, which come together for monthly meetings on conservation and dive-impact issues. They all observe common standards relating to the safety and number of their divers. They carry oxygen on their boats,

have working radios and dedicate time and resources to the preservation of the reefs, waters and shoreline. They also have a price agreement for fun dives, training and certification. Sample prices:

Introductory Dive 900,000Rp

Open Water Course 5,500,000Rp

Rescue Diver & EFR Course 7,000,000Rp

★**Blue Marlin Dive Centre** DIVING
(Map p320; ☎0370-613 2424; www.bluemarlindive.com; Jl Raya Trawangan; single dive 490,000Rp) This is Gili T's original dive shop and one of the best tech diving schools in the world. It's a GIDA member *and* home to one of Gili T's classic bars.

★**Freedive Gili** DIVING
(Map p320; ☎0370-619 7180; www.freedivegili.com; Jl Raya Trawangan; level I/level II course 3,995,000/5,495,000Rp; ⏰8am-8pm) Freediving is a breath-holding technique that

Gili Trawangan

Activities, Courses & Tours
1 Desha Spa ... C2
2 Lutwala Dive ... B1

Sleeping
3 Alam Gili ... C1
4 Coconut Garden ... B2
5 Eden Cottages ... B1
6 Gili Eco Villas ... B1
7 Gili Teak Resort ... B3
8 Gili Treehouses ... B2
9 Jali Resort ... C2
10 Kelapa Villas ... B2
11 Pondok Santi Estate ... B4
12 Wilson's Retreat ... B1

Eating
Jali Kitchen ... (see 9)
13 Pituq Waroeng ... B2

Drinking & Nightlife
14 Casa Vintage Beach ... A3
15 Exile ... B4

DIVING THE GILIS

The Gili Islands are an extremely popular dive destination, with plentiful and varied marine life to be encountered across about 25 closely packed sites. Turtles (green and hawksbill) and black- and white-tip reef sharks are common, and the macro life (small stuff) is excellent, with seahorses, pipefish and lots of crustaceans. Around the full moon, large schools of bumphead parrotfish appear to feast on coral spawn; at other times of year (generally February and March) manta rays cruise past dive sites.

Do note that while the Gilis have their share of virgin sites, years of bomb fishing, El Niño–induced bleaching, coral anchoring and poor tourist behaviour have damaged many corals above 18m, making deeper dives more visually appealing. Visibility is generally good (20m to 30m), temperatures range from 25°C to 30°C and usually calm stretches of water make the Gilis an excellent place to learn to dive. However, there are deeper waters, stronger currents and more challenging sites, too, catering to drift diving and more advanced practitioners.

Some of the best dive sites include the following:

Deep Halik A canyon-like site ideally suited to drift diving. Black- and white-tip sharks are often seen at 28m to 30m.

Deep Turbo At around 30m, this site is ideally suited to nitrox diving. It has impressive sea fans and leopard sharks hidden in the crevasses.

Japanese Wreck For experienced divers only (it lies at 45m), this shipwreck of a Japanese patrol boat (c WWII) is another site ideal for tech divers.

Mirko's Reef Named for a beloved dive instructor who passed away, this canyon was never bombed and has vibrant, pristine soft and table coral formations. It's also known as 'Secret Reef'.

Shark Point Perhaps the most exhilarating Gili dive: reef sharks and turtles are very regularly encountered, as well as schools of bumphead parrotfish and mantas. There's also a newly sunken tugboat to explore.

Sunset (Manta Point) Some impressive table coral; sharks and large pelagics are frequently encountered.

allows you to explore greater depths than snorkelling (to 30m and beyond). Owned by an expert diver who has touched 111m on a single breath, Freedive Gili offers two-day level I and three-day level II courses. After a two-day course many students are able to get down to 20m. It also has yoga and accommodation on site.

Manta Dive DIVING
(Map p320; ☎0370-614 3649; www.manta-dive.com; Jl Raya Trawangan; open-water courses 5,500,000Rp) The biggest SSI dive school and one of the best on the island, Manta has a large compound that spans the main road and a pool. It is a GIDA member and has instructor training and tech programs.

Trawangan Dive DIVING
(Map p320; ☎0370-614 9220; www.trawangandive.com; Jl Raya Trawangan; 5 guided nitrox boat dives from 2,700,000Rp) A top, long-running dive shop and GIDA member with a fun pool-party vibe. Ask how you can join the regular beach clean-ups with the Gili Eco Trust. Also runs Biorock coral gardening courses and a wide range of tech courses (including rebreather training).

Big Bubble DIVING
(Map p320; ☎0811 390 969; www.bigbubblediving.com; Jl Raya Trawangan; fun dive day/night 490,000/600,000Rp) The original engine behind the island's notable green-crusading NGO, Gili Eco Trust, and a long-running dive school and GIDA member, Big Bubble was in the midst of a complete rebuild after the 2018 earthquakes with plans to reopen in early 2019.

Lutwala Dive DIVING
(Map p317; ☎0877 6549 2615; www.lutwala.com; Jl Raya Trawangan; divemaster course 14,000,000Rp; ⏲8am-6pm) A nitrox and five-star PADI centre, this dive shop is a member of GIDA and rents top-quality snorkelling gear. There's accommodation on-site (rooms from 700,000Rp) plus a very nice garden cafe-bar

to relax in post-plunge. Make sure you say hello to the parrots.

Surfing

Trawangan has a fast right reef break off its southern tip that is best surfed December to March or on a windless high-season day. The beach nearby is lined with vendors renting boards.

Walking & Cycling

Trawangan is perfect for exploring on foot or by bike. You can walk around the whole island in a couple of hours – if you finish at the hill on the southwestern corner (which has the remains of an old Japanese gun placement circa WWII), you'll have terrific sunset views of Bali's Gunung Agung.

Bikes (per day from 40,000Rp to 70,000Rp; bargain hard) are a great way to get around. You'll find loads of rental outlets on the main strip, or your guesthouse can help you out. Beware the sandy, bike-unfriendly north coast and note that the paths across the interior of the island are usually in the best shape for cycling.

Sila CYCLING
(Map p320; 0878 6562 3015; Jl Raya Trawangan; bike rentals per day from 50,000Rp) Has a huge range of bikes for rent, including two-seaters. Also does boat trips.

Yoga & Wellness

Desha Spa MASSAGE
(Map p317; 0877 6510 5828; Jl Kelapa; 9am-9pm) Not as bare-bones as the massage parlours on the strip nor as posh and expensive as the hotel spas, this spot on the cross-island road is your happy medium. In addition to the standard massage options, there are coconut scrubs, pedicures, facials or aloe vera sunburn treatments.

Gili Yoga YOGA
(Map p320; 0370-619 7180; www.giliyoga.com; Jl Raya Trawangan; per person from 120,000Rp; 7am-6pm) Runs two daily vinyasa flow and hatha classes; attached to Freedive Gili (p317).

Courses

Sweet & Spicy Cooking School COOKING
(Map p320; 0878 6577 6429; www.facebook.com/gilicookingschool; Jl Raya Trawangan; classes from 385,000Rp) Learn how to transform chillis and myriad other seasonings into spicy and flavourful Indonesian dishes at these entertaining daily cooking classes. As always, you get to eat your work.

Sleeping

Gili T has reached a saturation point with hundreds of registered places to stay, ranging from thatched huts to sleek, air-conditioned villas with private pools. In peak season (July and August) the best places can book out, but with so much competition, prices have dropped considerably. You'll find steep low-season discounts.

Virtually all dive schools offer midrange accommodation; the cheapest digs are in the village.

Village

Gili La Boheme Sister HOSTEL $
(Map p320; 0853 3733 4339; Jl Ikan Duyung; dm with fan/air-con 130,000/150,000Rp;) Exposed brick walls, repurposed wood, tiled floors and a rainbow of colours – that's the design formula at this quirky, eye-pleasing hostel. Some beds are located in funky hexagonal rooms and there are several chill common areas.

Mango Tree Homestay HOMESTAY $
(Map p320; 0823 5912 0421; Jl Karang Biru; d 300,000Rp) This friendly homestay in a quieter part of the village offers eight simple doubles facing each other across a shady, fern-filled courtyard. The young staff are relaxed but competent, ukelele music frequently sweetens the air and bikes can be hired for 40,000Rp per day.

Madison Gili BUNGALOW $
(Map p320; 0878 6594 5554; www.madisongilli.com; Jl Kepiting; r 350,000-700,000Rp;) Twelve bungalow-style units are crowded

> **CULTURAL RESPECT**
>
> As almost all Gili Islanders are Muslim, visitors should keep these cultural considerations in mind:
>
> - It's not at all acceptable to wander the village lanes in a swimsuit, no matter how many others you see doing so. Cover up away from the beach or hotel pool.
> - Nude sunbathing anywhere is offensive.
> - During the month of Ramadan many locals fast during daylight hours and there are no all-night parties on Gili Trawangan.

Gili Trawangan East

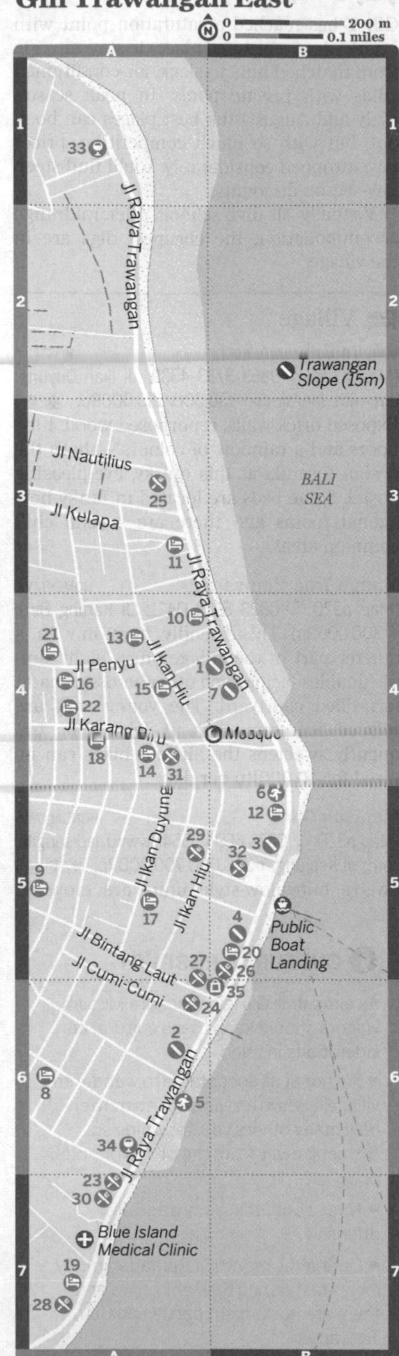

Gili Trawangan East

Activities, Courses & Tours

1 Big Bubble B4
2 Blue Marlin Dive Centre A6
3 Freedive Gili B5
Gili Yoga .... (see 3)
4 Manta Dive B5
5 Sila A6
6 Sweet & Spicy Cooking School B5
7 Trawangan Dive B4

Sleeping

8 Alexyane Paradise A6
9 Amora Villa A5
10 Balé Sampan A4
11 Blu d'aMare A3
12 Gili Beach Bum Hotel B5
13 Gili Joglo A4
14 Gili La Boheme Sister A4
15 Gili Mansion A4
16 Indigo Bungalows A4
17 Madison Gili A5
18 Mango Tree Homestay A4
19 Pearl of Trawangan A7
20 Sama Sama Bungalows B5
21 Villa Nero A4
22 Woodstock A4

Eating

23 Beach House A7
24 Fan A6
25 Hellocapitano A3
26 Kayu Café B5
27 La Dolce Vita A5
28 Pearl Beach Lounge A7
29 Regina A5
30 Scallywags A7
31 Thai Garden A4
32 Warung Dewi B5

Drinking & Nightlife

Blue Marlin .... (see 2)
33 La Moomba A1
34 Tir na Nog A6

Shopping

35 Abdi B6

into a tight site around a pool. However, through clever design, each unit feels private. The rooms are comfortable and have extras like fridges. Staff are helpful. It's got a quiet back-lane location.

Woodstock BUNGALOW $

(Map p320; ☎0878 6433 7237; www.woodstockgili.com; Jl Karang Biru; r with fan/air-con from 350,000/600,000Rp; ❄📶🏊) Should the vibe surprise you, given the name? Commune with the spirit of the Dead, drop out with Baez and turn on with Hendrix in 12 good-value rooms with tribal accents, private porches and outdoor bathrooms, all surrounding a laid-back pool area.

Gili Mansion HOSTEL $
(Map p320; 0852 3836 3836; https://gilimansion.com; Jl Ikan Hiu; dm/d from 80,000/200,000Rp;) Though the gimmicky castle theme is a real island buzzkill, this always-booming hostel is nevertheless one of the best budget bets in town with clean three-bed dorms, super cheap (if soulless) private rooms and a non-stop party vibe centred around the pool.

Indigo Bungalows GUESTHOUSE $$
(Map p320; 0818 0371 0909; www.facebook.com/indigogilit; Jl Penyu; r from 550,000Rp;) In the crowded Gili T midrange market, Indigo stands out for its attention to detail. The six rooms have hot water, patios and views of the pool or gardens. It's got a nice, quiet compound feel.

Alexyane Paradise BUNGALOW $$
(Map p320; 0878 6599 9645; oceaneparadise@hotmail.com; Jl Ikan Baronang; r 300,000-900,000Rp;) Five great-quality darkwood cottages (one is family-sized) with high ceilings, bamboo beds and lovely light-flooded outdoor bathrooms.

Amora Villa BUNGALOW $$
(Map p320; 0822 3521 5244; https://amoravillagili.com; off Jl Kepiting; bungalow incl breakfast 500,000-1,500,000Rp;) Thirteen *lumbung* (rice-barn) cottages, set deep in the village, tucked up against the hillside, surrounding a large pool. They're a great deal off season, but overpriced in peak times.

★ **Gili Joglo** VILLA $$$
(Map p320; 0813 5678 4741; www.gilijoglo.com; Jl Ikan Hiu; villas from 1,500,000Rp;) You'll find three fabulous villas here. One is crafted out of an *joglo* (traditional Javanese house) with polished concrete floors, two bedrooms and a massive indoor/outdoor great room. Though slightly smaller, we prefer the one built from two 1950s *gladaks* (middle-class homes). Rooms come with butler service.

Villa Nero VILLA $$$
(Map p320; 0819 0904 8000; www.thevillanero.com; Jl Penyu; villas incl breakfast from US$250;) One of the best-run (if totally overpriced) places to stay on Gili T. Each of the 10 large units has hardwood floors across multiple rooms and a large lounging patio. The scheme is refreshingly minimalist, with accents of art and green plants. Among the many amenities: free bike use.

Beachside

★ **Gili Beach Bum Hotel** HOSTEL $
(Map p320; 0877 6526 7037; www.gilibeachbum.com; Jl Raya Trawangan; dm 140,000-200,000Rp;) Formerly the Gili Hostel, this co-ed dorm complex has 19 triple rooms, some under a thatched Torajan-style roof. The rooms have concrete floors, high ceilings, lockers and their own bathrooms. Out front is the Lava Bar (open until 1am and often raucous) and there are weekly parties in the on-site pool. Breakfast is included.

Sama Sama Bungalows BUNGALOW $
(Map p320; 0811 399 649; Jl Raya Trawangan; dm/r/bungalow 100,000/350,000/550,000Rp;) A few metres from where the fast boats drop you on the beach, the two *lumbung* (rice-barn) units and seven rooms here are perfect if you want to be right in the heart of the action. Be warned that the music from the attached Sama Sama Reggae bar plays until 1am (to 3am on Saturday).

★ **Blu d'aMare** BUNGALOW $$
(Map p320; 0858 8866 2490; Jl Raya Trawangan; r from 500,000Rp;) At Blu d'aMare you can bed down in one of five lovely 1920s Javanese houses *(joglo)*. Features include gorgeous old wood floors, queen beds, and freshwater showers in a sunken bathroom. It has a fine, Euro-accented cafe.

Balé Sampan HOTEL $$
(Map p320; www.balesampanbungalows.com; Jl Raya Trawangan; r incl breakfast garden/pool 910,000/1,000,000Rp;) On a nice wide-open stretch of beach. The 13 fine modern-edge rooms have stone bathrooms and plush duvet covers. Other highlights include a freshwater pool and a proper English breakfast.

Pearl of Trawangan RESORT $$$
(Map p320; 0813 3715 6999; www.pearloftrawangan.com; Jl Raya Trawangan; r incl breakfast from 1,600,000Rp;) Sinuous bamboo and thatch architecture echo the curves of the pool at this upscale property at the south end of the strip. There are tidy bungalows with 91 rooms on the inland side of the beach walk. Terraces boast very comfortable loungers. On the actual beach, there's a plush beach club.

North, South & West Coast

★ **Eden Cottages** COTTAGE $$
(Map p317; 0819 1799 6151; www.edencottages.com; Jl Lili Laut; cottages 600,000-750,000Rp;

(❄📶🏊) Eden takes the form of six clean, thatched concrete bungalows wrapped around a pool, fringed by a garden and shaded by a coconut grove. Rooms have tasteful furnishings, stone bathrooms, TV-DVD and freshwater showers. The charming expat owner does all she can to ensure her guests' serenity (including installing wi-fi).

A new veggie cafe-bar was in the works at the time of research.

Coconut Garden BUNGALOW **$$**
(Map p317; ☎0819 0795 6926; www.coconutgardenresort.com; off Jl Kelapa; r incl breakfast from 750,000Rp; ❄📶🏊) An atmospheric spot with six bright and airy glass-fronted Javanese-style houses with tiled roofs connected to outdoor terrazzo bathrooms. Expect plush linens, queen beds, a rolling lawn dotted with coco palms and a small pool. It's on its own in a quiet inland quarter of the island and can be hard to find. Call ahead.

Gili Teak Resort BOUTIQUE HOTEL **$$**
(Map p317; ☎0853 3383 6324; www.giliteak.com; Jl Raya Trawangan; r incl breakfast from 1,000,000Rp; ❄📶🏊) New Age bungalows have teak walls and a stylish, simple design that lets in lots of light. Terraces for each of the 11 units have plush loungers, plus there's a lovely seating area down by the ocean, all of which begs guests to settle back, relax and let the days drift by. The grounds are attractive, the cafe good.

Alam Gili HOTEL **$$**
(Map p317; ☎0370-613 0466; www.alamgili.com; Jl Raya Trawangan; r from US$75; ❄📶🏊) A lush mature garden and a quiet beach location are the main draws here. The nine rooms and villas in a small compound boast elegant lashings of old-school Balinese style. A small pool and a cafe are on the beach.

Jali Resort BOUTIQUE HOTEL **$$**
(Map p317; ☎0817 000 5254; www.jaliresortgilitrawangan.com; Jl Nautilius; r incl breakfast 1,350,000Rp; ❄📶🏊) Sixteen turquoise-tiled rooms surround a frangipani-shaded pool in this exceedingly stylish and pleasantly compact boutique hotel.

★**Wilson's Retreat** RESORT **$$$**
(Map p317; ☎0878 6177 2111; www.wilsons-retreat.com; Jl Raya Trawangan; r/villa incl breakfast from 1,400,000/2,500,000Rp; ❄📶🏊) Wilson's has 16 rooms plus four villas with private pools. The setting is expansive, stylish and classy, but it still manages some Gili languor. The excellent cafe overlooks a fine stretch of beach.

★**Gili Treehouses** TREEHOUSE **$$$**
(Map p317; ☎0819 1601 6634; www.gilitreehouses.com; off Jl Kelapa; r incl breakfast 1,000,000-3,500,000Rp; ❄📶🏊) These five 'treehouses' (really stilted wooden villas) are a welcome change from the tried and true Gili T villa concept. Though tightly packed together, each feels remarkably secluded with cool chill spaces below the rooms that have kitchenettes, loungers and private pools. Perks include free bikes and portable wi-fi boxes.

Pondok Santi Estate RESORT **$$$**
(Map p317; ☎0819 0705 7504; www.pondoksanti.com; Jl Raya Trawangan; r incl breakfast from US$200; ❄📶🏊) Seventeen gorgeous bungalows are set well apart on this old coconut plantation. Lawns now cover the grounds, and this is easily one of the classier-looking resorts on Gili T. The units have outdoor showers and rich, traditional wood decor. It's on a great beach and *just* close enough to the strip. Huge pool.

Gili Eco Villas VILLA **$$$**
(Map p317; ☎0370-613 6057; www.giliecovillas.com; Jl Raya Trawangan; r/villa from US$120/250; ❄📶🏊) 🍃 Nineteen classy rooms and villas, made from recycled teak salvaged from old Javanese colonial buildings, are set back from the beach on Trawangan's relaxed north coast. Comfort and style are combined with solid green principles (water is recycled and there's an organic vegetable garden).

Kelapa Villas VILLA **$$$**
(Map p317; ☎0812 375 6003; www.kelapavillas.com; Jl Kelapa; villas from 1,500,000Rp; ❄📶🏊) Luxury development in an inland location with a selection of 18 commodious villas (all with private pools) that offer style and space in abundance. A tennis court and a gym are in the complex.

Eating

Gili T now rivals Bali in its culinary prowess with slick coffee shops, creative Indo fusion eateries and plenty of vegan and health-food cafes. In the evenings, numerous places on the main strip display and grill delicious fresh seafood. Pick by what looks good (it should all be superfresh), and by whose grilling skills seem to be superior.

★**Jali Kitchen** ASIAN **$**
(Map p317; ☎0817 000 5254; www.jaliresortgilitrawangan.com; Jl Nautilius; mains 45,000-

70,000Rp; 7am-11pm;) Distressed wood, gorgeous tiles and abundant foliage combine to give this eye-pleasing restaurant a chic and earthy vibe. The Asian-fusion dishes combine the familiar with the exotic in intriguing ways, and there are several options for vegetarians. Stand-out service to boot!

★ Warung Dewi INDONESIAN $

(Map p320; 0819 0763 3826; Jl Kardinal; mains 25,000-35,000Rp; 7am-8pm) The best traditional warung on Gili T is just a few steps back from the high-priced bustle of the main strip. The *nasi campur* is fantastic (coconut sambal, jackfruit curry, fried chicken and several vegetable sides is a common combination) while vegetarians will like the *plecing kangkung* (a spicy Sasak water spinach dish).

Hellocapitano CAFE $

(Map p320; 0853 3313 4110; www.hellocapitano.com; Jl Nautilius; mains 45,000-75,000Rp; 7am-9pm) A whimsical little pastel shack where you can order delicious smoothie bowls, iced lattes, burgers or local bites (try the chicken rendang!). Sit upstairs for a breezy sea view and be sure to ask the owner about his land- and water-based island tours.

★ Pituq Waroeng VEGAN $$

(Map p317; 0812 3677 5161; http://pituq.com; Jl Kelapa; small plates 20,000-30,000Rp; 9am-10pm;) Where else in the world will you find classic Indonesian fare reinterpreted as exquisite vegan tapas? Gather a group of friends (including any and all carnivores), sit together at one of the low-rise tables and order like there is no tomorrow. You can thank us later!

Fan CHINESE $$

(Map p320; 0852 5331 9394; www.facebook.com/fanchinesefood; Jl Cumi Cumi; mains 50,000-85,000; 9.30am-9.30pm) Home-made dumplings, wontons and broad noodles are the stars of this tiny Chinese restaurant that expats rave about as their secret spot. You'll dine at one long table and probably leave with new friends.

Beach House INTERNATIONAL $$

(Map p320; 0878 6440 4891; www.beachhousegilit.com; Jl Raya Trawangan; mains 70,000-250,000Rp; 3-11pm;) Boasts an elegant marina terrace, a wonderful nightly barbecue, a salad bar and fine wine. Among much competition, it's a contender for the best barbecued seafood in town.

Pearl Beach Lounge INTERNATIONAL $$

(Map p320; 0370-619 4884; www.pearlbeachlounge.com; Jl Raya Trawangan; mains 70,000-200,000Rp; 7am-11pm;) The bamboo flows only a little less fluidly than the beer at this high-concept beachside lounge and restaurant. During the day, spending 100,000Rp on food and drink from the burger- and salad-filled menu gets you access to comfy beach loungers. At night the striking bamboo main pavilion comes alive, and more complex steak and seafood mains are on offer.

Thai Garden THAI $$

(Map p320; 0878 6453 1253; Jl Karang Biru; mains 50,000-120,000Rp; 3-10pm Sun-Thu, from noon Fri & Sat) Who needs Bangkok when you have Gili T? The most authentic Thai food this side of Phuket is served up in a cute little garden. The flavours are spot on thanks to regular imports of key spices. This is the place to beat the Indo rice blues.

Regina PIZZA $$

(Map p320; 0877 6506 6255; Jl Ikan Hiu; pizza 40,000-100,000Rp; 5-11pm) The wood-fired oven rarely gets a break at this excellent Italian joint, just inland. At busy times there's a long line for takeaway pizzas, but a better option is to find a bamboo table in the garden and have some cold ones with the fine thin-crust pies. A sign announces: 'no pizza pineapple'. Ahh, the sound of authenticity...

Kayu Café CAFE $$

(Map p320; 0878 6547 2260; www.facebook.com/kayucafe; Jl Raya Trawangan; mains 65,000-70,000Rp; 7am-9pm;) Kayu is one of the original cafes on the inland side of the strip. It has an array of healthy baked goods, salads, sandwiches, rice bowls and the island's best juices, all served in air-con comfort.

La Dolce Vita ITALIAN $$

(Map p320; 0813 1772 0228; Jl Bintang Laut; piadinas 50,000Rp, mains 100,000-110,000Rp; 11am-10pm) There comes that moment when another nasi goreng will just make you turn nasty. Don't delay, hop right on over to this expanded cafe that's not much bigger than one of its excellent espressos. Slices of authentic pizza and a whole range of pastries are joined by daily specials cooked by the Italian chef-owner.

Scallywags INTERNATIONAL $$

(Map p320; 0819 1743 2086; www.scallywagsresort.com; Jl Raya Trawangan; mains 40,000-180,000Rp; 7am-10pm;) Scallywags offers

GREEN GILI

When you pay your hotel or diving bill on the Gilis you may be offered the chance to pay an 'Eco Donation' (50,000Rp per person). It's a voluntary donation, set up by the pioneering Gili Eco Trust (www.giliecotrust.com) to improve the islands' environment.

It's a worthy cause. The environmental pressure on the Gilis as their popularity has grown is enormous. Intensive development and rubbish plus offshore reef damage from fishers using cyanide and dynamite to harvest fish have been just some of the problems. Up to 10,000 visitors and workers arrive on the islands each day.

Gili Eco Trust has several initiatives to help:

- Selling reusable shopping bags to cut down on plastic-bag use, and encouraging restaurants to stop using plastic straws (we didn't see any when we visited!).
- An aggressive education campaign to get locals and business owners to recycle their rubbish. There are now over 1000 recycling bins on the islands.
- A long-term scheme to recycle virtually all the trash on the islands with a rubbish bank.
- Care of the islands' horses – vet clinics are offered and there are education programs in horse care for drivers.
- Biorock, an artificial reef-restoration program that now has over 150 installations around the islands.
- Installing more than 150 mooring buoys to stop coral anchoring.

There are many ways visitors to the Gilis can help, in addition to paying the Eco Tax:

Clean up the beach Gili Eco Trust organises regular beach clean-ups (typically on Fridays at 5pm). More hands are always needed and you'll be rewarded for your time with some free treats or a beer from the weekly sponsor.

Report horse mistreatment Anyone seeing a *cidomo* (horse-drawn cart) driver mistreating a horse can get the number of the cart and report it to the **Eco Trust** (☎0813 3960 0553), which will follow up with the driver. Unfortunately, many transport carts with their heavy loads of construction supplies and Bintang have no cart numbers for reporting.

Build a reef For 10,000,000Rp you'll get two dives a day for two weeks, the opportunity to help build a Biorock installation, and various specialist diving certifications. Gili Eco Trust has details.

Refill water bottles Help cut down on plastic waste by refilling your water bottle at designated stations all across the Gilis. Some places offer water refills for free; others for about 2000Rp or 3000Rp (way cheaper than buying a new bottle!). Download the app Refill Bali to find the closest tank.

casual yet stylish beach decor, polished glassware, switched-on service and superb cocktails. The dinner menu features tasty seafood – fresh lobster, tuna steaks, snapper and swordfish – and a great salad bar. The seafood barbecue lures many.

Drinking & Nightlife

Gili T has oodles of beachside drinking dens, ranging from sleek lounge bars to simple shacks. Parties are held several nights a week, shifting between mainstay bars such as Tir na Nog and various other upstarts. The strip south of the pier is the centre for raucous nightlife with places that were once bars now rapidly evolving into full-fledged clubs.

★Casa Vintage Beach LOUNGE

(Map p317; www.casavintagebeach.com; Jl Raya Trawangan; ⏲10am-midnight) Facing Bali's Gunung Agung and some superb sunsets, Casa Vintage is the best place to enjoy a sundowner on Trawangan. A brochure-perfect beach is littered with cushions and loungers, trees shelter hammocks and trestles, the Swedish-Jamaican owners do amazing Caribbean food (mains 70,000Rp to 115,000Rp), the soundtrack is just right (Billie Holiday, reggae, latin) and bonfires keep the atmosphere warm past sundown.

Exile BAR

(Map p317; ☎0819 0772 1858; http://theexilegilit.com; Jl Raya Trawangan; ⏲8am-late) This beach bar has a party vibe at all hours. It's locally owned and 20 minutes from the main strip on foot, or an easy bike ride. There is also a compound of 10 woven bamboo bungalows with rooms from 450,000Rp, just in case home seems too far.

Tir na Nog PUB
(Map p320; 0370-613 9463; www.tirnanogbar.com; Jl Raya Trawangan; 7am-2am Thu-Tue, to 3am Wed;) Known simply as 'the Irish', this hangar of hangovers has a sports-bar interior with big screens. Its shoreside open-air bar is probably the busiest meeting spot on the island. It serves bar chow such as fajitas and spicy wings (mains 50,000Rp to 100,000Rp). Jovial mayhem truly reigns on 'party night' every Wednesday. There's also live music Sunday nights.

La Moomba BAR
(Map p320; Jl Raya Trawangan; 7am-midnight) This beach bar straddles the road just north of Turtle Point. The Western and Indo fare is good (mains 65,000Rp to 85,000Rp), tables and loungers are dotted about the sand and there are great views across to Gili Meno and the cloud-capped heights of Gunung Rinjani beyond. After sundown the squid-fishing boats light up the nearby waters in eerie phosphorescent green.

Blue Marlin BAR
(Map p320; Jl Raya Trawangan; 8am-late) Of all the party bars, this upper-level venue has the largest dance floor and the meanest sound system – it pumps trance and tribal beats on Mondays.

Shopping

Abdi CLOTHING
(Map p320; Jl Raya Trawangan; 10am-8pm) Forgot your favourite frock? Shop for flouncy beachwear at this stylish shop.

Information

Gili T has abundant ATMs on the main strip and even on the west coast.

Blue Island Medical Clinic (Map p320; 0819 9970 5701; http://blueislandclinic.com; Jl Raya Trawangan; 24hr) Medical clinic among the shops immediately south of Hotel Vila Ombak. Also has clinics on Gili Air and Gili Meno.

Getting There & Away

You can buy tickets and catch public and island-hopping boats at the public boat landing. While you wait for your ship to sail, note the amazing number of Bintang bottles arriving full and leaving empty. Several of the fast-boat companies have offices on Gili T. These fast boats anchor all along the beach on the east side.

GILI MENO

0370 / POP 700

Gili Meno is the smallest of the three Gili Islands and a good setting for your desert-island fantasy. Ringed by gorgeous beaches and teeming reefs, Meno is also the quietest and most traditional of the three, beloved more of honeymooners and mature travellers than the full-moon-party set.

Most accommodation is strung out along the east coast, near the most picturesque beach. Inland you'll find scattered homesteads, coconut plantations and a salty lake. The once-lonely west coast is seeing some high-profile development, including an enormous beachside condo project called Bask (www.baskgilimeno.com) that is slated to have over 85 villas when it opens in 2020. It's got some powerful Australian backers and a high-profile pitchman, ex-*Baywatch* star David Hasselhoff (aka 'The Hoff'). The effect of this huge resort on little Gili Meno is likely to be profound.

Beaches

Ringed by sand, Gili Meno has one of the best strips of beach in the Gilis at its southeast corner. The beach is wide and the sand powdery white; swimming and snorkelling are excellent. The west coast is rockier, with outcrops and coral near the surface at low tide. Meno's northeast also has nice sand, although erosion is a problem in parts.

Activities

Like the other Gilis, most of the fun here involves getting wet. Additionally, walking around the island is scenic and takes less than two hours.

Diving & Snorkelling

Snorkelling is good off the northeast coast, on the west coast towards the north, and also around the site of the vast new Bask hotel on the west coast, where you'll find the underwater sculpture Nest (p326). Gear is available from 50,000Rp per day from guesthouses or dive shops (of which there are only a few on this island). **Meno Slope** and **Meno Wall** are two top dive sites.

Gili Meno

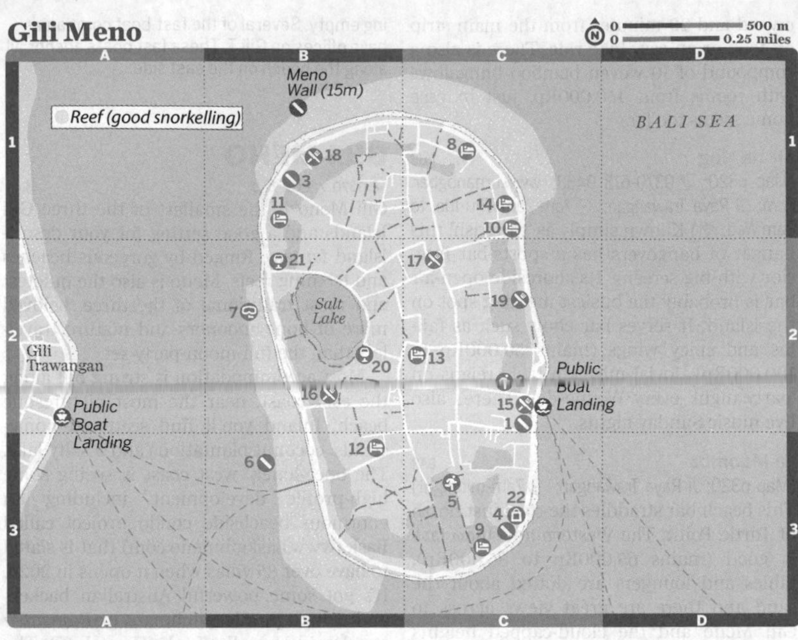

Gili Meno

Activities, Courses & Tours

1 Blue Marlin Dive C2
2 Blue Ocean C2
3 Divine Divers B1
4 Gili Meno Divers C3
5 Mao Meno C3
6 Meno Slope (21m) B3
7 Nest B2

Sleeping

8 Ana Bungalows C1
9 Biru Meno Beach Bungalows C3
10 Gili Meno Eco Hostel C1
11 Mahamaya B1
12 Meno Dream Resort B3
13 Rabbit Tree C2
14 Seri Resort C1

Eating

15 Rust Warung C2
16 Sasak Cafe B2
17 Warung Pak Man Buati C2
18 Webe Café B1
19 Ya Ya Warung C2

Drinking & Nightlife

20 Brother Hood B2
21 Diana Café B2

Shopping

22 Art Shop Botol C3

★ **Nest** SNORKELLING

Gili Meno's most photographed sight, Nest isn't even on the island itself, but rather just offshore from the BASK resort (set to open in 2020). BASK commissioned British artist Jason deCaires Taylor to create an underwater sculpture comprised of 48 life-sized human figures made from pH neutral, environmental grade concrete. Over time, the figures will provide a new home for soft corals and sponges, contributing to reef regeneration.

Nest is easily accessible from the shore in about 3m of water, though most of its visitors boat over from Gili T and Gili Air.

Gili Meno Divers DIVING

(☎0878 6409 5490; www.gilimenodivers.com; Kontiki Cottages; introductory dive from 900,000Rp; ⏰9am-5pm) French and Indonesian owned, this well-respected dive shop offers a range of courses, including freediving and underwater photography.

Blue Ocean WATER SPORTS

(☎0813 3950 9859; Fantastic Cottages; boat tours per person 150,000Rp) The irrepressible Mr Dean offers snorkelling boat tours of the rich waters around the Gilis. Tours are two to three hours. He'll drop you at another island, so you can check out underwater delights as you island-hop.

Divine Divers DIVING

(☎0852 4057 0777; www.divinedivers.com; guided dives from 490,000Rp) This Meno-only dive shop is on a sweet slice of beach on the west coast. It has six rooms, a pool and good dive-and-stay packages.

Blue Marlin Dive DIVING

(☎0370-639980; www.bluemarlindive.com; guided boat dives 490,000Rp) The Meno outlet of the Trawangan original, this is a well-respected mainstream dive shop.

Yoga

★Mao Meno YOGA

(☎0817 003 0777; www.mao-meno.com; classes from 120,000Rp) Offers two daily classes in styles that include hatha and vinyasa in a beautiful natural wood pavilion. It has cottages on its inland compound that range from simple to luxurious and rent from US$36 per night.

Cycling

Although you can rent bikes for 50,000Rp per day, you won't get far. The beach path from the southern tip right around up the west coast to the bottom of the salt lake is a shadeless dry sand path that may have you pushing your ride. You can go for a little jaunt to the northwest coast on the good path along the north side of the lake, but again, soft sand along the very north makes riding a chore.

Sleeping

Meno now leads the way in Gili growth, with prices climbing sharply alongside visitor numbers. As developers announce their posh new projects, older, more modest guesthouses have been literally wiped off the map. Though Meno skews more upmarket than its neighbours, it's also home to two of the best hostels in the Gilis.

★Gili Meno Eco Hostel HOSTEL $

(www.facebook.com/gilimenoecohostel; hammock/dm/r 60,000/100,000/250,000Rp;) A fantasy in driftwood, bamboo and coconut-palm thatch, this is the place you dream about when you're stuck in the freezing cold at home waiting for a train. A shady lounge, tree houses, beach bar and more open onto the sand, and there are trivia nights, pizza nights, music, bonfires and other social activities. It's also instrumental in humanitarian initiatives around the island.

★Rabbit Tree HOSTEL $

(☎0812 9149 1843; www.therabbittree.com; dm with fan/air-con 110,000/135,000Rp, d with air-con 240,000Rp;) You know you've tripped deep down the rabbit hole when you find yourself sleeping on a dorm bed in a technicolour ball pit, or when the floor you're walking on suddenly becomes a netted hammock. Such are the befuddling joys of the most bonkers hostel in the Gilis, a true Wonderland for every Alice wannabe.

★Meno Dream Resort BUNGALOW $$

(☎0819 1596 1251; http://gilimenobungalows.com; bungalows incl breakfast from 500,000Rp;) This intimate property has just five bungalows surrounding a central pool and tranquil garden. Each has a unique character with art on the walls, gorgeous sunken showers and covered verandas. Guests rave about the onsite restaurant, free bikes and friendly service from owners Made and Berni.

Biru Meno Beach Bungalows BUNGALOW $$

(☎0823 4143 4317; www.birumeno.com; d/f bungalow 1,000,000/1,500,000Rp;) Attractive bungalows in a tree-shaded compound are the headline feature in this unassuming but welcoming resort, which went through a major rebuild after the 2018 earthquakes. The beach is just over the shore path. The cafe has a wood-burning pizza oven.

Seri Resort RESORT $$

(☎0822 3759 6677; www.seriresortgilimeno.com; r 400,000-1,600,000Rp;) It's a tough call, but we think this beachfront resort is just *that* much whiter than the surrounding sand. There is an interesting range of 75 rooms here, from budget huts that share bathrooms to suites in three-storey blocks, to luxurious beach villas. Service is good, the atmosphere high end and there are activities including yoga.

Ana Bungalows BUNGALOW $$

(☎0878 6169 6315; www.anawarung.com; r with fan/air-con from 400,000/600,000Rp;) Four pitched-roof, thatch-and-bamboo bungalows with picture windows and outdoor bathrooms with pebbled floors. This family-run place has a cute used-book exchange on the beach next to its four lovely dining *berugas* (open-sided pavilions) lit with paper lanterns. Seafood dinners are excellent, as is the location.

Mahamaya BOUTIQUE HOTEL $$$

(☎0811 390 5828; www.mahamaya.co; r from 2,150,000Rp; ❄📶🏊) 🍃 A blindingly whitewashed modern pearl with resort service and 19 rooms featuring attractive rough-cut marble patios and white- and washed-wood furnishings. The restaurant is good; have dinner at the water's edge at your own private table.

Eating & Drinking

Meno's dining scene is not nearly as developed as that of neighbouring islands, but almost all of its restaurants have absorbing sea views (which is just as well as service can be painfully slow).

★Warung Pak Man Buati INDONESIAN $

(mains 25,000Rp; ⏲7am-9pm) Chef Juno became something of a local hero after the 2018 earthquakes when he tirelessly fed the Meno community with all the food he could muster. His homestyle Indonesian cooking remains the stuff of island legends. Though he was operating out of a makeshift tent when we passed through, he should have his warung up and running by the time you read this.

★Sasak Cafe INDONESIAN $

(☎0332-662379; mains 40,000-45,000Rp; ⏲kitchen 7am-9pm, bar to late) Set near Meno's quiet western shore, this island-casual resto does crispy fish and other yummy Sasak dishes. At sunset, it brings tables and chairs out onto the nearby beach for cocktails and live music as the sky takes on a rosy glow.

Ya Ya Warung INDONESIAN $

(dishes 15,000-30,000Rp; ⏲8am-10pm) Defining ramshackle, this beach food stall serves up Indonesian faves, curries, pancakes and plenty of pasta, along with the views you came to Meno to enjoy.

Webe Café INDONESIAN $

(☎0852 3787 3339; mains 30,000-75,000Rp; ⏲8am-8pm) Webe Café is a wonderful location for a meal, with low tables sunk in the sand (and some under shade) and the turquoise water just a metre away. It scores well for Sasak and Indonesian food such as *kelak kuning* (snapper in yellow spice); staff fire up a seafood barbecue most nights, too. Service can be slow.

Rust Warung INDONESIAN $

(☎0370-642324; mains 20,000-75,000Rp; ⏲8am-10pm) The most visible cog of the Rust empire (which includes Meno's one grocery) has a great waterfront position overlooking the beach. It's renowned for its grilled fish (with garlic or sweet-and-sour sauce), but also serves pizza and makes a very fine banana pancake any time of the day or night. Ask for the homemade sambal.

★Brother Hood BAR

(☎0819 0717 9286; www.facebook.com/anasasakbungalows; workshops by donation; ⏲workshops 9am-5pm, bar 5pm-late) 🍃 How to describe this place? On one hand, it's an educational hub promoting a cleaner island through garbage pick ups (each Sunday at 3.30pm) and recycling workshops where you can make dreamcatchers, glass cups, bamboo straws and other upcycled art. Come 5pm, however, it's a raging reggae bar where you can feel good about drinking since all those cocktails fund the daytime activities.

Diana Café BAR

(☎0819 3317 1943; ⏲8am-2pm & 5-10pm) If you find the pace of life on Meno too busy, head to this thoroughly chilled little tiki bar. Diana couldn't be simpler: a bamboo-and-thatch bar, a few tables, hammocks and huts on the sand, a whimsical coral garden and sweet reggae in the air. Happy hours are 5pm to 7pm and the food (mains 35,000Rp to 40,000Rp) is good.

Shopping

Art Shop Botol ARTS & CRAFTS

(⏲hours vary) Art Shop Botol is a large handicrafts stall just south of Kontiki Meno hotel. Choose from masks, Sasak water baskets, wood carvings and gourds. It's run by an elderly shopkeeper with 11 children and countless grandchildren.

Information

Meno has three ATMs.

Getting There & Away

The public boat landing is an increasingly busy place. None of the fast boats from Bali directly serve Meno, although some provide connections. Otherwise, you can go to Gili Trawangan or Gili Air and take the regular interisland fast boat. The beach landing is the choppiest of the three Gilis; sometimes a small lighter is required to get passengers out to the fast boats.

GILI AIR

0370 / POP 1800

Closest of the Gilis to Lombok, Gili Air blends Gili T's buzz and bustle with Meno's minimalist vibe. The white-sand beaches here are arguably the best of the Gili bunch and there's just enough nightlife to keep the sociable happy. Snorkelling is good right from the main strip along the east coast – a lovely sandy lane dotted with bamboo bungalows and little restaurants where you can eat virtually on top of a turquoise sea.

Though tourism dominates Gili Air's economy, coconuts, fishing and manufacturing of the fake distressed fishing-boat wood vital to any stylish Gili guesthouse are important income streams. Buzzy little strips have developed along the beaches in the southeast and the west, although the lanes are still more sandy than paved.

Beaches

The entire east side of the island has great beaches with powdery white sand and a gentle slope into beautiful turquoise water, with a foot-friendly sandy bottom. There are also good, private spots the rest of the way around Gili Air, but low-tide rocks and coral are a problem. For drinks and sunset, head north.

Activities

Diving & Snorkelling

The entire east coast has an offshore reef teeming with colourful fish; there's a drop-off about 100m to 200m out. Snorkelling gear is easily hired from guesthouses and dive shops for about 50,000Rp per day. Air Wall is a beautiful soft-coral wall off the island's west, while off the north there's **Frogfish Point** and **Hans Reef**. Snorkelling spots can be reached from the eastern and northeastern beaches.

Gili Air has an excellent collection of dive shops, which charge the standard Gili rates.

★Gili Air Divers DIVING

(0878 6536 7551; www.giliairdivers.com; Grand Sunset; guided diving boat trip 490,000Rp; 8am-8pm) This French-Indo-owned dive shop is long on charm and skill. Also offers introductory freediving classes and SSI Level 1 and 2 courses.

SNORKELLING THE GILIS

The Gilis are ringed by coral reefs and offer pleasant snorkelling. Masks, snorkels and fins are widely available and can be hired for about 50,000Rp per day. It's important to check your mask fits properly: just press it gently to your face, let go and if it's a good fit the suction should hold it in place.

Snorkelling trips – many on glass-bottomed boats – are very popular. Typically, you'll pay about 150,000Rp per person or about 650,000Rp for the entire boat. Expect to leave at about 10am and visit three sites, with a stop for lunch on another island. On Gili T there are many places selling these trips along the main strip; prices can be negotiable.

On Trawangan and Meno turtles very regularly appear on the reefs right off the beach. You'll likely drift with the current, so be prepared to walk back to the starting line. Over on Air, the walls off the east coast are good too.

It's not hard to escape the crowds. Each island has a less-developed side, usually where access to the water is obstructed by shallow patches of coral. Using rubber shoes makes it much easier to get into the water. Don't tread on the coral; ease yourself in, and then swim, keeping your body as horizontal as possible.

Don't expect the same prismatic reefs you may have seen elsewhere in Indonesia. The shallow reefs fringing all three Gilis ain't what they used to be, but an ever-growing collection of Biorock formations has helped with coral regeneration, ensuring a brighter future. Among the many reasons to snorkel in the Gilis are the high odds you'll encounter green sea turtles or even endangered hawksbill turtles. Top overall snorkelling spots include the following:

- Gili Meno's Nest (p326)
- The north end of Gili T's beach
- Gili Air Wall

Gili Air

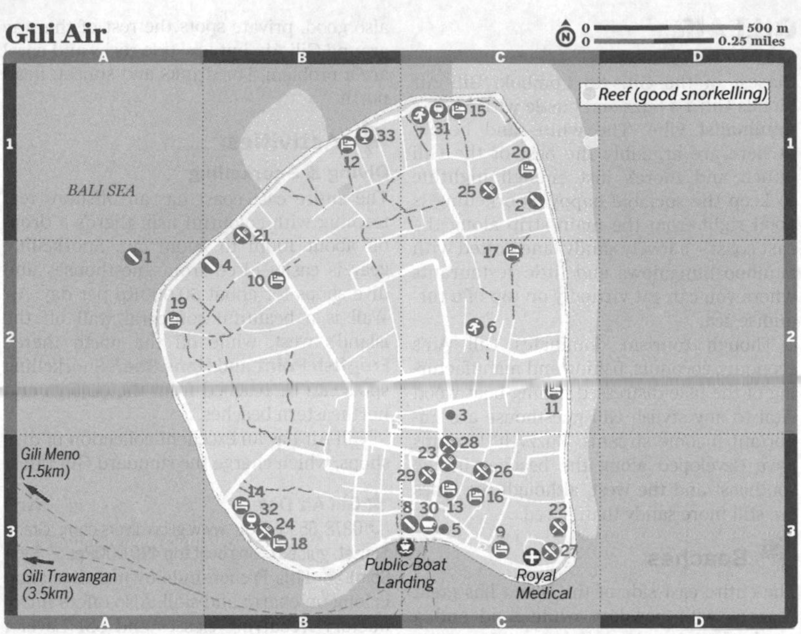

Gili Air

Activities, Courses & Tours

1 Air Wall (30m) A2
2 Blue Marine Dive Centre C1
3 Flowers & Fire Yoga C2
4 Gili Air Divers B2
5 Gili Cooking Classes C3
6 H2O Yoga C2
7 Harmony Spa C1
8 Oceans 5 .... C3

Sleeping

9 7 Seas C3
10 Begadang B2
11 Biba Beach Village C2
12 Bintang Beach 2 .... B1
Grand Sunset .... (see 4)
13 Hideout C3
14 Krishna Sunset Bungalow B3
15 Pelangi Cottages C1
16 Rival Village C3
17 Sejuk Cottages C2
18 Villa Casa Mio B3
19 Vyaana Resort A2
20 Youpy Bungalows C1

Eating

21 Boogils Sunset Lounge B1
22 Chill Out C3
23 Eazy Gili Waroeng C3
24 Mowie's B3
25 Pachamama C1
26 Ruby's C3
27 Scallywags Beach Club C3
28 Siti Shop C3
29 Warung Bambu C3

Drinking & Nightlife

30 Coffee & Thyme C3
31 K69 .... C1
32 Lucky's Bar B3
33 Pura Vida B1

Blue Marine Dive Centre DIVING
(☎0811 390 2550; www.bluemarinedive.com; night dive/10 dives 990,000/4,500,000Rp; ⏰7.30am-7.30pm) Blue Marine has a nice location on the beautiful northeast corner of the island, and also offers freediving, stand-up paddle-boarding and yoga (120,000Rp per class). The owner is active in reef preservation efforts.

Oceans 5 DIVING
(☎0813 3877 7144; www.oceans5dive.com; single dives from 490,000Rp) Has a 25m training pool, an in-house marine biologist and nice hotel rooms. Also offers a program of yoga diving and emphasises sustainable diving practices to its guests.

Surfing

Directly off the southern tip of the island there's **Play Gili**, a short, peeling right-hand break that can get big at times. May to October brings the best conditions.

Yoga & Wellness

★Flowers & Fire Yoga YOGA
(http://flowersandfire.yoga; 1/3/5 classes 120,000/330,0000/500,000Rp; ⏲9am-6pm) A welcoming, spiritual and serene yoga garden for pre- and post-beach classes. It also has a great health-food cafe, popular curry and movie nights, and on-site accommodation ranging from a luxe dorm (think Egyptian cotton sheets, 300,000Rp) to well-designed bungalows (1,000,000Rp). Guests get discounts on classes.

H2O Yoga YOGA
(☎0877 6103 8836; www.h2oyogaandmeditation.com; class/3hr workshop 120,000/300,000Rp) This wonderful yoga and meditation centre is found down a well-signposted track leading inland from Gili Air's eastern shore. Top-quality classes (at 7am, 9am, or 5pm for 'candlelight yoga') are held in one of two lovely thatched *shalas*. H2O also offers a day spa, a pool (with aqua yoga classes), accommodation (doubles from 270,000Rp) and seven-day retreats (from US$625).

H2O's Good Earth Cafe sells restorative and healthy post-yoga treats from 7am to 4.30pm.

Harmony Spa SPA
(☎0812 386 5883; www.facebook.com/harmonygiliair; massages from 120,000Rp; ⏲9am-8pm) The beautiful north-coast location alone will make you feel renewed. Facials, body treatments and more are on offer. Call first.

Cycling

Bikes can be rented for 40,000Rp to 70,000Rp a day, but large sections of the coastal path in the north and west are annoying to ride, as long slogs of deep sand swallow the trail at times and mud after rains can make it impassable. Inland lanes, however, are mostly concrete and very rideable. Some shops have fat bikes (bikes with huge tyres) that make sand a little more manageable.

Courses

Gili Cooking Classes COOKING
(☎0877 6506 7210; www.gilicookingclasses.com; classes from 290,000Rp) This slick operation has a large kitchen for daily classes right on the strip. You have a range of options for what you'll learn to cook – choose wisely as you'll be eating your work.

Sleeping

Gili Air's dozens of places to stay are mostly located on the east coast, though you'll find more isolation in the west. Bungalows, in one shape or another, are the uniting theme.

Begadang HOSTEL $
(begadangbackpackers@gmail.com; dm/d/tr from 200,000/250,000/350,000Rp; ❄📶🏊) This sprawling complex of basic bungalows in the northern interior of Gili Air is truly backpacker central, with a mushroom-shaped pool, heaps of inflatables, a hopping bar, a ping-pong table and even life-sized Connect Four. The cheaper doubles are little more than a mattress in a two-by-two-metre hut. The air-con triples are much nicer for small groups.

Bintang Beach 2 BUNGALOW $
(☎0819 742 3519; bungalow from 250,000Rp; ❄📶) On Gili Air's quiet northwest coast, this sandy but tidy compound has 25 basic bungalows (ranging from budget-friendly and fan-cooled to mildly snazzy) and an open-sided beach-bar/restaurant that's a delightful place to linger. This enterprising clan has a few other guesthouses nearby. It also rents bikes and snorkelling gear, and can take care of your laundry.

Hideout HOSTEL $
(www.giliairhostel.com; dm from 120,000Rp; ⏲reception 7.30am-7pm; ❄📶) Rooms at this fun hostel were newly refurbished after the 2018 earthquakes, with three beds and a bathroom apiece. The decor defines cheery and it has a cool bar, hot showers, free breakfast and a huge frangipani tree.

Krishna Sunset Bungalow BUNGALOW $
(☎0819 3675 0875; r 300,000-500,000Rp; @📶) There's a '60s vibe at this chilled place with sweeping views of Lombok, other Gilis, Bali and the technicolour sunsets. You can cheerfully let another day slip past from the beach loungers.

★Sejuk Cottages BUNGALOW $$
(☎0813 3953 5387; d from 450,000Rp, f 1,350,000Rp; ❄📶🏊) Thirteen well-built, tastefully designed thatched *lumbung* (rice-barn) cottages, and pretty two- and three-storey cottages (some have rooftop living rooms) scattered around a fine tropical

garden with a spring-fed pool. Some rooms are fan-only; others have rooftop hammocks.

★ Biba Beach Village BUNGALOW **$$**
(☎0819 1727 4648; www.bibabeach.com; bungalow incl breakfast 800,000-1,600,000Rp;) Biba offers nine lovely, spacious bungalows with large verandas, and grotto-like bathrooms that have walls inlaid with shells and coral. The gorgeous garden overlooks a great stretch of beach. Biba is also home to a good Italian restaurant (9am to 10pm). The best rooms have sea views.

Rival Village GUESTHOUSE **$$**
(☎0819 1749 8187; www.facebook.com/rivalvillagegiliair; r 300,000-600,000Rp;) This modest four-room guesthouse just gets everything right. The French owners have created a sparklingly clean little compound amid family houses off one of the village's main paths. Rooms are large, the bathrooms are open-air, breakfast is delicious, everything works. *Très bon!*

Youpy Bungalows BUNGALOW **$$**
(☎0852 5371 5405; rizkylily7@gmail.com; r 450,000-800,000Rp;) Among the outcrop of driftwood-decorated beach cafes and guesthouses strung along the coast north of Blue Marine Dive Centre, Youpy has some of the best-quality bungalows. Bathrooms have beachy designs, the beds are big and the ceilings are high.

Grand Sunset BUNGALOW **$$**
(☎0819 3433 7000; www.grandsunsetgiliair.com; r 600,000-1,900,000Rp;) These 25 sturdily built, bungalow-style rooms reflect the ethos of this modest resort: solid. Bathrooms are well designed and open-air, rooms have all the basic comforts, the pool is large and the beachside loungers have superb views. Plus there's the quietude that comes with the location on the sunset side of Air.

Pelangi Cottages BUNGALOW **$$**
(☎0819 3316 8648; pelangicottages@yahoo.co.id; r incl breakfast 500,000-700,000Rp;) Set on the north end of the island with coral reef out front, this place has 10 spacious but basic concrete and wood bungalows, friendly management and quality mountain bikes for rent.

7 Seas HOTEL **$$**
(☎0361-849 7094; www.7seas-cottages.com; r/bungalow from 550,000/750,000Rp;) Part of the 7 Seas dive empire, this is a decent bungalow compound just back from the beach. Rooms are tidy and have large balconies; cottages have soaring ceilings and thatch.

Villa Casa Mio BUNGALOW **$$$**
(☎0370-619 8437; www.giliair.com; cottages incl breakfast from 1,500,000Rp;) Casa Mio has fine cottages with pretty garden bathrooms, as well as a riot of knick-knacks from the artistic to the kitsch. The floridly named rooms ('Ocean of Love', 'Tropical Smile') have fridges, stereos and nice sun decks with loungers. It's on a great beach, plus there's a shade-fringed pool.

Vyaana Resort RESORT **$$$**
(☎0877 6538 8515; www.vyaanagiliair.com; r incl breakfast 1,600,000Rp;) The swath of beach on the sunset side of Gili Air is still fairly quiet, and this bungalow compound is a fine place to enjoy it. The eight (slightly overpriced) units are widely spaced for privacy, and cute little artistic touches abound.

Eating

Most places on Gili Air are locally owned and offer an unbeatable setting for a meal, with tables overlooking the water. Some of the most interesting new restaurants are opening on the backstreets of the village.

Warung Bambu INDONESIAN **$**
(☎0878 6405 0402; mains 20,000-30,000Rp; ⏲10am-10pm) A cheap, friendly and artfully decorated option for tasty local food (try the *tempe* curry!). It's two blocks in from the boat landing.

Eazy Gili Waroeng INDONESIAN **$**
(☎0819 0902 2074; mains 35,000-40,000Rp; ⏲8am-10pm) On a crossroads in the heart of the main village, this spotless corner cafe (the slightly Westernised adjunct of the more rootsy Warung Muslim, immediately to the east) serves up basic Indo fare aimed at visitors. It also does breakfasts, sandwiches and lip-smacking *pisang goreng* (banana fritters).

Siti Shop SUPERMARKET **$**
(⏲8am-8pm) A good general store in the village.

★ Ruby's INDONESIAN **$$**
(☎0878 6575 6064; mains 45,000-85,000Rp; ⏲noon-10pm) One of the finest places to eat in the Gilis. Candles flicker atop wooden tables at this back-lane eatery. The menu is short and there are daily specials; the secret here is the namesake genius in the kitchen.

The calamari is perfectly light and crispy, the green curry is flavourful and nuanced, the burgers are simply superb. Great desserts.

★ Pachamama HEALTH FOOD **$$**
(☎0878 6415 2100; www.pachamamagiliair.com; mains 70,000-85,000Rp; ⊙10am-10pm Mon-Sat; ✎) This oh-so-hip health-food restaurant brews its own kombucha, crafts exotic smoothies (or cocktails!) and has lots of flavourful veg, vegan and gluten-free options. It's a bit out of the way in the northern interior, but well worth the hike.

Boogils Sunset Lounge SEAFOOD **$$**
(☎0819 3301 7727; mains 40,000-120,000Rp; ⊙9am-11pm) More ambitious than your usual beachside bamboo hang-outs, Boogils offers a nightly seafood barbecue and an ever-changing line-up of fresh fare. Good pasta shows what the Italians can do with *mie* (noodles). Come for drinks, stay for sunset and then have a moonlit meal. (On a bike, buzz over via the paved interior lanes.)

Chill Out CAFE **$$**
(www.chilloutbargiliair.com; mains 35,000-90,000Rp; ⊙7.30am-11pm) Come for a swim and a sip with stunning views, and stay for dinner at a table on the sand. It puts on a full nightly seafood barbecue and cooks up some good pizzas in the wood-fired oven.

Scallywags Beach Club INTERNATIONAL **$$**
(☎0819 1743 2086; www.scallywagsresort.com; mains 50,000-150,000Rp; ⊙7am-11pm; 📶) Set on Gili Air's softest and widest beach, Scallywags offers elegant decor, upscale comfort food, great barbecue, homemade gelato and superb cocktails here. But the best feature is the alluring beach dotted with loungers. The choice of sambals is sublime.

Mowie's FUSION **$$**
(☎0878 6423 1384; www.mowiesbargiliair.com; mains 55,000-90,000Rp; ⊙8am-9pm) With a menu full of creative Indonesian and Western fusion fare, an ideal sunset location on the beach and chill EDM tunes after dark, Mowie's is the kind of place where you could show up for lunch and never leave.

Drinking & Nightlife

Gili Air is usually a mellow place, but there are full-moon parties and things can rev up at the sunset bars in high season. The largest concentration of bars is on the otherwise tranquil northern coast.

Pura Vida LOUNGE
(www.facebook.com/puravidagiliair; ⊙11am-11pm) A stylish bar with huge pillows and a rainbow of tables and chairs on the sand. Classy jazz plays over the sound system and some nights there's live reggae music. A wood-fired oven produces great thin-crust pizzas through the evening. Tops at sunset.

Coffee & Thyme CAFE
(☎0821 4499 3622; www.coffeeandthyme.co; ⊙7am-7pm) Right in the thick of things, where boats to Gili Air disgorge their sun-seeking seafarers, Coffee & Thyme is a bustling, part-open-air cafe that makes some of the best coffee in the Gilis. Also good if you're craving a Western-style breakfast, lunch wrap or muffin.

K69 BAR
(www.facebook.com/kopidarat; ⊙9am-11pm) This eccentric bar-cum-gallery is run by the Sulawesi-born artist Hardi, who also offers silkscreen workshops (150,000Rp). It's largely built out of recycled materials and has rotating exhibits of Indonesian art. Come for tea by day and wine by night.

Lucky's Bar BAR
(⊙7am-late) A great beach bar: lounge back on bamboo recliners and watch the sun set behind Gili Meno. There are DJs on Sundays and monthly full-moon parties with fire dancing.

Information

MEDICAL SERVICES

Royal Medical (☎0878 6442 1212; ⊙phone service 24hr) A simple clinic.

MONEY

There are ATMs scattered around the island, most notably in the south near the boat landing.

Getting There & Away

The public boat landing is busy. Gili Air's commerce and popularity mean that public boats fill rather quickly for the 15-minute ride to Bangsal. The ticket office has a shady waiting area.

Nusa Tenggara

Includes ➡

Best Places to Eat

- Sari Rasa (p364)
- Happy Banana (p355)
- Blue Corner (p354)
- Mopi's Place (p366)
- Depot Bambu Kuning (p376)

Best Places to Stay

- Ciao Hostel (p352)
- Villa Dominik (p354)
- Pantai Paris Homestay (p368)
- Ankermi Happy Dive (p372)
- Scuba Junkie Komodo Beach Resort (p354)

Why Go?

If you're seeking white sand, spectacular diving and surf, bubbling hot springs, majestic waterfalls and hidden traditional villages – away from Bali-esque crowds – then Nusa Tenggara is your wonderland. Spreading west from the Wallace Line dividing Asia from Australasia, this archipelago is jungle-green in the north and tending to drier savannah in the south and east. In between are limitless surf breaks and barrels, technicolor volcanic lakes, pink-sand beaches, swaggering dragons and underwater worlds filled with colour and creatures.

You'll also find a cultural diversity that's unmatched, even in multicultural Indonesia. Animist rituals and tribal traditions still thrive alongside minarets, convents and chapels, and though Bahasa Indonesia is the lingua franca, each island has at least one native language, often subdivided into dialects. From a beach-forward, tourist-ready vacation to stepping outside your comfort zone for the sort of experiences that leave an indelible mark on your memory, you're exactly where you're supposed to be.

When to Go

- The dry season (Apr-Sep) brings the best diving visibility; travellers flock to Komodo and other locales.
- May and October bring epic waves in Rote and Sumbawa.
- Komodo Dragons can usually be spotted at Komodo National Park from September to May.

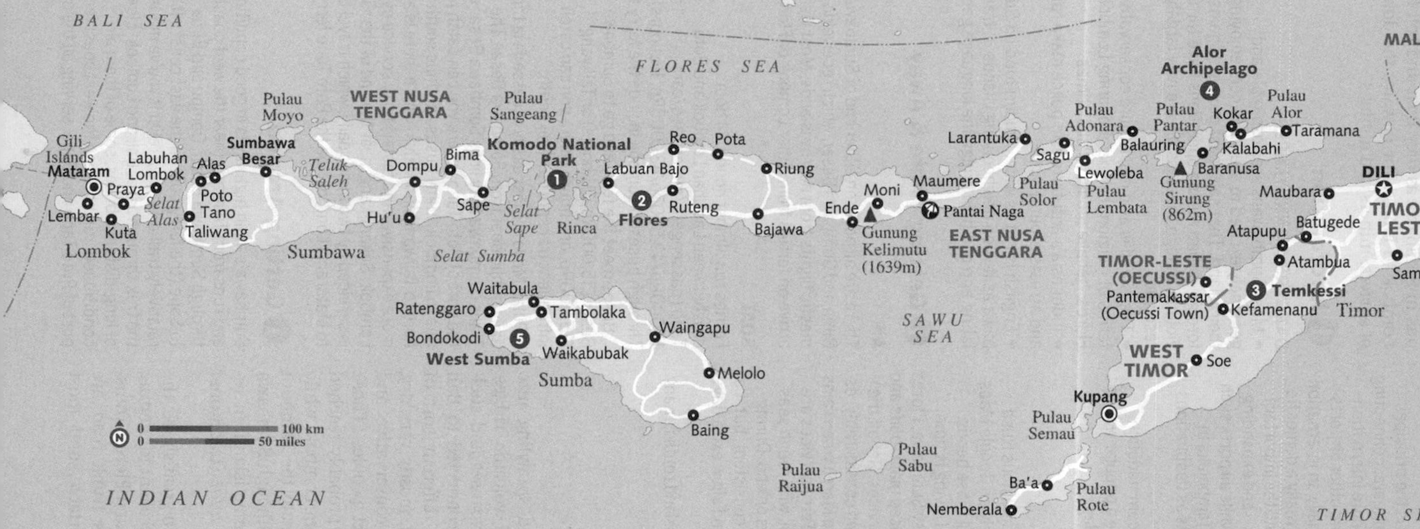

Nusa Tenggara Highlights

1 **Komodo National Park** (p344) Seeing dragons on land and then snorkelling or diving with underwater critters, big and small.

2 **Flores** (p348) Exploring a world of ancient cultures, volcanoes, lush rainforests and untrodden beaches from one end to the other.

3 **Temkessi** (p382) Discovering West Timor's remote villages characterised by beehive-shaped clan houses, like otherworldly Temkessi.

4 **Alor Archipelago** (p372) Diving this island chain that feels like one stop before the end of the world.

5 **West Sumba** (p388) Bouncing between one sensational scalloped beach and the next before pausing at the ancient village of Ratenggaro and breathtaking Weekuri Lagoon.

Getting There & Away

Lombok International Airport is the principal port of entry in West Nusa Tenggara, connecting with Kuala Lumpur and Singapore internationally, and Jakarta, Denpasar and other airports within Indonesia. While nominally an international airport, El Tari in Kupang is really a domestic hub for East Nusa Tenggara. All the important towns and cities have regular – and expanding – air service. Kupang is a hub, while airports such as Labuan Bajo in Flores and Tambolaka in Sumba are adding more flights as destinations increase in popularity.

Liveaboards (boats with accommodation; often used for diving trips) are a popular way to get from Lombok to Labuan Bajo.

Getting Around

Overland travel is slow in mountainous Nusa Tenggara and it's foolish to rely on Google Maps' estimated travel times with all those bends, potholes and road upgrades. Driving is time consuming, but beautiful. Busy Sumbawa, Flores and Timor have decent, surfaced main roads and relatively comfortable bus services. Get off the highways and things slow down considerably, especially between December to March when rains wallop gravel and dirt roads. Ferry services are also victims of the wet season, with rough seas causing cancellations for days on end. During the rest of the year boats are consistent, but it's always wise to check ahead and allow extra days in your itinerary.

Several airlines cover interisland routes, many of which start in Bali.

SUMBAWA

Elaborately contorted and sprawling into the sea, Sumbawa is all volcanic ridges, terraced rice fields, dry expanses and sheltered bays. Though well connected to Bali and Lombok, it's a very different sort of place – far less developed, mostly very dry, much poorer, extremely conservative and split between two distinct peoples. Those who speak Sumbawanese probably reached the west of the island from Lombok, while Bimanese speakers dominate the Tambora Peninsula and the east. Although Sumbawa is an overwhelmingly Islamic island, in remote parts underground *adat* (traditional law and lore) still thrives.

Mostly traffic-free and in great shape, the Trans-Sumbawa Hwy is excellent for getting quickly between Lombok and Flores. Transport connections off this trunk road are infrequent and uncomfortable, and most overland travellers don't even get off the bus in Sumbawa as they float and roll from Lombok to Flores. For now, it's the domain of surfers, miners and mullahs.

Information

DANGERS & ANNOYANCES

- Most Sumbawans are hospitable and genuinely excited to see foreigners enjoying their island. That said, past protests against foreign-owned mining operations have turned violent, though these issues are now largely resolved.
- The island is also much more conservative in terms of religion than neighbouring Lombok or Flores; behave modestly at all times.
- Indonesia's anti-terrorism police make raids and arrests around Bima.
- English is not as widely understood on Sumbawa as it is on neighbouring islands. A translating app can help bridge the language gap.

Getting There & Away

AIR

There are airports on either end of Sumbawa in Bima and Sumbawa Besar, which receive domestic flights from nearby islands. Most visitors arrive on ferries from either Lombok or Flores.

BOAT

Ferries run almost hourly, 24 hours a day, between Labuhan Lombok and Poto Tano (passengers/motorbikes/cars 17,000Rp/40,500Rp/431,000Rp, 1½ hours). Through buses to Lombok include the ferry fare.

Buses meet the ferry and go to Sumbawa Besar (35,000Rp, 2½ hours) or Taliwang (25,000Rp, one hour), where you can catch infrequent transport further south.

Pulau Moyo is most easily accessed via the daily public boat from Sumbawa Besar. The Trans-Sumbawa Hwy links Sumbawa Besar with the port of Poto Tano, where you can catch ferries to Lombok. Many buses continue south from here to Taliwang and Maluk, where there is a more expensive (and faster) ferry service over to Lombok. Sekongkang, near the end of the road, is serviced by two buses daily, which travel over to Mataram (Lombok) via the Poto Tano ferry.

Getting Around

Sumbawa's main highway is in good condition and runs from Taliwang (near the west coast) through Sumbawa Besar, Dompu and Bima to Sape (the ferry port on the east coast). It's relatively traffic-free – a relief if you've made the trek through Java, Bali and Lombok. Fleets of long-distance buses, some of them air-conditioned, run between the west coast ferry port of Poto Tano and Sape, serving all the major towns between. From Bima, you can catch buses or private transport to Calabai (for Gunung Tambora) or Hu'u (for Pantai Lakey). There are also frequent buses over to Sape for onward ferry journeys to Sumba and Flores.

Car hire is possible through hotels: depending on your destination, the cost will be about 600,000Rp to 800,000Rp per day, including a driver and fuel. Motorbikes cost 50,000Rp to 80,000Rp a day.

Jelenga

☎0372 / POP 200

Set along an enormous horseshoe bay, Jelenga is a humble country beach town with rice fields, goat farms and a world-class left break known as **Scar Reef**. It's one of the most serene beaches in Sumbawa and is the perfect base for low-key travellers to kick around in the sand for a few days. Find it by turning toward the coast in **Jereweh**, 11km south of the regional capital Taliwang.

Sleeping

A handful of quality lodges line the sand along Jelenga's shores. While most are aimed at surfers, non-surfers will feel more welcomed here than at any other surf town in West Sumbawa. All hotels along the beach in Jelenga have restaurants serving a combination of Western and Indonesian cuisine.

Wood Garden Bungalows BUNGALOW $

(☎0821 4721 4166; www.facebook.com/thewoodthaticould; bungalows 350,000Rp, r without bathroom 150,000Rp) These three bungalows built out of recycled teak (some of it from royal palaces, we're told) are set back about 100m from the beach on a leafy patch of land. They sleep up to three each and include outdoor bathrooms that are far more lavish than the plain interiors. There are also basic budget rooms with less glorious shared bathrooms.

★**Scar Reef Lodge** LODGE $$

(☎0812 3980 4885; www.scarreeflodge.com; r US$35-55, cabin for 6 from US$120; ❄📶) A modern lodge for surfers. The five rooms (two of which are air-conditioned) have soaring ceilings, wood furnishings and a common beachside restaurant and lounge area. It also has a cabin for groups, plenty of beach pouffes and a yoga *shala* for DIY sun salutations. Surf, SUP and motorbike rentals are all available.

Myamo Beach Lodge BOUTIQUE HOTEL $$

(☎0812 1598 1888; http://myamolodge.com; Jelenga; dm/d incl breakfast 450,000/650,000Rp; ❄📶) Bright white walls, distressed-wood furnishings and downtempo pop all combine to give this seafront surf lodge an airy beach-chic appeal. The spacious rooms have comfy mattresses and powerful showers, though dorm beds are totally overpriced. Nonsurfers can rent out paddleboards, kayaks, snorkels or spearguns for fishing.

Note that there's a 21% service fee at the restaurant.

Information

The nearest ATMs are along the main road through Taliwang.

Getting There & Away

The small, conservative town of Taliwang is the regional transport hub. Buses go from Taliwang to Poto Tano (25,000Rp, one hour) almost hourly, where you can hop on a bus to Mataram or Sumbawa Besar. Early morning and evening buses head to Maluk (30,000Rp, one hour).

The 45-minute *ojek* (motorcycle taxi) ride from Taliwang to Jelenga costs 50,000Rp. Most hotels in Jelenga can arrange private transfers from nearby destinations and will rent motorbikes for about 70,000Rp per day.

Maluk

☎0372 / POP 11,930

South of Taliwang, the beaches and bays try to outdo one another. Your first stop is the working-class commercial district of Maluk, 30km south of Taliwang. Yes, the town is ugly, but the beach is superb. The sand is a blend of white and gold, and the bay is buffered by two headlands. There's good swimming in the shallows, and when the swell hits, the reef further out sculpts perfect barrels.

Directly south of Maluk, within walking distance of the beach (though it is a long walk) is **Supersuck**, consistently rated the best left in the world. Surfers descend regularly from Hawaii's North Shore to surf here – which should tell you something – and many lifelong surfers have proclaimed it the finest barrel of their lives. It really pumps in the dry season (May to October).

Sleeping

Dreamtime Sumbawa Homestay GUESTHOUSE $

(☎0821 4523 9696; http://dreamtimesumbawa.com; Jl Pasir Putih; dm 55,000Rp, d with/without air-con 300,000/200,000Rp; ❄📶) The ultimate surf-bum crash-pad with a curtained-off dorm and cosy patio-facing rooms. Dreamtime is set a block back from the beach in the heart of the village, and staff are extremely knowledgeable about the nearby waves. Fast fibre-optic wi-fi is a plus.

★ **Merdeka House** GUESTHOUSE $$
(☎0822 4741 7866; www.merdekahouse.com; Jl Raya Balas; r 350,000Rp;) Wow! What a view you will have if you end a hard day in the waves at this hilltop guesthouse, whose communal lounge and kitchen overlook two stunning bays. The six rooms are spacious and spotless. Perks include an honesty bar, free snorkels, cheap board rentals (50,000Rp per day) and a helpful area guide typed up by the friendly Aussie owners.

Information

Banks and ATMs, such as **BNI** (☎0372-635146; Jl Raya Maluk; 8am-4pm Mon-Fri, ATM 24hr), cluster most thickly along Jl Raya Maluk, the road through the centre of town.

Getting There & Away

Two daily buses leave Terminal Maluk, north of town across from the entrance to the PT AMNT mine (look for the big gates and massive parking area), for Sumbawa Besar (40,000Rp, four hours). Departures are typically at 6am and 2pm, but you need to arrive well in advance to book a seat. This bus can also drop you off in Taliwang (25,000Rp, one hour).

Most people arrive here on the fast ferry from Lombok. From Benete Harbour, just north of Maluk, the ferry (135,000Rp, 90 minutes) goes to/from Labuhan Lombok two times daily. From Lombok, boats depart at 10am and 4.45pm. The return from Benete Harbour departs at 8am and 2.45pm. Transporting surf boards costs 25,000Rp extra.

Rantung Beach & Around

☎0372 / POP 8180

The spread-out settlement of Sekongkang includes three superb beaches with a handful of surf breaks. The best range of accommodation and restaurants is to be found along the coast a few kilometres from the centre of town, especially at Rantung Beach, a laid-back place with a classic surfer feel. Rantung is a secluded and majestic bay framed by 100m-high headlands. Almost everything is within easy walking distance.

The water is crystal-clear and waves roll in year-round at **Yo Yo's**, a right break at the north end of the bay. **Hook**, which breaks at the edge of the northern bluff, is also a terrific right. The next bay down is where you'll find **Tropical**, another phenomenal beach (named for the nearby resort) and home to great left and right breaks that beginners will enjoy. Immediately south of Tropical is **Remo's Left**, a solid A-frame.

North of Rantung is **Pantai Lawar**, a tree-shaded stretch of white sand on a turquoise lagoon sheltered by volcanic bluffs draped in jungle. When the surf is flat, come here to swim and snorkel. Further north at Pantai Balas is Supersuck. It's a consistent year-round break, though it gets heavy and delivers a long left when the swell comes in.

Sleeping & Eating

Beachside guesthouses and bungalows cater to the surfing set; most serve food to their guests.

Santai Beach Bungalows BUNGALOW $
(☎0878 6393 5758; Rantung Beach; r without/with bathroom 150,000/200,000Rp, with air-con & breakfast 300,000Rp;) The choice budget spot in the area offers a collection of 12 spacious, well-tended tiled rooms. Those with private bathroom have sensational sea views, which anyone can enjoy from the thatched restaurant (dishes 30,000Rp to 60,000Rp), where there's also a pool table to gather around for post-surf beers. Book ahead: when that swell hits it's full for weeks.

Yo Yo's Hotel RESORT $$
(☎0878 6695 0576; yoyoshotel@yahoo.co.id; Rantung Beach; s/d from 200,000/350,000Rp;) A vast beachfront complex with a range of 15 rooms. Deluxe rooms are quite large and well appointed with wood furnishings. Standard rooms are smaller and a bit worn. Monkeys wander the grounds and a large two-storey bar (with cocktails!) and cafe (dishes 30,000Rp to 80,000Rp) overlooks the surf.

Rantung Beach Bar & Cottages BUNGALOW $$
(☎0819 1700 7481; Rantung Beach; r from 200,000Rp, cottages from 400,000Rp;) The mining crowd has enjoyed more than a few sundowners at the vast and open beachside cafe here (dishes 40,000Rp to 60,000Rp); the food always delivers – we love the crunchy chips and huge burgers. Five refined, spacious cottages have queen beds and leafy private decks with sea views. Behind them is a row of cheaper rooms.

Lisa's Garden INTERNATIONAL $
(☎0822 3650 7340; Rantung Beach; mains 20,000-65,000Rp; 7am-10pm;) Those craving things like French-press coffee, avocado

toast, salads, granola or burritos – all exceptionally rare on Sumbawa – will love this cheap open-air eatery, which has an upstairs deck overlooking the waves.

Getting There & Away

The tourist-oriented minibuses of **Sekongkang Trans** (0853 3324 1931; www.facebook.com/sekongkangtrans; Jl Raya Sekongkang) leave every day at 7am and 7pm for the six-hour journey to Mataram via the Poto Tano ferry (120,000Rp). The air-conditioned bus can pick up in Maluk and Jereweh (15 and 30 minutes after departing from Sekongkang) if contacted in advance. Departures from Mataram to Sekongkang are also at 7am and 7pm.

Sekongkang Trans is the only bus that travels all the way to Sekongkang. At all other times you'll need to charter an *ojek* (around 20,000Rp) to get here from Maluk, the nearest town on the public-bus network.

Sumbawa Besar

0371 / POP 56,340

Sumbawa Besar, often shortened to 'Sumbawa', is the principal market town of the island's west. It's leafy, devoutly Muslim (oversupply of karaoke bars notwithstanding) and runs on the bushels of beans, rice and corn cultivated on the outskirts. It's a pleasant enough place for those transiting to Pulau Moyo, but there's not much to see here aside from the old palace and a lively morning market. Most travellers simply consider this town a respite while journeying along the Trans-Sumbawa Hwy.

Sights

Dalam Loka PALACE

(Sultan's Palace; Jl Dalam Loka 1; 8am-noon & 1-5pm Mon-Fri, 8-11am & 1.30-5pm Sat & Sun) FREE The Dalam Loka was built over 200 years ago for Sultan Mohammad Jalaluddin III and presently covers an entire city block. The remains of this once-imposing structure are in fair condition and are still used for political events. You can wander the grounds and scurry over the creaking floorboards inside to see old photos of the royal family, antique parasols and carriages.

Pasar Syketeng MARKET

(off Jl Dr Cipta; 7am-4pm) Rise early and hit the steamy, exotic Pasar Syketeng. Its dank alleyways come alive as young and old descend to barter and haggle for every conceivable item, from fish to household goods to live chickens.

Sleeping & Eating

Samawa Transit Hotel HOTEL $$

(0371-21754; Jl Garuda 41; s/d from 400,000/420,000Rp;) Conveniently located across the main road and to the left as you emerge from the airport is this low-rise, caramel-toned compound. Its rooms are spacious and spotless, with high ceilings, cheery bathroom tiles, flatscreen TVs, hot water and decent beds. VIP rooms are larger, quieter and have private balconies.

★ **Cipta Sari Bakery** BAKERY $

(0371-21496; Jl Hasanuddin 47; snacks from 4000Rp; 8am-7pm) Don't pass through town without a stop at this excellent bakery on a shady stretch of the main drag. Pause for coffee or a cold drink, and be sure to stock up for your journey: the various baked goods, pastries and savoury treats are the best you'll find between here and Bima.

Aneka Rasa Jaya CHINESE $

(0371-21291; Jl Hasanuddin 14; mains 25,000-50,000Rp; 8am-3pm & 6-9.30pm) Clean and popular, this Chinese seafood house plates tender fish fillets, prawns, squid, crab and scallops in oyster, Szechuan or sweet-and-sour sauce. The *soto kepiting* (crab soup) is good, as is anything with noodles.

Information

MEDICAL SERVICES

Klinik Surya Medika Sumbawa (0371-262 0023; Jl Hasanuddin 20A; 24hr) Hospital with 24-hour care.

OFF THE BEATEN TRACK

TRADITIONAL TEXTILES

Some of the best ikat and *songket* sarongs are made by members of a women's weaving *klompok* (collective) in the conservative mountain village of **Poto**, 12km east of Sumbawa Besar and 2km from the small town of Moyo. Traditional designs include the *prahu* (outrigger boat). You'll hear the clack of weavers' looms from the street and are welcome to duck into their humble huts. The most intricate pieces take up to 45 days to produce.

A return trip from Sumbawa Besar in an *ojek* should cost no more than 100,000Rp.

VISA EXTENSIONS

Kantor Imigrasi (Immigration Office; Jl Garuda 41; ⏲8am-3pm Mon-Thu, to noon Fri) Extend your tourist visa here; it'll take at least two days.

Getting There & Away

AIR

Sultan Muhammad Kaharuddin III Airport is very close to the centre. Garuda and Wings Air fly direct to Lombok daily, though more routes are planned when the airport expands in 2020.

BUS

Sumbawa Besar's main long-distance bus station is **Terminal Sumur Payung** (Jl Lintas Sumbawa), 5.5km northwest of town on the highway. Destinations served include the following:

Bima 100,000Rp, seven hours, several daily

Mataram 90,000Rp (including ferry ticket), six hours, several daily

Poto Tano 35,000Rp, 2½ hours, hourly from 8am to midnight

Getting Around

It's easy to walk into town from the airport – just turn to your right as you exit the terminal; the walk is less than 1km. Alternatively, you can arrange transport with local guesthouses.

Bemos cost 5000Rp for trips anywhere around town.

Pulau Moyo

☎0371

Moyo is a gently arcing crescent of jungled volcanic rock that floats atop the azure seas north of Sumbawa Besar. About half the size of Singapore, it's home to just 2000 people spread across six small villages. The largest, **Labuhan Aji**, is an authentic Sumbawanese town that has only recently opened up to tourism. It lies on a pebbly beach (better suited for snorkelling than swimming) and is the kind of throw-back island paradise where electricity only works in the evening and locals are still amused to see foreigners.

The majority of the island, and its rich reefs, form a nature reserve laced with trails, dripping with waterfalls and offering some of the best diving west of Komodo. Loggerhead and green turtles hatch on the beaches, long-tail macaques patrol the canopy, and wild pigs, barking deer and a diverse bird population all call Moyo home.

Sights

Mata Jitu Waterfall WATERFALL

Pulau Moyo's most famous attraction is this fairytale waterfall, whose cascading pools of turquoise water have entranced at least one princess (locals call it Lady Diana Waterfall because she visited in 1993). A sign in Labuhan Aji says it's 7km away, but this is a marketing ploy to get you on an *ojek* (100,000Rp). It's actually a relatively easy 4km hike (bring your swimsuit!).

If you go on your own, you'll need to pay a 25,000Rp 'island tax' to your hotel in advance.

Activities

Hiking and snorkelling are the big draws here. You can also charter local boats for trips to offshore dive sites or stunning beaches like **Tanjung Pasir** in the south of the island.

Diving

Good reefs with a plunging wall can be found all around the island. Those on a budget should book a dive with Maleo Moyo, while Amanwana Resort caters to the well-heeled set. If you join a Bali- or Lombok-based Komodo-bound liveaboard, you'll likely stop for a day or two in Moyo on the way.

Maleo Moyo DIVING

(DJL Diving; ☎0812 0472 9535; http://scubadivemoyo.com; Labuhan Aji; shore/boat dive 400,000/600,000K, discover scuba 800,000Rp; ⏲8am-5pm) The only PADI dive shop in Labuhan Aji with two comfortable boats, one of which is often used to take snorkellers to offshore reefs like Takat Sagele and Sengalo. Sign up for daily leisure diving or multiday dive safaris.

Maleo Moyo also has a row of bright and airy bungalows (400,000Rp to 600,000Rp) and a divers' crash pad with dorm beds (100,000Rp) and basic rooms (200,000Rp).

Sleeping & Eating

Labuhan Aji is the island's main village and the only place set up for tourism. You'll find basic homestays and midrange bungalows along its beach, while the island's long-running luxe resort lies in a secluded spot 7km to the south. Most accommodations along the beach have onsite restaurants and there are three simple warungs hidden away along the laneways of Labuhan Aji. Most businesses in the village only have electricity from 6pm to 6am.

Devi Homestay HOMESTAY $
(☎0853 3993 2815; Labuhan Aji; r without bathroom 100,000Rp, with full board 200,000Rp) The nicest of the ultra-basic homestays in town, set just back from the pier. All rooms have mattresses on the floor and shared bathrooms, but if you ask for the ones in the front you'll also get a patio overlooking the sea.

★ **Sunset Moyo Bungalows** BUNGALOW $$
(☎0852 0517 1191; http://sunsetmoyobungalows.com; Labuhan Aji; bungalow d/tr 650,000/750,000Rp) Everything is just so at this appropriately named getaway, whose terraced front deck is like a mini-amphitheatre for dreamy sunsets. The five bungalows are full of playful touches, like tree-trunk sinks and outdoor showers, while the overwater swing out front was surely built for Instagram travel porn. The friendly owners can arrange bikes, hikes, snorkelling and massages.

Maryan Moyo BUNGALOW $$
(www.facebook.com/moyobungalows; Labuhan Aji; bungalow with/without air-con 600,000/500,000Rp; ❄) Sleep to the sounds of lapping waves in one of five stilted bungalows, each with a sturdy wooden frame, stone-tiled bathroom and covered deck facing the sea. Umbrellas and sun loungers on the beach out front add to the soporific vibe.

★ **Amanwana Resort** RESORT $$$
(☎0371-22233; www.amanresorts.com; all-inclusive jungle/ocean-view tents from US$910/1090; ❄@📶) On Moyo's western side, 7km south of Labuhan Aji, Amanwana is the ultimate island hideaway. Guests stay in lavish permanent tents with antique wood furnishings, king-sized beds and air-con, but nature still rules here. The resort is built around diving, hiking and mountain biking. Guests arrive by private seaplane or helicopter from Bali, or from mainland Sumbawa on an Amanwana boat.

ℹ Getting There & Away

Public boats depart daily at noon from Sumbawa Besar for the two-hour journey to Labuhan Aji (75,000Rp). The normal departure point is Muara Kali, but when tides are low they will leave from Pantai Goa on the other side of town. The return trip from Labuhan Aji is at 7am each morning.

WORTH A TRIP

SNORKELLING SPOTS

There is decent coral in the waters just off Labuhan Aji. A better spot that's also accessible from the shore and has larger schools of fish is **Crocodile Head**. To reach it, hike or bike 5km south of Labuhan Aji on the path toward the Amanwana Resort until you see a sign indicating the turn-off.

Just northeast of Pulau Moyo is small **Pulau Satonda**, which also has good beaches and tremendous snorkelling. Maleo Moyo can arrange the two-hour boat ride to visit (2,000,000Rp).

The seas around Moyo get turbulent from December to March and boat captains understandably may refuse to risk a journey. They may also refuse to depart on the rare occasion when there are not enough passengers, in which case those in a rush may have to charter an entire boat for as much as 2,000,000Rp.

A popular alternative to the Sumbawa Besar route for those climbing Gunung Tambora is to arrange a boat over to the east side of the island, followed by a land transfer to Labuhan Aji. Rik Stoetman at **Visit Tambora** (☎0813 5337 0951; https://visittambora.com; near Pancasila) can make all the necessary arrangements.

Gunung Tambora

☎0373

Looming over central Sumbawa is the 2722m volcano Gunung Tambora. Its peak was obliterated during the epic eruption of April 1815 (p342). Two hundred years later much of the mountain was declared a national park.

Today from the summit you'll have spectacular views of the 6km-wide caldera, which contains a two-coloured lake, and endless ocean vistas that stretch as far as Gunung Rinjani (Lombok). A basic climb to the crater rim takes at least two days; if you want to venture down into the spectacular crater – one of the world's deepest – add another three days.

The base for ascents is the remote village of **Pancasila** near the town of **Calabai** on the western slope; here you can organise climbs. Contacts to organise climbs include **Pak Saiful** (☎0859 3703 0848, 0823 4069 3138; Pancasila) and Rik Stoetman. Both can rent rooms (from 150,000Rp to 300,000Rp) and handle transport and logistical issues.

THE YEAR WITHOUT SUMMER

After a few days of tremors the top blew off Gunung Tambora on 10 April 1815 in what is the most powerful eruption in modern history. Tens of thousands of Sumbawans were killed, molten rock was sent more than 40km into the sky, and the explosion was heard 2000km away (by comparison, the 1873 eruption of Krakatoa was one-tenth the size).

In the months and years that followed, weather was affected worldwide as the cloud of ash blotted out the sun. In Europe 1816 came to be known as 'the year without summer'. Crops failed, temperatures plummeted, disease spread and tens of thousands died across the globe. Historical evidence is everywhere, including in the works of JMW Turner, whose paintings from the period feature shocking orange colours in the dim, ash-filled skies.

Two books vividly illustrate how Tambora's eruption changed the planet: *Tambora* by Gillen D'Arcy Wood and *Tambora: Travels to Sumbawa and the Mountain that Changed the World* by Derek Pugh.

Activities

A two-day guided trek up Gunung Tambora should cost about 2,000,000Rp per person for groups of three or more, including guides, porters, camping equipment, meals and accommodation in Pancasila on either end. Also included is the 150,000Rp park entrance fee.

Getting There & Away

The road along the peninsula from the Trans-Sumbawa Hwy to Calabai is much improved. You can hire a private taxi from Bima Airport for 1,300,000Rp, or hop on a very crowded bus from Bima's Terminal Dara (70,000Rp, five hours, 6am and 3pm daily) to Calabai. From Calabai take an *ojek* (30,000Rp, 20 minutes) to Pancasila.

Pantai Lakey

0373

Pantai Lakey, a gentle crescent of golden sand, is where Sumbawa's tourist pulse beats, thanks to seven world-class surf breaks that curl and crash in one massive bay, and a string of modest beach guesthouses, all linked by a sandy path studded with bars. While there's an agreeable beach-bum ambience, Lakey isn't as polished as surf towns on neighbouring islands to the west, and nonsurfers may find little to hold their attention.

Hu'u is a small, poor, and very friendly fishing village, 3km north of Lakey. Neat and shady, suffused with the scent of drying fish and blessed with breathtaking pink sunsets, it's the nearest public-transport node to Lakey.

The area is the centre of a push to increase tourism on Sumbawa. New roads mean you can now easily drive east from Hu'u, and north to Bima via Parado, enjoying some superb sea views along the way.

Activities

This is one of Indonesia's best surfing destinations, blessed with almost-guaranteed surf. **Lakey Peak** and **Lakey Pipe** are the best-known waves and are within paddling distance of the various hotels and guesthouses. You'll need to rent a motorbike or hire an *ojek* to get to **Nungas**, **Cobblestone** and **Nangadoro**. **Periscope** is 150m from the sand at the far north end of the bay near **Maci Point**, which is another good spot. When the swell gets really big, there's a beach break at Hu'u as well.

Most surfers share the cost of a boat (from 800,000Rp, maximum five people) to get to the breaks and back. Waves can be very good (and very big) year-round, but the most consistent swell arrives between June and August. Inexperienced surfers should be cautious. Waves break over a shallow reef and serious accidents do happen, especially when the tide's out.

From August to October the wind gusts, which turns Pantai Lakey into Indonesia's best kitesurfing destination – it's regarded as one of the 10 best in the world. Kites descend on Lakey Pipe and Nungas when it's pumping.

Joey Barrel's Board Shop SURFING

(Jl Raya Hu'u; 7am-6pm) Out on the main drag, this small shop offers ding repairs, board rental (per day from 50,000Rp), surfing supplies and board sales. It's open when the owner isn't at the breaks.

Sleeping

There are plenty of decent-value digs strung along Pantai Lakey. A paved path skirts the beach, linking guesthouses.

Any Lestari BUNGALOW $
(0813 3982 3018; Jl Rya Hu'u; r 150,000-350,000Rp;) A vast bungalow complex that stretches back from the beach. All bungalows are spacious with tiled rooms and private patios, but some are in better shape than others. The most expensive rooms have Siberian air-con, hot water and satellite TV. The waterfront bar and restaurant, Blue Lagoon, draws a steady crowd.

Lakey Beach Inn GUESTHOUSE $
(0823 4011 6155; www.lakey-beach-inn.com; Jl Raya Hu'u; s/d with fan 150,000/200,000Rp, s/d with air-con 200,000/300,000Rp;) Rooms in this sprawling compound are basic but good value – the cheapest have fans and cold water. Overlooking two legendary breaks, Lakey Pipe and Lakey Peak, its open-sided, driftwoody cafe-bar is a great place to enjoy a post-surf beer, a pizza or Indo classics (mains 35,000Rp to 45,000Rp). French owner Rachel was one of the first foreign surfers to put down roots in Lakey.

★**Rock Pool Home Stay** HOMESTAY $$
(0813 3733 6856; http://rockpoolhomestay.com; Jl Pantai Nunggas Lakey; r 400,000-500,000Rp;) Set amid tropical gardens, the five rooms at Rock Pool are some of the nicest on Pantai Lakey, with air-con, decent wi-fi and fabulous views across the breaks towards the rolling hills of Sumbawa. The open-sided restaurant Ali's Bar, a great place to enjoy offshore breezes and beers after a day's surfing, serves Indonesian and Western food from 7am to 10pm.

Vivi's Lakey Peak Homestay HOMESTAY $$
(0823 4049 9139; www.lakeypeakhomestay.com; Jl Pantai Lakey; s/d/tr 250,000/350,000/450,000Rp;) Set along a little lane between the beach and the main road, this five-room compound offers the area's warmest welcome, with Vivian and her Sumbawanese-Australian family your generous hosts. Rooms are modern and large with nice furnishings, the yard is shaded by banana trees and there's a sociable, open-sided cafe. The cooking is excellent!

★**Lakey Peak Haven** HOTEL $$$
(0821 4413 6320; www.lakeypeakhaven.com; Jl Raya Hu'u; s/d from US$70/80;) Removed from the action on a hill above town, this highly manicured Bali-style 'haven' is easily the best accommodation option in town with two-storey surf 'shacks' overlooking a chequered pool deck and the distant breaks. Reserve in advance as it doesn't accept walk-ups.

Eating & Drinking

Most guesthouses have their own cafe-bars, and there are simple refreshment stalls and warungs along the beachfront path.

Mamat Warung INDONESIAN $
(Jl Raya Hu'u; mains 20,000-30,000Rp; 7am-10pm) While it lacks a sea view, this simple warung out on the main road serves up Lakey's cheapest and most authentic Indonesian fare, including *sate*, gado gado (a peanut-sauced salad) and plenty of tempe dishes for vegetarians.

Wreck INTERNATIONAL $$
(Jl Raya Hu'u; mains 50,000-65,000Rp; 8am-9pm) A beached Sumbawanese boat, its prow pointing to Lakey's famous breaks, has been turned into a breezy, open-sided restaurant that does surprisingly good 'Mexican' food, alongside Indonesian and Western standards. If the local interpretation of quesadillas, fajitas and burritos doesn't appeal, try the spicy fish in banana leaves, or simply sink a beer and some balls around the threadbare pool table.

Fatmah's INTERNATIONAL $$
(off Jl Raya Hu'u; mains 30,000-75,000Rp; 7am-9pm;) Once humble, Fatmah's has taken a slight turn upmarket in recent years. Tables sit in a raised bleached-wood house overlooking the beach where you can watch the sun set or the kitesurfers swoop, as you tuck into juices, *ayam lalapan* (fried chicken and sambal), or Western fare like pastas and Aussie meat pies ... all to the beat of EDM.

Balumba Shop COFFEE
(7am-6pm) This hole-in-the-wall shop on the beach walk in front of the Balumba Hotel offers the best coffees in East Sumbawa. All beans come from farms on the slopes of nearby Gunung Tambora and are manually pressed through a Rok Presso machine for silky espressos or creamy soy lattes.

Information

The nearest ATMs are 37km north in Dompu.

Getting There & Away

From Dompu there are two daily (slow) buses as far as Hu'u (25,000Rp, 1½ hours), where you can hire an *ojek* (20,000Rp) to Pantai Lakey. *Ojeks* to/from Dompu on the Trans-Sumbawa Hwy start at 80,000Rp.

Try doing this with a surfboard and you'll see why so many people take a taxi from Bima Airport (800,000Rp for up to four people). Buses to/from Bima cost 35,000Rp (one daily, usually at noon or 1pm). It's typically easier to travel via the more frequent Dompu route.

Getting Around

The *ojek* cartel is omnipresent in Lakey; rates to the breaks range from 30,000Rp to 80,000Rp. It's generally cheaper to rent your own motorbike from any shop on the main road (from 50,000Rp per day), all of which have special board racks.

Sape

0374 / POP 53,000

Sape's got a tumbledown port-town vibe, perfumed with the conspicuous scent of drying cuttlefish. The outskirts are quilted in rice fields backed by jungled hills, while *benhur* (horse-drawn carts) and early morning commerce whirl past the colourful wooden stilt homes in town. If you're catching a morning ferry, consider staying at **Losmen Mutiara** (0374-71337; Jl Pelabuhan Sape; r 70,000-160,000Rp;). Right next to the port gates and the last bus stop, it's a decent enough place with 20 rooms spread across two floors. Across the street is **Rumah Makan Citra Minang** (Jl Pelabuhan Sape; mains 30,000Rp; 8am-9pm), whose smiling chefs bring the finest and spiciest Padang dishes to life.

Getting There & Away

BOAT

The ferry port is 4km east of Sape's diminutive centre. Regular breakdowns and rough seas disrupt ferry services – always double-check the latest schedules in Bima and Sape. Ferries from Sape include the following:

Labuan Bajo (Flores) 60,000Rp, six hours, one daily

Waikelo (Sumba) 69,000Rp, eight hours, two weekly

BUS

Express buses with service to Lombok (250,000Rp, 12 to 15 hours) meet arriving ferries.

Buses leave almost every hour for Bima (30,000Rp, two hours), where you can catch local buses to other Sumbawa destinations.

Taxi drivers may claim that buses have stopped running and you must charter their vehicle to Bima (350,000Rp, 1½ hours); this is usually not true.

KOMODO & RINCA ISLANDS

Parked neatly between Sumbawa and Flores, the islands of Komodo and Rinca are the major draw cards of Unesco-recognised Komodo National Park. The islands' jagged hills, carpeted with savannah and fringed with mangroves, are home to prehistoric Komodo dragons or *ora*, the world's largest lizards.

Padar Island, conveniently positioned between Komodo and Rinca, is a highly prized photography perch, gifting those who climb the stairs an outlook of three perfect bays that transition from aquamarine to sapphire blue.

These isolated islands are surrounded by some of Indonesia's most tempestuous waters. Warm and cold currents converge and breed nutritious thermal climes and rip tides that attract large schools of pelagics, including dolphins, sharks, manta rays and blue whales. The coral here is mostly pristine. With some of the best diving in the world, it's no surprise that liveaboards ply these waters between April and September when diving is at its finest.

Komodo

POP 3,267

Spectacular Komodo, its steep hillsides jade in the short wet season (December to March) and frazzled by sun to a rusty tan that makes its crystal waters pop the rest of the year, is the largest island in Komodo National Park. A succession of peninsulas spread east, each providing a different perspective: some are even fringed in pink sand due to red coral offshore.

On its south coast is the entrance to **Loh Liang** and the PHKA office, where boats dock and guided walks and treks start. The fishing village of **Kampung Komodo** is a 30-minute boat ride south of Loh Liang. It's a friendly, stilted Bugis village filled with goats, chickens and children. The locals, said to be descendants of convicts exiled to the island by Sumbawanese Sultans in the 19th century, are used to seeing tourists. You can spend your time simply absorbing village life and gazing out over the water.

Activities

Walking & Trekking

The 150,000Rp entrance fee at Komodo includes a choice of three walks: the **short walk** (1.5km, 45 minutes), which includes a stop at an artificial waterhole that attracts diminutive local deer, wild boar and of course *ora;* the **medium walk** (2km, 1½ hours), which includes a hill with sweeping views and a chance to see colourful cockatoos; and the **long walk** (4km, two hours), which includes the features of the shorter hikes and gets you much further from the peak-season crowds.

You can also negotiate for adventure treks (from 500,000Rp for up to five people). These treks are up to 10km long and can last four or more hours, so bring plenty of water. There are two paths. One climbs the 538m-high **Gunung Ara**, with expansive views from the top. The other, **Poreng Valley**, has an out-in-the-wild feeling. Watch for wildlife on your way over **Bukit Randolph**, which passes a memorial to 79-year-old Randolph Von Reding who disappeared on Komodo in 1974, then head to **Loh Sebita**. It's challenging, the sea views are spectacular and you'll likely see a dragon or two – as well as buffalo, deer, wild boar and Komodo's rich bird life. Organise your boat to pick you up in Loh Sebita so you don't have to retrace your steps.

Water Sports

Almost everybody who visits Komodo hires a boat in Labuan Bajo or visits as part of a liveaboard itinerary. Day trips always offer snorkelling (gear included) as part of the itinerary as well as a stop at an island beach. Many snorkel around the small island of **Pulau Lasa** near Kampung Komodo, and just off the pink sands of **Pantai Merah** (Red Beach; although it's usually referred to as the Pink Beach).

People who stay on Komodo can arrange for kayaking and sunrise dolphin tours.

Sleeping & Eating

In the village of Kampung Komodo, you'll find a few very basic homestays that give you a bed and some meals. Either turn up and let locals guide you to one (rooms cost from about 200,000Rp per night) or arrange your stay in advance with **Usman Ranger** (☎0812 3956 6140). English is often minimal, so get your ranger to work out the nitty-gritty before you bed down for the night.

VISITING KOMODO NATIONAL PARK

Established in 1980 and declared a World Heritage Site and a Man and the Biosphere Reserve by Unesco in 1986, **Komodo National Park** (www.komodonationalpark.org) covers 1817 sq km. Within that area are Komodo, Rinca and Padar Islands: a constellation of smaller islands and an incomparably rich marine ecosystem.

Fees for visitors add up quickly:

- Landing fee per person for Komodo and Rinca islands: 150,000Rp (Monday to Friday); 225,000Rp (weekends and holidays)
- Boat fee: 100,000Rp
- Ranger-guided walk fee: 80,000Rp (maximum four people)
- Tourism tax: 100,000Rp
- Wildlife observation fee: 10,000Rp
- Hiking or trekking fee: 5,000Rp
- Diving fee per person per day: 25,000Rp
- Snorkelling fee per person per day: 15,000Rp

Note that these fees are often changing, with constant talk of increases. Tour operators (including dive shops) usually collect the fees in advance. If not, you pay them in the park offices on Komodo or Rinca, or at Labuan Bajo's PHKA Information Booth (p356).

At both Komodo and Rinca you have a choice of walks, from short to long, which you organise with a ranger when you arrive at the relevant island's park office. Longer walks demand a higher price.

Labuan Bajo in western Flores, with frequent air connections to Denpasar and Kupang and myriad tour- and dive-boats, is the gateway to the national park.

DIVING & SNORKELLING AROUND KOMODO & LABUAN BAJO

Komodo National Park (p345) has some of the most exhilarating scuba diving in Indonesia, if not the world. It's a region swept by strong currents and cold upswells, created by the convergence of the warmer Flores Sea with the cooler Selat Sumba (Sumba Strait). These conditions create a rich plankton soup that feeds an astonishing variety of marine life. Manta rays and whales are drawn here during their migration from the Indian Ocean to the South China Sea, dolphins are common in the waters between Komodo and Flores and you're likely to spot white-tip and reef sharks more fearful of you than you are of them.

Your diving instructor might have a penchant for seeking out pelagics and giant creatures of the deep, or take great pleasure in spotting tiny, colourful nudibranches – marine molluscs in extraordinary colours and patterns that are oddly adorable. With impressive muck diving and coral sites within 1½ hours of Labuan Bajo, scuba opportunities abound well before Komodo National Park, as well as when you pull up.

Whether you have thousands of dives under your weight belt or only know how to swim, dive operators line Labuan Bajo's main strip, Jl Soekarno Hatta, so you can take your pick. It's best to shop around, but not always possible to survey the equipment and boats before making a decision. Ask questions and to see photographs – staff should produce answers and a good gut feeling, but bring your own computer or anything else you deem essential.

A good place to start is with businesses that are members of Dive Operators Community of Komodo (DOCK; www.diveoperatorskomodo.com). The DOCK stickers you'll spot in windows are indicative of a quality diving experience that puts safety and the environment first. Members follow strict guidelines and also help combat illegal anchoring and fishing, working closely with the Komodo National Park authority to encourage sustainable tourism. Part of the membership fee includes donations to local NGOs, which support community initiatives like Trash Hero Komodo, where people don yellow T-shirts and help clean up the beaches.

Most shops also offer Divemaster and speciality courses. A handshake agreement between members of DOCK ensures similar prices: at the time of writing, 1,650,000Rp for three dives on a day trip is a common rate, as is 5,500,000Rp for a three-day Open Water Diver certification, which will open the oceanic doors to a whole new world. Snorkelling trips are also available (around 700,000Rp for three sites and a visit to the dragons). Your hotel will rent snorkelling gear or know who does. Local shops loan masks and fins for around 60,000Rp per day. July and August is peak season but in March, April and September visitor numbers thin and diving is magical. Dive operators tend to hit the northern dive sites between April and September and the south between October and March, when the currents are most conducive to safe and successful dives.

The following are among the several dozen dive sites mapped in the park and in the waters and islands around Labuan Bajo:

Batu Balong A split pinnacle with pristine coral and a relatively light current. The small rock jutting above the water only hints at the wealth of life below.

Crystal Bommie (aka Crystal Rock) Here advanced divers navigate the soft-coral covered sea mount and strong currents, spotting turtles and schooling pelagics.

Castle Rock (aka Tako Toko Toko) A tremendous sunrise dive site where, with a little luck, you'll be accompanied by dolphins or see magnificent pinwheels of tropical fish amid strong currents.

Karang Makassar (aka Manta Point) A shallow drift dive over moonscape rubble where massive manta rays school and clean themselves on the rocks. Multiple shark sightings are common.

Sebayur Kecil An almost current-free site where parrotfish, blue spotted rays and cuttlefish are common.

Siaba Besar (aka Turtle Town) A popular spot among both advanced divers and those just starting out, thanks to the local population of green turtles.

Any place you stay will provide you with simple meals, but be sure to confirm this with your ranger. Memorising the Bahasa Indonesia word for eat and food, *makan*, can get you a long way.

Komodo Guesthouse GUESTHOUSE **$$**
(☎0812 3956 6140; Loh Liang; r from 400,000Rp) Located on Komodo Island and just five-minutes' walk from the dock, this six-room guesthouse has a long, covered porch that's elevated and offers ocean views. Rooms are basic but have fans (there's electricity from 6pm to midnight) and you can organise meals through park rangers. Reserve when you arrive on the island or ahead by phone.

Getting There & Away

Competition for Komodo day trips from Labuan Bajo (p349) is fierce. Join one of the many tours hawked by operators in town, which cost from 500,000Rp per person, including a light lunch and stops for beach fun and snorkelling. As it takes 3½ hours to reach Komodo, day trips leave around 5.30am and return around 6pm.

You can also charter a local boat from 2,000,000Rp and pick your itinerary, which is a great deal when split between four to six people. Just be sure to make the proper safety checks before committing. Overnight charters leave around 7am and start at 2,000,000Rp per person.

A speedboat costing from 1,500,000Rp per person will cover the distance to Komodo in under an hour and arrive at hot spots before the crowds. Charter your own from around 7,000,000Rp for a full day out, which can include stops at both Komodo and Rinca. The many liveaboard schemes almost always include a stop at Komodo at some point, as do the private boats making the run between Flores, Lombok and Bali.

Rinca

Rinca is slightly smaller than nearby Komodo, closer to Labuan Bajo and easily done in a day trip. It packs a lot into a small space and for many it's a more convenient but just as worthy destination as Komodo.

The island combines mangroves, light forest, sun-drenched hills and – of course – Komodo dragons. Due to its smaller size and a tendency for *ora* to hang around Loh Buaya's camp kitchen, you're more likely to see the beasts on Rinca than Komodo.

Activities

From the boat dock it's a 10-minute walk across tidal flats, home to long-tail macaques and wild water buffalo, to the PHKA station camp at Loh Buaya. Three guided walks are included in the 80,000Rp admission fee: the **short walk** (500m, one hour) takes in mangroves and some *ora* nesting sites; the **medium walk** (1.5km, 90 minutes) is 'just right' as it includes the shady lowlands plus a trip up a hillside where the views across the arid landscape to achingly turquoise waters and pearly white specks of beach are spectacular; and the **long walk** (4km, three hours), which takes in all the island's attractions.

Besides dragons, you may see tiny Timor deer, snakes, monkeys, wild boar and an array of birds. There are supposedly no set dragon-feeding places on Rinca, but you're almost guaranteed to see the massive beasts near the camp kitchen at Loh Buaya, so you do the maths.

Sleeping & Eating

You can stay in a spare room in the ranger's dorm (from 300,000Rp), but there's little reason to as the site lacks charm and Labuan Bajo is nearby. There is a simple daytime cafe at the ranger station where you can stock up on water, have a snack and enjoy a cold beer while watching grazing deer.

Flores XPirates Dive Camp HUT **$$**
(☎0811 3985 344; http://xpiratesdivecamp.com; Pulau Sebayur; dm/d/bungalow per person all-inclusive 400,000/450,000/600,000Rp; wi-fi) In 2018 **Flores XP Adventure** opened its solar-powered island dive camp with new huts, breezy bungalows and a six-bed dorm. There's a restaurant with wi-fi, dive centre and brilliant snorkelling near the 180m jetty and reef, where a coral propagation program is underway. Prices include buffet meals and boat transfers. Full-board dive packages available from 3,700,000Rp per person.

Komodo Resort Diving Club RESORT **$$$**
(☎0385-42094, island number 0813 3761 6625, office 8am-5pm 0812 3810 3244; www.komodoresort.com; Pulau Sebayur; d/tr/f incl meals 2,820,000/9,548,000/10,936,800Rp; air-con, wi-fi) With 18 bungalows and four family rooms spread along a white-sand beach, this is a truly beautiful island resort. Bungalows have wooden floors, king beds, plush linen, 24-hour electricity, tented marble bathrooms with hot water and more. Rates include three excellent meals, but diving is separate. There's also a spa and beach bar. Minimum three-night stay.

KOMODO DRAGONS

The *ora* (Komodo dragon) is a monitor lizard, albeit one on steroids. Growing up to 3m in length and weighing up to 150kg, they are an awesome sight and must-see during any visit to Komodo National Park (p345). Standard day tours tend to arrive in the middle of the day, when *ora* lounge about lethargically. They're much more active at dawn and dusk, but even when resting, they can be as fearsome as their looks imply. Park rangers keep them from attacking tourists; random encounters are a bad idea. Some dragon details:

- They are omnivorous, and enjoy eating their young. Juvenile dragons live in trees to avoid becoming a meal for adults.
- *Ora* often rise up on their hind legs just before attacking, and the tail can deliver well-aimed blows that knock down their prey.
- Long thought to be a type of bacteria, venom (located in glands between the dragons' teeth) is their secret weapon. One bite from a dragon leads to septic infections that inevitably kill the victim. The venom is loaded with toxins that promote bleeding and the huge lizard lopes along after its victim waiting for it to die, usually within a week.
- Komodos can eat up to 80% of their body weight in a single sitting. They will then retire for up to a month to digest the massive meal.
- On Komodo, *ora* have been seen chasing deer into the ocean and then waiting on shore while the hapless mammal tries to return. Eventually the exhausted animal staggers onto the beach, where the dragon inflicts its ultimately deadly bite.
- There is no accepted reason why the dragons are only found in this small area of Indonesia, although it's thought that their ancestors came from Australia four million years ago.
- It's estimated that there are up to 5000 in the wild today, but there are concerns that only a few hundred or so are egg-laying females.
- In 2006, two female dragons kept isolated from other dragons their entire lives laid fertilised eggs, which hatched successfully. The process, parthenogenesis, is incredibly rare and occurs when an unfertilised egg develops into an embryo without being fertilised by a sperm.

Spotting Dragons

At both Komodo and Rinca your odds of seeing dragons are very good, with the exception of mating season on Komodo, which is between June and August, when the females go into hiding and the males spread out on the vast island trying to find them. Peak months for komodo-spotting are September to December, when both sexes are out and about. Mating season is less of a problem at Rinca, a smaller island where *ora* have a tendency to hang around the ranger stations, especially the kitchens.

You may get quite close to *ora* so a telephoto lens is handy but not essential. Rangers carry a forked, wooden staff as their only protection. Treat the seemingly slow-moving *ora* with great respect: so far five deaths have been recorded, including three villagers and two tourists.

Getting There & Away

Day trips to Rinca start at 400,000Rp and the choices are many. Chartering a speedboat to Rinca costs around 5,000,000Rp from Labuan Bajo and takes less than an hour each way. Boats usually return via small island beaches and snorkelling spots.

At Rinca, boats dock at the sheltered lagoon at Loh Kima, which at busy times may have over two dozen wooden vessels tied together.

FLORES

Flores, the island given a pretty but incongruous Portuguese name by its 16th-century colonists, has become Indonesia's Next Big Thing. The serpentine, 670km Trans-Flores Hwy runs the length of the island, skirting knife-edge ridges, brushing by paddy-fringed villages and opening up dozens of areas few tourists explore.

The island is a cacophony of smells, swinging between coffee roasting in the hills, clove cigarettes, exhaust fumes and the unmistakable scent of the ocean. In the west, Labuan Bajo is a booming tourist town combining tropical beauty with nearby attractions such as Komodo National Park, superb dive spots and white-sand islands.

The east is attracting an ever-greater number of travellers chasing smouldering volcanoes, emerald rice terraces, prehistoric riddles, exotic cultures, hot springs and hidden beaches. Away from the port towns most people are nominally Catholic. Many more are part of cultures dating back centuries, living in traditional villages seemingly unchanged in millennia.

Information

Foreign aid money has funded a string of useful tourist offices in key towns across Flores. Their enthusiastic assistance is backed by an excellent website (www.florestourism.com), free town maps and several publications well worth their modest prices, including a huge, detailed island map and books covering activities and culture.

Getting There & Away

AIR

You can easily get flights connecting Flores with Bali, Lombok and Kupang (West Timor), among other destinations. Labuan Bajo is the main gateway, while Maumere and Ende are also serviced by daily flights. It's easy to fly into Labuan Bajo, tour the island, and fly out of Maumere. Be aware that the booming popularity of Flores means that flights are booked solid at peak times.

BOAT

Daily ferries connect Labuan Bajo with Sape (Sumbawa), while weekly services go to Bira (Sulawesi) and Pulau Jampea (Sulawesi). From Larantuka (Flores), three weekly ferries go to Kupang (West Timor). From Ende, weekly boats will take you to Waingapu (Sumba) and Kupang (West Timor).

Getting Around

The Trans-Flores Hwy, the spine of the island, twists and turns through beautiful countryside and skirts photogenic volcanoes, but don't make the mistake of taking Google Maps' estimated journey times as gospel.

The improving roads mean that more and more visitors are hiring motorcycles in Labuan Bajo and heading east. This can cost from 75,000Rp per day plus petrol. It's not for the faint of heart: riding can be hazardous and exhausting.

Regular buses run between Labuan Bajo and Maumere. They're cheap and cramped. Much more comfortable and only somewhat more expensive are public minibuses (often a Toyota Kijang), which link major towns in air-con comfort.

Many travellers hire a car and driver, which costs from 800,000Rp to 1,200,000Rp per day, depending on English-speaking and tour-guiding capabilities. If you have a group of six, this is a fair deal. Many drivers also work as guides and can arrange detailed, island-wide itineraries. Your accommodation will usually be able to recommend someone reliable, but stop for a bite or drink anywhere in Flores and you're likely to meet someone who will recommend a friend.

Based in Labuan Bajo, Andy Rona (p352) is an excellent driver and guide, who has a network of reliable colleagues.

Labuan Bajo

☎0385 / POP 3000

This dusty, enchanting harbour town is perpetually being upgraded to cope with more travellers. It's the jumping-off point to see prehistoric dragons at Komodo National Park and be awed by world-class diving, and those who stay a little longer fall in love with 'Bajo' (attested to by a healthy expat community).

Everything you need is located on one-way Jl Soekarno Hatta, which is crammed with Western restaurants, local *rumah makans* and plenty of accommodation, travel agents and dive shops. The waterfront bustles with daily life, and connections to other parts of Indonesia are effortless.

A sparkly new marina and five-star AYANA resort opened in 2018; with more luxury accommodation confirmed by 2021, Labuan Bajo, the capital of Manggarai Barat regency, is officially no longer a low-key fishing town. As one local said when referring to a popular bar (p356), 'It's getting busy in Paradise.'

Activities

Labuan Bajo's pristine coastline is mostly occupied by hotels, making excursions to nearby islands essential day trips for snorkelling and lounging on palm-fringed beaches. **Pantai Waecicu** is on Bajo's mainland, where you can snorkel around the tiny islet of **Kukusan Kecil**. **Pulau Bidadari** (Angel Island) has crystalline water filled with fish and baby sharks. **Pulau Seraya** and **Pulau Kanawa** have postcard-perfect beaches and resorts taking advantage of them, while

Pulau Kalong is home to thousands of flying fox bats, active from dusk. Travellers with more time won't regret staying on a liveaboard boat and island-hopping further out from Labuan Bajo.

Diving & Snorkelling

Beneath the surface of Komodo lies one of the world's most biodiverse marine environments: vibrant reefs, mangroves, sand banks and drop-offs to teeming deep-water habitats supporting thousands of species of tropical fish, turtles, marine mammals, crustaceans and more.

Outstanding sites include: **Batu Bolong**, a tiny island surrounded by coral walls where you might see Napoleon wrasse and white-tip sharks; **Sebayur Kecil**, an almost current-free site where parrotfish, cuttlefish and blue spotted rays are common; **Karang Makassar** (Manta Point), which offers guaranteed sightings of graceful manta rays during rainy season from December to March (and often outside it); **Siaba Besar**, known as Turtle Town for its local residents; and **Crystal Rock**, where advanced divers navigate the soft coral-covered sea mount spotting sharks and larger fish.

An agreement between members of the Dive Operators Community of Komodo (DOCK) ensures similar prices: 1,650,000Rp for three dives on a day trip is a common rate, as is 5,500,000Rp for a three-day Open Water Diver certification. Many shops also offer Divemaster and speciality courses.

Dive operators line Jl Soekarno Hatta. It's best to shop around.

Snorkelling trips are also available (around 700,000Rp for three sites as well as a visit to the dragons). Your hotel will rent snorkelling gear or know who does. Local shops loan masks and fins for around 60,000Rp per day. July and August is peak season but in March, April and September visitor numbers thin and diving is magical.

CNDive DIVING
(☎0823 3908 0808, 0385-41159; www.cndivekomodo.com; Jl Mutiara 7; per diver per day from US$147; ⊙8am-5pm) Condo Subagyo, the Indonesian proprietor of CNDive, is the area's first dive operator (since 1987) and a former Komodo National Park ranger. Local staff are thoroughly trained and have intimate knowledge of more than 100 dive sites – some were 'discovered' and named by this outfit. Three-day liveaboard excursions are US$546 per person.

Divine Diving DIVING
(☎0813 5305 2200; www.divinediving.com; Jl Soekarno Hatta; day trips from 1,350,000Rp; ⊙6.30am-8pm) A proud supporter of numerous environmental and wildlife non-profit organisations, Divine Diving offers two- and three-dive day trips, PADI courses and liveaboard adventures capped at eight people.

Flores Diving Centre DIVING
(☎0822 4791 8573, 0812 3880 1183; www.floresdivingcentre.com; Jl Soekarno Hatta; day trip/eco-dive from 1,050,000/750,000Rp; ⊙8.30am-7.30pm) Offers all of the usual daily dive trips, courses and liveaboard safaris (on an impressive steel boat), but with the addition of an eco-dive – a not-for-profit initiative where people participate in a clean-up dive before two fun dives outside the national park.

Manta Rhei DIVING
(☎0812 9025 0791, 0821 4440 1355; www.mantarhei.com; Jl Soekarno Hatta 16; day trips from 1,650,000Rp; ⊙9am-7.30pm Mon-Sat, 2-7.30pm Sun) The only dive centre promising Belgian waffles after a day in the water, Manta Rhei specialises in themed day trips (Crazy Shark Day, Manic Manta Day, etc.) and PADI courses. Nitrox dives and *pinisi* (Sulawesi schooner) liveaboard (from 1,500,000Rp per person, per night), complete with hot tub, also available.

Uber Scuba DIVING
(☎0813 3961 9724; www.uberscubakomodo.com; Jl Soekarno Hatta; 3-dive fun dive 1,650,000Rp; ⊙8.30am-8pm) This dive shop is one of the best riding the wave of ever-increasing visitor numbers. Besides an extensive range of fun dives and courses, it offers all-inclusive liveaboard diving packages (three nights, 10 dives for US$815). The company owns the liveaboard, day-trip boats and a speedboat that accompanies the day-trip boats as an extra safety measure.

Blue Marlin DIVING
(☎0385-41789; www.bluemarlindivekomodo.com; Jl Soekarno Hatta; day trips from 1,400,000Rp; ⊙8am-8pm) Most dive schools in Bajo teach the basics in the ocean, but Blue Marlin makes a splash with the town's only purpose-built dive pool. Day-trip from a 15m-long custom fibreglass boat, or take *Toby* the speedboat

BOAT TOURS BETWEEN LOMBOK & FLORES

Travelling by sea between Lombok and Labuan Bajo is a popular way to get to Flores and you'll glimpse more of the region's spectacular coastline and dodge the slog by bus across Sumbawa. Typical three- and four-day itineraries take in snorkelling at Pulau Satonda or Pulau Moyo off the coast of Sumbawa, and throw in a dragon-spotting hike on Komodo or Rinca.

These are no luxury cruises – a lot depends on the boat, the crew and your fellow travellers. Some operators have reneged on 'all-inclusive' deals en route, and others operate decrepit old tugs without life jackets or radio. Plus this crossing can be hazardous when seas are rough.

Most travellers enjoy the journey though, whether it involves bedding down on a mattress on deck (recommended) or in a tiny cabin. The cost for a three- to four-day itinerary ranges from about US$170 to US$400 per person and includes all meals, basic beverages and use of snorkelling gear.

Other considerations:

➡ Carefully vet your boat for safety.

➡ Understand what's included and not included in the price. For instance, if drinking water is included, how much is provided? If you need more, can you buy it on the boat or do you need to bring your own?

➡ Taking snacks is a good idea as food might only be available during meal times.

➡ If you are flexible, you can often save money by travelling west from Flores, as travelling eastwards is more popular. Look for deals at agents once you're in Labuan Bajo.

Providers include:

➡ Kencana Adventure (p356) Offers basic boat trips between Lombok and Labuan Bajo with deck accommodation as well as cabins that sleep two.

➡ Perama Tour & Travel (p356) Runs basic boat trips between Lombok and Labuan Bajo with deck accommodation as well as small two-person cabins.

and arrive at dive sites before the crowds. There's a restaurant and bar onsite (mains 36,000Rp to 60,000Rp) and accommodation (dorms from 150,000Rp, doubles from 950,000Rp).

Wicked Diving DIVING
(☎0812 3964 1143; www.wickeddiving.com; Jl Soekarno Hatta; 3-/6-night trips from US$685/1125; ⏰9am-7pm) Wicked offers popular multiday liveaboard excursions, scouring the best dive sites on a *pinisi*. It also acts as an agent, organising day trips through local operators. The company wins plaudits for nurturing local guides and divers, promoting strong green practices and giving back to the community.

Komodo Dive Center DIVING
(☎0812 3630 3644, 0811 3897 007; www.komododivecenter.com; Jl Soekarno Hatta; day trips from 1,350,000Rp, 4-day liveaboard from €750; ⏰7am-7pm) Offers a full range of day trips, multiday tours and PADI courses. Promotes use of nitrox and extensive range of gear rentals. Do your due diligence from the beanbags on the wooden porch.

Current Junkies DIVING
(www.currentjunkies.com; 5-day, 5-night liveaboards from US$995) Liveaboard trips reserved for thrill seekers. Current Junkies doesn't shy away from Labuan Bajo's infamous currents; it dives into them for a chance to see pelagics. Five-day, five-night trips include 14 dives with a maximum of four experienced divers (five if you charter). Online bookings only; departs from Labuan Bajo.

Massage & Spa

★ Yayasan Ayo Mandiri SPA
(☎0385-41318; www.yam-flores.com; Jl Puncak Waringin; 60/90min massages 150,000/180,000Rp; ⏰9am-12.30pm & 3-8pm Mon-Sat) A not-for-profit foundation that trains locals with disabilities, ranging from vision to physical impairment, in massage therapy,

CLIMBING, CANYONING & CAVING

Shake off your sea legs by heading east of Labuan Bajo and exploring on land. Local tour operators on Jl Soekarno Hatta organise both best-of and custom itineraries.

Climbing up the rainforested slopes of **Gunung Mbeliling** (1239m) is popular. Leaving from Roe Village, 27km east of Bajo, the trip usually takes two days and includes six to eight hours of hiking through a fraction of the 150 sq km. Bonuses are a sunrise at the summit and a stop-off at **Air Terjun Cunca Rami**, a cooling cascade with freshwater swimming holes. A guide is recommended.

If you like canyoning, you'll enjoy the **Cunca Wulang Cascades**, 30km southeast of Bajo. Local guides lead you from Wersawe Village through rice fields, candlenut and coffee plantations to a winding canyon studded with rock water slides, swimming holes and waterfalls. Trips generally last half a day.

There are two caves worth exploring in Labuan Bajo. You only need an hour to visit **Gua Batu Cermin** (20,000Rp entry per person, guides optional but unnecessary for 50,000Rp), the 'Stone Mirror Cave' about 7km out of the town centre. Highlights include donning a hard hat and squeezing through tight spaces to see a whole fossilised turtle and coral gardens. Bring a torch. **Gua Rangko** (entry 20,000Rp) is more popular, an oceanic cave famed for its sunlit turquoise water (visit in the afternoon for the best light), stalagmites and stalactites. Drive from Labuan Bajo to Rangko Village, then don't pay more than 250,000Rp for the boat to get there.

providing employment to an otherwise marginalised community. The quality of treatments rivals the other spas in town. Visit for acupressure, hot stone and reflexology massages; manicures and pedicures; facials and more. Look for the big red 'massage' sign.

Flores Spa SPA
(☎0385-42089, WhatsApp 0813 5326 6199; www.floresspa.com; Jl Soekarno Hatta; 60/90 min massages from 144,000/188,000Rp; ⊙10am-8pm Mon-Sat, 1-8pm Sun) A bamboo-shopfront spa with treatments ranging from massages and facials to scrubs and ear candling. There are even massages tailored to sunburn and post-diving.

Tours

Alongside dedicated tour companies in Labuan Bajo, there are drivers that plan and lead trips. Budget between 800,000Rp to 1,200,000Rp per day – the price rises with guide qualifications and English-speaking capability. Perama Tour (p356) has a three-day/two-night 'Hunting Komodo by Camera' tour that takes you from Sengiggi (Lombok) to Labuan Bajo by bus and boat, with all meals provided and stops at islands, villages and scuba spots.

Andy Rona TOURS
(☎0813 3798 0855; andyrona7@gmail.com) An excellent guide and driver with a network of reliable colleagues and a penchant for reggae. He will point you in the right direction if he's booked up. Contact him by WhatsApp or email.

Wicked Adventures ADVENTURE
(☎0812 3607 9641; www.wickedadventures.com; Jl Soekarno Hatta; 1-day kayak trips from US$100; ⊙9am-7pm) An offshoot of the recommended Wicked Diving (p351) and located beneath it, this group runs kayak trips with local guides in Komodo National Park. Other adventures include Wae Rebo hikes and trips to Wicked's turtle conservation camp on a south Flores beach. Ask about their Wicked Good community and environment initiatives.

Sleeping

It seems every week there's a new place to stay in Labuan Bajo. Even so, during July and August travellers can outnumber beds, so book well ahead. Accommodation is concentrated around the centre of town. Don't settle for neglected hostels when spiffy new ones are the same price. Lush hotels are mostly outside the main drag, but if budget allows, nearby island resorts make for private paradises.

★**Ciao Hostel** HOSTEL $
(☎0852 2038 3641; www.ciaohostel.net; Jl Golo Silatey, off Jl Ande Bole; dm 160,000-230,000Rp; ❄📶) Labuan Bajo's best hostel has spacious ocean-view dorms with four to 12 beds – the latter in the popular, open-air room with

panoramic vistas and mosquito nets. There's plenty to love: the free shuttle to town and the airport, the rooftop bar, Pida Loca Reso (mains 47,000Rp to 85,000Rp), voting for nightly movies and Flores' friendliest staff. If only breakfast was included.

One Tree Hill HOSTEL $
(☎0812 4644 6414; onetreehill360@gmail.com; Jl Verhoeven, Pantai Klumpang, Desa Batu Cermin; dm with fan/air-con from 125,000/155,000Rp;) This 56-bed hostel from Tree Top (p355) should really provide transfers into town, but it's a must-visit for anyone with wheels. With both sunset and sunrise views, colourful wooden rooms summit at the open-air, beanbag-filled **Tre360 Bar** (4pm to 8pm weekdays, to 10pm weekends). Breakfast isn't included but there's a common kitchen. Limited wi-fi at the bar.

The Palm HOSTEL $
(☎0812 9655 2231; www.facebook.com/thepalmkomodo; Jl Puncak Waringin; dm 200,000Rp;) Peppered with quote decals ('Always remember, karma comes back') and adored for its pool and friendly staff, this five-room, 29-bed dorm nails the balance between backpacker fun and relaxation. There's a female-only room, individual power sockets and reading lights, air-con, pool parties and a restaurant (mains 50,000Rp to 150,000Rp, open 9.30am until 10pm). Speedboat day trips are competitively priced.

Green Hill Bed Station HOSTEL $
(☎0813 7429 3693; https://green-hill-bed-station.business.site; Jl Soekarno Hatta; dm 175,000Rp;) This central, 30-bed hostel from Green Hill Boutique Hotel (p354) is perfect for travellers who want a hostel set-up without the rowdy crowd. Immaculate and comfortable with privacy curtains and individual power outlets, reading lights and large lockers, the shared hot-water bathrooms wouldn't be out of place in a design magazine. Free airport transfers.

Le Pirate Boatel HOUSEBOAT $$
(☎0822 3724 4539; www.lepirate.com/boatel; Waecicu Bay; r 700,000Rp;) Halfway between staying in town and on a liveaboard, the charming, 10-room Boatel from Le Pirate (p355) is permanently docked a 10-minute, free boat shuttle from Bajo. Each room has a deck with a hammock and sun-bathing net over the water. Bathrooms are shared, breakfast is included and there's a restaurant on board. Take advantage of happy hour and free snorkelling.

Dragon Dive Komodo HOSTEL $$
(☎0385-2440421, 0822 4767 4874; www.dragondivekomodo.com; Jl Mutiara, Kampung Unjung; dm/d from 180,000/750,000Rp;) The drawcard at this hostel is the pool, flanked by a colourful ocean mural and shaded by a giant mango tree. Private rooms and dorms (mixed and female) are modern and air-conditioned, but the former are overpriced. The bar encourages a party atmosphere, while the pizza menu (50,000Rp to 90,000Rp) reenergises guests after daily dives (from 1,400,000Rp). Dive courses and liveaboard also available here.

Escape Bajo GUESTHOUSE $$
(☎0822 3532 6699, 0385-2440011; www.facebook.com/escapebajo.brewbitebed; Jl Binongko; dm/d 175,000/585,000Rp;) This swish, minimalist spot delivers on its tagline: brew (the trendy coffee shop opens 6am to 10pm), bite (there's a small menu of Indonesian and Western fare, 40,000Rp to 68,000Rp) and bed (six lush dorm beds boast individual power outlets, and two of the six ocean-view rooms are leased long term).

Join rooftop sunset yoga every Monday for 100,000Rp.

La Boheme Bajo HOSTEL $$
(☎0385-244 0442, WhatsApp 0813 3828 9524; www.backpacking-indonesia.com; Gang Perikanan Lama; dm/d 250,000/400,000Rp;) Laid-back beach vibes abound at this 90-something bed hostel, where free banana pancakes are available 24 hours. There's a restaurant (11am to 11pm, mains 35,000Rp to 70,000Rp), beanbags for chilling out, a cinema room, pool table, guest kitchen and strong wi-fi. A boat makes two daily trips to Pulau Micolo for 30,000Rp.

It's located about 1km from the centre of town, down a poorly marked side street on the right heading south, just after a small bridge and before the road forks to the MadeInItaly (p355) restaurant.

Palulu Garden Homestay HOMESTAY $$
(☎0822 3658 4279; www.palulugarden.wordpress.com; Jl Ande Bole; dm 85,000Rp, r with fan/air-con 250,000/350,000Rp;) Long-time local guide Kornelis Gega runs this four-room family homestay above the town centre. The basic, ramshackle dorm has six beds (two people can share the largest for 120,000Rp total) and there are three clean private rooms. Kornelis can help with trip planning, transport arrangements and motorbike hire (75,000Rp per day). Say hi to Charlie Chaplin, the cat.

Green Hill Boutique Hotel BOUTIQUE HOTEL **$$**
(☎0385-41289, 0813 3826 2247; www.greenhillboutiquehotel.com; Jl Soekarno Hatta; tw/d 525,000Rp; ❄📶) The view of town and sunset over the bay lifts these understated, spotless rooms. Set back from the main-street hubbub in the centre of town, entry to the 13 rooms with air-con and hot water is past Cafe in Hit (p356) and **Artomoro** restaurant, where breakfast is served (7am to 11pm, mains 40,000Rp to 150,000Rp).

There's a money changer on-site and free airport shuttles four times per day.

★ Scuba Junkie Komodo Beach Resort DIVE RESORT **$$$**
(☎0822 3724 8059, 0812 3651 7573; www.scubajunkiekomodo.com; Warloka Flores; 3-night all-inclusive packages bale/d from 4,740,000/6,250,000Rp) 🍃 A world-away from the bustle, this fantastic dive resort is on an isolated bay about an hour south of Bajo by boat. Rinca Island is nearby as are oodles of dive sites, which you'll get to explore with dives included in the accommodation packages. Stay in breezy beach bales or sea-view rooms and relax on the picturesque jetty.

★ Villa Domanik BUNGALOW **$$$**
(☎0852 3814 7795; www.villadomanik.com; Jl Belakang Pertamina, Pasar Baru, Desa Gorontalo; bungalows/2-bedroom villas from 1,100,000/2,300,000Rp; P❄📶🏊) Villa Domanik is bliss. On a hilltop outside Bajo, it has manicured gardens and a view of the Flores Sea from the pool. The three bungalows have outdoor bathrooms and wooden finishes, while a second, self-contained, two-bedroom villa is on the way. Food is a highlight, as is the sunset. In high season there's a two-night minimum stay.

Bayview Gardens Hotel INN **$$$**
(☎0385-41549; www.bayview-gardens.com; Jl Ande Bole; r from 850,000Rp; ❄📶🏊) Each of these 16 rooms tucked into the hillside – but still close to town – has a harbour view, best enjoyed during a balcony breakfast. Harbor Master Suites have day beds and outdoor showers; wooden Seaview Suits were crafted by a boat builder. Wi-fi only in the restaurant and by the picture-postcard perfect pool. Prices jump in high season.

Island Resorts

★ Angel Island Resort DIVE RESORT **$$$**
(☎0385-41443, WhatsApp 0812 3660 8475; www.angelisleflores.com; Pulau Bidadari; standard/deluxe cottages 4,784,000/5,152,000Rp; ❄📶) 🍃 Set on its own 15-hectare island linked to Labuan Bajo by private boat, this resort offers delightful garden-ensconced cottages behind one of three white-sand beaches. All meals are included and the food and service are casual and superb. Don't miss snorkelling in the protected reef, birdwatching and free kayaking. Minimum three-night stay.

Sudamala Resort Seraya RESORT **$$$**
(☎0361 288555, 0821 4647 1362; www.sudamalaresorts.com/seraya; Pulau Seraya; d per person from USD$325-450; ❄📶🏊) Get-away-from-it-all bliss exists on Pulau Seraya. Stay in flawless, whitewashed wood-and-thatch-bungalows set on a white-sand beach with offshore snorkelling. There's a spa, restaurant and rugged hilltop where you can wonder at spectacular sunsets for days on end. It's only 20 minutes by boat from Bajo. Minimum three-night stay.

🍴 Eating

Bajo's popularity has seen an influx of Western restaurants, from enviable Italian to Instagram-worthy seaside smoothie bowls. Hit the Pasar Malam for seafood, and Padang restaurants at the southern end of Jl Soekarno Hatta to eat beside locals. Further south the street forks left into the Trans-Flores Hwy, where street vendors sell *pisang goreng* (fried banana) and pancake-like *terang bulan*.

★ Pasar Malam INDONESIAN **$**
(Night Market; behind Jl Soekarno Hatta; mains 25,000-80,000Rp; ⏲6pm-midnight) Bajo town's most atmospheric dinner spot. Stalls with hand-painted names are fronted by tables of fresh seafood, with others specialising in more affordable nasi goreng, *mei goreng* and *bakso* (meatball noodle soup). Shop around before committing to a fish and BYO Bintang. At the time of research the market was due to move from its temporary, dusty soccer-field location back to the waterfront.

Rumah Makan Garuda INDONESIAN **$**
(Garuda; ☎0853 3864 2021; Jl Soekarno Hatta; mains 30,000-55,000Rp; ⏲7am-10pm) There are plenty of Padang restaurants at the southern end of Jl Soekarno Hatta, but Garuda is our pick. Point-and-order from the stacked window display: beef *rendang*, jackfruit curry, fried chicken or fish, tempe, egg and – if you're game – offal. Load up with garlicky sambal from tabletop jars.

Blue Corner INDONESIAN **$**
(☎0813 3762 0744; Jl Soekarno Hatta; mains 25,000-55,000Rp; ⏲10am-9pm) If you have

a predilection for local food, seek out this family-run warung with pink and blue walls. There's no English menu, but pictures on posters help. Juices are half the price of the Pasar Malam (p354) and *sop buntut* (oxtail soup) is the speciality – try the fried version.

Daily Market MARKET $

(Pasar Wae Kesambi; Jl Batu Cermin; 5am-4pm) Labuan Bajo's daily produce market is on the way to Batu Cermin. Things warm up after 7am, when you can browse the local bounty of fruits, vegetables and fish, and join the biggest queue to eat breakfast like a local. Shopkeepers are happy to have their picture taken and might demand it if they see you snapping someone else nearby.

★ **Happy Banana** JAPANESE $$

(0385-41467; happybananalb@gmail.com; Jl Soekarno Hatta; breakfast 46,000-120,000Rp, mains 84,000-105,000Rp; 7am-11pm) This inviting, wholesome spot has something for everyone, including vegans. Staff are trained in the art of sushi, with everything from udon noodles to gyoza made from scratch. The 'no rules' policy means you can start the day with a chia bowl and poached eggs or finish with fluffy gnocchi and tempura. Save room for vegan chocolate mousse.

★ **MadeInItaly** ITALIAN $$

(0385-244 0222; www.miirestaurants.com; Jl Pantai Pede; mains 84,000-169,000Rp; 11am-11pm) Bajo's best Italian is known for thin-crust pizza and fresh pasta. Sit in a stylish, semi-open dining room or air-conditioned cellar with river-stone walls. Ingredients are imported from Italy and grown on restaurant-owned organic farms, plus there's a bottle shop on-site and produce store on the way. For a luxury experience, enquire about the Culinary Journey island boat trip.

Bajo Taco TEX-MEX $$

(0821 4782 4697; Jl Soekarno Hatta; mains 45,000-100,000Rp; 9am-11pm Tue-Sun) Sharing a sea-view rooftop terrace with **Bajo Bakery** (0812 3878 8558; Jl Soekarno Hatta; breakfast 38,000-59,000Rp; 7am-7pm Mon-Sat, to 3pm Sun) is the town's only Tex-Mex restaurant. Tortillas are homemade and the fish tacos are some of the freshest you'll taste. Vegetarians, don't miss the barbecue jackfruit tacos.

La Cucina ITALIAN $$

(0812 3851 2172; lacucinakomodo@gmail.com; Jl Soekarno Hatta 46; mains 52,000-90,000Rp; 6.30am-10.30pm) This small, beachy dining room with its blue colour palette, fishing-net decorations and rustic wooden tables is a crowd favourite. Homemade pasta and pizza are the menu picks, but expect to join the end of a queue in peak season. Skip the line and take advantage of free delivery.

Bamboo Cafe CAFE $$

(0812 3697 4461; Jl Soekarno Hatta; breakfast 25,000-65,000Rp, mains 45,000-75,000Rp; 6am-9pm) Sit in white cane chairs and admire the hand-painted wall map while enjoying all-day breakfast made with vibrant ingredients from local farms. Booster juices and cold-brew coffee accompany smoothie bowls, eggs, toasties and wholefoods.

Tree Top INTERNATIONAL $$

(0385-41561, 0812 3803 9888; Jl Soekarno Hatta 22; mains 35,000-200,000Rp; 7am-11pm) This open-air, double-decker restaurant is a fantastic place to watch the sunset, especially if you nab the table that juts out to the harbour. While both Indonesian and Western food is better elsewhere, it's worth lingering for the view. There's a billiard table on the ground floor, shared with **Eco Tree O'tel** (double rooms from 680,000Rp).

Drinking & Nightlife

De'Flo Cafe & Ole-Ole COFFEE

(0822 8888 9118; https://deflocafeoleole.business.site; Jl Soekarno Hatta 22; snacks 20,000-45,000Rp; 7am-10pm) Owned and operated by enthusiastic university graduates from Jakarta, this tranquil coffee shop a level down from Tree Top is the best place in Bajo for a caffeine fix. De'Flo serves local Manggarai and limited-edition, single-origin coffee any way you like it, along with traditional cakes, snacks and ethical handicrafts, packaged for all your souvenir needs.

Le Pirate BAR

(0361-733493, 0385-41962, 0822 3724 4539; www.lepirate.com/labuan-bajo; Jl Soekarno Hatta; 7am-11pm) This colourful 1st-floor bar is a popular space for a drink after a day on the water. There's live music (8pm to 10pm Tuesday, Thursday and Saturday) and film nights (Monday and Wednesday). There's also a decent restaurant (mains 60,000Rp to 110,000Rp), rooftop bar and stylish but poky accommodation (private bunk from 500,000Rp, double from 650,000Rp).

Paradise Bar BAR
(☎0812 1341 5306; Jl Binongko; ⊙5pm-midnight Mon-Fri & Sun, to 2am Sat; ☜) 'Come to Paradise' is a common phrase in Bajo, referring to the bar-slash-nightclub famed for sea and sunset views. It's a preposterously lovely place for an *arak* cocktail, but come nightfall live music provides a party vibe. Saturdays demand a 65,000Rp cover charge, including a drink. Paradise is a 10-minute stroll uphill from central Labuan Bajo. *Ojeks* hang around to take you home after dark, though they charge a premium.

Catur'z Kopi Club COFFEE
(☎0812 4620 9890; caturzkopik@gmail.com; Jl Mutiara; veg food 35,000-55,000Rp; ⊙7.30am-10pm) Unwind at this rustic, double-storey coffee house in Bajo's backstreets. Try Indonesian spiced coffee while challenging staff to a game of chess. This is the town's only dedicated vegetarian and vegan cafe. For breakfast you can scramble eggs or tofu, and peruse the veggie bar later on.

Cafe in Hit CAFE
(☎0812 3642 4411; Jl Soekarno Hatta; coffee/light meals from 30,000/25,000Rp; ⊙7am-10pm; ☜) Labuan Bajo's answer to Starbucks, this casual coffee house serves ice-cold frappes alongside strong wi-fi. People-watch from above the street or browse shelves of local beans and second-hand books. Order from the giant blackboard.

Shopping

Magnolia Boutique Komodo FASHION & ACCESSORIES
(☎0812 3912 7007; hesty.hapsari@gmail.com; Jl Soekarno Hatta; ⊙8am-9pm) At Labuan Bajo's best fashion store, all pieces are locally made, with some also designed in Flores. There's plenty for the ladies, from linen clothing to contemporary caps made with naturally dyed ikat (patterned cloth), as well as shirts and tees for the blokes and adorable children's clothing. There are plans to move to the marina complex.

Carpe Diem Books & Bijoux BOOKS
(☎0812 3797 2275; Jl Soekarno Hatta; second-hand books 30,000-60,000Rp; ⊙10.30am-1.30pm & 4-9pm Thu-Tue) Blink and you'll miss this sweet, second-hand bookshop, which shares a space with a day-trip boat operator. Dive into a blind date with a mystery book wrapped in brown paper or trade pre-loved books for a discount or cash. Jewellery and postcards also available.

Information

PHKA Information Booth (☎0385-41005; Jl Soekarno Hatta; ⊙7-11am & 2-4pm Mon-Fri, 7-10am Sat & Sun) PHKA administers the Komodo National Park and provides information and permits for Komodo and Rinca islands.

Tourist Office (☎0361-271145, WhatsApp 0812 3746 9880; www.florestourism.com; Jl Mutiara; ⊙8.30am-4pm Mon-Sat) Friendly and helpful, this official office is set just back from Bajo's main drag.

Getting There & Away

AIR

Labuan Bajo's **Komodo Airport** (Bandar Udara Komodo) has a sizeable terminal and lengthened runway, a hint at expected tourism growth.

Garuda, Nam Air, TransNusa, Wings Air and Batik Air serve destinations including Denpasar, Jakarta and Kupang, and have counters in the terminal. There are several daily flights to/from Bali, although these are booked solid at busy times. Don't expect to just turn up and go.

BOAT

The ASDP ferry from Labuan Bajo to Sape runs every morning at 9.30am. It costs 60,000Rp and takes six hours. Confirm all times carefully. Buy your tickets the day of departure at the **ferry port office** (Jl Soekarno Hatta; ⊙8am-noon).

Agents for the boats running between Labuan Bajo and Lombok (p351) line Jl Soekarno Hatta.

Kencana Adventure (☎0812 2206 6065; www.kencanaadventure.com; Jl Soekarno Hatta, inside Beta Bajo Hotel; one-way deck/shared cabin per person 1,650,000/2,000,000Rp) and **Perama Tour & Travel** (☎0385-42016, 0385-42015; www.peramatour.com; Jl Soekarno Hatta; one-way/return from 1,500,000/3,300,000Rp; ⊙7.30am-10pm) offer multiday boat trips between Lombok and Labuan Bajo.

Easily missed on a side street leading uphill from Jl Mutiara, **Varanus Travel** (Pelni Agent; ☎0385-41106; ⊙9am-7pm Mon-Sat, 11am-6pm Sun) is the official Pelni agent and the place to get tickets for long-distance boat travel. Schedules posted in the windows outline services, including Makassar and the east coast of Sulawesi as well as Bima, Lembar and Benoa (Bali).

To get to Komodo, schedule in a day trip from Labuan Bajo. Join one of the many tours hawked by operators in town, which cost from 500,000Rp per person. Most leave around 5.30am and return around 6pm. Alternatively, charter a local boat or speedboat for a day or overnight.

BUS

The Labuan Bajo bus terminal is about 7km out of town, so most people book their tickets through a hotel or agency. If you get an advance ticket, the bus will pick you up from your accommodation. All eastbound buses run via Ruteng.

Ticket sellers for long-distance travel to Lombok and Bali work the ferry port office. The fares include all ferries, which can be unreliable due to weather conditions, and air-conditioned buses in between. The other option is to buy individual tickets for each leg of the journey yourself.

DESTINATION	TYPE	FARE (RP)	DURATION (HR)	FREQUENCY
Denpasar (Bali)	bus & ferry	580,000	36	1 daily
Bajawa	bus	210,000	10	2 daily
Mataram (Lombok)	bus & ferry	370,000	24	1 daily
Ruteng	bus	100,000	4	every 2hr, 6am-6pm

Getting Around

The airport is 1.5km from town. Some hotels offer free rides in and out. A private taxi to town and anywhere within town costs 50,000Rp.

Most places are walkable in Labuan Bajo. An *ojek* ride costs 5000Rp to 10,000Rp. Bemos do continual loops around the centre, following the one-way traffic, and cost 5000Rp per ride. The price may double if you have a sizeable bag.

Ruteng

0385 / POP 38,888

Surrounded by lush peaks and terraced rice fields, the staid and sprawling market city of Ruteng is the natural base for exploring Manggarai Regency. This predominantly Catholic town is a four-hour drive from Labuan Bajo. Should you take in a few sights, you'll be overnighting here. Fun fact: smaller streets here are named after animals, such as Jl Gajah (elephant), Jl Kelinci (rabbit) and Jl Kuda Belang (zebra).

Sleeping

Ruteng has a number of quiet, orderly homestays and some stale but reliable hotels. Remember it's somewhat elevated compared to Bajo and can get chilly at night.

Spring Hill Bungalows BUNGALOW $$

(0813 3937 2345, 0385-22514; springhillbungalowsruteng@gmail.com; Jl Kasturi 8; r from 750,000Rp;) Ruteng's nicest accommodation. Twelve deluxe bungalows set around a lily pond (with more on the way) have plush bedding and wooden feature walls inset with televisions. There's even a hairdryer in the bathroom, but the two-bedroom suite for four (1,750,000Rp) boasts a wooden deck with outdoor spa bath. The restaurant (mains 35,000Rp to 95,000Rp) has a snow ice machine.

D-Rima Homestay HOMESTAY $$

(0813 7951 188; deddydarung@gmail.com; Jl Kelinci; s/d 150,000/250,000-300,000Rp;) A cosy, three-room homestay run by a beautiful family brimming with information about the local area. The hot-water bathroom is shared between two rooms; the largest and most expensive has its own. Motorbike and car rental is available, as are home-cooked vegetarian dinners (45,000Rp per person).

Hobbit Hill Homestay GUESTHOUSE $$

(0812 4648 7553; www.ruteng.id; Jl Liang Bua Golobila; d/bungalow from 250,000/480,000Rp) Two kilometres from the centre of town towards Gua Liang Bua and surrounded by rice terraces is this welcoming, three-bedroom guesthouse. Two rooms have private toilets (only one is an ensuite), while the separate bungalow accommodates four people. The view from the property is especially impressive at sunrise. Generous breakfast included and home-cooked meals from 30,000Rp.

Eating & Drinking

Rumah Makan Cha Cha INDONESIAN $

(0385-21489, 0812 3698 9009; ywidianita@hotmail.com; Jl Diponegoro 12; mains 15,000-50,000Rp; noon-9pm;) Named after the owner's daughter, Ruteng's best restaurant is all wooden with framed Flores attractions on the walls and gingham table covers. The Indo standards are well prepared and it's a clean, relaxing place. *Nasi lontong opor* (chicken in coconut milk with rice) and *nasi soto ayam* (chicken soup with glass noodles, bean sprouts, egg, potato chips and rice) come recommended.

Street Vendors STREET FOOD $

(Jl Gajah; mains from 30,000Rp; 5-11pm) As the sun sets this small street fills with the scent of cooking over coals and half a dozen vendors sell *ayam goreng* (fried chicken), *ikan pepes* (fish grilled in banana leaf), *soto* (soup) and more. Pull up a plastic stool at our pick, Mas Ari; look for the colourful banners.

Kopi Mane Inspiration CAFE
(☎0821 4733 4545, 0813 8008 2778; Jl Yos Sudarso 12; mains 20,000-35,000Rp; ⏰8am-2am; 📶) A solid spot for a Manggarai coffee to power your day. Buy a bag of ground and roasted beans to take home or order cheap-eat Indonesian fare from a blackboard menu. Tourist information available, along with motorbikes rented at 100,000Rp per day.

ℹ Getting There & Away

Getting to the bus terminal for eastern destinations, found 3.5km out of Ruteng, costs 5000Rp to 10,000Rp by bemo or *ojek*. Local buses heading west run from an unofficial, central terminal near the **pasar** (Market; Jl Bhayangkara; ⏰7am-5pm). Regular buses head to Bajawa and Labuan Bajo (110,000Rp, five and four hours respectively).

Wae Rebo

Wae Rebo is the best of Manggarai's traditional villages. Road improvements have opened up the area, but it's still remote.

A village visit involves a splendid but challenging 9km hike that takes three to four hours and winds past waterfalls and swimming holes, as well as spectacular views of the Savu Sea. A donation of 200,000Rp per person is expected for a visit, or 320,000Rp if you stay overnight in a *mbaru tembong* (traditional home). The next morning retrace your steps or hike another six hours over a pass to another trailhead; arrange for pick up here in advance.

THE FLORES 'HOBBIT'

The Manggarai have long told folk tales of *ebo gogo* – hairy little people with flat foreheads who once roamed the jungle. Nobody paid them much attention until September 2003, when archaeologists made a stunning find. Excavating a limestone cave at Liang Bua, 14km north of Ruteng, they unearthed a skeleton the size of a three-year-old child but with the bone structure and worn-down teeth of an adult. Six more remains confirmed that the team had unearthed a new species of human, *Homo floresiensis*, which reached around 1m in height and was nicknamed the 'hobbit'.

Lab tests brought another surprise. The hominid with the nutcracker jaw and gangly, chimplike arms lived until 12,000 years ago, practically yesterday in evolutionary terms, when a cataclysmic volcanic eruption is thought to have wiped them out and devastated the island of Flores.

But not all scientists are convinced as to the origins of this Flores species. An Australian study in 2017 supposedly disproved the prevailing theory that the hobbits were descendants of *Homo erectus*, a species that fled Africa around two million years ago and spread throughout Asia. After analysing an array of Homo-related bones and dental samples from multiple countries, the research found the two had vastly different skeletal structures. *Homo floresiensis* could in fact be even more ancient than *Homo erectus*, most likely evolving from a common, African ancestor.

Rival anthropologists suggest that the Flores find could represent *Homo sapiens* (who were known to be travelling between Australia and New Guinea 35,000 years ago) that suffered from microcephaly – a neurological disorder causing stunted head growth, and often dwarfism, that runs in families. Others have suggested the hobbits are related to modern pygmy groups, but a 2018 study wholly refutes any link between the *Homo floresiensis* and *Homo sapiens*.

With every new piece of research comes another question about the origins of this species and its potential position on family trees. Unfortunately, tropical conditions are not conducive to recovering DNA from fossils and the jury is still out. The bones of at least eight more individuals have been found at the site with similar characteristics to those in the first discovery. With tools very similar to those found in Liang Bua reportedly unearthed in Timor, and possibly Sulawesi, more little people could yet emerge from the evolutionary backwoods, bringing with them more questions than answers.

The Liang Bua cave can be visited; local guides, whose service is included in the 30,000Rp entry fee, will meet you at the cave's entrance and explain why it is considered sacred. To get there take an *ojek* (100,000Rp) from Ruteng.

Arrange for guides (400,000Rp) and porters (250,000Rp) at the local guesthouses. Don't expect to be automatically treated to indigenous music, dance and weaving demonstrations – these cost extra and are usually organised for larger tour groups. Be sure to start very early, to avoid the sweltering heat of midday. Bring water.

Sleeping

Given that early morning is the optimal time to start the trek to Wae Rebo, you'll want to stay near the trailhead as opposed to in Ruteng.

Wae Rebo Lodge GUESTHOUSE $
(☎0852 3934 4046, 0812 3712 1903, WhatsApp 085 339 021 145; martin_anggo@yahoo.com; Dintor; r per person 250,000Rp) A purpose-built lodge run by Martin, a local from Wae Rebo. It sits serenely amid rice fields with views of both sunrise and sunset and is some 9km from the trailhead. Meals are included in the rate and you can make all trekking arrangements here. Ten per cent of Martin's profits go towards supporting the community.

Wae Rebo Homestay HOMESTAY $
(☎0813 3935 0775; Denge; r per person 200,000Rp) Right at the trailhead, this is the original place to sleep for people making the Wae Rebo trek. Friendly owner Blasius is a Wae Rebo expert and operates the small visitor centre as well as the 15-room homestay. Ask him about village visits and transport. If the phone signal is patchy, send him an SMS.

Getting There & Away

It's about a three-hour drive from Ruteng to the village trailhead in Denge. You'll need your own wheels for this.

Bajawa

☎0384 / POP 44,437

Framed by forested volcanoes and blessed with a cooler climate, Bajawa is a laidback and predominantly Catholic hill town. Perched at 1100m above sea level, it's the de facto trading post of the local Ngada people, a great base from which to explore dozens of traditional villages or to stay put and mingle with locals. Gunung Inerie (2245m), a perfectly conical volcano, looms to the south, where you'll also find active hot springs. **Wawo Muda** is another favourite thanks to its Kelimutu-esque lake, left behind after an eruption in 2001.

WORTH A TRIP

SPIDER WEB RICE FIELDS

These legendary rice fields, which are also known as the Lingko Fields, are vast creations shaped as implied, which is also the shape of Manggarai roofs that fairly divide property between families. For the best view, stop at the small pavilion, pay 25,000Rp and ascend a dirt path to the main viewing ridge. They're located 20km west of Ruteng, near the village of Cara, off the Trans-Flores Hwy.

Sights & Activities

★**Gunung Inerie** HIKING
A breathtakingly beautiful volcano looming above Bajawa, Gunung Inerie (2245m), just 10km from town, beckons all would-be climbers. The journey is difficult, but this spectacularly jagged cone is worth sweating for. You can do it as an eight-hour round trip, but it's also possible to camp by the lake. We recommend starting around 3am to catch the sunrise.

With an English-speaking guide and transport from Bajawa, expect to pay about 800,000Rp for one and 1,000,000Rp for two people. Bring water.

Air Panas Soa HOT SPRINGS
(per person 14,000Rp; ⏲7am-6pm) The most serviced hot springs in the region, situated east of town on the rough road to Riung. There are two man-made pools (one is a scintillating 45°C; the other a more pedestrian 35°C to 40°C) and one natural pool (25°C to 30°C). It has modern buildings and can get busy. Air Panas Malanage (p362) is a more natural option.

Sleeping

Thanks to a growth spurt in Bajawa tourism, locals are opening homestays all over town. Friendly and informative, they're the best accommodation option as hotels can be tired or soulless.

Madja Edelweis Homestay HOMESTAY $
(☎0812 3779 5490; austynobabtista@gmail.com; Jl Pipipodo; s/d from 150,000/200,000Rp; 📶) Not to be confused with the bland Edelweis Hotel on the main drag, this eight-room homestay has an assortment of comfortable and colourful rooms. The friendly owner is exceedingly helpful, loaning motorbikes for 100,000Rp a day and organising trips around Flores. The wi-fi is fast, a generous

THE NGADA

More than 60,000 Ngada people inhabit the upland Bajawa plateau and the slopes around Gunung Inerie. Most practise a fusion of animism and Christianity, worshipping Gae Dewa, a god who unites Dewa Zeta (the heavens) and Nitu Sale (the earth).

The most evident symbols of continuing Ngada tradition are pairs of *ngadhu* and *bhaga*. The *ngadhu* is a parasol-like structure about 3m high, consisting of a carved wooden pole and thatched 'roof', while the *bhaga* is a miniature thatched-roof house.

The *ngadhu* is 'male' and the *bhaga* is 'female'. Each pair is associated with a particular family group within a village. Some were built over 100 years ago to commemorate ancestors killed in long-past battles.

Agricultural fertility rites continue (sometimes involving gory buffalo sacrifices), as well as ceremonies marking birth, marriage, death and house building – always a communal event. The major annual festival is the six-day Reba ceremony held between late December to early January in the villages (in Bena, usually late December). Villagers wear specially made all-black ikat, sacrifice buffalo, and sing and dance through the night. Travellers are welcome to attend, but check in with the tourist office for more information on etiquette, as well as the locations and timings of each village celebration.

Although the Ngada are not matriarchal (the village elders are men), they are matrilineal, which means that property passes down through women.

breakfast is included and there's a guest kitchen. Pay extra for hot water.

Marselino's Homestay HOMESTAY **$**
(☎0852 3913 1331; www.floresholiday.wordpress.com; Jl Pipipodo; s/d/tr 150,000/170,000/210,000Rp; 📶) This is a simple affair with six rooms and a living and dining room as common space. Brave the cold, shared shower and enjoy nasi goreng and fruit for breakfast. The best thing about this place is the owner, an established tour guide worth calling on for all your Flores needs, from tours to tickets.

Hotel Happy Happy GUESTHOUSE **$$**
(☎0384-421763, 0853 3370 4455; www.hotelhappyhappy.com; Jl Sudirman; r from 350,000Rp; 📶) This purple guesthouse covered in smile emojis offers seven immaculate tiled rooms, furnished with decent linen and the odd dolphin painting. There's hot water, a sociable patio, free water-bottle refills and an excellent breakfast included. It's a short walk from the main cluster of tourist businesses.

★**Manulalu** BUNGALOW **$$$**
(☎0812 5182 0885; villamanulalu@gmail.com; Mangulewa; d/bungalows from 460,000/1,200,000Rp) Split into two nearby properties, Manulalu Hills and Manulalu Jungle are about 20km from Bajawa and 3km from Bena along a scenic, winding road. Hills has eight stylish rooms, but the seven Jungle bungalows, modelled on traditional houses, are something from a fairytale; think beautiful bathrooms and day beds on wooden decks perfect for admiring one of Flores' most spectacular outlooks.

Eating

Bajawa's best places to eat are clustered together around the tourist office, just south of the centre.

Rumah Makan Anugerah INDONESIAN **$**
(☎0812 1694 7158; Jl Sudirman; mains 25,000-50,000Rp; ⊙8am-10.30pm) This small and spotless family-run *rumah makan* (eating house) is a great choice for a cheap lunch. Some menu items veer into almost-Chinese territory, while others such as *nasi babi rica rica* (spicy pork with rice) keep it in the archipelago. Save room for sweets from the cabinet.

Lucas 2 INDONESIAN **$**
(☎0813 5390 7073; Jl Ahmad Yani; mains 20,000-35,000Rp; ⊙8am-10pm Fri & Sat, 3-10pm Sun) Not to be confused with other Lucas venues in the street, this one is on the 2nd storey of a wooden building. Yellow ceiling beams and painted tables up the decor ante in the dining room, which serves fine pork *sate* and other local faves.

Maiwali DESSERTS **$**
(☎0821 1942 1305; Jl Ahmah Yani; cakes 1000Rp; ⊙6am-7pm) On the main road beneath an unmarked white canvas gazebo, near the tourist office, is a smiling lady selling traditional sweets from a glass cabinet. Pick from

the likes of sesame balls, green pandan pancakes, fried 'flying saucers' sweetened with palm sugar and glutinous rice – everything is the same price.

Information

MONEY

BNI Bank (Jl Marta Dinata; 8am-4pm Mon-Fri, 7.30am-4pm Sat) In the centre; has an ATM and exchanges US dollars. There are several more ATMs around town.

TOURIST INFORMATION

Tourist Office (0852 3904 3771; www.welcome2flores.com; Jl Ahmad Yani 2; 8am-6pm) Small but highly useful; good for Ngada, transport and touring info.

Getting There & Away

There are buses and bemos to various destinations. Buses don't necessarily leave on time – only when the bus is almost full. Kijangs, or travel cars, also leave throughout the day from the **bemo terminal** (Jl Basoeki Rahmat). Rates are up to 30% more than bus fares. Bus services include the following:

Ende (80,000Rp, five hours, several times daily)

Labuan Bajo (210,000Rp, 10 hours, twice daily)

Ruteng (110,000Rp, five hours, regular services from 8am to 11am)

Getting Around

Bemos cruise town for 5000Rp a ride, but it is easy to walk almost everywhere except to the bus terminals.

Trucks serve remote routes; most leave traditional villages in the morning and return in the afternoon.

Motorcycles cost 100,000Rp a day. A private vehicle with a driver is 800,000Rp; expect to pay more the further out you explore. Most hotels can arrange rental.

Bajawa Turelelo Soa Airport is a small, domestic airport 25km from Bajawa and about 6km outside Soa. Wings Air and TransNusa both fly daily to Kupang in West Timor (one hour), while Wings also flies daily to Labuan Bajo (35 minutes).

Around Bajawa

Bajawa's big draw is the chance to explore villages in the gorgeous countryside. The fascinating architecture of the traditional houses features carved poles supporting conical thatched roofs. It's possible to visit the area alone, but you'll learn a lot more about the culture and customs with a guide. Some organise meals in their home villages, others suggest treks to seldom-visited villages accessible only by trail.

Locals and homestay owners can arrange car day trips from 600,000Rp per person, or you can jump on the back of a motorbike with a guide for between 400,000Rp to 500,000Rp. A classic one-day itinerary would start in Bajawa and include **Bena**, **Luba**, **Tololela** and **Air Panas Malange hot springs**. It's customary to make a donation to the head of traditional villages you visit. Make sure you do this directly, rather than through a guide, to ensure the money is received in full.

Bena

Resting on Inerie's flank, Bena is one of the most traditional Ngada villages. It's home to nine clans and its stone monuments are the region's best. Houses with high, thatched roofs line up in two rows on a ridge. They're interspersed with ancestral totems including megalithic tombs, *ngadhu* (thatched parasol-like structures) and *bhaga* (miniature thatched-roof houses). Most houses have male or female figurines on their roofs, while doorways are decorated with buffalo horns and jawbones – a sign of family prosperity.

Although the village is crowded when tour groups arrive during high season, and all villagers are now officially Catholic and

OFF THE BEATEN TRACK

PAULENI–BELARAGHI VILLAGE TREK

Most visitors to the Bajawa area rely on hired vehicles to whisk them between traditional villages. It's much more fulfilling to trek through the rainforest to villages such as **Belaraghi**, accessible only by trail. Your trek will begin in **Pauleni Village**, approximately 45km (90 minutes) from Bajawa by car. From there it's a steep 90-minute hike to a village of welcoming locals. There are more than a dozen traditional homes here. The hike can be done in a day trip, but you'll be tired by now, so you may as well stay the night. The *kepala kampung* (village head) offers a bed and meals for 250,000Rp per person. Ask a Bajawa area guide to help arrange the trip.

attend a local missionary school, traditional beliefs and customs endure. Sacrifices are held three times each year, and village elders still talk about a rigidly enforced caste system that prevented 'mixed' relationships, with those defying the *adat* facing serious consequences.

Bena is the most visited Ngada village, and weavings and souvenir stalls line the front of houses. It's so popular that an entrance fee has replaced donations – a set 25,000Rp per person – and there are official opening hours (6am to 6pm). Some travellers might prefer the atmosphere at lesser-visited villages nearby. You can spend the night at Bena for 150,000Rp per person, which includes meals of boiled cassava and banana. Bena is reached by a good 12km road from Langa, a traditional town 7km from Bajawa. An *ojek* ride here costs 100,000Rp return.

The natural hot springs of **Air Panas Malanage** (entry 10,000Rp) are 6km from Bena and unofficially staffed by friendly locals. At the base of one of the many volcanoes, two streams – one hot, one cold – mix together in a temperate pool. Soak amid the scents of coconut, hazelnut, vanilla and clove. Basic change facilities onsite; 10,000Rp entry per person.

Riung

☎0384 / POP 13,875

Riung is a charming and isolated little town, stilted with fishers' shacks and framed by coconut palms. Coming from Ende you'll drive along an arid coastline that skirts a spectacularly blasted volcano, before a burst of foliage swallows the road as it winds into town. The main reason to come here is to visit the offshore Seventeen Islands Marine Park.

Sights

Seventeen Islands Marine Park MARINE RESERVE

(Pulau Tujuh Belas) These uninhabited islands are as diverse as they are beautiful. The mangrove isle of Pulau Ontoloe hosts a massive colony of flying foxes and a few Komodo dragons, while Pulau Rutong and Pulau Temba boast picture-perfect white sand and turquoise waters. There's great snorkelling near Pulau Tiga, Pulau Laingjawa and Pulau Bakau, but wherever you visit, you won't be disappointed.

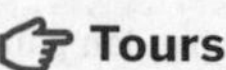

Tours

Tours to Seventeen Islands Marine Park can be organised at hotels and guesthouses, or at the waterfront. The standard is a day-long boat trip without a guide for four to six people, which should cost 500,000Rp to 600,000Rp. With a guide (a better option) you'll pay around 1,600,000Rp for up to four people and enjoy four snorkelling stops and a beach barbecue. Al Itchan of Del Mar Cafe is a recommended guide.

Before going to the islands you must sign in and pay 100,000Rp per person at a separate booth by the dock. Your captain or guide should pay the anchorage fees for your boat.

Sleeping & Eating

Guesthouses are few but comfortable. Book ahead from June to August during peak season.

Del Mar Cafe GUESTHOUSE $$

(☎0813 8759 0964, 0812 4659 8232; d/tr 400,000/500,000Rp; ❄) Off the main road heading to the pier, these 12 air-conditioned rooms with timber furniture and private bathrooms are owned by the area's top guide, Al Itchan. There's a small warung on-site, strung with shells and fairy lights, that rumbles with rock and roll, and grills fish over smouldering coconut husks (mains from 30,000Rp; open 7am to 11pm).

Nirvana Bungalows BUNGALOW $$

(☎0813 3710 6007; www.nirvanabungalows.doodlekit.com; d/tr/f 400,000/500,000/600,000Rp; ❄) Nine fun, detached hippy shacks with colourful walls, a smattering of inspirational sayings ('If life was easy where would all the adventures be?') and private patios where breakfast is served overlooking the tranquil garden. It's located near the port, and the engaging owner offers guided trips to the islands. Organise ahead for a grilled fish dinner.

Rumah Makan Murah Muriah INDONESIAN $

(☎0822 4714 6920; mains 25,000-45,000Rp; ⏲6am-9pm) The house speciality here is the *sop ikan asam pedas,* Nusa Tenggara Timor's endemic spicy-and-sour tamarind fish soup. This one, cooked by the ever-smiling Bernadetta, is as good as it gets. It also does grilled fish, fried squid and veggies, chicken *sate,* fried noodles and more. Located on the same gravel road as **Pondok SVD** (☎0813 3934 1572, 0813 3946 7082; pondoksvd@gmail.com; s/d from 225,000-275,000Rp; ❄).

Pato Resto INDONESIAN $
(☎0812 4698 7688; mains 25,000-55,000Rp; ⊙8am-11pm; ✎) One of Riung's best restaurants is also its most unassuming. This simple haunt with checkered tables and plastic chairs is the place to try local Indonesian food. Located on the main road, its succinct whiteboard menu (in English) changes with the seasons and daily catch. Seafood is a must, but there are plenty of veg dishes, too.

Information

INTERNET ACCESS

There's no useful internet and 3G data is patchy.

MONEY

There's a BRI ATM but no official currency exchange facilities in Riung. It's safest to bring ample rupiah.

Getting There & Away

Riung is 75km and about two hours over rough roads from the turn-off at Boawae on the Trans-Flores Hwy. There is a *much* worse 79km road to Riung from Bajawa that takes about four hours by a daily bus costing 35,000Rp. It's slightly quicker by car – a share taxi costs 60,000Rp per person while a private car is 700,000Rp total. Ende is also four hours by a daily bus at 70,000Rp per passenger.

If you can't bear the Trans-Flores Hwy for another second, consider chartering a boat from Riung all the way to Labuan Bajo from 3,000,000Rp, which takes seven to 10 hours. It's a bit pricey, but you'll enjoy a coastline most visitors never see, stopping in virgin coves and snorkelling along the way. Just bring headphones or earplugs. Those outboard motors are loud!

Ende

☎0381 / POP 103,987

The most apparent merit of this muggy port town is its spectacular surrounds. The eye-catching cones of **Gunung Meja** (661m) and **Gunung Iya** (627m) loom over the city and the black-sand and cobblestone coastline. Views get even better just northeast of Ende as the road to Kelimutu rises along a ridge, overlooking a roaring river and cliffs that tumble with waterfalls in the wet season from December to March. Throw in coffee and clove drying on tarps on the side of the road, jade rice terraces, and women picking macadamia nuts from bamboo ladders, and you have some of Flores' most jaw-dropping scenery.

You don't need long to cover Ende's compact and atmospheric centre. Most treat it as a pit stop on the way to elsewhere, but there's some intrigue to its grittiness. The central airport is a useful hub for connections to Labuan Bajo, Kupang (West Timor) and Tambolaka (Sumba).

Sights

There's less to see and more to 'soak up' in Ende. The black-sand beach is a morbid reminder of Indonesia's litter problem, but the views are dramatic and there's always something interesting happening at the waterfront.

Ikat Market MARKET
(cnr Jls Kathedral & Pasar; ⊙5am-5pm) The ikat market sells hand-woven tapestries from across Flores and Sumba. Bargaining is acceptable, but bear in mind you're expected to make good on any offer that's accepted. Shops can be closed during lunch.

Pasar MARKET
(Market; Jl Pasar; ⊙7am-6pm) Meander through the aromatic market that stretches from the waterfront into the streets. Expect plastic tubs of vegetables, fruit and an astonishing selection of fish.

Sleeping

Accommodation is plentiful and spread around town, but lacklustre. Many people blow through Ende on their way east to Moni, but an overnight stay will result in a good feed, a little atmosphere and a well-rested start onward to Moni in the morning.

The Roomz HOMESTAY $
(☎0812 4900 0901; Jl Woloare Km1; r 100,000-200,000Rp; ❄@) This five-bedroom budget homestay is run by a sweet, young family. The cheapest room shares a toilet, there's a 150,000Rp fan room with its own bathroom and the three spacious deluxe rooms have air-con, lounge space and televisions. There's no sign, so look for the concrete steps up to the ochre house.

F Hostel Ende HOSTEL $
(☎0812 8294 6977; Jl Gatot Subroto Km4; dm 145,000Rp; ❄📶) There are eight beds in this single-dorm hostel, each with its own privacy curtain, power socket, reading light and hooks. Staff are friendly and the place is clean, albeit further from the centre of town in the direction of Kelimutu (p365). Only toast is provided for breakfast.

★ Dasi Guest House GUESTHOUSE $$
(☎0852 1863 8432, 0381-262 7049; yosdam@yahoo.co.id; Jl Durian Atas 2; dm/s/d 100,000/200,000/250,000Rp; ❄📶) This friendly guesthouse fulfils its motto, 'feel like home', thanks to incredibly helpful staff. Although 15 basic rooms came before the 11 private dorm beds, each in its own cubicle, there's a definite hostel vibe here. The common room has views to the south. Free airport transfers and pick up from town if the weather's bad or you get lost.

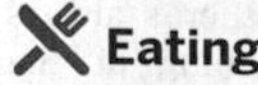

Eating

★ Sari Rasa INDONESIAN $
(☎0812 3925 3699; Jl Ahmad Yani; mains 25,000-45,000Rp; ⏲6.30-10pm) This sparkling-clean, bare-walled restaurant is filled with travellers out for a taste of local food, but who come back for Martin, the charismatic owner and self-appointed 'captain of the boat'. He'll explain the short, whiteboard-scrawled menu cooked by his wife as jazz plays in the background. The *ayam goreng* (fried chicken) uses free-range village chickens, marinated, tenderised then fried. *Empal* is the Javanese answer to brisket – a hunk of tender, spiced fried beef. Both come with a mound of addictive *serundeng* (spiced, grated coconut) on top.

Pasar Malam SEAFOOD $
(Night Market; Jl Bakti; mains from 15,000Rp; ⏲5pm-midnight) At sunset the smell of grilled fish wafts through the air at this beachside market. Browse the many stalls and feast on what looks best. Remember to shop around before settling; a bigger fish equals a bigger price.

Depot Se'i Babi Melati Indah INDONESIAN $
(☎0813 3903 2791; Jl Melati Atas; mains 25,000-45,000Rp; ⏲10am-10pm Mon-Sat) This thatched, open-air dining room specialises in *se'i babi*, succulent smoked pork hailing from Kupang. Meal deals are 35,000Rp and include pork, white rice, a porky kidney-bean soup and *rumpu rampe* (stir-fried vegetables).

ℹ Information

There are two tourist information centres in Ende, both with enthusiastic staff who dispense up-to-date information.

Ende Tourism Office (☎0381-21303; www.florestourism.com; Jl Soekarno; ⏲8am-3pm Mon-Fri)

Flores DMO Tourist Office (☎0381-23141; www.florestourism.com; Jl Bhakti; ⏲8am-5pm Mon-Fri)

ℹ Getting There & Away

Air and ferry schedules in East Nusa Tenggara are historically fluid and it's best to confirm all times and carriers prior to planning your trip.

AIR

Wings, Garuda, Nam Air, TransNusa and Susi Air serve **Ende Airport** (H Hasan Aroeboesman Airport; Jl Ahmad Yani), which is located almost in the centre of town.

DESTINATION	AIRLINE	FREQUENCY
Kupang	Nam Air, TransNusa, Wings Air, Garuda	daily
Labuan Bajo	Wings Air, Lion Air, Garuda	daily
Tambolaka	Wings Air	daily

BOAT

Pelni has boats every two weeks to Waingapu, Benoa and Surabaya, then east to Kupang and Sabu. Visit the helpful **Pelni office** (☎0381-21043; Jl Kathedral 2; ⏲8am-noon & 2-4pm Mon-Sat) for tickets, including to Waingapu (for 65,000Rp), which takes nine hours.

BUS & CAR

East-bound buses leave from the Roworeke terminal, 8km from town. Buses heading west leave from the Ndao terminal, 2km north of town on the beach road.

DESTINATION	TYPE	FARE (RP)	DURATION (HR)	FREQUENCY
Bajawa	bus	80,000	5	several daily
Labuan Bajo	bus	200,000	12-15	daily, 6am
Maumere	bus	80,000	5	regularly, 7am-4pm
Maumere	car	150,000	4½	regularly, 7am-4pm
Moni	bus	50,000	2	several daily
Moni	car	100,000	1½	hourly, 6am-4pm

ℹ Getting Around

Airport taxis to most hotels cost around 50,000Rp per car. Bemos and *ojeks* run frequently to just about everywhere for a flat rate of 5000Rp.

Kelimutu

Kelimutu (1639m), a sacred and extinct volcano, is the centrepiece of the mountainous, jungle-clad **national park** (admission per person Mon-Sat/Sun 150,000/225,000Rp, per ojek/car 5000/10,000Rp; ⏲ ticket office 5am-5pm) of the same name. There aren't many better reasons to wake up before dawn than to witness the sun cresting Kelimutu's western rim, filtering mist into the sky and revealing three deep, volcanic lakes – nicknamed the tri-coloured lakes because for years each one was a different striking shade. Less than 30 minutes by car from Moni, the park shelters endangered flora and fauna (including 19 rare avian species) and other peaks such as Mount Kelibara (1731m).

Alert local guides if you dream about the sacred lakes – apparently siren-like spirits have lured people to their demise, which can be avoided if the right prayers and offerings are made.

Kelimutu is sacred to the local Lio people, who believe the souls of the dead migrate here: young people's souls go to the warmth of Tiwu Koo Fai Nuwa Muri; old people's to the cold of Tiwu Ata Bupu; and those of the wicked to Tiwu Ata Polo. Pork, betel nuts, rice and other valuable offerings are left on ceremonial rocks beside the lakes, amid the dancing of the Lio's annual 'Feed the Spirit of the Forefathers' ceremony, on 14 August.

Ever since locals led early Dutch settlers here, sightseers have been making the sunrise trek. Most visitors glimpse the lakes at dawn, leaving nearby Moni at 4am for early morning views after the pre-dawn mist rises and before clouds drift in. Afternoons are usually empty and peaceful at the top of Mt Kelimutu, and when the sun is high, the colours sparkle.

There's a staircase up to the highest lookout, Inspiration Point, from where all three lakes are visible. It's not advisable to scramble around the craters' loose scree. The footing is so bad and the drop so steep that hikers have perished here in the past.

It's worth staying in Moni rather than attempting Kelimutu as a day trip, should bad weather obscure the view or close the road to the top. Remain flexible with onward travel plans, especially during wetter months.

Activities

For a beautiful walk through the lush local landscape, hire transport one-way to the lakes and then walk back to Moni. The stroll down the mountain, through the village, past rice fields and along cascading streams, takes about three hours and isn't too taxing. A *jalan potong* (shortcut) leaves the road back to Moni 3km south of the ticket office and goes through Manukako village, then meanders back to the main road 750m uphill from Moni.

A second path diverges from the trail and goes through Tomo, Mboti, Topo Mboti, Kolorongo and Koposili villages, skirts a waterfall and returns to Moni without rejoining the highway. It's possible (although not essential) to hire a guide in Moni (350,000Rp) to show you the way.

OFF THE BEATEN TRACK

SIKKA

The charming seaside village of Sikka was one of Flores' first Portuguese settlements. Its kings dominated the Maumere region until the 20th century. The big draw is the gorgeous, narrow Catholic cathedral that dates from 1899. The open windows in the arched, beamed eaves allow the sound of crashing waves to echo through the sanctuary.

You'll be swarmed by ikat-wallahs as soon as you enter town, but they're a charming bunch. For a 150,000Rp donation you can watch them work the looms. The village is 4km past Lela, some 6km off the Trans-Flores Hwy (the paved access road is about 20km south of Maumere).

Getting There & Away

The ticket office is 8.5km up the paved access road, which connects to the Trans-Flores Hwy 2km west of Moni. The parking area for the lake is another 4km. From the car park it's a nice 20-minute walk up through the pines to Inspiration Point. To get here from Moni, hire an *ojek* (60,000Rp/100,000Rp one way/return) or car (250,000Rp/350,000Rp one way/return), maximum five people.

Moni

0361 / POP 7604

People often skip Moni, making a beeline for Kelimutu and treating its volcanic lakes as a day trip. These people miss out. If you're not in a rush, a couple of nights in Moni – a lovely, picturesque hill town fringed by rice fields, lush volcanic peaks and hot springs – will bring you back down to earth. It's slow-paced and easy-going thanks to friendly locals and an unexpected Rasta community, who live to play music and invite travellers to join in at every turn. The Tuesday market, held on the soccer pitch, is a major local draw and good place to snare local ikat.

Activities

Apart from the trek to/from Kelimutu (p365), there are several other walks from Moni. About 750m along the Ende road from the centre of Moni, paths lead down to a 10m **air terjun** (waterfall), with a swimming hole and **air panas** (hot springs) near the falls. The trail branches to the left of **Rainbow Cafe** (0813 3947 7300; ana.rainbow@ovi.com; Jl Trans Flores; mains 30,000-80,000Rp; 9am-9pm). A must-visit is the breathtaking hot spring in the middle of the rice fields at **Kolorongo** (3.5km from Moni) on the way to Kelimutu. Or walk south past the church to **Potu** and **Woloara** (about 2.5km from Moni).

Sleeping

It seems every local in Moni is building a homestay along the Trans-Flores Hwy. Most are budget to midrange, but prices will jump in the near future – already there's a discrepancy between accommodation of the same standard. Do your research so you don't get ripped off. Booking ahead from June to August is recommended, but locals should know someone with a bed if you get stuck.

Legend Guest House GUESTHOUSE $
(0813 9831 3581; ino.alexander99@gmail.com; off Jl Trans Flores, behind market; r 200,000Rp) You'll feel like family at this budget, three-bedroom guesthouse. Rooms are simple, spotless and share a bathroom (with a pebbled shower). Ask owner Ino about booking day trips...and to hear him sing at Mopi's Place (p366). The guesthouse is next to the market, which makes for a great atmosphere but not the best sleep-in.

Bintang by Tobias GUESTHOUSE $$
(0812 3761 6940, WhatsApp 0823 4103 6979; www.bintang-lodge.com; Jl Trans Flores; s/d/f 385,000/440,000/800,000Rp) Bintang is one of the best guesthouses in town, and offers five large, centrally located and renovated rooms. It has hot water (a blessing in chilly Moni) and the cafe (mains 30,000Rp to 99,000Rp) has an open terrace with views over the green surrounds. Owner Tobias is a super-friendly fount of local information and can organise motorbike hire, tours and transport.

Mahoni Guest House GUESTHOUSE $$
(0813 7212 3313; Jl Trans Flores; r 350,000Rp) Look for a friendly group of Rastas sitting under a dried grass umbrella in front of a white house and you've found Mahoni. Owner Galank is incredibly welcoming to all who stay in the four sparkling rooms, all of which have hot showers. Banana pancakes and fresh fruit included for breakfast; a taste of local life all day.

Estevania Lodge GUESTHOUSE $$
(0812 3791 5480; Jl Trans Flores; r 400,000-500,000Rp) Five spacious and spotless rooms, with those on the second floor commanding a higher price thanks to the verdant view. With hot water and chatty Jenny calling the shots (ask her about home-cooked meals and local culture), you won't feel swindled by the slightly higher guesthouse price point.

★**Kelimutu Crater Lakes Ecolodge** LODGE $$$
(0852 3324 8518, 0361-747 4205; www.ecolodgesindonesia.com; Jl Ende-Maumere Km54; r/villas from 800,000/1,000,000Rp;) Easily the nicest spot in Moni. Nestled by the riverside east of town are 21 rooms and villas, all with pebbled tiles, hot water, some solar power and outdoor sitting areas. Cross the bridge over a babbling stream and check out the rice terraces. The restaurant (mains from 40,000Rp to 65,000Rp) serves local specialities.

Eating

Local specialities tend to be hearty, to ward off chilly nights. Try a 'Moni cake', a starchy mashed-potato pie similar to a croquette and topped with cheese.

★**Mopi's Place** CAFE $
(0813 3736 5682, 0812 3956 4019; Jl Trans Flores; breakfast 25,000-35,000Rp, mains 35,000-55,000Rp; 8am-10pm;) Moni has a surprisingly contagious vibe, and this is the heart of it. The open-sided Indo-Australian affair starts with local coffee, house soy milk and freshly baked bread; it progresses to exceptional Indonesian mains with plenty of veg options and – if the musically gifted locals are around – morphs into a dance floor as live reggae rings through the mountains.

Order by noon and you can be sitting down to an evening *nasi bamboo* buffet of *tapa kolo* – coconut rice cooked over coals in a bamboo tube, with chicken (and/or fish), veggies and accompaniments (150,000Rp per person, for a minimum of two).

Chenty Restaurant & Cafe INDONESIAN $
(☎0852 8114 1320; Jl Trans Flores; dishes 15,000-50,000Rp; ⏲8am-10pm) Long-running, popular place with a nice porch overlooking the rice fields. The special here is the Moni cake. The gado gado comes recommended and there are two, shiny rooms with hot water available (350,000Rp). The friendly family can help with Kelimutu tours.

Good Moni INDONESIAN $$
(☎0813 5377 5320; Jl Trans Flores; mains 40,000-80,000Rp; ⏲8am-9pm; 📶) With a friendly chef-owner and misty view of the hills, this open-air restaurant at the top of town is worth a stop. Indonesian food is the speciality, but there's pasta available, too. Check out the blackboard for the daily special and be sure to try the Moni croquette. Perhaps the only place in Moni for wi-fi.

Drinking & Nightlife

Thanks to Mopi's Place, a cafe that morphs into an evening bar with live music, Moni has nightlife.

If you're here during First Communion (June, August or September) there will be all-night parties with food, *moke* (palm alcohol) and dancing to massive sound systems. Wander on up and you'll no doubt be invited in (a gift of 50,000Rp is appropriate).

Getting There & Away

It's always best to travel in the morning, when buses are often half empty; afternoon buses are usually overcrowded. Don't book through your homestay – hail the bus as it passes through town.

A private car from Ende airport to Moni costs 500,000Rp one way. Book via the stand near baggage collection.

Motorbikes (100,000Rp) and cars with a driver (800,000Rp) are available per day from Bintang by Tobias.

Always organise drivers and transport through trusted locals, accommodation and homestays – avoid opportunists hawking transport on the street as there have been reports of scams. If you're unsure, ask Tobias at Bintang.

DESTINATION	TYPE	FARE (RP)	DURATION (HR)	FREQUENCY
Ende	bus	50,000	2	several daily
Ende	car	100,000	1½	hourly, 6am-4pm
Maumere	bus	50,000	3	several daily
Maumere	share taxi	80,000	2½	several daily

Paga

☎0382 / POP 15,598

Halfway between Moni and Maumere you'll find a string of beaches that are the stuff of Flores fantasy. The Trans-Flores Hwy swoops down to the shore at this rice-farming and fishing hamlet, where the wide rushing river meets the placid bay.

Beaches

The lush scenery lures you inland from beautiful beaches such as **Pantai Paga**. You can hike to megalithic stone graves and amazing ocean views at the nearby village of **Nuabari**. Agustinus Naban (www.floresgids.com) of Restaurant Laryss (p368) will guide you for 500,000Rp per day.

★Pantai Koka BEACH
(entry per person/car 10,000/20,000Rp) About 5km west of Pantai Paga, look for a small, partially paved road that runs for 2km through a cocoa plantation to a stunning double bay. Facing a promontory are two perfect crescents of sand; one protected and another with views out to sea. Eat grilled fish (50,000Rp) at **Blasius Homestay**, or stay in the basic bamboo accommodation (rooms 200,000Rp).

Sleeping & Eating

Inna's Homestay HOMESTAY $$
(☎0813 3833 4170; innanadoke@gmail.com; Jl Maumere-Ende, Pantai Paga; r 300,000-450,000Rp) An absolute beachfront, four-room homestay with a back porch and hammock for maximum ocean enjoyment. Rooms are basic but spotless. One has an impressively renovated bathroom. Fan cooling assists the ocean breeze.

Paga Beach Bungalow BUNGALOW $$
(☎0823 3912 5221; Jl Maumere-Ende; r 250,000Rp) Changing ownership and shape a few times in as many years, there are now five beachfront bungalows here. They're a basic affair with tiled floors and mosquito nets, a tad pricey and only two rooms have Western toilets. The food (15,000Rp to 25,000Rp) cooked by the loveable family owners is a steal.

★**Restaurant Laryss** SEAFOOD $$
(☎0852 5334 2802; www.floresgids.com; Jl Raya Maumere-Ende; mains 30,000-35,000Rp, fish up to 150,000Rp; ⏰kitchen 9am-10pm) Don't miss this beachside fish shack. Sit at a tree-shaded table on the sand and order the catch of the day or a soul-stirring *ikan kuah assam* (tamarind fish soup). The sambal here demands second helpings. Owner and guide Agustinus Naban's wife, Cecilia, rubs fish with turmeric and ginger, douses it with lime and then roasts it over coconut shells.

Two very basic rooms (200,000Rp) match the ad hoc architecture and open directly onto the sand.

Getting There & Away

Flag down passing buses, which run regularly during daylight hours. East to Maumere costs 15,000Rp; west to Moni costs 30,000Rp.
A share taxi from Moni to Paga costs from 50,000Rp per person.

Maumere

☎0382 / POP 54,000

Blessed with a long, languid coastline backed by layered hills and fringed with islands, Maumere is a logical terminus to a trans-Flores tour. With good air connections to Bali and Timor, it's a gateway to Flores Timur (East Flores). Largely razed in the devastating earthquake of 1992, it's been thoroughly rebuilt and is now a busy, dusty urban hub. Thankfully, you don't have to stay in the city, with the nicest accommodation options along the coast to the east. Divers will appreciate Maumere's 'sea gardens', destroyed in the quake but now recovered, as well as the diving hot spot accessible from Waiara.

Sleeping & Eating

★**Pantai Paris Homestay** HOMESTAY $
(☎0812 3895 8183; www.pantaiparishomestay.wordpress.com; Pantai Paris, Jl Larantuka-Maumere; dm/d 110,000/300,000Rp; @) Run by an environmentally and socially conscious family, this tropical garden setting beside the sea is our pick for budget accommodation. There are four private rooms with bamboo furniture and mosquito nets and the spacious, nine-bed dorm shares a lovely, semi-outdoor bathroom. Join in a Sunday beach or snorkelling clean-up or support locals with disabilities by buying organic, homemade tea.

Wailiti Hotel HOTEL $$
(☎0382-23416, 0821 4717 5576; wailitihotel@yahoo.co.id; Jl Da Silva; r/bungalow from 400,000/450,000Rp; ❄📶🏊) Maumere's most pleasant accommodation offers tidy rooms and bungalows in spacious grounds on a narrow black-sand beach, complete with novelty animal paddle boats for hire. The simple restaurant serves acceptable seafood and Indonesian standards (mains 35,000Rp to 60,000Rp), and there's a dive shop on-site. It's 6.5km west of the centre; a taxi from the airport costs 100,000Rp.

Pasar Malam INDONESIAN $
(Night Market; off Jl Slamet Riyadi; mains from 15,000Rp; ⏰5-11pm) As well as dirt-cheap Indonesian favourites like nasi goreng, Maumere's large night market, unsurprisingly, has plenty of stalls grilling fresh fish.

Golden Fish Restaurant SEAFOOD $$
(☎0382-21667; Jl Hasanuddin; mains 40,000-150,000Rp; ⏰9am-10pm) Walk through the open kitchen and peruse the day's live catch in blue tanks – including crab and lobster – on your way to the second-storey dining room with a classic harbour view.

Getting There & Away

AIR

Maumere is connected to Bali and Kupang. Airline offices and travel agents are clustered in the centre on Jl Pasar Baru Timur. Maumere's **Frans Seda Airport** (Wai Oti Airport) is 3km east of town, 800m off the Maumere–Larantuka road.

A taxi to/from town is a non-negotiable, flat fee of 60,000Rp.

DESTINATION	AIRLINE	DURATION (HR)	FREQUENCY
Bali	Garuda, Wings Air	2	daily
Kupang	Nam Air, Wings Air	1	daily

BUS

There are two bus terminals. Buses and Kijang heading east to Larantuka leave from **Terminal Lokaria** (Jl Raja Centis), 3km east of town. **Terminal Madawat** (Jl Gajah Mada), 1km southwest of town, is the place for westbound departures. Schedules are rarely precise – be prepared to wait around until there are sufficient passengers, and watch out for buses that pick up passengers from the streets adjoining the terminals, without actually entering them.

DESTINATION	TYPE	PRICE (RP)	DURATION (HR)	FREQUENCY
Ende	bus	80,000	5	regularly, 7am-4pm
Ende	car	150,000	4½	regularly, 7am-4pm
Larantuka	bus	60,000	4	several daily
Larantuka	car	80,000	3	several daily
Moni	bus	50,000	2½	several daily
Moni	car	80,000	3	several daily

Getting Around

Car rental, including driver and fuel, costs 800,000Rp to 1,000,000Rp per day, depending on your destination. You can organise vehicle and motorbike rental at hotels for 100,000Rp.

Waiara

Waiara is the departure point for the Maumere 'sea gardens', once regarded as one of Asia's finest dive destinations. The 1992 earthquake and tsunami destroyed the reefs around Pulau Penman, Pulau Besar and Pulau Babi but they've now recovered – with the exception of 'The Crack' near Pulau Babi, a consequence of the earthquake and now a diving hot spot where sea life flourishes.

Sleeping

Sea World Club RESORT **$$**
(Pondok Dunia Laut; ☎0382-242 5089, 0821 47770 0188; www.flores-seaworldclub.com; Jl Nai Roa; d/tr cottages from 600,000/650,000Rp, beachfront bungalows from 1,100,000Rp; ❄📶) Just off the Larantuka road is this modest black-sand beach resort, established to provide local jobs and build tourism. There are simple, thatched cottages and more modern and comfortable air-conditioned bungalows. Expect to add up to an additional 200,000Rp per night to listed prices during busy months.

There's an adequate restaurant (mains 45,000Rp to 95,000Rp) and dive shop (1,000,000Rp for two dives including gear).

Budi Sun Flores Diving Resort DIVE RESORT **$$**
(☎0813 5323 7327; www.budi-sun-resort.com; Jl Nairoa Km16, Wairita; d/bungalows from 600,000/750,000Rp; ❄🏊) This Indonesian-German venture sits on a strip of grey sand with lovely views. There's a large pool and the restaurant has decent local and European food (mains 30,000Rp to 60,000Rp). The bungalow-style rooms are pristine, but expect to pay more for sea views. The dive operation is outsourced and unreliable – safer elsewhere.

Coconut Garden Beach Resort RESORT **$$$**
(☎0821 4426 0185; www.coconutgardenbeachresort.com; Jl Nasional Larantuka Km15; d/bungalow 450,000/1,250,000Rp; ❄📶) Set among coconut palms, this resort is so spotless it feels like someone's raking the sand as you walk. Eight bamboo bungalows have undulating roofs and gorgeous outdoor bathrooms, but you're paying mostly for the setting with the pricey budget rooms (shared bathroom). There's a restaurant (mains 33,000Rp to 77,000Rp) and water sports, but we love the little details most.

Getting There & Away

To get to Waiara, catch any Talibura- or Larantuka-bound bus from Maumere 12km to Waiara. It will cost 10,000Rp and take around 20 minutes. Resorts are signposted from the highway.

Wodong

The pod of beaches and resorts just east of Waiara centres on Wodong, 26km east of Maumere. The narrow, palm-dappled beaches here, which include Ahuwair, Wodong and Waiterang, are tranquil and beautiful.

There's an impressive variety of dive and snorkelling sites with plenty of marine life offshore around Pulau Babi, Pulau Besar and Pulau Pangabatang, a sunken Japanese WWII ship, and colourful microlife in the 'muck' (shallow mudflats). Damage to the reefs from a devastating tsunami in 1992 has largely been overcome by new coral growth. In November whale-watching trips are also offered, although you'll probably see migrating sperm whales spout from the beach.

1

WOLFGANG POELZER/GETTY IMAGES ©

MUNDOSEMFIMV/SHUTTERSTOCK ©

1. Komodo National Park (p344)
Hiking in the park, including on Padar Island, rewards with stunning views.

2. Flores (p348)
Traditional methods are used to create beautiful fabrics.

3. Sumba (p385)
This island offers pristine beaches, hilltop villages, waterfalls and rugged savannah.

4. Alor Archipelago (p372)
Crystal-clear bays in this chain of islands offer spectacular diving.

DWI PRAYOGA/SHUTTERSTOCK ©

Sleeping

Most accommodation options are basic but tasteful beach hideaways located down trails 10m to 500m from the road; they are signposted from the highway.

Sante Sante HOMESTAY **$**
(☎0813 3734 8453; www.santesante-homestay-flores.com; Wairterang Beach; r 200,000-350,000Rp, camping s/d 80,000/120,000Rp) This homestay and beach bar has two basic rooms and beach tents available. Both have private, outdoor bathrooms; the more expensive room sleeps up to four people. Food is around 35,000Rp to 50,000Rp and proprietor Marleno organises tours and transfers.

Sunset Cottages BUNGALOW **$**
(☎0812 4602 3954, 0821 4768 7254; sunsetcottages@yahoo.com.uk; Jl Maumere-Larantuka Km28; d/f 250,000/350,000Rp) Nestled on a secluded black-sand beach with island views, Sunset Cottages is shaded by swaying coco palms. The thatched, coconut-wood-and-bamboo bungalows have Western toilets and *mandis* (ladle baths), with decks overlooking the sea. Snorkel gear is available for hire (25,000Rp per day) and there's a restaurant (mains 25,000Rp to 40,000Rp). Pop next door to Sante Sante for a sunset drink.

Lena House BUNGALOW **$**
(☎0813 3940 7733; www.lenahouseflores.com; Jl Maumere-Larantuka Km28; r from 175,000Rp) Lena House has 10 clean bamboo bungalows spread across two properties (Lena 2 is reached by boat) on a spectacular bay framed by jungled mountains. The sweet family arranges snorkelling trips (100,000Rp per person) and treks up Gunung Egon (100,000Rp), although you may choose just to stretch out under the palms and let your mind drift.

★**Ankermi Happy Dive** BUNGALOW **$$**
(☎text only 0821 4778 1036; www.ankermi-happydive.com; Jl Larantuka-Maumere, Watumita; s/d bungalow from 295,000/365,000Rp; ❄☒) Run by Claudia and Kermi, Balinese-influenced Ankermi has eight cute, tiled and thatched bungalows with private porches and stunning sea views (fan only) or garden views (with air-con). The dive shop is the best in the Maumere area (shore/night/boat dives from €25/35/35). Locally grown, organic rice and vegetables feature in the restaurant (mains 42,000Rp to 95,000Rp).

Getting There & Away

Wodong, the main village in the area, is on the Maumere–Larantuka road. Take any Talibura, Nangahale or Larantuka bemo or bus from the Lokaria (p368) terminal in Maumere for 5000Rp.

A bemo from Wodong to Waiterang costs another 5000Rp. A car from Maumere is around 150,000Rp to 200,000Rp and an *ojek* 75,000Rp to 100,000Rp one way. Buses pass by throughout the day.

ALOR ARCHIPELAGO

The final link of the Lesser Sunda Islands – the chain stretching east of Java – is wild, volcanic and drop-dead gorgeous. There are crumbling red-clay roads, jagged peaks, white-sand beaches and crystal-clear bays offering remarkable diving.

Isolated from the outside world and one another by rugged terrain, the 212,000 inhabitants of this tiny archipelago are divided into 134 tribes speaking 18 languages and 52 dialects. Although the Dutch installed local rajas along the coastal regions after 1908, they had little influence, with people still taking heads into the 1950s. These days animist traditions have been mostly replaced by Muslim and Christian ones. In more populated areas mosques dot the coast beside eye-catching, pastel-tiled graves.

Though a network of simple roads now covers Pulau Alor, boats are still a common form of transport. The few visitors who land here tend to linger on nearby Pulau Kepa or dive these waters from liveaboards.

Getting There & Away

There are two 45-minute flights from Kupang in West Timor to Alor Island Airport, costing around 750,000Rp. The price has jumped due to reduced flights, but is the easiest way to access the archipelago. The airport is on the island's northwest corner and Kalabahi is only 16km and 25 minutes by taxi for 50,000Rp. A taxi to Alor Kecil is 150,000Rp to 200,000Rp, or take an *ojek* for 100,000Rp.

There are also ferries from Kupang to Kalabahi that cost 168,000Rp and take 15 to 18 hours, leaving on Tuesday, Thursday and Saturday. The ferry returns on Wednesday, Friday and Sunday.

Major upgrades are underway at the airport – a sure sign of things to come.

Kalabahi

☎0386 / POP 61,000

Kalabahi is the chief town on Pulau Alor, located at the end of a spectacular 15km-long, palm-fringed bay on the south coast. Travellers come here to explore its coasts and nearby islands, using the town as a base that pales in comparison to the beaches and promise of diving. Other than some impressive banyan trees that make great points of reference, there's not much to see in the town's dusty main drag, unless *you* happen to be passing by – expect locals to yell out and stop for a chat. Keep an eye out for school children and government officials wearing woven ikat vests over their uniforms on Thursdays to upkeep tradition.

Sights & Activities

Pasar Kedelang MARKET

(Kedelang; ⊙7.30am-7.30pm) Mingle with locals at Alor's most exciting fresh-produce market. Pyramids of vegetables are piled on tables; betel nut, flower and leaves are arranged on tarps on the ground; and *kenari* (almond-like nut) is everywhere. Pick up nasi and accompaniments wrapped up for 5000Rp and bring your bargaining hat to purchase local ikat.

Alor Dive DIVING

(☎0813 3964 8148, 0386-222 2663; www.alor-dive.com; Jl Suka Maju; 2-dive day trips from €79; ⊙8am-4pm) This dive shop run by a German expat organises all manner of diving trips, from half-day to a week or more. It has years of experience in the beautiful local waters.

Mila Salim TOURS

(☎0822 3619 2859; milanur266@yahoo.com) Mila Salim is a wonderful English teacher and local guide who can help with trips across Alor. She opened Kalabahi's first *oleh-oleh* (souvenir) art shop supporting local craftspeople.

Sleeping & Eating

Cantik Homestay GUESTHOUSE $

(☎0821 4450 9941, 0386-21030; Jl Dahlia 12; s/d 150,000/200,000Rp; ❄) These 12 tiled rooms with private bathrooms and air-con are basic but quiet, located in a shady residential neighbourhood. Rent a motorbike for the day (75,000Rp) and stick around for communal meals (from 25,000Rp per person) as the co-owner is a wonderful cook. At breakfast, Jacob the caged bird will wish you good morning in both English and Indonesian.

Dinda Home Stay across the road is a good alternative (singles and doubles cost 200,000Rp and 250,000Rp).

Pulo Alor Hotel HOTEL $$

(☎0386-21727, 0852 3380 0512; puloalorhotel@gmail.com; Jl Eltari 12; r from 549,000Rp; ❄📶🏊) Although a little bland, this is the best option for travellers used to hotel accommodation. There are 30 rooms with televisions, desks and bottled water, plus a terrace with a view of Alor Bay and the green hills beyond. Pool and restaurant on-site. Free airport pick up.

Rumah Makan Jember INDONESIAN $

(☎0813 5392 9118; Jl Pamglima Polim 20; mains 15,000-30,000Rp; ⊙7am-7.30pm) Before you turn down Jl Suka Maju to reach Alor Dive,

ALOR OFFSHORE

Alor's dive operators regularly visit upwards of 42 dive sites, sprinkled throughout the archipelago. There are wall dives, slopes, caves, pinnacles, reefs and impressive muck diving in the Alor bay. What makes Alor special are its completely unspoiled reefs with vibrant soft and hard coral intact. Dive sites are never crowded, the water is crystal clear and you may well see a thresher shark, pod of dolphins or, come November, migrating sperm whales. Just know the current is frequently unpredictable and the water can be as low as 22°C. The cool temperature is what keeps the coral nourished, and spectacular. It's best to have 30 dives under your belt before venturing into these waters.

All divers must pay a marine park fee of 50,000Rp per day to fund the management of a 4000-sq-km marine park. The WWF works with the government to help manage and take care of this unique marine environment.

Sandwiched between Pulau Pantar and Alor is **Pulau Pura**, which has some of Alor's best dive sites. **Pulau Ternate**, not to be confused with the Maluku version, also has some magnificent dive and snorkel sites. **Uma Pura** is an interesting weaving village on Ternate, with a rather prominent wooden church. To get there, charter a boat from Alor Besar or Alor Kecil (150,000Rp), or take a motorbike to the Padang location of Alor Besar Village and pay 10,000Rp each way.

stop at this fantastic local haunt. Make a beeline for the counter, piled with *sayur* (vegetables), chicken *sate*, noodles, tempe and more. Make your decision and then pull up a chair in what feels like someone's tiled dining room, complete with garish green curtains.

Resto Mama INDONESIAN $$
(0822 1320 2525; Jl Buton 15; mains 25,000-65,000Rp; 10am-10pm Mon-Fri & Sun, to 11pm Sat;) This wood-and-bamboo dining room is perched over the bay on stilts, 50m west of Pasar Kedelang (p373). There's plenty of seafood and Indo fare, but the house speciality is *ikan kuah assam mama*, a sweet and sour fish soup with a fiery, tamarind-inflected broth. Service can be painfully slow.

Information

MEDICAL SERVICES

Hospital (0386-21008; Jl Dr Soetomo 8; 24hr) Centrally located and open 24 hours.

MONEY

Bank BNI (Jl Sudirman; 8am-4pm Mon-Fri) has an ATM; other banks dot the centre.

Getting There & Away

AIR

Wings Air makes the 45-minute flight to Kupang. The tiny airport is comically disorganised, and 16km from Kalabahi. Check in early to avoid the mad scrum.

BOAT

ADSP ferries serve Kupang and Larantuka. Ferries leave from the ferry terminal 1km southwest of the town centre; it's a 10-minute walk or a 3000Rp bemo ride. There are two weekly to Kupang (114,000Rp to 168,000Rp, 18 hours), and one to Larantuka (107,000Rp, 12 hours). Pelni ships leave from the main pier in the centre of town and visit Kupang, Sabu, Rote, Ende, Waingapu, Bima and more on a monthly schedule serviced by three ships. The **Pelni office** (0386-21195; www.pelni.co.id; Jl Cokroaminoto 5; 8am-5pm) is near the pier.

BUS

Buses and bemos to Alor Kecil cost 5000Rp and take 30 minutes. To Alor Besar it's 7000Rp for the 40-minute journey. Both leave from the central Kalabahi Pasar Tabakar and Pasar Kedelang (p373) (markets). You can also take a taxi from the airport from 150,000Rp to 200,000Rp.

Getting Around

The airport is 16km from town. Taxis cost a fixed 100,000Rp, or 50,000Rp for one person.

Transport around town costs 3000Rp by bemo. To get out to the villages, look for blue bemos that cost between 5000Rp and 10,000Rp. Rent a motorbike at Cantik Homestay (p373) for 75,000Rp per day, elsewhere they're 100,000Rp. *Ojeks* are easily hired for 150,000Rp per day.

Local guide Mila Salim (p373) can help with trips across Alor.

WEST TIMOR

It doesn't take much for West Timor to get under your skin. A smile in someone's direction will see their face erupt in one, too. It might reveal teeth stained red from chewing betel; one framed by wrinkles in the rugged countryside; or a yelp and wave from a music-thumping bemo in Kupang – the coastal capital and East Nusa Tenggara's metropolis.

Within its mountainous, *lontar* palm-studded land, animist traditions persist alongside tribal dialects and chiefs preserve *adat* in traditional beehive-hut villages. Hit up one of the many weekly markets and you'll not only get a feel for rural Timor life, but be the star attraction as you eavesdrop on one of 14 different languages spoken on the island. Although West Timor is a relatively undiscovered gem, you'll still be welcomed wherever you go.

History

The Tetun (or Tetum) of central Timor are one of the largest ethnic groups on the island and boast the dominant indigenous language. Before Portuguese and Dutch colonisation, they were fragmented into dozens of small states led by various chiefs. Conflict was common, and headhunting a popular pastime.

The first Europeans in Timor were the Portuguese, who prized its endemic *cendana* (sandalwood) trees. When the Dutch landed in Kupang in the mid-17th century, a prolonged battle for control of the sandalwood trade began, which the Dutch eventually won. The two colonial powers divvied the island in a series of treaties signed between 1859 and 1913. Portugal was awarded the eastern half plus the enclave of Oecussi, the island's first settlement.

Neither European power penetrated far into the interior until the 1920s, and the island's political structure was left largely intact. The colonisers spread Christianity and ruled through the native aristocracy, but some locals claim Europeans corrupted Timor's royal bloodlines by aligning with imported, and eventually triumphant, Rotenese kingdoms. When Indonesia won independence in 1949 the Dutch left West Timor, but the Portuguese still held East Timor. In 1975 East Timor declared itself independent from Portugal and shortly afterwards Indonesia invaded, setting the stage for the tragedy that continued until 2002 when East Timor's independence was officially recognised.

During August 1999, in a UN-sponsored referendum, the people of East Timor voted in favour of independence. Violence erupted when pro-Jakarta militias, backed by the Indonesian military, destroyed buildings and infrastructure across the East, leaving up to 1400 civilians dead before peacekeepers intervened. Back in West Timor, the militias were responsible for the lynching of three foreign UN workers in Atambua in 2000, making Indonesia an international pariah. After several turbulent years, relations normalised by 2006 and road and transport links were restored.

Getting There & Away

West Timor is easily accessed through the principal city, Kupang, site of El Tari Airport (p378), the regional gateway to East Nusa Tenggara. Technically an international airport, it also offers daily flights to Jakarta, Denpasar, Alor, Sumba and Flores.

Ferries also sail to Kalabahi, Larantuka, Rote and Waingapu but their running times and ability are weather dependant.

Kupang

0380 / POP 334,516

Kupang is the capital of Nusa Tenggara Timur (NTT). Despite the city's scruffy waterfront, sprawling gnarl of traffic and the almost complete lack of endearing cultural or architectural elements, this is a place you can get used to. Besides, there are atmospheric markets in the centre, spots to relax beside locals and a smattering of nearby natural wonders. The chaos can be contagious – it's a university town, after all – even if you're just popping in and out.

Kupang's a regional transport hub, but don't be surprised if between trips to the interior, Alor or Rote you discover that it grows on you. England's Captain Bligh had a similar epiphany when he spent 47 days here after that emasculating mutiny on the *Bounty* in 1789.

Sights

The heart of old Kupang centres on the **old port area** and its surrounding cacophonous market. Look closely and you'll see a few traces of Dutch colonial times, when Kupang was considered a genteel tropical idyll.

Pantai Tedis BEACH

(cnr Jl Soekarno & Siliwangi; snacks/smoothies from 7000/10,000Rp; from 5pm) Don't miss the atmosphere – or sunset – at this local hangout where Jl Soekarno intersects with the oceanfront. The sand vendors set up stalls and seating, while those in the know chow down on grilled corn and *pisang goreng* (fried plantain banana), the latter served with chocolate and grated *keju* (cheese). This is also the best place for smoothies, from mango and dragonfruit to avocado spiked with chocolate sauce.

Museum Nusa Tenggara Timur MUSEUM

(0380-832471; Jl Frans Seda 64; by donation; 8am-3.30pm Mon-Fri) This regional museum has skulls, seashells, stone tools, swords, gourds and antique looms from across the province, plus an entire blue whale skeleton in a separate building. Displays (some

SIGHTS AROUND KUPANG

On Kupang's west coast, south of the centre, lies a local haunt not often visited by international travellers: **Gua Kristal** (Bolok), the Crystal Cave, where locals swim and partake in photo shoots. If you take the coastal road to get to Gua Kristal, you'll pass **Gua Monyet**, the Monkey Cave. It's well signposted, but you're likely to see monkeys on the side of the road without entering. Unfortunately it seems that they're drawn to the area more by trash than by habitat.

Continue out of Kupang city on Jl Alfons Nisnoni for around 25km to arrive at **Pantai Tablolong**, a lovely sandy beach. Relatively nearby is **Air Terjun Oenesu** (3000Rp), a three-stage, turquoise-tinted waterfall with a popular swimming hole and an unfortunate accumulation of litter.

in English), cover historical moments and cultural topics, including plants that create dyes for traditional fabrics.

Tours

Kupang is a gateway to West Timor's fascinating and welcoming traditional villages. Bahasa Indonesia, let alone English, is often not spoken. The villages can also be a minefield – albeit a friendly minefield – of cultural dos and don'ts. A local guide is essential.

Oney Meda (0813 3940 4204; onymeda@gmail.com; ½ day tour 300,000Rp) is an English-speaking guide with nearly two decades of experience organising anthropological tours and treks throughout West Timor and Alor.

Eben Oematan (0852 3795 8136; per day from 400,000Rp) is from Kapan, which means he speaks several dialects spoken in the villages you'll want to visit.

Edwin Lerrick (0812 377 0533; lavalonbar@gmail.com; per day from 400,000Rp), the irrepressible owner of Kupang's Lavalon Bar & Hostel, is also a guide, with deep regional knowledge and connections throughout West Timor.

Recommended by Lonely Planet in 1995, **Willy Kadati** (0812 5231 0678; willdk678@gmail.com) took time off to do research for various organisations and universities; he is now back with more cultural, botanic and ikat knowledge than ever.

Kefamenanu-based guide **Aka Nahak** (0813 3820 0631, 0852 346 3104; timorguide@gmail.com) has been touring Timor since 1988. He's enthusiastic and will proudly show you his handwritten guestbooks.

Sleeping

Near the airport and the new commercial district there are several large and bland chain hotels, such as the Neo Aston and the Amaris. Properties on the waterfront are more atmospheric and come with ocean breezes, views and sometimes pools. There are budget-friendly homestays, too.

★Lavalon Bar & Hostel HOSTEL $

(0812 377 0533; www.lavalontouristinfo.com; Jl Sumatera 44; dm from 70,000Rp, r from 100,000-260,000Rp;) Run by living Nusa Tenggara encyclopedia and former Indonesian film star, Edwin Lerrick, Lavalon is Kupang's best-value accommodation. Rooms are worn but clean (some with Western bathrooms). Pay extra for the corner one with air-con, hot water and a window that opens to the sea. Edwin goes well out of his way to help guests with information and bookings.

Also an avid cook, Edwin has put together a small but tasty menu of speciality Indonesian dishes and Western comfort food, which can be enjoyed in the small common area by the ocean. He also runs the attached (private) visitor information office, arranges cars, motorcycles (75,000Rp per day) and drivers and can advise on onward connections. Phone or message ahead to guarantee a booking.

Hotel Maliana GUESTHOUSE $

(0380-821879; Jl Sumatera 35; r with fan/air-con 175,000/250,000Rp;) These 13 basic, comfy and clean motel rooms could do with a refurb, but remain a popular budget choice. There are ocean glimpses from the vine-shrouded front porch and it's next to a bank.

★Sotis HOTEL $$

(0380-843 8000, 0380-8438 888; www.sotishotels.com; Jl Timor Raya Km3; r from 650,000Rp;) One of Kupang's newer, nicer accommodation options, these 88 rooms are stylish with pops of colour instead of the usual beige palette. Expect toiletries, a rain shower, fridge, desk and more. There are two pools (only one is open to the public), a spa, salon, restaurant with live music, bar with pool tables and cake shop. Ask for a sea view.

Hotel La Hasienda HOTEL $$

(0380-855 2717, SMS or WhatsApp 0812 3841 7459; www.hotellahasienda.com; Jl Adi Sucipto, Penfui; d from 395,000-500,000Rp;) You've got to feel for whoever covered this three-storey, family-run hotel in mosaic tiles. It adds to the Mexican vibe, with a rooftop terrace and bar, faded-ochre walls and cowboy paraphernalia. The 22 rooms are spotless with air-con and hot water and on-site restaurant (mains 25,000Rp to 85,000Rp). Note that it's closer to the airport than town.

Eating

As you'd expect, seafood is big in Kupang. Another local speciality is succulent *se'i babi* (pork smoked over kesambi wood and leaves); it's used as the base for various sauces and is served with noodles, rice and plenty of sambal.

★Depot Bambu Kuning INDONESIAN $

(0813 3336 8812, 0813 3910 9030; Jl Perintis Kemerdekaan 4; se'i babi portion/kg 20,000/170,000Rp; 10am-10pm) A popular place for authentic Kupang *se'i babi*. Choose from chopped up meat or ribs, both served with rice and a rich pork soup with red

TIMOR-LESTE VISA RUN

Crossing the border into Timor-Leste is not nearly as complicated or lengthy as it used to be. You can still make the 12-hour, one-way journey to the considerably more expensive Dili for 225,000Rp, but it's no longer necessary to visit the Indonesia Consulate.

Instead, the easiest way to do the visa run is to cross the border at Napan, just over 20km north of Kefamenanu; Atapupu, which will only cost 50,000Rp by *ojek* from Atambua; or catch the bus to Batugade via Mota'ain. Once at the border, present your authorisation letter, US$30 and proof of an onward journey, and continue with a free 90-day visa. If you're short on time, you could conceivably catch the 45-minute morning Wings Air flight from Kupang to Atambua, cross the border and then fly back to Kupang in time for lunch. A one-way flight starts at around 350,000Rp.

But first you need to get an approved visa application letter. Apply at the Timor-Leste Consulate (p378) in Kupang with a valid passport, a photocopy of it, passport photos and either proof or return tickets or a bank statement. You'll receive the letter and stamp within one to three working days. If you attempt this a few days before Christmas, you're likely to be out of luck as staff go on holiday. Also be aware that the consulate is closed on weekends.

Note that since 2015, some European citizens who fall into the Schengen Agreement can stay in Timor-Leste without a visa for up to 90 days, every 180 days.

Timor Tour & Travel (☎0380-881543, 0812 3794 199; Jl Timor Raya Km8, Oesapa) and **Paradise Tour & Travel** (☎0813 3935 6679; Jl Pulau Indah, Oesapa) operate buses. Departures can be as early as 5am, so brace yourself. Call for a hotel pick up or ask Edwin from Lavalon to lend a hand.

It's also worth checking the daily cost of the visa overstay fine – at the time of writing, it's 300,000Rp per day, so it's worth weighing up cost and convenience (accommodation and a bus fare will be more expensive than paying a fine for a couple of days). Check the current price of the fine to avoid being caught out; rumours are circulating that it could jump significantly.

beans. *Sate* and a couple of veg dishes are also available. Check out the outdoor cooking area piled with *kesambi* leaves for smoking the meat.

★ Pasar Malam MARKET $

(Night Market; Jl Kosasih; fish from 50,000Rp; ⊙6pm-midnight) As tiny tailor shops finish up for the day, stallholders begin setting up this lamp-lit market. You're here for seafood, whether *ikan* (fish), *cumi* (squid), *kepiting* (crab) or *udang* (prawns), but you can also pick up Indo standards like grilled chicken, *bakso* and gado gado for a steal.

Depot Se'i Aroma INDONESIAN $

(☎0822 3667 1755; Jl Cak Doko 35L; mains 18,000-50,000Rp) This contemporary Kupang chain wouldn't be out of place in a Western city, except it specialises in *se'i babi* (smoked pork), not burgers. Spotless and buzzing, it's a great place to try local food at competitive prices, with locals, if you're not into street eats.

There are two stores in Kupang, but this one is on the main road instead of inside a shopping mall.

Rumah Makan Palembang INDONESIAN $

(☎0821 4689 1137; Jl Cak Doko; 30,000-75,000Rp; ⊙7am-2pm & 5-11pm Mon-Sat, 5.30-10pm Sun) This is first-rate Chinese Indonesian food. It's spotless with an enormous range of veg, chicken, seafood, noodle and rice dishes. Get the *ikan bakar rica rica* (grilled fish with chilli sauce) and don't miss the cucumber sambal. Local honey sold at the counter.

🍷 Drinking & Nightlife

As the largest city in a predominantly Christian region, Kupang has decent drinking options. You'll find karaoke bars on Jl Sudirman and a few 'pubs' on Jl Timor Raya.

999 Restaurant & Bar BAR

(☎0380-802 0999; www.999-kupang.com; Jl Tongkol 3; mains 38,000-140,000Rp; ⊙10am-midnight; 📶) In the shadow of an old fort, this tropical outdoor bar has an expansive thatched roof, views of the shabby beach and the ever-present sound of rolling surf. There's a pool table, comfortable repurposed tyre seats, a full bar including plenty of cocktails and a decent menu, too. There is regular live music and a full band on Saturday nights.

Shopping

Sandalwood oil is trickier to find than it used to be, thanks to strict regulations that only allow harvest on one's own land. Some shops still sell it, and the purest oils are upwards of 300,000Rp for a small vial.

Ina Ndao TEXTILES
(☎0380-821178, 0812 378 5620; ina_ndao@yahoo.com; Jl Kebun Raya II; ⏲8am-7pm Mon-Sat, 7-11am Sun) It's worth seeking out this neighbourhood ikat shop. Textile lovers will be pleased with the wares sourced from across Nusa Tenggara, and you can take home a neat pair of ikat espadrilles. It offers naturally and chemically dyed varieties, and staff demonstrate the weaving process upon request. Accepts credit cards.

Pasar Inpres MARKET
(off Jl Soeharto; ⏲4am-7pm) The main market is the rambling Pasar Inpres, south of the city. It's mostly fruit and vegetables, but *ti'i langga* (*lontar*-leaf hats with a centre plume) from Rote make an authentic, but novel souvenir.

For more variety, check out **Pasar Oeba** off Jl Ahmed Yani, in between Lavalon and Swiss-Belinn, about 1km from each and walking distance to the Pasar Ikan (fish market).

Information

EMBASSIES & CONSULATES

Timor-Leste Consulate (☎0380-855 4552; Jl Frans Seda; ⏲8-11.30am & 1.30-3.30pm Mon-Thu, to 3pm Fri) The visa office for Timor-Leste. See p377 for more information.

MEDICAL SERVICES

Siloam Hospital (☎1 500 911, 0380-853 0900; www.siloamhospitals.com; Jl R W Monginsidi, off Jl Eltari; ⏲24hr) This is an upscale hospital attached to the Lippo Plaza shopping mall.

TOURIST INFORMATION

Edwin Lerrick (☎0812 377 0533; lavalonbar@gmail.com; per day from 400,000Rp), the proprietor of Lavalon Bar & Hostel (p376), is a vital source for the latest transport information, as well as cultural attractions throughout Nusa Tenggara.

Getting There & Away

AIR

Kupang is the most important hub for air travel in Nusa Tenggara, thanks to **El Tari Airport** (☎0380-882031; www.kupang-airport.com/en; Jl Adi Sucipto). There are frequent flights to Bali and a web of services across the region.

Kupang's El Tari Airport is 15km east of the town centre.

Taxis from the airport to town cost a fixed 70,000Rp. An *ojek* will cost 30,000Rp. For public transport, turn left out of the terminal and walk 1km to the junction with the main highway, from where bemos to town cost 3000Rp (possibly 5000Rp with a bag).

Going to the airport, take the Penfui or Baumata bemo to the junction and walk.

PT Stindo Star (☎0380-809 0583, 0380-809 0584; Jl Urip Sumohardjo 2; ⏲9am-6pm) is an efficient travel agency that sells airline tickets.

DESTINATION	AIRLINE	DURATION (HR)	FREQUENCY
Alor Island	Wings Air	¾	two daily
Bajawa	Wings Air, TransNusa	1	two daily
Denpasar	Garuda, Lion Air, Nam Air	1¾	several daily
Jakarta	Batik Air, Garuda, Citilink Indonesia	3	several daily
Labuan Bajo	Wings Air, Garuda, Nam Air	1½	several daily
Maumere	Nam Air, Wings Air, TransNusa	1	1-2 daily
Tambolaka	Nam Air, Wings Air, Garuda	1½	several daily
Waingapu	Nam Air, Wings Air	1	several daily

BOAT

Tenau Harbor, 7km west of the centre, is where the fast ferry to Rote and Pelni ships dock. Bolok Harbour, where you get regular ferries to Kalabahi, Larantuka, Rote and Waingapu, is 11km west of the centre.

Pelni (☎0380-821944; www.pelni.co.id; Jl Pahlawan 7; ⏲8am-4pm) serves Kupang on a twice-monthly loop that includes Larantuka and Maumere. Its office is near the waterfront.

DESTINATION	TYPE	FARE (RP)	DURATION (HR)	FREQUENCY
Kalabahi	ferry	114,000-168,000	18	noon Tue & Sat
Larantuka	ferry	105,000	15	three weekly
Rote	ferry	55,000	5	6am daily
Rote	Bahari Express	138,000-168,000	2	9am daily
Waingapu	ferry	176,000	28	three weekly

BUS

Kupang's intercity bus terminal, **Terminal Oebobo** (Jl Frans Seda), is located around 7km from the airport, but people tend to use the shadow terminal in Oesapa, tour agencies or get picked up from hotels.

DESTINATION	FARE (RP)	DURATION (HR)	FREQUENCY
Kefamenanu	50,000	5½	several times daily
Niki Niki	35,000	3½	hourly 5am-6pm
Soe	30,000	3	hourly 5am-6pm

Getting Around

BEMO

A ride in one of Kupang's bass-thumping bemos (3000Rp, or 5000Rp with luggage) is one of the city's essential experiences (Kupang is too spread out to walk). Each bemo has an entertaining Western name, like Man Tap, Cold Play or City Car. Windscreens are festooned with soft toys, girlie silhouettes and Jesus. The lowrider paint job is of the *Fast & Furious* colourful variety, while banks of subwoofers will have your butt involuntarily shaking. Clap loudly when you want to stop.

Bemos stop running by 8pm. The bemo hub is the Terminal Kota terminal. Useful bemo routes:

1 & 2 Kuanino–Oepura; passing many popular hotels.

5 Oebobo–Airnona–Bakunase; passing the main post office.

6 Goes to the Flobamora shopping mall and the post office.

10 Kelapa Lima–Walikota; from Kota Kupang terminal to the tourist office, Oebobo bus terminal and Museum Nusa Tenggara Timur.

Bemos running outside Kupang use names instead of numbers. Tenau and Bolok Harbour bemos run to the docks; Penfui and Baumata bemos link to the airport.

CAR & MOTORCYCLE

It's possible to rent a car with a driver from 750,000Rp to 1,000,000Rp per day, depending on the destination. Motorcycles cost 75,000Rp a day at Lavalon Bar & Hostel (p376), but 100,000Rp or more elsewhere. Your accommodation will be able to organise it for you.

Soe

0388 / POP 39,031

About 110km northeast from Kupang, the cool, leafy market town of Soe (800m) makes a decent base from which to explore West Timor's interior, even if there's not a lot to see in town. The traditional villages scattered throughout the interior are some of the most intriguing in Nusa Tenggara Timor.

Sleeping & Eating

Hotel Bahagia I GUESTHOUSE $

(0853 3830 3809; Jl Diponegoro 22; s/d/VIP r 150,000/200,000/300,000Rp) Right in the centre of Soe, and not to be confused with Bahagia II on the outskirts, Bahagia I offers a range of rooms from small, dark cubbies to spacious suites. It's a compact courtyard building with a little breezy terrace, but don't expect air-con, hot water, wi-fi or English.

If you're in transit but not staying overnight, you can drop 125,000Rp on a room for two hours of rest. There's a bank across the road.

WORTH A TRIP

AIR TERJUN OEHALA

The gushing water diffusing over huge boulders in a silvery sheen at this waterfall is a magnificent sight. Though the infrastructure in the jungle setting hasn't seen maintenance for years, it does make the whole thing feel very Jurassic Park. Look for a road going north off the main highway, drive 6km and turn east at a sign for 'Oehala'. After 3km is a parking area, from which it's a short walk down steep steps. Sadly, crowds leave rubbish behind on weekends.

Dena Hotel HOTEL $$
(☎0812 3696 9222, 0388-21616; hotel_dena@yahoo.com; Jl Hayam Wuruk, Pasar Inpres; s/d from 200,000/225,000Rp; ❄) Although these beige rooms aren't about to win design awards, they're as clean and serviced as they come in Soe. Some have Indonesian toilets, so inspect before you decide. The most expensive have air-con (350,000Rp for a double). It's across the road from the market, ATM and a great little Padang restaurant.

★**Depot Remaja** INDONESIAN $
(Jl Gajah Mada; mains from 20,000Rp; ⏲10am-10pm; 🖉) This modest and clean diner specialises in succulent *se'i babi*, the iconic Kupang pork smoked over *kesambi* wood. But the fun doesn't stop there; try the warming pork soup – which is more of a stew – and one of the many veg options, like *jantung pisang* (banana flower salad).

Warung Putra Lamongan INDONESIAN $
(☎0823 4096 4969; Jl El Tari; mains 15,000-30,000Rp; ⏲10am-10pm) You'll smell this place before you see it, thanks to the grill charring *sate* out the front. Within the orange walls are a handful of large tables populated by locals digging into grilled and fried chicken, fish, tempe and *tongseng*, a Javanese stew with goat or beef. The *sambal terasi*, made with shrimp paste, is addictive.

Bundo Kanduang INDONESIAN $
(☎0813 3947 0806; Jl Gajah Mada; meals 20,000-30,000Rp; ⏲6.30am-10.30pm) If you've been waiting to find a fresh spot to try Padang food, originally hailing from West Sumatra, this is it. Point-and-choose from dishes stacked in the window, which come with rice and veg. There are chilli devilled eggs, fried and curried fish, *rendang*, *perkadel* (potato cakes) and more. Everything's as tasty as it is spicy. It's located 1.5km west of Soe centre.

Shopping

Timor Art Shop ARTS & CRAFTS
(☎0853 3783 5390; Jl Bill Nope 17; ⏲6am-8pm) If you're interested in antiques and handicrafts, don't miss this shop that could double as a museum. You'll find Timor's best selection of masks, sculpture, handspun fabrics and carvings at unbelievable prices. There's no sign, so call owner Alfred Maku first. He speaks excellent English. Opening hours can vary.

Information

Tourist Information Centre (☎0368-21149; Jl Diponegoro 39; ⏲7am-4pm Mon-Fri) Has information on the surrounding area and is a good place to arrange guides, should you catch someone there who speaks English.

Getting There & Away

The Haumeni bus terminal is 4km west of town and 3000Rp by bemo, but people tend to flag down buses on the side of the road instead. Regular buses go from Soe to Kupang, taking three hours and costing 30,000Rp. Knock off half an hour for buses to Kefamenanu and Oinlasi, both 25,000Rp. Bemos cover Niki Niki for 10,000Rp.

None

POP 238

None is one of the area's best attractions, despite fires destroying three *ume bubu* (traditional windowless beehive huts that are home to local Dawan people) in as many years. A compact, gravel trail runs for 1km from where the bemo drops you on the main road, so you can walk or drive past corn, pumpkin and bean fields to the entrance. None is home to 56 families that have lived here for 10 generations and the village is protected by a native rock fort that abuts a sheer cliff.

At the cliff's edge you'll find a 300-year-old banyan tree and a totem pole where shamans once met with warriors before they left on headhunting expeditions. The wise ones consulted chicken eggs and a wooden staff before predicting if the warriors would prevail. If there was a speck of blood in the egg, a sign of poor fortune, they'd delay their attack.

DON'T MISS

IKAT MARKETS

Women in small villages across West Timor produce some of the most beautiful traditional ikat cloth in all of Indonesia. They sell their wares at weekly markets at prices one tenth of what you'll pay at a boutique in Bali, although it's always cheapest to buy directly from the villages. Top ikat markets include the following:

Oinlasi – Tuesday

Niki Niki – Wednesday

Ayotupas – Thursday

Villagers might break out their looms at the village *lopo* (meeting place) for weaving demonstrations upon request. It's so peaceful here that it's hard to believe they were taking heads just two generations ago (the last conflict was in 1944). You can also arrange for traditional dances. Leave an offering of 50,000Rp for up to a few people.

You can reach None, 18km east of Soe, on an *ojek* (30,000Rp), or hop on a Soe–Niki Niki bemo for 5000Rp.

Kefamenanu

0388 / POP 42,840

A former Portuguese stronghold, Kefamenanu is a quiet hill town. Still, it remains devoutly Catholic and has a couple of impressive colonial churches. Most importantly it's the jumping-off point for Temkessi (p382), one of West Timor's 'can't miss' villages. Known locally as Kefa, the town lies at the heart of an important weaving region. Prepare to haggle with the ikat cartel. Note that the town mostly shuts up shop on Sundays.

Just 3.5km from Kefamenanu is the traditional village of **Maslete**, known for its *sonaf* (palace). Made from wood carved with mythical birds and an imposing grass roof with hanging dried corn, you'll find the king sitting on its sheltered porch. Although his eyes are cloudy blue from blindness and he doesn't speak English ('We are like the cow and buffalo talking,' he might observe) a guide will translate as you're quizzed by the Catholic animist about life in your part of the world.

Sleeping & Eating

Hotel Ariesta HOTEL $

(0388-31007; Jl Basuki Rahman 29; r standard/superior/ste 120,000/290,000/385,000Rp;) Set on a leafy backstreet, this longtime budget joint sprawls across 42 rooms in a modern annex and weathered original block. Economy rooms are best avoided, the all-suite annex boasts plenty of light and a private porch, and the midrange deluxe rooms with air-con and hot water have the Goldilocks effect – just right. BYO loo paper. The hotel rRents motorbikes for 70,000Rp per day.

New Victory Hotel HOTEL $$

(Hotel Victory II; 0388-243 0090; Jl Kartini 199; r 350,000Rp;) The newer of the Victory hotels opened in 2017 with 23 clean rooms with questionably patterned wallpaper, air-conditioning, TV, hot water and breakfast included. Strangely, there is an enormous gym and exercise hall here, with Zumba and aerobics. There are plans to double in size.

Hotel Victory I HOTEL $$

(0823 3946 9998, 0388-31349; victoryhotelkefa@gmail.com; Jl Sudirman 10; r 250,000-450,000Rp;) Still shiny and clean, this two-storey block has 20 rooms ranging from windowless cells to spacious, light-filled retreats. All have hot water and air-con. The small breakfast buffet is above average and reception doubles as a jewellery shop.

Rumah Makan Pondok Selera INDONESIAN $

(Jl El Tari; mains 15,000-30,000Rp; 10am-9pm Mon-Sat;) A tiny, delicious menu served in a big, dining-room space. This *rumah makan* boasts some of the best tempe and tofu in Nusa Tengarra, a giant serve that comes with *lalapan* (raw veg nibbles) and sweet, chunky sambal made with fresh tomato. There's also gado gado and *ikan kua asam* (sour fish soup).

Rumah Makan Padang 2 INDONESIAN $

(0388-31841; Jl El Tari; mains 20,000-30,000Rp; 9am-9pm) Motorbikes pull up outside this corner Padang restaurant and hint at its popularity. Specialities such as *ayam rica rica* (chicken fried in a sweet, spicy sauce), *rendang*, boiled cassava leaves and fish curry are piled onto plates in this green-walled establishment. Cool down with *sirsak* (soursop) juice.

THE VILLAGE MIDWIFE

Traditionally every village has a nurse or midwife to help deliver babies. Discouraged by the government, it can still happen in remote villages where hospitals are far away. In None, the husband of a pregnant woman is invited into the house of the village midwife, where he arrives with a chicken as a down payment for her services (a larger animal is expected when the baby arrives safely). She then tells him to prepare firewood and fetch water. His wife gives birth on a rock with the assistance of the midwife, after which a fire is lit under the bed of the new mother and child for warmth and protection. The placenta is buried inside the home with objects to propel the future of the child (books for intelligence, weaving tools for craft etc).

OFF THE BEATEN TRACK

MAUBESI

Located 19km from Kefamenanu, the village of Maubesi is known for its textile market. Market day is Thursday, when along with produce, animals and pottery, ikat is displayed beneath tamarind trees. Pieces using natural dye are the most prized and can fetch between 1,000,000Rp and 5,000,000Rp, depending on the technique. Some take over six months to make. If you're not passing by on a Thursday, **Maubesi Art Shop** (☎0852 8508 5867; ⏰hours vary) has a terrific selection of local ikat and handicrafts. Bargaining is acceptable despite price tags. Look for the 'ART SHOP' sign. If it appears closed, just knock.

Information

The tourist office, **Dinas Pariwisata** (☎0388-21520; Jl Sudirman; ⏰7am-3pm Mon-Fri), is opposite the field north of the highway and can help locate a guide.

Getting There & Away

The bus terminal is in Kefamenanu's centre, 50m from the Jl El Tari market, which blooms most days. From here between about 6am and 4pm there are regular buses to Kupang (50,000Rp, five hours) and Soe (25,000Rp, two hours); Atambua (20,000Rp) on the Timor-Leste border is only 20,000Rp and 1½ hours away.

Hotel Ariesta (p381) rents motorbikes for 70,000Rp per day. Rental cars in Kefa cost 650,000Rp per day with driver.

Timor Tour & Travel (☎0388-243 0624; Jl Ahmad Yani) You can join express minibuses running between Kupang (95,000Rp, five hours) and Dili in Timor-Leste (180,000Rp, 7½ hours). Tickets are sold at an office 4km east of the centre on the main highway; pick ups are made at hotels.

Temkessi

Accessible through a keyhole between jutting limestone cliffs, 50km northeast of Kefa, Temkessi is one of West Timor's most isolated and best-preserved villages. The drive across wind-swept ridges, with distant views out to sea, sets the otherworldly mood, but upon arrival you'll be met by giggling children and perhaps a puppy or piglet.

Sights

Temkessi is one of West Timor's most isolated and best-preserved villages. There are two entrances: one is reserved for royalty but often used by travellers; the correct entrance has a sign reading 'Eno Fatnai Naimnune' on a stone platform, from which it's a short uphill walk along a cobblestone pathway under a canopy of trees.

The **raja's house** overlooks the village, with the east and west pillars representing male and female respectively. Clamber up the stone steps to meet the day's designated dignitary, where you'll offer betel nut (buy it in Manufui, the last village off the main road before you turn off for Temkessi) and make a donation (50,000Rp per person). After that you can shoot pictures of the low-slung beehive huts built into the bedrock, connected by red clay paths that ramble to the edge of a precipice. Just don't take pictures of the conical hut where the village's mysterious sacred objects are stored, unless you want bad juju. The same goes if you drop something; don't pick it up immediately, alert local villagers who will first pray to the ancestors for forgiveness.

You can't miss the soaring and utterly alien-looking limestone rocks. At least once every seven years, young warriors climb the face of **Tapenpah**, sans rope, with a goat, rooster, branches of betel nut, bamboo, coconut, sugar cane and cotton. Depending on the size of the offering, this is done in multiples of seven. Other members of the community also ascend in multiples of seven. They slaughter the goat (but not the rooster), chew betel nut and only come down once everything has been eaten. This Natamamausa ritual is performed to give thanks for a good harvest or to stop or start the rain.

A young villager will likely ask if you want to climb the other notable rock face, **Oepuah**. It's a crumbly, craggy affair, so only attempt it if you're comfortable. The view back over the village from the top, not to mention the 360-degree views, is invigorating. Tip your adventurous leader 20,000Rp when you reach the bottom again.

Very little Bahasa Indonesia is spoken here, so a guide is essential. The overall mood is warm and welcoming and once you're settled into this surreal place, with the wind rustling the trees in what feels like the top of the world, you might find it hard to leave.

Getting There & Away

Regular buses run from Kefa to Manufui, about 8km from Temkessi. On market day in Manufui (Saturday), trucks or buses should run through to Temkessi. Otherwise, charter an *ojek*, or better, secure your own wheels.

ROTE

A slender, rain-starved limestone jewel with powdery white-sand beaches and epic surf, Rote floats southwest of West Timor, but has an identity of its own. For tourists it's all about the surf, which can be gentle enough for beginners and wild enough for experts.

Ba'a, Rote's commercial centre, is a sleepy port town on the west coast where fast ferry and flights land, but people don't tend to linger. Stunning Pantai Nemberala is home to the world-renowned T-Land break, and there are dozens of hidden beaches to the south and north. To find them you'll roll through villages, over natural limestone bridges and through undulating savannah that turns from green in the December to March wet season to gold in the dry season, which is also when offshore winds fold swells into barrels. Don't overlook the tiny offshore islands where you can find gorgeous ikat, turquoise bays and more surf.

Information

INTERNET ACCESS

Internet access is sparse, but you can get 3G data in some places, including Nemberala.

MONEY

There's a BRI ATM in Ba'a but it usually refuses foreign cards. Bring plenty of rupiah as exchanging cash is difficult.

Getting There & Away

AIR

Wings Air operates flights between Kupang and Ba'a twice daily. They take 30 minutes and the afternoon flight allows for a same-day connection from Bali, although transporting surfboards can complicate the transfer and add to the costs (Wings Air charges 200,000Rp per board).

BOAT

The swiftest and most comfortable way to reach Rote is via the Baharai Express (executive/VIP 138,000Rp/168,000Rp, two hours), a fast ferry that departs from Kupang at 9am daily (and sometimes at 2pm between Wednesday and Monday), docks at Ba'a and returns at 11am. Book your ticket in advance and arrive at the dock at least half an hour early. Be warned, this service is often cancelled due to rough seas.

There's also a daily slow ferry (55,000Rp, five hours) that docks at Pantai Baru, north of Ba'a, but by the time you charter transport to Nemberala, it will cost you more than the fast ferry.

Getting Around

Local touts will try to convince you that to get to Nemberala from the fast-boat port in Ba'a you'll have to charter a bemo (from 300,000Rp, two hours). This is only a good option if you are sharing with a group, but just outside the harbour gates you can easily flag down a public bemo (with/without surfboard 100,000/50,000Rp). You can also arrange with your hotel for a car to pick you up for about 400,000Rp.

Many of the resorts offer transfer packages from Kupang's airport via the fast ferry and on to the resort. These are undeniably seamless, but can cost US$100 or more.

Nemberala

Nemberala is a chilled-out fishing village on an exquisite white-sand beach. It's sheltered by a reef that helps form the legendary 'left', T-Land. Don't expect an isolated vibe here as an influx of visitors, expats and vacation home owners have bought up large swatches of beachfront in the area. New businesses are opening to serve these devotees.

Still, Nemberala hasn't gone all flash: the local pigs, goats, cows, chickens and other critters still freely wander the beach and resorts, and you still need to avoid getting conked on the head by a falling coconut. Explore the surrounding lonely limestone coast by motorbike in order to absorb its majesty.

Activities

The **T-Land** wave gets big, especially between June and August, but it's not heavy, so the fear factor isn't ridiculous. Like other once-undiscovered waves in east Indo, the line-up gets busy in the high season. If you prefer a heavier, hollow wave, your first stop should be 3km north of Nemberala at **Suckie Mama's**.

Many resorts rent high-quality boards from about 100,000Rp per day.

Sleeping & Eating

The surf season peaks between June and September. Accommodation range and value are solid, but there aren't a lot of rooms so book ahead.

While most of the lodges and guesthouses are all inclusive, some local warungs have appeared, so you have options to vary your vittles.

Ti Rosa BUNGALOW $
(☎0823 3915 2620; per person incl meals from 250,000Rp) Run by sweet Ibu Martine and her son, this fine collection of eight lime-green, concrete bungalows is super clean, shaded by palms and is the cheapest beach option available. Budget surfers love it so much that some book rooms for the whole season. Turn right at the first intersection in town and head north along the dirt road for 500m.

Anugerah Surf & Dive Resort BUNGALOW $$
(☎0811 382 3441, 0813 5334 3993; www.surfdiverote.com; s/d incl meals from 565,000/904,000Rp;) The 40 cute and compact *lontar*-palm bungalows range from newish to older, and come with a variety of patios and *mandis,* wooden furniture, outdoor bathrooms and more. It's right on the beach opposite T-Land. The restaurant, with ikat tablecloths, serves *ikan bakar* (grilled fish) amid a menu that changes daily. Reserve ahead during surf season.

Scuba diving is also offered; per person, all gear included is 1,470,000Rp for two dives.

Lualemba Bungalows BUNGALOW $$
(☎0812 3740 4137, 0812 3947 8823; www.lualemba.com; s/d incl meals 770,000/1,370,000Rp;) This highly recommended spot is set 500m inland from the beach. Attractive, thatched *lontar* bungalows feature stone foundations and private verandahs strung with hammocks, and they share a natural swimming pool. Rates include boat rides to the surf break, three meals and use of mountain bikes.

★ **Malole Surf House** SURF CAMP $$$
(☎0813 5317 7264, 0813 3776 7412; www.rotesurfhouse.com; s/d per person incl 3 meals from US$105/126;) Built by surf legend Felipe Pomar, this lodge blends comfort, cuisine and style better than anywhere else in Rote. Four rooms are set in a large wooden house and guesthouse with day beds, ikat bedspreads, limitless laundry and more. You'll hit the right waves at the right time via three boats. Closed during wet season; mid-November to March.

Sublime international seafood is but one highlight of the kitchen, which carves fresh sashimi, bakes fresh bread and blends spectacular soups and curries. Mountain bikes, fishing trips and island excursions are also on offer.

The level of comfort and elegance here feels effortless (it isn't) and belies its extremely remote location.

ℹ Getting Around

You should be able to hire a motorbike (100,000Rp per day) through your hotel or guesthouse.

Around Nemberala

If you rent a motorbike and drive the spectacularly rutted coastal road north or south, you'll notice that you're within reach of a half-dozen other desolate beaches and a few superb, uncharted surf breaks. Beginners take note: just north of the Nemberala fishing-boat harbour is a terrific novice break called **Squealers**. The village of **Boni** lies about 15km from Nemberala, near the northern coast, and is one of the last villages on Rote where traditional religion is still followed. Market day is Thursday.

About 8km south of Nemberala, **Bo'a** has a spectacular white-sand beach and consistent off-season surf. Set on a notch in the headland that bisects this absurdly wide and almost unjustly beautiful bay, **Bo'a Hill Surf House** (☎0822 7771 7774, 0822 7771 7775; www.surfrote.com; per person incl meals from 800,000Rp) has beautiful bungalows set on a three-hectare site with stunning views. The eco-cred is strong here. The owner grows fruit and herbs, raises pigs and ducks, collects honey, and is a superb guide to local delights on land and sea.

From Bo'a continue south over the dry rocky road – look out for monkeys – and after you traverse the natural limestone bridge, negotiate the descent and reach **Oeseli** village. Then make a right on the dirt road, which leads to another superb beach with some good waves, and a huge natural tidal lagoon that shelters local fishing boats and floods limestone bat caves. There's an ideal kitesurf launch here, too.

The southernmost island in Indonesia, **Pulau Ndana**, can be reached by a local fishing boat from Nemberala. Although it's currently a military camp it can still be visited, but for years it was uninhabited. Legend has it that the entire population was murdered in a 17th-century revenge act, staining the island's small lake with the victims' blood. Ndana is known for its wildlife and superb snorkelling. Look out for wild deer and a wide variety of birds, as well as for nesting turtles on the beaches.

Pulau Ndao has more powdery white-sand beaches, limestone bluffs and a tidy, charming ikat-weaving, *lontar*-tapping (collecting sap from *lontar* palm-tree flowers) fishing village that's home to nearly 600 people who speak their own indigenous dialect, Bahasa Ndao. There are some fantastic swimming beaches up the west and east coasts, and good though inconsistent surf off the southern point.

Ndao is 10km west of Nemberala. To get here you'll have to charter a boat (800,000Rp to 1,000,000Rp, maximum five people). You could easily combine a visit here with nearby **Pulau Do'o**, a flat spit of pale golden sand with terrific though finicky surf. You can see Do'o from Pantai Nemberala.

SUMBA

☎0387

There's something truly enchanting about Sumba. With its rugged, undulating savannah and low limestone hills growing maize and rice, it's nothing like Indonesia's northern volcanic islands. Scattered throughout the countryside are hilltop villages with tall, symbolic grass roofs clustered around megalithic tombs, where nominally Protestant villagers still respect indigenous *marapu* with bloody sacrificial rites.

Encircling Sumba are white-sand beaches that are the stuff of dreams, as are the island's secret swimming spots and waterfalls further inland. Throw in some of Indonesia's most prized ikat and you have one of the most diverse islands in Indonesia. Here *adat* runs deep and small children with big smiles shout 'hello mister', irrespective of your gender.

This is one of Indonesia's poorest islands, though an influx of investment has seen villages swap thatched roofs for tin. Traditional dress is reserved for special occasions and remote villagers expect larger donations from visitors.

Getting There & Away

Sumba's links to greater Indonesia are ever-improving. Airports in Tambolaka and Waingapu have daily flights to Denpasar (Bali), Kupang (West Timor) and Ende (Flores). Ferries run to Flores, Kupang and Sape in Sumbawa. Time your travel so you can fly into Waingapu and out of Tambolaka – or the other way around – so you don't have to double back when exploring sizeable Sumba.

Waingapu

☎0387 / POP 34,811

Waingapu is a laid-back town with a split personality: there's the leafy, dusty centre interspersed with accommodation and small *toko* (stores), the old harbour that becomes redolent with the smell of grilled fish after sundown when the Pasar Malam (p386) kicks off, and villages in the middle of it all, where chickens bolt between *marapu* tomb stones adorned with carved crocodile and deer statues.

Waingapu also has some ikat stores and workshops, and traders lugging bundles of textiles and carvings hang around hotels touting for rupiah. It's a mostly walkable place, and you'll spot grazing buffalo and horses as you explore. Since becoming an administrative centre after the Dutch military 'pacified' the island in 1906, Waingapu remains Sumba's main trading post for textiles, prized Sumbanese horses, dyewoods and lumber.

Tours

Erwin Pah TOURS
(☎02 813 3933 7971; erwinpah9@gmail.com) If you need a knowledgable driver and guide, look no further than Erwin Pah. Based in Waingapu, he has his own car and seems to know everyone in Sumba. If you're into adventure, ask him about tailored trips that include everything from rock climbing to caving. His daily rate is 1,200,000Rp, including transport, petrol and guiding services.

SUMBA'S BEST WEBSITE

A true labour of love by German Matthias Jungk, www.sumba-information.com is a vast compendium for all things Sumba. You can buy a pdf version of the website for €5. Jungk has also created a superbly detailed *and* accurate map of Sumba, which you can use online or buy. Best of all, this invaluable resource is continually updated.

Sleeping

Breakfast and free airport transfers (if you call in advance) are usually included in accommodation rates. There's a decent range of options and budgets, from rooms with a view to rooms in the village.

Mr. R. Home Stay GUESTHOUSE $
(0853 3744 6164; Kandara Belankang SMP Kristen; r 200,000Rp) A plain, clean guesthouse with an out-of-place dolphin water feature, overlooking a rice paddy with grazing buffalo. There are six rooms with air-con, TV and long pillows to hug should you get lonely. Food is ordered from nearby **Sacca Resto** (0851 0270 7222, 0387-62677; saccacellular@gmail.com; Jl S Parman 88, Tandarotu Waingapu; r from 350,000Rp) and if you're lucky, the hot water will be working.

★ **Morinda Villa & Resto** CABIN $$
(0812 379 5355; freddy_ikat@yahoo.com; Bendungan Lambanapu; r from 650,000-750,000Rp) About 11km south of the airport and perched on a hill, Morinda Villa has five cabins with eye-popping views. Each has a traditional grass roof, huge windows and a balcony for a peek into local life on the river. There's hot water, a restaurant (mains 25,000Rp to 100,000Rp, open 11am until 9pm) and an ikat shop on-site.

★ **Praikamarru Guest House** BUNGALOW $$
(0813 3809 3160; www.prailiu.org; Jl Umbu Rara Meha 22; r/bungalow 250,000/275,000Rp) Run by an Australian who married a local king and now welcomes guests into village life. Stay in one of two spacious bamboo bungalows with *alang alang* grass roofs, comfortable beds with ikat throws and even a fridge; or in one of two basic rooms (shared squat toilet) in a traditional house with bamboo mats and a people-watching porch.

Enjoy freshly baked bread and fruit every morning and delicious local food with the family for 50,000Rp per meal. Ask owners Sarah and Umbu anything you like about local culture and the *marapu* religion – they're more than happy to share. Look for the tree adorned in animal skulls, remnants of sacrificial ceremonies. Motorbike rental for 75,000Rp per day.

Tanto Hotel GUESTHOUSE $$
(0812 8181 6484, 0387-62500; www.tantohotel.com; Jl Prof Yohanes 14; s/r/ste from 250,000/350,000/650,000Rp) Fifty-seven bright, fresh rooms and good service set Tanto apart from most of the Waingapu competition. The decor is primarily white with wood and vivid-red accents. Many rooms have fridges, all have hot water and air-con, and the breakfast is good. There's free airport transfers at certain times and they can arrange car hire from 575,000Rp for 12 hours.

There's a decent lobby restaurant (open 6am to 9.30pm, mains 25,000Rp to 75,000Rp).

OFF THE BEATEN TRACK

AIR TERJUN TANGGEDU

Head northwest of Waingapu to find this extraordinary sight: two rivers running between time-layered limestone cliffs and converging into waterfall terraces that feed into multiple pools. Expect to spend two hours or more making the 60-or-so-km journey along roads that leave a lot to be desired, followed by a 40-minute trek through savannah or grasslands, depending on the time of year.

Eating

★ **PC Corner** INDONESIAN $
(0387-256 0142, 0812 2317 1725, 0852 3702 8401; lusijowin@gmail.com; Jl Radamata 1; mains 25,000-50,000Rp; 8am-10pm Mon-Fri, 9am-11pm Sat, 4-10pm Sun) Pause for a photo in front of the bohemian 'dream big, work hard, stay focus' mural before continuing up stairs to this open-air cafe with vintage furniture and dreamcatchers. Eat veg dishes like papaya flower with *kangkung* (water spinach) and free-range *kampung* chicken. There's a band from 7pm on Saturday, a killer view and charging points at every table.

★ **Pasar Malam** INDONESIAN $
(Night Market; off Jl Yos Sudarso; mains from 15,000Rp; 6-11pm) The best dinner options turn up at dusk: a couple of warungs and half a dozen gas-lit carts at the old wharf grill and fry seafood on the cheap. In the centre of town at the southern fork of Jl Ahmad Yani are more street eats, such as *sate ayam* (chicken satay) and *bakso*, from 10,000Rp.

Warung Enjoy Aja SEAFOOD $
(0852 3027 2104; Pelabuhan Lama; mains 15,000-70,000Rp; 6pm-midnight) The last warung before the pier on the east side. Pick your fish caught fresh that day from a cool

OFF THE BEATEN TRACK

SOUTH CENTRAL SUMBA

It's worth toughing out access issues to get to this part of Sumba, especially if you're a keen surfer. Although there are daily buses from Waingapu to Tarimbang and trucks to Praingkareha, getting around may require a 4WD, motorcycle and even some hiking.

If you're looking for deserted waves, check out **Pantai Tarimbang**, a gorgeous crescent of white sand framed by a massive limestone bluff 95km southwest of Waingapu. The beach thumps with terrific surf, there's snorkelling nearby and beach-shack accommodation is available at **Marthen's Homestay** (0852 8116 5137; Jl Gereja Tarimbang; dm/s/d incl all meals from 300,000/400,000/700,000Rp). The *kepala desa* had just started building a traditional village accommodation concept when we last visited, set to offer three seven-room houses and a bungalow.

Daily trucks to Tarimbang leave Waingapu in the morning and take five hours. They cost 40,000Rp, but don't be surprised if the local sitting beside you is only charged 25,000Rp – you get the *bule* price.

box, then enjoy it with rice, local veg and three types of sambal. In the yellow building next door is a second 'dining room' with less lurid light and the opportunity to sit on the floor while eating.

El Cafe INDONESIAN $
(0812 3766 2611, 0387 61875; elcafesubma@gmail.com; Jl Pemuda 10; mains 25,000-50,000Rp; 9am-10pm Mon-Fri, to 11pm Sat, noon-10pm Sun;) Clean but over-styled (cue wallpaper scrawled with country names and both ikat and guitars on the walls) El Cafe has strong wi-fi, live music on Saturday night and karaoke. Try *otak otak bandeng* (fish stuffed with its own sweet flesh, mixed with coconut and spices and steamed in banana leaves).

Shopping

There are a few 'art shops' selling Sumbanese ikat and artefacts. Vendors also squat patiently all day outside hotels. Prices are fair and there's more choice here than in the countryside. East Sumbanese is renowned across East Nusa Tengarra for having some of the most detailed ikat motifs – buy here before venturing west, where it can look more basic and modern.

Praikundu Ikat Centre TEXTILES
(0812 3758 4629; kornelis.ndapakamang@gmail.com; Jl S Parman, Kelurahan Lambanapu; hrs vary) This small weaving centre is 2.5km off the main road, sticking to the left fork. Run by Kornelis Ndapakamang, it's hung with some of Sumba's most prized ikat, all naturally dyed with detailed motifs. Kornelis will happily chat in Bahasa Indonesia, explaining how his members are keeping Sumbanese traditions alive. Lengthier ikat workshops available upon request.

There are also three rooms available in the on-site homestay; two doubles and another with two single beds off a sweet communal living and dining space. The cost is 200,000Rp per night, per person. Rooms share a clean squat toilet and *mandi*. Kornelis' wife cooks traditional meals for 60,000Rp a pop.

Ama Tukang TEXTILES
(0812 3622 5231; Jl Hawan Waruk 53; 24hr) A series of rooms and houses championing ikat and jewellery, where guests can see everything from motif design to colouring and weaving. The collection features *marapu*, animals and village scenes – all hung on display beside dried corn in the rafters. There's also decent accommodation from 250,000Rp per night.

There are currently four rooms with air-con available and another eight on the way, which will have hot water. Motorbike rental is available for 150,000Rp per day, as are cars from 600,000Rp to 800,000Rp. To get here, head south of the bridge on the southern side of Waingapu and turn right onto the street.

Getting There & Away

AIR

The airport is 6km south on the Melolo road. A taxi into town costs a standard 60,000Rp, but most hotels offer a free pick-up and drop-off service. It's 5000Rp for a bemo ride to any destination around town, and 10,000Rp to the western bus terminal, although there are fewer bemos than there used to be. An *ojek* around town is between 5000Rp to 10,000Rp.

OFF THE BEATEN TRACK

A SLICE OF HEAVEN

About 39km east of Waingapu's airport, French-run **Wera Beach Resort** (☎0812 3758 1671; www.sumbaeastresort.com; Jl Melolo, Pantai Wera; bungalow/house from 750,000/1,500,000Rp) is a peaceful oasis with two houses that have kitchens and are decked out in rattan furniture; both are available as one- or two-bedroom stays. There's also a neat bamboo bungalow on the beach. The open-air restaurant (mains 45,000Rp to 220,000Rp) serves French food while wind chimes tinkle in the breeze.

TX Waingapu (☎0821 4509 5477, 0812 1718 1930, 0387-61534; www.txtravel.com; Jl Beringin 12; ⏲8.15am-5pm Sun-Fri, to 4pm Sat) is a travel agency that books airline tickets.

Nam Air and Wings Air have flights to Denpasar (1½ hours, 1-2 daily) and Kupang (one hour, several daily)

BOAT

Pelni ships leave from the newer Darmaga dock to the west of town but their **ticket office** (☎0387-61665; www.pelni.co.id; Jl Hasanuddin 1; ⏲7am-noon, 1.30-5pm) is at the old port. Schedules are subject to change: check with **ASDP** (☎0214-288 2233; www.indonesiaferry.co.id; Pelabuhan Waingapu) or see the timetables at the port.

DESTINATION	COMPANY	FARE (RP)	DURATION (HR)	FREQUENCY
Aimere (Flores)	ASDP	81,000	10	two weekly
Ende (Flores)	ASDP	83,000	13	weekly
Kupang (West Timor)	ASDP	176,000	28	three weekly
Sabu	ASDP	97,000	12	weekly

BUS & BEMO

Bemos from Waingapu's Terminal Kota run to Londolima and Prailiu.

Three daily buses head northwest to Puru Kambera (15,000Rp to 20,000Rp, one hour). There are also several daily buses to Waikabubak (50,000Rp, five hours).

The terminal for eastbound buses is in the southern part of town, close to the market. The West Sumba terminal, aka Terminal Kota, is about 5km west of town.

ℹ Getting Around

Sumba has some of the highest car-rental rates in Nusa Tenggara. Even after bargaining, 800,000Rp is a good price per day, including driver and petrol. Expect to pay more if you want your driver to double as a guide – 1,200,000Rp is a good price. As is the case across Indonesia, bargaining is acceptable and multiday tours are great leverage. Virtually any hotel can arrange motorcycle rental but Praikamarru Guest House (p386) has the best rate at 75,000Rp per day; expect to pay around 100,000Rp elsewhere.

West Sumba

☎0387

If you're hungry for traditional Sumbanese culture, head west into the rice fields that crawl up blue mountains, carved by rivers and sprouting with bamboo and coconut palms. *Kampung* of high-roofed houses are still clustered on their hilltops, surrounding the imposing stone tombs of their ancestors. Rituals and ceremonies involve animal sacrifices and can take place at any time. Outsiders are welcome, but make a donation – your guide will know how much (usually 20,000Rp to 50,000Rp). Even though *kampung* seem accustomed to visiting foreigners, gifts of betel nut help warm the waters and are a sign of respect.

West Sumba is most easily traversed and experienced with a guide, especially if you don't speak Bahasa Indonesia. In the west, locals get around with giant knives called *parang* strapped to their waist, but it's mostly for show. Still, it is ill-advised to travel after dark in West Sumba.

ℹ Information

Although relatively safe, those on the ground will strongly advise you not to travel after dark in the west, and some drivers will refuse to take you until light. Best not mess with locals carrying *parang* knives, just in case.

ℹ Getting There & Away

Tambolaka is the transport hub of the west, thanks to a modern airport with daily flights to Denpasar in Bali and Kupang in West Timor with Garuda, Nam Air and Wings Air. Note that some still refer to Tambolaka as 'Waikabubak'. Ferries depart from Pelabuhan Waikelo, about 6km north of the city centre, to Sape in Sumbawa. They leave three times per week, take nine hours and cost 52,000Rp.

Getting Around

If you have limited time and want to explore remote villages and the wild coast without having to worry about transport schedules and language barriers, call Sumba Adventure Tours & Travel (p391). The team of drivers (most speak English) have good cars, are trustworthy and know Sumba well. An SUV with driver is between 800,000Rp to 1,000,000Rp for up to four people per day; guide services are extra. Combine the two by giving Erwin Pah (p385) a call; based in Waignapu, he has his own 4WD and charges 1,200,000 per day for transport, petrol and guide services.

For a much cheaper drive around the west, you can hire an *ojek* for the day for between 100,000Rp and 150,000Rp, but again, don't travel at night.

Waikabubak

0387 / POP 28,760

A country market town, home to thatched clan houses and rows of concrete shops, administrative buildings and tin-roof homes sprouting satellite dishes, Waikabubak makes Waingapu feel like a metropolis. It's a welcoming place, surrounded by thick stands of mahogany and lush rice fields. At about 600m above sea level, it's cooler than the east and a good base for exploring the traditional villages of West Sumba.

The food market is on daily from 7am until 10pm. On your way here from Waingapu, about 15km out of town, look out for **Bukit Raksasa Tidur** (Sleeping Giant Hill) – no prizes for guessing what the landscape looks like, but it's a great photo opportunity.

Sights & Tours

Within the town are some friendly and quite traditional *kampung* (villages) with stone-slab tombs and thatched houses. You can tell the wealthier families by the detail and intricacy – or otherwise – of the tombs. You don't need a guide here if you're just looking around. Locals are happy to show off their spacious homes lashed with old ironwood columns and beams. Some children mug for the camera, others giggle and disappear around corners. Old folks will offer betel nut. Bring your own to share and offer a donation (minimum 20,000Rp to 50,000Rp).

Kampung Tambelar (off Jl Sudirman) has very impressive *kubur batu* (stone graves), but the most interesting *kampung* are on the western edge of town. It's only a short stroll from most hotels to **Kampung Prai Klembung** (off Jl Manda Elu) and then up the hill that juts from the centre of town to **Kampung Tarung** (off Jl Manda Elu) and **Kampung Waitabar** (Jl Manda Elu).

Other interesting *kampung* occupying ridge or hilltop positions outside town include **Praijing**, with traditional huts set around some cool, primitive stone tombs and surrounded by coconut palm and bamboo groves. **Bondomarotto**, **Kampung Prairami** and **Kampung Praikateti** are also beautifully located on adjacent hilltops. You can take a bemo to the turn-off for Praijing (5000Rp).

Yuliana Leda Tara TOURS
(0822 3621 6297; yuli.sumba@gmail.com; Kampung Tarung; per day from 500,000Rp) Yuliana is a wonderful local English- and French-speaking guide who lives in Tarung – Waikabubak's traditional hilltop village – and can organise village tours throughout West Sumba, where she can find out about funerals and sacrifices, organise horse tours

VISITING VILLAGES

Many Sumbanese villagers are now accustomed to tourists. If you're interested in their weavings or other artefacts, the villagers put you down as a potential trader. If all you want to do is chat and look around, use basic manners and ask first, or risk them being confused or offended. Often the tables turn, and you might feel under the microscope.

On Sumba, offering *pinang* (betel nut) is the traditional way of greeting guests or hosts. You can buy it at most markets in Sumba, and it's a respectful ice breaker. Offer it to the *kepala desa* (village head) or to whoever gives you their time.

Many villages keep a visitors book, which villagers will produce for you to sign, and you should donate between 2000Rp and 5000Rp per person, placed in the book when signing and handed back. Hiring a guide to isolated villages is a big help and offers some protection from falling into the wrong situation. Take the time to chat with the villagers to be seen as a guest, rather than a customer or visiting alien.

WORTH A TRIP

WEEKURI LAGOON

Almost as far west as you can get on Sumba is one of the island's most magical spots, Weekuri Lagoon. On one side, locals and tourists rent black rubber rings for 10,000Rp and float in the cool, crystal water; on the other, the Indian Ocean rages against rocks and bursts through cracks and blowholes, best viewed from the bisecting bridge. Allow at least half a day to enjoy it, at a bargain price of 20,000Rp per person. It's about 45km from Tambolaka.

There are more than half a dozen small dirt roads leading off Jl Waitabula-Bondokodi that eventually get you to the aquamarine waters of this jaw-droppingly beautiful wonder. There are vendors selling cup noodles, coconuts and other snacks, but avoid purchasing bracelets illegally made from turtle shells.

through rice fields and arrange village stays. Book ahead and note that her guide fee excludes transport.

Sleeping & Eating

Mona Lisa Cottages GUESTHOUSE **$$**
(0387-21364, 0813 3943 0825; Jl Adhyaska 30; s from 200,000, d from 300,000 750,000Rp;) Named after a disco in Surabaya from the owner's party days, the best night's sleep is 2km northwest of town opposite rice fields. It includes fan-cooled budget rooms, higher-end units and freshly renovated cottages with peaked tin roofs, private patios and bamboo furnishings. Some have air-con.

Hotel Manandang HOTEL **$$**
(0812 3620 5222, 0387-21197; hotelmanandang@yahoo.com; Jl Pemuda 4; r 327,000-500,000Rp;) These tidy, good-value rooms cluster around a pleasant back garden. The cheapest, fan-only rooms have cold water; more money brings air-con and even more brings hot water. Staff speak perfect English and can help with airline tickets. Mains at the canteen-like restaurant start at 20,000Rp.

Rumah Makan Fanny INDONESIAN **$**
(0387-21389; Jl Bhayangkara 55; mains 20,000-50,000Rp; 8am-9pm Mon-Sat) A pint-sized Waikabubak staple, favoured for flavourful but crazy-spicy *ikan kuah assam* – one is enough to feed two. It also has assorted Chinese-Indo seafood dishes and a house-special fried chicken. There's a BNI with an ATM across the road.

D'Sumba Ate INTERNATIONAL **$$**
(0812 3868 3588; Jl Ahmad Yani 148A; mains 30,000-80,000Rp; 10am-11pm;) This cool, bamboo restaurant cooks up wood-fired pizzas, pasta and burgers alongside the usual Indo suspects. If you know what's good for you, you'll eat *ayam betutu kampung dan urap,* a Balinese-spiced village chicken with plenty of condiments and coconut greens. It's also the only place in town where you'll get a latte fix.

Take the wooden bridge over the pond to **Kakitangan Spa**, a simple operation by the same folk with massages from 50,000Rp per hour.

Information

BNI Bank (0387-21549, 0387-321540; Jl Bhayangkara 48; 8am-4pm Mon-Thu, 7.30am-4pm Fri) Has an ATM and offers fair exchange rates.

Getting There & Away

Tambolaka, about 45km northwest of Waikabubak, has the closest airport. A bus to the terminal at Waitabula (an older town being swallowed by Tambolaka) and a bemo or *ojek* from there is the cheapest option, but most people get a taxi from Waitabula or charter a bemo (around 150,000Rp) from Waikabubak.

Bemos, trucks and minibuses service most other towns and villages in West Sumba. Generally, it's best to leave early in the day, when they tend to have more passengers and depart quickly, instead of waiting until they're full. There are several daily buses to Waingapu (60,000Rp, five hours).

Waikabubak is the place to rent a motorcycle for exploring West Sumba. Expect to pay 100,000Rp per day. Hotels can set you up with motorbike or car rental. The latter costs 500,000Rp with a driver if you're sticking to town, otherwise it's from 800,000Rp to 1,000,000Rp.

Tambolaka

0387

Located 45km northwest of Waikabubak, this once-sleepy market town has become West Sumba's main transport hub – it's booming and the name of the airport, Tambolaka, has been transferred to the rest of town, including in tourism brochures and other government literature. We've followed suit, even if many locals still refer to it as

Waitabula. While still in the early stages of growth, Tambolaka is easily accessible from Bali and is the gateway to the island's sensational western half.

Sights & Tours

Tambolaka has a daily market opposite **Hotel Sinar Tambolaka** (☎0387-253 4088; www.sinartambolaka.com; Jl Tambolaka; r 200,000-450,000Rp, 1-bed villa 750,000Rp; ❄📶🗷).

Lembaga Studi & Pelestarian Budaya Sumba MUSEUM
(Rumah Budaya Culture House; ☎0813 3936 2164; museum by donation; ⏲8am-4pm Mon-Sat) Just 3km west of town, this Catholic-run NGO is in a working coconut plantation and has an excellent cultural museum. It was developed by Fr Robert Ramone, who noticed how, once baptised, Sumbanese frequently break clean from their old culture and develop negative associations with the *marapu* and other totems. There are displays of old photographs, money, pottery, ikat, stone carvings and more.

The complex also has 10 basic rooms for rent (300,000Rp to 600,000Rp). Sit on one of the private porches and let the quiet envelop you. An ikat museum opened on-site in 2018.

Sumba Adventure Tours & Travel TOURS
(☎0813 3710 7845; www.sumbaadventuretours.com; Jl Timotius Tako Geli 2; guide services per day 300,000Rp, car & driver per day 800,000-1,000,000Rp; ⏲8am-5pm) With an office close to the airport, experienced guide Philip Renggi and his team of guides lead trips into seldom-explored villages, including his native Manuakalada and Waiwarungu, where there are several sacred *marapu* houses that only shaman can enter. He can arrange itineraries, rent cars and more. Look for his office near Rumah Makan Richard.

Sleeping & Eating

New hotels are shooting up in Tambolaka, a contrast against more timeworn guesthouses. There are some pleasant, quiet – and in some cases more expensive – options 20 minutes outside of town.

Penginapan Melati GUESTHOUSE $
(☎0813 5396 6066; Jl Sapurata; r with fan/air-con 175,000/250,000Rp; ❄📶) With 14 simple rooms that are much cleaner than the gloomy fish tank in reception, you can expect plenty of images of the host family, Virgin Mother and Il Papa to brighten things up. There are rain shower heads in the bathrooms and a Padang-style restaurant next door. Look for the green and orange stripes in lieu of signage.

★Oro Beach Houses & Restaurant BUNGALOW $$
(☎0813 3911 0060, WhatsApp 0813 3978 0610; www.oro-beachbungalows.com; Weepangali; villa/bungalow 665,000/850,000Rp) 🍃 Think: four wild beachfront hectares where you can nest in a circular thatched bungalow with canopied driftwood beds and outdoor bathrooms. Oro offers excellent meals, mountain bikes and snorkelling (50,000Rp each) just off their stunning 200m-long beach. There are six rooms, including two bungalows with air-con and fan-only beach houses and villas. Motorbikes available for 150,000Rp per day.

Ella Hotel HOTEL $$
(☎0821 4583 7745, 0387-252 4150; ellahotelsumba@gmail.com; Jl Jenderal Sudirman; r from 350,000Rp; 🅿❄) Set around a manicured courtyard are 54 immaculate, modern rooms. All have air-con and the only difference between a standard and deluxe is hot water. Two VIP rooms and suites have views. For those wondering, we were told in a deadly serious tone that 'Ella' comes from 'umbrella'.

★Maringi Eco Resort by Sumba Hospitality Foundation RESORT $$$
(☎0822 366 15505; www.sumbahospitalityfoundation.org; Jl Mananga Aba, Desa Karuni; pavilions/deluxe r 1,000,000/1,500,000Rp; ❄📶🗷) 🍃 Where to start with this incredible complex: that it's a not-for-profit NGO where students from Sumba learn the art of hospitality before landing top hotel jobs in Indonesia? Or the brilliantly designed bamboo pavilions with giant glass oval doors and outdoor bathrooms? Maybe its sustainability, reusing water in the garden and harnessing solar. This is so much more than accommodation.

Warungku INDONESIAN $
(☎0812 5250 5000; Jl Ranggaroko; mains 20,000-40,000Rp; ⏲8am-11pm) Set back from the main road in a walled compound, this open-air restaurant, complete with water feature and karaoke, has excellent versions of Indo classics. It's a pretty garden setting, and you can while away a few hours grazing and sipping *jus semangka* (watermelon juice).

Warung Gula Garam INTERNATIONAL **$$**
(☎0812 3672 4266, 0387-252 4019; gulagaram sumba@gmail.com; Jl Soeharto; mains 26,000-110,000Rp; ⏰10am-10pm; 📶) Run by expat Frenchman Louis, this open-air cafe near the airport plays funky-fresh R&B tunes and serves surprisingly good wood-fired pizza, plus other Western dishes like chicken cordon bleu and sausages with mash and veg. There's also good Indo fare, like locally approved beef *rendang*, and more than passable coffee and juices. Stay tuned for a new venue.

ℹ Information

BNI Bank (Jl Jenderal Sudirman; ⏰8am-1pm Mon-Thu, 7.30am-4pm Fri) Has an ATM and exchanges money.

ℹ Getting There & Away

AIR

Tambolaka's airport is shiny and modern. There are daily flights to Denpasar in Bali and Kupang in West Timor with Garuda, Nam Air and Wings Air. Note that on some airline and booking websites the destination is listed as 'Waikabubak'.

BOAT

Waikelo, a small and predominantly Muslim town north of Tambolaka, has a little, picturesque harbour that's the main port for West Sumba and offers a ferry service to Sape in Sumbawa (52,000Rp, three weekly). It takes nine hours, depending on the weather.

BUS

Buses leave throughout the day for Waikabubak, which takes an hour and costs between 15,000Rp to 20,000Rp, departing from the centre of town.

Wanokaka

☎0361 / POP 14,163

The Wanokaka district south of Waikabubak has stunning mountain scenery, coastline and several traditional *kampung*. It's a gorgeous drive from Waikabubak taking a sealed, narrow road that splits at Padede Weri junction, 6km from town. This is where white-headed eagles soar over mountains that tumble to the azure sea. Turn left at the junction and the road passes through the riverside settlement of **Taramanu**, 5km further on.

Downhill from Taramanu is **Kampung Waigalli** on a promontory above the sea, and beyond that a nearly 200-year-old Watu Kajiwa tomb in the deeply traditional village of **Praigoli**. About 5km onwards is **Waeiwuang**, featuring a stone tomb with a 2.5m-tall fleur-de-lis.

Take the right fork before Sumba Nautil and you'll reach **Litikaha**, where a gravel road leads to the panoramic villages of **Tokahale**, **Kahale** and **Malisu**. It's a 15-minute 4WD drive, or park on the road and walk to all three in about two hours.

🛏 Sleeping

★ **Sumba Sunset Home Stay** BUNGALOW **$$**
(☎0852 0591 7662, WhatsApp 0821 47546538; www.sumbasunset.com; Kerewe Beach; per person incl meals 400,000Rp) When you see the surfboard sign, turn into this homestay roosting above Kerewe Beach. Each of the four, traditional bungalows has a different bed set up to accommodate couples, friends or families. All have mosquito nets and share two *mandis*. Owner Petu worked for Nihi Sumba for eight years and can tell you all about surf break Occy's Left.

Boat trips are available for 150,000Rp per person for three people, or 300,000Rp for solo travellers. Pull up a hammock or hire a bike for 100,000Rp per day and explore. In bad weather there's the option of going camping with Petu. In good weather, organise a fish barbecue on the beach for 50,000Rp per person.

Nihi Sumba RESORT **$$$**
(☎0361-757149; www.nihi.com; bungalows & villas from US$845; ❄📶🏊) Formerly Nihiwatu, few luxuries are excluded from this celebrity-favoured resort, where you might bump into the Beckhams. Hefty price tag aside (we've listed the low-season rate), you can understand the draw to this stunning accommodation, where every detail is considered and there's a virgin beach crashing with surf that folds into turquoise barrels on Sumba's ruggedly beautiful coast.

Sumba Surf Camp BUNGALOW **$$$**
(☎0821 4647 5974; www.sumbasurfcamp.com; Kerewe Beach, Patiala Bawa, Lamboya; r/bungalows per person incl meals US$85/95) 🍃 Consisting of a main house with four rooms and three private bungalows decked out in natural materials, Sumba Surf Camp is all about – you guessed it – surfing. The rate includes transport to a dozen breaks accessible within 30 minutes by boat. Meals are served family-style using produce from the organic garden. Electricity is solar powered and day trips easily arranged.

WEST SUMBA BEACHES

The beaches on West Sumba's south coast remain largely undiscovered, except by surfers in search of the perfect break and those with deep pockets staying at Nihi Sumba. The world-class surf spot known as **Occy's Left**, featured in the film *The Green Iguana*, is on **Pantai Nihiwatu**, an achingly stunning stretch of sand buffered by a limestone headland. Unfortunately only Nihi Sumba's guests are allowed onto it and the number of surfers is capped at 10. Thankfully homestay owners are experts on where to find the best lefts and rights, with more scattered along the coast. That being said, you might be able to get to Occy's anyway if you stay with Petu from Sumba Sunset Home Stay.

From Pantai Nihiwatu, the magic starts at **Pantai Wanokaka**'s craggy palm-dotted cliffs, a bay bobbing with fishing boats and a beachfront Pasola site. Here most of the action gathers around the concrete public fishers house, where you can see the catch in the morning and watch fisherfolk mend nets come late afternoon. **Rua**, the next in a series of luscious south Sumba beaches, is 10km southwest of the Padede Weri junction, or continue along the road from Waeiwuang Village until you hit the coast. Expect more lovely pale golden sand, turquoise water and great waves when the swell hits between June and September.

Heading west again, the road passes through the village of Lamboya, with rice fields scalloped into the inland side of the rugged coastal mountains and a Pasola field set on rolling grassland that attracts thousands of people in February. From here there's yet another turn-off south to surf hot spot **Pantai Kerewe** and the glassy seas of **Pantai Tarakaha**. Here you'll find **Magic Mountain** if you know where to look – a coral-draped, underwater volcano that is Sumba's best dive site. Next is **Pantai Watubela** (Patiala Bawa, Waikabubak), another nearby beach with perfect sand and limestone caves. Further along the coast are the idyllic white sands of **Pantai Marosi**, about 35km from Waikabubak.

Getting There & Away

A few buses run between Waikabubak and the many Wanokaka villages, but by far the best way to visit the area is by car or motorbike. Most roads are sealed and traffic is minimal. The hills south of Waikabubak are a taxing yet exhilarating ride for cyclists, but travelling by any vehicle in West Sumba at night is not recommended.

Rua Beach Resort RESORT **$$$**
(☎0811 3865 891; www.ruabeachresort.com; Rua Beach; r from 900,000Rp; ❄) This beach resort has 12 rooms and bungalows, all beautifully furnished with whitewashed wooden furniture, local stone, *alang alang* grass and ikat. It's even feng shui certified. There's a guest-only lounge and restaurant beside three pools, but the upmarket beachfront warung (mains 65,000Rp to 90,000Rp) is open to all. Ask about tours to Kodi, surfing trips and nearby snorkelling.

Ratenggaro

One of Sumba's most attractive and interesting villages, Ratenggaro is known for its prime real-estate position on a grassy bluff above a river with breathtaking views of the sea. Across the river you'll spot Wainyapu and on the way to Ratenggaro, the roadside tombs of Kampung Ranggabaki and Kampung Paronambaroro through the trees.

The remarkable village hasn't had much luck: in 1964 a fire burnt 57 traditional houses to the ground, while another in 2004 flattened 13 more. Government assistance helped to rebuild the 12 houses (and make them a tourist hot spot). They're supported by intricately carved columns, one for each cardinal point. Children are well-trained to welcome visitors and you're likely to see puppies just as adorable as the kids. Bapa Lucas is the man in charge, and he's all too happy to share his knowledge, translator permitting.

Sights

The tall, peaked-roof homes are situated on a grassy lawn on a bluff above the mouth of **Sungai Ratewoya** (Crocodile River), with an absolutely breathtaking view along the coconut palm-fringed shoreline. You can easily pass hours watching the waves of **Miller's Point** (a famous surf break) pound the rocks, with the high roofs of **Wainyapu**, a collection of 12 *kampung* and more than 40 homes, peeking out above the trees across the river. On the near side of the river mouth, Wainyapu's unusual stone tombs occupy a small headland; these are remnants of where the village was formerly located before the ancestors moved further inland to escape exposure to the weather.

Visitors are asked to contribute a donation of 50,000Rp, and you can expect a lack of personal space and some intense staring until you pay up. Unfortunately some of the effects of tourism are becoming apparent – don't be surprised if this is the only place in Sumba where instead of waving, people gesture for cigarettes, or even something more vulgar.

On the way to Ratenggaro, look out for the impressive, roadside tombs of **Kampung Ranggabaki** and the thinner, high-peaked roofs of **Kampung Paronambaroro** through the trees, about 1km inland. The best of these have enormous timber columns intricately carved and cured by an almost perpetually smouldering cooking fire in the centre of the raised bamboo platform. Stone statues decorate the public space. During the day women are often weaving and are happy to chat. During ceremonial times you may see pig jaws and buffalo horns displayed on the front porch.

Getting There & Away

Take the paved road from Bondokodi, or go off-road for about 3km along Pantai Radakapal – a sliver of white sand along a pasture – and you'll get here.

Understand Bali, Lombok & Nusa Tenggara

Bali, Lombok & Nusa Tenggara Today

Can you love a place to death? That's the question being asked more and more on these Indonesian islands. As visitor numbers continue to soar, many are wondering if Bali in particular has finally reached saturation point. Other topics being debated include the effectiveness of the government's response to the devastating 2018 earthquakes on Lombok and the Gilis, and the likelihood of a major volcanic eruption on Bali in the near future.

Best on Film

Act of Killing (director Joshua Oppenheimer, 2013) A searing documentary about the 1965 slaughter of accused communist sympathisers in Indonesia (including tens of thousands on Bali).

Secrets of Desert Point (2017) Surf doc about the pioneers who discovered 'the world's best wave' and kept it a secret for more than a decade.

A Fish Full of Dollars (2016) Documentary exposing the ongoing shark trade at Tanjung Luar.

Best in Print

Island of Bali (Miguel Covarrubias, 1937) The classic work about Bali and its civilisation.

Bali Soul Journals (Clare McAlaney, 2013) Written by a Bali expat and lavishly illustrated, the book looks for Bali's soul in the modern age.

Bali Daze: Freefall Off the Tourist Trail (Cat Wheeler, 2011) Daily life in Ubud makes for an illuminating romp.

Secrets of Bali: Fresh Light on the Morning of the World (Jonathan Copeland and Ni Wayan Murni, 2010) A fun read about Bali and its people.

East of Bali: From Lombok to Timor (Kal Müller; 1991) An illuminating travelogue charting one man's voyage through Nusa Tenggara.

An Unshakable Spirit

Three separate earthquakes rocked Lombok and the Gili Islands in July and August 2018, leaving more than 500 people dead and hundreds of thousands more homeless. The sheer force of the event lifted the island by as much as 25cm and damaged some 80% of all structures in North Lombok.

As with any earthquake, the level of damage depended greatly on the distance from the epicentre and the building materials involved. In general, buildings made in the traditional style with wood or bamboo survived, while those built using unreinforced concrete crumbled to the ground. Towns north of Gunung Rinjani took the hardest hit, followed by the Gili Islands, Senggigi and, to a lesser extent, Mataram. Most places in South Lombok sustained little more than cosmetic damages.

Rebuilding was relatively swift in economically important tourist centres, including the Gili Islands and Senggigi. The trekking hubs on the north side of Gunung Rinjani were far slower to recover, particularly after the most popular routes up Gunung Rinjani were closed for reparations. A new two-day, one-night trek up the volcano from the south side near Aik Berik opened in late 2018 to provide an alternative route that could lure back tourists.

Indonesian President Joko Widodo promised payments of between 10 million and 50 million rupiah to those whose homes were damaged or destroyed. However, as of December 2018, only a fraction of those eligible for the money had actually received it.

Frustrated by the government's response to the disaster, residents from all across the region banded together to raise money for their neighbours, rebuild homes and chart a new path forward.

Successful Environmental Campaigns

In August 2018, environmental activists on Bali rejoiced when the permit for the 30-trillion-rupiah Benoa Bay Reclamation Project expired after PT Tirta Wahana Bali Internasional (TWBI), Indonesian tycoon Tomy Winata's Artha Graha conglomerate property development unit, failed to acquire government approval on environmental impact assessments for the project.

The reclamation project would have potentially devastated the bay and its mangroves, which play an important role in filtering out trash and pollutants from five of the island's rivers.

Though TWBI lost the government's concession, its officials claim that the project's termination sets a bad precedent for Indonesia's investment climate due to uncertainty over acquiring permits. The claim is that development of Benoa Bay is inevitable and that ongoing proposals for expansion of the Benoa Port and Ngurah Rai airport, plus construction of another airport in north Bali, will necessitate coastal reclamation.

There has been a number of other environmental campaigns on the islands in recent years. In the Gilis, dive shops have been actively working to protect the islands' fragile ecosystem, educating visitors about responsible behaviour and placing more than 150 Biorock installations around the islands to stimulate reef restoration. The Gili Eco Trust has also been at the forefront of change, placing 1000 recycling bins on the islands, encouraging restaurants to use bamboo or steel straws, and installing more than 150 mooring buoys to stop coral anchoring.

Halal Tourism on the Rise

Though it's still possible to find alcohol at major tourist centres, mainland Lombok has become increasingly conservative in recent years. The Ministry of Tourism's Halal Tourism Development Acceleration Team, formed in 2016, has worked hard to position the island as Indonesia's premier destination for Muslim families. One of the most visible moves in this direction was the creation of the massive Islamic Center in Mataram in 2016. The stunning green and gold mosque towers over the city, with observation decks and a minaret rising to a height of 114 metres. This is but one of nearly a thousand mosques scattered across the island, and the government is betting that Lombok's devout population can play a starring role in its plan to attract 5 million Muslim visitors by 2020.

Bali's predominantly Hindu population has no cultural taboo on drinking, and so the push for Halal Tourism isn't as strong there. That said, Muslim conservatives in the national legislature would like to see a country-wide ban of alcohol.

AREA: **BALI 5780 SQ KM, LOMBOK 5435 SQ KM**

LANGUAGES SPOKEN: **BAHASA INDONESIA, BALINESE AND SASAK (LOMBOK & THE GILIS)**

POPULATION: **BALI 4.3 MILLION, LOMBOK 3.4 MILLION, GILI ISLANDS 4000**

if Bali were 100 people

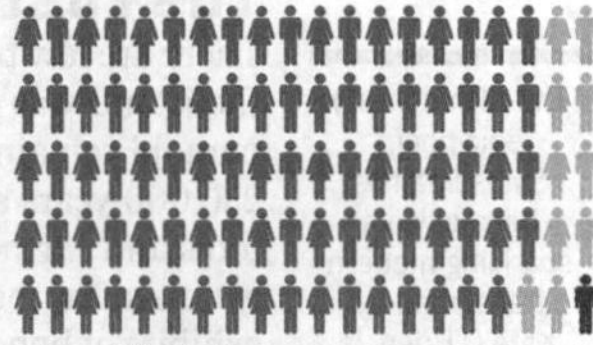

89 would be Balinese
7 would be other Indonesians
3 would be other nationalities
1 would be a tourist

belief systems – Bali

(% of population)

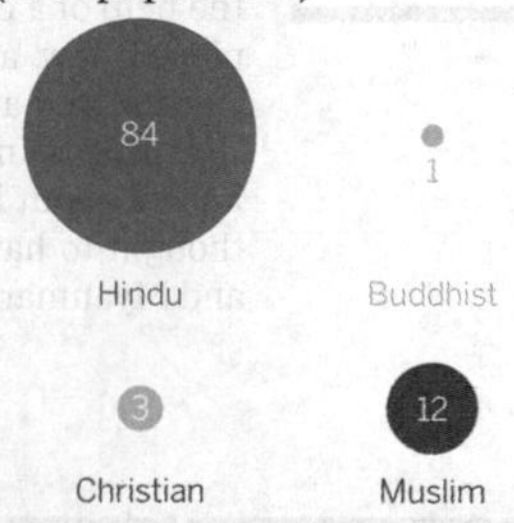

population per sq km

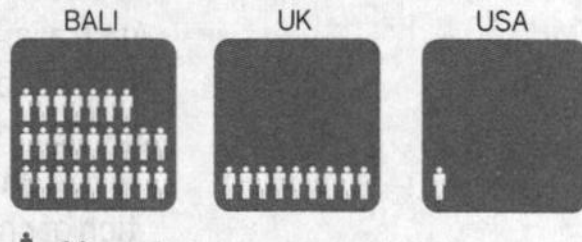

History

When Islam swept through Java in the 12th century, the kings of the Hindu Majapahit kingdom moved to Bali while the priest Nirartha established temples, including Rambut Siwi, Tanah Lot and Ulu Watu. In the 19th century, the Dutch formed alliances with local princes and eventually conquered the island. Westerners began celebrating Balinese arts in the 1930s; surfers arrived in the 1960s. As tourism has boomed, Bali's unique culture has proved to be remarkably resilient.

The First Balinese

There are few traces of Stone Age people in Bali, although it's certain that the island was populated very early in prehistoric times – fossilised humanoid remains from neighbouring Java have been dated to as early as 250,000 years ago. The earliest human artefacts found in Bali are stone tools and earthenware vessels dug up near Cekik in west Bali, which are estimated to be 3000 years old. Discoveries continue, and you can see exhibits of bones that are estimated to be 4000 years old at the Museum Manusia Purbakala Gilimanuk. Artefacts indicate that the Bronze Age began in Bali before 300 BC.

Little is known of Bali during the period when Indian traders brought Hinduism to the Indonesian archipelago, although it is thought it was embraced on the island by the 7th century AD. The earliest written records are inscriptions on a stone pillar near Sanur, dating from around the 9th century; by that time, Bali had already developed many similarities to the island you find today. Rice, for example, was grown with the help of a complex irrigation system, probably similar to the one employed now, and the Balinese had already begun to develop their rich cultural and artistic traditions.

If little is known about the earliest inhabitants of Bali, then even less is known about Lombok until about the 17th century. Early inhabitants are thought to have been Sasaks from a region encompassing today's India and Myanmar (Burma) rather than migrating Balinese.

The 14th-century epic poem *Sutasoma* has been given a sparkling modern translation by Kate O'Brien. It follows the life of a Javanese prince as he becomes king and defeats the ultimate demon using the mystical beliefs that underpin Balinese faith today.

TIMELINE

50 million BC

A permanent gap in the earth's crust forms between Asia and Australia. The Wallace Line keeps Australian species from crossing to Bali until the invention of cheap Bintang specials.

2000 BC

A Balinese man passes away. One of the first known inhabitants of the island, he rests peacefully until his bones are found and placed on display in Gilimanuk.

7th century

Indian traders bring Hinduism to Bali. Little is known about what was traded, although some speculate that they left with lots of wooden carvings of penises and bootleg *lontar* books.

Javanese Influence

Java began to spread its influence into Bali during the reign of King Airlangga (1019–42), or perhaps even earlier. At the age of 16, when his uncle lost the throne, Airlangga fled into the forests of western Java. He gradually gained support, won back the kingdom once ruled by his uncle and went on to become one of Java's greatest kings. Airlangga's mother had moved to Bali and remarried shortly after his birth, so when he gained the throne, there was an immediate link between Java and Bali. It was at this time that the courtly Javanese language known as Kawi came into use among the royalty of Bali; the rock-cut memorials seen at Gunung Kawi, near Tampaksiring, provide a clear architectural link between Bali and 11th-century Java.

After Airlangga's death, Bali remained semi-independent until Kertanegara became king of the Singosari dynasty in Java two centuries later. Kertanegara conquered Bali in 1284, but the period of his greatest power lasted a mere eight years, until he was murdered and his kingdom collapsed. The great Majapahit dynasty was then founded by his son, Wijaya. With Java in turmoil, Bali regained its autonomy, and the Pejeng dynasty rose to great power. Temples and relics of this period can still be found in Pejeng, near Ubud.

Oldest Sites

Goa Gajah (east of Ubud)

Gunung Kawi (north of Ubud)

Tirta Empul (north of Ubud)

Stone Pillar (Sanur)

Exit Pejeng

In 1343, Gajah Mada, the legendary Majapahit prime minister, defeated the Pejeng king Dalem Bedaulu, and Bali was brought back under Javanese influence.

Although Gajah Mada brought much of the Indonesian archipelago under Majapahit control, this was the furthest extent of their power. The 'capital' of the dynasty was moved to Gelgel, in Bali, near modern Semarapura, around the late 14th century; this was the base for the 'king of Bali', the Dewa Agung, for the next two centuries. The Gelgel dynasty in Bali, under Dalem Batur Enggong, extended its power eastwards to the neighbouring island of Lombok and even westwards across the strait to Java.

The collapse of the Majapahit dynasty into weak, decadent petty kingdoms opened the door for the spread of Islam from the trading states of the north coast into the heartland of Java. As the Hindu states fell, many of the intelligentsia fled to Bali. Notable among these was the priest Nirartha, who is credited with introducing many of the complexities of Balinese religion to the island, as well as establishing the chain of 'sea temples', which includes Pura Luhur Ulu Watu and Pura Tanah Lot. Court-supported artisans, artists, dancers, musicians and actors also fled to Bali at this time and the island experienced an explosion of cultural activity that has not stopped to this day.

9th century

A stone carver creates an account in Sanskrit of now long-forgotten military victories. Bali's oldest dated artefact proves early Hindu influence and ends up hidden in Sanur.

1019

Airlangga is born in Bali. He lives in the jungles of Java until he gains political power and becomes king of the two islands, unifying both cultures.

12th century

Ten incredible 7m-high statues are carved from stone cliffs at Gunung Kawi, north of Ubud. Further monuments are created in nearby valleys.

1292

Bali gains complete independence from Java with the death of Kertanagara, a powerful king who had ruled the two islands for eight years. Power shifts frequently between the islands.

ARTISTS IN CHARGE

The lasting wholesale change to Balinese life because of the mass exodus of Hindu elite from Javanese kingdoms in the 16th century cannot be overstated. It's as if all the subscribers to the opera were put in charge of a town – suddenly there would be a lot more opera. The Balinese had already shown a bent for creativity but once the formerly Javanese intelligentsia exerted control, music, dance, art and more flowered like the lotus blossoms in village ponds. High status was accorded to villages with the most creative talent, a tradition that continues today.

This flair for the liberal arts found a perfect match in the Hinduism that took full hold then. The complex and rich legends of good and evil spirits found ample opportunity to flourish, such as the legend of Jero Gede Macaling, the evil spirit of Nusa Penida.

Dutch Dealings

In 1597, Dutch seamen were among the first Europeans to appear in Bali. Setting a tradition that has prevailed to the present day, they fell in love with the island and when Cornelis de Houtman, the ship's captain, prepared to set sail from the island, two of his crew refused to come with him. At that time, Balinese prosperity and artistic activity, at least among the royalty, was at a peak, and the king who befriended de Houtman had 200 wives and a chariot pulled by two white buffalo, not to mention a retinue of 50 dwarfs, whose bodies had been bent to resemble the handle of a kris (traditional dagger). By the early 1600s, the Dutch had established trade treaties with Javanese princes and controlled much of the spice trade, but they were interested in profit, not culture, and barely gave Bali a second glance.

Locks of hair from Nirartha, the great priest who shaped Balinese Hinduism in the 16th century, are said to be buried at Pura Rambut Siwi, an evocative seaside temple in west Bali.

In 1710, the 'capital' of the Gelgel kingdom was shifted to nearby Klungkung (now officially called Semarapura), but local discontent was growing; lesser rulers were breaking away, and the Dutch began to move in, using the old strategy of divide and conquer. In 1846, the Dutch used Balinese salvage claims over shipwrecks as a pretext to land military forces in northern Bali, bringing the kingdoms of Buleleng and Jembrana under their control. Their cause was also aided by the various Balinese princes who had gained ruling interests on Lombok and were distracted from matters at home, unaware that the wily Dutch would use Lombok against Bali.

In 1894, the Dutch, the Balinese and the people of Lombok collided in battles that would set the course of history for the next several decades.

With the north of Bali long under Dutch control and the conquest of Lombok successful, the south was never going to last long. Once again, it was disputes over the ransacking of wrecked ships that gave the Dutch

1343
The legendary Majapahit prime minister, Gajah Mada, brings Bali back under Javanese control. For the next two centuries, the royal court is just south of today's Semarapura (Klungkung).

1520
Java fully converts to Islam, leaving Bali in isolation as a Hindu island. Priests and artists move to Bali, concentrating and strengthening the island's culture against conversion.

1546
The Hindu priest Nirartha arrives in Bali. He transforms religion and builds temples by the dozen including Rambut Siwi, Tanah Lot and Luhur Ulu Watu.

1579
Sir Francis Drake, while looking for spice, is thought to be Bali's first European visitor.

an excuse to move in. In 1904, after a Chinese ship was wrecked off Sanur, Dutch demands that the rajah of Badung pay 3000 silver dollars in damages were rejected, and in 1906 Dutch warships appeared at Sanur.

Bali Loses Lombok

In 1894, the Dutch sent an army to back the Sasak people of eastern Lombok in a rebellion against the Balinese rajah, who controlled Lombok with the support of the western Sasak. The rajah quickly capitulated, but the Balinese crown prince decided to fight on.

The Dutch camp at the Mayura Water Palace was attacked late at night by a combined force of Balinese and western Sasak, forcing the Dutch to take shelter in a temple compound. The Balinese also attacked another Dutch camp further east at Mataram and soon the entire Dutch army on Lombok was forced back to Ampenan where, according to one eyewitness, the soldiers 'were so nervous that they fired madly if so much as a leaf fell off a tree'. These battles resulted in enormous losses of men and arms for the Dutch.

Although the Balinese had won the first battles, they had begun to lose the war. They faced a continuing threat from the eastern Sasak, while the Dutch were soon supported with reinforcements from Java.

The Dutch attacked Mataram a month later, fighting street-to-street against Balinese and western Sasak soldiers and civilians. Rather than surrender, Balinese men, women and children opted for the suicidal *puputan* (a warrior's fight to the death) and were cut down by rifle and artillery fire.

In late November 1894, the Dutch attacked Sasari and, again, a large number of Balinese chose the *puputan*. With the downfall of the dynasty, the local population abandoned its struggle against the Dutch.

Balinese Suicide

In 1906, the Dutch mounted a large invasion of Bali in order to subdue it once and for all. The Dutch forces landed despite Balinese opposition and, four days later, had marched 5km to the outskirts of Denpasar. On 20 September, the Dutch mounted a naval bombardment of Denpasar and began their final assault. The three princes of Badung realised that they were completely outnumbered and outgunned, and that defeat was inevitable. Surrender and exile, however, would have been the worst imaginable outcome, so they decided to take the honourable path of a suicidal *puputan*. First the princes burned their palaces, and then, dressed in their finest jewellery and waving ceremonial golden kris, the rajah led the royalty, priests and courtiers out to face the modern weapons of the Dutch.

A Short History of Bali: Indonesia's Hindu Realm (2004), by Robert Pringle, is a thoughtful analysis of Bali's history from the Bronze Age to the present, with excellent sections on the 2002 bombings and ongoing environmental woes caused by tourism and development.

With staff reviews, hard-to-find titles and stellar recommendations, *the* place for books about Bali is Ganesha Books (www.ganeshabooksbali.com) in Ubud. The website offers a vast selection and the shop does mail orders.

1580

The Portuguese also come looking for spice but, in a foreshadowing of today's surfers, they wipe out on rocks at Ulu Watu and give up.

1597

A Dutch expedition arrives off Kuta. A contemporary describes the skipper, Cornelis de Houtman, as a braggart and a scoundrel.

1795–1815

European wars shift the control of Indonesia from the Dutch to the French to the British and back to the Dutch.

1830

The Balinese slave trade ends. For over two centuries, squabbling Balinese royal houses helped finance their wars by selling some of their most comely subjects.

The Dutch implored the Balinese to surrender rather than make their hopeless stand, but their pleas went unheeded and wave after wave of the Balinese nobility marched forward to their death, or turned their kris on themselves. In all, nearly 4000 Balinese died. The Dutch then marched northwest towards Tabanan and took the rajah of Tabanan prisoner – he also committed suicide rather than face the disgrace of exile.

For much of the 19th century, the Dutch earned enormous amounts of money from the Balinese opium trade. Most of the colonial administrative budget went to promoting the opium industry, which was legal until the 1930s.

The kingdoms of Karangasem (the royal family still lives in the palaces of Amlapura) and Gianyar had already capitulated to the Dutch and were allowed to retain some of their powers, but other kingdoms were defeated and their rulers exiled. Finally, in 1908, the rajah of Semarapura followed the lead of Badung, and once more the Dutch faced a *puputan*. As had happened at Cakranegara on Lombok, the beautiful palace at Semarapura, Taman Kertha Gosa, was largely destroyed.

With this last obstacle disposed of, all of Bali was under Dutch control and became part of the Dutch East Indies. There was little development of an exploitative plantation economy in Bali, and the population noticed little difference between Dutch rule and the rule of the rajahs.

WWII

In 1942 the Japanese landed unopposed in Bali at Sanur (most Indonesians saw the Japanese at first as anticolonial liberators). The Japanese established headquarters in Denpasar and Singaraja, and their occupation became increasingly harsh for the Balinese. When the Japanese left in August 1945 after their defeat in WWII, the island was suffering from extreme poverty. The occupation had fostered several paramilitary, nationalist and anticolonial groups that were ready to fight the returning Dutch.

Bali's airport is named for I Gusti Ngurah Rai, the national hero who died leading the resistance against the Dutch at Marga in 1946. The text of a letter he wrote in response to Dutch demands to surrender ends with 'Freedom or death!'

Independence

In August 1945 just days after the Japanese surrender, Sukarno, the most prominent member of the coterie of nationalist activists, proclaimed the nation's independence. It took four years to convince the Dutch that they were not going to get their great colony back. In a virtual repeat of the *puputan* nearly 50 years earlier, Balinese freedom fighters led by the charismatic I Gusti Ngurah Rai (namesake of the Bali airport) were wiped out by the Dutch in the battle of Marga in west Bali on 20 November 1946. The Dutch finally recognised Indonesia's independence in 1949 – though Indonesians celebrate 17 August 1945 as their Independence Day.

At first, Bali, Lombok and the rest of Indonesia's eastern islands were grouped together in the unwieldy province of Nusa Tenggara. In 1958 the central government recognised this folly and created three new governmental regions from the one, with Bali getting its own and Lombok becoming part of Nusa Tenggara Barat.

1856

Mads Lange, a Danish trader, dies mysteriously in Kuta after earning a fortune selling goods to ships anchored off the beach. His death is blamed on poisoning by jealous rivals.

1891–94

Years of failed Sasak rebellions in eastern Lombok finally take hold after a palace burning. With Dutch assistance the Balinese rulers are chased from the islands within three years.

1908

The Balinese royalty commit suicide. Wearing their best dress and armed with 'show' daggers, they march into Dutch gunfire in a suicidal *puputan* (warrior's fight to the death) in Klungkung.

1912

A German, Gregor Krause, photographs beautiful Balinese women topless. WWI intervenes, but in 1920 an 'art book' of photos appears and Dutch steamers docking in Singaraja now bring tourists.

THE TOURIST CLASS

Beginning in the 1920s, the Dutch government realised that Bali's unique culture could be marketed internationally to the growing tourism industry. Relying heavily on images that emphasised the topless habits of Bali's women, Dutch marketing drew wealthy Western adventurers, who landed in the north at today's Singaraja and were whisked about the island on rigid three-day itineraries that featured canned cultural shows at a government-run tourist hotel in Denpasar. Accounts from the time are ripe with imagery of supposedly culture-seeking Europeans who really just wanted to see a boob or two. Such desires were often thwarted by Balinese women who covered up when they heard the Dutch jalopies approaching.

But some intrepid travellers arrived independently, often at the behest of members of the small colony of Western artists, such as Walter Spies in Ubud. Two of these visitors were Robert Koke and Louise Garret, an American couple who had worked in Hollywood before landing in Bali in 1936 as part of a global adventure. Horrified at the stuffy strictures imposed by the Dutch tourism authorities, the pair built a couple of bungalows out of palm leaves and other local materials on the otherwise deserted beach at Kuta, which at that point was home to only a few impoverished fishing families.

Word soon spread, and the Kokes were booked solid. Guests came for days, stayed for weeks and told their friends. At first, the Dutch dismissed the Kokes' Kuta Beach Hotel as 'dirty native huts', but soon realised that increased numbers of tourists were good for everyone. Other Westerners built their own thatched hotels, complete with the bungalows that were to become a Balinese cliché in the decades ahead.

WWII wiped out both tourism and the hotels (the Kokes barely escaped ahead of the Japanese), but once people began travelling again after the war, Bali's inherent appeal made its popularity a foregone conclusion.

In 1987, Louise Koke's long-forgotten story of the Kuta Beach Hotel was published as *Our Hotel in Bali*, illustrated with her incisive sketches and her husband's photographs.

Coup & Backlash

Independence was not an easy path for Indonesia to follow. When Sukarno assumed more direct control in 1959 after several violent rebellions, he proved to be as inept as a peacetime administrator as he was inspirational as a revolutionary leader. In the early 1960s, as Sukarno faltered, the army, communists and other groups struggled for supremacy. On 30 September 1965, an attempted coup – blamed on the Partai Komunis Indonesia (PKI; Communist Party) – led to Sukarno's downfall. General Suharto emerged as the leading figure in the armed forces, displaying great military and political skill in suppressing the coup. The PKI was outlawed and a wave of anticommunist massacres followed throughout Indonesia.

1925

The greatest modern Balinese dancer, Mario, first performs the Kebyar Duduk, his enduring creation. From a stooped position, he moves as if in a trance to the haunting melody of gamelan.

1936

Americans Robert and Louise Koke build a hotel of thatched bungalows on then-deserted Kuta Beach. Gone is stuffy, starched tourism; replacing it is fun in the sun followed by a drink.

1945

Following the Japanese surrender at the end of WWII, nationalists, Sukarno among them, proclaim independence from the Netherlands. It sets off an intense period of revolution.

1946

Freedom fighter Ngurah Rai dies with the rest of his men at Marga. But this *puputan* slays the Dutch colonial spirit, and soon Indonesia is independent.

In Bali, the events had an added local significance as the main national political organisations, the Partai Nasional Indonesia (PNI; Nationalist Party) and the PKI, crystallised existing differences between traditionalists, who wanted to maintain the old caste system, and radicals, who saw the caste system as repressive and were urging land reform. After the failed coup, religious traditionalists in Bali led the witch-hunt for the 'godless communists'. Eventually, the military stepped in to control the anticommunist purge, but no one in Bali was untouched by the killings, estimated at between 50,000 and 100,000 out of a population of about two million, a percentage many times higher than on Java. Even as late as 2017, mass graves were still being discovered.

Kuta was never a part of mainstream Bali. During royal times, the region was a place of exile for malcontents and troublemakers. It was too arid for rice fields, the fishing was barely sustainable and the shore was covered with kilometres of useless sand...

The 1963 Eruption

Amid the political turmoil, the most disastrous volcanic eruption in Bali in 100 years occurred in 1963. Gunung Agung blew its top in no uncertain manner, at a time of considerable prophetic and political importance.

Eka Dasa Rudra, the greatest of all Balinese sacrifices and an event that takes place only every 100 years on the Balinese calendar, was to culminate on 8 March 1963. It had been well over 100 Balinese years since the last Eka Dasa Rudra, but there was dispute among the priests as to the correct and most favourable date.

Naturally, Pura Besakih was a focal point for the festival, but Gunung Agung was acting strangely as final preparations were made in late February. Despite some qualms, political pressures forced the ceremonies forward, even as ominous rumblings continued.

On 17 March, Gunung Agung exploded. The catastrophic eruption killed more than 1000 people (some estimate 2000) and destroyed entire villages – 100,000 people lost their homes. Streams of lava and hot volcanic mud poured right down to the sea at several places, completely covering roads and isolating the eastern end of Bali for some time. You can still see some lava flows from the main road near Tulamben.

A woman of many aliases, K'tut Tantri breezed into Bali from Hollywood in 1932. After the war, she joined the Indonesian Republicans in their postwar struggle against the Dutch. As Surabaya Sue, she broadcast from Surabaya in support of their cause. Her book, *Revolt in Paradise*, was published in 1960.

Suharto Comes & Goes

Following the failed coup in 1965 and its aftermath, Suharto established himself as president and took control of the government. Under his 'New Order' government, Indonesia looked to the West for its foreign and economic policies.

Suharto ensured that his political party, Golkar, with strong support from the army, became the dominant political force. Other political parties were banned or crippled. Regular elections maintained the appearance of a national democracy, but until 1999, Golkar won every election hands down. This period was also marked by great economic development in Bali and later on Lombok as social stability and maintenance of

1949

South Pacific, the musical, opens on Broadway and the song 'Bali Hai' fixes a tropical cliché of Bali in the minds of millions (even though it's based on Fiji).

1960s

The lengthening of the airport runway for jets, reasonably affordable tickets and the opening of the Bali Beach Hotel in Sanur mark the start of mass tourism.

1963

The sacred volcano Gunung Agung erupts, destroying a fair bit of east Bali, killing a thousand or more, leaving 100,000 homeless and sending out large lava flows.

1965

Indonesia's long-running rivalry between communists and conservatives erupts after a supposed coup attempt by the former. The latter triumph and in the ensuing purges, tens of thousands are killed in Bali.

a favourable investment climate took precedence over democracy. Huge resorts – often with investors in government – appeared in Sanur, Kuta and Nusa Dua during this time.

In early 1997, the good times ended as Southeast Asia suffered a severe economic crisis, and within the year, the Indonesian currency (the rupiah) had all but collapsed and the economy was on the brink of bankruptcy.

Unable to cope with the escalating crisis, Suharto resigned in 1998, after 32 years in power. His protégé, Dr Bacharuddin Jusuf Habibie, became president. Though initially dismissed as a Suharto crony, he made the first notable steps towards opening the door to real democracy, such as freeing the press from government supervision.

Bali's history is reduced to miniature dramas with stilted dolls at the delightfully unhip Bajra Sandhi Monument in Denpasar. Meaning 'Struggle of the People', the museum brings cartoon-like, 3D veracity to important moments in the island's history.

Peace Shattered & Democracy Dawns

In 1999, Indonesia's parliament met to elect a new president. The front-runner was Megawati Sukarnoputri, who was enormously popular in Bali, partly because of family connections (her paternal grandmother

THE BALI BOMBINGS

On Saturday 12 October 2002, two bombs exploded on Kuta's bustling Jl Legian. The first blew out the front of Paddy's Bar. A few seconds later, a far more powerful bomb obliterated the Sari Club.

The number of dead, including those unaccounted for, exceeded 200, although the exact number will probably never be known. Many injured Balinese made their way back to their villages, where, for lack of adequate medical treatment, they died.

Indonesian authorities eventually laid the blame for the blasts on Jemaah Islamiah, an Islamic terrorist group. Dozens were arrested and many were sentenced to jail, including three who received the death penalty. But most received relatively light terms, including Abu Bakar Ba'asyir, a radical cleric who many thought was behind the explosions. His convictions on charges relating to the bombings were overturned by the Indonesian supreme court in 2006, enraging many in Bali and Australia. (In 2011 he was sent back to prison for 15 years after a new conviction on terrorism charges.)

On 1 October 2005, three suicide bombers blew themselves up: one in a restaurant on Kuta Square and two more at beachfront cafes in Jimbaran. It was again the work of Jemaah Islamiah and, although documents found later stated that the attacks were targeted at tourists, 15 of the 20 who died were Balinese and Javanese employees of the places bombed.

Umar Patek was convicted in 2012 of helping to assemble the 2002 Bali bombs and sentenced to 20 years in jail. But threats continue: in 2012 police on Bali shot dead five suspected terrorists and there have been occasional arrests of suspected terrorists through 2018.

1970

A girl ekes out a living selling candy in Kuta. Surfers offer advice, she posts a menu, then she builds a hut and calls it Made's Warung. She prospers.

1972

Filmmaker Alby Falzon brings a band of Australians to Bali for his surfing documentary *Morning on Earth*, which proves seminal for a generation of Australians who head to Kuta.

1979

Australian Kim Bradley, impressed by the gnarly surfing style of locals, encourages them to start a club. Sixty do just that (good on an island where people fear the water).

1998

Suharto, who always had close ties to Bali, resigns as president after 32 years. His family retains control of several Bali resorts, including the Pecatu Indah resort.

was Balinese) and partly because her party was essentially secular (the mostly Hindu Balinese are very concerned about any growth in Muslim fundamentalism). However, Abdurrahman Wahid, the moderate, intellectual head of Indonesia's largest Muslim organisation, emerged as president.

Hotel Kerobokan (2009) is a lurid book detailing conditions inside Bali's notorious Kerobokan jail. Journalist Kathryn Bonella, who has written about noted former inmate Schapelle Corby, details the goings on behind the walls. The jail was nearly destroyed during riots in 2012.

On Lombok, religious and political tensions spilled over in early 2000 when a sudden wave of attacks starting in Mataram burned Chinese and Christian businesses and homes across the island. The impact on tourism was immediate and severe, with some visitors also shunning Bali.

After 21 months of growing ethnic, religious and regional conflicts, parliament had enough ammunition to recall Wahid's mandate and hand the presidency to Megawati in 2001. In 2004 she was replaced by Indonesia's first democratically elected president, Susilo Bambang Yudhoyono (SBY). He had gained international recognition after he led the hunt for the 2002 Bali bombers.

The reign of SBY proved very successful. Indonesia's economy expanded at a rapid pace and he was easily re-elected in 2009 for another five-year term during which the nation (and Bali in particular) enjoyed rising fortunes and political calm. In 2014, Joko Widodo, the governor of Jakarta, won the presidency. Seen as a man of the people, he enjoyed widespread support. Although this included Bali – where he won the popular vote – there was some concern on the island that Jokowi (as he's known) was the first Indonesian leader in several generations to have no blood and/or marriage ties to Bali.

In recent years, visitors have been big news on Bali. As fears sparked by the bombings faded, international arrivals have increased by 10% to 15% a year on average. Where a short time ago two million visitors was a big deal, now that number hovers well above five million. Tourism is literally taking over many aspects of Balinese life, especially economic ones.

2000

Indonesian rioting spreads to Lombok and hundreds of Chinese, Christian and Balinese homes and businesses are looted and burnt, particularly after a Muslim-sponsored rally to decry violence turns ugly.

2002

Bombs in Kuta kill more than 200, many at the Sari Club. Bali's economy is crushed as tourists stay away and there is economic devastation across the island.

2005

Three suicide bombers blow themselves up in Kuta and Jimbaran, killing 20 mostly Balinese and Javanese.

2017

Bali tops five-and-a-half million foreign tourists for the year, a new record that continues many years of growth that averages more than 15% a year.

Local Life & Religion

The peoples of this region have deep cultural heritage and belief systems. All of the islands have distinct traditions, dress, food and architecture, and have fought hard to keep them. In Bali in particular, religion plays a role in so much of what makes the island appealing to visitors: the art, the music, the offerings, the architecture, the temples and more.

Bali

Ask any traveller what they love about Bali and, most times, 'the people' will top their list. Since the 1920s, when the Dutch used images of bare-breasted Balinese women to lure tourists, Bali has embodied the mystique and glamour of an exotic paradise.

For all the romanticism, there is a harsher reality. For many Balinese, life remains a near hand-to-mouth existence, even as the island prospers due to tourism and the middle class grows. And the idea of culture can sometimes seem misplaced as overzealous touts test your patience in their efforts to make a living.

But there's also some truth to this idea of paradise. There is no other place in the world like Bali, not even in Indonesia. Being the only surviving Hindu island in the country with the largest Muslim population in the world, Bali's distinctive culture is worn like a badge of honour by a fiercely proud people. After all, it's only in the last century that 4000 Balinese royalty, dressed in their finest, walked into the gunfire of the Dutch army rather than surrender and become colonial subjects.

True, development has changed the landscape and prompted endless debate about the displacement of an agricultural society by a tourism-services industry. And the upmarket spas, clubs, boutiques and restaurants in Seminyak and Kerobokan might have you mistaking hedonism, not Hinduism, for the local religion. But scratch the surface and you'll find that Bali's soul remains unchanged.

The island's creative heritage is everywhere you look, and the harmonious dedication to religion permeates every aspect of society, underpinning the strong sense of community. There are temples in every house, office and village, on mountains and beaches, in rice fields, trees, caves, cemeteries, lakes and rivers. Yet religious activity is not limited to places of worship. It can occur anywhere, sometimes smack-bang in the middle of peak-hour traffic.

A great resource on Balinese culture and life is www.murnis.com, the website for one of Ubud's original restaurants. Find explanations on everything from kids' names to what one wears to a ceremony, to how garments are woven; see the 'Culture' section.

Balinese Tolerance

The Balinese are famously tolerant of and hospitable towards other cultures, though they rarely travel themselves, such is the importance of their village and family ties. The financial cost is also prohibitive for many Balinese families. If anything, the Balinese are bemused by all the attention, which reinforces their pride; the general sense is, whatever we're doing, it must be right to entice millions of people to leave their homes for ours.

The Balinese are unfailingly friendly, love a chat and can get quite personal. English is widely spoken but they love to hear tourists attempt Bahasa Indonesia or, better still, throw in a Balinese phrase such as *'sing ken ken'* (no worries); do this and you'll quickly make some friends. They have a fantastic sense of humour and their easygoing nature is hard to ruffle. They generally find displays of temper distasteful and laugh at 'emotional' foreigners who are quick to anger.

Lombok & the Gilis

While Lombok's culture and language are often likened to those of Bali, this does justice to neither island. True, Lombok's language, animist rituals and music and dance are reminiscent of the Hindu and Buddhist kingdoms that once ruled Indonesia, and of its time under Balinese rule in the 18th century. But the majority of Lombok's Sasak people are Muslim – they have very distinct traditions, dress, food and architecture, and have fought hard to keep them. While the Sasak peasants in western Lombok lived in relative harmony under Balinese feudal control, the

WHAT'S IN A NAME?

Far from being straightforward, Balinese names are as fluid as the tides. Everyone has a traditional name, but their other names often reflect events in each individual's life. They also help distinguish between people of the same name, which is perhaps nowhere more necessary than in Bali.

Traditional naming customs seem straightforward, with a predictable gender non-specific pattern to names. The order of names, with variations for regions and caste, is:

First-born Wayan (Gede, Putu)

Second-born Made (Kadek, Nengah, Ngurah)

Third-born Nyoman (Komang)

Fourth-born Ketut (or just Tut, as in 'toot')

Subsequent children reuse the same set, but as many families now settle for just two children, you'll meet many Wayans and Mades.

Castes also play an important role in naming and have naming conventions that clearly denote status when added to the birth order name. Bali's system is much less complicated than India's.

Sudra Some 90% of Balinese are part of this, the peasant caste. Names are preceded by the title 'I' for a boy and 'Ni' for a girl.

Wesya The caste of bureaucrats and merchants. Gusti Bagus (male) and Gusti Ayu (female).

Ksatria A top caste, denoting royalty or warriors. I Gusti Ngurah (male) and I Gusti Ayu (female), with additional titles including Anak Agung and Dewa.

Brahman The top of the heap: teachers and priests. Ida Bagus (male) and Ida Ayu (female).

Traditional names are followed by another given name – this is where parents can get creative. Some names reflect hopes for their child, as in I Nyoman Darma Putra, who's supposed to be 'dutiful' or 'good' *(dharma)*. Others reflect modern influences, such as I Wayan Radio who was born in the 1970s, and Ni Made Atom who said her parents just liked the sound of this scientific term that also had a bomb named after it.

Many are given nicknames that reflect their appearance. For example, Nyoman Darma is often called Nyoman Kopi (coffee) for the darkness of his skin compared with that of his siblings. I Wayan Rama, named after the Ramayana epic, is called Wayan Gemuk (fat) to differentiate his physique from his slighter friend Wayan Kecil (small).

aristocracy in the east remained hostile and led the rebellion with the Dutch that finally ousted their Balinese lords in the late 1800s. To this day, the Sasaks take great joy in competing in heroic trials of strength, such as the stick-fighting matches held every August near Tetebatu.

Lombok remains poorer and less developed than Bali, and is generally more conservative. Its Sasak culture is not as prominently displayed as Bali's Hinduism, but you'll see evidence of it, such as in the proud mosques that stand in every town.

On the Gilis, the local people practise a very moderate form of Islam.

Flores

Flores' 1.9 million people are divided into five main linguistic and cultural groups. From west to east, these are the Manggarai (main town Ruteng), the Ngada (Bajawa), the closely related Ende and Lio people (Ende), the Sikkanese (Maumere) and the Lamaholot (Larantuka). In remote areas, some older people don't speak a word of Bahasa Indonesia, and their parents grew up in purely animist societies.

Animist rituals are still used for births, marriages and deaths, and to mark important points in the agricultural calendar. Even educated, English-speaking Florinese participate in the animal sacrifice to the ancestors when rice is planted and on special occasions.

Balinese culture keeps intimacy behind doors. Holding hands is not customary for couples in Bali, and is generally reserved for small children; however, linking arms for adults is the norm.

Family Ties

Through their family temple, Balinese have an intense spiritual connection to their home. As many as five generations share a Balinese home, in-laws and all. Grandparents, cousins, aunties, uncles and various distant relatives all live together. When the sons marry, they don't move out – their wives move in. Similarly, when daughters marry, they live with their in-laws, assuming household and child-bearing duties. Because of this, Balinese consider a son more valuable than a daughter. Not only will his family look after them in their old age, but he will inherit the home and perform the necessary rites after they die to free their souls for reincarnation, so they do not become wandering ghosts.

A Woman's Work is Work

Men play a big role in village affairs and helping to care for children, and only men plant and tend to the rice fields. But women are the real workhorses in Bali, doing everything from manual labour jobs (you'll see them carrying baskets of wet cement or bricks on their heads) to running market stalls and almost every job in tourism. In fact, their traditional role of caring for people and preparing food means that women have established many successful shops and cafes.

In between all of these tasks, women also prepare daily offerings for the family temple and house, and often extra offerings for upcoming ceremonies; their hands are never idle. You can observe all of this and more when you stay at a classic Balinese homestay, where your room is in the family compound and everyday life goes on about you. Ubud has many homestays.

Religion

Hinduism

Bali's official religion is Hindu, but it's far too animistic to be considered in the same vein as Indian Hinduism. The Balinese worship the trinity of Brahma, Shiva and Vishnu, three aspects of the one (invisible) god, Sanghyang Widi, as well as the *dewa* (ancestral gods) and village founders. They also worship gods of earth, fire, water and mountains; gods of fertility, rice, technology and books; and demons who inhabit the world

RELIGIOUS ETIQUETTE

- Cover shoulders and knees if visiting a temple or mosque; in Bali, a *selandang* (traditional scarf) or sash plus a sarong is usually provided for a small donation or as part of the entrance fee.
- Women are asked not to enter temples if they're menstruating, pregnant or have recently given birth. At these times women are thought to be *sebel* (ritually unclean).
- Don't put yourself higher than a priest, particularly at festivals (eg by scaling a wall to take photos).
- Take off your shoes before entering a mosque.

underneath the ocean. They share the Indian belief in karma and reincarnation, but much less emphasis is attached to other Indian customs. There is no 'untouchable' caste, arranged marriages are very rare, and there are no child marriages.

Bali's unusual version of Hinduism was formed after the great Majapahit Hindu kingdom that once ruled Indonesia evacuated to Bali as Islam spread across the archipelago. While the Bali Aga (the 'original' Balinese) retreated to the hills in places such as east Bali's Tenganan to escape this new influence, the rest of the population simply adapted it for themselves, overlaying the Majapahit faith on their animist beliefs incorporated with Buddhist influences. A Balinese Hindu community can be found in west Lombok, a legacy of Bali's domination of its neighbour in the 19th century.

The ancient Hindu swastika seen all over Bali is a symbol of harmony with the universe. The German Nazis used a version where the arms were always bent in a clockwise direction.

The most sacred site on the island is Gunung Agung, home to Pura Besakih and frequent ceremonies involving anywhere from hundreds to sometimes thousands of people. Smaller ceremonies are held across the island every day to appease the gods, placate the demons and ensure balance between *dharma* (good) and *adharma* (evil) forces.

The significant Balinese population on Lombok means you can often glimpse a Hindu ceremony while there; the minority Wektu Telu, Chinese and Buginese communities add to the diversity.

Islam

Islam is a minority religion in Bali; most followers are Javanese immigrants, Sasak people from Lombok or descendants of seafaring people from Sulawesi.

Most muslims on Bali practise a moderate version of Islam, as in many other parts of Indonesia. They generally follow the Five Pillars of Islam; the pillars decree that there is no god but Allah and Muhammad is His prophet; that believers should pray five times a day, give alms to the poor, fast during the month of Ramadan and make the pilgrimage to Mecca at least once in their lifetime. However, in contrast to other Islamic countries, Muslim women are not segregated, head coverings are not compulsory (although they are becoming more common) and polygamy is rare. A stricter version of Islam is beginning to spread from Lombok, which in turn is being influenced by ultra-conservative Sumbawa.

On Lombok, *adat* (tradition, customs and manners) underpins all aspects of daily life, especially regarding courtship, marriage and circumcision. Friday afternoon is the official time for worship, and government offices and many businesses close. Many, but not all, women wear headscarves, very few wear the veil, and large numbers work in tourism. Middle-class Muslim girls are often able to choose their own partners. Circumcision of Sasak boys normally occurs between the ages of six and 11 and calls for much celebration following a parade through their village.

Wektu Telu

Believed to have originated in Bayan, north Lombok, Wektu Telu is an indigenous religion unique to Lombok. Now followed by a minority of Sasaks, it was the majority religion in northern Lombok until as recently as 1965, when Indonesia's incoming president Suharto decreed that all Indonesians must follow an official religion. Indigenous beliefs such as Wektu Telu were not recognised. Many followers thus state their official religion as Muslim, while practising Wektu traditions and rituals. Bayan remains a stronghold of Wektu Telu; you can spot believers by their *sapu puteq* (white headbands) and white flowing robes.

Wektu means 'result' in Sasak and *telu* means 'three', and it probably signifies the complex mix of Balinese Hinduism, Islam and animism that the religion is. The tenet is that all important aspects of life are underpinned by a trinity. Like orthodox Muslims, they believe in Allah and that Muhammad is Allah's prophet; however, they pray only three times a day and honour just three days of fasting for Ramadan. Followers of Wektu Telu bury their dead with their heads facing Mecca and all public buildings have a prayer corner facing Mecca, but they do not make pilgrimages there. Similar to Balinese Hinduism, they believe the spiritual world is firmly linked to the natural; Gunung Rinjani is the most revered site.

Huge decorated *penjor* (bamboo poles) appear in front of homes and line streets for ceremonies such as Galungan. Designs are as diverse as the artists who create them, but always feature the signature drooping top – in honour of the Barong's tail and the shape of Gunung Agung. The decorated tips, *sampian*, are exquisite.

Marapu

In Sumbawa, the basis of traditional religion is *marapu,* a collective term for all of Sumba's spiritual forces including gods, spirits and ancestors. At death the deceased join the invisible world, from where they can influence the world of the living. *Marapu mameti* is the collective name for all dead people. The living can appeal to them for help, especially their own relatives, though the dead can be harmful if irritated. The *marapu maluri* are the original people placed on earth by god and their power is concentrated in certain places or objects, which are often kept safe in the family's thatched loft.

Christianity

On Flores, around 85% of people are Catholic, but in rural areas Christianity is welded onto *adat* (traditional laws and regulations).

Balinese Ceremonies & Rituals

Between the family temple, village temple and district temple, a Balinese person takes part in dozens of ceremonies every year, on top of their daily rituals. Most employers allow staff to return to their villages for

DOS & DON'TS

➡ You'll see shorts and short skirts everywhere on locals but overly revealing clothing is still frowned upon, as is wandering down the street shirtless quaffing a beer.

➡ Many foreign women go topless on beaches, offending locals who are embarrassed by foreigners' gratuitous nudity.

➡ Don't touch anyone on the head; in Bali, it's regarded as the abode of the soul and is therefore sacred.

➡ Do pass things with your right hand. Even better, use both hands. Just don't use only your left hand, as it's considered unclean.

➡ Beware of talking with hands on hips – a sign of contempt, anger or aggression (as displayed in traditional dance and opera).

➡ Beckon someone with the hand extended and using a downward waving motion. The Western method of beckoning is considered very rude.

Balinese wedding ceremony

these obligations, which consume a vast chunk of income and time (and although many bosses moan about this, they have little choice unless they wish for a staff revolt). For tourists, this means there are ample opportunities to witness ceremonial traditions.

Ceremonies are the unifying centre of a Balinese person's life and a source of much entertainment, socialisation and festivity. Each ceremony is carried out on an auspicious date determined by a priest and often involves banquets, dance, drama and musical performances to entice the gods to continue their protection against evil forces. The most important ceremonies are Nyepi, which includes a rare day of complete rest, and Galungan, a 10-day reunion with ancestral spirits to celebrate the victory of good over evil.

The Ubud tourist office (www.fabulousubud.com) is an excellent source for news of cremations and other Balinese ceremonies that occur at erratic intervals. Another good source is www.ubudnowandthen.com.

Under their karmic beliefs, the Balinese hold themselves responsible for any misfortune, which is attributed to an overload of *adharma* (evil). This calls for a *ngulapin* (cleansing) ritual to seek forgiveness and recover spiritual protection. A *ngulapin* requires an animal sacrifice and often involves a cockfight, satisfying the demons' thirst for blood.

Ceremonies are also held to overcome black magic and to cleanse a *sebel* (ritually unclean) spirit after childbirth or bereavement, or during menstruation or illness.

On top of all these ceremonies, there are 13 major rites of passage throughout every person's life. The most extravagant and expensive is the last – cremation.

Birth & Childhood

The Balinese believe babies are the reincarnation of ancestors, and they honour them as such. Offerings are made during pregnancy to ensure the minideity's well-being, and after birth, the placenta, umbilical cord, blood and afterbirth water – representing the child's four 'spirit' guardian brothers – are buried in the family compound.

Newborns are literally carried everywhere for the first three months, as they're not allowed to touch the 'impure' ground until after a purification ceremony. At 210 days (the first Balinese year), the baby is blessed in the ancestral temple and there is a huge feast. Later in life, birthdays lose their significance and many Balinese couldn't tell you their age.

A rite of passage to adulthood – and a prerequisite to marriage – is the tooth-filing ceremony at around 16 to 18 years. This is when a priest files a small part of the upper canines and upper incisors to flatten the teeth. Pointy fangs are, after all, distinguishing features of dogs and demons. Balinese claim the procedure doesn't hurt, likening the sensation to eating very cold ice: it's slightly uncomfortable, but not painful. Most tooth-filings happen in July and August.

Another important occasion for girls is their first menstrual period, which calls for a purification ceremony.

The Balinese tooth-filing ceremony closes with the recipient being given a delicious *jamu* (herbal tonic), made from freshly pressed turmeric, betel-leaf juice, lime juice and honey.

Marriage

Marriage defines a person's social status in Bali, making men automatic members of the *banjar* (local neighbourhood organisation). Balinese believe that when they come of age, it's their duty to marry and have children, including at least one son. Divorce is rare, as a divorced woman is cut off from her children.

The respectable way to marry, known as *mapadik*, is when the man's family visits the woman's family and proposes. But the Balinese like their fun and some prefer marriage by *ngrorod* (elopement or 'kidnapping'). After the couple returns to their village, the marriage is officially recognised and everybody has a grand celebration.

Marriage ceremonies include elaborate symbolism drawn from the island's rice-growing culture. The groom will carry food on his shoulders like a farmer while the bride will pretend to peddle produce, thus showing the couple's economic independence. Other actions need little explanation: the male digs a hole and the female places a seed inside for fertility, which comes after the male unsheathes his kris (knife) and pierces the female's unblemished woven mat of coconut leaves.

Death & Cremation

The body is considered little more than a shell for the soul, and upon death it is cremated in an elaborate ceremony befitting the ancestral spirit. It usually involves the whole community, and for important people, such as royalty, it can be a spectacular event involving thousands of people.

Because of the burdensome cost of even a modest cremation (estimated at around 7,000,000Rp), as well as the need to wait for an auspicious date, the deceased is often buried, sometimes for years, and disinterred for a mass cremation.

The body is carried in a tall, incredibly artistic, multitiered pyre on the shoulders of a group of men. The tower's size depends on the deceased's importance. A rajah's or high priest's funeral may require hundreds of men to tote the 11-tiered structure.

Along the way, the group sets out to confuse the corpse so it cannot find its way back home; the corpse is considered an unclean link to the material world, and the soul must be liberated for its evolution to a higher state. The men shake the tower, run it around in circles, simulate war battles, hurl water at it and generally rough-handle it, making the trip anything but a stately funeral crawl.

At the cremation ground, the body is transferred to a funeral sarcophagus reflecting the deceased's caste. Finally, it all goes up in flames

Black magic is still a potent force and spiritual healers known as *balian* are consulted in times of illness and strife. There are plenty of stories floating around about the power of this magic. Disputes between relatives or neighbours are often blamed on curses, as are tragic deaths.

BALI PLAYS DEAD

Nyepi

This is Bali's biggest purification festival, designed to clean out all the bad spirits and begin the year anew. It falls around March or April according to the Hindu *caka* calendar, a lunar cycle similar to the Western calendar in terms of the length of the year. Starting at sunrise, the whole island literally shuts down for 24 hours. No planes may land or take off, no vehicles of any description may be operated, and no power sources may be used. Everyone, including tourists, must stay off the streets. The cultural reasoning behind Nyepi is to fool evil spirits into thinking Bali has been abandoned so they will go elsewhere.

For the Balinese, it's a day for meditation and introspection. For foreigners, the rules are more relaxed, so long as you respect the 'Day of Silence' by not leaving your residence or hotel. If you do sneak out, you will quickly be escorted back to your hotel by a stern *pecalang* (village police officer).

As daunting as it sounds, Nyepi is actually a fantastic time to be in Bali. Firstly, there's the inspired concept of being forced to do nothing. Catch up on some sleep, or if you must, read, sunbathe, write postcards, play board games…just don't do anything to tempt the demons! Secondly, there are colourful festivals the night before Nyepi.

Ogoh-Ogoh

In the weeks prior to Nyepi, huge and elaborate papier-mâché monsters called *ogoh-ogoh* are built in villages across the island. Involving everybody in the community, construction sites buzz with fevered activity around the clock. If you see a site where *ogoh-ogoh* are being constructed, there'll be a sign-up sheet for financial support. Contribute, say, 50,000Rp and you'll be a fully fledged sponsor and receive much street cred.

On Nyepi eve, large ceremonies all over Bali lure out the demons. Their rendezvous point is believed to be the main crossroads of each village, and this is where the priests perform exorcisms. Then the whole island erupts in mock 'anarchy', with people banging on *kulkuls* (hollow tree-trunk drums), drums and tins, letting off firecrackers and yelling *'megedi megedi!'* (get out!) to expel the demons. The truly grand finale is when the *ogoh-ogoh* all go up in flames. Any demons that survive this wild partying are believed to evacuate the village when confronted with the boring silence on the morrow.

Christians find unique parallels to Easter in all this, especially Ash Wednesday and Shrove Tuesday, with its wild Mardi Gras–like celebrations the world over.

In coming years, dates for Nyepi are 7 March 2019, 25 March 2020, and 14 March 2021.

and the ashes are scattered in the ocean. The soul is then free to ascend to heaven and wait for the next incarnation, usually in the form of a grandchild.

In classic Balinese fashion, respectful visitors are welcome at cremations. It's always worth asking around or at your hotel to see if anyone knows of one going on. The Ubud tourist office is a good source too.

Although illegal because it involves gambling, cockfighting is the top sport on Bali. It's easy to spot one when you know the main clue: lots of cars and motorbikes parked by the side of the road but no real sign of people. Or, just go to Pantai Masceti in east Bali where there is a huge cockfighting arena.

Offerings

No matter where you stay, you'll witness women making daily offerings around their family temple and home, and in hotels, shops and other public places. You're also sure to see vibrant ceremonies, where whole villages turn out in ceremonial dress, and police close the roads for a spectacular procession that can stretch for hundreds of metres. Men play the gamelan (traditional Balinese and Javanese orchestral music) while women elegantly balance magnificent tall offerings of fruit and cakes on their heads.

There's nothing manufactured about what you see. Dance and musical performances at hotels are among the few events 'staged' for tourists, but they do actually mirror the way Balinese traditionally welcome visitors, whom they refer to as *tamu* (guests). Otherwise, it's just the Balinese going about their daily life as they would without spectators.

Village Life

Village life doesn't just take place in rural villages. Virtually every place in this region is a village in its own way. This is particularly pronounced in Bali, with the *banjar* (local neighbourhood organisation) being particularly important.

Local Rule Bali-Style

Within Bali's government, the more than 3500 *banjar* wield enormous power. Comprising the married men of a given area (somewhere between 50 and 500), a *banjar* controls most community activities, whether it's planning for a temple ceremony or making important land-use decisions. These decisions are reached by consensus, and woe to a member who shirks his duties. The penalty can be fines or worse: banishment from the *banjar*. (In Bali's highly socialised society where your community is your life and identity – which is why a standard greeting is 'Where do you come from?' – banishment is the equivalent of the death penalty.)

Although women and even children can belong to the *banjar*, only men attend the meetings where important decisions are made. Women, who often own the businesses in tourist areas, have to communicate through their husbands to exert their influence. One thing that outsiders in a neighbourhood quickly learn is that one does not cross the *banjar*. Entire streets of restaurants and bars have been closed by order of the *banjar* after it was determined that neighbourhood concerns over matters such as noise were not being addressed.

Motorbikes are an invaluable part of daily life. They carry everything from towers of bananas and rice sacks headed to the market, to whole families in full ceremonial dress on their way to the temple, to young hotel clerks riding primly in their uniforms. You'll even see school children as young as six years old riding solo in small villages.

Rice Farming

Rice cultivation remains the backbone of rural Bali's strict communal society. Traditionally, each family makes just enough to satisfy their own needs and offerings to the gods, and perhaps a little to sell at market. The island's most popular deity is Dewi Sri, goddess of agriculture, fertility and success, and every stage of cultivation encompasses rituals to express gratitude and to prevent a poor crop, bad weather, pollution or theft by mice and birds.

Subak: Watering Bali

The complexities of tilling and irrigating terraces in mountainous terrain require that all villagers share the work and responsibility. Under a centuries-old system, the four mountain lakes and criss-crossing rivers irrigate fields via a network of canals, dams, bamboo pipes and tunnels bored through rock. More than 1200 *subak* (village irrigation associations) oversee this democratic supply of water, and every farmer must belong to his local *subak*, which in turn is the foundation of each village's powerful *banjar*.

Although Bali's civil make-up has changed with tourism, from a mostly homogenous island of farmers to a heterogeneous population with diverse activities and lifestyles, the collective responsibility rooted in rice farming continues to dictate the moral code behind daily life, even in the urban centres. *Subak*, a fascinating and democratic system, was placed on Unesco's World Heritage List in 2012.

The Arts

Bali's vibrant arts scene makes the island so much more than just a tropical beach destination, and the same can be said about the other islands of the region. In paintings, sculpture, dance and music, you will see artistry that will leave a lasting impression.

An Island of Artists

Colin McPhee's iconic book about Balinese dance and culture, *A House in Bali* (1946), has been made into an opera of the same name. It's the creation of Evan Ziporyn, a composer who spends much time in Ubud.

It's telling that there is no Balinese equivalent for the words 'art' or 'artist'. Until the tourist invasion, artistic expression was exclusively for religious and ritual purposes, and was almost always done by men. Paintings and carvings were used purely to decorate temples and shrines, while music, dance and theatrical performances were put on to entertain the gods who returned to Bali for important ceremonies. Artists did not strive to be different or individual as many do in the West; their work reflected a traditional style or a new idea, but not their own personality.

That changed in the late 1920s when foreign artists began to settle in Ubud; they went to learn from the Balinese and to share their knowledge, and helped to establish art as a commercial enterprise. Today, it's big business. Ubud remains the undisputed artistic centre of the island, and artists come from near and far to draw on its inspiration, from Japanese glass-blowers to European photographers and Javanese painters.

Galleries and craft shops are all over the island; the paintings, stone carvings and woodcarvings are stacked high on floors and will trip you up if you're not careful. Much of it is churned out quickly, and some is comically vulgar (you're not thinking of putting that 3m-high vision of a penis as Godzilla in your entryway, are you?) but there is also a great deal of extraordinary work.

Dance

There are more than a dozen different dances in Bali alone, each with rigid choreography, requiring high levels of discipline. Most performers have learnt through painstaking practice with an expert. No visit is complete without enjoying this purely Balinese art form; you will be delighted by the many styles, from the formal artistry of the Legong to crowd-pleasing antics in the Barong. One thing Balinese dance is not is static. The best troupes, such as Semara Ratih in Ubud, are continually innovating.

You can catch a quality dance performance at any place where there's a festival or celebration, and you'll find exceptional performances in and around Ubud. Performances are typically at night and last about 90 minutes, and you'll have a choice of eight or more performances a night.

With a little research and some good timing, you can attend performances that are part of temple ceremonies. Here you'll see the full beauty of Bali's dance and music heritage in the context of how it is meant to be seen. Performances can last several hours. Absorb the hypnotic music and the alluring moves of the performers, as well as the rapt attention of the crowd. Music, theatre and dance courses are also available in Ubud.

With the short attention spans of tourists in mind, many hotels offer a smorgasbord of dances – a little Kecak, a taste of Barong and some Legong to round it off. These can be pretty abbreviated, with just a few musicians and a couple of dancers.

Kecak

Probably the best-known dance for its spellbinding, hair-raising atmosphere, the Kecak features a 'choir' of men and boys who sit in concentric circles and slip into a trance as they chant and sing 'chak-a-chak-a-chak', imitating a troupe of monkeys. Sometimes called the 'vocal gamelan', this is the only music to accompany the dance re-enactment from the Hindu epic Ramayana, the familiar love story about Prince Rama and Princess Sita.

The tourist version of Kecak was developed in the 1960s. This spectacular performance is easily found in Ubud (look for Krama Desa Ubud Kaja with its 80 shirtless men chanting hypnotically) and also at the Pura Luhur Ulu Watu.

Balinese Dance, Drama and Music: A Guide to the Performing Arts of Bali, by I Wayan Dibia and Rucina Ballinger, is a lavishly illustrated and highly recommended in-depth guide to Bali's cultural performances.

Legong

Characterised by flashing eyes and quivering hands, this most graceful of Balinese dances is performed by young girls. Their talent is so revered that in old age, a classic dancer will be remembered as a 'great Legong'.

Peliatan's famous dance troupe, Gunung Sari, is often seen in Ubud and is particularly noted for its Legong Keraton (Legong of the Palace). The very stylised and symbolic story involves two Legong girls dancing in mirror image. They are elaborately made up and dressed in gold brocade, relating a story about a king who takes a maiden captive and consequently starts a war, in which he dies.

MONKEYS & MONSTERS

The Barong and Rangda dance rivals the Kecak as Bali's most popular performance for tourists. Again, it's a battle between good (the Barong) and bad (the Rangda).

The Barong is a good but mischievous and fun-loving shaggy dog-lion, with huge eyes and a mouth that clacks away to much dramatic effect. Because this character is the good protector of a village, the actors playing the Barong (who are utterly lost under layers of fur-clad costume) will emote a variety of winsome antics. But as is typical of Balinese dance, it is not all lighthearted – the Barong is a very sacred character indeed and you'll often see one in processions and rituals.

There's nothing sacred about the Barong's buddies. One or more monkeys attend to him and these characters often steal the show. Actors are given free rein to range wildly. The best aim a lot of high jinks at the audience, especially members who seem to be taking things a tad too seriously.

Meanwhile, the widow-witch Rangda is bad through and through. The Queen of Black Magic, the character's monstrous persona can include flames shooting out her ears, a tongue dripping fire, a mane of wild hair and large breasts.

The story features a duel between the Rangda and the Barong, whose supporters draw their kris (traditional daggers) and rush in to help. The long-tongued, sharp-fanged Rangda throws them into a trance, making them stab themselves. It's quite a spectacle. Thankfully, the Barong casts a spell that neutralises the power of the kris so it cannot harm them.

Playing around with all that powerful magic, good and bad, requires the presence of a *pemangku* (priest for temple rituals), who must end the dancers' trance and make a blood sacrifice using a chicken to appease the evil spirits.

In Ubud, Barong and Rangda, dance troupes have many interpretations of the dance: everything from eerie performances that will give you the shivers (until the monkeys appear) to jokey versions that could be a variety show or Brit pantomime.

Barong masks are valued objects; you can find artful examples in the village of Mas, south of Ubud.

Sanghyang & Kecak Fire Dance

These dances were developed to drive out evil spirits from a village – Sanghyang is a divine spirit who temporarily inhabits an entranced dancer. The Sanghyang Dedari is performed by two young girls who dance a dreamlike version of the Legong in perfect symmetry while their eyes are firmly shut. Male and female choirs provide a background chant until the dancers slump to the ground. A *pemangku* (priest for temple rituals) blesses them with holy water and brings them out of the trance.

In the Sanghyang Jaran, a boy in a trance dances around and through a fire of coconut husks, riding a coconut palm 'hobby horse'. Variations of this are called the Kecak Fire Dance and are performed in Ubud almost daily.

Women often bring offerings to a temple while dancing the Pendet their eyes, heads and hands moving in spectacularly controlled and coordinated movements. Every flick of the wrist, hand and fingers is charged with meaning.

Other Dances

The warrior dance, the Baris, is a male equivalent of the Legong – grace and femininity give way to an energetic and warlike spirit. The highly skilled Baris dancer must convey the thoughts and emotions of a warrior first preparing for action and then meeting the enemy: chivalry, pride, anger, prowess and, finally, regret are illustrated.

In the Topeng, which means 'pressed against the face', as with a mask, the dancers imitate the character represented by the mask. This requires great expertise because the dancer cannot convey thoughts and meanings through facial expressions – the dance must tell all.

Dance on Lombok

Lombok has its own unique dances, but they are not widely marketed. Performances are staged in some top-end hotels and in Lenek village, known for its dance traditions. If you're in Senggigi in July, you might catch dance and *gendang beleq* (big drum) performances. The *gendang beleq*, a dramatic war dance also called the Oncer, is performed by men and boys who play a variety of unusual musical instruments for *adat* (traditional customs) festivals in central and eastern Lombok.

Music

Balinese music is based around an ensemble known as a gamelan, also called a *gong*. A *gong gede* (large orchestra) is the traditional form, with 35 to 40 musicians. The more ancient gamelan *selunding* is still occasionally played in Bali Aga villages such as Tenganan.

The popular modern form of a *gong gede* is *gong kebyar*, with up to 25 instruments. This melodic, sometimes upbeat and sometimes haunting percussion that often accompanies traditional dance is one of the most lasting impressions for tourists to Bali.

The prevalent voice in Balinese music is from the xylophone-like *gangsa,* which the player hits with a hammer, dampening the sound just after it's struck. The tempo and nature of the music is controlled by two *kendang* (drums), one male and one female. Other instruments are the deep *trompong* drums, small *kempli* gong and *cengceng* (cymbals) used in faster pieces. Not all instruments require great skill and making music is a common village activity.

Many shops in south Bali and Ubud sell the distinctive gongs, flutes, bamboo xylophones and bamboo chimes. Look online for downloads.

Preserving and performing rare and ancient Balinese dance and gamelan music is the mission of Mekar Bhuana (www.balimusicanddance.com), a Denpasar-based cultural group. They sponsor performances and offer lessons.

Genggong

The *genggong*, a performance seen on Lombok, uses a simple set of instruments, including a bamboo flute, a *rebab* (two-stringed bowed lute) and knockers. Seven musicians accompany their music with dance movements and stylised hand gestures.

Wayang Kulit

Much more than sheer entertainment, *wayang kulit* (shadow puppetry) has been Bali's candlelit cinema for centuries, embodying the sacred seriousness of classical Greek drama. (The word drama comes from the Greek *dromenon,* a religious ritual.) The performances are long and intense – lasting six hours or more and often not finishing before sunrise.

Originally used to bring ancestors back to this world, the shows feature painted buffalo-hide puppets believed to have great spiritual power, and the *dalang* (puppet master and storyteller) is an almost mystical figure. A person of considerable skill and even greater endurance, the *dalang* sits behind a screen and manipulates the puppets while telling the story, often in many dialects.

Stories are chiefly derived from the great Hindu epics, the Ramayana and, to a lesser extent, the Mahabharata.

You can find performances in Ubud, which are attenuated to a manageable two hours or less.

An *arja* drama is not unlike *wayang kulit* puppet shows in its melodramatic plots, offstage sound effects and cast of easily identifiable goodies (the refined *alus*) and baddies (the unrefined *kras*). It's performed outside and a small house is sometimes built on stage and set on fire at the climax!

Painting

Balinese painting is probably the art form most influenced by Western ideas and demand. Traditional paintings, faithfully depicting religious and mythological subjects, were used for temple and palace decoration; the set colours were made from soot, clay and pigs' bones. In the 1930s, Western artists introduced the concept of paintings as artistic creations that could also be sold for money. To target the tourist market, they encouraged deviance to scenes from everyday life and the use of the full palette of modern paints and tools. The range of themes, techniques, styles and materials expanded enormously, and women painters emerged for the first time.

A loose classification of styles is classical, or Kamasan, named for the village of Kamasan near Semarapura; Ubud style, developed in the 1930s under the influence of the Pita Maha; Batuan, which started at the same time in a nearby village; Young Artists, begun postwar in the 1960s and influenced by Dutch artist Arie Smit; and finally, modern or academic, free in its creative topics, yet strongly and distinctively Balinese.

INFLUENTIAL WESTERN ARTISTS

Besides Arie Smit (who died on Bali at age 99 in 2016), several other Western artists had a profound effect on Balinese art in the early and middle parts of the 20th century. In addition to honouring Balinese art, they provided a critical boost to its vitality at a time when it might have died out.

Walter Spies (1895–1942) German artist Walter Spies first visited Bali in 1925 and moved to Ubud in 1927, establishing the image of Bali for Westerners that prevails today.

Rudolf Bonnet (1895–1978) Bonnet was a Dutch artist whose work concentrated on the human form and everyday Balinese life. Many classical Balinese paintings with themes of markets and cockfights are indebted to Bonnet.

Miguel Covarrubias (1904–57) *Island of Bali,* written by this Mexican artist, is still the classic introduction to the island and its culture.

Colin McPhee (1900–65) Canadian musician Colin McPhee wrote *A House in Bali*. It remains one of the best written accounts of Bali, and his tales of music and house building are often highly amusing. His patronage of traditional dance and music cannot be overstated.

Adrien-Jean Le Mayeur de Merpres (1880–1958) This Belgian artist arrived on Bali in 1932 and did much to establish the notions of sensual Balinese beauty, often based on his wife, the dancer Ni Polok. Their home is now an under-appreciated museum in Sanur.

Classical Painting

There are three basic types of classical painting – *langse, iders-iders* and calendars. *Langse* are large decorative hangings for palaces or temples that display *wayang* figures (which have an appearance similar to the figures used in shadow puppetry), rich floral designs and flame-and-mountain motifs. *Iders-iders* are scroll paintings hung along temple eaves. Calendars are, much as they were before, used to set dates for rituals and predict the future.

Langse paintings helped impart *adat* (traditional customs) to ordinary people in the same way that traditional dance and *wayang kulit* puppetry do. The stylised human figures depicted good and evil, with romantic heroes like Ramayana and Arjuna always painted with small, narrow eyes and fine features, while devils and warriors were prescribed round eyes, coarse features and facial hair. The paintings tell a story in a series of panels, rather like a comic strip, and often depict scenes from the Ramayana and Mahabharata. Other themes are the Kakawins poems, and demonic spirits from indigenous Balinese folklore – see the ceilings of the Kertha Gosa (Hall of Justice) in Klungkung (Semarapura) for an example.

A carefully selected list of books about art, culture and Balinese writers, dancers and musicians can be found at www.ganeshabooksbali.com, the website for the excellent Ubud bookstore (with a branch in Sanur).

The Pita Maha

In the 1930s, with few commissions from temples, painting was virtually dying out. European artists Rudolf Bonnet and Walter Spies, with their patron Cokorda Gede Agung Surapati, formed the Pita Maha (literally, 'Great Vitality') to take painting from a ritual-based activity to a commercial one. The cooperative had more than 100 members at its peak in the 1930s and led to the establishment of Museum Puri Lukisan (p162) in Ubud, the first museum dedicated to Balinese art.

The changes Bonnet and Spies inspired were revolutionary. Balinese artists such as the late I Gusti Nyoman Lempad, I Wayan Ketig, I Ketut Regig and Gus Made started exploring their own styles. Narrative tales were replaced by single scenes, and romantic legends by daily life: the harvest, markets, cockfights, offerings at a temple or a cremation. These paintings were known as Ubud style.

Meanwhile, painters from Batuan retained many features of classical painting. They depicted daily life, but across many scenes – a market, dance and rice harvest would all appear in a single work. This Batuan style is also noted for its inclusion of some very modern elements, such as sea scenes with the odd windsurfer.

The painting techniques also changed. Modern paint and materials were used and stiff formal poses gave way to realistic 3-D representations. More importantly, pictures were not just painted to fit a space in a palace or a temple.

In one way, the style remained unchanged – Balinese paintings are packed with detail. A painted Balinese forest, for example, has branches, leaves and a whole zoo of creatures reaching out to fill every tiny space.

This new artistic enthusiasm was interrupted by WWII and Indonesia's independence struggle, and stayed that way until the development of the Young Artists style.

The Young Artists

Arie Smit was in Penestanan, just outside Ubud, in 1956, when he noticed an 11-year-old boy drawing in the dirt. Smit wondered what the boy could produce if he had the proper equipment. As the legend goes, the boy's father would not allow him to take up painting until Smit offered to pay somebody else to watch the family's ducks.

Other 'Young Artists' soon joined that first pupil, I Nyoman Cakra, but Smit did not actively teach them. He simply provided the equipment and encouragement, unleashing what was clearly a strong natural talent.

TODAY'S BALINESE PAINTERS

Numerous Balinese artists are receiving international recognition for their work, which often has a strong theme of social justice and a questioning of modern values. Still, being Balinese and all, the works have a sly wit and even a wink to the viewer. Some names to watch for:

Nyoman Masriadi Born in Gianyar, Masriadi is easily the superstar of Bali's current crop of painters, and his works sell for upwards of a million dollars. He is renowned for his sharp-eyed observations of Indonesian society today and his thoroughly modern techniques and motifs.

Made Djirna Hailing from the comparatively wealthy tourist town of Ubud, Djirna has the perfect background for his works, which criticise the relationship between ostentatious money and modern Balinese religious ceremonies.

Agung Mangu Putra This painter from the deeply green hills west of Ubud finds inspiration in the Balinese being bypassed by the island's uneven economic boom. He decries the impact on his natural world.

Wayan Sudarna Putra An Ubud native, Putra uses satire and parody in his works, which cross media to question the absurdities of current Indonesian life and values.

Ketut Sana A resident of Keliki, a village near Ubud, Sana knew noted artists Gusti Nyoman Sudara Lempad and Wayan Gerudug when he was young. He started his impressionistic work by adapting scraps from their work.

Gede Suanda Sayur Sayur's works are often dark as he questions the pillaging of Bali's environment. He joined Putra to create an installation in a rice field near Ubud that featured huge white poles spelling out 'Not for sale'.

Today this style of rural scenes painted in brilliant Technicolor is a staple of Balinese tourist art.

I Nyoman Cakra still lives in Penestanan, still paints, and cheerfully admits that he owes it all to Smit. Other Young Artists include I Ketut Tagen, I Nyoman Tjarka and I Nyoman Mujung.

Other Styles

There are some other variants to the main Ubud and Young Artists' painting styles. The depiction of forests, flowers, butterflies, birds and other naturalistic themes, for example, sometimes called Pengosekan style, became popular in the 1960s. It can probably be traced back to Henri Rousseau, who was a significant influence on Walter Spies. An interesting development in this particular style is the depiction of underwater scenes, with colourful fish, coral gardens and sea creatures. Somewhere between the Pengosekan and Ubud styles sit the miniature landscape paintings that are popular commercially.

The new techniques also resulted in radically new versions of Rangda, Barong, Hanuman and other figures from Balinese and Hindu mythology. Scenes from folk tales and stories appeared, featuring dancers, nymphs and love stories, with an understated erotic appeal.

The Bali Arts Festival (www.baliartsfestival.com) showcases the work of thousands of Balinese from mid-June to mid-July in Denpasar. It is a major event that draws talent and audiences from across the island.

Crafts

You'll find crafts from around Indonesia in this part of the country. Better-quality tourist shops sell puppets and batiks from Java, ikat garments from Sumba, Sumbawa and Flores, and textiles and woodcarvings from Bali, Lombok and Kalimantan. The kris, important to a Balinese family, will often have been made in Java.

On Lombok, where there's less money, traditional handicrafts are practical items, but are still skillfully made and beautifully finished. Finer examples of Lombok weaving, basketware and pottery are highly valued by collectors.

Craftsperson making batik

Textiles & Weaving

Textiles here are woven by women for ceremonies, as well as for gifts. They are often part of marriage dowries and cremations, where they join the deceased's soul as it passes to the afterlife.

Batik

Traditional batik sarongs, which fall somewhere between a cotton sarong and *kamben* for formality, are handmade in central Java. The dyeing process has been adapted by the Balinese to produce brightly coloured and patterned fabrics. Watch out for 'batik' that's been screenprinted: the colours will be washed out and the pattern is often only on one side (the dye in proper batik should colour both sides to reflect the belief that the body should feel what the eye sees).

Ikat

Ikat involves dyeing either the warp threads (those stretched on the loom) or weft threads (those woven across the warp) before the material is woven. The resulting pattern is geometric and slightly wavy. The colouring typically follows a similar tone – blues and greens; reds and browns; or yellows, reds and oranges. Gianyar, in east Bali, has a few factories where you can watch ikat sarongs being woven on a hand-and-foot-powered loom. A complete sarong takes about six hours to make.

Bali

The most common material in Bali is the sarong, which can be used as an article of clothing, a sheet or a towel, among other things. The cheap cottons, either plain or printed, are for everyday use and are popular with tourists for beachwear.

For special occasions, such as a temple ceremony, Balinese men and women use a *kamben* (a length of *songket* wrapped around the chest). The *songket* is silver- or gold-threaded cloth, handwoven using a floating weft technique, while another variety is the *endek* (like *songket,* but with predyed weft threads). The men pair the *kamben* with a shirt and the women pair it with a *kebaya* (long-sleeved lace blouse). A separate slim strip of cloth known as a *kain* (or known as *prada* when decorated with a gold-leaf pattern) is wound tightly around the hips and over the sarong like a belt to complete the outfit.

The magazine/comic *Bog Bog,* by Balinese cartoonists, is a satirical and humorous insight into the contrast between modern and traditional worlds in Bali. It's available in warungs (food stalls), bookshops and supermarkets or online at www.facebook.com/bogbogcartoon.

Lombok

Lombok is renowned for traditional weaving on backstrap looms, the techniques handed down from mother to daughter. Abstract flower and animal motifs such as buffalo, dragons, crocodiles and snakes sometimes decorate this exquisite cloth. Several villages specialise in weaving cloth, while others concentrate on fine baskets and mats woven from *rotan* (hardy, pliable vine) or grass. You can visit factories around Cakranegara and Mataram that produce weft ikat (patterned textiles) on old hand-and-foot-operated looms.

Sukarara and Pringgasela are centres for traditional ikat and *songket* weaving (silver- or gold-threaded cloth, handwoven using floating weft technique). Sarongs, Sasak belts and clothing edged with brightly coloured embroidery are sold in small shops.

Sumba

East Sumbanese ikat is the most dramatic and arguably the best executed in Indonesia. Natural dyes are still preferred by weavers who sell their wares to serious collectors in Bali and beyond. The earthy orange-red

OFFERINGS

Traditionally, many of Bali's most elaborate crafts have been ceremonial offerings not intended to last: *baten tegeh* (decorated pyramids of fruit, rice cakes and flowers); rice-flour cookies modelled into entire scenes with a deep symbolic significance and tiny sculptures; *lamak* (long, woven palm-leaf strips used as decorations in festivals and celebrations); stylised female figures known as *cili,* which are representations of Dewi Sri (the rice goddess); and intricately carved coconut-shell wall hangings.

Tourists in Bali may enjoy being welcomed as honoured guests, but the real VIPs are the gods, ancestors, spirits and demons. They are presented with these offerings throughout each day to show respect and gratitude, or perhaps to bribe a demon into being less mischievous. Marvel at the care and energy that goes into constructing huge funeral towers and exotic sarcophagi, all of which will go up in flames.

A gift to a higher being must look attractive, so each offering is a work of art. The most common is a palm-leaf tray little bigger than a saucer, artfully topped with flowers, food (especially rice, and modern touches such as Ritz crackers or individually wrapped lollies) and small change, crowned with a *saiban* (temple or shrine offering). More important shrines and occasions call for more elaborate offerings, which can include the colourful towers of fruits and cakes called *baten tegeh,* and even entire animals cooked and ready to eat, as in Bali's famous *babi guling* (suckling pig).

Once presented to the gods an offering cannot be used again, so new ones are made each day, usually by women. You'll see easy-to-assemble offerings for sale in markets, much as you'd find quick dinner items in Western supermarkets.

Offerings to the gods are placed on high levels and to the demons on the ground. Don't worry about stepping on these; given their ubiquity, it's almost impossible not to (just don't try to). In fact, at Bemo Corner in Kuta offerings are left at the shrine in the middle of the road and are quickly flattened by cars. Across the island, dogs with a taste for crackers hover around fresh offerings. Given the belief that gods or demons instantly derive the essence of an offering, the critters are really just getting leftovers.

colour comes from *kombu* tree roots and *loba* leaves, while intense blues are derived from *wura* (indigo) leaves. You'll see more detailed motifs and natural dyes in the east than west. Some are a record of tribal wars and precolonial village life, while others depict symbolic animals and mythical creatures.

Traditionally, ikat cloth was only worn ceremonially. Around a century ago, only members of Sumba's highest clans and their personal attendants could make or wear it. Dutch conquest broke the Sumbanese royal ikat monopoly and opened up an external market, which increased production. In the late 19th century ikat was collected by Dutch ethnographers and museums, and by the 1920s visitors were already noting the introduction of nontraditional designs, such as lions from the Dutch coat of arms and dragons from Chinese influence.

Woodcarving

Woodcarving in Bali has evolved from its traditional use for doors and columns, religious figures and theatrical masks to modern forms encompassing a wide range of styles. While Tegallalang and Jati, on the road north from Ubud, are noted woodcarving centres, along with the route from Mas through Peliatan, you can find pieces in any souvenir store.

The common style of a slender, elongated figure reportedly first appeared after Walter Spies gave a woodcarver a long piece of wood and commissioned him to carve two sculptures from it. The carver couldn't bring himself to cut it in half, instead making a single figure of a tall, slim dancer.

The nonprofit Lontar Foundation (www.lontar.org) works to get Indonesian books translated into English so that universities around the world can offer courses in Indonesian literature.

Other typical works include classical religious figures, animal caricatures, life-size human skeletons, picture frames and whole tree trunks carved into ghostly 'totem poles'. In Kuta there are various objects targeting beer drinkers: penis bottle openers (which are claimed to be Bali's bestselling souvenir) and signs to sit above your bar bearing made-to-order slogans.

Almost all carving is of local woods including *belalu* (quick-growing light wood) and the stronger fruit timbers such as jackfruit wood. Ebony from Sulawesi is also used. Sandalwood, with its delightful fragrance, is expensive and soft, and is used for some small, very detailed pieces, but beware of widespread fakery.

On Lombok, carving usually decorates functional items such as containers for tobacco and spices, and the handles of betel-nut crushers and knives. Materials include wood, horn and bone, and you'll see these used in the recent trend: primitive-style elongated masks. Cakranegara, Sindu, Labuapi and Senanti are centres for carving on the island.

Wooden articles lose moisture when moved to a drier environment. Avoid possible shrinkage – especially of your penis bottle opener – by placing the carving in a plastic bag at home, and letting some air in for about one week every month for four months.

Masks used in theatre and dance performances such as the Topeng require a specialised form of woodcarving. The mask master – always a man – must know the movements each performer uses so the character can be accurately depicted in the mask. These masks are believed to possess magical qualities and can even have the ability to stare down bad spirits.

Other masks, such as the Barong and Rangda, are brightly painted and decorated with real hair, enormous teeth and bulging eyes.

Puaya near Sukawati, south of Ubud, is a centre of mask carving. You can visit workshops there and see all manner of ceremonial art being created. The Museum Negeri Propinsi Bali (p117) in Denpasar has an extensive mask collection so you can get acquainted with different styles before buying.

KRIS: SACRED BLADES

Usually adorned with an ornate, jewel-studded handle and a sinister-looking wavy blade, the kris is Bali's traditional ceremonial dagger, dating back to the Majapahit era. A kris is often the most important of family heirlooms, a symbol of prestige and honour and a work of high-end art. Made by a master craftsperson, it's believed to have great spiritual power, sending out magical energy waves and thus requiring great care in its handling and use. Many owners will only clean the blade with waters from Sungai Pakerisan (Pakerisan River) in east Bali because it is thought to be the magical 'River of Kris'.

Balinese men will judge each other in a variation of 'show me your kris'. The size of the blade, the number owned, the quality, the artistry of the handles and much more will go into forming a judgement of a man and his kris. Handles are considered separately from a kris (the blade). As a man's fortunes allow, he will upgrade the handles in his collection. But the kris itself remains sacred – often you will see offerings beside ones on display. The undulations in the blade (called *lok*) have many meanings and there's always an odd number – three, for instance, means passion.

The Museum Negeri Propinsi Bali (p117) in Denpasar has a rich kris collection.

Stone Carving

Traditionally for temple adornment, stone sculptures now make popular souvenirs ranging from frangipani reliefs to quirky ornaments that display the Balinese sense of humour: a frog clutching a leaf as an umbrella, or a weird demon on the side of a bell clasping his hands over his ears in mock offence.

At temples, you will see stone carving in set places. Door guardians are usually a protective personality such as Arjuna. Kala's monstrous face often peers out above the main entrance, his hands reaching to catch evil spirits. The side walls of a *pura dalem* (temple of the dead) might feature sculpted panels showing the horrors awaiting evildoers in the afterlife.

Among Bali's most ancient stone carvings are the scenes of people fleeing a great monster at Goa Gajah, the so-called 'Elephant Cave', believed to date to the 11th century. Inside the cave, a statue of Ganesha, the elephant-like god, gives the rock its name. Along the road through Muncan in east Bali you'll see roadside factories where huge temple decorations are carved in the open.

Much of the local work is made in Batubulan from grey volcanic stone called *paras,* so soft it can be scratched with a fingernail (which, according to legend, is how the giant Kebo Iwa created the Elephant Cave).

Treasures of Bali, by Richard Mann (2006), is a beautifully illustrated guide to Bali's museums, big and small. It highlights the gems often overlooked by group tours.

Jewellery

Silversmiths and goldsmiths are traditionally members of the *pande* caste, which also incudes blacksmiths and other metalworkers. Bali is a major producer of fashion jewellery and produces variations on currently fashionable designs.

Very fine filigree work is a Balinese speciality, as is the use of tiny spots of silver to form a pattern or decorative texture – this is considered a very skilled technique because the heat must be perfectly controlled to weld the delicate wire or silver spots to the underlying silver without damaging it. Balinese work is nearly always handmade, rarely involving casting techniques.

Expat John Hardy built an empire worth hundreds of millions of dollars by adapting old Balinese silver designs along with his own beautiful innovations before he sold his company and started building bamboo buildings. Ubud has numerous creative silver jewellery shops, especially along upper Jl Hanoman.

Architecture

Design is part of Bali's spiritual heritage and this heritage contributes to the look of traditional homes, temples and even modern buildings, such as the myriad resorts. Bali style is timeless, whether it is centuries old or embodied in a new hip villa. And it's not static – Bali is the site of world-renowned architecture made with renewable materials like bamboo.

Architecture & Life

Architecture brings together the living and the dead, pays homage to the gods and wards off evil spirits, not to mention the torrential rain. As spiritual as it is functional, as mystical as it is beautiful, Balinese architecture has a life force of its own.

The various open-air *bale* in family compounds are where visitors are received. Typically, drinks and small cakes will be served and friendly conversations will ensue for possibly an hour or more before the purpose of the visit is discussed.

On an island bound by deep-rooted religious and cultural rituals, the priority of any design is appeasing the ancestral and village gods. This means reserving the holiest (northeast) location in every land space for the village temple, the same corner in every home for the family temple, and providing a comfortable, pleasing atmosphere to entice the gods back to Bali for ceremonies.

So while it exudes beauty, balance, age-old wisdom and functionality, a Balinese home is not a commodity designed with capital appreciation in mind; even while an increasing number of rice farmers sell their ancestral land to foreigners for villa developments, they're keeping the parcel on which their home stands.

Preserving the Cosmic Order

A village, a temple, a family compound, an individual structure – and even a single part of the structure – must all conform to the Balinese concept of cosmic order. It consists of three parts that represent the three worlds of the cosmos – *swah* (world of gods), *bhwah* (world of humans) and *bhur* (world of demons). The concept also represents a three-part division of a person: *utama* (the head), *madia* (the body) and *nista* (the legs). The units of measurement used in traditional buildings are directly based on the anatomical dimensions of the head of the household, ensuring harmony between the dwelling and those who live in it.

The design is traditionally done by an *undagi* (a combination architect-priest); it must maintain harmony between god, man and nature under the concept of *Tri Hita Karana*. If it's not quite right, the universe may fall off balance and no end of misfortune and ill health will visit the community involved.

Building on the Bale

The basic element of Balinese architecture is the *bale*, a rectangular, open-sided pavilion with a steeply pitched roof of thatch. Both a family compound and a temple will comprise a number of separate *bale* for specific functions, all surrounded by a high wall. The size and proportions of the *bale*, the number of columns and the position within the compound are all determined according to tradition and the owner's caste status.

The focus of a community is a large pavilion, called the *bale banjar,* used for meetings, debates and gamelan (traditional orchestra) practice, among many other activities. You'll find that large modern buildings such as restaurants and the reception areas of resorts are often modelled on the larger *bale,* and they can be airy, spacious and very handsomely proportioned.

The Family Compound

The Balinese house looks inward – the outside is simply a high wall. Inside there is a garden and a separate small building or *bale* for each activity – one for cooking, one for washing and the toilet, and separate buildings for each 'bedroom'. In Bali's mild tropical climate people live

TYPICAL FAMILY COMPOUND

The following are elements commonly found in family compounds. Although there are variations, the designs are surprisingly similar, especially given they occur thousands of times across Bali.

Sanggah or Merajan Family temple, which is always at the *kaja–kangin* (sunrise in the direction of the mountains) corner of the courtyard. There will be shrines to the Hindu 'trinity' of Brahma, Shiva and Vishnu, and to *taksu* (the divine intermediary).

Umah Meten Sleeping pavilion for the family head.

Tugu Shrine to the god of evil spirits in the compound but at the far *kaja–kuah* (sunset in the direction of the mountains) corner; by employing the chief evil spirit as a guard, others will stay away.

Pengijeng Small shrine amid the compound's open space, dedicated to the spirit who is the guardian of the property.

Bale Tiang Sanga Guest pavilion, also known as the *bale duah*. Literally the family room, it's used as a gathering place, offering workplace or temporary quarters of lesser sons and their families before they establish their own home.

Natah Courtyard with frangipani or hibiscus shade trees, with always a few chickens pecking about, plus a fighting cock or two in a basket.

Bale Sakenam or Bale Dangin Working and sleeping pavilion; may be used for important family ceremonies.

Fruit Trees & Coconut Palms Serve both practical and decorative purposes. Fruit trees are often mixed with flowering trees such as hibiscus, and caged songbirds hang from the branches.

Vegetable Garden Small; usually just for a few spices such as lemongrass not grown on larger plots.

Bale Sakepat Sleeping pavilion for children; highly optional.

Paon Kitchen; always in the south, as that is the direction associated with Brahma, god of fire.

Lumbung Rice barn – the domain of both the precious grain and Dewi Sri, the rice goddess. It's elevated to discourage rice-eating pests.

Rice-Threshing Area Important for farmers to prepare rice for cooking or storage.

Aling Aling Screen wall requiring visitors to turn a sharp left or right. This ensures both privacy from passers-by and protection from demons, which the Balinese believe cannot turn corners.

Candi Kurung Gate with a roof, resembling a mountain or tower split in half.

Apit Lawang or Pelinggah Gate shrines, which continually receive offerings to recharge the gate's ability to repel evil spirits.

Pigsty or garbage pit Always in the *kangin–kelod* (sunrise in the direction away from the mountains) corner, the compound's waste ends up here.

Pura Luhur Ulu Watu (p141)

outside, so the 'living room' and 'dining room' will be open verandah areas, looking out into the garden. The whole complex is oriented on the *kaja–kelod* (towards the mountains–towards the sea) axis.

Analogous to the human body, compounds have a head (the family temple with its ancestral shrine), arms (the sleeping and living areas), legs and feet (the kitchen and rice-storage building), and even an anus (the garbage pit or pigsty). There may be an area outside the house compound where fruit trees are grown or a pig is kept.

The gate to a traditional Balinese house is where the family gives cues as to its wealth. They range from the humble – grass thatch atop a gate of simple stones or clay – to the relatively grand, including bricks heavily ornamented with ornately carved stone and a tile roof.

There are several variations on the typical family compound. For example, the entrance is commonly on the *kuah* (sunset side), rather than the *kelod* (away from the mountains and towards the sea) side, but *never* on the *kangin* (sunrise) or *kaja* (in the direction of the mountains) side.

Traditional Balinese homes are found in every region of the island; Ubud remains an excellent place to see them simply because of the concentration of homes there. Many accept guests. South of Ubud, you can enjoy an in-depth tour of the Nyoman Suaka Home in Singapadu.

Temples

Every village in Bali has several temples, and every home has at least a simple house-temple. The Balinese word for temple is *pura,* from a Sanskrit word literally meaning 'a space surrounded by a wall'. Similar to a traditional Balinese home, a temple is walled in – so the shrines you see in rice fields or at 'magical' spots such as old trees are not real temples. These simple shrines or thrones often overlook crossroads, to protect passers-by.

All temples are built on a mountains–sea orientation, not north–south. The direction towards the mountains, *kaja,* is the end of the temple, where the holiest shrines are found. The temple's entrance is at the *kelod. Kangin* is more holy than the *kuah,* so many secondary shrines are on the *kangin* side. *Kaja* may be towards a particular mountain – Pura Besakih in east Bali is pointed directly towards Gunung Agung – or towards the mountains in general, which run east–west along the length of Bali.

Temple Types

There are three basic temple types found in most villages. The most important is the *pura puseh* (temple of origin), dedicated to the village founders and at the *kaja* end of the village. In the middle of the village is the *pura desa*, for the many spirits that protect the village community in daily life. At the *kelod* end of the village is the *pura dalem* (temple of

TYPICAL TEMPLE ELEMENTS

No two temples on Bali are identical. Variations in style, size, importance, wealth, purpose and much more result in near-infinite variety. But there are common themes and elements. Use this as a guide and see how many design elements you can find in each Balinese temple you visit.

Candi Bentar The intricately sculpted temple gateway, like a tower split down the middle and moved apart, symbolises that you are entering a sanctum. It can be quite grand, with auxiliary entrances on either side for daily use.

Kulkul Tower The warning-drum tower, from which a wooden split drum *(kulkul)* is sounded to announce events at the temple or warn of danger.

Bale A pavilion, usually open-sided, for temporary use or storage. It may include a *bale gong,* where the gamelan orchestra plays at festivals; a *paon,* or temporary kitchen, to prepare offerings; or a *wantilan,* a stage for dances or cockfights.

Kori Agung or Paduraksa The gateway to the inner courtyard is an intricately sculpted stone tower. Entry is through a doorway reached by steps in the middle of the tower and left open during festivals.

Raksa or Dwarapala Statues of fierce guardian figures who protect the doorway and deter evil spirits. Above the door will be the equally fierce face of a Bhoma, with hands outstretched against unwanted spirits.

Aling Aling If an evil spirit does get in, this low wall behind the entrance will keep it at bay, as evil spirits find it difficult to make sharp turns. Also found in family compounds.

Side Gate (Betelan) Most of the time (except during ceremonies), entry to the inner courtyard is through this side gate, which is always open.

Small Shrines (Gedong) These usually include shrines to Ngrurah Alit and Ngrurah Gede, who organise things and ensure the correct offerings are made.

Padma Stone Throne for the sun god Surya, placed in the most auspicious *kaja–kangin* (sunrise in the direction of the mountains) corner. It rests on the *badawang* (world turtle), which is held by two *naga* (mythical snakelike creatures).

Meru A multiroofed shrine. Usually there is an 11-roofed *meru* to Sanghyang Widi, the supreme Balinese deity, and a three-roofed *meru* to the holy mountain Gunung Agung. However, *meru* can take any odd number of steps in between, depending on where the intended god falls in the pecking order. The black thatching is made from sugar-palm fronds and is very expensive.

Small Shrines (Gedong) At the *kaja* end of the courtyard, these may include a shrine to the sacred mountain Gunung Batur; a Maospahit shrine to honour Bali's original Hindu settlers (Majapahit); and a shrine to the *taksu,* who acts as an interpreter for the gods. (Trance dancers or mediums may be used to convey the gods' wishes.)

Bale Piasan Open pavilions used to display temple offerings.

Gedong Pesimpangan A stone building dedicated to the village founder or a local deity.

Paruman or Pepelik Open pavilion in the inner courtyard, where the gods are supposed to assemble to watch the ceremonies of a temple festival.

the dead). The graveyard is also here, and the temple may include representations of Durga, the terrible side of Shiva's wife Parvati. Both Shiva and Parvati have a creative and destructive side; their destructive powers are honoured in the *pura dalem*.

Hard-wearing terracotta tiles have been the traditional roofing material since the Dutch era. Thatch in various forms, or bamboo, is now reserved for the most traditional and ceremonial sites.

Other temples include those dedicated to the spirits of irrigated agriculture. Because rice growing is so important in Bali, and the division of water for irrigation is handled with the utmost care, these *pura subak* or *pura ulun suwi* (temple of the rice-growers association) can be of considerable importance. Other temples may also honour dry-field agriculture, as well as the flooded rice paddies.

In addition to these 'local' temples, there is also a smaller number of great temples. Often a kingdom would have three of these temples that sit at the very top of the temple pecking order: a main state temple in the heartland of the state (such as Pura Taman Ayun in Mengwi, western Bali); a mountain temple (such as Pura Besakih, eastern Bali); and a sea temple (such as Pura Luhur Ulu Watu, southern Bali).

Every house in Bali has its house-temple, which is at the *kaja–kangin* corner of the courtyard and has at least five shrines.

TOP TEMPLE VISITS

Over 10,000 temples are found everywhere on Bali – from cliff tops and beaches to volcanoes – and are often beautiful places to experience. Visitors will find the following especially rewarding.

Directional Temples

Some temples are so important they are deemed to belong to the whole island rather than particular communities. There are nine *kahyangan jagat* (directional temples), including the following:

Pura Luhur Batukau (p250) One of Bali's most important temples is situated magically up the misty slopes of Gunung Batukau.

Pura Luhur Ulu Watu (p141) As important as it is popular, this temple has sweeping Indian Ocean views, sunset dance performances and monkeys.

Pura Goa Lawah (p215) See Bali's own Bat Cave at this cliff-side temple filled with the winged critters.

Sea Temples

The legendary 16th-century priest Nirartha founded a chain of temples to honour the sea gods. Each was intended to be within sight of the next, and several have dramatic locations on the south coast. They include the following:

Pura Tanah Lot (p277) Sacred as the day begins, it becomes a temple of mass tourism at sunset.

Other Important Temples

Some temples have particular importance because of their location, spiritual function or architecture. The following reward visitors:

Pura Maduwe Karang (p255) An agricultural temple on the north coast, famous for its spirited bas-reliefs, including one of possibly Bali's first bicycle rider.

Pura Pusering Jagad (p179) One of the famous temples at Pejeng, which dates to the 14th-century empire that flourished here. It has an enormous bronze drum from that era.

Pura Taman Ayun (p279) This vast and imposing state temple was a centrepiece of the Mengwi empire and has been nominated for Unesco recognition.

Pura Tirta Empul (p198) The beautiful temple at Tampaksiring, with holy springs discovered in AD 962 and bathing pools at the source of Sungai Pakerisan.

Temple Decoration

Temples and their decoration are closely linked on Bali. A temple gateway is not just erected; every square centimetre of it is carved in sculptural relief and a diminishing series of demon faces is placed above it as protection. Even then, it's not complete without several stone statues to act as guardians. The level of decoration inside varies. Sometimes a temple is built with minimal decoration in the hope that sculpture can be added when more funds are available. The sculpture can also deteriorate after a few years because much of the stone used is soft and the tropical climate ages it very rapidly (that centuries-old temple you're looking at may in fact be less than 10 years old!). Sculptures are restored or replaced as resources permit – it's not uncommon to see a temple with old carvings, which are barely discernible, next to newly finished work.

Sculpture often appears in set places in Bali's temples. Door guardians – representations of legendary figures such as Arjuna or other protective personalities – flank the steps to the gateway. Above the main entrance to a temple, Kala's monstrous face often peers out, sometimes a number of times, and his hands reach out beside his head to catch any evil spirits foolish enough to try and sneak in.

Look for carved wooden *garudas*, the winged bird that bears the god Wisnu, in the most surprising places – high up in pavilion rafters, at the base of columns, pretty much anywhere.

Temple Design

Although overall temple architecture is similar in both northern and southern Bali, there are some important differences. The inner courtyards of southern temples usually house a number of *meru* (multitiered shrines), together with other structures, whereas in the north, everything is grouped on a single pedestal. On the pedestal you'll find 'houses' for the deities to use on their earthly visits; they're also used to store religious relics.

While Balinese sculpture and painting were once exclusively used as architectural decoration for temples, you'll see that sculpture and painting have developed as separate art forms influencing the look of every aspect of the island. And the art of temple and shrine construction is as vibrant as ever: more than 500 new ones in all sizes are built every month.

The Birth of Bali Style

Tourism has given Balinese architecture unprecedented exposure and it seems that every visitor wants to take a slice of this island back home with them. Shops all around Denpasar churn out prefabricated, knock-down *bale* for shipment to far-flung destinations. Furniture workshops in Denpasar and handicraft villages near Ubud are flat out making ornaments for domestic and export markets.

The craze stems back to the early 1970s, when Australian artist Donald Friend formed a partnership with Manado-born Wija Waworuntu, who had built the Tandjung Sari on Sanur beach a decade earlier. With a directive to design traditional, village-style alternatives to the Western multistoreyed hotels, they brought two architects to Bali – Australian Peter Muller and the late Sri Lankan Geoffrey Bawa – who took traditional architecture and adapted it to Western standards of luxury.

When you stay in a hotel featuring *lumbung* design, you are really staying in a place derived from rice storage barns – the 2nd floor is meant to be airless and hot!

Before long, the design sensation known as 'Bali Style' was born. Then, the term reflected Muller and Bawa's sensitive, low-key approach, giving precedence to culture over style, and respect for traditional principles and craftspeople, local renewable materials and age-old techniques. Today, the development of a mass market has produced a much looser definition.

Contemporary Hotel Design

For centuries, foreign interlopers, such as the priest Nirartha, have played an intrinsic part in the island's myths and legends. These days, tourists are making an impact on the serenity of Balinese cosmology and its seamless translation into the island's traditional architecture. And while these visitors with large credit limits aren't changing the island's belief system – much – they are changing its look.

THE POWER OF BAMBOO

Bali has always had natural cathedrals of bamboo. In the dense tropical forests of the east and west, soaring stalks arch together in ways that lift the soul. Now bamboo, one of the world's great renewable resources, is being used to create inspirational buildings whose sinuous designs are simply awe-inspiring.

Much credit for the current bamboo revolution goes to famed jeweller John Hardy, who had bamboo used in the revolutionary structures that formed the landmark Green School (p202) in 2007. People took one look at the fabulous fantasy of its bridge and came away inspired. Since then bamboo's use in buildings has taken off across Bali. There are some beautiful examples of its use, including the following:

Fivelements (p202) A health resort, not far from the Green School.

Power of Now Oasis (p127) A striking beachside yoga studio in Sanur.

Hai Bar & Grill (p155) A beachside bar on Nusa Lembongan.

Sardine (p91) The lauded restaurant on its own rice field in Kerobokan.

Finns Beach Club (p104) A high-style, upscale beach lounge and restaurant near Canggu.

Most hotel designs on Bali and Lombok are purely functional or pastiches of traditional designs, but some of the finest hotels on the islands aspire to something greater. Notable examples:

Tandjung Sari (p128) Located in Sanur, it is Wija Waworuntu's classic prototype for the Balinese boutique beach hotel.

The rule that no building shall exceed the height of a coconut palm dates back to the 1960s when the 10-storey Bali Beach Hotel caused much consternation. However, soaring land prices in the south and ineffectual enforcement of building codes mean that this 'rule' is being increasingly challenged.

Amandari (p181) The crowning achievement of architect Peter Muller, who also designed the two Oberois. Located near Ubud, the inclusion of traditional Balinese materials, crafts and construction techniques, as well as Balinese design principles, respects the island's approach to the world.

Oberoi (p86) The very first luxury hotel, located in Seminyak, remains Muller's relaxed vision of a Balinese village. The *bale agung* (village assembly hall) and *bale banjar* form the basis for common areas.

Oberoi Lombok (p300) Lombok's most luxurious and traditionally styled hotel.

Hotel Tugu Bali (p102) In Canggu, exemplifies the notion of instant age, the ability of materials in Bali to weather quickly and provide 'pleasing decay'.

Four Seasons Resort (p182) A striking piece of aerial sculpture near Ubud, with a huge elliptical lotus pond sitting above a base structure that appears like an eroded and romantic ruin set within a spectacular river valley.

Alila Villas Uluwatu (p144) In far south Bali, Alila employs an artful contemporary style that's light and airy, conveying a sense of great luxury. Set amid hotel-tended rice fields, it embodies advanced green-building principles.

Katamama (p93) The same architectural derring-do that makes neighbouring Potato Head much copied is on display at the club's hotel. However, here the details are lavish and artful. Designed by Indonesian Andra Martin, it's a lavish confection of Javanese bricks, Balinese stone and other indigenous materials.

Lombok Architecture

Traditional laws and practices govern Lombok's architecture. Construction must begin on a propitious day, always with an odd-numbered date, and the building's frame must be completed on that day. It would be bad luck to leave any of the important structural work until the following day.

There are some picturesque traditional Sasak villages in Rembitan and Sade, near Kuta.

A traditional Sasak village layout is a walled enclosure. There are three types of buildings: the *beruga* (open-sided pavilion), the *bale tani* (family house) and the *lumbung* (rice barn). The *beruga* and *bale tani* are both rectangular, with low walls and a steeply pitched thatched roof; of course, the *beruga* is much larger. A *bale tani* is made of bamboo on a base of compacted mud. It usually has no windows and the arrangement of rooms is very standardised. There is a *serambi* (open veranda) at the front and two rooms on two different levels inside – one for cooking and entertaining guests, the other for sleeping and storage.

Environment

This region has rich and varied natural environments. Volcanoes, beaches and reefs are just some of the prominent features. Along with this are an array of creatures, from ducks in the rice fields to one of the world's rarest birds. Ever-growing tourist numbers mean that the threats to these unique environments are many, but there's much each visitor can do to lessen their impact.

The Landscape

Bali is a small island, midway along the string of islands that makes up the Indonesian archipelago. It's adjacent to the most heavily populated island of Java, and immediately west of the chain of smaller islands comprising Nusa Tenggara, which includes Lombok and the Gili Islands.

Bali is visually dramatic – a mountainous chain with a string of active volcanoes and several peaks around 2000m. The agricultural lands are south and north of the central mountains. The southern region is a wide, gently sloping area, where most of the country's abundant rice crop is grown. The northern coastal strip is narrower, rising rapidly into the foothills of the central range. It receives less rain, but coffee, copra, rice and cattle are farmed there. Bali also has beaches in all shapes, characters and colours, from hidden coves to dramatic sweeps, from lonely strands to party scenes, and from pearly white to sparkling black.

The Indonesian Ecotourism Centre (www.indecon.or.id) is devoted to highlighting responsible tourism; Bali Fokus (www.balifokus.asia) promotes sustainable community programs on Bali for recycling and reuse.

Bali's arid, less-populated regions include the western mountain region and the eastern and northeastern slopes of Gunung Agung. The Nusa Penida islands are dry and cannot support intensive rice agriculture. The Bukit Peninsula is similarly dry, but with the growth of tourism, it's become very populous.

Volcanoes

This region is volcanically active and extremely fertile. The two go hand-in-hand as eruptions contribute to the land's exceptional fertility, and high mountains provide the dependable rainfall that irrigates complex and amazingly beautiful patchworks of rice terraces. Of course, the volcanoes are a hazard as well – Bali has endured disastrous eruptions in the past, the worst of which occurred in 1963, when Gunung Agung, the island's 3142m high 'Mother Mountain', erupted and almost 2000 lives were lost. Less dramatic eruptions occurred in 2017 and 2018. Also active is the comparatively diminutive 1717m Gunung Batur, which rises from a lake that itself is set in a vast crater.

Animals & Plants

Since Bali is geologically young, most of its living things have migrated from elsewhere and true native wild animals are rare. This is not hard to imagine in the heavily populated and extravagantly fertile south of Bali, where the orderly rice terraces are so intensively cultivated they look more like a work of sculpture than a natural landscape.

In fact, rice fields cover under 20% of the island's surface area, and there is a great variety of other environmental zones: the dry scrub of the northwest, the extreme northeast and the southern peninsula; patches of dense jungle in the river valleys; forests of bamboo; and harsh volcanic regions that are barren rock and volcanic tuff at higher altitudes.

Animals

Wild Animals

Bali has lots and lots of lizards, and they come in all shapes and sizes. The small ones (onomatopoeically called *cecak*) that hang around light fittings in the evening, waiting for an unwary insect, are a familiar sight. Geckos are lizards often heard but less often seen. The loud and regularly repeated two-part cry 'geck-oh' is a nightly background noise that many visitors soon enjoy.

Bali has more than 300 species of birds, but the one that is truly native to the island is the Bali starling. Much more common are colourful birds such as the orange-banded thrush, numerous species of egrets, kingfishers, parrots, owls and many more.

Bali's only wilderness area, Bali Barat National Park (Taman Nasional Bali Barat), has a number of wild species, including grey and black monkeys (which you will also see in the mountains, Ubud and east Bali), *muncak* (barking deer), squirrels, bats and iguanas.

The plight of Bali's dogs and the irony of the important role they play in island life is captured by filmmakers Lawrence Blair and Dean Allan Tolhurst in *Bali: Island of the Dogs* (2010).

Bali Starling

Also known as the Bali myna, Rothschild's mynah, or locally as *jalak putih,* the Bali starling is perhaps Bali's only endemic bird (opinions differ – as other places are so close, who can tell?). It is striking white in colour, with black tips to the wings and tail, and a distinctive bright-blue mask. These natural good looks have caused the bird to be poached into virtual extinction. The wild population is thought to number under 100. In captivity, however, there are hundreds if not thousands.

RESPONSIBLE TRAVEL

To visit Indonesia responsibly, try to tread lightly as you go, with respect for both the land and the diverse cultures of its people.

Watch your use of water Water demand outstrips supply in much of Indonesia – even in seemingly green places like Bali. Take your hotel up on its offer to save water by not washing your sheets and towels every day. At the high end you can also forgo your own private plunge pool, or a pool altogether.

Don't hit the bottle Those bottles of Aqua (a top local brand of bottled water, owned by Danone) are convenient but they add up. The zillions of such bottles tossed away each year are a serious blight. Since tap water is unsafe, ask your hotel if you can refill from their huge containers of drinking water. Some businesses already offer this service.

Support environmentally aware businesses The number of businesses committed to good environmental practices is growing fast in Indonesia.

Conserve power Turn off lights and air-con when not using them.

Bag the bags Refuse plastic bags and say no to plastic straws too.

Leave the animals be Reconsider swimming with captive dolphins, riding elephants and patronising attractions where wild animals are made to perform for crowds; these interactions have been identified by animal-welfare experts as harmful to the animals. And don't try to pet, feed or otherwise interact with animals in the wild as it disrupts their natural behaviour and can make them sick.

THE WALLACE LINE

The 19th-century naturalist Sir Alfred Wallace (1822–1913) observed great differences in fauna between Bali and Lombok – as great as the differences between Africa and South America. In particular, there were no large mammals (elephants, rhinos, tigers etc) east of Bali, and very few carnivores. He postulated that during the ice ages, when sea levels were lower, animals could have moved by land from what is now mainland Asia all the way to Bali, but the deep Lombok Strait would always have been a barrier. He drew a line between Bali and Lombok, which he believed marked the biological division between Asia and Australia.

Plant life does not display such a sharp division, but there is a gradual transition from predominantly Asian rainforest species to mostly Australian plants, such as eucalypts and acacias, which are better suited to long, dry periods. This is associated with the lower rainfall as one moves east of Java. Environmental differences – including those in the natural vegetation – are now thought to provide a better explanation of the distribution of animal species than Wallace's theory about limits to their original migrations.

Near Ubud, the Bali Bird Park (p202) has large aviaries where you can see Bali starlings. The park was one of the major supporters of efforts to reintroduce the birds into the wild. Efforts to reintroduce the species include a breeding program run by the NGO Friends of the National Parks Foundation (p157) on Nusa Penida.

Marine Animals

There is a rich variety of coral, seaweed, fish and other marine life in the coastal waters off the islands; in fact Indonesia's entire marine territory has been declared a manta ray sanctuary. Much of the marine life can be appreciated by snorkellers, but you're only likely to see the larger marine animals while diving.

Dolphins

Dolphins can be found right around the islands and have been made into an attraction off Lovina. But you're just as likely to see schools of dolphins if you take a fast boat between Bali and the Gilis.

Sharks

There are very occasional reports of large sharks, including great whites, throughout the region, although they are not considered a massive threat.

Sea Turtles

Both green and hawksbill turtles inhabit the waters around Bali, and both species are supposedly protected by international laws that prohibit trade in anything made from sea turtles.

In Bali, however, green sea turtle meat *(penyu)* is a traditional and very popular delicacy, particularly for Balinese feasts. Bali is the site of the most intensive slaughter of green sea turtles in the world – no reliable figures are available, although in 1999 it was estimated that more than 30,000 are killed annually. It's easy to find the trade on the backstreets of waterside towns such as Benoa.

Still, some progress is being made, especially by groups like ProFauna (www.profauna.net), which is raising awareness on Bali about sea turtles and other animals across Indonesia.

A broad coalition of divers and journalists supports the SOS Sea Turtles (www.sos-seaturtles.ch) campaign, which spotlights turtle abuse in

The only national park on Bali is Bali Barat National Park. It covers 190 sq km at the western tip of Bali, plus a substantial area of coastal mangrove and the adjacent marine area, including the excellent dive site at Menjangan.

Bali. It has been instrumental in exposing the illegal poaching of turtles at Wakatobi National Park in Sulawesi for sale in Bali. This illegal trade is widespread and, like the drug trade, hard to prevent. Bali's Hindu Dharma, the body overseeing religious practice, has decreed that turtle meat is essential in only very vital ceremonies.

Some turtle hatcheries open to the public do a good job of educating locals about the need to protect turtles and think of them as living creatures (as opposed to satay), but these operations have their own complexities, and many environmentalists are opposed to them because they keep captive turtles. There are also hatcheries that are ostensibly conservationist, but in reality are run as commercial tourist attractions with little concern for the welfare of the turtles. Environmental groups recommend you do not visit certain hatcheries in Tangung Benoa and around Sanur.

One hawksbill turtle that visited Bali was tracked the following year. He travelled to Java, Kalimantan, Australia (Perth and much of Queensland) and then back to Bali.

Two that win praise are the Bali Sea Turtle Society (p67) in Kuta and Proyek Penyu (p200) in Pemuteran.

On Nusa Penida, volunteers can join the efforts of Green Lion Bali (p158), which runs a turtle hatchery.

Fish

Smaller fish and corals can be found at a plethora of spots around the islands. Everybody's favourite first stop is Bali's Menjangan. Fish as large as whale sharks have been reported, but what thrills scores daily is the coloured beauty of an array of corals, sponges, lacy sea fans and much more. Starfish abound and you'll easily spot clownfish and other polychromatic characters.

Plants

Trees

Much of the island is cultivated. As with most things in Bali, trees have a spiritual and religious significance, and you'll often see them decorated with scarves and black-and-white chequered cloths (*poleng,* a cloth signifying spiritual energy) signifying their sacred status. The *waringin* (banyan tree) is the holiest Balinese tree and no important temple is complete without a stately one growing within its precincts. The banyan is an extensive, shady tree with an exotic feature: creepers that drop from its branches to take root to propagate a new tree. *Jepun* (frangipani or plumeria trees), with their beautiful and sweet-smelling white flowers, are found everywhere.

Balinese Flora & Fauna (1999), published by Periplus, is a concise and beautifully illustrated guide to the animals and plants you'll see on your travels. The feature on the ecology of a rice field is excellent.

Bali's forests cover 127,000 hectares, ranging from virgin land to tree farms to densely forested mountain villages. The total is constantly under threat from wood poaching for carved souvenirs and cooking fuel, and from development.

Bali has monsoonal rather than tropical rainforests, so it lacks the valuable rainforest hardwoods that require rain year-round. Nearly all the hardwood used for carving furniture and high-end artwork is imported from Sumatra and Kalimantan.

A number of plants have great practical and economic significance. *Tiing* (bamboo) is grown in several varieties and is used for everything from satay sticks to hip and stylish resorts.

Flowers & Gardens

Balinese gardens are a delight. The soil and climate can support a huge range of plants, and the Balinese love of beauty and the abundance of cheap labour means that every space can be landscaped. The style is generally informal, with curved paths, a rich variety of plants and usually a water feature. Who wouldn't be enchanted by a frangipani tree dropping a carpet of fragrant blossoms?

You can find almost every type of flower in Bali, but some are seasonal and others are restricted to the cooler mountain areas. Many of the flowers will be familiar to visitors – hibiscus, bougainvillea, poinsettia, oleander, jasmine, water lily and aster are commonly seen in the southern tourist areas.

Less-familiar flowers include Javanese *ixora (soka, angsoka),* with round clusters of red-orange flowers; *champak (cempaka),* a fragrant member of the magnolia family; flamboyant, the flower of the royal poinciana flame tree; *manori (maduri),* which has several traditional uses; and water convolvulus *(kangkung),* whose leaves are commonly used as a green vegetable. There are thousands of species of orchid.

Bali's climate means that gardens planted today look mature – complete with soaring shade trees – in just a couple of years. Good places to see Bali's plant bounty include Bali Botanic Garden (p245), Bali Orchid Garden (p125) and the many plant nurseries (north from Sanur and along the road to Denpasar).

Despite water shortages, villa construction and other loss of rice fields, Bali's rice production hit a record in 2015 (the last year with detailed records available) of 853,710 tonnes. With island consumption at 455,000 tonnes, that keeps Bali as a rice exporter.

Environmental Issues

Bali

Fast-growing populations, limited resources, pressure from the increasing number of visitors and lax or nonexistent environmental regulations mean that Bali is under great threat. And some of Bali's environmental

GROWING RICE

Rice cultivation has shaped the social landscape in Bali – the intricate organisation necessary for growing rice is a large factor in the strength of community life. Rice cultivation has also changed the environmental landscape – terraced rice fields trip down hillsides like steps for a giant, in shades of gold, brown and green, green and more green. Some date back 1000 years or more.

Subak, the village association that deals with water rights and irrigation, makes careful use of all the surface water. The fields are a complete ecological system, home for much more than just rice. In the early morning you'll often see the duck herders leading their flocks out for a day's paddle around a flooded rice field; the ducks eat various pests and leave fertiliser in their wake.

A harvested field with its leftover burnt rice stalks is soaked with water and repeatedly ploughed, often by two bullocks pulling a wooden plough. Once the field is muddy enough, a small corner is walled off and seedling rice is planted there. When it is a reasonable size, it's replanted, shoot by shoot, in the larger field. While the rice matures, there is time to practise the gamelan, watch the dancers or do a little woodcarving. Finally, the whole village turns out for the harvest – a period of solid hard work. While it's only men who plant the rice, everybody takes part in harvesting it.

In 1969, new high-yield rice varieties were introduced. These can be harvested a month sooner than the traditional variety and are resistant to many diseases. However, the new varieties also require more fertiliser and irrigation water, which strains the imperilled water supplies. More pesticides are also needed, causing the depletion of the frog and eel populations that depend on the insects for survival.

Although everyone agrees that the new rice doesn't taste as good as the traditional rice, the new strains now account for more than 90% of the rice grown in Bali. Small areas of traditional rice are still planted and harvested in traditional ways to placate the rice goddess, Dewi Sri. Temples and offerings to her dot every rice field.

Recently, a few farmers have been trying to grow organic rice and you may see it on menus in top restaurants and at better markets.

worries are larger than the island: climate change is causing increased water levels that are damaging the coast and beaches.

Meanwhile, a fast-growing population in Bali has put pressure on limited resources. The tourist industry has attracted new residents, and there is a rapid growth in urban areas and of resorts and villas that encroach onto agricultural land. Concerns include:

A study showed that the average occupied hotel room in south Bali accounted for 1000L to 1500L of water a day for use by its occupants and to service their needs. In contrast the average local required less than 120L a day for all needs.

Water usage A major concern. Typical top-end hotels use 1000L to 1500L of water a day per room, and the growing number of golf courses – the ones on the arid Bukit Peninsula in the Pecatu Indah development and at Nusa Dua, for example – put further pressure on an already stressed resource. The many huge new resorts on the Bukit's south coast are also massive water users.

Water pollution A major problem, both from deforestation brought on by firewood collecting in the mountains and lack of proper treatment for the waste produced by the local population. Streams that run into the ocean at popular spots like Double Six Beach in Legian are very polluted, often with waste water from hotels. The vast mangroves along the south coast near Benoa Harbour are losing their ability to filter the water that drains here from much of the island and are themselves threatened with development.

Air pollution As anyone stuck behind a smoke-belching truck or bus on one of the main roads knows, south Bali's air is often smoggy. The view of south Bali from a hillside shows a brown blanket hanging in the air that could be LA in the 1960s.

Waste The problem is not just all those plastic bags and water bottles but the sheer volume of waste produced by the growing population – what to do with it? The Balinese look with sadness at the enormous amounts of waste – especially plastic – that have accumulated in their once pristine rivers.

On the upside, there is a nascent effort to grow rice and other foods organically. A sewage treatment program in the south is operating in certain areas, though some businesses still refuse to connect in objection to costs.

In Pemuteran, artificial reef-growing programs have won universal praise. This is important, as a study by the World Wide Fund for Nature found that less than 5% of Bali's reefs were fully healthy.

Lombok & the Gilis

On Lombok, environmental disaster in the gold-rush town of Sekotong is ongoing. Gold mining using mercury in huge open-cast pits is causing enormous damage to once-pristine areas. Development in the south, especially around the beaches in the Kuta region, is accelerating with often enormous and unchecked environmental effects.

Coastal erosion is a problem here, just as it is on Bali. The Gilis are naturally concerned. On the plus side, the reefs around the Gilis are on the road to recovery as tourism has spurred intense preservation efforts.

Survival Guide

Directory A–Z

Accessible Travel

Bali

Bali, with its wide range of tourist services and facilities, is the favoured destination for travellers with disabilities since it is much easier to find suitable amenities and adapted accommodation. Sanur and Nusa Dua – where the higher-end hotels and resorts are located – are more wheelchair-accessible than Kuta, Legian and Seminyak, although there are accessible beach walks in all of these locations. But expect high kerbs, few kerb cuts, badly maintained and crowded pavements (sidewalks), and steps into many establishments. Help, however, is always readily at hand.

Most temples are only partially wheelchair accessible at best, stairs being an integral philosophical part of every Hindu temple. However, there is often a way around these stairs – ask a caretaker or a local.

Pura Ulun Danu Bratan (p245) is entirely accessible, and Pura Taman Ayun (p279), Pura Luhur Ulu Watu (p141) and Pura Tirta Empul (p198) have ramps to most areas. Taman Tirta Gangga (p225), Taman Ujung (p224) and Jatiluwih rice terraces (p250) are also accessible to a great extent, making them well worth a visit.

Bali One Care (balionecare.com) Can arrange accessible transport and supplies a wide range of mobility and medical equipment, as well as care, nursing and even babysitting services.

Bali Beach Wheels (☎877 6508 5812; balibeachwheels.com) This brand-new company has three Hippocampe beach/all-terrain wheelchairs for hire by the day, week or month for easier access to the beach and rice paddies.

Download Lonely Planet's free Accessible Travel guides from http://lptravel.to/AccessibleTravel.

Lombok

Lombok is not well set up to cater to those with any visual, mobility or hearing impairments. It'd be wise to consult with a local specialist like **Accessible Indonesia** (www.accessibleindonesia.org) or **Bali Access Travel** (www.baliaccesstravel.com), who can assist with trip planning and advice.

SLEEPING PRICE RANGES

The following price ranges refer to a double room with a bathroom. Unless otherwise stated, taxes are included in the price.

$ less than 450,000Rp (under US$30)

$$ 450,000–1,400,000Rp (US$30–95)

$$$ more than 1,400,000Rp (over US$95)

Accommodation

Bali has a huge range of great-value accommodation for any budget. If visiting in the peak periods of August and Christmas, book three or more months ahead.

Homestays & Guesthouses Bali's family-run accommodation is comfortable and puts you right in the middle of fascinating local life.

Hotels Many of Bali's hundreds of hotels are located near the action and offer good deals.

Resorts Bali has some of the world's best resorts at prices that would be a bargain elsewhere. You can stay on the beach or be nestled in a lush mountain valley.

Villas Enjoy a sybaritic escape and private pool.

Booking Services

Websites such as homeaway.com and airbnb.com have hundreds of listings for Bali villas and private accommodation. However, many listed properties are not licensed,

BOOKING HOTELS

When booking a south Bali hotel room, be careful where you book.

As tourist numbers on Bali have exploded, so have the number of chain hotels. The number of available rooms has more than doubled since 2005. The boom in the construction of large hotels in Kuta, Legian, Seminyak, Kerobokan and Canggu is changing the area's character in fundamental ways, especially as the many family-run, cheap and cheerful small inns are pushed out.

While some of these large new hotels are appearing in traditionally appealing areas of south Bali, not far from the beaches and nightlife, scores more are opening far from the areas visitors consider desirable. Many chains have properties in both good and unappealing areas and it is easy to get misled about a hotel's actual location, especially on booking websites. In the tradition of real estate agents everywhere, 'Seminyak' is now the address used for hotels far into Denpasar.

So when you see that great web bargain for a midrange room for US$40, carefully consider the following:

➡ Anything west of the Jl Legian–Jl Seminyak–Jl Kerobokan spine will be close to both beaches and nightlife.

➡ East of the spine things begin to get inconvenient fast. There will be less to walk to, beaches can be far and cruising cabs hard to come by.

➡ Jl Ngurah Rai Bypass and Jl Sunset are both noisy major streets that lack charm and are hard to cross. Many new chain hotels are located right on these traffic-choked thoroughfares.

➡ East of Jl Ngurah Rai Bypass and Jl Sunset and you are deep into suburban Denpasar, where it will be hard to find cabs or much else you'll be interested in.

➡ In Sanur, which is also getting an influx of chain hotels, Jl Ngurah Rai Bypass should be the absolute western border in your room hunt.

➡ With careful shopping, you can usually find great room deals in the most appealing parts of south Bali, and often you can end up at a small or family-run guesthouse with oodles more charm and character than a generic cheap hotel.

which makes for an unregulated market with all the associated pros and cons. Local agents include the following:

Bali Discovery (☎0361-286283; www.balidiscovery.com) The main local source for hotel deals (it's always worth comparing their rates to the major websites); also books villas.

Bali Private Villas (☎0361-844 4344; www.baliprivatevillas.com) Handles a variety of top-end villas.

Bali Ultimate Villas (☎0851 0057 1658; www.baliultimatevillas.net) A villa agent that also offers wedding services.

Lonely Planet (www.lonelyplanet.com/hotels/) Recommendations and bookings.

Budget Hotels

The cheapest accommodation on Bali is in small places that are simple but clean and comfortable. Names often include the word 'losmen', 'homestay', 'inn' or '*pondo*'. Many are built in the style of a traditional Balinese home.

There are budget hotels all over Bali, and they vary widely in standards and price. Expect the following:

➡ Maybe air-con

➡ Maybe hot water

➡ Private bathroom with shower and Western-style toilet

➡ Often a pool

➡ Simple breakfast

➡ Carefree and cheery staff

International budget chains are making a splashy entry into south Bali, but note that a tiny US$9 room quickly hits US$40 when you add various extras such as taxes and fees for items included elsewhere, like internet and towels.

Midrange Hotels

Older midrange hotels are often constructed in Balinese bungalow style or in two-storey blocks and are set on spacious grounds with a pool. Many have a sense of style that is beguiling and may help postpone your departure. In addition to what you'll get at a budget hotel, expect the following:

➡ Balcony, porch or patio

➡ Satellite TV

➡ Small fridge

➡ Often wi-fi

BOOK YOUR STAY ONLINE

For more accommodation reviews by Lonely Planet authors, check out http://lonelyplanet.com/hotels/. You'll find independent reviews, as well as recommendations on the best places to stay. Best of all, you can book online.

Note that dozens of mid-range chain hotels have appeared across south Bali. Rooms are often small and the sites cramped, although standards are reliable. But beware of properties far from the beach and nightlife.

Top-End Hotels

Top-end hotels and resorts in Bali are world-class. Service is refined and you can expect decor plucked from the pages of a glossy magazine, along with the following:

- Superb service
- Views – ocean, lush valleys and rice fields or private gardens
- Spa
- Maybe a private pool
- Not wanting to leave

Villas

Villas are scattered around south Bali and Ubud, and are now appearing in the east. They're often built in the middle of rice paddies, seemingly overnight. The villa boom has been quite controversial for environmental, aesthetic and economic reasons. Many skip collecting government taxes from guests, which has raised the ire of their luxury hotel competitors and brought threats of crackdowns.

Large villas, such as those found in the Canggu area, can be bacchanalian retreats for groups of friends. Others are smaller, more intimate and part of larger developments – common in Seminyak and Kerobokan – or top-end hotels. Expect the following:

- Private garden
- Private pool
- Kitchen
- Air-con bedroom(s)
- Open-air common space

Villas will also potentially include:

- Your own staff (cook, driver, cleaner)
- Lush grounds
- Private beachfront
- Isolation (which can be good or bad)

Rates range from around US$200 per night for a modest villa to US$2000 per week and beyond for your own tropical estate. There are often deals, especially in the low season, and several couples sharing can make something grand affordable. You can sometimes save quite a bit by waiting until the last minute, but during the high season the best villas book up far in advance.

VILLA RENTAL QUESTIONS

It's the Wild West out there. There are myriad agents, some excellent, others not. It is essential to be as clear as possible about what you want when arranging a rental. Some things to keep in mind and ask about when renting a villa:

- How far is the villa from the beach and stores?
- Is a driver or car service included?
- If there is a cook, is food included?
- Is there an electricity surcharge?
- Are there extra cleaning fees?
- Is laundry included?
- What refunds apply on a standard 50% deposit?
- Is there wi-fi and is it free?

Long-Term Accommodation

For longer stays, you can find flats for US$300 to US$1200 a month and much more. Sources include the following:

- Facebook groups. There are scores with rentals on Bali; Bali Rooms for Rent (www.facebook.com/baliroomsforrent) is one large board. You can also try looking for groups with names like '[name of town] Housing'.
- Bali Advertiser (www.baliadvertiser.biz)
- Noticeboards in cafes such as Bali Bhudda in Ubud and Umalas, plus the many Cafe Moka locations. Bintang supermarkets in Seminyak and Ubud are also good.
- Word of mouth. Tell your new Bali friends you're looking, as everybody seems to know someone with a place for rent.

Climate

Denpasar

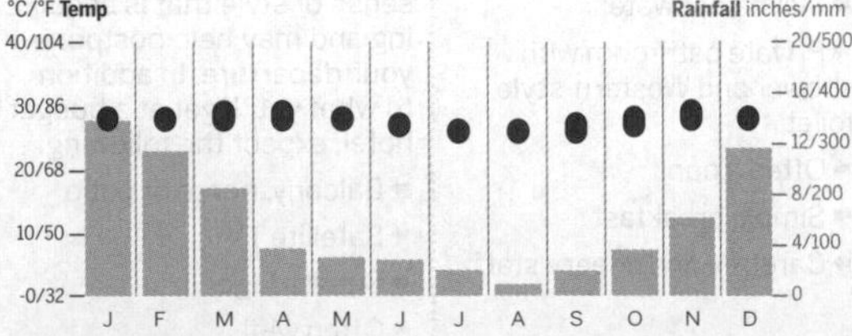

Customs Regulations

Indonesia's list of prohibited imports includes drugs, weapons, fresh fruit and anything remotely pornographic. Items allowed include the following:

- 200 cigarettes (or 50 cigars or 100g of tobacco)
- a 'reasonable amount' of perfume
- 1L of alcohol

Surfers with more than two or three boards may be charged a fee, and this can apply to other items if the officials suspect that you intend to sell them in Indonesia. There is no restriction on foreign currency, but the import or export of rupiah is limited to 5,000,000Rp. Greater amounts must be declared.

Electricity

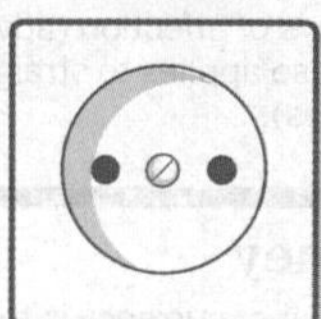

Type C
220V/50Hz

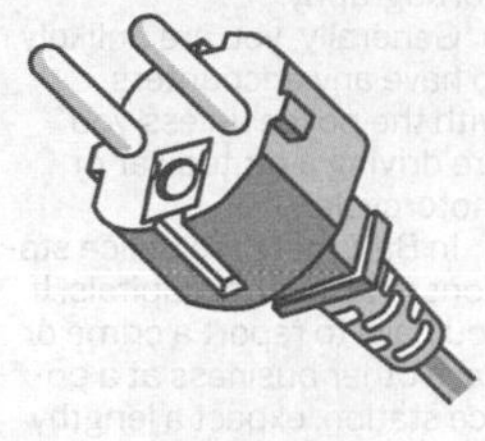

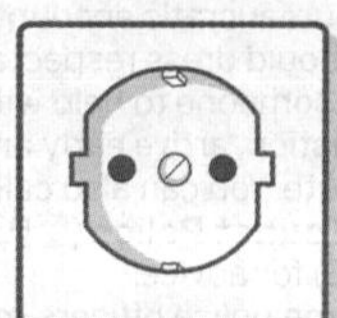

Type F
230V/50Hz

Embassies & Consulates

Foreign embassies are in Jakarta, the national capital. Most of the foreign representatives in Bali are consular agents (or honorary consuls) who can't offer the same services as a full consulate or embassy. A lost passport may mean a trip to an embassy in Jakarta.

The USA, Australia and Japan have formal consulates in Bali (citizens from these countries make up half of all visitors).

Indonesian embassies and consulates abroad are listed on the website of Indonesia's Ministry of Foreign Affairs (www.kemlu.go.id). There is a handy search function under the 'Mission' menu item, which also gives contact details for other nations' embassies and contacts in Indonesia.

Australian Consulate (Map p120; ☎0361-200 0100; www.bali.indonesia.embassy.gov.au; Jl Tantular 32, Denpasar; ⊙8am-4pm Mon-Fri) The Australian consulate has a consular sharing agreement with Canada.

Japanese Consulate (Map p120; ☎0361-265066; www.denpasar.id.emb-japan.go.jp; Jl Raya Puputan 170; ⊙10am-3pm Mon-Fri)

US Consulate (☎0361-233605; https://id.usembassy.gov; Jl Hayam Wuruk 310, Renon, Denpasar; ⊙9am-noon & 1-3.30pm Mon-Fri)

Food

Bali is a splendid destination for food. The local cuisine, whether truly Balinese or influenced by the rest of Indonesia and Asia, draws from the bounty of fresh local foods and is rich with spices and flavours. Savour this fare at roadside warungs (simple local cafes) or top-end restaurants. For tastes further afield, you can choose from restaurants offering some of the best dining in the region.

The following price ranges represent the average cost of a main course or meal.

$ less than 60,000Rp (under US$4)

$$ 60,000–250,000Rp (US$4–17)

$$$ more than 250,000Rp (over US$17)

Insurance

A travel-insurance policy to cover theft, loss and medical problems is essential. There is a wide variety of policies, most sold online; make certain your policy will cover speedy medical evacuation from anywhere in Indonesia.

Theft is a potential problem on Bali and elsewhere in Indonesia, so make sure that your policy covers expensive items adequately. Many policies have restrictions on laptops and expensive camera gear, and refunds are often for depreciated value, not replacement value.

Worldwide travel insurance is available at www.lonelyplanet.com/travel-insurance. You can buy, extend and claim online anytime – even if you're already on the road.

Internet Access

➡ Free wi-fi is common in cafes, restaurants, hotels and malls. Internet cafes are uncommon.

➡ Internet speeds are reasonably fast, especially in south Bali, Ubud and mainland Lombok.

➡ 3G data and faster is universal.

Language Courses

Many visitors to Bali like to learn at least the basics of Bahasa Indonesia. South Bali and Ubud have many tutors who advertise in the same places you'll find rental listings. Otherwise, the best place for courses in Bahasa Indonesia is the **Indonesia Australia Language Foundation** (IALF; ☎0361-225243; www.ialf.edu; Jl Raya Sesetan 190).

Legal Matters

The Indonesian government takes the smuggling, using and selling of drugs very seriously and the drug laws are unambiguous. If caught with drugs, you may have to wait for up to six months in jail before trial. As seen in high-profile cases involving foreigners, multiyear prison terms are common for people caught with illegal drugs, including marijuana. Those found guilty of dealing can be subject to the death penalty.

Gambling is illegal (although it's common, especially at cockfights), as is pornography.

Generally, you are unlikely to have any encounters with the police unless you are driving a rented car or motorcycle.

In Bali, there are police stations in all district capitals. If you have to report a crime or have other business at a police station, expect a lengthy and bureaucratic encounter. You should dress respectably, bring someone to help with translation, arrive early and be polite. You can also call the **Bali Tourist Police** (☎0361 224111) for advice.

Some police officers may expect to receive bribes, either to overlook some crime, misdemeanour or traffic infringement (whether actual or not), or to provide a service that they should provide anyway. Generally, it's easiest to pay up – and the sooner this happens, the less it will cost. Travellers may be told there's a 'fine' to pay on the spot, while others may offer to pay a 'fine' to clear things up. How much? Generally, 50,000Rp can work wonders and the officers are not proud. If things seem unreasonable, however, ask for the officer's name and write it down.

LGBT+ Travellers

Bali

Bali is a popular spot for LGBT travellers owing to the many ways it caters to a rainbow of visitors. There is a large gay and lesbian expat community and many own businesses that – if not gay-specific – are very gay-friendly. In south Bali and Ubud, couples have few concerns, beyond remembering that the Balinese are quite modest. Otherwise, there's a rollicking strip of very gay-friendly nightclubs in the heart of Seminyak, and there's no part of Bali any LGBT person should avoid.

Having said that, gay travellers in Bail (and Indonesia) should follow the same precautions as straight travellers and avoid public displays of affection. As the nation becomes more religiously conservative, any form of closeness between people of the same sex may be unwise.

➡ Gay men in Indonesia are referred to as homo or gay; lesbians are *lesbi*.

➡ Indonesia's community of transvestite and transsexual *waria* – from the words *wanita* (woman) and *pria* (man) – has always had a very public profile; they are also known by the less polite term *banci*.

➡ Islamic groups proscribe homosexuality, but physical harassment is uncommon.

➡ GAYa Nusantara (www.gayanusantara.or.id) has a very useful website that covers local LGBT issues.

➡ Bali's gay organisation is Gaya Dewata (www.gayadewata.com).

Lombok

On Lombok, LGBT+ travellers should refrain from public displays of affection (advice that also applies to straight couples).

Money

The unit of currency is the rupiah (Rp). Coins of 50Rp, 100Rp, 200Rp, 500Rp and 1000Rp are in circulation. Notes come in 1000Rp (rare), 2000Rp, 5000Rp, 10,000Rp, 20,000Rp, 50,000Rp and 100,000Rp denominations.

STOPPING CHILD-SEX TOURISM

Strong laws exist in Indonesia to prosecute people seeking to sexually exploit local children, and many countries also have extraterritorial legislation that allows nationals to be prosecuted in their own country for these crimes.

Travellers can help stop child-sex tourism by reporting suspicious behaviour. Reports can be made to the **Anti Human Trafficking Unit** (☎021-721 8098) of the Indonesian police. If you know the nationality of the individual, you can contact their embassy directly.

ATMs

There are ATMs all over Bali. In Lombok they are common on the mainland – you may find them hard to source on smaller satellite islands (like Gili Gede) and in more isolated interior villages. Most accept nonlocal ATM cards and major credit cards for cash advances.

- The exchange rates for ATM withdrawals are usually quite good, but check to see if your home bank will hit you with outrageous fees.
- Most ATMs allow a maximum withdrawal of one million to 2.5 million rupiah per transaction.
- ATMs have stickers indicating whether they issue 50,000Rp or 100,000Rp notes (the former are easier to use for small transactions).
- Most ATMs return your card last instead of before dispensing cash, so it's easy to forget your card.
- Card skimming is a widespread problem in Bali – try to use ATMs attached to banks if possible and keep an eye on your bank balance after making withdrawals.

Credit Cards

Accepted at midrange and better hotels and resorts. More expensive restaurants and shops will also accept them, but there is often a surcharge of around 3%.

Moneychangers

US dollars are by far the easiest currency to exchange. Try to have new US$100 bills.

Follow these steps to avoid getting ripped off when exchanging money:

- Find out the going exchange rate online. Know that anyone offering a better rate or claiming to charge no fees or commissions will need to make a profit through other means.
- Stick to banks, airport exchange counters or large and reputable operations such as the Central Kuta Money Exchange (www.centralkutabali.com), which has locations across south Bali and Ubud.
- Avoid exchange stalls down alleys or in otherwise dubious locations (it sounds obvious but scores of tourists are ripped off daily).
- Common exchange scams include rigged calculators, sleight-of-hand schemes, 'mistakes' on the posted rates, and demands that you hand over your money before you have counted the money on offer.
- Use an ATM to obtain rupiah.

RUPIAH REDENOMINATION

Indonesia has plans to redenominate the rupiah by removing three digits from the currency, although the timing of this has been debated for years. For example, the 20,000Rp note would become the 20Rp note. The exchange value of the new notes would remain the same. Changing the national currency is likely to be a very complex process.

Opening Hours

Typical opening hours are as follows:

Banks 8am–2pm Monday to Thursday, 8am–noon Friday, 8am–11am Saturday

Government offices 8am–3pm Monday to Thursday, 8am–noon Friday (although these are not standardised)

Post offices 8am–2pm Monday to Friday, longer in tourist centres

Restaurants & cafes 8am–10pm daily

Shops & services catering to visitors 9am–8pm or later daily

Post

Bali

Every substantial town has a *kantor pos* (post office). In tourist centres, there are also postal agencies, which provide postal services and are often open long hours. Sending postcards and normal-sized letters (ie under 20g) by airmail is cheap, but not very fast.

From Bali, mail delivery takes two weeks to the US and Australia, and three weeks to the UK and the rest of Europe.

Most post offices will properly wrap parcels over 20g for shipping for a small fee. Don't use the post for anything you'd miss.

International express companies like DHL, Fedex and UPS operate on Bali and offer reliable, fast and expensive service.

Lombok

Major tourist towns like Kuta and Senggigi have a *kantor pos* (post office), but don't expect to ship anything from the Gilis. As with Bali, sending postcards and normal-sized letters by airmail is cheap, but not very fast. From Lombok, mail delivery takes about two to three weeks to Australia, Europe or North America. Don't post anything you'd miss.

Public Holidays

The following holidays are celebrated throughout Indonesia. Many of the dates change according to the phase of the moon (not by month) or by religious calendar, so the following are estimates only.

Tahun Baru Masehi (New Year's Day) 1 January

Tahun Baru Imlek (Chinese New Year) Late January to early February

GOVERNMENT TRAVEL ADVICE

Government advisories often are general and guaranteed to allow for bureaucratic cover should trouble occur. However, the following sites also have useful tips.

Australia (www.smartraveller.gov.au)

Canada (www.travel.gc.ca)

New Zealand (www.safetravel.govt.nz)

UK (www.gov.uk/foreign-travel-advice)

US (www.travel.state.gov)

Wafat Yesus Kristus (Good Friday) Late March or early April

Hari Buruh (Labour Day) 1 May

Hari Waisak (Buddha's birth, enlightenment and death) May

Kenaikan Yesus Kristus (Ascension of Christ) May

Hari Proklamasi Kemerdekaan (Independence Day) 17 August

Hari Natal (Christmas Day) 25 December

The following Islamic holidays are celebrated by Bali's large Muslim population; in addition, many Indonesians travel to Bali at these times. Dates change each year.

Isra Miraj Nabi Muhammad (Ascension of the Prophet Muhammad) Around April

Idul Fitri (Also known as Lebaran) This two-day national public holiday marks the end of Ramadan; avoid travel due to crowds. Around June.

Idul Adha (Islamic feast of the sacrifice) Around September

Muharram (Islamic New Year) Around September

Maulud Nabi Muhammad (Birthday of the Prophet Muhammad) Around December

Safe Travel

It's important to note that compared to many places in the world, this part of Indonesia is fairly safe. There are some hassles from the avaricious, but most visitors face many more dangers at home. There have been some high-profile cases of visitors being injured or killed, but in many cases these tragedies have been inflamed by media sensationalism.

Boat travel carries risks. Take precautions (p452).

Drugs

Numerous high-profile drug cases on Bali and Lombok should be enough to dissuade anyone from having anything to do with illicit drugs. As little as two ecstasy tabs or a bit of pot have resulted in huge fines and multiyear jail sentences in Bali's notorious jail in Kerobokan. Try smuggling and you may pay with your life (remember the Bali Nine?). Kuta is filled with cops posing as dealers.

In the Gilis, the drug trade remains endemic in Trawangan, where you'll get offers of everything from meth to ecstasy and mushrooms. The latter is also openly advertised in cafes on Meno and Air. Those found in possession of or taking drugs risk jail or worse.

Alcohol Poisoning

Outside of reputable bars and resorts, avoid *arak*, the locally produced fermented booze made from rice or palm. Deaths and injuries happen – especially on Bali and the Gilis – when unscrupulous vendors stretch stocks with poisonous chemicals.

Hawkers & Touts

Many visitors regard hawkers and touts as *the* number one annoyance in Bali (and in tourist areas of Lombok). Visitors are frequently, and often constantly, hassled to buy things. The worst places for this are Jl Legian in Kuta, Kuta Beach, the Gunung Batur area, Lovina and the temples at Besakih and Tanah Lot. And the cry of 'Transport?!?' – that's everywhere. Many touts employ fake, irritating Australian accents ('Oi! Mate!').

Use the following tips to deflect attention.

- Completely ignore touts/hawkers.
- Don't make any eye contact.
- A polite *tidak* (no) actually encourages them.
- Never ask the price or comment on the quality of their goods unless you're interested in buying.

Keep in mind, though, that ultimately they're just people trying to make a living, and if you don't want to buy anything, you are wasting their time trying to be polite.

Theft

Violent crime is uncommon, but bag- and phone-snatching from motorbikes, pickpocketing and theft from rooms and parked cars occurs. Take the same precautions you would in any urban area. Other common-sense tips:

- Secure money before leaving an ATM (and don't forget your card!).
- Don't leave valuables on a beach while swimming.
- Use front-desk/in-room safes.

If you are the victim of a theft in the Gili Islands, immediately report thefts to the island *kepala desa* (village head), who will deal with the issue; staff at the dive schools will direct you to him.

While police used to only visit the Gilis sporadically, they set up shop on all three islands following the 2018 earthquakes due to the subsequent looting. Many predict that they are now here to stay.

Scams

It's hard to say when an 'accepted' practice such as overcharging becomes an unacceptable rip-off, but be warned that there are people in Bali (not always Balinese) who will try to rip you off.

Most Balinese would never perpetrate a scam, but some can be reluctant to get involved and warn travellers when one is happening. Be suspicious if you notice that bystanders are uncommunicative and perhaps uneasy, and one person is doing all the talking.

ORPHANAGES

Bali has a number of 'fake' orphanages designed to extract money from well-meaning tourists. If you are considering donating anything to an orphanage, carefully research its reputation online. Orphanages using cab drivers as hawkers are especially suspect.

CAR CON

Locals (often working in pairs) discover a 'serious problem' with your car or motorcycle – it's blowing smoke, leaking oil or petrol, a wheel is wobbling or a tyre is flat (problems that one of the pair creates while the other distracts you). Coincidentally, a brother/cousin/friend nearby can help and soon they're demanding an outrageous sum for their trouble.

CASH SCHEMES

Many travellers are ripped off by money changers who use sleight of hand and rigged calculators. Always count your money at least twice in front of the money changer, and don't let them touch the money again after you've finally counted it. The best defence is to use a bank-affiliated currency exchange or ATMs (although there has been a rash of fake card skimmers attached to ATMs, so check their authenticity and cover your hand as you enter your PIN).

Swimming

Kuta Beach and those to the north and south are subject to heavy surf and strong currents – always swim between the flags. Trained lifeguards are on duty, but only at Kuta, Legian, Seminyak, Nusa Dua, Sanur and (sometimes) Senggigi. Other beaches can have strong currents, even when protected by reefs.

Be careful when swimming over coral and never walk on it. It can be very sharp and coral cuts are easily infected. In addition, you are damaging a fragile environment.

Water pollution is a problem, especially after rain. Swim far away from any open streams you see flowing into the surf, including the often foul and smelly ones at Double Six Beach and Seminyak Beach. The seawater around Kuta is commonly contaminated by run-off from built-up areas.

Do not try to swim between the Gili Islands as currents can be deadly.

Traffic & Footpaths

Apart from the dangers of driving in Bali, the traffic in most tourist areas is often annoying and frequently perilous to pedestrians. Footpaths can be rough, even unusable, and sometimes motorbikes will recklessly swerve on to them. Gaps in the pavement are also a cause of injury. Carry a torch (flashlight) at night.

Telephone

The international access code can be any of three versions; try all three. Mobile phone numbers in Indonesia start with ☎08.

Indonesia's country code ☎62

International access codes ☎001/008/017

Mobile Phones

Cheap local SIM cards (from 5000Rp with no calling credit) are sold everywhere. Data speeds of 3G and faster are the norm across Bali and Lombok. Any modern mobile phone will work.

➡ SIM cards come with cheap rates for calling other countries, starting at US$0.20 per minute.

➡ SIM cards are widely available and easily topped up with credit.

➡ Watch out for vendors who sell SIM cards to visitors for 50,000Rp or more. If they don't come with at least 45,000Rp in credit you are being ripped off. Go elsewhere.

➡ Data plans average about 150,000Rp for 10GB of data.

➡ Telkomsel, a major carrier, often has reps selling SIM cards in the airport

WRONG NUMBER?

Some of Bali's landline phone numbers (those with area codes that include 0361, across the south and Ubud) are being changed on an ongoing basis. To accommodate increased demand for lines, a digit is being added to the start of the existing six- or seven-digit phone number. So 0361-761 XXXX might become 0361-4761 XXXX. The schedule and plans for the new numbers change regularly, but usually you'll hear a recording first in Bahasa Indonesia and then in English telling you what digit to add to the changed number.

PRACTICALITIES

- Bali has a smoking ban that covers most tourist facilities, markets, shops, restaurants, hotels, taxis and more. In practice, adoption is uneven.
- Indonesia uses the metric system.

arrivals area just before the 'duty-free' shop. They cost 50,000Rp and come with credit, plus they offer good data deals. This is an easy way to get set up, but make sure you're not dealing with a faux vendor charging outlandish rates.

Time

Bali is on Waktu Indonesian Tengah or WIT (Central Indonesian Standard Time), which is eight hours ahead of Greenwich Mean Time/Universal Time or two hours behind Australian Eastern Standard Time. Java is another hour behind Bali.

Not allowing for daylight-saving time elsewhere, when it's noon in Bali, it's 11pm the previous day in New York, 8pm in Los Angeles, 4am in London, and 2pm in Sydney and Melbourne.

Toilets

Western-style toilets are pretty universal at cafes and hotels in tourist areas. Public toilets are a rare find.

Tourist Information

The tourist office in **Ubud** (Map p164; ☎0361-973285; www.fabulousubud.com; Jl Raya Ubud; ⏰8am-9pm; 📶) is an excellent source of information on cultural events. Otherwise, the tourist offices in Bali are not useful.

Some of the best information is found in the many free publications and websites aimed at tourists and expats. There are also numerous Facebook groups, although some are simply forums for the intolerant.

Bali Advertiser (www.baliadvertiser.biz) Has excellent columns with info for visitors including 'Greenspeak' by journalist Cat Wheeler and 'Bali Explorer' by legendary travel writer Bill Dalton.

Bali Discovery (www.balidiscovery.com) The weekly online news report by Jack Daniels is a must-read of events in Bali.

The Beat Bali (http://thebeatbali.com) Useful website and biweekly publication with extensive entertainment and cultural listings.

GU Guide (https://cangguguide.com) Female-run website highlighting the hippest happenings in Canggu.

Ubud Now and Then (http://ubudnowandthen.com) Run by famous photographer Rio Helmi and other luminaries; has Ubud-centric info and features, as well as excellent Bali-wide cultural listings.

The Yak (www.theyakmag.com) Glossy, cheeky mag celebrating the expat swells of Seminyak and Ubud.

Visas

Visas are easily obtained but can be a hassle if you hope to stay longer than 30 days.

Visa Types

There are three main visa types for visitors:

Visa in Advance Visitors can apply for a visa before they arrive in Indonesia. Typically this is a visitor's visa, which is valid for 30 or 60 days. Details vary by country; contact your nearest Indonesian embassy or consulate to determine processing fees and times. Note: this is the only way to obtain a 60-day visitor visa, even if you qualify for Visa on Arrival (VOA).

Visa on Arrival Citizens of most countries may apply for a 30-day visa when they arrive at major airports and harbours. The cost is 528,000Rp, payable by cash (no coins) or credit card; other currencies are accepted in amounts equivalent to the fee in Rp. VOA renewals for 30 days are possible.

Visa Free Citizens of most countries can receive a 30-day visa for free upon arrival. This visa cannot be extended.

If you have obtained one of the coveted 60-day visas in advance, be sure the immigration official at the airport gives you a 60-day tourist card.

For further info on Indonesia's visa situation, contact an Indonesian embassy.

Renewing Your Visa

You can renew a 30-day Visa on Arrival once (but not a Visa Free). The procedures are complex:

- At least seven days before your visa expires, go to an immigration office. These can usually be found in larger cities and regional capitals. The best one for south Bali is the **immigrasi office** (☎0361-935 1038; Jl Raya Taman Jimbaran; ⏰8am-4pm Mon-Fri) near Jimbaran.
- Bring your passport, a photocopy of your passport and a copy of your ticket out of Indonesia (which should be for a date during the renewal period).
- Wear modest clothes (eg men may be required to wear long pants).
- Pay a fee of 355,000Rp.
- You may have to return to the office twice over a three- to five-day period for fingerprinting, photos and other procedures.

One way to avoid the renewal hassle is to use a visa agent such as **ChannelOne**

(Map p82; ☎0878 6204 3224; www.channel1.biz; Jl Sunset 100X) on Bali, who (for a fee) will do most of the bureaucratic work for you.

Fines for overstaying your visa expiration date are 300,000Rp per day and include additional hassles.

Social Visas

If you have a good reason for staying longer (eg study or family reasons), you can apply for a *sosial/budaya* (social/cultural) visa. You will need an application form from an Indonesian embassy or consulate, and a letter of introduction or promise of sponsorship from a reputable person or school in Indonesia. It's initially valid for three months, but it can be extended for one month at a time at an immigration office within Indonesia for a maximum of six months. There are fees for the application and for extending the visa.

Volunteering

There's a plethora of opportunities to lend a hand in Bali. Information sources include the Bali Advertiser (www.baliadvertiser.biz), under 'Community Info', and Bali Spirit (www.balispirit.com/ngos). There are also Ubud organisations helping Bali's dogs (p194).

Local Organisations

The following organisations need donations, supplies and often volunteers. Check their websites to see their current status.

Amicorp Community Centre (www.amicorpcommunitycentre.com) This organisation is building a community centre in the village of Les in northeast Bali; it has tours and programs including culinary classes, permaculture training, Balinese gamelan and dance workshops.

Bali Children's Project (www.balichildrensproject.org) Funds education and offers English and computer training.

East Bali Poverty Project (www.eastbalipovertyproject.org) Works to help children in the impoverished mountain villages of east Bali.

Friends of the National Parks Foundation (www.fnpf.org) Has volunteer programs on Nusa Penida aimed at wildlife conservation.

IDEP (www.idepfoundation.org) The Indonesian Development of Education & Permaculture has projects across Indonesia; works on environmental projects, disaster planning and community improvement.

JED (Village Ecotourism Network; ☎0361-366 9951; www.jed.or.id; tours US$75-150) Organises highly regarded tours of small villages, some overnight. Often needs volunteers to improve its services and work with the villagers.

ROLE Foundation (www.rolefoundation.org) Works to improve well-being and self-reliance in underprivileged Bali communities; has environmental projects.

Smile Foundation of Bali (www.senyumbali.org) Organises surgery to correct facial deformities; it operates the **Smile Shop** (Map p168; www.senyumbali.org; Jl Nyuh Kuning; ⊙10am-5pm) in Ubud to raise money.

Yayasan Bumi Sehat (www.bumisehatfoundation.org) Operates an internationally recognised clinic and gives reproductive services to disadvantaged women in Ubud; accepts donated time from medical professionals. Founder Robin Lim has had international recognition.

Yayasan Rama Sesana (www.yrsbali.org) Dedicated to improving reproductive health for women across Bali.

YKIP (www.ykip.org) Established after the 2002 bombings, it organises and funds health and education projects for Bali's children.

Women Travellers

Bali

Bali is generally safer for women than many areas of the world and, with the usual care and common sense, women should feel secure travelling alone.

Lombok

Traditionally, women on Lombok and the Gilis are treated with respect, but in the touristy areas, harassment of single foreign women may occur. Would-be guides/boyfriends/gigolos are often persistent in their approaches and can be aggressive when ignored or rejected. Clothes that aren't too revealing are a good idea – beachwear should be reserved for the beach. Two or more women together are less likely to experience problems, and women accompanied by a man are unlikely to be harassed.

Gili Islands

Although it's rare, some foreign women have experienced sexual harassment and even assault while on the Gilis – it's best not to walk home alone to the quieter parts of the islands.

Transport

GETTING THERE & AWAY

Most visitors to this part of Indonesia will arrive by air. Island-hoppers can catch frequent ferries between eastern Java and Bali, between Bali and Lombok, and between many destinations in Nusa Tenggara.

Flights, cars and tours can be booked online at lonelyplanet.com/bookings.

Entering the Region

The two major points of arrival are Bali's Ngurah Rai International Airport and Lombok International Airport.

Passport

Your passport *must* be valid for six months after your date of arrival in Indonesia. Before passing through immigration you may fill out a disembarkation card, half of which you must keep to give to immigration when you leave the country.

Air

Departure tax is included in the price of a ticket.

Bali

Ngurah Rai International Airport (http://bali-airport.com), just south of Kuta, is the only airport in Bali. It is sometimes referred to internationally as Denpasar or on some internet flight-booking sites as Bali.

Bali's current airport terminal opened in 2013. Unfortunately, it has many problems:

- Outrageous food and drink prices, even by airport standards.
- A serpentine layout that forces departing passengers to walk a very long narrow path amid shops.
- Long lines at immigration and customs. Immigration officials may offer passengers a chance to cut the queue for an unsanctioned fee of 750,000Rp.
- Nonoperating escalators.
- Touts offering dubious accommodation and transport services in the arrivals area.

International airlines flying to and from Bali have myriad flights to Australia and Asian capitals. The present runway is too short for planes flying nonstop to/from Europe.

Note that domestic airlines serving Bali from other parts of Indonesia change frequently.

Arrival procedures at the airport are straightforward, although it can take some time for planeloads of visitors to clear immigration; afternoons are typically worst.

At baggage claim, porters are keen to help get your luggage to the customs tables and beyond, and they've been known to ask up to US$20 for their services – if you want help with your bags, agree on a price beforehand. The formal price is 10,000Rp per piece. Luggage carts are always free.

Once through customs, you're out with the tour operators, touts and taxi drivers. Ignore the touts as they offer no service of value, except to themselves.

TRANSPORT HUBS

Ngurah Rai International Airport Flights to/from many international and domestic destinations.

Lombok International Airport Flights to/from Kuala Lumpur and Singapore internationally, and Jakarta, Denpasar and other airports within Indonesia.

Benoa Harbour (Bali) Pelni ships from ports throughout Indonesia dock here.

Gilimanuk (West Bali) Ferry service to and from Java.

Padangbai (Bali) Boat service to Lombok and the Gili Islands.

CLIMATE CHANGE & TRAVEL

Every form of transport that relies on carbon-based fuel generates CO_2, the main cause of human-induced climate change. Modern travel is dependent on aeroplanes, which might use less fuel per kilometre per person than most cars but travel much greater distances. The altitude at which aircraft emit gases (including CO_2) and particles also contributes to their climate change impact. Many websites offer 'carbon calculators' that allow people to estimate the carbon emissions generated by their journey and, for those who wish to do so, to offset the impact of the greenhouse gases emitted with contributions to portfolios of climate-friendly initiatives throughout the world. Lonely Planet offsets the carbon footprint of all staff and author travel.

Nusa Tenggara (Including Lombok)

Lombok International Airport (www.lombok-airport.co.id) is the main port of entry in West Nusa Tenggara, connecting with Kuala Lumpur and Singapore internationally, and Jakarta, Denpasar and other airports within Indonesia. While nominally an international airport, El Tari in Kupang is really a domestic hub for East Nusa Tenggara.

All the important towns and cities have regular – and expanding – air service. Lombok and Kupang are hubs, while airports such as Labuan Bajo in Flores and Tambolaka in Sumba are adding more flights as destinations increase in popularity.

Land

Any trip to Bali over land will require a ferry crossing.

Bus

The ferry crossing from Bali is included in the services offered by numerous bus companies, many of which travel overnight to Java. It's advisable to buy your ticket at least one day in advance from a travel agent or at the terminals in Denpasar (Ubang) or Mengwi. Note that flying can be almost as cheap as the bus.

Fares vary between operators; it's worth paying extra for a decent seat (all have air-con). Destinations include Yogyakarta (350,000Rp, 20 hours) and Jakarta (500,000Rp, 24 hours). You can also get buses from Singaraja in north Bali.

Train

Bali doesn't have trains but the State Railway Company does sell tickets through travel agents in Denpasar. From here buses leave for eastern Java where they link with trains at Banyuwangi for Surabaya, Yogyakarta and Jakarta, among other destinations.

Fares and times are comparable to the bus, but the air-conditioned trains are more comfortable, even in economy class. Note: Google Translate works well on the website.

Sea

Pelni (www.pelni.co.id), the national shipping line, operates large boats on infrequent long-distance runs throughout Indonesia. For Bali, Pelni ships stop at the harbour in Benoa. Schedules and fares are found on the website. You can enquire and book at the **Pelni ticket office** (Map p74; ☎0623 6175 5855, 0361-763963; www.pelni.co.id; Jl Raya Kuta 299; ⌚8am-noon & 1-4pm Mon-Fri, 8am-1pm Sat) in Tuban.

You can reach Java, just west of Bali, via the ferries that run between Gilimanuk in west Bali and Ketapang (Java), and then take a bus all the way to Jakarta.

GETTING AROUND

Air

There are regular flights between Bali's Ngurah Rai International Airport and Lombok International Airport. Regional airlines also service an array of airports across Nusa Tenggara. Airlines include Garuda, Nam Air, Transnusa, Wings Air and Batik Air.

Regional Flights

Regional airlines service the following routes:

To/From Denpasar (Bali)

- ➡ Labuan Bajo (Flores)
- ➡ Kupang (West Timor)
- ➡ Maumere (Flores)
- ➡ Tambolaka (West Sumba)
- ➡ Waingapu (East Sumba)
- ➡ Bima (East Sumbawa)

To/From Lombok

- ➡ Bima (East Sumbawa)
- ➡ Sumbawa Besar (West Sumbawa)

To/From Bajawa, Ende, Labuan Bajo & Maurere (Flores)

- ➡ Kupang (West Timor)

To/From Tambolaka & Waingapu (Sumba)

- ➡ Kupang (West Timor)

To/From Sumbawa

- ➡ Makassar (Sulawesi)
- ➡ Labuan Bajo (Flores)

To/From Ba'a (Rote)

➡ Kupang (West Timor)

To/From Kupang (West Timor)

➡ Alor Island

Bicycle

Increasingly, people are touring the island by *sepeda* (bike) and many visitors are using bikes around towns and for day trips.

There are plenty of bicycles for rent in tourist areas, but many are in poor condition. Ask at your accommodation. Prices are from 30,000Rp per day.

Boat

Fast boats link Bali with Lombok and Gili Trawangan in the Gili Islands. There are also services between Lombok and the Gilis. Liveaboards are a popular way to get from Lombok to Labuan Bajo in Flores.

Services can be unreliable during the wet season, with rough seas causing cancellations for days on end. During the rest of the year boats are consistent, but it's always wise to check ahead and allow extra days in your itinerary.

TRAVELLING SAFELY BY BOAT

Safety regulations are nonexistent and accidents happen regularly. In 2016 two tourists were killed when a fast boat to the Gilis exploded.

Crews on these boats may have little or no training: in one accident, the skipper admitted that he panicked and had no recollection of what happened to his passengers. And rescue is far from assured: a volunteer rescue group in east Bali reported that they had no radio.

Conditions are often rough in the waters off Bali. Although the islands are in close proximity and are easily seen from each other, the ocean between can get more turbulent than is safe for the small speedboats zipping across it.

With these facts in mind, it is essential that you take responsibility for your own safety because no one else will.

Bigger is better It may add half an hour or more to your journey, but a larger boat will simply deal with the open ocean better than the overpowered small speedboats. Also, trips on small boats can be unpleasant because of the ceaseless pounding through the waves and the fumes coming from the screaming outboard motors. Avoid anything under 30 seats except between Nusa Lembongan and Nusa Penida.

Check for safety equipment Make certain your boat has life preservers and that you know how to locate and use them. In an emergency, don't expect a panicked crew to hand them out. Also, check for lifeboats. Some promotional materials show boats with automatically inflating lifeboats that have later been removed to make room for more passengers.

Avoid overcrowding Some boats leave with more people than seats and with aisles jammed with stacked luggage, to the point where the captain can't see oncoming boats (this resulted in a boat crash off Nusa Penida in 2017 that killed one person and left six more injured). Don't use the boat if it's too full of luggage or passengers.

Look for exits Cabins may have only one narrow entrance, making them death traps in an accident. Sitting at the open back may seem safer but fuel explosions regularly injure passengers at the back of boats.

Avoid fly-by-nighters Taking a fishing boat and jamming too many engines on the rear in order to cash in on booming tourism is a recipe for disaster.

Don't ride on the roof It looks like carefree fun but travellers are regularly bounced off when boats hit swells and crews may be inept at rescue. Rough seas can drench passengers and ruin their belongings.

The ferry isn't safer One of the big Padangbai–Bangsal, Lombok car ferries caught fire and sank in 2014. A Gilimanuk, Bali–Java ferry capsized and sank in 2016.

Use common sense There are good operators on the waters around Bali but the line-up changes constantly. If a service seems sketchy before you board, go with a different operator. Try to get a refund but don't risk your safety for the cost of a ticket.

Ferries service the following regional routes:

To/From Lembar (Lombok)

- ➡ Padangbai (Bali)

To/From Senggigi (West Lombok)

- ➡ Gili Islands
- ➡ Padangbai (Bali)
- ➡ Nusa Lembongan (Bali)
- ➡ Sanur (Bali)

To/From Labuan Lombok (East Lombok)

- ➡ Poto Tano (Sumbawa)
- ➡ Bira (Sulawesi)
- ➡ Pulau Jampea (Sulawesi)
- ➡ Maluk (West Sumbawa)

To/From Lembar (West Lombok)

- ➡ Padangbai (Bali)

To/From Bangsal (North Lombok)

- ➡ Gili Islands
- ➡ Seminyak (Bali)
- ➡ Senaru (North Lombok)

To/From Gili Islands

- ➡ Serangan (Bali)
- ➡ Padangbai (Bali)
- ➡ Jemeluk (Bali)

To/From Ende (Flores)

- ➡ Waingapu (Sumba)
- ➡ Kupang (West Timor)

To/From Larantuka (Flores)

- ➡ Kalabahi (Alor Archipelago)
- ➡ Kupang (West Timor)

To/From Labuan Bajo (Flores)

- ➡ Sape (Sumbawa)

Waingapu (East Sumba)

- ➡ Sabu Island

Sape (Sumbawa)

- ➡ Tambolaka (West Sumba)
- ➡ Waikelo (Sumba)

Within Alor Archipelago

- ➡ Kalabahi–Pantar

➡ To/From Ba'a (Rote)

- ➡ Kupang

To/From Sape (Sumbawa)

- ➡ Tambolaka (West Sumba)
- ➡ Waikelo (Sumba)

Within West Sumbawa

- ➡ Sumbawa Besar–Pulau Moyo

To/From Kupang (West Timor)

- ➡ Waingapu (East Sumba)
- ➡ Kalabahi (Alor Archipelago)

Bus

Bali

PUBLIC BUS

Larger minibuses and full-size buses ply the longer routes, particularly on routes linking Denpasar, Singaraja and Gilimanuk. They operate out of the same terminals as bemos. However, with everybody riding motorbikes, there are long delays waiting for buses to fill up at terminals before departing.

TRANS-SARBAGITA BUS

Trans-Sarbagita (Map p68; ☎0811 385 0900; Jl Imam Bonjol; 3000Rp; ⏰5am-9pm) runs large, air-con commuter buses like you find in major cities the world over. It is suited more to locals due to long wait times and unreliable schedules; however, it's handy if you're heading along any of the following four routes: the bypass linking Sanur to Nusa Dua; Denpasar to Jimbaran; Tabanan to Bandara; or Mahendradata to Lebih via Sanur.

TOURIST BUS

Tourist buses are economical and convenient ways to get around. You'll see signs offering services in major tourist areas. Typically a tourist bus is an air-conditioned eight- to 20-passenger vehicle. Service is not as quick as with your own car and driver, and stops are often outside the centre, requiring another shuttle or taxi. That said, taking one of these is usually far easier than using public bemos and buses. Note that buses may not provide a direct service – stopping, say, at Ubud between Kuta and Padangbai.

Kura-Kura Bus (Map p68; ☎0361-757070; www.kura2bus.com; Jl Ngurah Rai Bypass, ground fl, DFS Galleria; rides 20,000-80,000Rp, 3-/7-day pass from 150,000/250,000Rp; wi-fi) This innovative expat-owned tourist-bus service covers important areas of south Bali and Ubud. Buses have wi-fi and run during daylight and early evening, from every 20 minutes to over two hours. Check schedules online or with the app. There are eight lines and the hub is the DFS Galleria duty-free mall.

Perama (☎0361-751170; www.peramatour.com) The major tourist-bus operator. It has offices or agents in Kuta, Sanur, Ubud, Lovina, Padangbai and Candidasa as well as Gili T and Senggigi on Lombok.

Lombok

Mandalika Terminal (Jl Pasar Bertais B8) in Mataram is the departure point for major cities in Bali, Sumbawa, and Flores, via inter-island ferries. For long-distance services, book tickets a day or two ahead at the terminal, or from a travel agent.

If you get to the terminal before 8am without a reservation, there may indeed be a spare seat on a bus going in your direction, but don't count on it, especially during holidays.

There are direct buses from Denpasar on Bali that connect to the Padangbai–Lembar ferry and then continue on to the Mandalika Terminal in Mataram (225,000Rp). Buses also connect to Bima via the Lombok–Sumbawa ferry (225,000Rp).

TOURIST SHUTTLE BUS

There are tourist shuttle-bus services between the main tourist centres in Lombok (Senggigi and Kuta) and most tourist centres in south Bali and the Gilis. Typically these combine a minibus with public ferries. Tickets can be booked directly or with a travel agent.

Bemo

Bemos are normally minibuses or vans with a row of low seats down each side and which carry about 12 people in very cramped conditions.

Bali

Bemos were once the dominant form of public transport in Bali, but widespread motorbike ownership (which is often cheaper than daily bemo use) has caused the system to wither. Getting to many places by bemo is both time-consuming and inconvenient. It's uncommon to see visitors on bemos in Bali.

FARES

Bemos operate on a standard route for a set (but unwritten) fare. The minimum is about 5000Rp. If you get into an empty bemo, always make it clear that you do not want to charter it.

TERMINALS & ROUTES

Most towns have at least one terminal *(terminal bis)* for all forms of public transport. There are often several terminals in larger towns. Terminals can be confusing, but most bemos and buses have signs, and if you're in doubt, people will usually help you.

To travel from one part of Bali to another, it is often necessary to go via one or more terminals. For example, to get from Sanur to Ubud by bemo, you go to the Kereneng terminal in Denpasar, transfer to the Batubulan terminal and then take a third bemo to Ubud. This is circuitous and time-consuming, which is why so few visitors take bemos in Bali.

Lombok

Mandalika Terminal (Jl Pasar Bertais B8) is 3km east of central Mataram; other regional terminals are in Praya, Anyar and Pancor (near Selong). You may have to go via one or more of these terminals to get from one part of Lombok to another, although you can flag bemos from the roadside. Fixed fares should be displayed, and short trips start at 5000Rp. Public transport becomes scarce in the late afternoon and normally ceases after dark.

Car & Motorcycle

Renting a car or motorbike can open up this region for exploration – and can also leave you counting the minutes until you return it; driving conditions on the islands can be harrowing at certain times and Bali's main roads are often clogged with traffic.

Most people don't rent a car for their entire visit but rather get one for a few days of meandering. Note that very few agencies in Bali will allow you to take their rental cars or motorcycles to Lombok.

Overland travel is slow in mountainous Nusa Tenggara and it's foolish to rely on Google Maps' estimated travel times with all those bends, potholes and road upgrades. Driving is time-consuming, but beautiful. Lombok, Sumbawa, Flores and Timor have decent, surfaced main roads but when you get off the highways things slow down considerably, especially between December and March when rains wallop gravel and dirt roads.

Driving Licences

CAR LICENCES

If you plan to drive a car, you're supposed to have an International Driving Permit (IDP). You can obtain one from your national motoring organisation if you have a normal driving licence. Bring your home licence as well. Without an IDP, add 50,000Rp to any fine you'll have to pay if stopped by the police (although you'll have to pay this fine three times to exceed the cost and hassle of getting the mostly useless IDP).

MOTORCYCLE LICENCES

If you have a motorcycle licence at home, get your IDP endorsed for motorcycles too; with this you will have no problems. Otherwise you have to get a local licence – something of an adventure.

Officially, there's a 2,000,000Rp fine for riding without a proper licence and your motorcycle can be impounded. Unofficially, you may be hit with a substantial 'on-the-spot' payment (50,000Rp seems average) and allowed to continue on your way. Also, if you have an accident without a licence your insurance company might refuse coverage.

To get a local motorcycle licence in Bali (valid for a year), go to the Polresta Denpasar Station (www.polrestadenpasar.org), which is northwest of Kerobokan on the way to Denpasar. Bring your passport, a photocopy of your passport (just the page with your photo on it) and a passport photo. Then take the following steps.

➡ Ignore the mobbed hall filled with jostling permit seekers.

➡ Look helpless and ask uniformed officials 'motorcycle licence?'.

➡ Be directed to cheery English-speaking officials and pay 300,000Rp.

➡ Take the required written test (in English, with the answers provided on a sample test).

➡ Get your permit.

Sure it costs more than in the hall of chaos, but who can argue with the service?

Fuel

Bensin (petrol) is sold by the government-owned Pertamina company and costs a cheap (subsidised) 8000Rp per litre. Bali has scads of petrol stations. On Lombok there are stations in major towns. Motorbike fuel is often sold from roadside stands out of Absolut vodka bottles.

Car

The most popular rental vehicle is a small 4WD – they're compact and well suited to exploring back roads. Automatic transmissions are unheard of.

Rental and travel agencies in tourist centres rent vehicles, though prices have gone up recently. A small 4WD starts at around 200,000Rp per day, with unlimited kilometres and very limited insurance. Extra days often cost less than the first day.

There's no reason to book rental cars in advance or with a tour package; doing so will almost certainly cost more than arranging it locally. Any place you stay can set you up with a car, as can the ever-present touts in the street.

Motorcycle

Motorbikes are a popular way of getting around – locals ride pillion almost from birth. A family of five all riding cheerfully along on one motorbike is called a Bali minivan. Rentals cost around 60,000Rp a day, less by the week. This should include minimal insurance for the motorcycle but not for any other person or property. Some have racks for surfboards.

Think carefully before renting a motorbike. It is dangerous and every year visitors go home with lasting damage – this is no place to learn to ride. Helmet use is mandatory.

Insurance

Rental agencies and owners usually insist that the vehicle itself is insured, and minimal insurance should be included in the basic rental deal – often with an excess of as much as US$100 for a motorcycle and US$500 for a car (ie the customer pays the first US$100/500 of any claim).

Check to see what your own vehicle, health and travel insurance covers, especially if you are renting a motorbike.

Road Conditions

Bali traffic can be horrendous in the south, up to Ubud, and as far as Padangbai to the east and Gilimanuk to the west. Finding your way around the main tourist sites can be a challenge because roads are only sometimes signposted, maps are unreliable and lots of streets are one-way, particularly in Ubud. Off the main routes, roads can be rough but they are usually surfaced.

Avoid driving at night or at dusk. Many bicycles, carts and vehicles do not have proper lights and street lighting is limited.

Road Rules

Visiting drivers commonly complain about crazy local drivers, but often it's because the visitors don't understand the local conventions of road use. For instance, the constant use of horns doesn't mean 'Get the @£*&% out of my way!'; rather, it is a local way of saying 'Hi, I'm here'.

- Watch your front – it's your responsibility to avoid anything that gets in front of your vehicle. In effect, a car, motorcycle or anything else pulling out in front of you has right of way.
- Often drivers won't even look to see what's coming when they turn left at a junction – they listen for the horn.
- Use your horn to warn anything in front that you're there, especially if you're about to overtake.
- Drive on the left side of the road.

Traffic Police

Some police will stop drivers on very slender pretexts. If a cop sees your front wheel half an inch over the faded line at a stop sign, if the chinstrap of your helmet isn't fastened, or if you don't observe one of the ever-changing and poorly signposted one-way traffic restrictions, you may be waved down.

The cop will ask to see your licence and the vehicle's registration papers, and they'll also tell you what a serious offence you've committed. Stay cool and don't argue. Don't offer a bribe. Eventually they'll suggest that you can pay them some amount of money to deal with the matter. If it's a very large amount, tell them politely that you don't have that much. These matters can be settled for something between 10,000Rp and 100,000Rp, although it will be more if you argue.

Hiring a Vehicle & Driver

An excellent way to travel anywhere around Bali is by hired vehicle, allowing you to leave the driving and inherent frustrations to others. If you're part of a group, it can make sound economic sense as well. This is also possible on Lombok but less common.

It's easy to arrange a charter: just listen for one of the frequent offers of 'transport?' in the streets around the tourist centres. Approach a driver yourself or ask at your hotel, which is often a good method, because it increases accountability. Also consider the following:

- Although great drivers are everywhere, it helps to talk with a few.
- Get recommendations from other travellers.
- You should like the driver and their English should be sufficient for you to communicate your wishes.

- Costs for a full day should average 500,000Rp to 800,000Rp.
- The vehicle, usually a late-model Toyota Kijang seating up to seven, should be clean.
- Agree on a route beforehand.
- Make it clear if you want to avoid tourist-trap restaurants and shops (smart drivers understand that tips depend on following your wishes).
- On the road, buy the driver lunch (they'll want to eat elsewhere, so give them 20,000Rp) and offer snacks and drinks.
- Many drivers find ways to make your day delightful in unexpected ways. Tip accordingly.

Local Transport

Ojek

Around towns and along roads, you can always get a lift by *ojek* (a motorcycle or motorbike that takes a paying passenger). Formal *ojek* are less common now that anyone with a motorbike can be a freelance *ojek* (stand by the side of the road, look like you need a ride and people will stop and offer). They're OK on quiet country roads, but a risky option in the big towns. *Ojek* are more common on Lombok.

Fares are negotiable, but about 30,000Rp for 5km is fairly standard.

In heavily developed parts of Bali, Go-Jek is a popular mobile application that allows you to order on-demand motorcycle rides (in addition to just about anything you'd like delivered to you). Note that you must have an Indonesian SIM card, and it may be hard to get picked up or dropped off in heavily touristed areas due to territory rivalries between local drivers.

Taxi

BALI

Metered taxis are common in south Bali and Denpasar (but not Ubud). They are essential for getting around and you can usually flag one down in busy areas. They're often a lot less hassle than haggling with drivers offering 'transport!'

The best taxi company by far is **Blue Bird Taxi** (☎0361-701111; www.bluebirdgroup.com), which uses blue vehicles with a light on the roof bearing a stylised bluebird. Drivers speak reasonable English and use the meter at all times. Many expats will use no other firm. Blue Bird has a slick app that summons a taxi to your location just like Uber. Watch out for fakes – there are many. Look for 'Blue Bird' over the windscreen and the phone number.

- Taxis are fairly cheap: Kuta to Seminyak can be 80,000Rp.
- Avoid any taxis where the driver won't use a meter, even after dark when they claim that only fixed fares apply.
- Other taxi scams include lack of change, 'broken' meter, fare-raising detours and offers for tours, massages, prostitutes etc.

LOMBOK

Reliable metered taxis operated by **Blue Bird Lombok Taksi** (☎0370-645000; www.bluebirdgroup.com) are found in west Lombok. Motorbike ride-hailing app **Go-Jek** (www.go-jek.com) is useful for cheap short trips around Mataram and west Lombok.

Health

Treatment for minor injuries and common traveller's health problems is easily accessed in Bali and in larger towns across Nusa Tenggara. For serious conditions, you will need to leave the region.

Travellers tend to worry about contracting infectious diseases when in the tropics, but infections are rarely a cause of serious illness or death in travellers. Pre-existing medical conditions, such as heart disease, and accidental injury (especially traffic accidents) account for most life-threatening problems. Becoming ill in some way is relatively common, however; ailments you may suffer include gastro, overexposure to the sun and other typical traveller woes.

It's important to note certain precautions you should take here, especially in regard to rabies, mosquito bites and the tropical sun.

The advice we provide is a general guide only and does not replace the advice of a doctor trained in travel medicine.

BEFORE YOU GO

Make sure all medications are packed in their original, clearly labelled containers. A signed and dated letter from your physician describing your medical conditions and medications (including generic names) is also a good idea. If you are carrying syringes or needles, be sure to have a physician's letter documenting their medical necessity. If you have a heart condition ensure you bring a copy of an electrocardiogram taken just prior to travelling.

If you take any regular medication bring double your needs in case of loss or theft. You can buy many medications over the counter without a doctor's prescription, but it can be difficult to find some of the newer drugs, particularly the latest antidepressant drugs, blood-pressure medications and contraceptive pills.

Insurance

Unless you are definitely sure that your health coverage at home will cover you here, you should take out travel insurance; bring a copy of the policy as evidence that you're covered. It's a good idea to get a policy that pays for medical evacuation if necessary (which can cost US$100,000).

Some policies specifically exclude 'dangerous activities', which can include scuba diving, renting a local motorcycle and even trekking. Be aware that a locally acquired motorcycle licence isn't valid under some policies.

Worldwide travel insurance is available at www.lonelyplanet.com/bookings. You can buy, extend and claim online anytime – even if you're already on the road.

Medical Checklist

Recommended items for a convenient personal medical kit (other items can be easily obtained on Bali if needed):

- antibacterial cream (eg muciprocin)
- antihistamine – there are many options (eg cetirizine for daytime and promethazine for night)
- antiseptic (eg Betadine)
- contraceptives
- DEET-based insect repellent
- first-aid items such as scissors, bandages, thermometer (but not a mercury one) and tweezers
- ibuprofen or another anti-inflammatory
- steroid cream for allergic/itchy rashes (eg 1% to 2% hydrocortisone)
- sunscreen and hat
- throat lozenges
- thrush (vaginal yeast infection) treatment (eg clotrimazole pessaries or diflucan tablet)

Websites

It's usually a good idea to consult your government's travel-health website before departure, if one is available.

RECOMMENDED VACCINATIONS

Specialised travel-medicine clinics are your best source of information; they stock all available vaccines and will be able to give specific recommendations for you and your trip.

Your doctor may also recommend vaccines against the following:

- tetanus (single booster)
- hepatitis A
- typhoid
- rabies

Australia (www.smarttraveller.gov.au)

UK (www.gov.uk/foreign-travel-advice)

USA (www.travel.state.gov)

There is a wealth of travel health advice on the internet.

World Health Organization (www.who.int/ith) Publishes a superb book called *International Travel & Health,* which is revised annually and is available online at no cost.

Centers for Disease Control & Prevention (www.cdc.gov) Good general information.

IN BALI, LOMBOK & NUSA TENGGARA

Availability of Health Care

Bali

In south Bali and Ubud there are clinics catering to tourists, and just about any hotel can put you in touch with an English-speaking doctor.

INTERNATIONAL MEDICAL CLINICS

For serious conditions, foreigners are best served in the costly private clinic **BIMC** (Map p68; ☎0361-761263; www.bimcbali.com; Jl Ngurah Rai 100X; ⏰24hr), which caters mainly to tourists and expats. Confirm that your health and/or travel insurance will cover you. In cases where your medical condition is considered serious, you may be evacuated by air ambulance to Singapore or beyond; this is where proper insurance is vital because these flights can cost more than US$50,000.

BIMC is on the bypass road just east of Kuta near the Bali Galleria. It's a modern Australian-run clinic that can do tests, hotel visits and arrange medical evacuation. Visits can cost US$100 or more. It has a branch in Nusa Dua.

HOSPITALS

There are two facilities in Denpasar that offer a good standard of care. Both are more affordable than the international clinics.

BaliMed Hospital (☎0361-484748; www.balimedhospital.co.id; Jl Mahendradatta 57) On the Kerobokan side of Denpasar, this private hospital has a range of medical services. A basic consultation is 220,000Rp.

RSUP Sanglah Hospital (Rumah Sakit Umum Propinsi Sanglah; Map p120; ☎0361-227911; www.sanglahhospitalbali.com; Jl Diponegoro; ⏰24hr) The city's general hospital has English-speaking staff and an ER. It's the best hospital on the island, although standards are not the same as at those in developed countries. It has a special wing for well-insured foreigners, **Paviliun Amerta Wing International** (Map p120; ☎0361-247250, 0361-232603; off Jl Pulau Bali).

PHARMACIES

Many drugs requiring a prescription in the West are available over the counter in Indonesia, including powerful antibiotics.

The **Kimia Farma** (www.kimiafarma.co.id) chain is recommended. It has many locations, charges fair prices and has helpful staff. The Guardian chain of pharmacies has appeared in tourist areas, but the selection is small and prices can be shocking even to visitors from countries with high prices. Elsewhere you need to be more careful as fake medications and poorly stored or out-of-date drugs are common.

Lombok

Rumah Sakit Harapan Keluarga (☎0370-617 7009; www.harapankeluarga.co.id; Jl Ahmad Yani 9; ⏰24hr) is the best private hospital on Lombok and the only place with a recompression chamber. It's just east of central Mataram and has English-speaking doctors.

The tourist-oriented Blue Island Medical Clinic has outposts in Lombok's main resort areas, including **Kuta** (Map p305; ☎0819 9970 5700; http://blueislandclinic.com; Jl Raya Kuta; ⏰24hr) and **Gili Trawangan** (Map p320; ☎0819 9970 5701; http://blueislandclinic.com; Jl Raya Trawangan; ⏰24hr).

Infectious Diseases

Bird Flu

Otherwise known as avian influenza, the H5N1 virus remains a risk to be aware of when travelling in Southeast Asia. It has claimed more than 100 victims in Indonesia; most cases have been in Java.

Dengue Fever

This mosquito-borne disease is a major problem on Bali. As there is no vaccine available it can only be prevented by avoiding mosquito bites. The mosquito that carries dengue bites day and night, so use insect avoidance measures at all times. Symptoms include high fever, severe headache and body ache (dengue was previously known as 'breakbone fever'). Some people develop a rash and experience diarrhoea. It's vital to see a doctor to be diagnosed and monitored.

Hepatitis A

A problem throughout the region, this food- and water-borne virus infects the liver, causing jaundice (yellow skin and eyes), nausea and lethargy. There's no specific treatment for hepatitis A; you just need to allow time for the liver to heal. All travellers to Southeast Asia should be vaccinated against hepatitis A.

Hepatitis B

The only sexually transmitted disease that can be prevented by vaccination, hepatitis B is spread by body fluids.

HIV

HIV is a major problem in many Asian countries, and Bali has one of the highest rates of HIV infection in Indonesia. The main risk for most travellers is sexual contact with locals, prostitutes and other travellers.

The risk of sexual transmission of HIV can be dramatically reduced by the use of a *kondom* (condom). These are available from supermarkets, street stalls and drugstores in tourist areas, and from the *apotik* (pharmacy) in almost any town. Don't buy a cheap brand.

Malaria

The risk of contracting malaria is greatest in rural areas of Indonesia. Generally malaria is not a concern on Bali or in the main touristed areas of Lombok. Consider precautions if you are going into remote areas or on side trips beyond Bali.

Two strategies should be combined to prevent malaria: mosquito avoidance and antimalarial medications. Most people who catch malaria are taking inadequate or no antimalarial medication.

Rabies

Rabies is a disease spread by the bite or lick of an infected animal, most commonly a dog or monkey. Once you are exposed, it is uniformly fatal if you don't get the vaccine very promptly. Bali has had a major outbreak dating to 2008 and people continue to die each year.

To minimise your risk, consider getting the rabies vaccine, which consists of three injections. A booster after one year will then provide 10 years' protection. This may be worth considering given Bali's rabies outbreak. The vaccines are often unavailable on Bali, so get them before you go.

Also, be careful to avoid animal bites. Especially watch children closely.

Having the pretravel vaccination means the postbite treatment is greatly simplified. If you are bitten or scratched, gently wash the wound with soap and water, and apply an iodine-based antiseptic. It is a good idea to also consult a doctor.

Those not vaccinated will need to receive rabies immunoglobulin as soon as possible. Clean the wound immediately and do not delay seeking medical attention. Note that Bali is known to run out of rabies immunoglobulin, so be prepared to go to Singapore immediately for medical treatment.

Typhoid

This serious bacterial infection is spread via food and water. Its symptoms are a high and slowly progressive fever, headache and possibly a dry cough and stomach pain. It is diagnosed by blood tests and treated with antibiotics. Vaccinations are 80%

AVOIDING MOSQUITO BITES

Travellers are advised to prevent mosquito bites by taking these steps:

- Use a DEET-containing insect repellent on exposed skin. Wash this off at night, as long as you are sleeping under a mosquito net. Natural repellents such as citronella can be effective, but must be applied more frequently than products containing DEET.
- Sleep under a mosquito net impregnated with permethrin.
- Choose accommodation with screens and fans (if not air-conditioned).
- Impregnate clothing with permethrin in high-risk areas.
- Wear long sleeves and trousers in light colours.
- Use mosquito coils.
- Spray your room with insect repellent before going out for your evening meal.

If you are going to an area where there is a malaria problem, consult with a clinic about the various prescription drugs you can use to reduce the odds that you'll get it.

effective and should be given one month before travelling to an infected area.

Traveller's Diarrhoea

Traveller's diarrhoea (aka Bali belly) is by far the most common problem affecting travellers – between 30% and 50% of people will suffer from it within two weeks of starting their trip. In over 80% of cases, traveller's diarrhoea is caused by bacteria (there are numerous potential culprits) and therefore responds promptly to treatment with antibiotics.

Traveller's diarrhoea is defined as the passage of more than three watery bowel actions within 24 hours, plus at least one other symptom such as fever, cramps, nausea, vomiting or feeling generally unwell.

Treatment

Loperamide is just a 'stopper' and doesn't get to the cause of the problem. However, it can be helpful, for example, if you have to go on a long bus ride. Don't take Loperamide if you have a fever or blood in your stools. Seek medical attention quickly if you do not respond to an appropriate antibiotic.

- Stay well hydrated; rehydration solutions such as Gastrolyte are the best for this.
- Antibiotics such as Norfloxacin, Ciprofloxacin or Azithromycin will kill the bacteria quickly.

Giardiasis

Giardia lamblia is a parasite that is relatively common in travellers. Symptoms include nausea, bloating, excess gas, fatigue and intermittent diarrhoea. The parasite will eventually go away if left untreated but this can take months. The treatment of choice is Tinidazole, with Metronidazole being a second-line option.

Environmental Hazards

Diving

Divers and surfers should seek specialised advice before they travel to ensure their medical kit contains treatment for coral cuts and tropical ear infections, as well as the standard problems. Divers should ensure their insurance covers them for decompression illness – get specialised dive insurance if necessary.

Divers should note that there is a decompression chamber in Sanur, which is a fast-boat ride from Nusa Lembongan. Getting here from north Bali can take three to four hours.

Heat

Bali is hot and humid throughout the year. It takes most people at least two weeks to adapt to the hot climate. Swelling of the feet and ankles is common, as are muscle cramps caused by excessive sweating. Prevent these by avoiding dehydration and excessive activity in the heat. Be careful to avoid the following conditions:

Heat exhaustion Symptoms include weakness, headache, irritability, nausea or vomiting, sweaty skin, a fast, weak pulse and a normal or slightly elevated body temperature. Treatment involves getting out of the heat and/or sun, fanning the victim and applying cool wet cloths to the skin, laying the victim flat with their legs raised, and rehydrating with water containing one-quarter of a teaspoon of salt per litre. Recovery is usually rapid and it is common to feel weak for some days afterwards.

Heatstroke A serious medical emergency. Symptoms come on suddenly and include weakness, nausea, a hot dry body with a body temperature of over 41°C, dizziness, confusion, loss of coordination, fits and eventually collapse and loss of consciousness. Seek urgent medical help and commence cooling by getting the person out of the heat, removing their clothes, fanning them and applying cool wet cloths or ice to their body, especially to hot spots such as the groin and armpits.

Prickly heat A common skin rash in the tropics, caused by sweat being trapped under the skin. The result is an itchy rash of tiny lumps. Treat by moving out of the heat into an air-conditioned area for a few hours and by having cool showers.

WATER

Tap water in this region is never safe to drink.

Widely available and cheap, bottled water is generally safe but check that the seal is intact when purchasing. Look for places that allow you to refill containers, thus cutting down on landfill.

Most ice in restaurants is fine if it is uniform in size and made at a central plant (standard for large cities and tourist areas). Avoid ice that is chipped off larger blocks (more common in rural areas).

Avoid fresh juices outside of tourist restaurants and cafes.

The website **Refill My Bottle** (www.refillmybottle.com) will direct you to hotels and restaurants in Bali and Lombok where you can refill your water bottle for free or for a negligible fee.

Bites & Stings

During your time in Indonesia, you may make some unwanted friends.

Bedbugs These don't carry disease but their bites are very itchy. They live in the cracks of furniture and walls and then migrate to the bed at night to feed on you as you sleep. You can treat the itch with an antihistamine.

Jellyfish Most are not dangerous, just irritating. Stings can be extremely painful but rarely fatal. First aid for jellyfish stings involves pouring vinegar onto the affected area to neutralise the poison. Do not rub sand or water onto the stings. Take painkillers, and anyone who feels ill in any way after being stung should seek medical advice.

Ticks Contracted after walking in rural areas, ticks are commonly found behind the ears, on the belly and in armpits. If you have had a tick bite and experience symptoms such as a rash at the site of the bite or elsewhere, fever or muscle aches, you should see a doctor.

Skin Problems

Fungal rashes There are two common fungal rashes that affect travellers. The first occurs in moist areas that get less air such as the groin, armpits and between the toes. It starts as a red patch that slowly spreads and is usually itchy. Treatment involves keeping the skin dry, avoiding chafing and using an antifungal cream such as Clotrimazole or Lamisil. *Tinea versicolor* is also common – this fungus causes small, light-coloured patches, most commonly on the back, chest and shoulders. Consult a doctor.

Cuts & scratches These can easily get infected in tropical climates so take meticulous care of any cuts and scratches. Immediately wash all wounds in clean water and apply antiseptic. If you develop signs of infection see a doctor. Divers and surfers should be careful with coral cuts because they become easily infected.

Sunburn

Even on a cloudy day, sunburn can occur rapidly, especially near the equator. Don't end up like the dopey tourists you see roasted pink on Kuta Beach. Instead:

- Use a strong sunscreen (at least SPF 30).
- Reapply sunscreen after a swim.
- Wear a wide-brimmed hat and sunglasses.
- Avoid baking in the sun during the hottest part of the day (10am to 2pm).

ALCOHOL POISONING

There are ongoing reports of injuries and deaths among tourists and locals due to *arak* (the local spirits that should be distilled from palm or cane sugar) being adulterated with methanol, a poisonous form of alcohol. Although *arak* is a popular drink, it should be avoided outside established restaurants and cafes.

Women's Health

In the tourist areas and large cities, sanitary napkins and tampons are easily found. This becomes more difficult the more rural you go. Birth-control options may be limited so bring adequate supplies of your own form of contraception.

Language

Indonesian, or Bahasa Indonesia as it's known to the locals, is the official language of Indonesia. It has approximately 220 million speakers, although it's the mother tongue for only about 20 million. Most people in Bali and on Lombok also speak their own indigenous languages, Balinese and Sasak respectively. The average traveller needn't worry about learning Balinese or Sasak, but it can be fun to learn a few words, which is why we've included a few in this chapter. For practical purposes, it probably makes better sense to concentrate your efforts on learning Bahasa Indonesia.

Indonesian pronunciation is easy to master. Each letter always represents the same sound and most letters are pronounced the same as their English counterparts, with *c* pronounced as the 'ch' in 'chat'. Note also that *kh* is a throaty sound (like the 'ch' in Scottish *loch*), and that the *ng* combination, which is found in English at the end or in the middle of words such as 'ringing', also appears at the beginning of words in Indonesian.

Syllables generally carry equal emphasis – the main exception is the unstressed *e* in words such as *besar* (big) – but the rule of thumb is to stress the second-last syllable.

In written Indonesian there are some inconsistent spellings of place names. Compound names are written as one word or two, eg Airsanih or Air Sanih, Padangbai or Padang Bai. Words starting with 'Ker' sometimes lose the *e*, eg Kerobokan/Krobokan. Some Dutch variant spellings also remain in use, with *tj* instead of the modern *c* (eg Tjampuhan/Campuan), and *oe* instead of *u* (eg Soekarno/Sukarno).

Pronouns, particularly 'you', are rarely used in Indonesian. *Anda* is the egalitarian form used to overcome the plethora of words for 'you'.

WANT MORE?

For in-depth language information and handy phrases, check out Lonely Planet's *Indonesian Phrasebook*. You'll find it at **shop.lonelyplanet.com**.

BASICS

Hello. — *Salam.*
Goodbye. (if leaving) — *Selamat tinggal.*
Goodbye. (if staying) — *Selamat jalan.*
How are you? — *Apa kabar?*
I'm fine, and you? — *Kabar baik, Anda bagaimana?*
Excuse me. — *Permisi.*
Sorry. — *Maaf.*
Please. — *Silahkan.*
Thank you. — *Terima kasih.*
You're welcome. — *Kembali.*
Yes./No. — *Ya./Tidak.*
Mr/Sir — *Bapak*
Ms/Mrs/Madam — *Ibu*
Miss — *Nona*
What's your name? — *Siapa nama Anda?*
My name is ... — *Nama saya ...*
Do you speak English? — *Bisa berbicara Bahasa Inggris?*
I don't understand. — *Saya tidak mengerti.*

ACCOMMODATION

Do you have any rooms available? — *Ada kamar kosong?*
How much is it per night/person? — *Berapa satu malam/orang?*
Is breakfast included? — *Apakah harganya ter masuk makan pagi?*
I'd like to share a dorm. — *Saya mau satu tempat tidur di asrama.*
campsite — *tempat kemah*
guesthouse — *losmen*
hotel — *hotel*
youth hostel — *pemuda*

a ... room — *kamar ...*
single — *untuk satu orang*
double — *untuk dua orang*

air-conditioned	*dengan AC*
bathroom	*kamar mandi*
cot	*velbet*
window	*jendela*

DIRECTIONS

Where is ...?	*Di mana ...?*
What's the address?	*Alamatnya di mana?*
Could you write it down, please?	*Anda bisa tolong tuliskan?*
Can you show me (on the map)?	*Anda bisa tolong tunjukkan pada saya (di peta)?*

at the corner	*di sudut*
at the traffic lights	*di lampu merah*
behind	*di belakang*
in front of	*di depan*
far (from)	*jauh (dari)*
left	*kiri*
near (to)	*dekat (dengan)*
next to	*di samping*
opposite	*di seberang*
right	*kanan*
straight ahead	*lurus*

EATING & DRINKING

What would you recommend?	*Apa yang Anda rekomendasikan?*
What's in that dish?	*Hidangan ituisinya apa?*
That was delicious.	*Ini enak sekali.*
Cheers!	*Bersulang!*
Bring the bill/check, please.	*Tolong bawa kuitansi.*

I don't eat ...	*Saya tidak mau makan ...*
dairy products	*susu dan keju*
fish	*ikan*
(red) meat	*daging (merah)*
peanuts	*kacang tanah*
seafood	*makanan laut*

a table ...	*meja ...*
at (eight) o'clock	*pada jam (delapan)*
for (two) people	*untuk (dua) orang*

KEY PATTERNS

To get by in Indonesian, mix and match these simple patterns with words of your choice:

When's (the next bus)?
Jam berapa (bis yang berikutnya)?

Where's (the station)?
Di mana (stasiun)?

How much is it (per night)?
Berapa (satu malam)?

I'm looking for (a hotel).
Saya cari (hotel).

Do you have (a local map)?
Ada (peta daerah)?

Is there (a toilet)?
Ada (kamar kecil)?

Can I (enter)?
Boleh saya (masuk)?

Do I need (a visa)?
Saya harus pakai (visa)?

I have (a reservation).
Saya (sudah punya booking).

I need (assistance).
Saya perlu (dibantu).

I'd like (the menu).
Saya minta (daftar makanan).

I'd like (to hire a car).
Saya mau (sewa mobil).

Could you (help me)?
Bisa Anda (bantu) saya?

Key Words

baby food (formula)	*susu kaleng*
bar	*bar*
bottle	*botol*
bowl	*mangkuk*
breakfast	*sarapan*
cafe	*kafe*
children's menu	*menu untuk anak-anak*
cold	*dingin*
dinner	*makan malam*
dish	*piring*
drink list	*daftar minuman*
food	*makanan*
food stall	*warung*
fork	*garpu*
glass	*gelas*
highchair	*kursi tinggi*
hot (warm)	*panas*
knife	*pisau*

SIGNS

Buka	Open
Dilarang	Prohibited
Kamar Kecil	Toilets
Keluar	Exit
Masuk	Entrance
Pria	Men
Tutup	Closed
Wanitai	Women

lunch *makan siang*
menu *daftar makanan*
market *pasar*
napkin *tisu*
plate *piring*
restaurant *rumah makan*
salad *selada*
soup *sop*
spicy *pedas*
spoon *sendok*
vegetarian food *makanan tanpa daging*
with *dengan*
without *tanpa*

Meat & Fish

beef *daging sapi*
carp *ikan mas*
chicken *ayam*
duck *bebek*
fish *ikan*
lamb *daging anak domba*
mackerel *tenggiri*
meat *daging*
pork *daging babi*
shrimp/prawn *udang*
tuna *cakalang*
turkey *kalkun*

Fruit & Vegetables

apple *apel*
banana *pisang*
beans *kacang*
cabbage *kol*
carrot *wortel*
cauliflower *blumkol*
cucumber *timun*
dates *kurma*
eggplant *terung*
fruit *buah*
grapes *buah anggur*
lemon *jeruk asam*
orange *jeruk manis*
pineapple *nenas*
potato *kentang*
raisins *kismis*
spinach *bayam*
vegetable *sayur-mayur*
watermelon *semangka*

Other

bread *roti*
butter *mentega*
cheese *keju*
chilli *cabai*
chilli sauce *sambal*
egg *telur*
honey *madu*
jam *selai*
noodles *mie*
oil *minyak*
pepper *lada*
rice *nasi*
salt *garam*
soy sauce *kecap*
sugar *gula*
vinegar *cuka*

Drinks

beer *bir*
coconut milk *santan*
coffee *kopi*
juice *jus*
milk *susu*
palm sap wine *tuak*
red wine *anggur merah*
soft drink *minuman ringan*
tea *teh*
water *air*
white wine *anggur putih*
yogurt *susu masam kental*

EMERGENCIES

Help!	*Tolong saya!*
I'm lost.	*Saya tersesat.*
Leave me alone!	*Jangan ganggu saya!*
There's been an accident.	*Ada kecelakaan.*
Can I use your phone?	*Boleh saya pakai telpon genggamnya?*
Call a doctor!	*Panggil dokter!*
Call the police!	*Panggil polisi!*
I'm ill.	*Saya sakit.*
It hurts here.	*Sakitnya di sini.*
I'm allergic to (antibiotics).	*Saya alergi (antibiotik).*

SHOPPING & SERVICES

I'd like to buy ...	*Saya mau beli ...*
I'm just looking.	*Saya lihat-lihat saja.*
May I look at it?	*Boleh saya lihat?*
I don't like it.	*Saya tidak suka.*
How much is it?	*Berapa harganya?*
It's too expensive.	*Itu terlalu mahal.*
Can you lower the price?	*Boleh kurang?*
There's a mistake in the bill.	*Ada kesalahan dalam kuitansi ini.*
credit card	*kartu kredit*
foreign exchange office	*kantor penukaran mata uang asing*
internet cafe	*warnet*
mobile/cell phone	*hanpon*
post office	*kantor pos*
signature	*tanda tangan*
tourist office	*kantor pariwisata*

TIME & DATES

What time is it?	*Jam berapa sekarang?*
It's (10) o'clock.	*Jam (sepuluh).*
It's half past (six).	*Setengah (tujuh).*

QUESTION WORDS

How?	*Bagaimana?*
What?	*Apa?*
When?	*Kapan?*
Where?	*Di mana?*
Which	*Yang mana?*
Who?	*Siapa?*
Why?	*Kenapa?*

in the morning	*pagi*
in the afternoon	*siang*
in the evening	*malam*

today	*hari ini*
tomorrow	*besok*
yesterday	*kemarin*
Monday	*hari Senin*
Tuesday	*hari Selasa*
Wednesday	*hari Rabu*
Thursday	*hari Kamis*
Friday	*hari Jumat*
Saturday	*hari Sabtu*
Sunday	*hari Minggu*

January	*Januari*
February	*Februari*
March	*Maret*
April	*April*
May	*Mei*
June	*Juni*
July	*Juli*
August	*Agustus*
September	*September*
October	*Oktober*
November	*Nopember*
December	*Desember*

TRANSPORT

Public Transport

bicycle-rickshaw	*becak*
boat (general)	*kapal*
boat (local)	*perahu*
bus	*bis*
minibus	*bemo*
motorcycle-rickshaw	*bajaj*
motorcycle-taxi	*ojek*
plane	*pesawat*
taxi	*taksi*
train	*kereta api*

I want to go to ...	*Saya mau ke ...*
How much to ...?	*Ongkos ke ... berapa?*
At what time does it leave?	*Jam berapa berangkat?*
At what time does it arrive at ...?	*Jam berapa sampai di ...?*
Does it stop at ...?	*Di ... berhenti?*

NUMBERS

1	*satu*
2	*dua*
3	*tiga*
4	*empat*
5	*lima*
6	*enam*
7	*tujuh*
8	*delapan*
9	*sembilan*
10	*sepuluh*
20	*duapuluh*
30	*tigapuluh*
40	*empatpuluh*
50	*limapuluh*
60	*enampuluh*
70	*tujuhpuluh*
80	*delapanpuluh*
90	*sembilanpuluh*
100	*seratus*
1000	*seribu*

What's the next stop? *Apa nama halte berikutnya?*
Please tell me when we get to ... *Tolong, beritahu waktu kita sampai di ...*
Please stop here. *Tolong, berhenti di sini.*

the first *pertama*
the last *terakhir*
the next *yang berikutnya*

a ... ticket *tiket ...*
  1st-class *kelas satu*
  2nd-class *kelas dua*
  one-way *sekali jalan*
  return *pulang pergi*

aisle seat *tempat duduk dekat gang*
cancelled *dibatalkan*
delayed *terlambat*
platform *peron*
ticket office *loket tiket*
timetable *jadwal*
train station *stasiun kereta api*
window seat *tempat duduk dekat jendela*

Driving & Cycling

I'd like to hire a ... *Saya mau sewa ...*
  4WD *gardan ganda*
  bicycle *sepeda*
  car *mobil*
  motorcycle *sepeda motor*

child seat *kursi anak untuk di mobil*
diesel *solar*
helmet *helem*
mechanic *montir*
petrol/gas *bensin*
pump (bicycle) *pompa sepeda*
service station *pompa bensin*

Is this the road to ...? *Apakah jalan ini ke ...?*
(How long) Can I park here? *(Berapa lama) Saya boleh parkir di sini?*
The car/motocycle has broken down. *Mobil/Motor mogok.*
I have a flat tyre. *Ban saya kempes.*
I've run out of petrol. *Saya kehabisan bensin.*

LOCAL LANGUAGES

Balinese

How are you? *Kenken kabare?*
What's your name? *Sire wastene?*
My name is ... *Adan tiange ...*
I don't understand. *Tiang sing ngerti.*
How much is this? *Ji kude niki?*
Thank you. *Matur suksma.*
What do you call this in Balinese? *Ne ape adane di Bali?*
Which is the way to ...? *Kije jalan lakar kel ...?*

Sasak

What's your name? *Saik aranm side?*
My name is ... *Arankah aku ...*
I don't understand. *Endek ngerti.*
How much is this? *Pire ajin sak iyak?*
Thank you. *Tampak asih.*
What do you call this in Sasak? *Ape aran sak iyak elek bahase Sasek?*
Which is the way to ...? *Lamun lek ..., embe eak langantah?*

GLOSSARY

adat – tradition, customs and manners

adharma – evil

aling aling – gateway backed by a small wall

alus – identifiable 'goodies' in an *arja* drama

anak-anak – children

angker – evil power

apotik – pharmacy

arja – refined operatic form of Balinese theatre; also a dance-drama, comparable to Western opera

Arjuna – a hero of the *Mahabharata* epic and a popular temple gate guardian image

bahasa – language; Bahasa Indonesia is the national language of Indonesia

bale – an open-sided pavilion with a steeply pitched thatched roof

bale banjar – communal meeting place of a *banjar;* a house for meetings and *gamelan* practice

bale tani – family house in Lombok; see also *serambi*

balian – faith healer and herbal doctor

banjar – local division of a village consisting of all the married adult males

banyan – a type of ficus tree, often considered holy; see also *waringin*

bapak – father; also a polite form of address to any older man; also *pak*

Barong – mythical lion-dog creature

baten tegeh – decorated pyramids of fruit, rice cakes and flowers

batik – process of colouring fabric by coating part of the cloth with wax, dyeing it and melting the wax out; the waxed part is not coloured, and repeated waxing and dyeing builds up a pattern

batu bolong – rock with a hole

belalu – quick-growing, light wood

bemo – popular local transport in Bali and on Lombok; usually a small minibus but can be a small pick-up in rural areas

bensin – petrol (gasoline)

beruga – communal meeting hall in Bali; open-sided pavilion on Lombok

bhur – world of demons

bhwah – world of humans

Brahma – the creator; one of the trinity of Hindu gods

Brahmana – the caste of priests and the highest of the Balinese castes; all priests are Brahmanas, but not all Brahmanas are priests

bu – mother; shortened form of *ibu*

bukit – hill; also the name of Bali's southern peninsula

bulau – month

candi – shrine, originally of Javanese design; also known as *prasada*

candi bentar – entrance gates to a temple

cendrawasih – birds of paradise

cengceng – cymbals

cidomo – horse cart with car wheels (Lombok)

cili – representations of Dewi Sri, the rice goddess

dalang – puppet master and storyteller in a *wayang kulit* performance

Dalem Bedaulu – legendary last ruler of the Pejeng dynasty

danau – lake

desa – village

dewa – deity or supernatural spirit

dewi – goddess

Dewi Sri – goddess of rice

dharma – good

dokar – horse cart; known as a *cidomo* on Lombok

Durga – goddess of death and destruction, and consort of Shiva

dusun – small village

endek – elegant fabric, like *songket,* with predyed weft threads

Gajah Mada – famous *Majapahit* prime minister who defeated the last great king of Bali and extended *Majapahit* power over the island

Galungan – great Balinese festival; an annual event in the 210-day Balinese *wuku* calendar

gamelan – traditional Balinese orchestra, with mostly percussion instruments like large xylophones and gongs; may have one to more than two dozen musicians; also used to refer to individual instruments such as drums; also called a *gong*

Ganesha – Shiva's elephant-headed son

gang – alley or footpath

Garuda – mythical man-bird creature, vehicle of Vishnu; modern symbol of Indonesia and the national airline

gedong – shrine

genggong – musical performance seen in Lombok

gili – small island (Lombok)

goa – cave; also spelt *gua*

gong – see *gamelan*

gong gede – large orchestra; traditional form of the *gamelan* with 35 to 40 musicians

gong kebyar – modern, popular form of a *gong gede,* with up to 25 instruments

gua – cave; also spelt *goa*

gunung – mountain

gunung api – volcano

gusti – polite title for members of the *Wesia* caste

Hanuman – monkey god who plays a major part in the *Ramayana*

homestay – small, family-run accommodation; see also losmen

ibu – mother; also a polite form of address to any older woman

Ida Bagus – honourable title for a male Brahmana

ikat – cloth where a pattern is produced by dyeing the individual threads before weaving

jalak putih – local name for Bali starling

jalan – road or street; abbreviated to Jl

jepun – frangipani or plumeria trees

Jl – *jalan;* road or street

kahyangan jagat – directional temples

kain – a length of material wrapped tightly around the hips and waist, over a sarong

kain poleng – black-and-white chequered cloth

kaja – in the direction of the mountains; see also *kelod*

kaja-kangin – corner of the courtyard

kaki lima – mobile food carts

kala – demonic face often seen over temple gateways

kamben – a length of *songket* wrapped around the chest for formal occasions

kampung – village or neighbourhood

kangin – sunrise

kantor – office

kantor imigrasi – immigration office

kantor pos – post office

Kawi – classical Javanese; the language of poetry

kebyar – a type of dance

Kecak – traditional Balinese dance; tells a tale from the *Ramayana* about Prince Rama and Princess Sita

kelod – in the direction away from the mountains and towards the sea; see also *kaja*

kempli – gong

kendang – drums

kepala desa – village head

kori agung – gateway to the second courtyard in a temple

kras – identifiable 'baddies' in an *arja* drama

kris – traditional dagger

kuah – sunset side

kulkul – hollow tree-trunk drum used to sound a warning or call meetings

labuhan – harbour; also called *pelabuhan*

laki-laki – boy

lamak – long, woven palm-leaf strips used as decorations in festivals and celebrations

langse – rectangular decorative hangings used in palaces or temples

Legong – classic Balinese dance

legong – young girls who perform the *Legong*

lontar – specially prepared palm leaves

losmen – small Balinese hotel, often family-run

lulur – body mask

lumbung – rice barn with a round roof; an architectural symbol of Lombok

Mahabharata – one of the great Hindu holy books, the epic poem tells of the battle between the Pandavas and the Kauravas

Majapahit – last great Hindu dynasty on Java

mekepung – traditional water buffalo races

meru – multi-tiered shrines in temples; the name comes from the Hindu holy mountain Mahameru

mobil – car

moksa – freedom from earthly desires

muncak – barking deer

naga – mythical snake-like creature

nusa – island; also called *pulau*

Nusa Tenggara Barat (NTB) – West Nusa Tenggara; a province of Indonesia comprising the islands of Lombok and Sumbawa

nyale – worm-like fish caught off Kuta, Lombok

Nyepi – major annual festival in the Hindu *saka* calendar; this is a day of complete stillness after a night of chasing out evil spirits

ogoh-ogoh – huge monster dolls used in the *Nyepi* festival

ojek – motorcycle that carries paying passengers

open – tall red-brick buildings

padi – growing rice plant

padmasana – temple shrine resembling a vacant chair

pak – father; shortened form of *bapak*

pantai – beach

paras – a soft, grey volcanic stone used in stone carving

pasar – market

pasar malam – night market

pecalang – village or *banjar* police

pedagang – mobile traders

pemangku – temple guardians and priests for temple rituals

perempuan – girl

plus plus – a combined tax and service charge of 21% added by midrange and top-end accommodation and restaurants

pondok – simple lodging or hut

prada – cloth highlighted with gold leaf, or gold or silver paint and thread

prahu – traditional Indonesian boat with outriggers

prasasti – inscribed copper plates

propinsi – province; Indonesia has 27 *propinsi* – Bali is a *propinsi,* Lombok and its neighbouring island of Sumbawa comprise *propinsi* Nusa Tenggara Barat (NTB)

pulau – island; also called *nusa*

puputan – warrior's fight to the death; an honourable but suicidal option when faced with an unbeatable enemy

pura – temple

pura dalem – temple of the dead

pura desa – village temple for everyday functions

pura puseh – temple of the village founders or fathers, honouring the village's origins

pura subak – temple of the rice growers' association

puri – palace

pusit kota – used on road signs to indicate the centre of town

rajah – lord or prince

Ramadan – Muslim month of fasting

Ramayana – one of the great Hindu holy books; these stories form the keystone of many Balinese dances and tales

Rangda – widow-witch who represents evil in Balinese theatre and dance

raya – main road, eg Jl Raya Ubud means 'the main road of Ubud'

RRI – Radio Republik Indonesia; Indonesia's national radio broadcaster

rumah makan – restaurant; literally 'eating place'

saiban – temple or shrine offering

Sasak – native of Lombok; also the language

sate – satay

sawah – rice field; see also *subak*

selat – strait

sepeda – bicycle

Shiva – the creator and destroyer; one of the three great Hindu gods

songket – silver- or gold-threaded cloth, handwoven using a floating weft technique

stupas – domes for housing Buddha relics

subak – village association that organises rice terraces and shares out water for irrigation

Sudra – common caste to which the majority of Balinese belong

sungai – river

swah – world of gods

tahun – year

taksu – divine interpreter for the gods

tanjung – cape or point

teluk – gulf or bay

tika – piece of printed cloth or carved wood displaying the Pawukon cycle

tirta – water

toya – water

undagi – designer of a building, usually an architect-priest

Vishnu – the preserver; one of the three great Hindu gods

wantilan – large *bale* pavilion used for meetings, performances and cockfights; community hall

waria – female impersonator, transvestite or transgendered person; combination of the words *wanita* and *pria*

waringin – large shady tree with drooping branches which root to produce new trees; see banyan

wartel – public telephone office; contraction of *warung telekomunikasi*

warung – food stall

wayang kulit – leather puppet used in shadow puppet plays; see also *dalang*

Wektu Telu – religion peculiar to Lombok; originated in Bayan and combines many tenets of Islam and aspects of other faiths

wuku – Balinese calendar made up of 10 different weeks, between one and 10 days long, all running concurrently; see also *saka*

yeh – water; also river

yoni – female symbol of the Hindu god Shiva

Behind the Scenes

SEND US YOUR FEEDBACK

We love to hear from travellers – your comments keep us on our toes and help make our books better. Our well-travelled team reads every word on what you loved or loathed about this book. Although we cannot reply individually to your submissions, we always guarantee that your feedback goes straight to the appropriate authors, in time for the next edition. Each person who sends us information is thanked in the next edition – the most useful submissions are rewarded with a selection of digital PDF chapters.

Visit **lonelyplanet.com/contact** to submit your updates and suggestions or to ask for help. Our award-winning website also features inspirational travel stories, news and discussions.

Note: We may edit, reproduce and incorporate your comments in Lonely Planet products such as guidebooks, websites and digital products, so let us know if you don't want your comments reproduced or your name acknowledged. For a copy of our privacy policy visit lonelyplanet.com/privacy.

OUR READERS

Many thanks to the travellers who used the last edition and wrote to us with helpful hints, useful advice and interesting anecdotes:

Michael Beukema, Alex Boladeras, Catherine Burns, Kim Cox, Michael Gillespie, Barbara Hardy, Laura Hartshorne, Linnea Hedlund, Pierre Jaeger, Emily Lois, Mark McKnight, Martina Míková, Jennie Murray, Robert Pilger, Summer Read, Daniel Ribas, Anniek Schellen

WRITER THANKS

Virginia Maxwell

Thanks to Ryan Ver Berkmoes for the Bali briefing, Hanafi Dharma for the expert driving and navigation, and Niamh O'Brien for monitoring the safety situation. My support team of Peter and Max Handsaker stayed calm when they saw the earthquake reports and made regular Skype calls to check up on me. I couldn't work as a travel writer without them.

Mark Johanson

Thanks to all the people on Lombok and Sumbawa who steered me in the right direction and helped me to navigate the post-earthquake islands, even when their personal lives were in shambles. I owe a debt of gratitude to Rudy Trekker, Gemma Marjaya, Kelly Goldie and Andy Wheatcroft for being fountains of knowledge along the way. A special thanks to my partner Felipe Bascuñán for tolerating my long absences and to my editor Niamh O'Brien for tirelessly ensuring I was OK!

Sofia Levin

Erwin, Willy and Andy – thank you for your guidance on the road, but most of all, your friendship. To my husband, Matt, this job would be impossible without your constant support and encouragement, both when I'm away and by your side. And to my parents (aka my biggest fans), thank you for instilling me with curiosity, appetite and the travel bug from the moment I was born.

MaSovaida Morgan

Deepest thanks to the wonderful souls who provided assistance, insight and companionship throughout my time on Bali: Rob, Margie, Max, Kristy and the Outsite crew; Gigi and Annette; Ty and Jeff; and especially to my dear brother Bayu for an efficient and unforgettable journey.

ACKNOWLEDGMENTS

Climate map data adapted from Peel MC, Finlayson BL & McMahon TA (2007) 'Updated World Map of the Köppen-Geiger Climate Classification', *Hydrology and Earth System Sciences*, 11, 1633–44.

Cover photograph: Pura Ulun Danu Bratan, Marco Bottigelli/AWL ©.

THIS BOOK

This 17th edition of Lonely Planet's *Bali, Lombok & Nusa Tenggara* guidebook was curated by Virginia Maxwell, who also researched and wrote it along with Mark Johanson, Sofia Levin and MaSovaida Morgan. The previous edition was researched and written by Ryan Ver Berkmoes and curated by Kate Morgan. This guidebook was produced by the following:

Destination Editors Niamh O'Brien, Tanya Parker

Senior Product Editor Kate Chapman

Product Editor Carolyn Boicos

Regional Senior Cartographer Julie Sheridan

Book Designer Mazzy Prinsep

Assisting Editors Kate Daly, Melanie Dankel, Carly Hall, Lou McGregor, Maja Vatrić, Simon Williamson

Cartographer Rachel Imeson

Assisting Book Designer Clara Monitto

Cover Researcher Wibowo Rusli

Thanks to Andrea Dobbin, Andi Jones, Claire Naylor, Karyn Noble, Victoria Smith, Angela Tinson, Amanda Williamson

Index

Map Pages **000**
Photo Pages **000**

Map Pages **000**
Photo Pages **000**

U

V

W

Y

Map Legend

Sights

- Beach
- Bird Sanctuary
- Buddhist
- Castle/Palace
- Christian
- Confucian
- Hindu
- Islamic
- Jain
- Jewish
- Monument
- Museum/Gallery/Historic Building
- Ruin
- Shinto
- Sikh
- Taoist
- Winery/Vineyard
- Zoo/Wildlife Sanctuary
- Other Sight

Activities, Courses & Tours

- Bodysurfing
- Diving
- Canoeing/Kayaking
- Course/Tour
- Sento Hot Baths/Onsen
- Skiing
- Snorkelling
- Surfing
- Swimming/Pool
- Walking
- Windsurfing
- Other Activity

Sleeping

- Sleeping
- Camping
- Hut/Shelter

Eating

- Eating

Drinking & Nightlife

- Drinking & Nightlife
- Cafe

Entertainment

- Entertainment

Shopping

- Shopping

Information

- Bank
- Embassy/Consulate
- Hospital/Medical
- Internet
- Police
- Post Office
- Telephone
- Toilet
- Tourist Information
- Other Information

Geographic

- Beach
- Gate
- Hut/Shelter
- Lighthouse
- Lookout
- Mountain/Volcano
- Oasis
- Park
- Pass
- Picnic Area
- Waterfall

Population

- Capital (National)
- Capital (State/Province)
- City/Large Town
- Town/Village

Transport

- Airport
- Border crossing
- Bus
- Cable car/Funicular
- Cycling
- Ferry
- Metro station
- Monorail
- Parking
- Petrol station
- Subway station
- Taxi
- Train station/Railway
- Tram
- Underground station
- Other Transport

Routes

- Tollway
- Freeway
- Primary
- Secondary
- Tertiary
- Lane
- Unsealed road
- Road under construction
- Plaza/Mall
- Steps
- Tunnel
- Pedestrian overpass
- Walking Tour
- Walking Tour detour
- Path/Walking Trail

Boundaries

- International
- State/Province
- Disputed
- Regional/Suburb
- Marine Park
- Cliff
- Wall

Hydrography

- River, Creek
- Intermittent River
- Canal
- Water
- Dry/Salt/Intermittent Lake
- Reef

Areas

- Airport/Runway
- Beach/Desert
- Cemetery (Christian)
- Cemetery (Other)
- Glacier
- Mudflat
- Park/Forest
- Sight (Building)
- Sportsground
- Swamp/Mangrove

Note: Not all symbols displayed above appear on the maps in this book

OUR STORY

A beat-up old car, a few dollars in the pocket and a sense of adventure. In 1972 that's all Tony and Maureen Wheeler needed for the trip of a lifetime – across Europe and Asia overland to Australia. It took several months, and at the end – broke but inspired – they sat at their kitchen table writing and stapling together their first travel guide, *Across Asia on the Cheap*. Within a week they'd sold 1500 copies. Lonely Planet was born.

Today, Lonely Planet has offices in Franklin, London, Melbourne, Oakland, Dublin, Beijing and Delhi, with more than 600 staff and writers. We share Tony's belief that 'a great guidebook should do three things: inform, educate and amuse'.

OUR WRITERS

Virginia Maxwell

Ubud Region, East Bali Although based in Australia, Virginia spends at least half of her year updating Lonely Planet destination coverage across the globe. The Mediterranean is her major area of interest – she has covered Spain, Italy, Turkey, Syria, Lebanon, Israel, Egypt, Morocco and Tunisia for Lonely Planet – but she also covers Bali, Finland, Armenia, the Netherlands, the USA and Australia. Follow her @maxwellvirginia on Instagram and Twitter.

Mark Johanson

Lombok, West Nusa Tenggara Mark grew up in Virginia and has called five different countries home over the last decade while circling the globe reporting for British newspapers *(The Guardian)*, American magazines *(Men's Journal)* and global media outlets (CNN, BBC). When not on the road, you'll find him gazing at the Andes from his current home in Santiago, Chile. Follow his adventures at www.markjohanson.com.

Sofia Levin

East Nusa Tenggara A Melbourne-based food and travel journalist, Sofia believes that eating in a country other than one's own is the simplest way to understand a culture. She has a stomach of steel and the ability to sniff out local haunts. Aside from trawling Melbourne as the Lonely Planet local, she also co-authors guidebooks and writes for Fairfax newspapers and travel magazines. When she's not travelling or eating, Sofia runs copywriting and social-media company Word Salad and spreads smiles with her Insta-famous poodle, @lifeofjinkee. Find her on Instagram and Twitter (@sofiaklevin).

MaSovaida Morgan

Bali MaSovaida is a travel writer and multimedia storyteller whose wanderlust has taken her to more than 40 countries and all seven continents. Previously, she was Lonely Planet's Destination Editor for South America and Antarctica for four years, and worked as an editor for newspapers and NGOs in the Middle East and the United Kingdom. Follow her on Instagram @MaSovaida.

Published by Lonely Planet Global Limited
CRN 554153
17th edition – Jul 2019
ISBN 978 1 78657 510 4

10 9 8 7 6 5 4 3 2 1
Printed in Singapore